NELL HEATON'S
COOKING DICTIONARY

NELL HEATON'S
COOKING
DICTIONARY

Compiled by
NELL HEATON

PRINTED IN POLAND

Published by Murray's Sales and Service Co.
Cresta House,
63, St. Paul's Road, London N. 1.

FOREWORD

THERE are certain people who can so transform rooms which are utterly devoid of beauty that, within a few hours, all the ugliness is disguised and there is an air of homeliness. These same *home-makers*, however far they may be from the shops, can serve delicious food on an attractively appointed table. Some women (and men) are born home-makers. Others can acquire the art. One does not need costly things to make a beautiful home. Nor does one require to be a slave to the home. Everlasting talk of domestic details and chores can become a bore—and it also shows inefficiency. Housekeeping is an exact science and one is either a good housekeeper or a bad one. The aim should be to produce the best of nourishment, comfort, and beauty on an economical basis and with no waste of energy.

Hard and fast rules cannot be laid down. A good housekeeper, who today is frequently cook and waitress as well as the gracious wife and hostess, plans her details according to schedule. She knows just how long the shopping and the preparing of the food will take, and she gets down to it and does her job skilfully.

The difference between perfect food and bad food is one which is dependent upon the cooking. The choice of dishes depends upon the purse. The raw material, as purchased, is the same, but the preparation of dishes finally served may differ vastly. One of the great secrets of culinary success is to make the most of what you have—by care in cooking and dishing up, and by neatness and spotlessness both in table-setting and serving.

It has not been possible for me to extend every recipe in this book as much as I should have liked to do so, because space would not allow. In certain places, certain recipes will be found grouped together under a convenient sub-heading. Other recipes have been given as variations of basic recipes. Our basic cooking processes, as we all know, are traditional recipes of our forbears but, although no cooking recipe is original, we each have our own way of suggesting its present-day adaptation. Throughout the Dictionary I have indicated approximate oven heats and cooking times.

I hope you will find this book easy to use and that you will enjoy using it as much as I have enjoyed compiling it.

NELL HEATON

"The following recipes are not a mere marrowless collection of shreds, and patches and cuttings and pastings but a *bona fide* register of Practical Facts. . . . Moreover, the author has submitted to a labour no preceding cookery-book maker, perhaps, ever attempted to encounter, having EATEN each receipt, before he set it down in his book."

The Cook's Oracle
(Kitchener, 1822)

Abbreviations used in this book

Arab. . . .	Arabian
bicarb. soda . .	bicarbonate of soda
c.c.	cubic centimetre
C.H. . . .	carbohydrates
dr (s). . . .	dram (s)
dsp.	dessertspoon (s)
F.	Fahrenheit
Fr.	French
gall.	gallon (s)
grm. . . .	gram (s)
hr (s). . .	hour (s)
"	inch (es)
lb.	pound (s)
min (s). . . .	minute (s)
wk (s). . . .	week (s)
mth (s). . . .	month (s)
oz.	ounce (s)
pl.	plural
pt.	pint (s)
qt.	quart (s)
tbsp.	tablespoon (s)
Therm. . . .	Thermostat
tsp.	teaspoon (s)

All cups unless otherwise stated are B.S.I. (8 oz.) cups.
All spoonfuls are level unless otherwise stated.
All flour should be plain flour unless otherwise stated.
Fahrenheit temperatures and the standardised thermostat figures (Therm.) are given throughout this book (see Table, p. 357). If your cooker is not a current model, your figures will vary from those given, but this can easily be adjusted by referring to the table of comparative oven heats.

A

ABBATTAGE. Term especially applied to a pile of "game pieces".

ABERDEEN SANDWICHES

Ingredients
2 oz. cold chicken
1 oz. cold ham or tongue
Slices of stale bread
2 tbsp. good sauce
1 tbsp. curry paste
Watercress to garnish

Method
Dice the chicken and ham or tongue and place in a saucepan with the sauce and curry paste. Simmer gently for 5 mins. stirring all the time, then turn the mixture into a basin to cool. Cut some slices of stale bread about ⅛″ thick, stamp into rounds the size of a penny, and fry in boiling oil until lightly browned. Place on kitchen paper to drain, then spread the mixture thickly on one round, placing another on top, until all are used. Put them into a hot oven for a few minutes, arrange on a pre-heated dish and serve hot. The remains of fish and game may be used in this recipe. Five or 6 sandwiches should be allowed for each person.

ACAJU. See **CASHEW**.

ACANTHUS. The young and tender leaves of this spiny grass, which grows freely in the lands of the Mediterranean basin, are used in salads.

ACETIC ACID. This acid is an essential constituent of vinegar. Dilute acetic acid has been known as vinegar since the earliest times. It is also used in confectionery for boiled sugar foods, etc.

ACID. Biting, piquant, sharp or sour to the taste. Chemically, a substance usually soluble in water, which reddens vegetable substances such as litmus. See **ACETIC ACID, CITRIC ACID, MALIC ACID, TARTARIC ACID**.

ACID BRINE OR ACID SOLUTION. This is used in sterilisation both of canned and bottled vegetables to prevent cloudiness.

ACID ICE FOR PUDDINGS

Ingredients
Juice of 1 large lemon
3 oz. sugar
4 egg whites

Method
Beat the whites of eggs to a stiff froth and add to the strained lemon juice and sugar. Pile this over the pudding after it is cooked. Bake at 350° F. Therm. 4 for about 10 mins.; leave to set. This will serve 4 or 5 persons.

ACIDIMETER. This is used in cheese-making to test the milk for acidity. Put 10 c.c, milk into a dish and add 3 drops phenolphthalein as an indicator. Add caustic soda

[1]

ACIDIMETER (*continued*)

($\frac{N}{9}$) solution slowly, stirring continually, until the mixture turns a permanent pink. The proportion of lactic acid can be measured by the amount of soda needed to neutralise it. For a quick-ripening cheese 0·2° is needed: for a hard cheese 0·22°.

ACID RINSE. When peeled, quartered or stoned and exposed to the air, the surface of many fruits, e.g. apples and pears, goes brown, and though their flavour is not affected by discolouration, their appearance is often spoilt. By immersing the fruit in salted water or lemon juice and water for a short time, this will be prevented. See FRUIT, p. 230.

ACIDULATED ALKALI

Ingredients

2 oz. bicarb. soda
2 oz. tartaric acid
4 oz. powdered lump sugar
Few drops lemon essence

Method

Mix all together. Keep the mixture in a bottle well corked. When required use 1 tsp. to a tumbler three parts full of water and drink during effervescence.

ACIDULATED LEMONADE

Ingredients

4 oz. fresh lemon juice
4 oz. sugar
3 pt. boiling water
½ oz. thinly and freshly cut lemon peel

Method

Put the lemon juice in a bowl or jug, add peel, sugar and water. Cover with clean cloth and leave to cool. When cold, strain and, if not required immediately, bottle and cork securely.

ACIDULATED WATER

Ingredients

1 tsp. lemon juice or vinegar
1½ qt. water

Method

Mix together and use as desired.

ACORN COFFEE. This may be used as a substitute for real coffee. The acorns are gathered in the autumn when they are ripe. After shelling, cut into pieces the size of coffee berries, and dry at 200° F. Therm. ¼. They should then be roasted, like ordinary coffee, until they become cinnamon-brown colour. To prevent the acorns from becoming tough, they should be ground or pounded immediately after roasting. A little butter may be added during the pounding. Place in airtight bottles, and use ½ oz. coffee to every pint of water. Acorn coffee may be mixed with ordinary coffee.

ADIRONDACK PANCAKES. Use the recipe for French Pancakes (see p. 363). Make them about the size of a large plate, but do not roll them. Pile them on top of each other, with butter and powdered maple sugar between. Cut as you would a layer cake.

ADJUSTING RECIPES. See RECIPES, CHECKING AND BUILDING.

ADMIRAL. A hot drink (punch) made with claret, sugar, vanilla, cinnamon; egg yolk is added to thicken it.

ADMIRAL'S SAUCE. See SAUCES.

ADULTERATION. Certain substances (mostly foodstuffs) can be adulterated by the addition of another substance of similar consistency and colour and a neutral flavour. The aim is to increase the bulk and reduce the cost with intent to defraud the public. Examples of adulterants are: water in milk or butter, starch in cocoa, ground husk in pepper. The Ministry of Food has in some measure protected the

ADULTERATION (*continued*)
public by the passing of food-labelling regulations by which a manufacturer is compelled by law to list the ingredients of his product according to the proportion in which they are present.

AERATED BREAD. Bread made without leaven or yeast, water charged with carbonic acid gas being mixed with the flour.

AERATED WATER. Used to add "sparkle" to drinks or consumed alone.

AERATION. Charging a substance with air or gas (carbon dioxide unless otherwise indicated). The air or gas may be incorporated in any liquid containing gelatinous matter by simply beating with some open utensil such as a fork or whisk. The air is imprisoned as the liquid opens out, and the gelatinous substance forms innumerable small gas-filled cells. It is thus that eggs, or a liquid containing eggs, or containing gelatine or albumen, can be beaten to a froth. Mixtures which contain fat and sugar, particularly if the fat, like butter, contains albuminous matter, can be aerated, but to a less degree than if eggs or egg albumen are in the mixture. Water can be aerated by incorporating gas under pressure, the gas escaping by effervescence when the pressure is removed.

AFRICANS. Small French dessert biscuits.

AFTERS. A North-country term meaning "pudding".

AGAMI. Known in England as Trumpeter; one of the best South American game birds.

AGAR-AGAR. A transparent-leafed seaweed used extensively for soups and stews. Sold in thin strips, leaves or powdered. The Salanganese or Chinese swallows use agar-agar to build their nests, hence Bird's Nest Soup.

AGARIC. This French word is the family name of over two thousand different types of fungi. There are about sixteen varieties of edible agarics, also some deadly ones, the Aniatites, which are very dangerous as they greatly resemble the field mushroom.

AGNELLOTO. Small paste envelopes, filled with vegetable purée or minced meat, or any other suitable stuffing. They differ in shape from ravioli as they are cut in half-moons whilst ravioli is cut into squares.

AGRIMONY. A common perennial weed also known as Church Steeple, Cockly Burr and Sticklewort. The rich green leaves are about 6″ long and arise from root stalk. They are used to make a tonic tea, and also astringent gargles. Yellow dye is extracted from the leaves.

Agrimony Tea. The whole herb, including root, may be infused, or, if preferred, just the leaves. In the latter case, place 1 tsp. leaves in a jug or bowl, pour over 1 pt. water, and leave to infuse.

AIGUILLETTES. This literally means "like needles". By some cooks this term is applied to the very thin strips into which fish and meat is cut. But Soyer and others adapt the term to indicate a mode of serving, that is, on small silver skewers. Soyer says: "For this kind of hors d'œuvres it is necessary to have 12 small silver (or electro-plated) skewers about 4″ long and the thickness of a packing needle, with a fancy ring or design on the top. The person eating what is served upon them taking the head of the skewer with the thumb and fingers of the left hand and picking it up with a fork." See FISH.

AITCHBONE (Fr. *culotte*). A low-priced joint which is cut from between the rump and buttocks of beef. Sometimes called by its own name "edge-bone". H-bone = haunch bone. Boiled or used for stews.

ALBRAN, ALEBRAN or HALEBRAN. Young wild duck; after the month of October is called Canardeau, and the month following, Canard.

ALBUMEN. A nitrogenous substance contained in white of egg and lean meat, principally beef.

[3]

Albumen Lemonade
Ingredients
- 6 tsp. orange juice
- 1 tsp. lemon juice
- 1 tsp. sugar
- ½ glass crushed ice
- 1 egg white
- Water

Method

Sweeten the fruit juices and pour over ice. Break the egg white into a saucer and clip with scissors. Strain into fruit juice through two or three thicknesses of butter muslin or gauze, wetted in cold water and wrung dry. Lift fork through to see there are no strings. Fill glass with water and stir.

Albumen Milk
Ingredients
- ¾ cup whole milk
- 1 egg white

Method

Chill the milk thoroughly, clip egg white and strain, then stir into chilled milk or, if preferred, shake for a foamy milk.

Albumen Water
Ingredients
- 1 egg white
- 1½ pt. water
- 1 tsp. brandy

Method

Mix the strained clipped egg white with the cold water; add brandy very slowly to prevent the egg white coagulating.

ALCOHOL (from Arab. *alkohl*, essence, spirits). Alcohol is the product of fermenting sugar and gives to wines, spirits and beers an intoxicating quality. It is highly inflammable, and used as "spirits of wine" for heating purposes. It also evaporates freely, so in some instances it is used for cooling. Dilute alcohol may be procured by distillation from all saccharine liqueurs after fermentation: brandy from wine; rum from the refuse juice of the sugar cane; whisky from fermented malt; arrack from fermented rice or from palm wine, etc. Spirits of wine is diluted alcohol, and may be either *rectified* or *proof*. *Proof spirit* contains in 100 parts about 57 of alcohol and 47 of water, the 4% over disappearing by the condensation that follows the admixture of spirit and water. *Rectified spirit* is usually sold at from 54 to 64 over-proof, reckoning proof as 100. Alcohol cannot replace food, but it can be used to yield energy and to supply the fuel needed by the body in certain cases of illness.

ALDERMAN'S WALK. The name given to the centre cut (long incision) of a haunch of mutton or venison, where the most delicate slices are to be found. It also denotes the best part of the under-cut (fillet) of a sirloin of beef. The name is supposed to be derived from a City company's dinner, at which a City alderman showed a special liking for this cut.

ALE. "A liquor brewed from malt, to be drunk fresh." (Dr. Johnson's *Dictionary*.) Ale is sometimes used as a medium for boiling fish, e.g. eels, or giving body to thin soup and stews. It has also been used as a substitute for sherry in sauces and invalid foods. See also **BEER.**

Ale Berry
Ingredients
- 2 tbsp. oatmeal
- Water
- ½ pt. beer or porter
- Grated ginger
- Sugar

Method

Soak the oatmeal in a little water for an hour. Strain, and add the boiling beer or porter. Pour mixture into a saucepan, add a little grated ginger, and sweeten as desired. Simmer for 10 mins. Sufficient for 1 person.

[4]

Ale Cup

Ingredients
Juice of 1 lemon
Slice hot, dry toast
Thin slice lemon rind
1 tbsp. sugar
2 wineglasses sherry
Little grated nutmeg or powdered allspice
Sprig of balm
Wineglass of brandy
3 pt. mild ale

Method
Squeeze the lemon juice on to the slice of toast, lay on the rind, add sugar, sherry, nutmeg or allspice and balm. Pour over the brandy and mild ale. Do not allow the balm to remain many minutes. Sufficient for 5 or 6 persons.

Ale Flip

Ingredients
3 pt. ale
1 tbsp. sugar
Blade of mace
1 clove
Small piece of butter
1 egg white
2 egg yolks
1 tbsp. cold ale

Method
Put the ale into a saucepan, add sugar, mace, clove and butter, and bring the liquid to the boil. Beat the white of egg, then the yolks, and mix them with ale. Mix all together, then pour the whole rapidly from one jug to another from a good height for some minutes, to froth it accordingly, but do not allow to cool. Sufficient for 5 or 6 persons.

Ale, Mulled

Ingredients
2 eggs
½ pt. ale
1 clove
Little whole ginger
Marble of butter
1 tsp. sugar

Method
Beat the eggs with 1 tbsp. cold ale. Put the remainder of ale, clove, ginger, butter and sugar into a saucepan and bring to boiling point, then pour mixture on to eggs. Turn into a jug and pass the whole from one jug to another for some minutes, and at a good height. Return it to the saucepan, heat it again, but do not allow to boil. Time about 15 mins. Sufficient for 1 person.

Ale Posset (*an old-fashioned remedy for colds*)

Ingredients
½ pt. new milk
1 egg yolk
Walnut of butter
Sugar
½ pt. ale
1 slice toasted bread

Method
Bring the milk just to the boil, stir in the beaten egg yolk and butter. Add sugar to taste, and mix with the warmed ale. Return to the heat and boil until the scum rises (this will take about 5 mins.). Remove from heat and pour over well-toasted slice of bread (crusts removed). Serve steaming hot in a basin.

[5]

Ale Punch

Ingredients

1 qt. mild ale
1 wineglass sherry
1 wineglass brandy
1 tbsp. icing sugar
Peel and juice of 1 lemon
Little grated nutmeg
Small piece of ice

Method

Put the ingredients into a bowl, mix well together, and serve in small tumblers.

Ale Sangaree

Ingredients

½ pt. ale
1 tsp. icing sugar
Dusting of grated nutmeg

Method

Bring the ale to the boil, then pour into a small jug. Add the icing sugar and nutmeg. If preferred, this drink may be served cold with a small lump of ice.

ALECOST. See COSTMARY.

ALEVIN. The first stage of salmon.

ALF. WIFE. A member of the herring family.

ALEXANDER. This perennial herb can be used as a vegetable. It is best when blanched before cooking. Sometimes called locally Alisander, Blackpot Herb, Monk's Salad, Stanmarch.

ALGAE. See SEAWEED.

ALISANDER. See ALEXANDER.

ALKALI. An agent which neutralises acids. The chief alkalis used in cookery and confectionery are ammonia, potash and soda. Alkaline (base) forming elements predominate in apples, bananas, beans (dried and fresh), beef (fresh), cantaloup, carrots, citron, dates, lemons, olives, onions, oranges and orange peel, pears (fresh), potatoes, radishes, sweet potatoes, tomatoes, turnips and water melon. In pregnancy, a good alkaline balanced diet is essential.

ALKANET. A plant of the bugloss tribe. A beautiful crimson dye is obtained from the dried root, which is used for colouring fats, oils, wax, spirits, essences and other things in which it can be infused. Commercially it is used for colouring cheese, and wine merchants add it to inferior port to heighten the colour.

ALLELUIA. See WOOD SORREL.

ALLEMANDE SAUCE. See SAUCES.

ALLIGATOR PEAR. See AVOCADO PEAR.

ALLOWANCES FOR CATERING

ITEM	APPROXIMATE AMOUNTS PER HEAD AS SERVED (unless otherwise stated)
BEVERAGES	
Cider	½ cup
Coffee } Cocoa }	1–2 cups
Lemonade	1 glass
Orange juice	¾ glass
Tea (Hot)	1–2 cups
Tea (Iced)	13-oz. glass
Tomato juice	4–6-oz. glass

ALLOWANCES FOR CATERING (*continued*)

ITEM	APPROXIMATE AMOUNTS PER HEAD AS SERVED (unless otherwise stated)
CEREALS AND PASTE	
Cornflakes	$\frac{5}{8}$ cup
Grapenuts	$\frac{1}{4}$ cup
Puffed Wheat	1 cup
Rice Krispies	$\frac{2}{3}$ cup
Shredded Wheat	2 biscuits
Barley } Oatmeal porridge } Farinoca }	1 oz. plus water
Rice	$\frac{2}{3}$ cup
Wheat, Cream of	$\frac{2}{3}$ cup
Milk pudding	$\frac{1}{2}$ pt.
Macaroni (cooked) } Noodles ,, } Spaghetti ,, }	$\frac{1}{3}$ cup
DAIRY PRODUCTS	
Butter	1–2 pats
Cheese	1$\frac{1}{2}$ oz.
Cream	2 tbsp.
Cream (for whipping)	1 tbsp.
Cream cheese	$\frac{1}{3}$ cup
Ice cream	$\frac{1}{4}$ cup or 4 tbsp.
Milk	1 glass
FISH (*as purchased*)	
Cutlets	1 lb.
Dressed fish	$\frac{1}{2}$ lb.
Fillets	$\frac{1}{4}$–$\frac{1}{2}$ lb.
Whole or Round	$\frac{3}{4}$–1 lb.
FISH (*Dried*)	
Smoked	4 oz.
FISH (*Shell*)	
Clams	4–6
Clams in liquid	$\frac{1}{2}$ pt.
Crab meat	$\frac{1}{2}$ lb.
Crayfish	2
Frog's legs	4
Lobster, boiled	2–3 lb.
Lobster meat	$\frac{1}{2}$ lb.
Mussels	1 doz.
Oysters in liquor	1 pt.
Oysters on shell	6–12
Prawns for cocktail	1 doz.
Prawns, cooked	$\frac{1}{4}$–$\frac{1}{2}$ lb.
Scallops	$\frac{1}{4}$–$\frac{1}{2}$ lb.
Shrimps	1–2 doz
Snails	$\frac{1}{2}$–1 lb.
Turtle meat	$\frac{1}{2}$ lb.

ALLOWANCES FOR CATERING (*continued*)

Item	Approximate Amounts per Head as Served (unless otherwise stated)
FLOUR MIXES	
Breads	3–4 oz. or 2–6 slices
Cake	4–5 oz.
Pastry	6 oz.
Scones	4–6
FRUITS	
Apricots	3
Apples (fresh)	1
Bananas	1
Blackberries	½ lb.
Blackcurrants	½ lb.
Cherries	½ lb.
Cranberries (for sauce)	¼ lb.
Dates	5–6
Figs	2
Melon	1 slice
Nectarines	1
Oranges	1
Peaches	1 fresh or 3 oz. canned fruit
Plums	½ lb.
Pineapple	½ cup diced or 1 slice
Prunes	3 oz.
Raspberries	½ lb.
Strawberries	½ lb.
For fruit pies	An 8″ pie cuts into 6–7 pieces
For fruit fools	⅓ cup
For stewing	6 oz.
Dried fruits	3 oz.
MEATS	
Bacon	2 oz.
Beef	
Roast	2–2½ oz.
Fried	3 oz.
Creamed mince	3 oz.
Patties	3 oz.
Steaks grilled	6–8 oz.
Stewed with vegetables	5½ oz.
Ham	
Boiled, sliced	2 oz.
Grilled	3 oz.
Lamb and Mutton	
Chops	4 approx. to 1 lb.—2 each
Roast	2½ oz.
Pork	
Boiled	2½ oz.
Chops	1 each
Roast loin	3 oz.
Sausage	4 or 5 to 1 lb.—2–3 each
Poultry and Game	¾ lb. (as bought). ½ lb. (as cooked)

ALLOWANCES FOR CATERING (*continued*)

ITEM	APPROXIMATE AMOUNTS PER HEAD AS SERVED (unless otherwise stated)
Veal	
Breast and neck	$\frac{1}{2}$ lb.
Chops	1 each
Cutlets	3 oz.
MEATS COOKED	4–6 oz.
OFFAL	
Brains	1 pair
Head (calf's, pig's, sheep's)	6 servings
Kidney (pig's, sheep's)	3–4
Kidney (Veal)	2
Liver	6–8 oz.
Oxtail	2 servings
Ox tongue	6 servings
Sausages	$\frac{1}{2}$–$\frac{3}{4}$ lb.
Sweetbreads	1 pair
Tripe	$\frac{1}{2}$–$\frac{3}{4}$ lb.
Trotters	2
PRESERVES AND PICKLES	
Honey	2 tbsp.
Jam	2 tbsp.
Jelly	2 tbsp.
SALADS	
Cabbage	$\frac{1}{2}$ cup
Fish or Meat	$\frac{3}{4}$ cup
Mixed or Fruit	$\frac{1}{2}$ cup
Potato	$\frac{1}{2}$ cup
Vegetable	$\frac{1}{2}$ cup
SALAD DRESSING	
French	$\frac{3}{4}$–1 tbsp.
Mayonnaise	1–$1\frac{1}{2}$ tbsp.
SAUCES	
Gravy	2 tbsp.
Sauce with meat	1 tbsp.
Sauce with pudding	2 tbsp.
Sauce for vegetables	2–3 tbsp.
SOUPS	1 cupful = $\frac{1}{2}$ pt.
SUGAR AND SYRUP	
Granulated	$1\frac{1}{2}$ tsp.
Loaf	$1\frac{1}{2}$ cubes
Syrup	$\frac{1}{4}$ cup = 2 oz.
VEGETABLES (*as purchased*)	
Artichokes (Globe)	1
Artichokes (Jerusalem)	1–2
Aubergine	1–2

ALLOWANCES FOR CATERING (*continued*)

ITEM	APPROXIMATE AMOUNTS FOR TWO PEOPLE
Beans (French)	
Beans (Runner)	
Beetroot	
Broccoli	
Brussels Sprouts	1 lb.
Cabbage (raw)	
Cabbage (to cook)	
Canned vegetables	
Carrots	
Cauliflower	1 small
Celery	1 head
Cucumber	1 small
Dried vegetables	½ lb.
Kale	1 lb.
Lettuce	1 medium-sized head
Lettuce (garnish)	
Parsnips	1 lb.
Peas	
Potatoes (to mash)	1½ lb.
Potatoes (to brown)	
Radishes	1 Bunch
Spinach	1½ lb.
Swede	1 lb.
Tomato (small)	4–6
Tomato (sliced)	
Turnips	1 lb.
Vegetable marrow	1½ lb.
Watercress	½ lb.

ALLSPICE (Fr. *piment épice*). Also called Jamaica pepper and Pimento. The ripe berries dried and ground of an evergreen tree of the myrtle species; called "allspice" because it not only resembles in flavour and smell the three chief spices, cloves, cinnamon and nutmeg, but is said to combine them. The ripe berries look rather like ripe black peppers, but are larger in size and less pungent to taste. Used whole in pickles, and ground in baking and sweets, etc.

Allspice, Essence of

Ingredients

2 drs. oil of pimento
3 oz. spirits of wine

Method

Put the oil of pimento very gradually into the spirits of wine. Leave to stand for a few minutes. Put into a bottle, cork closely. When using for flavouring, 5 or 6 drops will flavour a pint.

Allspice, Tincture of

Ingredients

2 oz. allspice
1 pt. brandy

Method

Put the allspice in a bottle with the brandy. Let it soak for 14 days. Shake every 3 days, then pour off into a clean, dry bottle, leaving the sediment, and cork closely. To flavour 1 pt. use ½ tsp.

ALLUMETTES. See PASTE AND PASTRY.

ALMACK'S CONFECTION (Fr. *confiture d'almack*)

Ingredients	Method
2 doz. apples 4 doz. plums 2 doz. pears 1 lb. sugar to each 1 lb. fruit	Peel, core and slice the apples and pears; slit the plums and remove the stones, weigh and place in a stone jar in layers and put the jar in the oven and bake at 250° F. Therm. ¼ until the fruit is tender. Pass through a coarse sieve and then put into a preserving pan, add the sugar, and sift over a moderate heat until the jam sets when tested. Put into small jars, cover and store. (This jam is as thick as damson cheese.) Cut into slices when used.

ALMOND (Fr. *amande*). The almond is the fruit of the tree belonging to the genus *Prunus* of the family *Rosaceae*. There are two kinds; the one with the pink flowers produces sweet almonds and the one with the white flowers produces bitter almonds. The kernel of the sweet almond is largely used in cooking and confectionery because of its delicate and sweet flavour. The sweet almonds and bitter almonds resemble each other closely in appearance, but are distinguishable in taste. The sweet variety is harmless, but the bitter almond is said to contain a trace of prussic acid, and therefore must be used with discretion. The best almonds are the Jordan almonds; these are chiefly imported from Malaga and Almeria, and are preferable for dessert. There are two kinds; one which is about an inch long, flat and of a clear brown skin, sweet or mucilaginous and rather tough. The other, more pointed at one end, brittle, sweet in flavour as before. Valencia almonds are reckoned second quality; they are under an inch long, round at the one end, and bluntly pointed at the other, flat, of a dingy brown colour and with dirty skins. The Barbary or Italian almonds are smaller and less flattened. Almonds should never be bought if they are dry, broken or smell in the least rancid. See also SEASONING (p. 458).

TO BLANCH. Throw the almonds into a pan of boiling water and allow them to remain over a gentle heat until the skins will slip off readily when rubbed between finger and thumb. Drain and plunge into cold water for a minute or two; drain again and rub in a cloth, when the skins will be easily removed. Then throw into salted water, leave 2 hrs. and drain and dry. Split each one lengthwise and shred as desired.

TO COLOUR. Whether the almonds are whole or shredded or chopped, it is only necessary to rub them together with the colouring matter until all are saturated. They should be dried on a screen or sieve.

ALMONDS, BURNT—I. Chop or shred the blanched almonds, put them on a baking sheet, bake to a golden brown in a slow oven (250° F. Therm. ¼).

ALMONDS, BURNT—II

Ingredients	Method
1 lb. almonds 1¾ lb. granulated sugar Cold water	Blanch the almonds and dry in a cool oven. Put 1 lb. sugar and ½ pt. water into a saucepan, bring to the boil and boil over a low heat until the almonds make a cracking noise; remove pan from heat and stir until the sugar granulates. Turn the mix on to a sieve, shake and let the sugar that drains off drip into the saucepan. Add 1½ gills water and ¾ lb. sugar

ALMONDS, BURNT—II (*continued*)

and boil to soft ball (237° F.). Add the almonds, stir till well coated, remove as soon as almonds show signs of sticking and strain on sieve. (If desired, colour and flavour this second-stage coating sugar.)

ALMONDS, DEVILLED
Ingredients
  Almonds
  Butter
  Salt
  Cayenne

Method
Put sufficient butter in a small pan to give a depth of 1″ when melted. Bring to boiling point. After blanching the almonds throw them in all together. Mix salt and cayenne together on a piece of paper. Remove almonds from pan, roll them in salt and shake till cold.

ALMONDS, SALTED
Ingredients
  ½ lb. almonds
  1 tbsp. butter
  Salt

Method
Place the butter in a frying pan over a low heat, and when melted, add almonds. Shake the pan from time to time, to cook the almonds till they are light brown. Then sprinkle them with salt and drain them on brown paper. Change the paper after the first few minutes.

Almond and Cucumber Dressing (*for salads*)
Ingredients
  ½ pt. salad dressing
  ½ cucumber
  4 oz. almonds

Method
Make a salad dressing (see **SALAD DRESSINGS**). Peel and dice the cucumber. Blanch and shred or grate the almonds; combine all the ingredients.

Almond Cakes. See CAKES.

Almond Candy (Hard Bake)
Ingredients
  1 lb. sugar
  ½ pt. water
  4 oz. almonds
  Juice of ½ lemon
  1 oz. butter

Method
Boil the sugar in the water until it becomes brittle when dropped in cold water. Add the almonds blanched and split, the lemon juice and butter. Boil until the candy hardens at once in water. Pour it out on a well-oiled tin.

Almond Cream
Ingredients
  ½ lb. ground almonds
  ¼ pt. sour cream
  ½ pt. orange juice
  4 oz. cornflakes

Method
Mix together the almonds, sour cream, orange juice and beat well. Add the cornflakes and serve in individual cups.

[12]

Almond Cream Filling (*for cakes*)
Ingredients

Method

3 tbsp. apricot marmalade
1 tsp. maraschino or lemon
   juice
3 tbsp. ground almonds
2 tbsp. whipped cream

Put the apricot marmalade into a small basin, add flavouring and the ground almonds. Then lightly fold in the whipped cream.

Almond Filling (*for cakes*)
Ingredients

Method

3 tbsp. butter or unsalted
   margarine
4 oz. sugar
¾ tsp. grated lemon or orange
   peel (or ½ tsp. vanilla)
4 oz. ground almonds
1 egg

Cream the butter and sugar. Add lemon rind or orange rind and the ground almonds. Beat the egg slightly and add. Beat lightly all together. Sufficient for one 6″–8″ cake.

Almond Iced Fingers
Ingredients

Method

3 pieces Victoria Sandwich,
   3″ × 9″ (see **CAKES**, p. 118)
Apricot marmalade
   (see p. 31)
Almond paste (see p. 14)
Chopped browned almonds
Crystallised flower petals

Make the sandwich mixture a day before required for use; cut into strips, and cut off the brown outside layer. Cut through each strip transversely and spread the inside of each piece thinly with apricot marmalade. Make the almond paste, cut into 3 pieces and roll out each piece to fit the size of the cake. Put a layer between each 2 pieces of the sandwich and press well. Trim off the sides and ends and spread the top of each piece of cake with a thin layer of apricot marmalade. Cover with chopped almonds and press well. Cut into fingers about an inch wide and dust some crystallised flower petals over.

Almond Macaroons
Ingredients

Method

¼ lb. ground almonds
½ lb. caster sugar
2 egg whites
½ oz. ground rice
½ tsp. vanilla essence
Wafer paper
Shredded blanched almonds

Put the ground almonds, sugar and unbeaten egg whites into a mixing bowl and cream them together for about 10 mins. Add the ground rice and vanilla. If the mixture is too thick add a few drops of water. Put the mixture into a forcing bag with a ½″ plain pipe and pipe on to small squares of wafer paper, making 12 from each sheet of paper, dividing it into 3 along the narrow way, and 4 lengthwise.

[13]

Almond Macaroons (*continued*)

Brush slightly with beaten egg white and put 2 pieces of almond on to the top. Bake at 350° F. Therm. 4 for about 20 mins. until evenly golden brown. This quantity should make about 15 macaroons.

Almond Paste, Boiled
Ingredients
- 1 lb. sugar
- ½ pt. water
- 1 lb. blanched and ground almonds
- 6 tsp. orange juice
- Few drops rose or orange flower water

Method
Put the sugar and water into a saucepan and cook until just past the thread stage (240° F.) (See SUGAR.) Add the ground almonds and orange juice and rosewater and stir till the ingredients are well blended and creamy. Knead them towards the end. Flatten them out on a board, dusted with icing sugar. Leave the paste to cool, pack it into a jar or tin, cover closely and leave it to ripen for about a week. Use as desired. This will make about 2 lb. almond paste.
See also **MARZIPAN**.

Almond Paste, Unboiled
Ingredients
- 8 oz. blanched and ground almonds
- 8 oz. icing or caster sugar
- 1 fresh egg
- Juice of ½ lemon

Method
Mix the ground almonds and sugar together, add the lightly beaten egg and lemon juice. Mix to a stiff paste. Knead till pliable and smooth, then roll. Use as required. If the paste breaks, work for a few more minutes.

Almond Paste, Mock
Ingredients
- 4 oz. butter
- 8 oz. sugar
- 2 tbsp. water
- 8 oz. soya bean flour
- Smallest pinch salt
- 2 tsp. almond essence

Method
Melt butter, sugar and water in a saucepan. Remove from the heat, add soya flour, salt, and beat well together. Add the almond essence. Turn on to a board and knead well until smooth and pliable. Cool slightly before using.

Almond Petits Fours
Ingredients
- ¼ lb. ground almonds
- 2 oz. caster sugar
- 1½–2 egg whites
- Few drops almond essence
- Wafer paper
- Cherries and angelica

Method
Mix the almonds and sugar and fold in lightly the stiffly whisked whites of egg. Add the almond essence, put the mixture into a forcing bag fitted with a rose biscuit forcer. Place the wafer paper on a baking sheet, smooth side to the tin, and force the mixture into small rosettes and short finger lengths. Brush lightly

Almond Petits Fours (*continued*)

with slightly beaten egg white and decorate with small pieces of cherry and angelica. Bake at 350° F. Therm. 4 for about 15 mins. until golden brown. Break off any superfluous wafer paper when the biscuits are cold.

Almond Pound Cake

Ingredients

4½ oz. flour
½ tsp. baking powder
Smallest pinch of salt
¼ lb. fresh butter or margarine
¼ lb. caster sugar
2 eggs
2 oz. ground almonds
1 tbsp. sherry
Few drops almond essence
½ oz. whole almonds

Method

Sift the flour, baking powder and salt together. Cream the butter, add sugar, and cream together very thoroughly. Whisk the eggs and add gradually, beating well between each addition. Mix in the ground almonds lightly, add the sherry and essence, and sifted flour mixture (about one-third at a time). Put the mixture into a 6″ paper-lined tin and scatter evenly the shreds of almond over the top. Bake at 350° F. Therm. 4 for 1½ hr.

Almond Purée. See SOUPS.

Almond Sauce. See SAUCES.

Almond Tartlets (Fr. *tartlettes aux amandes*)

Ingredients

½ lb. short crust (see p. 375)
¾ oz. cornflour
1 whole egg
1 egg yolk
¼ lb. caster sugar
Little grated nutmeg
½ oz. butter
Strawberry or raspberry jam

Method

Roll out the paste to about ⅛″ thick. Stamp out some rounds and line a number of buttered patty pans. Prick the bottom of each pan to prevent blisters in baking. Mix the cornflour with the whole egg and egg yolk. Add the sugar and work in the ground almonds. Add the nutmeg and melted butter. Put a teaspoonful of jam into each lined mould, fill up with the mixture. Bake to a golden brown, at 350° F. Therm. 4 (about 15 mins.).

Almond (Burnt) Soufflé (Fr. *soufflé aux amandes pralinées*)

Ingredients

1 oz. caster sugar
1½ gills milk
1 oz. butter
1 oz. flour
2 oz. burnt almonds
3 eggs
10 drops vanilla essence

Method

Dissolve half the sugar with a few drops of water in a saucepan; stir until it is light brown in colour. Then add milk and boil up, stirring frequently. Melt the butter in another saucepan, stir in the flour, mixing well with a wooden spoon, and add gradually the prepared milk. Stir until it forms a smooth paste, then mix in the chopped burnt almonds and sugar mix. Allow to cool a little, then stir in one by

Almond (Burnt) Soufflé (*continued*)

one the 3 egg yolks, beat the mixture well, add the vanilla essence. Whisk the egg whites to a stiff froth; fold in with a metal spoon. Pour into a well-buttered mould, which has a buttered paper band round the edge. Steam for about 40 mins. Turn on to a hot dish, and serve with a suitable sweet sauce.

ALUM. Alum is a white transparent mineral salt having a very astringent quality. It is sometimes used to whiten flour. It can be used to clear gin which has become turbid by the addition of water.

Alum Whey

Ingredients
½ pt. milk
4 tbsp. raisin wine
½ pt. water
1 tsp. alum (powder)
Sugar

Method
Put the milk in a saucepan and bring to the boil. Add the raisin wine. If the milk does not turn, add a little more raisin wine. Return to heat, reboil and then remove from the heat until the curd has settled at the bottom. Pour the whey from the curd, and boil it up once more with the water, to which the alum and a little sugar to taste have been added.

AMBROSIA

Ingredients
6 seedless oranges
¼ lb. icing sugar
Madeira wine
½ lb. coconut

Method
Combine sliced oranges or orange segments, sugar, wine to taste for moistening, and grated coconut (fresh or canned). Sufficient for 3 or 4 persons.

AMERICAN CRESS or Land cress is a native of England and other parts of Europe. It is pleasant to taste, and is used in salads.

AMERICAN WEIGHTS See Weights and Measures, American.

ANCHOVY (Fr. *anchois*). A small fish, native to the Mediterranean. Though caught as far as the Black Sea, this fish is also obtained from the coasts of France, Portugal, Spain and the Channel Islands. The Gorgona fish are considered the best, while the Dutch, Russian and Norwegian varieties are distinguished by having no scales. Gorgona anchovies are imported both in brine and in oil, the Dutch in brine only, the Russian in brine and highly spiced vinegar, and the Norwegian in spiced brine.

ANCHOVY ESSENCE. Used for flavouring, generally a basic white sauce. Allow ½ tsp. (or more according to taste) to ¼ pt. sauce. A few drops of this essence greatly improve a beef gravy.

Anchovy and Caper Sauce

Ingredients
1 oz. butter
½ oz. flour
¼ pt. water
1 tbsp. chopped capers
2 anchovies
Lemon juice

Method
Melt the butter in a saucepan, add the flour, stirring the whole time with a wooden spoon. Then add the water, bring to the boil and add the boned and chopped anchovies and the bruised capers. Add a few drops of lemon juice and serve.

[16]

Anchovy Butter
Ingredients
5 tbsp. butter
1 tbsp. anchovy essence
Lemon juice

Method
Melt the butter in a small pan, combine with the anchovy essence, add a few drops of lemon juice and serve with fish or steak.

Anchovy Butter, Black
Ingredients
4 oz. butter
1 tsp. anchovy essence
1 tbsp. tarragon vinegar

Method
Put the butter in a saucepan, and let it become brown. Add the anchovy and tarragon vinegar. Cook for about 10 mins. and serve with broiled fish or lobsters.

Anchovy Eggs
Ingredients
2 hard-boiled eggs
2 oz. butter
Few drops anchovy essence
Cayenne pepper
Carmine if needed

Method
Remove egg shells, cut eggs in half and remove yolk. Rub yolk through a fine wire sieve, pound with the other ingredients. Pipe or pile this mixture into whites of egg. Serve on round of cucumber or beetroot, and garnish with watercress or lettuce.

Anchovy Fritters
Ingredients
2 doz. anchovies
Salad oil
Parsley
Batter (see p. 50)

Method
Cleanse, bone and fillet anchovies; steep them in vinegar for an hour or two, then dry them with a cloth. Take up the fillets and remove all the small bones. Spread them on a plate and add a little olive oil and chopped parsley. Five minutes before they are required, roll up each fillet, then dip them into batter, and plunge into a pan of fat so hot that, when water is dropped into it, it splutters and hisses. In a very short time the batter will be fried to a light brown, when the fritters must be removed with a skimmer. Place them on a strainer to dry, then arrange on a neatly folded napkin or ornamental dish-paper. Serve garnished with fried parsley.

Anchovy Salad
Ingredients
Garlic
¼ pt. olive oil
2 tins anchovy fillets
Chopped parsley
1½ tbsp. wine vinegar

Method
Rub the salad bowl with garlic; open tins of anchovy fillets and drain the oil into the salad bowl. Combine the olive oil, finely chopped parsley and wine vinegar. Add the anchovy fillets and green peppers

[17]

Anchovy Salad (*continued*)

2 green peppers
3 tomatoes
6 shallots
12 ripe olives

sliced into fine strips, and the blanched and seeded tomatoes cut into fifths (removing the small seed sections with a small sharp knife). Add the peeled, diced shallots and the ripe olives. Toss the ingredients and allow to stand for an hour at least before serving.

Anchovy Sauce. See SAUCES.

Anchovy Stuffing (*for Scoter or Waterfowl*)

Ingredients

2 large onions
2 handfuls breadcrumbs
Small piece of liver (of the bird)
Pinch of parsley
7 or 8 fillets of salted anchovies
Few capers
Pepper
1 egg yolk
Little milk

Method

Peel and chop the onions and fry in a little oil or butter till lightly browned. Add the two handfuls of breadcrumbs that have been dipped into water, and squeezed quite dry. Add a small piece of the bird's liver chopped finely, the parsley, the chopped anchovies and capers. Work well together, season with pepper and bind with lightly beaten egg yolk and a little milk.

Anchovy Toast

Ingredients

5 or 6 anchovies
2 rounds well-buttered toast
Mustard and cayenne pepper to season

Method

Wash anchovies and cut off their heads and fins. Fillet them (take out the backbone) and divide into two from shoulder to tail. Put a little mustard and cayenne on each slice of toast to suit the palate.

ANCHUSA. The leaves of this deciduous herbaceous plant are used in wine cups like borage, which they resemble.

ANEMONE. See PASQUE FLOWER.

ANEURIN. Vitamin B_1.

ANGELICA. The tender green tubular stems are preserved in sugar and used for decorating and flavouring sweet dishes. Used medicinally for making tea.
Angelica Jam. To each 2 lb. angelica allow $1\frac{1}{2}$ lb. sugar. Choose tender stems of angelica and cut them into strips of even length. Blanch them in boiling water for a few minutes to soften and then soak them in cold water for 12 hrs. Make the sugar into a syrup with $\frac{1}{2}$ teacup water, put the angelica in and cook until done. Afterwards pot in the usual way.

ANGEL'S BREAD. See COCONUT CAKE.

ANGELS ON HORSEBACK (Fr. *anges à cheval*)

Ingredients

2 doz. large oysters
12 bacon rashers
$\frac{1}{2}$ tsp. salt
$\frac{1}{8}$ tsp. pepper
$\frac{1}{8}$ tsp. paprika

Method

Drain the oysters, open and beard. Remove from shells. Cut the bacon rashers into half and lay an oyster in centre of each. Sprinkle with salt, pepper, paprika and chopped parsley. Roll the

[18]

ANGELS ON HORSEBACK (continued)

2 tbsp. chopped parsley	bacon round each oyster and fasten with
Lemon quarters	toothpick; place in a shallow baking dish.

bacon round each oyster and fasten with toothpick; place in a shallow baking dish. Bake at 450° F. Therm. 8 for 6 to 8 mins. or until the bacon is slightly browned and crisp. Serve very hot on preheated individual plates, and garnish with lemon quarters.

ANISE (Fr. *anis*). An aromatic plant, the seed of which is used for flavouring creams, pastries, puddings, salads, tea and liqueur, e.g. Kummel.

Aniseed Cakes

Ingredients
- 5 eggs
- 1 lb. sugar
- 1 lb. flour
- 1 dr. essence of aniseed

Method

Break the eggs into a basin, add sugar, beat well, then add gradually the flour and aniseed. Take small quantities up with a fork and drop lightly on to buttered baking sheets. Leave a small space between each. Set in a warm place to rise for 25 mins. Bake at 350° F. Therm. 4 for 25 mins.

ANNATTO. This colouring, made from the seeds of an evergreen tree, is used at times for colouring butter. See BUTTER (p. 93).

ANTIPASTO. Assorted appetisers of fish, cold meats, and/or vegetables.

APÉRITIF. A short drink taken before a meal to sharpen the appetite.

APPETISERS. Titbits of highly flavoured savoury foods served with sherry or cocktails. Appetisers need careful preparation and garnishing. Many hostesses find them useful for buffet meals and, in some instances, they may be easily adapted and used as savouries, or made in larger proportions and used as light luncheon and supper dishes. Choose the plates and dishes used for service in a colour scheme which is attractive to the eye; also ensure that an assortment of flavours is provided. Never overcrowd the dishes; rather use an extra dish than squash the food. Remember to serve hot appetisers piping hot, and cold appetisers really chilled. A simple platter of these titbits mixed makes an attractive and appetising dish instead of serving the different items individually. The smallest titbits may be served on sticks stuck into an orange or grapefruit pincushion-wise: cut a slice off the bottom of the fruit so that it will stand.

Biscuits with Foie Gras and Bacon. Take some small round biscuits or cracker biscuits, divided into halves, and spread them with foie gras. Garnish with small pieces of bacon and a little chopped chive.

Celery Stalks Stuffed. Take the young stalks of celery and, having pulled off the stringy parts, fill with scrambled egg and garnish with paprika. Serve carefully arranged on a dish of lettuce leaves or round the edge of a large platter.

Cheese and Parsley. Grate some cheese, add chopped parsley and a sprinkle of dry mustard and mix well together with a little melted margarine. Serve on small biscuits garnished with parsley.

Cheese Fluffs. Grate some cheese and add to cream cheese. Mix with a little cold fluffy mashed potato. Form into small balls and roll in grated cheese. Serve on lettuce leaves and garnish with slices of tomato, paprika and celery salt.

Cheese Straws. Roll out thinly about 2 oz. puff pastry, and cut it into two strips. Make a paste with a beaten egg, 1 oz. melted butter, 2 oz. grated cheese and ¼ tsp. each dry mustard, salt and cayenne. Spread this paste over one half of the pastry and cover with the other half. Brush with egg or milk and sprinkle with grated cheese and a little red pepper. Cut into fingers and bake at 400° F. Therm. 6 for about 10 mins. Serve piled high on a dish and garnish with cress.

Chutney Rolls. After cutting off the crusts, spread some thin slices of brown bread with chutney and at one end pile a little mustard and cress or cream cheese. Roll up lightly and cut into halves.

Cream Cheese Cubes. Put a little cream cheese on top of some pineapple or beetroot cubes, garnish with paprika and serve on small rounds of bread or toast, or on lettuce leaves.

Creamed Beetroct. Grate half a medium-sized beetroot into a small bowl of stiffly whisked cream. Fold together till the cream is pink. Serve well chilled on small biscuits garnished with chopped parsley.

Crisps and Ribbons. Remove the skin from some good-sized old potatoes and peel the potatoes into ribbons, as in peeling an apple. Cook in very hot fat. When brown, drain, reheat the fat and plunge in the potatoes and cook quickly to crisp. Drain again, sprinkle with celery salt and serve. For crisps, the potatoes should be cut into flat rounds about the size of a penny.

Egg Savoury. Break an egg into a bowl and beat up with 1 tbsp. milk, pour into a pan with a little melted butter and add chopped chives or onions, and sliced tomato. When set, serve on small fingers of toast or rounds of brown bread and garnish with watercress.

Flavoured Butters. These can be used on the smallest rounds of pastry, toast or bread. See BUTTERS.

Haddie Toasts. Take a little cooked finnan haddock, remove the skin and bones and pound the fish with a little melted margarine. If available add a little stiffly whisked cream or mayonnaise. Serve on small puff pastry slices, garnished with paprika.

Mock Caviare. Mix well together some chopped black olives and the roe of salted herrings, add a little oil or melted butter to moisten and season with pepper and salt and a little paprika. Serve spread on buttered toast fingers or cracker biscuits.

Prawns. Dissolve enough gelatine with a little warm water to make ¼ cup thick liquid. Shell some prawns, dip each in turn into the liquid and leave them to dry. Serve on a small mound of cold mashed potato—the prawns sticking out all over it—and garnish with lettuce leaves.

Sardine Rolls. Take 4 oz. puff pastry and roll out thinly. Cut into small squares and on each square place a sardine. Roll up, brush with a little milk and seal the edges. Place on a baking sheet. Bake at 400° F. Therm. 6. When the pastry has risen, brush with egg or milk and sprinkle with grated cheese and return to the oven to brown. Serve very hot piled high on a dish and garnished with cress.

Sausage Balls. Add a little mashed potato to ½ lb. sausage meat. Work well together and form into small balls. Dip into egg or milk and roll in grated cheese and oatmeal. Place on a baking sheet. Bake at 375° F. Therm. 5. Serve hot with a garnish of red pepper or chopped parsley.

Stuffed Olives. Place the stuffed olives on small mounds of cream cheese and serve with the smallest lettuce leaves.

Stuffed Prunes—I. Remove the stones from cooked prunes and stuff with cream cheese or grated cheese mixed with a little mayonnaise. Place each prune on a small round of thinly buttered brown bread with a cocktail stick through it.

Stuffed Prunes—II. Remove the stones of the prunes and roll lightly in thin rashers of bacon. Place them on a skewer and cook in a hot oven or under the grill. Remove the skewer, insert cocktail stick, and serve on small rounds of grilled cooked beetroot, garnished with watercress.

APPLE (Fr. *pomme*). The apple can be said to be the cook's friend because it is in season from one year's end to the other. Its sweet-acid flesh renders it particularly delicious in sweet foods, but when used as a sauce for meats its piquant flavour is, in the opinion of epicures, unequalled by that of any other fruit. The original apple in this country was a "crab", which is astringent and bitter.

Dessert apples take first place for quality; they are characterised by a firm juicy pulp, piquant flavour, regular form and colour. Cooking or kitchen apples are characterised by their property of "falling" into a pulpy mass of equal consistency when subjected to heat and, to a degree, by their large size and keeping qualities.

Some apples will "fall" in cooking when green, such as the codlins, and others will only do so when ripe, as the russets. Others again are equally good for dessert

APPLE (*continued*)

or cooking, and amongst these are some of the pippins. The addition of apples to some foods gives a wonderful zest to their appetising qualities. For instance, with pork and goose, apple sauce is essential to the gourmet's table, and in some parts of the country apple pie or pudding. With apple pie in Yorkshire a piece of cheese is often served. It is an old Yorkshire saying that "Applecake without cheese is like a kiss without a squeeze."

There are many varieties of apples, among them the following:

VARIETY	SEASON
Dessert or Cooking Apples	
Charles Ross	Oct. to end Dec.
Blenheim Orange	Nov. to end Feb.
Bramley's Seedling	Nov. to end March
Cooking Apples	
Early Victoria (Emneth Early)	Aug. to end Sept.
Lord Suffield	,, ,, ,,
Lord Grosvenor	,, ,, ,,
Bismark	Sept. to end Oct.
Stirling Castle	,, ,, ,,
Peasgood's Nonesuch	,, ,, ,,
Grenadier	,, ,, ,,
Lord Derby	Oct. to end Dec.
Ecklinville	,, ,, ,,
Golden Spire	,, ,, ,,
Royal Jubilee	,, ,, ,,
Gascoyne's Scarlet	Oct. to end Jan.
Lane's Prince Albert	Nov. to end March
Dessert Apples	
Gladstone	July to end Aug.
Beauty of Bath	Aug. to end Sept.
King of Pippins	
James Grieve	Sept. to end Oct.
St. Everard	,, ,, ,,
Wm. Crump	,, ,, ,,
Ellison's Orange	,, ,, ,,
Low Lambourne	,, ,, ,,
Worcester Pearmain	,, ,, ,,
Allington Pippin	Oct. to end Dec.
Laxton's Superb	Nov. to end Feb.
Cox's Orange Pippin	,, ,, ,,
Belle de Boskoop	,, ,, ,,
Roundway Magnum **Bonum**	,, ,, ,,
Baumann's Reinette	Nov. to end March
Sturmer Pippin	Feb. to end May
Warner's King	Nov. to end March
Newton Wonder	,, ,, ,,

TO PEEL AND CORE. If scalding water is poured over the apples they will peel more easily. Use a very sharp knife or peeler, and peel thinly and evenly. To core, use a corer. This will remove the core without breaking or damaging the apple.

TO PRESERVE. See **FRUIT** and **BIFFINS**.

TO PRESERVE COLOUR. If peeled apples are soaked for 15 mins. in cold water to which a little lemon juice has been added, they will retain their colour during cooking.

TO STORE. Lay the apples on the floor or shelf so that they do not touch one another. They should be frequently examined and any that show signs of decay should be removed. Rough-skinned apples and russets keep best.

APPLES FOR DESSERT. See **FRUIT** (p. 228).

[21]

Apples with Apricot Jam
Ingredients
12 small apples
Apricot jam
Sugar

Method
Peel and core the apples, cut into slices about the thickness of a halfpenny piece. Place a layer of apricot jam on a dish, cover with apples, and then more jam. Continue in this way in layers forming a dome. Sprinkle freely with caster sugar. Bake at 350° F. Therm. 4 for about 20 mins. Sufficient for 4 to 6 persons.

Apples, Baked
Ingredients
Apples
Brown sugar or syrup
Butter
Jam or sultanas or cinnamon

Method
Core the apples and wipe clean. With a darning needle prick a few holes in the skin or with a knife make a ring round, cutting the skin only, as if to divide into half crosswise. Put on baking tray or oven-glass dish, then fill the centres with a little sugar or syrup, butter and a few sultanas or jam or sprinkle cinnamon over. Bake at 350° F. Therm. 4 till tender. The time depends on the kind of apple as some take longer than others.

Apple Batter Pudding
Ingredients
½ lb. flour
Pinch of salt
½ pt. milk
2 eggs
Apples
Sugar
Lemon rind

Method
Put the sifted flour and salt into a bowl, and stir in the milk very gradually. Beat till quite smooth, then add the eggs. Well butter a pie-dish and pour half the batter into it. Bake at 400° F. Therm. 6 until quite firm. Nearly fill the dish with apples pared, cored and sliced, and slightly stewed with a little sugar and lemon rind. Pour remaining batter in and return to oven for 1½ hr. Sufficient for 6 persons.

Apple Bavoise
Ingredients
4 lb. sweet apples
Juice of 2 lemons
1 or 2 wineglasses sherry
8 oz. caster sugar
1 oz. isinglass
1 gill warm water
1 pt. whipped cream or evaporated milk

Method
Peel the apples and cut into quarters, place in a preserving pan with the lemon juice, sherry and sugar. Dissolve the isinglass in warm water, strain and add. Place the pan over a moderate heat, stirring occasionally with a wooden spoon, stew till the apples are quite tender, and rub them through a tammy sieve into a basin. Place this on ice or in a refrigerator until upon the point of setting, when the whipped cream must be

Apple Bavoise (*continued*)

stirred in, and the whole poured into a wetted mould. Turn out when set. If desired, a wineglass of maraschino or noyau can be added; it gives a considerably richer flavour. Sufficient for 6 persons.

Apple Black Caps
Ingredients

Firm juicy apples
Cloves or mixed spice or cinnamon
Sweet wine
Sugar
Lemon rind

Method

Peel and core the apples, and fill each with a little pounded sugar and 2 cloves or flavouring. Place them in a shallow dish with a little sweet wine, sugar to taste, and a little lemon rind. Let them cook very slowly at 350° F. Therm. 4 until soft (about 30 mins.) though not broken. Then place under hot grill for few minutes to darken them on top. Serve hot or cold. Allow 1 apple per person.

Apple and Blackberry Jam. See BLACKBERRY.

Apple Butter
Ingredients

Small quantity of apples
Cider
Little mixed spice or a few cloves
Demerara sugar

Method

Peel and quarter the apples. Place in preserving pan with cider and seasoning over a low heat, and bring to the boil. Then reduce heat and simmer slowly until the whole is of a thick, smooth consistency. A little demerara sugar may then be added.

Apple Cake Pudding
Ingredients

6 large apples
3 large boiled potatoes
8 oz. sugar
Rind and juice of 2 lemons
4 eggs

Method

Peel and core the apples and boil them in just sufficient water to cover. Reduce to a pulp, strain, add the dry mashed potatoes, the sugar and lemon rind and juice, and the well-beaten eggs. Stir to a smooth batter, pour into a buttered pudding basin and steam for 2 hrs. Serve with Lemon sauce.

Apple Charlotte (Fr. *charlotte de pommes*)
Ingredients   *Method*

Several slices of white bread
4 tbsp. melted butter
Apple sauce
1 tbsp. rum
6 oz. apricot jam

Remove the crusts from the bread, and cut 12 long triangles. Fry gently in the melted butter. Line the bottom of a smooth mould with these triangles (with the points meeting in the centre). Line the sides with rectangles which have been cut to the height of the mould and lightly fried. Fill the mould with apple sauce.

Apple Charlotte (*continued*)

Bake at 375° F. Therm. 5. Turn upside-down on a dessert dish and serve with sauce made by heating the apricot jam and adding rum to flavour. Sufficient for 5 to 6 persons.

Apple Cheese Cakes

Ingredients
Apple pulp
Lemon juice
Grated lemon rind
1 egg yolk
Sugar
Butter
Puff pastry

Method
Beat together with a wooden spoon the apple pulp, lemon juice, grated lemon rind and egg yolk with sufficient sugar to sweeten; add a little warmed butter and turn into lined patty tins. Bake at 400° F. Therm. 6 for 15–20 mins. Turn on to dish and serve.

Apple Chutney

Ingredients
6 apples
4 small onions
6 oz. sultanas
½ tsp. each salt and essence of anchovy
1 tbsp. olive oil
2 tbsp. tomato sauce
1 tsp. ground ginger
½ tsp. cayenne
1 tbsp. vinegar

Method
Peel and core apples, mince finely, add peeled and minced onions, sultanas, and place in a mortar and pound. Add salt, essence of anchovy, olive oil, tomato sauce, ground ginger, and cayenne. Pound fine, add vinegar, then put into jars. Cover securely until required.

Apple and Crumb Pudding

Ingredients
Apples
Breadcrumbs
Cinnamon
Sugar

Method
Cover the bottom of a well-greased deep dish with breadcrumbs. Over that put a layer of apples, peeled, cored and cut into thin slices; sprinkle lightly with cinnamon and sufficient sugar to taste. Continue in this way till the dish is full. Bake at 240° F. Therm. ¼ for 30 mins. Turn on to a hot dish, pour round a little cream or custard. See also **BROWN BETTY.**

Apple and Currant Soup

Ingredients
12 apples
Few slices bread
Lemon peel
Water
6 oz. currants
½ pt. milk
Sugar to taste
Cloves

Method
Peel and core the apples and place in saucepan with bread, lemon peel, and sufficient water to cover. Place over a low heat and stew until the apples are soft and pulpy. Pass through a sieve and return to saucepan with currants, milk, sugar and cloves. Reheat, simmer for a few minutes, and serve.

Apple Dumplings, Baked. Apple dumplings may be baked or boiled (see below); in each case the pastry is made to suit the method of cooking.

Ingredients

Apples
Sugar
Butter
Cinnamon
Short crust

Method

First peel and core the apples and fill up the cavity with sugar, butter and a sprinkle of cinnamon. Cut some rounds of ¼″ thick paste rather larger than the apples and cover the fruit, leaving no cracks. (Put each apple on a round of pastry, close the pastry round it and pinch together.) Bake the dumplings on an oven tin at 360° F. Therm. 5 for about 1 hr. and then just before they are done, damp the tops with a little milk, and sprinkle lightly with sugar. Return to oven for a few minutes to glaze. Any juice which has oozed out may be used as a sauce by adding a little sugar, butter and nutmeg.

Apple Dumplings, Boiled. Use suet crust for these dumplings and proceed as above. Drop the dumplings into boiling water and keep them boiling the whole time, or they will be heavy. Sometimes the dumplings are boiled in a fish net to make a pattern over them, or in a floured cloth. When done, remove net cloth or cloth and serve with sugar, lemon and butter.

Apple Fritters. See FRITTER.

Apple Ginger

Ingredients

4 lb. apples (all green or all yellow)
4 lb. sugar
1 qt. water
2 oz. essence of ginger

Method

Pare the fruit and remove the core; cut into shapes as like a ginger root as possible. Boil the sugar and water for 25 mins. to a nice syrup. Then place the apples in the syrup, keeping it boiling the whole time, stirring as little as possible. Add the ginger; it will take about an hour to clear and become yellow. Skim well.

Apple Jam—I

Ingredients

4 lb. apples
4 lb. sugar
¼ oz. ground ginger
Juice and rind of 2 lemons
Few cloves

Method

Peel and cut the apples as for a pie. Place in saucepan with other ingredients. Boil for 1½ hr. without adding water. Pour into warm jars and seal when cool.

Apple Jam—II

Ingredients

4 lb. green cooking apples
Sugar
Water

Method

Peel and core apples, weigh fruit and allow an equal amount of sugar. Boil sugar in as little water as possible; add

C.C.D.—2

[25]

Apple Jam—II (*continued*)
Grated rind of 4 lemons
1 tsp. grated ginger

chopped apples, lemon rind and ginger. Allow to simmer until the apples are tender and clear. Test for setting, then bottle and cover.

Apple Jelly
Ingredients
3 lb. apples
Approximately 1 qt. water
Sugar

Method
Quarter and core apples, but do not peel. Simmer gently in water until tender. Strain, without squeezing, through a hair sieve or muslin. Measure juice and allow 1 lb. sugar to every pint of juice. Place juice and preheated sugar in saucepan and boil for 25 mins. Pour into glass jars and cover when cold.

Apple (Crab) Jelly
Ingredients
3 lb. crab apples
1 qt. water
Sugar

Method
Take ripe crab apples, core them but do not remove peel. Bring them to the boil with the water, and when pulped, strain through a jelly bag. Measure and return to pan. Allow ¾ lb. sugar to each pint of juice. Boil juice with sugar until jelly sets, about 20 mins. Pour into warm jars and cover when cool.

Apple Marmalade
Ingredients
2 lb. good apples
1 lb. sugar
1 pt. sweet cider

Method
Peel, core and quarter apples, and place in saucepan with cider and sugar. Allow to cook gently for 3 hrs., until the fruit is soft enough to put through a sieve. More sugar may be added if not sweet enough. Pour into warmed jars and seal as jam.

Apple Meringue
Ingredients
12 apples
2 oz. sugar
Apricot jam
5 egg whites
Caster sugar

Method
Peel and core the apples, cut them into quarters and put into a saucepan with the sugar. Cook until tender. Turn on to a sieve over a basin to drain off all the juice. Arrange the pulp at the bottom of a dish and put a layer of apricot jam over it. Beat the whites of egg to a snowy froth and spread over the dish; dust this with caster sugar and bake at 350° F. Therm. 4 for a few minutes to dry the egg froth. Remove from the oven before it colours, and serve at once.

Apple Plate Pies
Ingredients
- ½ lb. short crust
- Apples
- Sugar
- Nutmeg
- Butter
- Water

Method

Peel, core and slice the apples across the core-hole, making rings. Line some patty tins with good puff paste and fill with 2 layers of apple slices, sprinkle with caster sugar and nutmeg, and put into each a piece of butter the size of a walnut and 1 tbsp. cold water. Bake at 360° F. Therm. 4. The apples soon become transparent and dry and the crust lightly browned.

Apple Pudding, Boiled
Ingredients
- ½ lb. suet crust
- 1½ lb. apples
- Sugar
- Cloves
- Water

Method

Line a greased pie-dish with suet pastry (see p. 375). Fill with prepared fruit, add a little sugar, a few cloves and 4 tbsp. water. Damp the edges and cover with a small round of pastry, pressing together and folding the edges well over. Cover with scalded, floured and pleated cloth. Tie on firmly and boil as directed. See **PUDDINGS,** TO BOIL and TO STEAM.

Apple Pupton. A kind of apple pudding made with apple pulp, breadcrumbs, butter, eggs and sugar, baked in a mould and served with fruit syrup (hot).

Apple Salad
Ingredients
- Apples
- Lettuce leaves
- Cream cheese
- Chopped parsley
- Celery, if desired

Method

Peel, core and dice the apples. Dress with Lemon dressing (see **SALAD DRESSINGS**). Serve on lettuce leaves, garnish with cream cheese and diced celery and a little finely chopped parsley.

Apple Sauce. See SAUCES.

Apple Snow. This is the name of a sweet dish composed of apple pulp or purée, mixed with sugar and combined with some stiffly whipped cream and white of egg. The mixture is piled high in a glass dish, and decorated with fruit jelly.

Apple Sponge Pudding
Ingredients
- 1 lb. cooking apples
- 4 oz. sugar
- 3 oz. butter
- 1 egg
- 5 oz. flour
- ½ tsp. baking powder
- Pinch of cinnamon
- Small pinch of salt

Method

Peel, core and slice the apples. Place in a greased pie-dish and sprinkle over 1 oz. sugar. Cream the butter with the remaining sugar, beat in the egg, then add the flour previously sifted with the baking powder, cinnamon and salt. Spread evenly over the apples. Bake at 360° F. Therm. 4 for 45 mins.

[27]

Apple Tansy. This is a kind of apple fritter; the batter is made with cream and eggs, and poured over the partially stewed apples. These fritters are fried in butter and served very hot.

Apple One Crust and Two Crust Pies. See **PASTE AND PASTRY** (p. 369).

APRICOT (Fr. *abricot*). There are many varieties of apricot. The coarser ones do well for cooking, and the green fruit, or thinnings, can be used for tarts, like gooseberries. The Chinese preserve apricots and make lozenges of the clarified juice, which, when dissolved in water, make a pleasant beverage. Tinned or dried apricots are also much used, often combined with other fruits. Fresh apricots, halved, peeled and sliced may be served with sugar and cream. Slice or halve the apricots and cover with sugar; add Kirsch, cognac or apricot liqueur, or combine the apricots with raspberries or strawberries, adding sugar and Kirsch.

TO PEEL. Dip the apricots into boiling water for one or two minutes. The skin can then be taken off easily with a sharp knife.

TO DRY AND USE DRIED. Blanch the apricots, halve and remove stones. Lay on baking tins and bake at 200° F. Therm. ¼ for 4–6 hrs. When using this fruit dried, allow 2 pt. water to each 1 lb. dried fruit. Place the fruit in a bowl, cover with water and allow to stand overnight. Next day make a syrup of 2 oz. sugar to each pint water, simmer fruit gently for 30–35 mins. and use as desired.

Apricot D'Artois. Roll out puff paste rather thinly, to about the size of the baking sheet. Lay the paste on the sheet and spread apricot jam all over it. Roll out another piece the same size, pick up by winding over the rolling pin, and cover. Decorate by using the back of a knife to mark out equal-sized diamonds, about 2″ × 1″. Bake at 360° F. Therm. 4.

Apricot Bonnes Bouches. Use a biscuit crust (see **PASTE AND PASTRY**). Put through piping bag and squeeze out into rounds about 1½″ diameter on to a sheet of stiff paper spread over a baking tin. Sprinkle with a little caster sugar and bake at 360° F. Therm. 4 till light golden brown. When cooked remove from the oven and trim. Remove paper by inverting and damping and cool biscuits on a wire sieve. Place half an apricot on each, glaze with Noyau-flavoured icing, leave in warmth to dry. Use as required.

Apricot Brandy

Ingredients
2 doz. apricots
½ lb. sugar
Water
Brandy

Method
Place the apricots in a saucepan with syrup made with the sugar and water. Boil them up in this, then remove fruit, place in jars and when cool cover with brandy. Cover securely and leave for several days. Use as desired.

Apricot Charlotte Russe

Ingredients
Finger biscuits
1 pt. apricot marmalade
1 oz. gelatine
1 gill water
1 qt. whipped cream

Method
Line a plain mould with the finger biscuits, pack in ice and place in refrigerator. Rub the marmalade through a sieve, put into a basin and stir in the gelatine, dissolved in the water. Then strain, put the basin on ice, and work until the mixture begins to freeze. Add the cream. Mix well and fill the mould with mixture. Place to chill. Turn out charlotte before serving.

[28]

Apricot Cheese. Take any kind of apricot, parboil, reduce to pulp by beating in a mortar, or with a fork. Pass through a sieve. Add ½ lb. caster sugar to each 1 lb. purée and the kernels of the half stones, nicely blanched. Boil until thickened, then pour into buttered moulds. Bake at 200° F. Therm. ¼. When firm, serve with whipped cream.

Apricot Chips

Ingredients
2 lb. sugar
1 pt. water
1 lb. unpeeled apricots

Method
Make a thick syrup by boiling the sugar and water together until it is nearly candied. Put in the fruit and allow to stand for 2 hrs. Simmer very gently but on no account allow to boil. Remove from heat and allow to stand overnight. Next day remove chips from the syrup, spread them on plates to dry.

Apricots, Compôte of. Divide and remove the kernels from a dozen ripe apricots and stew the fruit in a little light syrup until done, with the rind of a lemon pared very thinly. Next prepare a border of rice round a dish, fill in the centre with the apricots, then pour some whipped cream over the top and sprinkle with pistachio nuts chopped finely.

Apricot Cream

Ingredients
12 ripe apricots
¼ lb. caster sugar
Water
½ oz. gelatine
1 pt. whipped cream

Method
Divide and remove the kernels from the apricots, and put fruit into a saucepan with the sugar and a little water. Stew gently until soft, then add the gelatine. Rub through a sieve and mix with the cream, adding a little extra sugar if required. Pour into a fancy mould and leave to set. To serve, dip the mould into warm water to loosen the cream, and turn on to a glass dish.

Apricot Flawn. Butter a flawn circle, place on a baking sheet, line with puff pastry (see p. 374) and trim level to the rim. Mask the bottom with sugar, and arrange halves of peeled or tinned apricots, sufficient to fill it to the rim of paste. Sprinkle over with sugar, bake at 260° F. Therm. ½ for 35 mins.

Apricot Fritters—I (Fr. *beignets d'abricots*)

Ingredients
1 lb. brioche paste
Apricot jam

Method
Make 1 lb. brioche paste (see p. 81), using only ¼ lb. butter, and allow to stand for 3 hrs. to rise. Then lay paste on board, fold it over and roll out thickly. Fold over again, leave in a cool place, then when firm roll out to ⅛″ thickness. Stamp into rounds with 2″ cutter; moisten the top edge of the rounds with a little brush dipped into water, and place ½ tsp. apricot jam in the centre of each. Cover with a second round of paste and press two together, taking care to make the

[29]

Apricot Fritters—I (*continued*)

edges stick fast. Prick round the top, about ⅛″ from edge and fry the fritters in warm fat. Drain and sprinkle with some fine sugar. Pile on a napkin on a dish garnished with cherries and angelica.

Apricot Fritters—II
Ingredients
4 oz. flour
Pinch of salt
½ pt. water
½ pt. milk
2 egg whites
1 lb. apricots

Method
Make a light batter with the flour, salt and water. Stir briskly till quite smooth, then add the milk, and the whites of eggs beaten to a froth. Peel, halve and stone the apricots, draw them through the batter, and fry them in boiling oil or butter until they are nicely browned. Drain and pile on to a folded napkin and serve with sifted sugar. Sufficient for 4 or 5 persons. See also FRITTER.

Apricot Gâteau
Ingredients
3 eggs and 3 oz. caster sugar for Genoese Paste (see p. 113)
1 tbsp. apricot jam
2 tbsp. apricot marmalade
Ratafia biscuits
Few pistachio nuts
Half a crystallised or glacé apricot

Method
Prepare the Genoese pastry and bake it in a 6″ paper-lined cake tin for about ¾ hr. in a moderate oven (350°F. Therm. 4). Allow the pastry to cool, split in half transversely and spread with a layer of apricot jam. Fit together again and mask completely with apricot marmalade. Put the half of preserved apricot in the centre and arrange the pistachios (halved lengthwise) radiating from it. Arrange the ratafia biscuits in rows around the edge of the cake.

Apricot Ice
Ingredients
1 lb. chopped apricots
1 pt. water
Kernels from ½ lb. apricots
½ lb. sugar
2 egg whites
3 ripe apricots

Method
Stew the chopped apricots in the water for a few minutes, with the kernels and sugar. Rub the fruit through a strainer with the back of a spoon; mix in the syrup and freeze. When it is nearly set, add the stiffly whipped egg whites and put to freeze. Just before serving cut up 2 or 3 very ripe apricots and stir into the ice. (Tinned apricots can be used if desired.)

Apricot Jam—I
Ingredients
3 lb. fresh apricots
2½ lb. sugar

Method
Peel and halve the apricots, remove stones and lay fruit in a dish; sprinkle over 1 lb. sugar and allow to stand for

Apricot Jam—I (*continued*)

24 hrs. Next day place fruit, syrup and remaining sugar in preserving pan with a few blanched kernels, thinly sliced. Bring to boil, stirring gently, and boil gently for 30 mins. until the fruit is tender. Test for setting, pour into warmed jars and cover.

Apricot Jam—II (*from dried fruits*)
Ingredients
  2 lb. dried apricots
  6 lb. loaf sugar
  6 pt. water
  Few almonds

Method
Cut each apricot in half, place in large bowl with water and allow to stand for three days and three nights. Then place all in preserving pan with few finely chopped almonds. Bring to boil slowly, and allow to boil for 30 mins. until jam thickens. Test for setting, pour into warmed jars and cover.

Apricot Marmalade
Ingredients
  1 lb. apricot jam
  1 tbsp. lemon juice

Method
Sieve the apricot jam through a wire sieve; this will cause the jam to become cloudy, but the clearness is easily restored by placing the sieved jam in a saucepan with the lemon juice and bringing to the boil over a low heat. Stir gently the whole time. Pour the marmalade into a jar and tie down unless required for immediate use.

Apricot Omelet
Ingredients
  6 egg yolks
  4 egg whites
  Pinch of salt
  Apricot jam

Method
Put the yolks and whites of eggs into a basin, sprinkle over salt and beat well together. Pour the mixture into an omelet pan (see OMELET) which has a little melted butter in it. As soon as it is set turn out carefully on to a well-heated dish, spread with apricot jam or marmalade and fold omelet. Sprinkle with caster sugar and glaze in oven before serving.

Apricot Pie
Ingredients
  Pastry
  Apricots
  Sugar
  2 or 3 oz. butter

Method
Take a pie-dish and make sufficient pastry to cover it. Lay closely pressed round the border of the dish (previously wetted) a band of pastry 3″ wide and ½″ thick. Fill the dish with halves of apricots (unripe fruit can be used if desired). Add sugar to sweeten and the butter. Roll out

Apricot Pie (*continued*)

pastry to make a crust, having wetted the band with pastry brush. Cover the pie, press edges down, trim off with an upright knife and notch round with back of knife or ornament if desired. Brush top with egg white and milk, sprinkle on caster sugar and bake at 350° F. Therm. 4 for 1¼ hrs. If to be served cold, omit the butter.

Apricot Pudding
Ingredients
   2 doz. apricots
   6 oz. sugar
   ¾ pt. water
   Suet crust.

Method
Divide the apricots and remove stones. Place the halves in a saucepan with the sugar and water and parcook over a low heat. Turn into pudding basin which has been previously well buttered and lined with suet crust (see p. 374). Cover top, pinch edges together and tie over a pudding cloth. Plunge into boiling water and boil for 2 hrs. Remove from saucepan and untie cloth. Turn out on to a pre-heated dish and serve. By running the edge of a small knife round the edge of the basin between it and the pudding, the latter turns out more easily.

Apricot Sauce. See SAUCES.

Apricot Soufflé (Fr. *soufflé aux abricots*)
Ingredients
   12 large ripe apricots
   3 tbsp. sugar
   3 tbsp. ground rice or flour
   Walnut of butter
   ½ pt. new milk or cream
   4 eggs

Method
Peel, stone and slice apricots, place them in a saucepan with sugar and add a little water. Place over a low heat and simmer until reduced to pulp. Then mix in smoothly the rice or flour, butter and new milk or cream. When the liquid boils, add to it the lightly beaten egg yolks. Well oil a soufflé tin and line with paper (see SOUFFLÉ). At the last moment fold in with a metal spoon the stiffly whisked whites of eggs. Bake at 400° F. Therm. 6 for 30 mins. Let the soufflé be taken out and eaten at once or it will be ruined.

Apricot Tart, Green
Ingredients
   Green apricots
   Sugar (half weight of fruit)
   Puff paste

Method
Place the apricots in a saucepan with a little water and stew gently with the sugar. When they are soft and tender, place fruit and syrup in a pie-dish which

Apricot Tart, Green (*continued*)

has been lined with puff paste. Cover with paste and bake in a moderate oven 350° F. Therm. 4 for 30 mins. If desired, stiffly beaten whites of eggs, with a little caster sugar added, may be spread over top of tart, and placed in oven for 5 mins. Do not allow topping to become coloured.

Apricot Tartlets. See PASTE AND PASTRY (p. 374).

Apricot Wine

Ingredients
- 12 lb. apricots
- 3 gall. water
- 1 lb. sugar
- 1 tbsp. brewer's yeast
- 1 pt. Rhenish or other white wine

Method
Boil the sliced apricots in the water with the sugar for 30 mins. Then strain off the liquor into a pan. Add a few kernels from the fruit, cover the vessel and allow the liquid to cool. When cool, mix in the brewer's yeast and leave for 3–4 days to ferment. Then pour off the clear liquid into a cask, which must be scrupulously clean and allow to remain until the fermentation is ended. Add the white wine and close the cask for 6 mths. At the end of that time it should be decanted into bottles, and kept for a year longer before being used. Sufficient to make 3 gall.

AROMATIC CORDIAL

Ingredients
- 2 oz. ground ginger
- ½ oz. pepper
- 1 oz. cardamom seeds
- ½ oz. bruised cinnamon
- ½ oz. mace
- ½ oz. orange peel in 1 qt. good whisky

Method
Mix together ingredients. Allow to stand for 2 wks. tightly corked. Then strain and bottle. It is good to take 2 or 3 tsp. in wine or water when suffering from indigestion or debility.

ARROWHEAD. This water plant, the roots of which are dried and powdered, is used in the same way as arrowroot in invalid cookery.

ARROWROOT. This is prepared from the root or tuber of the maranta, a plant which grows in the West Indies and India. It bears pretty spikes of small white flowers. It is called "arrowroot" because it was at one time confused with the roots of another plant with which the Indians used to poison their arrows.

TO PREPARE. Mix 1 dsp. arrowroot with a little cold water. Pour on it, very gradually, ½ pt. water boiled with a little lemon rind. Stir briskly, and allow to boil for a few minutes. Add sugar to taste, and a little sherry or port wine. For infants, a drop of cinnamon water or essence of caraway seeds may be added. Fresh milk may be substituted for the water, and the wine omitted.

TO THICKEN SAUCES. Arrowroot may be used to thicken sauces for those who object to butter, as invalids often do. Mix 1 dsp. arrowroot with a little cold water until it is a smooth paste. Add to 1 pt. liquid, and continue boiling for 4–5 mins. stirring continually.

2*   [33]

Arrowroot Blancmange

Ingredients

1 tbsp. arrowroot
2 tbsp. cold water
1½ pt. milk
1 bay leaf or rind of 1 lemon
1 dsp. sugar

Method

Mix the arrowroot and water into a smooth paste. Place the milk in a saucepan with the sugar and bay leaf or lemon rind, and when it boils, strain and pour over the arrowroot. Return to heat and allow to thicken, then pour into a wetted mould. A little brandy may be added, if desired, before placing the mixture in the mould. To obtain a glistening appearance the mould should be oiled instead of rinsed with cold water. Garnish with bright red jelly or jam.

Arrowroot Custard

Ingredients

1 pt. milk
2 oz. caster sugar
1 tbsp. arrowroot
2 egg yolks
Vanilla or other flavouring

Method

Place the milk in a saucepan and bring to boil with sugar. Mix the arrowroot to a smooth paste with a little cold milk. Pour over the boiling milk, add flavouring, return to heat and boil until mixture thickens. Remove from heat, beat in eggs and stir until they thicken.

Arrowroot Jelly

Ingredients

Rind of 1 lemon
1 tbsp. sugar
1 cup water
3 tbsp. arrowroot
1 tbsp. brandy
Juice of 4 lemons
3 drops almond flavouring

Method

Soak the lemon rind and sugar in cupful of cold water. Allow it to stand for 4 hrs. Then strain the liquid and mix with the arrowroot to a smooth paste. Add the brandy, lemon juice and almond flavouring. Place in a saucepan, stir until it is thick. Pour into wetted moulds and allow to cool.

Arrowroot, Nourishing (*for invalids and sick children*). Boil ½ oz. hartshorn shavings and a little lemon rind in 1 pt. water for 15 mins. Strain, and pour the liquid on 2 dsp. arrowroot which has been previously mixed with a little cold water. Stir briskly, and boil for a few minutes. Add 1 tsp. sugar and a glass of wine.

Arrowroot Pudding, Baked

Ingredients

2 tbsp. arrowroot
1½ pt. milk
Little grated nutmeg
1 tbsp. sugar
Walnut of butter

Method

Mix the arrowroot with a little water. Place the milk in a saucepan with the nutmeg and sugar and bring to the boil. When boiling, pour over the arrowroot and add the butter. Pour into well-greased fireproof dish, bake at 350° F. Therm. 4 for 1–1¼ hr.

[34]

Arrowroot Pudding, Steamed

Ingredients

- 2 tbsp. arrowroot
- 2 pt. milk
- Flavouring (cinnamon, lemon, orange or almond)
- 3 eggs
- 1 tbsp. sugar
- 1 tbsp. brandy

Method

Mix the arrowroot to a smooth paste with a cupful of the milk. Place remaining milk in a saucepan, add desired flavouring and bring to boil. Pour over the arrowroot, stirring well, and when cool add the well-beaten eggs, sugar and brandy. Place in a well-greased fireproof dish and steam for 1½ hr. Serve garnished with a ring of jam.

Arrowroot Sauce. See SAUCES.

Arrowroot Soufflé

Ingredients

- 4 tbsp. arrowroot
- 1½ pt. milk
- 2 tbsp. sugar
- Grated rind of ½ lemon
- 6 egg yolks
- 6 egg whites

Method

Mix the arrowroot with a cupful of the milk until it is a smooth paste. Stir gradually into a saucepan containing remaining milk which has been boiled. Add the sugar and finely grated lemon rind. Allow to simmer for 15 mins. and stir frequently. Remove from heat and allow to cool. Then stir in well-beaten yolks of eggs. Oil a plain mould, then whisk to a stiff froth the whites of eggs and fold in with a metal spoon. Fill the mould three parts full, and bake at 400° F. Therm. 6 for 20 mins. Serve immediately. Sufficient for 5 or 6 persons.

Arrowroot Water (*a drink for invalids*)

Ingredients

- Rind of 1 lemon
- 1 qt. water
- 1 tbsp. arrowroot
- 2 tbsp. wine or brandy or water

Method

Boil the thinly peeled lemon rind in the water. When boiling, pour over the arrowroot, which has been previously mixed with the wine, brandy or water. Sweeten to taste, and, stirring frequently, allow to boil for a further 2 or 3 mins. A little lemon juice may be added if desired.

ARTICHOKE (Fr. *artichaut*). There are two kinds of artichoke frequently used in this country. In the Green or Globe artichoke the flower is the edible part and in the Jerusalem artichoke it is the tuberous root. The latter is most common. There are three kinds of fresh Globe artichokes commonly cultivated, but the variety with the green (not purplish) head is generally reckoned the best, and it is the largest. In France they are eaten raw as a salad. The very small may be trimmed and used as "artichoke hearts" forming small cups to hold hot or cold food. The Chinese artichoke, a native of Japan and North China, is rather a rarity in this country; it possesses small irregular tubers which are edible, slightly resembling the Jerusalem artichoke in flavour. The stringy ends should be cut off before cooking. When cooked, serve with butter as the Globe artichokes.

TO DRY. Wash the artichokes in two or three waters. Put them for ¼ hr. in plenty

Artichoke

ARTICHOKE (*continued*)

of fast-boiling water. Drain and bake at 300° F. Therm. 2 for about 1 hr. Allow them to cool. Repeat this several times, until they are quite dry. They should be kept in a dry place, well covered.

ARTICHOKES (GLOBE), BOILED. Soak the artichokes, and wash them in several waters to expel the insects. Cut the stalks even, and trim away the lower leaves and the ends from the upper ones. Boil in plenty of salted water for 30–40 mins., with the tops downwards and allow to remain over heat until leaves can be easily drawn out. Prepare a little white sauce to be served separately, or remove the "choke", the core of the artichoke, and fill hollow with sauce. The leaves of the artichokes are pulled out, dipped in sauce and eaten. Or the artichokes may be quartered and the "choke" removed. When these quarters are thoroughly cleaned they should be rubbed with lemon, and then half boiled in acidulated salted water. After draining they are placed in a flat stewpan with a knob of butter, and a little seasoning, and boiled over a low heat. They are served with brown or white sauce (see SAUCES), finished with chopped parsley and the juice of a lemon.

ARTICHOKES (JERUSALEM), BOILED. Wash and pare the artichokes and throw each root into cold water, to which a squeeze of lemon juice may be added, to preserve the colour. Cut a little piece off one end, so that each one will stand, and taper the other end. Boil in milk and water until tender (20–40 mins.) then stand on a dish with points uppermost, and pour over them a good white sauce.

ARTICHOKES (JERUSALEM), FRICASSÉED. Boil some artichokes in boiling water until they are tender enough to allow a fork to be passed through. Remove from water and drain. Place a cupful of milk in a saucepan with a little salt, pepper, powdered cinnamon, and thicken with a little butter rolled in flour. Turn the artichokes in this and allow to simmer gently for 5–6 mins.

ARTICHOKES (GLOBE), FRIED. Wash and trim three young, freshly cut artichokes. Cut into thin slices, and place in bowl of water to which a cupful of vinegar has been added (this is to preserve the colour). Drain and season with a pinch of salt and pepper. Make a batter with 3 eggs, 2 tbsp. oil and 2 tbsp. flour. When well mixed, put the slices of artichokes into it and stir gently for 3 or 4 mins. until every piece of artichoke is covered. Fry gently in hot fat, until the vegetable is thoroughly cooked and browned. Drain, pile on a napkin and garnish with fried parsley.

ARTICHOKES (JERUSALEM), FRIED. Pare and cut the artichokes in slices about $\frac{1}{8}''$ thick, and fry in boiling oil or lard until rich brown. Sprinkle with salt, pile on a dish and serve hot.

ARTICHOKES (GLOBE), STEWED. Strip off the leaves from the artichokes, remove the chokes, and soak them in lukewarm water for 3 hrs., changing the water 3 or 4 times. Place in a saucepan with enough gravy to cover them, 1 tbsp. mushroom ketchup, the juice of 1 lemon, knob of butter rolled in flour. Allow to simmer gently for 30 mins. and serve with the gravy poured over.

ARTICHOKES FOR SALAD. See SALADS.

Artichoke Bottoms. Take a few artichoke bottoms, dried. Soak them and boil in sufficient clear stock to cover. When tender, which may be ascertained by sticking a fork into them, take them out and drain. Place a little forcemeat into each one and serve on a napkin. Allow 1 for each person.

Artichokes à la Lyonnaise. Wash, blanch and trim four globe artichokes. Then place them in a stewpan with 2 oz. butter, the juice of 1 lemon, a pinch of salt and a pinch of pepper. Simmer gently until sufficiently cooked, then drain from the fat and place in oven to brown lightly. Put a cupful of good stock into the saucepan in which the artichokes were stewed. Stir gently for a few minutes, add a glass of white wine and serve. Sufficient for 3 persons.

Artichokes à l'Italienne. Well wash, trim and quarter some globe artichokes, and boil them in salt and water until tender. Remove the chokes, drain thoroughly, arrange them on a dish with the leaves outwards and intersperse them with watercress. Pour good white sauce, flavoured with stewed mushrooms, over them. Allow 1 artichoke per person.

Artichokes (Jerusalem), Soup or Purée of. See SOUPS.

Artichokes (Globe), Stuffed. Thoroughly wash the artichokes. Boil them till nearly

Artichokes (Globe), Stuffed (*continued*)
tender, drain and remove the middle leaves and chokes. Fill each with a little good forcemeat, and bake at 360° F. Therm. 4 until the meat is cooked. Serve with a little melted butter.

ASCORBIC ACID. Water-Soluble Vitamin C. Antiscorbutic. See **FOOD VALUES.**

ASHBERRY JELLY. See **ROWAN JELLY.**

ASPARAGUS (Fr. *asperge*). An excellent plant, originally a wild seaplant of Great Britain, of which three varieties are grown, white, violet and green. It is in season from April to October. It grows in temperate regions of both hemispheres, and in the tropics to a gigantic size. The tender shoots of this plant make an excellent table vegetable. The shoots when young can be eaten raw in salad, while the larger, coarser shoots require cooking.

ASPARAGUS BOILED. Choose freshly cut bunches with straight heads. If the cut end is brown and dry, and the heads bent on one side, the asparagus is stale. It may be kept a day or two with the stalks in cold water, but is much better freshly cut. Scrape off the white skin from the lower end and cut the stalks of equal length. Let them lie in cold water until it is time to cook them. Put a handful of salt into a gallon of water and let it boil. Tie the asparagus in bundles and put them into it, tips upwards. Toast a slice of bread brown on each side, dip it in water, and lay it on a dish. When the asparagus is sufficiently cooked, dish it on to the toast, leaving the white ends outwards each way. Serve with melted butter.

ASPARAGUS, A FRENCH METHOD OF COOKING. Wash and boil the asparagus about 20 mins. Then drain and cut off the heads and about 2″ of the stalks. Mince small, and mix with a chopped onion. Add well beaten yolk of an egg, salt and pepper. Heat through, and serve with a good sauce over it, and sippets of toasted bread.

ASPARAGUS FRICASSÉED. Wash 25 heads of asparagus, cut off the tender portions and lay them in cold water until they are required. Drain, and chop with young lettuce, half a head of endive and a small onion. Put 1 tbsp. butter into a saucepan and, when melted, mix with 1 tsp. flour and ½ pt. stock. Add the chopped vegetables, season with pepper and salt and allow to stew gently until thick. Serve hot.

Asparagus Omelet. Boil in the usual way 25 heads of asparagus and cut the green ends, when tender, into pieces the size of peas. Asparagus that has been previously cooked may be used in this way, first heating it in a little boiling water. Mix with them 4 well-beaten eggs, and add a little pepper and salt. Melt 1 tbsp. butter in an omelet pan, pour in the mixture, stir till it thickens, and serve immediately with sauce and vinegar.

Asparagus Pudding

Ingredients	*Method*
25 heads asparagus 1 tbsp. butter ¼ lb. flour 2 tbsp. finely chopped ham 4 eggs Pepper and salt Milk	Cut the green parts into pieces the size of peas. Beat the butter to a cream, add flour, ham, eggs, asparagus and seasoning. Mix well together, and add sufficient milk to make a stiff batter. Put into a well-oiled mould, wrap it in floured cloth and place in a saucepan of boiling water. Boil for 2 hrs. Turn on to a hot dish and serve with melted butter.

Asparagus Salad. See **SALADS.**

Asparagus and Sour Cream Salad. Use tender parts of young asparagus and cut them into small pieces. Dress with a little sour cream. Arrange on crisp lettuce leaves and serve with new potatoes.

Asparagus Sauce. See **SAUCES.**

Asparagus Soup

Ingredients

25 heads asparagus
1½ pt. stock
Cup of milk

Method

Remove tops of asparagus and soak them in water for some time. Then place in saucepan with the stock, to which has been added a cupful of milk. Boil for 10 mins. If desired a little spinach juice may be added to colour. Sufficient for 6 to 8 persons.

Asparagus Soup (Cream). See SOUPS.

ASPIC. A jelly made from clarified meat stock flavoured with meat, vegetables, tomato juice and herbs. It is boiled to reduce and become firm when cold or fortified with calves' feet or gelatine. Used for cold entrées, savouries, garnishes, a decorative glaze, etc.

TO MAKE. Place a knucklebone of veal, knucklebone of ham, a calf's foot, four cloves stuck into 1 large onion, 1 large carrot, a bunch of savoury herbs in 2 qt. water, and boil gently until it is reduced rather more than half. Strain and put aside to cool. Very carefully remove every particle of fat or sediment and place jelly in saucepan with a glass of white wine, 1 tbsp. tarragon vinegar, salt and pepper to taste, and two egg whites. Keep stirring until it nearly boils and becomes white; remove from heat and allow to just simmer for 15 mins. Cover and allow to stand for a while until sediment has settled. Strain through a jelly bag two or three times until quite clear. Place in mould which has been soaked in cold water. Aspic jelly may also be bought in powder form. Directions for the use of this are given on packets. See also JELLY.

VARIATIONS AND USES. Aspic may be used either plain or with added flavouring, e.g. mayonnaise, Worcester sauce, or other piquant sauce, or a small amount of cider, to mask cooked meat or fish, or to set meat, fish, vegetables or eggs in moulds or small individual shapes. When making moulds, the mould should be soaked and then lined with the jelly, then the food put in and more jelly poured in to cover it. These moulds may be garnished with lettuce, cress, and other shredded green leaves, or chopped parsley or chives. Other suggestions for moulds are: assorted parboiled vegetables and chopped parsley; baked rice and diced vegetables; cold fish or tinned fish with rounds of cucumber and French beans; macaroni and vegetables or tomatoes; oddments of meat, with boiled rice, garnished with cress and tomato; sardines, tomatoes, fresh young peas and new potatoes; minced ham or cooked sausage meat placed in a mould garnished with cucumber; asparagus tips; spaghetti and small whole tomatoes.

Aspic Game or Poultry. Cut up what is left of game or poultry into meat joints. Pour some aspic jelly into the bottom of a mould which has been soaked in cold water. Next a layer of stars or diamonds cut out of cold hard-boiled white of egg, a few leaves of parsley, and the red part of cold boiled tongue dotted here and there. Let it become nearly stiff, then arrange the cold game or poultry, taking care to leave room for the jelly, which should be cool when it is poured in. When quite stiff (after about 12 hrs.) turn out the mould and garnish with parsley.

ASTRACHAN. Name of a caviare.

ATHOL BROSE. Scottish drink composed of whisky, honey, etc.

ATTELETTES. Small skewers with ornamental heads.

AUBERGINE. Also known as egg-plant. Egg-shaped, from yellowish-white to violet in colour, it is a native of the West Indies. The aubergine is an annual plant and seldom more than 2 ft. in height. It can be cultivated in temperate regions under favourable conditions. Aubergines are usually served stuffed, either baked or boiled, as an entrée. They should only be eaten when quite ripe, otherwise they may prove to be indigestible.

Aubergines Farcies. Cut aubergines in halves from end to end (not across) and remove centre. Place them in a basin with seasoning of salt and pepper and

Aubergines Farcies (*continued*)

vinegar. Leave about an hour. Then cook very carefully for a few minutes in a little oil with a few mushrooms, 2 small onions, a chopping each of chives and parsley. Mix well and fill the scooped-out centres of the aubergines with this mixture. Sprinkle with breadcrumbs and dot with small knobs of butter. Place in a fireproof dish and bake at 400° F. Therm. 6 for about 20 mins.

Aubergine Fritters. Peel and cut rounds about ½" thick, dip in batter and fry. Drain and serve sprinkled with salt or sugar.

AURORA SAUCE. See SAUCES.

AUSTRALIAN WINES. There is a wide range of these wines. They are available both in red and white varieties, and among them will be found wine with good flavour and choice bouquet.

AVOCADO PEAR. This fruit grows in the West Indies, Mexico, Central America, Columbia, the South Sea Islands and the Southern States of the U.S.A. The name is a corruption of the Aztec word *Ahuacatel*. The fruits, which are round or pear-shaped, vary in size, weighing from 3 oz. to 3 lb., and their skin varies in colour and in texture. Some varieties are red, some green and others purple-black; the green are considered best. Some have thin tissue-paper-like skin, and others a quarter of an inch of thick horny shell. Avocado is richer in protein than any other fruit and contains large proportions of mineral salts and fat. It should never be cooked or refrigerated. It is eaten with pepper and salt, and a squeeze of lime or lemon juice; sometimes Worcester sauce is added. Half an avocado may also be served on a bed of lettuce leaves with a vinaigrette sauce in the well from which the seed has been removed.

Avocado with Lettuce and Orange. Arrange crisp young lettuce leaves in a salad bowl; peel, stone and halve two avocados. Arrange on lettuce. Fill centre with orange quarters, a little French dressing, and garnish with grating of onion.

Avocado Salad

Ingredients	*Method*
Avocados	Cut avocados into halves and fill with a dressing made with the other ingredients well mixed in a bowl which has been rubbed with the clove of garlic. Allow to stand for ½ hr. before serving.
Small clove of garlic	
2 oz. fresh lime juice	
½ tsp. sugar	
½ tsp. dry mustard	
¼ tsp. salt	
⅛ tsp. ground pepper	
2 tbsp. chopped chives	
1 tbsp. Worcester sauce	
Pinch of paprika	

Avocado Stuffed. Stuff the avocado halves with shrimp, crabmeat or lobster. Serve with Russian dressing.

AVOIRDUPOIS WEIGHT. See WEIGHTS AND MEASURES.

AYOLI. The name given to butter of garlic which is so much used for culinary purposes in Provence and in the south of France, and wherever garlic is held in esteem. It is especially coveted as a sauce for codfish, whether served hot or cold. Ayoli is made by pounding a few cloves of garlic in a mortar and gradually adding olive oil until the whole is reduced to the consistency of paste.

B

BABA. A sweet unleavened cake, somewhat like brioche.

Baba au Rhum

Ingredients

  ½ oz. yeast
  5 tbsp. warm milk
  8 oz. flour
  2 eggs
  6 oz. sugar
  ¼ tsp. salt
  2 oz. butter
  1 tsp. sugar
  2 oz. currants
  2 oz. chopped citron
  Small pinch saffron

Method

Dissolve yeast in milk and add to flour and unbeaten eggs; beat the dough for 3 mins. (hands are the best for this). Cover and let the dough rise in a warm place. Add sugar, salt, butter which is softened but not melted. Beat again vigorously for 10 mins. Mix the remaining ingredients and turn the dough into a buttered Angel Cake tin; cover with a cloth, and let the dough rise for 1 hr. until it is doubled in bulk. Bake at 375° F. Therm. 5 for 1 hr. Should the baba be difficult to unmould, wrap the pan in a clean teacloth so that no steam escapes; after about 6 mins. it will easily slip out.

FOR THE RUM SYRUP

Ingredients

  4 oz. sugar
  4 tbsp. water
  2 tbsp. rum

Method

Boil together sugar and water for 10 mins. and then add the rum. The syrup should be cool before pouring over cake. Serve hot or cold.

Baba au Madère. Make a Baba as above, but do not glaze.

FOR THE SYRUP

Ingredients

  1 pt. cold water
  8 oz. sugar
  ½ lemon
  ½ gill curaçao
  1 gill sherry

Method

Place the water and sugar into a saucepan, add the lemon and bring to the boil. Simmer for 3 mins., then remove from heat. Remove lemon. Add the sherry and curaçao. Slit the cake into halves and remove the top piece. Lay it in a round flat-bottomed vessel (if placed in a wire basket it makes it easier to remove), and pour the sauce over it gradually. Allow to stand for 2 mins. then remove and place carefully over lower half of cake. Serve garnished with candied cherries and candied pineapple sliced thinly.

BACON (Fr. *lard*). The word "bacon" is derived from the German *bachen*, plural of *bache*, a wild sow. Bacon may be salted and dried only (green), or salted, dried and smoked. This name is restricted to the sides and belly so prepared. Other parts of the pig are cured in a similar manner, but they have distinctive names—ham, bath chaps, etc. (see under those headings).

TO CUT UP A PIG FOR BACON. In a pig of fair size, the chine, which is excellent for roasting or boiling, is cut from between the sides of flitches. But if the pig is small, the flitches should be divided down the chine. The shoulders may be left attached to the sides, or separated, according to the size of the pig. The legs are made into hams, and the sides form what is bacon proper. The head or cheek is either boiled, collared, or pickled. The inner fat is melted for lard, and the pieces cut off in trimming the joints are used for sausages, pies, brawn and other purposes.

SIDE OF BACON: HOW TO CUT

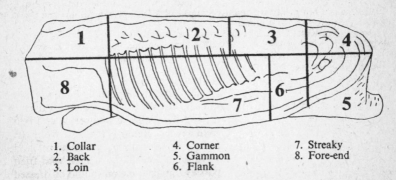

1. Collar   4. Corner   7. Streaky
2. Back   5. Gammon   8. Fore-end
3. Loin   6. Flank

TO CURE BACON. Take two sides or flitches of bacon, rub the insides with salt, then place one on the other, the flesh side uppermost, in a salting trough which has a gutter round its edges to drain away the brine; to have sweet and fine bacon the flitches must not be sopping in brine, which gives an objectionable taste. Change the salt often, once in 4 or 5 days—let it melt and sink in, but not lie too long; change the position of the flitches every 10 days—putting the top to the bottom and the bottom on the top. The time required in salting the flitches sufficiently depends on circumstances. It takes a longer time to cure a thick than a thin flitch, and they both take longer to dry in damp weather, or in a damp place; but for the flitches of a 7–8 stone hog about 6 wks. may do.

TO CURE HAM. Draw away all the slime and blood from two hams by rubbing them well with salt for 2 days before they are put into the pickle. Drain them, lay them in a pan, and pour over them boiling hot the following ingredients:

2 lb. treacle
2 oz. saltpetre
1 lb. common salt
1 pt. good vinegar.

Turn and baste them every day for a month, then drain and smoke.

TO CURE BACON OR HAM THE WILTSHIRE WAY. The excellence of bacon depends to a great degree upon the care with which the meat is drained of blood and slime before it is salted. The amount of salt used is not so important if this be well attended to, as will be seen by the Wiltshire method. The quantity of salt for a whole pig is 1½ lb. bay salt, and 1 lb. common salt to 6 oz. saltpetre, and 1½ lb. brown sugar or treacle. Strew common salt over the bacon, and let it drain a day and night. Powder the bay salt and saltpetre, and mix thoroughly with the other salt and sugar. When well blended, rub each piece of bacon and lay them together in a trough. Turn every alternate day for a month. Smoke for 9 days. Sufficient for the flitches of 10–12 stone pig.

BACON (continued)

TO SMOKE BACON AND HAM. Bacon and hams may be smoked at home by being hung up in the chimney of a fire on which wood only is burnt. Fir or deal must not be used; the best is oak, and its sawdust, if this can be obtained.

TO CHOOSE BACON. The fat of bacon should have a clear white appearance and the lean be firm. The rind, like the skin of good pork, should be thick. Should it look yellow and crusted with salt, it should be rejected, as it will probably be rancid and unpalatable.

BACON, TO BOIL. Place the piece of bacon to be boiled in a saucepan with sufficient cold water to cover. Allow it very gradually to come to the boil, removing all scum as it arises, and allow to simmer until thoroughly done. For a 2 lb. piece allow 1½ hr. Remove outer skin, dress with breadcrumbs and serve.

BACON, TO FRY. Place the bacon in a cold frying pan and heat slowly until cooked. For crisp bacon, pour off dripping while cooking.

BACON, TO GRILL. Cut streaky bacon into thin slices and lay on a grill tray. Place under a hot grill, turn repeatedly until of a light brown colour, and serve hot. Time to broil, 3 or 4 mins.

BACON, TO WARM UP. Cut it into thin slices, sprinkle each slice with fine breadcrumbs with which a very little cayenne has been mixed, and toast quickly. A common wire toaster that can be turned without disturbing the bacon answers best.

Bacon and Beans

Ingredients

2 lb. bacon
1 qt. broad beans
Breadcrumbs
Parsley

Method

Place the bacon in a pan with cold water, nearly full. When it has boiled for over 1 hr. add the shelled broad beans, and boil until tender. Remove the skin from the bacon, sprinkle with breadcrumbs, and serve on the beans, garnished with fried parsley. Smoked bacon should be dressed separately and placed on the beans when ready.

Bacon and Bread Fricandelle

Ingredients

8 oz. bacon rashers
Slices of bread
Batter made with flour, egg and milk (see p. 51)

Method

Lay the rashers between slices of bread of the same size, press them together and dip into the batter. Fry in hot fat for 8–10 mins. over a moderate heat. Garnish with parsley and serve with a sharp sauce.

Bacon and Calf's Liver

Ingredients

Bacon rashers
Sliced liver
Flour
Pepper
1 tbsp. lemon juice
Lemon slices

Method

Fry the bacon rashers first, place on a hot dish and keep hot whilst the liver, after coating in flour seasoned with a sprinkle of pepper, is fried. Turn this frequently until it is done, then place a slice of bacon on each slice of liver. Make a gravy by pouring off the fat and dredging a little flour into the pan; pour in enough water to supply the quantity of gravy desired, add the lemon juice, boil and pour upon the dish. Garnish with lemon slices, or with forcemeat if desired.

[42]

Bacon or Ham Omelet

Ingredients
6 eggs
1 tbsp. water or milk
1 tsp. flour
Salt and pepper
8 oz. minced bacon or ham
Butter

Method
Beat the eggs thoroughly, add the flour mixed with the milk or water, and pepper and salt to taste. Add the minced boiled bacon or ham, and stir in gently. Melt some butter in an omelet pan, pour in the mixture and cook for 3–4 mins. When cooked the sides may be folded over and the omelet turned on to a hot dish. Some cooks prefer to place the ham or bacon in the middle of the omelet and fold it over.

Bacon and Potato Salad

Ingredients
4–6 medium-sized potatoes
Pinch of salt
Pepper
3 rashers bacon, diced
1 small onion, thinly sliced
Head of celery, finely shredded
1 tbsp. finely chopped parsley
1 hard-boiled egg, shelled and grated

Method
Peel, cook and slice the potatoes into a deep salad bowl. Add pepper and salt to season. Sauté bacon and onion until bacon is lightly cooked and the onion tender. Add celery and mix well; add dressing and stir well; garnish with the hard-boiled egg and parsley.

FOR THE DRESSING

Ingredients
2 cloves garlic or shallots
½ tsp. each salt and dry mustard
¼ tsp. each pepper and paprika
⅛ pt. vinegar or onion sauce
¼ pt. salad oil

Method
Cut the garlic or shallots into small pieces into a bowl; add other ingredients and leave an hour. Beat well with a rotary beater before use.

BACTERIA. A group of widely distributed vegetable micro-organisms. In yeast and the making of cheese they are used beneficially. Cooking and preserving processes aim to destroy them by heat as they cause food to decay.

BAIN MARIE. By using a *bain marie* or hot-water bath, all the stewpan is placed in water, which must be kept very hot, but must not boil. In this, every dish is kept warm without altering the quantity or quality. Used for baking custards and soufflés.

BAKE. See COOKING TERMS.

BAKEWELL TART. See PASTE AND PASTRY (p. 375).

BAKING POWDER. As soon as water is added to baking powder or similar substances, there is a chemical reaction and carbon dioxide is given off, aerating the mixture; it is therefore essential that any mixture containing baking powder should be cooked immediately after being moistened, as in many cases the action

BAKING POWDER (*continued*)

will pass off before the mixture is in the oven. Allow 2–2¾ level tsp. baking powder to each pound of flour.

Baking Powder, Home-Made. Mix and sift together six times, 4 oz. cream of tartar, 2 oz. bicarbonate of soda, 4 oz. ground rice (this prevents lumps forming). Store in airtight tins or jars.

BALLACHONY

Ingredients	*Method*
8 doz. prawns	Shell and clean the prawns, pound in a pestle and mortar, using a little vinegar to keep them moist. Turn into a basin, add the green ginger, chillies, lemon rind, and pound together. Add the strained lemon juice and in the meantime cut the onions into rings, and fry in the butter. When they are golden brown, add the mixture, and cook until dry. Remove from heat; when cold, pot and use as required.
1 oz. green ginger	
½ oz. chillies	
Grated rind of 4 lemons	
Lemon juice	
4 small onions	
2 oz. butter	

BALM. Lemon Balm, Sweet Balm. This was a favourite stewing herb in olden days. The fragrant sweet-scented leaves are used to flavour tea, soups, salads, summer drinks, egg dishes, and also sometimes added to tarragon vinegar. Also used in Chartreuse, Benedictine and medicinally. A little balm may be added to a partridge stew. Finely chopped, freshly gathered Lemon balm mixed with a suspicion of onion or chives gives a salad a specially delectable scent and taste.

Balm Tea. Pour 1 pt. boiling water on 1 oz. herbs; infuse for 15 mins., strain and drink freely as desired. This tea may be sweetened to taste and lemon juice may be added if desired.

BAMBOO. The young shoots of the bamboo form favourite dishes in the East: they can be had in Chinese restaurants in this country. They are also used in pickles.

BANANA (Fr. *banane*). The fruit of the banana tree grows in bunches or "hands"; for shipping it is picked when green and allowed to ripen in transit from tropical climes. The ripe fruit of the banana may also be preserved, like the fig, by drying in the sun. Never peel bananas until they are wanted as they discolour quickly; this may be prevented by covering the peeled bananas with lemon juice. This fruit is served raw in salads, with cream or in custard, but see also the recipes following.

Bananas, Baked. Peel firm ripe bananas and place in a buttered baking dish. Sprinkle lightly with brown sugar and a little lemon or lime juice. If desired, add a sprinkling of coconut. Dot with butter. Bake at 350° F. Therm. 4 for 15 mins. or until the bananas are soft but not mushy. A little rum may be poured over just before serving and ignited before carrying to table.

Bananas, Compôte of. Peel a dozen or so bananas, cut them in halves, place in a saucepan with sufficient sweet sauce to cover, and parboil. Put a thick layer of well-sweetened rice on a dish, lay the bananas on it, pour over sauce, and serve.

Banana Cream Pie

Ingredients	*Method*
1½ oz. butter	Place the butter in a basin, warm and add the sugar, egg yolks, milk and sherry, and the peeled, mashed bananas. Mix thoroughly. Pour the mixture into a fireproof dish, stir in the well-whisked egg whites.
2 tbsp. crushed loaf sugar	
2 egg yolks	
½ pt. milk	
1 wineglass sherry	

Banana Cream Pie (*continued*)

1¼ cups bananas mashed
2 egg whites
Angelica

Bake at 350° F. Therm. 4 until done. To prevent burning, cover the pie with paper, and do not let it bake too quickly. Decorate with angelica.

Banana Fritters. See FRITTER.

Banana Ice Cream. Peel 2 large bananas, rub them through a sieve into a basin; mix with 1 pt. boiling sweet cream, leave to heat together for 5 mins. When cool, freeze.

Banana Jam

Ingredients

6 lb. bananas
2 lb. pears
Juice of 2 lemons
4½ lb. sugar

Method

Peel and cut bananas into small pieces. Put 1 lb. sugar and lemon juice into preserving pan, add pears and when they boil add rest of sugar and bananas. Stir carefully till the jam boils. Then boil rapidly for about 1 hr. Skim well, pour into hot jars at once.

Banana Marmalade

Ingredients

3 lb. bananas
3 lemons
3 lb. sugar

Method

Peel and slice bananas into ½" rounds. Add sugar and grated rind and juice o lemons. Place in crock bowl and leave until the sugar dissolves. Then turn into preserving pan, heat gradually, stirring well, and skim. When the mixture boils, boil fast until it thickens and sets. Pour into jars and cover when cool.

Banana Omelet. Proceed as for other omelets (see p. 350), but put a few thinly-sliced rounds of banana into batter. When omelet is cooked and before folding, fill with warm sliced banana steeped in wine.

Banana Pie. Line a pie-dish with rich puff paste, having it thinner in the centre of the dish than at the outside. This can be easily done by folding over the paste and rolling it. Remove the peel from 4 or 5 mellow bananas, cut them lengthwise in slices, place in the dish, cover with sugar, a few dots of butter, and pour over 4 or 5 tbsp. white wine. Bake at 350° F. Therm. 4 for 20 mins.

Banana Purée. Peel bananas, remove strings, and beat until light and fluffy. Flavour with a squeeze of lemon juice and add sugar if desired.

Banana Salad—I. Combine with any fresh fruit, adding a little sugar, using tinned, bottled or frozen fruit if desired. Bananas and strawberries make a good combination.

Banana Salad—II. Combine with pineapple, cream cheese and lettuce to make an excellent salad.

Banana Soufflé

Ingredients

⅓ oz. butter
¾ oz. flour
1 gill milk
3 eggs
4 bananas
1 dsp. sugar

Method

Melt the butter in a thick saucepan, stir in the flour, and cook the mixture slowly for a couple of minutes. Add the milk, and stir until the mixture leaves the sides of the pan clean. Remove from heat, add gradually the egg yolks and the bananas,

[45]

Banana Soufflé (*continued*)
½ tsp. vanilla essence

which should be sliced and rubbed through a sieve. Add the sugar and vanilla and beat the mixture well, and then stir in the stiffly-whisked egg whites. Turn the mixture into a fireproof dish and bake about 40 mins. at 350° F. Therm. 4.

BANBURY CAKES. The Oxfordshire town of Banbury has for generations been famous for these delicious cakes.

Ingredients
8 oz. butter
1 lemon
1 orange
1 lb. currants
½ oz. cinnamon
2½ oz. allspice
1 lb. pastry
1 egg

Method
Beat the butter to a cream, add the chopped rinds of the lemon and orange, currants, cinnamon and allspice. Mix all together thoroughly, and keep in a covered jar for use. The paste for these buns should be tolerably rich, rolled out thin, and cut into rounds or squares. Put a layer of the mince on one round, cover over with another. Flatten with the hand, and moisten the edges with white of egg to make them adhere. Before putting into the oven brush the cakes over with the froth of eggs and sprinkle with sugar. Bake at 350° F. Therm. 4 for 15 mins. They may be eaten hot or cold.

BANBURY MINCEMEAT
Ingredients
¾ lb. currants
2 oz. beef suet
Little nutmeg
¼ lb. candied orange peel
3 oz. ratafias
Sliced lemon peel

Method
Wash and dry the currants, and mix with the suet, chopped very finely. Add the grated nutmeg, the finely shredded orange peel, crushed up ratafias, and a slice of lemon peel. Mix all well together. Keep in a covered jar until required.

BANNOCKS. History tells us that in the days of King Alfred bannocks were indigenous to all parts of England, Scotland and Wales, but custom has led us to regard these cakes as of Scottish origin.

Bannocks, Barley
Ingredients
½ lb. barley meal
4 oz. flour
½ tsp. salt
3 teacups buttermilk
2 small tsp. bicarb. soda

Method
Put the barley meal, flour and salt together into a bowl. Mix well. Mix the buttermilk and bicarb. soda together. Stir briskly and as the mixture fizzes up, pour on to the flour mixture. Make into a soft dough. Turn on to a floured board; roll out to about ½″ thickness; cut into rounds the size of a meat plate. Bake on a hot girdle; when the underside browns, turn and brown the other side.

[46]

BAR. This fish is sometimes mistaken for the haddock. Some Continental cooks prefer it for culinary purposes to the salmon. It is used as a substitute for these fish in any recipes.

BARBECUE. To roast an animal or fowl whole on a spit or over coals, frequently basted with a highly seasoned sauce. The term is derived from the French *barbe à queue*, beard to tail.

Barbecue Sauce—I

Ingredients

½ pt. tomato juice
½ pt. consommé
Sprig tarragon
Sprig thyme
2 or 3 cloves
1 tsp. each salt and pepper
2 tbsp. onion juice
2 tbsp. wine vinegar
1 tbsp. brown sugar
1 clove garlic
1 tbsp. chopped parsley
¼ pt. sherry

Method

Heat the tomato juice and consommé, with the tarragon, thyme and cloves. Just before it boils, add the salt, pepper, onion juice, wine vinegar, brown sugar, the garlic grated, parsley and sherry. This sauce is good with grilled or roast meats. If preferred, thicken with a little blended flour and water.

Barbecue Sauce—II

Ingredients

2 cloves garlic
¼ lb. lean bacon
¼ pt. olive oil
1 onion
Sprig rosemary
Pinch thyme
1 tsp. salt
¼ tsp. pepper
¼ tsp. cayenne
¼ tsp. ground cloves
2 lb. tomatoes
2 cups consommé
1 tbsp. sugar
¼ cup celery
1 green pepper
1 tbsp. chopped parsley

Method

Sauté the bacon and garlic together in a large pan with the olive oil. Add onion finely chopped, rosemary, pinch thyme, salt, pepper, cayenne and cloves. Cook together for 5 mins. then add tomatoes, consommé, sugar and celery and simmer for 40 mins. Add green pepper, diced and chopped parsley. Cook for a further 5 mins. This sauce is delicious with pork chops and most meats.

BARBEL (Fr. *barbeau* or *barbillon*). This fish belongs to the carp and goldfish tribe, but differs in that its upper jaw extends considerably in front of the lower, and has 4 soft barbules attached to it. It is not considered a delicacy, but much improves if kept in water for a few days before cooking. The best method of preparation is to score and soak in oil for 30 mins. Sprinkle with salt and pepper and broil each side from 8–10 mins. over a moderate heat. Serve on a hot dish with Maître d'Hôtel butter (see **BUTTERS**).

BARBERRY. This fruit used to grow profusely in the hedgerows in olden times. The red berries are acid to taste and used in preserves, tarts, sauce and for flavouring. The roots when boiled yield a yellow dye.

TO CANDY. Take some preserved barberries, wash them in warm water to cleanse them from the syrup, and cover with dry, finely powdered sugar. Put them quickly

BARBERRY (*continued*)

to bake at 350° F. Therm. 4, keeping them sprinkled with sugar and turning frequently.

TO DRY. Take bunches of barberries and hang them for $\frac{1}{4}$ hr. in a vessel of boiling water; remove carefully without bruising and simmer for 10 mins. in a boiling syrup made with 2 lb. sugar and 1 pt. water. Remove from heat but let the bunches remain in it for several hours. Then hang them up to drain and dry. Remove when sufficiently dry and store with care. Barberries may be had without stones, but should there be any they must be removed before commencing.

TO PICKLE FOR GARNISHING. Gather the clusters before they are fully ripe; carefully pick off any unsound or very ripe berries, and lay the remainder in bottles. Cover them with a strong brine, made by boiling $\frac{1}{4}$ lb. salt with each pint of water, and add a small nut of alum to the whole. The brine must not be put over the fruit until it is quite cold. Store the bottle in a cool, dry place and examine occasionally. If at any time a scum should be observed on the surface, pour off the liquid, and put freshly boiled brine in its place, made not quite so salt. Keep the jars closely covered.

TO PRESERVE. To every 2 lb. fruit take $4\frac{1}{2}$ lb. powdered loaf sugar, throw some of it over the barberries to be preserved, and with the remainder make a strong syrup in the proportion of 1 pt. water to 1 lb. sugar. Put the barberries into it, and make them boil as quickly as possible, that they may not lose colour; then fill jars for use.

Barberry Ketchup

Ingredients

3 qt. barberries
4 qt. cranberries
1 qt. water
1 cup stoned raisins
1 large quince
4 small onions
$\frac{1}{4}$ pt. vinegar
$\frac{3}{4}$ cup salt
$\frac{1}{2}$ lb. sugar
1 dsp. each ground cloves and ground allspice
2 tbsp. black pepper
2 tbsp. celery seed
1 tbsp. ground mustard
1 tsp. cayenne
1 tsp. cinnamon
1 tsp. ginger
1 tsp. grated nutmeg

Method

Stew the barberries and strain. Stew the cranberries in the water with the raisins, quince, onions, and strain. Mix these ingredients with the barberries, add rest of ingredients and let whole boil for 1 min. If too thick, add vinegar or water. Bottle for future use.

BARCELONA NUTS. These are cultivated in Spain, especially in the Catalan provinces; they are used as dessert nuts and also in confectionery.

BARLEY (Fr. *orge*). Barley in its natural state is chiefly used for malting. Barley, we are told, was extensively cultivated by the Romans and many other nations of antiquity, as well as by the ancient inhabitants of Gaul, and the Greeks are said to have trained their athletes upon it.

Pearl barley is plain barley deprived of its husks, then steamed, rounded and polished. Scotch barley just has the husks removed and is not as rounded as the pearl. Scotch Pot and French barley are much about the same but smaller, and prepared from winter grain.

Barley Bannocks. See BANNOCKS.

Barley Beverage
Ingredients
1 tbsp. ground barley
1 qt. boiling water
1 tbsp. cold water
Juice of ½ lemon
Small piece of lemon rind
Sugar or honey

Method
Put the ground barley into a basin and mix to a smooth paste with the cold water. Place in a saucepan and pour over gradually the boiling water and boil for 10 mins. Stir frequently and strain off liquor. Pour into basin or bowl, and add the lemon juice and piece of rind. Sweeten with sugar or honey, leave an hour, strain and use as desired.

Barley Cream Soup. See SOUPS.

Barley Gruel
Ingredients
1 oz. pearl barley
2 pt. cold water

Method
Wash and soak the barley, put in into saucepan, add the cold water and simmer for 3 hrs. Strain and serve as desired with lemon to flavour or diluted with milk. Sweeten to taste.

Barley Meal Scones. Take as much good fresh barley meal as is required, season with a little salt and mix with hot milk until it forms a stiff paste. Roll this out into thick round cakes, and quarter with a knife into scones. Bake in a hot oven (375° F. Therm. 5). 1 tsp. baking powder may be added if desired.

Barley Milk
Ingredients
2 tbsp. pearl barley
1 pt. milk
½ tsp. salt

Method
Wash the pearl barley in several waters, then put into a large jar; place this in stewpan of water. Stir in milk and salt, and boil the water until the milk is reduced to half its original volume. Strain off milk, and sweeten to taste. The barley itself is very good when served on a plate with a wineglass of sherry poured over it and sprinkled with caster sugar if desired.

Barley Pudding. See MILK PUDDINGS.

Barley Water. Place 1 teacup washed pearl barley in 1 qt. cold water. Place over a low heat and when it boils skim carefully. Leave to simmer a further ½ hr. Strain off liquid and leave to cool. Sweeten and flavour as desired.

BARLEY SUGAR. Dissolve lump sugar, boil and skim until it is crisp and clear and no scum rises; test the crispness by drop-lemon. Pour the sugar on to a marble slab or a tin which has been rubbed with butter or salad oil, cut into strips and before it is cold, twist. If marked with a knife it will break easily, and may be made into any form. If making drops, when cold, sprinkle with pounded sugar to dry up any moisture.

BARM. The yeast which is formed on brewing liquor.

BARON OF BEEF. A double sirloin joined together at the backbone.

BARREL. A barrel holds 36 gallons. See also **WEIGHTS AND MEASURES**.

BASIL. Any one of the five varieties of basil may be used in cooking: Sweet basil, with the clove-pepperish odour and taste, or the Sweet basil with purplish-red leaves; the green leaf dwarf variety; the variety of the purple leaf; or the Italian

BASIL (*continued*)

or Curly basil. The culinary uses are in vinegar, soup, stew, some salads and creams or cream cheese. Also used in tomato dishes and some egg dishes, in butter sauce or in vegetable juice cocktails, or chopped and sprinkled over potatoes or peas.

BASS. This fish belongs to the perch tribe. Known in France as *loup de mer* (sea-wolf). Rock bass is the poorest bass for culinary purposes. Black Sea bass is gastronomically important.

Bass, Fried

Ingredients
2 lb. bass
Flour
2 tsp. salt
¼ tsp. pepper
3 tbsp. butter or margarine
1 tbsp. chopped chives
1 lemon sliced

Method
Dress the fish, removing fins, tail and entrails (remove head if desired). Wipe well with damp cloth. Sift flour (or flour and cornflour mixed in equal proportions) and seasoning and roll fish in mixture. Melt butter in frying pan, brown fish very quickly on both sides but do not overcook. Serve on very hot dish, garnished with chives and lemon, accompanied by sauce if desired.

Bass, Stuffed. Scale and clean the bass. Wash well and stuff with highly seasoned veal stuffing. Sew it up and put it into a saucepan with 1 oz. butter or margarine. Pour over it a cupful of stock or water. Cook over a low heat until tender, turning frequently. Serve with Mushroom sauce.

BATH BUNS. See BUNS.

BATH CHAP. The cheek and jawbone of the pig, salted and smoked. Thus called because those coming from Bath were the first known, and the first to obtain a reputation as being the very finest. See also **PIG'S CHEEKS.**

TO COOK. The excellence of this well-prepared meat depends greatly on the soaking and boiling. If these are not properly attended to, it will be hard and unsatisfactory. Lay it in a pail of cold water, skin downwards, and let it remain one night. Scrub the chap with a small brush to cleanse it. Pour it into plenty of cold water to boil. Bring to the boil quickly, then draw the pan aside to a low heat and simmer for 2–3 hrs. Skin, and garnish with any boiled green vegetable.

BATTER. This signifies a mixture of flour and milk or water. The addition of eggs, yeast, spirits, etc., depends on the use to which it is to be put. Many novel, well-flavoured batters may be made by the introduction of liqueurs, such as ratafia, noyau, maraschino or brandy, but they should be used with discretion. Small slices of meat, cold cooked vegetables, such as carrots and celery, joints of fowl, etc., are excellent fried in batter, and many seemingly useless remnants may be dressed again in this way, in a pleasing shape, and used to ornament and accompany other dishes.

BATTER FOR FRYING MEAT, FISH, FRUIT AND VEGETABLES

Ingredients
4 oz. flour
1 gill water
Pinch of salt
2 tbsp. salad oil
2 egg whites

Method
Mix the flour, water, salt and salad oil together, and allow to stand for a while. Just before using, dash in the whites of the eggs, whisked till firm.

BATTER, FRENCH
Ingredients
1 oz. butter
⅛ pt. boiling water
¾ pt. cold water
6 oz. flour
1 egg white
Pinch of salt

Method
Melt the butter by pouring over it the boiling water, and cool it by adding the cold water. Mix it gradually and smoothly with the flour. If the batter is savoury, add a good pinch of salt, less if it is for fruit. If the batter is too thick, add a little more water. Beat up the egg white to a froth and stir into batter. This batter is excellent for apple, peach, or orange fritters.

BATTER, ITALIAN
Ingredients
2 eggs
½ pt. French wine or cider
Orange-flower water
¾ lb. flour
2 tbsp. Lucca oil
1 tsp. salt
2 or 3 egg whites

Method
Mix and beat the eggs with the French wine or cider and a little orange-flower water. Add this to the flour, and the Lucca oil and salt. Blend the batter with a spoon until it is like cream. Allow to stand 1–2 hrs. before use, and at the last minute add, very lightly, the stiffly whisked egg whites.

Batter Fritters
Ingredients
Batter as given in following recipe
Apples
3 oz. currants

Method
Peel, core and mince some apples, add to the batter, and if desired 3 oz. currants. The addition of a little suet to the apples is an improvement but it must be very judiciously used, as too much will make the fritters greasy. 1 large tbsp. batter is sufficient for one fritter. Fry in boiling dripping and serve with sugar sprinkled over.

Batter Pudding, Baked
Ingredients
2 or 4 eggs
8 oz. flour
Pinch of salt
1 pt. milk

Method
Separate the yolks from the whites of the eggs, beat them separately, then put them in a basin together. Mix in gradually the flour and salt. Blend to a creamy consistency and gradually add the milk. Bake in a well-greased oven-dish for ¾ hr. at 375° F. Therm. 5. This pudding is much improved by careful mixing. If the eggs, flour and milk are not well blended together, the pudding is often a failure. Serve with jam and sugar. For a variation fruit may be added to the batter.

Batter Pudding, Boiled

Ingredients

1 oz. butter
1 pt. milk
3 tbsp. flour
3 eggs
Pinch of salt

Method

Melt the butter. Mix the flour with a little milk, then add gradually the whole pint, blending carefully. Stir in the melted butter, and, still stirring, add the beaten eggs, and pinch of salt. Put the mixture into a well-greased basin, tie a cloth over it, and put it to boil at once or the batter will settle at the bottom. It will take 1¼ hr. and should be moved in the saucepan for a few minutes after it is put to boil.

BEANS. Of those cultivated in this country there are two distinct kinds: Broad or Windsor and the Kidney bean. The Broad bean has many varieties all having more or less the same characteristics, whereas the Kidney bean includes the French, the Dwarf and the Runner. For culinary purposes it is best to treat them as three distinct sorts, and then include the Dried Haricot beans, the Lima or Butter beans and the little black beans known as "frijoles". Scarlet Runners are also obtainable in a variety. See also **FLAGEOLET.**

BEANS, BROAD (Fr. *fèves*).

BEANS, BROAD, BOILED. When very young these beans are cooked like peas. When they are older they should be boiled in plenty of salted water until the skins are detachable from the beans. They should then be drained, skinned, and stirred over a low heat in a sauté-pan with 1 oz. butter or dripping for each pint of beans, and a seasoning of pepper and salt added. Sprinkle with finely chopped parsley before serving.

Broad Beans with Cream. Boil full-grown shelled broad beans in salted water with sprig of summer savory. When almost done, drain, and remove thin shells (French cooks call them *robes*). Put in a stewpan with a lump of butter the size of a walnut, a dusting of flour, and the same sugar, a little finely chopped parsley and summer savory. Toss together over a low heat, then add a cupful of cream. When well-heated remove beans, pile on to a hot dish and thicken cream with egg yolk. Pour over beans and serve immediately.

BEANS, FRENCH (Fr. *haricots verts*). French beans are best when gathered young so that the pod is simply peeled the whole way round to remove the delicate fibre, and then the ends nipped off. When the beans are old and sliced the whole way through much of the flavour is lost. They should be plunged into boiling salted water, to which 1 tsp. sugar has been added. When cooked, drain in a colander, then shake in the hot pan with a knob of butter, season with pepper and salt, and serve. These beans may be served with a dressing of Hollandaise or Bearnaise sauce, or, if preferred, Tomato sauce. Boiling time for young beans 15–20 mins; for old, 20–30 mins. Stewing time, 30 mins. Beans stewed should be served with sauce made from the stock, thickened with butter, flour and an egg yolk, and a squeeze of lemon juice added.

BEANS (FRENCH), To SALT. To each 3 lb. beans allow 1 lb. salt. Wash and dry the beans and remove the string. Put a good layer of salt in the bottom of a glass or stone jar and then place on a layer of prepared beans. Continue to fill the jars with alternate layers of beans and salt, then cover and leave for a few days. When the beans shrink, continue to add more beans and more salt until the jar is full and tightly packed. If not tightly packed with plenty of salt, the beans will become slimy and will not keep. A final layer of salt should cover the top layer of beans. Before using them, soak the beans for about 2 hrs. and wash them well. Cook in boiling water, without salt, drain and serve.

Beans (French) à la Crême. Sprinkle the cold cooked beans with tarragon vinegar and pour over ¼ cupful cream or top of milk. Garnish with finely chopped chives.

Beans (French) à la Maître d'Hôtel. Stir a little Maître d'Hôtel butter (see BUTTERS) into the cooked beans and serve very hot.

Beans (French) à la Milanaise. Make ½ pt. white sauce, enrich with the yolk of an egg, add a little cream or milk and 1 tbsp. grated cheese; sharpen with a squeeze of lemon juice and pour over the beans.

Beans (French) aux Fines Herbes. Turn the cooked beans out into a hot dish, melt 1 oz. butter in a saucepan, add 1 tbsp. each finely chopped parsley, chervil, tarragon and green stem of an onion or chives, pepper and salt to season and a grating of nutmeg. Pour over beans and serve at once.

Haricots Verts Panaches. This dish is composed of the young, green pods and the shelled beans boiled together in salted water and, when tender, drained. They are seasoned with freshly ground black pepper, and a small piece of butter is added just before serving.

Haricots Verts Soubise. Drain the water from the beans and stir in ½ pt. Soubise sauce (after passing this carefully through a fine sieve). Reheat and add 1 dsp. cream. Serve at once.

Haricots Verts Sautés. Drain the cooked beans and turn them into a sauté-pan with 1 oz. butter. Stir them gently over a low heat (using a 2-pronged fork) to allow the beans to absorb the butter. Season with salt and pepper and serve.

BEANS, HARICOT (Ff. *haricots secs*). These are the dried seeds of the Kidney bean. White (*soissons*), Red haricots, and Butter beans must be well washed and any beans that float thrown away. After this they should be soaked for 12 hrs. at least and then put into cold water slightly salted, brought slowly to the boil and simmered very gently until they are quite tender. Add an onion to each 1 pt. measure of beans (it greatly improves the flavour) also a small bouquet garni. Always allow 3 pt. water to 1 pt. beans; this when drained from the cooked beans can be used in soups, etc. The beans when cooked can be finished off in any of the ways for *haricots verts* above, or if desired:

1. Toss in butter and sprinkle a little finely chopped parsley over.
2. Add 1 pt. brown onion purée to each pint beans and stir over gentle heat till the purée is reduced to half.
3. Add 1 pt. tomato purée, a dried onion and a rasher of bacon diced. Stir over a gentle heat till the purée is reduced to half.
4. Add 1 pt. Soubise sauce and a little finely chopped parsley and heat till the purée is reduced by half.

Beans and Bacon

Ingredients

2 cups cooked beans
2 tbsp. minced onion
2 shelled hard-boiled eggs, chopped
1 chopped gherkin
1 cup dried celery
4 rashers bacon, diced and fried to golden brown (or corned beef)
½ oz. mayonnaise
1 head lettuce
Salt and pepper
Tomatoes to garnish

Method

Combine beans, onion, egg, gherkin and celery in bowl, add fried bacon (or corned beef), season with salt and pepper. Add mayonnaise and serve on lettuce leaves. Garnish with tomatoes.

Haricot Bean Soufflé

Ingredients

¼ lb. cooked beans
¼ pt. white sauce

Method

Put the beans in white sauce and cook to a purée. When cool add the beaten yolks

[53]

Haricot Bean Soufflé (*continued*)

2 eggs
Pepper
Salt
2 tbsp. grated cheese

of eggs and seasoning. Next add the grated cheese and fold in the stiffly whisked whites of egg. Turn into a well-buttered mould and bake at 350° F. Therm. 4 till set, about 20 mins. Serve garnished with a little chopped parsley or dusting of paprika.

BEARNAISE SAUCE. See SAUCES.

BEAT. See COOKING TERMS.

BÉCHAMEL SAUCE. See SAUCES.

BEDSTRAW. Yellow bedstraw, also called Lady's bedstraw or Cheese Rennet. White bedstraw, also called False Baby's Breath or Wild Maddle. The stem and leaf can be used for curdling milk for cheese, the flower for colouring cheese and butter yellow.

BEE WINE. Take 1 oz. "Bees" (these are yeasts bought at the chemists). Add 2 pt. warm water, 1 level tsp. sugar and stand in a warm room or in the open air. Cover with muslin, then the "bees" begin to work. Feed them each day with 1 tsp. sugar for 7 days. Then pour off liquid into a bottle, cork and use as desired. This makes a strong heady mead. It is good when flavoured with fruit juice.

BEEF (Fr. *bœuf*). TO CHOOSE. Good beef should be bright red in colour; if almost dark brown it is of inferior quality. The flesh should be firm, fine-grained and well marbled or with streaks of fat. (Lean beef may prove to be tough.) The fat which surrounds the flesh should be brittle or crumbly, and creamy white. Meat should

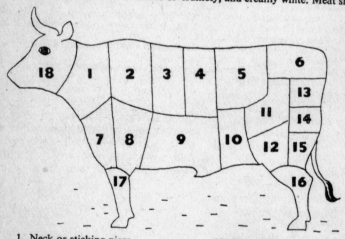

1. Neck or sticking piece	10. Thin Flank
2. Fore Ribs	11. Topside
3. Middle Ribs	12. Thick Flank
4. Chuck Ribs	13. Aitchbone
5. Sirloin	14. Mouse Buttock
6. Rump	15. Veiny Piece
7. Clod	16. Leg or Shin
8. Brisket or Shoulder	17. Hough or Shin
9. Nine Holes	18. Head including Cheek

BEEF (*continued*)

be hung in a cool place if not kept in a refrigerator. Always allow meat to stand at room temperature for an hour or more if possible before cooking.

CUTS OF BEEF. *Sirloin*. Prime roasting joint. The chump end is the finest part, as it contains the largest portion of the undercut or fillet. Excellent steaks may be cut from this fillet, and are considered by some superior to rump steak. The sirloin should be hung as long as possible before it is cooked. Two sirloins cut together form a baron of beef.

Rump. Upper part or chump end roasted. Lower or silverside salted and boiled. Middle part cut into steaks.

Aitchbone (or *top*). Salted and boiled or stewed, sometimes roasted.

Buttock or Round (Silverside). Boiled, stewed, or cut into steaks. The upper side if hung for a few days makes an excellent and economical roasting joint.

Mouse Round. Boiled or stewed.

Veiny Piece. Steaks. Inferior in quality to the rump.

Thick Flank. Fine boiling piece and roasts well.

Thin Flank. Makes good puddings and pies.

Leg (or *hock*). Stewed and good for soup.

Fore Ribs. (Five ribs.) Roasted. Prime roasting part. Some people prefer this joint to sirloin.

Middle Ribs. (Four ribs.) Economical roasting part.

Chuck Ribs. (Three ribs.) Steaks. Second quality. The worst cut of this joint is recognised by the piece of yellow gristle running round it between the muscles about an inch from the outside.

Shoulder or leg of mutton piece. Boiled or stewed.

Brisket. Boiled or stewed. Excellent when salted and pressed.

Neck. Soups, gravies, etc.

Shin. Soups and gravies. Also for stewing.

Cheeks. Brawn, soup, etc.

Tail. Soup. Stewed.

Tongue. Salted and boiled.

Liver. Stewed and fried.

TO ROAST. Wipe the meat over with a damp cloth, then put into melted dripping in the roasting tin. Cook meat in a very hot oven for the first 10–15 mins. to seal the juices, then reduce oven heat to cook joint through. Baste well while cooking. Allow 15 mins. per lb. and 15 mins. over, a little longer for the thicker joints. Beef should be served slightly underdone and run red when cut. Serve with gravy (made with the sediment in the roasting pan), Yorkshire pudding and Horseradish sauce.

Beef à la mode

Ingredients

2 or more lb. rump steak
Some good stock well fla- voured with vegetables and herbs
2 or 3 oz. good dripping
Little flour
Pepper and salt to taste
1 doz. or more medium- sized mushrooms

Method

Make the dripping hot in a stewpan. Fasten the meat into a nice shape, and flour it; fry it a nice brown on either side. Then pour in enough stock barely to cover it, add the mushrooms, which should be peeled and rinsed, and cut in half. Simmer gently over a low heat or bake at 200° F. Therm. ¼. Then place it on a hot dish, with the mushrooms round it, or if preferred serve in casserole. Remove any fat from the gravy, thicken it with the flour, and pour it over the meat.

[55]

Sirloin   Thin Flank   Silverside   Heuk Bone

Beef, Brisket, Stewed

Ingredients
  4 lb. beef
  2 carrots
  2 turnips
  2 onions
  2 head of celery
  1 sprig each parsley, mar-
      joram and thyme
  2 bay leaves
  6 cloves
  12 peppercorns
  3 qt. hot water

Method
Put the meat into a saucepan with the
vegetables and other ingredients, and
simmer gently for 3 hrs. Serve on a hot
dish with some of the liquor for gravy.
The remainder can be made into soup.
If to be eaten cold, remove the bones and
press the beef. Strain the meat liquor and
boil it down to a glaze. Brush the meat
over with it, giving it as many coats of
glaze as necessary.

Beef, Fillet, Braised

Ingredients
  4 lb. fillet beef
  Larding bacon
  Some stiff second stock
  3 large mushrooms
  1 carrot
  1 turnip
  2 onions
  Sprig of parsley
  Thyme
  Marjoram
  1 bay leaf
  Pepper and salt to taste

Method
Roll up the fillet and tie it securely with
string, lard it neatly (see **LARDING**). Put
it in the braising-pan and cover it with
buttered paper; put it into the pot, with
herbs and vegetables, and enough stock
to come halfway up the fillet. Cook it
gently, keeping it well basted. It will take
2 hrs. or longer. When cooked place it on
a hot dish in the oven. Strain the gravy
and rapidly boil it to a glaze. Remove the
string from the fillet and substitute silver
skewers. Pour the glaze over, and garnish
with vegetables. The following vegetables
may be used as a garnish: carrots and
turnips, cut into fancy shapes, cooked and
glazed; a macedoine of vegetables; sauté
mushrooms or truffles; cauliflower, brussels sprouts, asparagus, peas, etc. Serve
half-glaze in a sauceboat.

Beef Fillets with Mushrooms (Fr. *fillets de bœuf aux champignons*).

Ingredients
  Fillet of beef
  Brown mushroom sauce
  Button mushrooms sautéed
      in butter

Method
Cut the fillet into slices, beat these with a
wet cutlet-bat and cut into neat round or
oval shapes. Fry in clarified butter or fat
skimmings. Dish on a border of mashed

Round   Salt Round   Fresh Brisket   Salt Brisket

Beef Fillets with Mushrooms (*continued*)

Butter or fat skimmings off the stockpot

Mashed potatoes or a fried croustard of bread

potatoes or on fried croustard of bread. Pour Mushroom sauce round the fillets, and put the mushrooms in the centre of the dish.

Beef Jelly

Ingredients
2 lb. beef
¼ cupful water

Method
Scrape and mince up the beef finely. Put it in a jar and cover closely. Put the jar to stand in a tin of water, and put that into a slow oven for 6 hrs. Then pass the meat and liquid through a sieve and strain it through filtering-paper until clear.

Beef Olives (Fr. *olives de bœuf*)

Ingredients
1½ lb. rump steak
Sausage meat
1½ pt. stock
1 oz. butter
1 oz. flour
Few drops lemon juice
Pepper and salt
Mashed potatoes
Macedoine of tomatoes, or other suitable vegetables

Method
Cut the meat into thin strips; lay a little sausage meat on each and roll up; tie up each roll with fine string. Put rolls in a stewpan, close together, and cover with the stock. Stew them gently for 2 or 3 hrs. until quite tender. Then remove the string and place them in a circle on a border of mashed potatoes or spinach. Remove any fat from the stock, and stir in the butter and flour thoroughly mixed together. Cook the flour well, then add the lemon juice and seasoning, strain or tammy the sauce and pour it over the olives. Put the vegetables in the centre of the dish.

Beef Rump, Stewed

Ingredients
Rump of beef
½ pt. beer
4 tbsp. vinegar
2 tbsp. mushroom catsup
Little powdered mace
Bouquet garni
Onion stuck with 3 cloves
Little cayenne pepper
Pepper and salt

Method
Half-roast the rump, then put it in a large stewpan with the beer, vinegar, catsup, herbs, etc., and enough water or stock to cover it. Stew over a low heat until the meat is tender, about 3½ hrs., then place on a hot dish. Strain and thicken the gravy and pour over.

C.C.D.—3

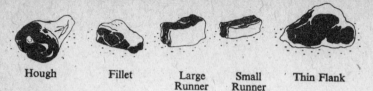

Hough   Fillet   Large   Small   Thin Flank
                           Runner   Runner

Beef Shin, Stewed. This may be cooked according to the directions given for stewed steak. Being gelatinous, it makes an excellent stew.

Beef Spiced

Ingredients	Method
Round of beef, or rolled ribs of beef	Mix dry ingredients together, then heat
¾ lb. coarse salt	gently in the oven for about 5 mins. Rub
2 oz. saltpetre	over the meat. Leave 2 days, then pour in
1½ oz. sal prunelle	the treacle. Baste well each day for a
½ lb. moist sugar	week, then boil the meat until tender (so
½ oz. cloves and peppercorns mixed and pounded	that the bones will pull out); press between two dishes with a weight on top.
½ cup treacle	Trim and glaze before serving.

Beef Steak, Broiled or Grilled. The steak should be cut from well-hung beef. Rump is the best part for the purpose. It should not be less than ¾″ in thickness. Broil or grill it according to the directions for broiling meat. It will probably take about 10 mins. to cook. Serve at once, very hot, with, if liked, Maître d'Hôtel butter, or Mushroom, Piquant, Oyster, or Horseradish sauce.

Beef Steak, Fried. Put a very little butter or dripping or some of the fat skimmings of the stockpot into a frying-pan, make it quite hot, put in the steak, fry it for one minute on either side. Then moderate the heat, either by reducing or removing the pan further from the fire. Cook steak gently, turning occasionally, for about 15 mins. The flavour of fried steak is not so fine as that of broiled. It may be served with any of the sauces recommended for broiled steak. Fried or sauté potatoes are an excellent accompaniment to broiled or fried steaks, so are also tomatoes cut in slices and cooked in the oven. Steak which is to be broiled or fried must be tender to be satisfactory.

Beef Steak Pie

Ingredients	Method
1 lb. flaky or rough puff paste	Roll the paste to ¼″ thickness. Invert the
2 lb. beef steak	pie-dish, and cut the paste to the right size
1 tbsp. flour	and shape for the crust. Roll out the
Pepper and salt	remainder, cut a band 1″ wide, wet the
½ lb. bullock's kidney	edge of the dish and place this round it.
Mushrooms or oysters if desired	Cut the beef into thin strips, dip them in flour, and season with pepper and salt.
½ pt. water	Roll each of the strips round a tiny piece of fat. Put them in the pie-dish alternately

with pieces of kidney, adding, if desired, mushrooms or oysters. Raise them in the middle of the dish in a dome form, and pour in the water. Wet the paste round

Shoulder   Rib Roast   Nine Holes

Beef Steak Pie (*continued*)

the dish, and lay the cover over. Press the edges lightly together, and trim round with a knife. Make a hole in the middle of the paste to let the gases from the meat escape. Brush the crust with beaten egg, and decorate with leaves cut from the trimmings. Bake for about 2 hrs. The pie should be baked at 400° F. Therm. 6 until the pastry is cooked, then reduce heat to 300° F. Therm. 2, to cook the meat thoroughly without drying up the pastry. Some people prefer stewing the meat before using it in the pie. If this is done, it must be allowed to get cold before the pie is made and the cooking time of the pie will be less. It is an improvement to the pie to put layers of oysters, bearded, or mushrooms, alternately with the rolls of beef. See also **SAILOR'S PIE.**

Beef Steak Pudding
Ingredients
    1 lb. flour
    ¼ tsp. salt
    ½–¾ lb. suet or cooking fat
    1½ lb. beef steak
    ½ lb. bullock's kidney
    Seasoning
    Mushrooms or oysters if
        desired
    Water

Method
Sift flour and salt, add chopped suet, or cut and rub in cooking fat. Mix to a paste with cold water. Roll it out, and line a greased quart basin, reserving one-third for the cover. Cut the steak into thin strips, and the kidney into slices. Mix some pepper and salt on a plate and season the meat nicely. Roll each piece of meat round a tiny piece of the fat, and place the rolls and the pieces of kidney in the basin, and add the mushrooms (if desired). Pour in rather more than ¼ pt. water. Roll out the remaining piece of paste. Wet the edges of that in the basin, lay the cover on, and trim round neatly. Tie over a well-scalded and floured cloth, and boil for 4 hrs. Oysters are sometimes

[59]

Beef Steak Pudding (*continued*)

put in these puddings; they should be bearded and the hard white part removed. Rabbit or chicken puddings may be made in the same manner. To these add ¼ lb. lean ham or bacon or pickled pork. Less suet may be used in making the crust if desired. Serve the pudding in the basin with a napkin folded round it, and directly the pudding is cooked pierce the crust with a fork to prevent the steam bursting it.

Beef Steak, Rolled

Ingredients
    Beef steak
    Veal forcemeat or sausage-meat
    Pepper and salt
    Stock
    Dripping
    Pickled mushrooms
    Little catsup

Method
Take care that the steak is a tender one, and beat it well with a bat or rolling-pin. Lay on it the forcemeat or sausage-meat, roll and secure with skewers and tape. Fry it brown in a frying-pan in a little dripping, then put it into a stewpan with the stock, mushrooms and catsup, and a little pepper and salt, and simmer until the steak is tender. Put on a hot dish, remove the tape, pour the gravy over. If preferred, the steak may be roasted in a moderate oven 360° F. Therm. 4. Baste thoroughly.

Beef Steak, Stewed

Ingredients
    2 lb. beef steak (less tender steak will answer for stewing)
    2 oz. dripping
    1 carrot
    1 turnip
    1 onion
    Half-head of celery, or 1 tsp. celery-seed tied in muslin
    1 sprig of parsley
    Thyme
    Marjoram
    1 bay leaf
    2 pt. hot water
    Pepper and salt
    2 oz. flour

Method
Fry the steak in the dripping, either whole, or cut in pieces, then put it into a stewpan with the vegetables, herbs, hot water, pepper and salt. Simmer gently until tender. It will take from 2 to 4 hrs. to cook, according to the kind of steak used, baked at 250° F. Therm. ½. When tender, place it on a hot dish, thicken the gravy with the flour, and strain over the steak. If liked, the steak may be garnished with vegetables prepared as for Julienne soup; or the vegetables stewed with the steak may be served with it, the herbs being removed. Oysters are very good served with stewed steak, and may be prepared thus: Beard the oysters, and stew the beards with the steak to extract the flavour. These must afterwards be strained out of the gravy. When the gravy is ready

Beef Steak, Stewed (*continued*)

to serve, scald the oysters in it, and serve them on top of the steak. In economical stews, tinned oysters may be used, and these do not require to be bearded. The gravy for the steak will be improved if half a wineglass of porter or ale is cooked with it, or a glass of red wine added before serving.

Beef Tea (Quick)

Ingredients
½ lb. beef
1 pt. water

Method
Make like raw beef tea, then put into a jar and place that in a saucepan of boiling water until the tea is cooked.

Beef Tea (Raw)

Ingredients
Equal quantities of raw beef and cold water

Method
Scrape the meat finely, soak it in water for ½ hr. or more, stirring occasionally. When all the juices are drawn into the water and it has become a deep red colour, strain it, pressing the meat well. This tea should be made from the best rump or beef steak. It is not advisable to make it in too large quantities, especially in hot weather. This tea is a most valuable remedy in many cases of extreme exhaustion.

Beef Tea (Savoury). As above with vegetables and small bunch of herbs added.

BEEFSTEAK. An edible fungi which may be as large as two feet across jutting out in half circles frequently one above the other on tree trunks. Purply red top changing to brown on underside, pale brown to dark red but without gills. Reddy and juicy flesh.

BEER (Fr. *bière*). A fermented liquor brewed from barley. It is seldom used in cooking, but see **SAUSAGES** cooked in beer.

Beer Caudle. Mix some fine oatmeal with good beer in the place of water; turn it into a saucepan, and for every quart of gruel, put in ½ tsp. allspice and ⅓ tsp. ground ginger. Sweeten it to taste with moist sugar. Stir the gruel over heat till thick and cooked, then turn into a bowl or soup plate and serve.

Beer Soup with Milk

Ingredients
1 qt. milk
2 tbsp. flour
1 qt. beer
Grated peel of ½ lemon
½ tsp. ground ginger
Sugar
4 eggs

Method
Boil the milk in a saucepan, mix the flour with a little of the beer and add to remainder with the grated lemon rind, ginger and sugar to taste. Beat the eggs and stir the boiling milk into them. Return to saucepan, add the beer and bring to boiling point, stirring all the time. Turn into tureen and serve.

BEETROOT (Fr. *betterave*). Out of a great number of varieties, the red and white beets only are concerned in culinary operations. The leaves of the beetroot are cooked and served like spinach, and the foot-stalks and midribs are eaten under

BEETROOT (*continued*)

the name of Swiss chard or *poirée aux carottes*, but the root of the red beetroot is of the greatest value to us. When cooked it should be tender, well flavoured, of rich crimson colour throughout and therefore of supreme service for these reasons in salads, pickles and as a garnish. It is sometimes made into jam. When cooking beetroot, basil, fennel, caraway, coriander or summer savory may be used.

BEETROOT, To BAKE. Cleanse the root carefully from the mould about it, wash carefully and dry; bake, unpeeled, at 350° F. Therm. 4 until tender.

BEETROOT, To BOIL. Select, if possible, small smooth varieties; thoroughly clean, but do not break the skin in any way. Place in saucepan with water to cover, and boil for 2–4 hrs. according to size. When cool, carefully remove peel, trim nicely, slice and serve as a vegetable alone, or with salads.

BEETROOT, To MACERATE. Peel and mince one or two boiled beetroots. Put a layer of the minced beetroot at the bottom of a jar, cover with minced horseradish and a few peppercorns and continue in this way until ingredients are used up. Fill the jar with vinegar and allow to stand for a day. It is then ready for use as garnish for cooked salads.

BEETROOT, To PICKLE. Boil ½ oz. peppercorns, cloves, mace, and ginger in 1 pt. vinegar, and add another pint when cold. Well clean six beetroots, boil for 2 hrs.; when cold slice and place in spiced vinegar.

Beetroot à la Poitreine. Put a little brown thickening into a saucepan with a small quantity of chopped onion and ground mixed spice. Heat and add a cold boiled sliced beetroot. Warm through, over a low heat, add tsp. vinegar, stir gently, turn on to a heated dish and serve.

Beetroot in Butter Sauce

Ingredients
1 lb. beetroot
1 pt. water
¼ pt. vinegar
4 oz. butter
½ tsp. salt
Button onions or parsley

Method
Put the beetroot in a saucepan and boil for 1 hr., then place in a basin of cold water and rub off the skin. Put in a saucepan the water, vinegar, butter and salt. Warm over a low heat and when it boils add a little flour to thicken. Cut beetroot into pieces and add to sauce and reheat. Turn the whole out into a heated dish and serve garnished with button onions or chopped parsley.

Beetroot Pie. Cut up sufficient red beetroot to fill the dish to be used, season with vinegar, sugar and spices to taste. Put into a dish lined with paste, cover over with more paste, bake at 350° F. Therm. 4, allowing the same time as for an apple pie. It is better to have the beetroot boiled before using in the pie.

Beetroot Preserve

Ingredients
6 peeled beetroots
1½ pt. cold water
4 lb. loaf sugar
Peel of 4 lemons
Juice of 6 lemons
Vanilla essence
Cinnamon
4 cloves

Method
Peel the beetroots and boil in the water for 20 mins. Then add the sugar well broken, lemon juice, lemon rind chopped small, vanilla, half a finger's length of cinnamon stick and the cloves. Allow to boil for 1 hr. Skim well and when the beetroots are quite tender remove from pan and place in a jar, but leave the syrup to boil until it is thick, when it may be strained over the beetroots. This preserve and syrup will be found useful for colouring creams, jellies, etc.

Beetroot Salad. Boil and slice some beetroots, and lay with alternate rows of boiled sliced onion; pour over them any salad sauce, or simply oil and vinegar if preferred. Garnish with parsley. See also SALADS.

Beetroots Sautéed in Butter. Boil the beetroots, peel and cut into heart-shaped slices. Put into a saucepan with 1 oz. butter, season with pinch of pepper, and sprinkle over a very little sugar. Allow to cook over low heat for 6 mins., carefully tossing from time to time. Arrange on preheated dish and serve.

Beetroot Soup (Bortsch)

Ingredients
2 large beetroots
2 onions
4 tbsp. vinegar
½ gall. gravy soup
1 tbsp. brown sugar

Method
Cleanse carefully, boil and peel the beetroots. Also boil the onions and mince them together with the beetroot. Place the vinegar and brown sugar and gravy soup into a saucepan, add the beetroot and onion and some small pieces of cold veal, or other meat, if desired, and heat together. Serve hot.

BEL PAESE CHEESE. This is a semi-hard, whole-milk cheese made in different parts of Italy, mostly from October to June. It is of the Port-du-Salut type.

BENNET. The yellow avens of Europe. The roots are sometimes used as a substitute for cloves in both sweet and savoury dishes. Name also of a small walnut.

BERGAMOT. From the rind of the Bergamot orange, a citrus fruit, a very fragrant essential oil is obtained; sometimes this is used in high-class confectionery. The name Bergamot also belongs to a very choice variety of pear, shaped like an apple and very juicy.

BETEL. A climbing species of pepper.

BETONY. Also called Purple or Wood betony. This member of the mint family is used medicinally.

BEXHILL CHEESE. A small round flat cream cheese of excellent quality, known locally.

BICARBONATE OF SODA. A white, crystallised substance, commonly known as cooking soda, *salcratus*. When used as a raising agent with cream of tartar, allow 2 level tsp. cream of tartar and 1 level tsp. bicarbonate of soda, to each pound flour. If a pinch is used when cooking rhubarb or other very acid fruit, less sugar will be needed. When cooking green vegetables, a pinch is added to tenderise and preserve the colour.

BIFFINS. Apples which have been peeled, partly baked and dried under pressure. Select as many good cooking apples as are required. Peel and place them on oven sheet and bake at 300° F. Therm. 2 for a few minutes. Remove and place a board on them and weights on top and allow to stand till the apples are cold. Repeat this process until the biffins are reduced to half their original thickness. In this condition they can be preserved for any length of time, and if well dried retain all the flavour of the fresh fruit.

BIGARADE SAUCE. See SAUCES.

BIGOS. A Polish dish which is much esteemed in Germany. Cook 2 lb. good sauerkraut, drain and arrange it in layers in an earthenware stewpan, alternating each layer with slices of cooked meats, such as mutton, chicken, ham, duck, sausages or bacon. Pour over a little good gravy, cover and keep in a slow oven for ¼ hr. Serve hot or cold.

BILBERRY. The shrub grows wild, and the berries, which make rich wine, are known by a variety of names in different parts of the world, e.g. blueberries, blaeberries, whortleberries, huckleberries, as well as other local names.

Bilberry–Whortleberry Hurt's Jam

Ingredients

6 lb. ripe berries
6 lb. sugar

Method

Place the fruit without water into a saucepan and simmer until reduced and thick. Add sugar and dissolve. Boil for 3 mins., pour into warmed jars and cover.

Bilberry Pie. See FRUIT (p. 228).

Bilberry Wine

Ingredients

2 gall. bilberries
3 gall. water
5 lb. sugar
1 oz. powdered ginger
1 qt. brandy
1 oz. tartar
Rosemary
Lavender leaves

Method

Remove the stalks and leaves from the bilberries, place in a large tub, pour over the water, or half cider and half water, and add the sugar. When the liquor has fermented, add the brandy, powdered ginger and tartar, and a little rosemary and lavender leaves. Allow to stand for 2 days, then strain through a fine sieve into a cask, place the bung in lightly and as soon as the fermenting is over, and the hissing noise has ceased, bung it down tightly. Bottle after 3 mths. Leave for 8 or 9 mths. before use. It will keep for a long time.

BINDING. Liquid used to bind ingredients together as in forcemeat, e.g. egg, catsup, cream, fruit juice and pulp, gravy, milk, mayonnaise. See **COOKING TERMS** and also **ROUX** used as a binding sauce.

BIRCH BEER. The bark of the Black birch is sometimes used to manufacture beer. It is made this way:

Ingredients

1 lb. Black birch bark
1 gall. water
2 handfuls hops
½ lb. pimento
½ lb. ginger
6 qt. golden syrup
20 gall. water
1 pt. fresh yeast
1 pt. warm water

Method

Make a liquid extract of the bark by boiling 1 lb. of it in a gallon of water, straining and reducing the liquor rapidly until it is as thick as treacle. Next boil the hops, pimento and ginger in 3 gall. water for ¾ hr. Strain and stir into the birch extract. Boil up and stir in the golden syrup. Put this into a cask and add 20 gall. water and the yeast dissolved in the warm water. In a short time the beer will show signs of fermenting. Allow this to continue for two days, leaving the bung out, and the bung hole tightly covered with a piece of stout cloth. When the fermentation begins to flag, draw off the beer into bottles, passing it first through a flannel strainer, cork securely and store in a cool place. As only a little of this beer is usually drunk at a time, small-sized bottles are best.

BIRD'S FOOT. See FENUGREEK.
BIRT or BYRT. A small turbot.

BISCOSCHA. An Arabian dish, very popular in Turkey, but believed to be of Spanish origin.

Ingredients
6 eggs
½ lb. fine sugar
Few drops of vanilla essence
6 oz. cornflour

Method
Put the eggs and fine sugar into a large bowl and beat thoroughly with a whisk for 15–25 mins. This should double or even treble the original contents. Add slowly the vanilla essence and cornflour, only stirring enough to mix the ingredients. Put the mixture into a well-oiled deep turban-shaped mould. Bake at 350° F. Therm. 4 for about 30 mins.

BISCUITS. Originally, it is said, biscuits were a variety of hard unleavened bread made in flat cakes. They may be cut into special shapes with cutters, or piped in fancy designs.

BISCUIT POWDER. Biscuits may be made into a fine powder by drying the biscuits in low oven and then rolling them with a rolling pin. Pass through a sieve, and store in an airtight tin. They are useful for charlottes and other sweet dishes requiring crumbs.

Abernethy Biscuits

Ingredients
1 oz. butter or margarine
1 lb. sifted flour
1 oz. caraway seeds
1 dsp. sugar
2 eggs
Little milk

Method
Rub the butter or margarine into the sifted flour, add the sugar and caraway seeds. Add the eggs and mix well; if necessary add a little milk. Roll out, knead into small round cakes, prick with fork and bake at 350° F. Therm. 4 for 15 mins. This is sufficient for 8 biscuits.

American Biscuits, Hot

Ingredients
¼ lb. flour
2½ tsp. baking powder
1 tsp. salt
2 oz. lard
1½ gills milk and water

Method
Sift the flour, baking powder and salt together. Cut and rub in the lard with the fingertips; mix to a soft dough with the milk and water (the exact amount will vary because of the absorbability of the flour). Toss the dough lightly on a floured board, roll out, and pat it into ¾″ thickness. Using a 2″ cutter, cut into rounds and place the rounds on a greased tin. Bake at 375° F. Therm. 5 for 12–15 mins. Serve hot with butter.

Biscuit Drops

Ingredients
8 oz. flour
½ tsp. baking powder
4 oz. dripping
2 oz. sugar
2 oz. chopped peel
4 oz. currants
Grated rind of ½ lemon
1 egg
Little milk

Method
Sieve the flour with baking powder. Rub in the dripping, add the sugar, chopped peel, currants and lemon rind. With the egg and a little milk mix to a very stiff paste. Prepare a floured tin, and drop the mixture in teaspoonfuls on to it. Bake at 375° F. Therm. 5 until golden brown.

3*

Chocolate Rice Biscuits
Ingredients
- 8 oz. sugar
- Pinch of salt
- 4 oz. butter, melted
- 2 eggs
- 4 oz. melted chocolate
- 4 oz. chopped nuts
- Vanilla essence
- 2 oz. flour
- 2 oz. ground rice

Method

Mix together the sugar, salt, melted butter, eggs, melted chocolate, nuts, a few drops of vanilla essence. Next add the ground rice and flour and mix together. Place in a flat baking tin, sprinkle the top with chopped nuts and bake at 350° F. Therm. 4 for 20–30 mins. Remove from oven, and mark in strips whilst still warm.

Coconut Biscuits. See COCONUT.

Digestive Biscuits
Ingredients
- 1½ lb. flour
- 6 oz. fat
- 1½ pt. milk and water
- ½ oz. yeast

Method

Place the flour in basin, rub the fat into it with fingertips. Pour the milk and water into a hollow in the flour, add the yeast. Work a little of the flour into the liquid, and allow to stand until it sponges. Then work in remainder of the flour and allow to stand in a warm place to rise. When it has risen, work the mixture until it is quite smooth. Turn on to floured board and roll out ¼″ thick. Cut into rounds with biscuit cutter and bake at 400° F. Therm. 6 until golden brown.

Ginger Biscuits
Ingredients
- 8 oz. flour
- 2 oz. butter or lard
- 2 oz. caster sugar
- ½ tsp. baking powder
- ½ oz. ground ginger
- 1 egg
- Little milk

Method

Place the flour in a basin and rub in butter or lard with fingertips until like fine breadcrumbs. Next add the sugar, baking powder, ginger, the well-beaten egg and enough milk to make a stiff paste. Turn on to a floured board, roll out and cut into biscuits with a round cutter. Place on a greased baking sheet. Bake at 350° F. Therm. 4 for 20 mins.

Gingerbread Nuts
Ingredients
- 6 oz. flour
- 1 oz. ground ginger
- 3 oz. sugar
- 1½ oz. butter
- 3 oz. treacle

Method

Place the flour in a basin with the ginger and sugar. Melt the butter or margarine in a saucepan with the treacle, pour into flour mixture and mix thoroughly. Form the mixture into little round balls the size of marbles, place on a baking sheet covered with greased paper and bake at 350° F. Therm. 4 for 10 mins. See also **GINGERBREAD**.

Hard Biscuits
Ingredients
2 oz. butter
Skimmed milk
1 lb. flour

Method
Warm the butter and add to as much skimmed milk as will make a very stiff paste when added to the flour. Beat with a rolling pin and work until it becomes smooth. Turn on to a floured board, roll very thin, and cut the biscuits with a round cutter. Prick with a fork, place on a baking sheet and bake at 350° F. Therm. 4 for 8 mins.

Macaroon Biscuits. See MACAROONS.

Nursery Biscuits
Ingredients
4 oz. semolina
4 oz. rolled oats
1 oz. fat
Golden syrup
Pinch of salt

Method
Mix the semolina and rolled oats, rub in fat, add pinch of salt and enough golden syrup to bind to a stiff dough. Roll out and cut into rounds. Bake at 350° F. Therm. 4 until crisp.

Oatmeal Biscuits
Ingredients
3 oz. oatmeal
7 oz. flour
3 oz. caster sugar
¼ tsp. baking powder
½ tsp. salt
3 oz. dripping, lard or butter
1 egg
1 tbsp. water

Method
Put the oatmeal, flour, sugar, baking powder and salt into a basin and mix thoroughly. Melt the fat and add to flour mixture, then the egg beaten with the water. Knead lightly, turn on to floured board, roll out and cut into round shapes. Place on well-greased baking tin and bake at 350° F. Therm. 4 for 20 mins.

Plain Biscuits
Ingredients
1 egg yolk
Milk
1 lb. flour

Method
Beat the egg yolk with a little milk and add to the flour. Beat and knead until the dough is smooth. Turn on to floured board, roll out thin and cut into rounds. Place on greased baking tin at 320° F. Therm. 2 for about 20 mins.

Shortbread. See under this heading.

Shrewsbury Biscuits (Shrewsbury Cakes)
Ingredients
12 oz. flour
4 oz. fat
4 oz. sugar
1 tsp. mixed spice
1 egg
Milk

Method
Place the flour in a basin, rub in fat with fingertips, make a hollow in it, add the sugar, spice, egg and sufficient milk to mix a stiff dough. Mix thoroughly and turn on to a floured board. Roll out to ½″ thickness and cut into rounds. Bake on a floured baking sheet at 300° F. Therm. 2 until the biscuits are slightly coloured round the edge.

[67]

BISMARK. American doughnut made with stewed fruit inside.

BITTERN. A small or medium-sized bird of the heron family, which is noted for its booming cry. A protected bird.

BITTERS. An essence or liqueur made from different kinds of aromatic plants, herbs or fruits.

BLACKBERRY. The fruit of the common bramble is known by this name, although it is not strictly speaking a berry but a cluster of small fruits, each of which contains its own seed. The blackberry and several other berries of the raspberry species, such as the dewberry and cloudberry, are found growing in all parts of the country. Blackberries are frequently used with apples in a boiled suet pudding to give added flavour.

Blackberry Jam

Ingredients

Equal amounts of black-berries and sour apples

¾ lb. sugar to 1 lb. combined fruit

Method

Peel, core and slice the apples, weigh and place in large jar with the blackberries. Cover the jar and bake at 350° F. Therm. 4 for about 1 hr. until the fruit is soft. Turn all into a saucepan, add the sugar and boil for 20 mins. or until the jam will set when tested. Pour into warmed jars and cover.

Blackberry Jelly

Ingredients

3 lb. sour apples

6 lb. blackberries

¾ lb. sugar to every pint of juice

Method

Wipe the apples, core, slice and place them in a preserving pan and cover with cold water. Add blackberries and simmer until the fruit is quite cooked. Strain juice through hair sieve or muslin. Allowing ¾ lb. sugar to every pint of juice, boil together for 1¼ hrs. Stir and skim and pour into warmed jars.

Blackberries, Pickled

Ingredients

1 gall. blackberries

1 lb. sugar

2 cups vinegar

1 tsp. each allspice, cinnamon, cloves, nutmeg

Method

Put the sugar, vinegar, and spices into a saucepan, place over a low heat and simmer for 15 mins. Then add the blackberries, carefully picked and stalked, and cook without boiling for 10 mins. Pour the mixture into jars and use as desired.

Blackberry Pie. See FRUIT (p. 228).
Blackberry Pudding. See FRUIT (p. 229).

Blackberry Syrup

Ingredients

2 qt. blackberry juice

1 lb. sugar

½ oz. powdered nutmeg

¼ oz. powdered cloves

½ oz. powdered cinnamon

¼ oz. allspice

1 pt. good brandy

Method

Place the juice, sugar and spices into a saucepan and boil gently for a short time. Allow to cool and then add the brandy.

[68]

Blackberry Tarts

Ingredients
  Puff paste (see p. 374)
  8 oz. apple marmalade
  2 oz. sugar
  1 pt. blackberries
  1½ oz. apple jelly

Method
Line the tart moulds with puff paste, put a little apple marmalade into each one, bake at 350° F. Therm. 4 for 20 mins. Without removing from the oven, sprinkle with sugar and bake for further 2 mins. when the sugar should have melted. When cool fill up each case with blackberries mixed with soft sugar, spread over a little apple jelly and serve.

Blackberry Wine

Ingredients
  Blackberries
  Boiling water
  Gin or brandy
  Sugar

Method
Place the blackberries in a jar or pan, cover with boiling water. Bake at 200° F. Therm. ¼ to draw out the juice. Measure and strain through a sieve and put the juice in a jar or cask. Allow to ferment for a fortnight. Next add 1 lb. sugar to each gallon of juice with ¼ pt. gin or brandy.

BLACK BRYONY. The young shoots are eaten in the spring. After soaking in salted water and then cooking in fast-boiling water till tender, they are served with White or Vinaigrette sauce like asparagus.

BLACK-COCK (Fr. *coq de bruyère*). This bird of the grouse species is plentiful in parts of the Continent, on the moors and mountains of northern England, in Russia, Siberia and Scandinavia. The female, which rarely weighs more than 2 lb., is a rust colour, commonly known as the "grey-hen". Black cock is also known as Heath Fowl or Black Grouse.

Black-Cock, Roasted

Ingredients
  Black cock
  Butter
  Piece thick toast
  Lemon juice
  Brown gravy
  Bread sauce

Method
The bird should be hung until it is obvious that it has hung long enough. Pick, draw, and wipe the inside with a dry cloth. Truss like a fowl. Bake at 375° F. Therm. 5 and baste with butter until it is done. Ten minutes before the bird is cooked place under it a thick piece of toast dipped in lemon juice. Serve the bird on the toast, with brown gravy and bread sauce.

Black-Cock, Stewed

Ingredients
  Black cock
  Clove of garlic
  Salt and pepper
  Butter
  Wineglass of stock
  2 wineglasses port wine

Method
Joint the bird as an ordinary fowl, fry in butter until nicely browned. A clove of garlic may be added if desired. Remove the joints, put the stock, wine, salt and pepper into the frying pan with the butter and make a good gravy. Then place the black cock into a saucepan, pour over the

[69]

Black-Cock, Stewed (*continued*)

gravy and simmer for 30 mins. Serve on dish with gravy round, and sippets of toast.

BLACK FISH. These dark fish are caught in deep water in the Mediterranean Sea, off the west coast of Europe and occasionally along the south coast of Great Britain.

BLACK JACK. Caramel or burnt sugar used to colour brown stews, soups, sauces and gravies, also wines and spirits.

BLACK PEPPER. The dried, ground whole berry. See **PEPPER.**

BLACK PUDDING (Fr. *boudin noir*). This nondescript sort of sausage is made chiefly from pig's blood or sheep's blood and suet. Known in some parts of Scotland as "black pot". Well clean and steep pig's entrails in cold water until required. To 1 pt. fresh-drawn pig's blood take 3 onions, chopped very fine and cooked until nearly done in a very little water. Chop up finely 2 lb. fresh pork, mix with the onions, pig's blood, salt, pepper, allspice. Tie one end of a sausage-skin and by means of a funnel fill it at the other with the mixed ingredients. Fasten the upper end of the pudding, coil it into the desired shape or tie it into short lengths, and throw it into boiling water, which must be kept boiling for 20–25 mins. Remove from water, and allow to cool. Keep in cold water until it is wanted for use. So prepared it will keep good for 2 or 3 days in the summer, and a week in the winter. When required to serve, broil gently over a low heat, but this requires great care to prevent the skin cracking.

BLADDERLOCK. See **SEAWEED.**

BLANCH. See **COOKING TERMS.**

BLANCHED OR SOLID PACK FOR APPLES. See **PRESERVATION.**

BLANCMANGE. The literal meaning of this French word is "something white to eat", but in this country it is used with no reference to colour.

Blancmange with Cornflour

Ingredients
  3 oz. cornflour
  1 qt. milk
  3 oz. caster sugar
  Flavouring

Method
Mix the cornflour to a smooth paste with a little cold milk. Add the smallest pinch of salt. Put the remainder of the milk with the sugar in a saucepan over a low heat. Just before it boils stir in the cornflour and allow to boil for 10 mins. stirring all the time to prevent burning. Flavour with vanilla or any other essence, pour into a wetted mould and allow to cool. Jam or stewed fruit should be served with blancmange of this kind.

Blancmange with Isinglass

Ingredients
  1 oz. isinglass
  1 pt. milk
  4 oz. sugar
  1 pt. cream
  Flavouring essence

Method
Dissolve the isinglass in the milk, add sugar and stir over a low heat until all dissolves. Pour in the cream, stir at intervals until cold. Add the flavouring essence and pour into a wetted mould.

BLAZE. See **COOKING TERMS.**

BLEACHING. The surface of many fruits, peeled and quartered or stoned, goes brown when left to the air. The colour may be maintained by immersing in cold water with a squeeze of lemon juice added (see APPLES). Also by boiling or steaming, brine bath, sulphuring or acid rinse.

BLEAK (Fr. *ablette*). A small European river fish of the carp family, used and dressed in the same way as sprat.

BLEND. See COOKING TERMS.

BLEWITT. An edible fungi resembling the field mushroom. It has a moist and smooth cap, with the edges turning inwards, which is browny-grey, at times with a lilac tinge. Stem is violet-coloured and the blewitt has a very faint scent.

BLOATERS. Bloaters are lightly salted and smoked herrings, in the preparation of which Great Yarmouth has no rival.

TO COOK. Open the bloaters down the back and bone them. Lay the fish under a hot grill. When cooked lay on a heated dish, rub with a little butter and serve immediately. Alternatively, split open, remove backbone, head, tail and fins, fold double and broil for 6 mins.

Bloater Fillets. Place 3 or 4 bloaters in a saucepan with water and boil until the skin peels off easily. Carefully remove the flesh in strips or fillets, place on strips of hot buttered toast, rub over with a little butter, a dust of cayenne, and stand in oven until heated through. Serve immediately.

BLONDE. The sluggish ray which is found near Plymouth.

BLUEBERRY. See BILBERRY.

BLUE VINNEY CHEESE. A hard, blue-veined cheese which is made in Dorset from skimmed milk.

BOAR (Fr. *porc*). The wild swine or domestic male pig. In some places on Christmas Day, the Boar's Head Ceremony takes place, i.e. Queen's College, Oxford. To dress a boar's head handsomely is regarded as proof of culinary skill.

Boar's Head, Boiled. Remove the snout, hair, and bones. Cleanse it thoroughly, scald and place in a boiling pot containing vinegar and water. Add 2 oz. salt, a few peppercorns, some parsley, thyme, eschalot and sage, and allow to steep for 3 days with the tongue and 2 lb. meat. When drained, fill up the cavities made by the removal of the bones, etc., with thin slices of the meat and tongue rolled together. Fasten up the opening with strong thread as soon as the head has been well filled and the form is good. Place the head, tied in a cloth, in a stewpan with the herbs and add a pint of wine, 4 cloves, a carrot, 1 oz. salt and simmer for 6–7 hrs. Remove from stewpan and allow to cool. When quite cold, remove the cloth, undo the fastenings, ornament and glaze the head. Replace the tusks, and insert eyes made of white of egg and beetroot.

FOR THE SAUCE. Rub the rind from 2 oranges and slice them. Rub 2 or 3 lumps of sugar on 2 more oranges, put the sugar into a basin with 6 tbsp. redcurrant jelly, a little white pepper, a shallot, 1 tsp. mixed mustard and enough port wine to make the sauce as thick as good cream. Add the orange rind slices, which should be cut very thin, and bottle for use. This sauce may be used for nearly every kind of cold meat.

BOAR, YOUNG WILD. This can be baked, roast or braised or cooked as any other form of pork. Serve with Demi-glace or Madeira sauce, redcurrant jelly and sour cream. Barbecued Wild Boar is especially good; the meat should be well basted with hot Barbecue sauce (see p. 47).

Boar, Haunch of Young Wild. Take a quarter of young wild boar, remove the rind, take out the thigh bone and saw off the thin end; rub it with salt, put it into a pan and pour marinade to cover it. Allow to soak for 3 days. Then drain, wipe dry with a cloth and place in a deep baking dish with a quantity of lard, cover with greaseproof paper and bake at 400° F. Therm. 6 for ¾ hr. Baste frequently. Then add 2 cups of the marinade, cook for 30 mins. longer, basting with the stock. When cooked, remove from the oven, drain and spread over a thick layer of bread raspings, dried and pounded, mixed with a little caster sugar and powdered

Boar, Haunch of Young Wild (*continued*)

cinnamon, and sufficiently moisten this with red wine to make it into a paste. Over this layer sprinkle dry breadcrumbs. Put the haunch back into the baking-dish, reduce heat, bake at 200° F. Therm. ¼ for 20 mins., basting often with the fat. Remove, place a paper frill on end of bone and serve with Orange sauce.

BOARFISH. A fish allied to the red mullet found in the North Atlantic and the Mediterranean.

BOBOTEE. Cut an onion into slices, and fry in butter. Soak a small thin slice of bread in milk and mix it up with the onion and add 8 grated sweet almonds and 2 eggs beaten up in ¼ pt. milk. Now stir in 1 lb. chopped meat, 1 tbsp. curry powder and 1 oz. butter. Brush a pie-dish with butter, squeeze over a little lemon juice, pour the mixture into the dish and bake for 30 mins. Put a border of boiled rice round the hot dish, pour over Curry sauce (see p. 442) and serve.

BOLOGNA SAUSAGE. Take equal quantities of beef and pork, pound to a paste and season it very highly with pepper, salt, mace, cloves and a little garlic. When this mixture is put into the skins, add a strip or two of fat bacon; it may be boiled for 1 hr., or smoked for 2–3 mths., when it will be fit for use. The Italians eat it in its uncooked state.

BOMBAY DUCK. Also called Bummelo, Bumbalo, or Bumaloe fish. A fish found in Indian waters. It is very nutritious, and possesses a peculiar yet delicate flavour. For exportation it is salted and cured and is usually served with curry.

BOMBES. These ices may be made in different colours and flavours and with various ingredients, but they are always cast in a spherical shape in special moulds.

BONDON. A small loaf-shaped, whole-milk, soft cheese similar to gournay; made round about Rouen. Normandy is famous for this cheese, which gets its name from its resemblance in shape to a bung (*bondon*).

BONE, TO. To remove the bones. Like every other process of cooking, boning requires some practical experience. A small boning knife is required; it should have a sharp, short, pointed blade so that the external flesh may be removed and the space left when the bone has been taken out stuffed with forcemeats and other things. The boning of joints of meat is mostly done by the butcher. See **FISH, CHICKEN, GAME,** and various meats.

BONELESS BIRDS. Get the butcher to cut 1 lb. veal or steak in one thin piece, which will divide into four. For the stuffing, take 3 tbsp. each diced celery, finely minced onion, mushrooms and chopped parsley. Sauté them in a little butter for about 5 mins. over a low heat. Then add 1½ cups breadcrumbs, seasoned with ½ tsp. salt and a little pepper. Add a sprinkling of thyme, tarragon and basil and stir all together. Remove from heat and divide mixture into 4 heaps in the centre of each slice of meat. Roll up and wrap each in a rasher of bacon and fasten with a small toothpick and a piece of thread. Then brown in a hot frying-pan. Add ¾ pt. water, to which 1 tsp. meat extract has been added. Add a few drops of Worcester sauce or 1 tbsp. mango chutney. Cover closely and simmer for ¾ hr. Should you wish to use this dish some hours later, remove the rolls and make a gravy in the pan by adding 2 tbsp. flour, blended with a little cold water, stirring slowly into the hot liquid, and cook until thick. Put the rolls back again and cover, and leave till about 20 mins. before use. Heat gently and serve with boiled rice or noodles or fluffy mashed potato, garnished with watercress. This is sufficient for 4 persons. If desired, the boneless birds may be simmered in a Tomato sauce or Mushroom sauce instead of the above.

BONES. The composition of bones is half earthy salts and half gelatine, and these salts can be extracted by soaking bone. Add a little vinegar to the soaking water or soak the bone in vinegar or hydrochloric acid. When the process is completed nothing will remain of the substantial bone, and it will be soft as india-rubber. Bones are used to make stock for soups.

Bones, Devilled. Make a mixture of mustard, salt, cayenne pepper and a little mushroom ketchup; lay a coating of butter over the bones, then rub the mixture well in and broil brown over a gentle heat. See **MARROW BONES.**

BONNE FEMME SOUP. See SOUPS. "Bonne Femme" is used generally to mean simply cooked with a garnish of fresh vegetables or herbs, usually including mushrooms.

BORACIC OINTMENT. This can be used to preserve eggs when they are very fresh. Rub the boracic ointment in the shell, covering the whole surface.

BORAGE. The culinary uses of borage, which has a cucumber flavour, are: the leaves as a cooling summer drink, young leaves as a vegetable, or in salads and pickles. Also used medicinally. The flowers are sometimes candied and used for confectionery. Also called Bee Bread and Star Flower.

BORDEAUX, BORDELAISE. The capital of the Gascon country, which is famous for its wine (claret), gives its name to a brown sauce, Bordelaise (see SAUCES), and to a method of serving the entrecôte, or ribsteak, and to the cooking of crayfish.

BORTSCH. See BEETROOT SOUP (p. 63).

BOTARGO. Roe of the grey mullet. See FISH ROES for uses.

BOTTLING FRUIT. See FRUIT.

BOUCHÉE. Small patty of puff pastry or vol-au-vent filled with a salpicon of chicken, game or fish, well moistened with white sauce. Bouchées may also be made sweet, filled with preserves. For Bouchées with Game, Lobster, Shrimp, etc., see PASTE AND PASTRY (p. 376).

BOUDINADE. The French term for a boned quarter of lamb stuffed with white and black puddings, roasted and served with rich sauce.

BOUILLABAISSE. Sometimes written *Bouille-abaisse* or *Bouille-a-baisse.* A fish soup which is a great favourite among the Provençal French. It is so called because it is boiled up, and then removed from heat and boiled over and over again. It is said to be best prepared at Marseilles. Some five or six kinds of fish are used, in addition to the shellfish.

BOUILLIE. The name given in France to flour or other farinaceous food boiled in milk.

BRACE. A pair of game birds, usually composed of a cock and hen.

BRAINS (Fr. *cerveaux*). Brains must be thoroughly cleansed of blood and skin before use.

Brain Cakes

Ingredients	*Method*
Brains	Blanch the brains by soaking in salted water for 3 hrs., then boil for 15 mins. to get them firmer. Chop up, place in a mortar with the parsley, mace, cayenne, salt, pepper and eggs. Pound together until a stiff paste is formed. Lay out the paste in small rounds 1½″ in diameter, dip in egg and breadcrumbs, and fry to a light brown.
2 eggs	
Salt and pepper	
1 tsp. chopped parsley	
1 saltspoon each mace and cayenne	

Brain Fritters

Ingredients	*Method*
1 large brain	Wash a large brain in salted water and boil for 15–18 mins. in a good stock. Allow to get cold, cut into very thin slices; make a batter by mixing the flour
1 cup flour	
1 gill water	
1 tbsp. olive oil	

[73]

Brain Fritters (*continued*)

1 egg yolk
Pepper and salt
1 egg white

vith the water and adding the olive oil, egg yolk, and a seasoning of pepper and salt. Allow this to stand for 1½ hrs., then beat the white of egg to stiff froth and fold in. Dip the slices of brain into the batter and fry one or two at a time. Allow to drain on kitchen paper and serve garnished with dried parsley dipped in the fat.

Brains, Scrambled

Ingredients

1 lb. brains
1 oz. butter
4 eggs
Chopped parsley
Salt and pepper
8 oz. puff paste

Method

Place the brains in a saucepan with water and a little vinegar and simmer gently for 20 mins. Remove the dark outside, and place in a frying pan with the butter, eggs, parsley, salt and pepper. Place over a gentle heat and cook until eggs are soft. Fill patty tins with the puff paste, take a cutter smaller than the pans and cut the centre of the paste half through, so as to form a lid. Place in the oven for a few minutes to cook before adding the brains. When the paste is set, remove the centre lids, fill up the central cavities with brain mixture, replace the lids and return to oven for a few seconds to heat. Garnish each with a sprig of parsley.

Brains, Stewed. Put the brains into salted water for 3 hrs. to get the blood out, then boil for 30 mins. in a saucepan with sufficient water to cover. Pour off water, add a cupful of milk or cream, pinch of salt, little pepper, and 1½ oz. butter. Boil quickly for 12 mins., add 1 tsp. vinegar and serve.

BRAMBLE. See BLACKBERRY.

Bramble Tip Wine. Gather the green shoots in May or early June whilst still tender, and boil together 1 gall. tips in 1 gall. water with 4 lb. demerara sugar. Strain off the liquid and leave to ferment, then bottle. Do not use for 12 mths.

BRAN. The husks of ground corn. Not much used in cooking, although it forms an important item in brown bread.

Bran Muffins

Ingredients

1 cup flour
¾ cup bran
½ tsp. salt
2 tsp. baking powder
⅓ cup molasses
⅔ cup milk
2 eggs

Method

Put the flour into a basin, add bran, salt and baking powder, and mix together. Add molasses, milk, eggs, well beaten; blend together, put into greased muffin tins and bake at 350° F. Therm. 4 for 15 mins. This makes 12 muffins.

Bran Tea. Take 1 lb. fresh wheat bran and boil in 3 qt. water; reduce to 1 qt.; strain, add sugar, honey or treacle to taste.

Bran Yeast. A good serviceable yeast can be made from 1 pt. bran boiled in 2 qt. water for 10 mins. with a handful of hops added. Strain the liquor and, when lukewarm, add 3 or 4 tbsp. best yeast and 2 tbsp. brown sugar or treacle. Put into a jar or wooden cask, and place in a warm place to ferment. When well worked it may be bottled, corked tightly and kept in a cool place.

BRANDADE. This name is applied to dishes of codfish cut into little pieces pounded with the addition of garlic, parsley, lemon juice and pepper, and beaten up with olive oil to form a paste about the consistency of cream cheese. Also known as Branlade.

Ingredients

1½ lb. salted codfish
3 shallots
1 large onion
2 tbsp. oil
2 cups salad oil
Juice of 3 lemons
3 tbsp. cream
Nutmeg
Pepper and salt
1 tsp. chopped parsley

Method

Divide the codfish into squares and soak for 2 or 3 days in fresh water, changing the water repeatedly. Clean and place in a saucepan with plenty of cold water, cover and bring to boil, reduce the heat and allow to simmer for ¼ hr. Remove the fish, take out all bones, and place fish in a basin. Peel and fry the shallots and onion in 2 tbsp. oil and, when a golden colour, add the cod, warm it and put into a mortar. Pound it well and then place in a saucepan and work in a cupful of salad oil. Continue to work until all the oil is absorbed, add the juice of two lemons, add a further cupful of oil gradually. When this is creamy, add the cream, season with salt, pepper, nutmeg and parsley. Now add the juice of a third lemon and thoroughly incorporate all the ingredients to a smooth paste. Warm up, pile on a dish in a dome shape, and sprinkle with chopped truffles, top with a whole truffle, and garnish with crayfish, scallops of fish and truffles alternately and pyramids of oyster patties.

BRANDY (Fr. *eau-de-vie*). Brandy is a great acquisition to the cook, and finds its way into many a sweet and savoury dish. Pure brandy should be clear, and sparkling, of a light colour when new, yellow if a few years old, and brownish yellow if very old. Its flavour should be sweet, mellow, slightly vinous, and not in any degree fiery from raw alcohol.

Brandy Bitters. Take 2 lb. dry orange peel, 1 lb. cardamom seeds, 3 lb. gentian root, 2 oz. cochineal and 2 oz. cinnamon, and grind to a coarse powder. Pour over them 1 gall. brandy and 8 gall. water, leave for 10 days and then filter.

Brandy Butter. See BUTTERS.

Brandy, Lemon. Take the thin or yellow rinds only of 2 small lemons, and cover them with ½ pt. best French brandy. Let them stand in a closed-up bottle for 2 wks., then strain off the spirit and keep it corked closely for use. A syrup of 2 oz. loaf sugar and ¼ pt. water may be added if a sweet brandy is desired.

Brandy Mince for Pies. Take 1 lb. each fresh beef suet, sugar, currants and apples. Wash, pick and dry the currants, and mince the suet and peeled, cored apples with ¼ lb. citron and the same of orange peel, the juice of 1 lemon and the grated peel of 2. When all these ingredients are well mixed, add a glass of brandy gradually. Keep closely covered until required for use.

Brandy Sauce. See SAUCES

Brandy Snaps. Brandy snaps are flat, but are often confused with Jumbles, which are curled round the finger or a stick before cooling.

Ingredients	*Method*
1 lb. flour	Place the flour in a basin and rub in the
½ lb. butter	butter, then mix in the sugar, ginger, all-
½ lb. sugar	spice, grated lemon rind, and strained
2 oz. ground ginger	lemon juice; beat in the treacle, spread
1 dsp. allspice	the paste thinly over some well-greased
Grated rind of ½ lemon	baking sheets and bake at 325° F. Therm.
Strained juice of 1 lemon	4. When cool cut into squares.
½ lb. treacle	

BRAWN. The literal meaning of this term from A.S. *bawr-en* is "the flesh of the boar" (easily corrupted to "brawn").

Ingredients	*Method*
The meat, ears and tongue of	Soak the meat, ears and tongue in salt
a pig's head	water overnight. Cleanse and boil for
1 large onion	3 hrs. in very little water, but care must
25 peppercorns	be taken not to allow the meat to burn.
2 bay leaves	Remove the bones, cut the ears into
2 blades of mace	strips and the tongue into slices. Put the
1 tsp. allspice	bones into the saucepan with the liquor,
½ tsp. thyme	the onions and herbs and boil for 30 mins.
	Strain the liquor and put with the meat,
	boil once more and pour into a brawn
	mould. When required, either dip the
	mould into hot water, or wrap it round
	with a hot towel for a few minutes.

BRAZIL NUT. The seed of a native tree of Brazil. It is sometimes called "chestnut of Brazil" and has a delicate flavour, not unlike our hazel-nut in taste.

BREAD (Fr. *pain*). Bread is generally white or brown; sometimes spiced currant bread or "granny" bread is made. Also bread without leaven, e.g. rye loaf, barley bannocks, oaten cakes.

When making bread it is essential to work in a warm even temperature, keeping the dough lukewarm and avoiding all draughts, both while mixing and proving, or a sad loaf will result. In making bread in small quantities it is necessary to guard against over-kneading. Before beginning to make the bread, have your tins prepared: floured *and* greased if you want crisp crust; floured *or* greased if you want a soft crust.

YEASTS. There are two kinds of yeast available to the housewife: (1) Fresh yeast, which is the kind that is moist and crumbly and looks like putty and is bought from the bread shop, dairy or grocer; (2) Tins of yeast, which contain a granulated form of the product. This type needs careful reconstituting. It must never be hurried while regaining life and should be softened in lukewarm liquid, all the liquid stated in the recipe being put into a warm bowl with a sprinkle of sugar and gently stirred to allow the yeast germ to come to life again. Then the flour is added, a slack dough is left to rise, and the remainder of the flour and salt added after 1 hr.

In breadmaking, the yeast and sugar are creamed together, then a little tepid milk and tepid water are added. The mix is allowed to froth, and poured into the centre of the warmed flour; a little flour is sprinkled over the top, the yeast allowed to bubble through, then the mixture is ready to knead. This process is known as "sponging".

YEASTS (*continued*)

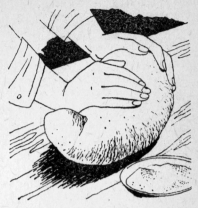

Testing heat of water   Getting the dough into convenient lumps
                                                for proving

The rising time is dependent on the amount of yeast used:

½ oz. yeast to	1 lb. flour	about 1–2	hrs.
1 ,, ,,	3½ ,, ,,	,, 3	,,
1 ,, ,,	5–7,, ,,	,, 12	,,

TO PROVE. Bread is proved by placing the dough in the warmth after mixing
and kneading it well, and allowing it to rise, with a clean cloth on the top of the
bowl. The dough is left until it doubles its size. The time allowed for the dough to
rise will vary not only according to the proportion of yeast used (see above) but
also according to other circumstances. If the yeast is fresh it will rise quicker
than "old" yeast. Again, the rising varies according to the weather; in hot
weather it will rise more quickly than in cold. Should the yeast be good, a quartern
loaf should be light in about 2 hrs. Experience is necessary to enable anyone to
judge when the dough is ready. It looks light and "risen". If the bread is left too
long to "over-prove" it will be spoilt. Also, should the bread be put into too cool
an oven, it will continue to prove long after it is in the oven and it will be full of
holes like a sponge when it is cooked: always have the oven ready heated. After
making it into loaves or shapes the bread is again left covered with a clean cloth
in a warm place to rise and again double its size. The bread is then brushed over
with lukewarm milk and placed in the oven to bake. Small loaves bake the best.
By adding 1 oz. fat to each 1 lb. flour and rubbing the fat into the flour before
adding the yeast, the bread usually keeps moist a few days longer.

TO BAKE. The dough should be baked at 400° F. Therm. 6 for the first 10 mins.
then the temperature should be reduced to 350° F. Therm. 4 till the bread is cooked
through. For a soft crust, bake the whole time in a moderate oven at 350° F.
Therm. 4, but if a crisp crust is required, bake at 400° F. Therm. 6 till the crust
is formed, then reduce heat to 350° F. Therm. 4.

When you think the bread should be ready, test it to see that it is thoroughly,
cooked; the loaves should be well risen and when tapped should sound hollow;
they should be baked to a good brown colour. The usual time for baking bread
is between 45 and 60 mins. for a 1-lb loaf.

TYPES OF LOAVES

Brown Bread. Make like ordinary bread. What is generally called brown bread is made from flour with the bran in it.

Coburg loaf is sometimes made with only one cut or crease in the centre of the loaf, but more generally with cuts at right angles on top; these are made just

Testing the rise   Dividing

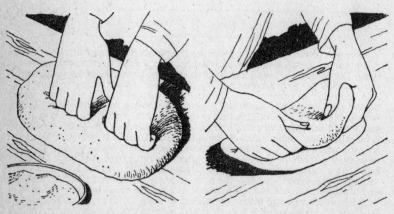

Kneading   Folding

before the loaves are set in the oven and the dough spreads out where the cuts have been made, producing a surface of two textures and colours.

Cottage loaf. Divide the dough into two pieces, one less than a fourth the size of the other. Make them both smooth and round, drawing the edges underneath. Place the small one on the top of the large one and press down the centre of it with a floured finger. Mark the sides of the loaf here and there with a knife. drawing it upwards and slightly cutting them.

Crusty Brick is somewhat like a cottage loaf, crusty all round but oblong in form instead of being round. A similar shape but baked close to another loaf is the *Sister Brick* which is crusty on one side.

Farm House is the name given to loaves made of rather soft flour or soft dough, usually flat and round in form and well dusted with flour before baking.

Long loaves are about 12″ long proved on the baking sheets, and cut four times slat-wise just before baking.

Pan or *Tin loaves* are made all shapes and sizes.

"Plait" Collar or *Collars*. A loaf made shuttle-shaped.

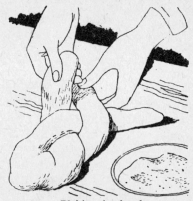

Plaiting the dough

Tinned loaf. After kneading the bread, put into a floured tin which it should only half fill. When it has risen to the top, bake it.

Undertins or *Underpans* are those loaves baked either on the oven bottom or a baking sheet covered with a long pan which the loaf fills as it springs. These are generally made for sandwich bread.

Wholemeal Bread. This is also made like other bread, but with wholemeal flour, and it requires rather more yeast to lighten it.

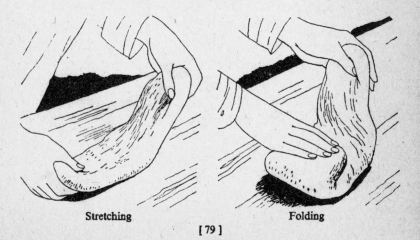

Stretching   Folding

TO MAKE 2 LARGE OR 3 SMALL LOAVES

Ingredients

3½ lb. flour
1 level tsp. salt
1 oz. yeast
1 dsp. sugar
1½ pt. water
½ pt. milk

Method

Sift the flour and salt into a basin. Make a hollow in the flour and pour into it the yeast which has been creamed with the sugar and stirred into the milk and hot water. Sprinkle a little flour over the liquid and leave till the yeast begins to bubble. Then knead thoroughly but lightly, cover with a cloth and set in the warmth to rise. After about an hour the dough should have doubled itself and

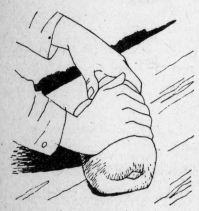

Rolling

Putting into tins

Putting baked loaf to cool

then it should be kneaded again. Divide into even-sized lumps and lay them in well-greased tins; put to rise again until double their size. Bake at 375–400° F. Therm. 6 for 30–35 mins., reducing the heat for the last 20 mins. Do not remove the loaves from the oven till they are firm and crisp and sound hollow when tapped.

For *Brown Bread* use recipe above but substitute wholemeal flour for white flour.

BAKING POWDER BREAD

Ingredients

1 lb. flour
2 tsp. baking powder
1 tsp. salt
Milk to mix
1 tbsp. sugar (if desired)

Method

Mix flour, salt and baking powder well and add 1 tbsp. sugar if desired. Moisten to a fairly stiff dough with about ½ pt. milk, knead very quickly and divide into 2 square loaves. Place in well-greased tins and bake at 425° F. Therm. 7, keeping the oven heat up the whole time for 1 hr.

BREAD CROÛTONS FOR SOUP

Ingredients

Slices of stale bread ¼" thick
Fat for frying

Method

Remove the crust from the bread, and cut the slices into dice about ¼" square. Have a pan of deep fat heated, and when the blue smoke rises from it, plunge the diced bread into it (a wire frying basket is useful for this) and fry till a golden brown. Drain on kitchen paper and serve with soup. Sometimes the sippets are put into the soup tureen and the soup poured over them.

BREADCRUMBS I. Take slices of stale white bread and rub through a sieve or remove the crusts from a loaf of bread and grate on a grater.

BREADCRUMBS II. Put the crumbs into a tin or frying-pan and allow 1 oz. butter or margarine to each ¼ lb. crumbs. Stir frequently over the heat till the crumbs are well browned. When cool, store in airtight glass jar. If carefully prepared, these crumbs will keep about 7 days.

BREAD RASPINGS. Put slices of bread on a tin. Bake at 250° F. Therm. ½ and leave them till they are crisp and dry. Remove and crush with a rolling pin. Rub through a sieve and store in an airtight jar. Bread that has become too stale may be utilised in the same way, and will thus be useful for the preparation of puddings and stuffings.

BRIOCHE. A light French yeast cake, which is a favourite at breakfast, eaten hot with coffee or tea. It requires both time and patience and it cannot be hurried. It should be made the day before it is required for use, as follows:

Ingredients

1 oz. yeast dissolved in ¼ pt. water
4 oz. flour
3 large eggs

Method

Dissolve the yeast in warm water and add the ¼ lb. flour. Make a gash in the top and set the basin in a large bowl in warm water to sponge. This will double its bulk.

[81]

BRIOCHE (*continued*)
¾ lb. flour
8 oz. butter
1 tsp. salt
1 tbsp. sugar

Meanwhile work the unbeaten eggs in the remaining flour, add a little extra warm water if necessary and beat with the hands for 10 mins. Add butter, salt and sugar, beat a further 5 mins. Next add the yeast mixture, but do not mix any longer than necessary. Cover and leave to rise for 3–4 hrs. Knead down and leave in a cool place overnight. Next day break down gently so that it remains light. It may be baked in a loaf on a buttered baking sheet or buttered ring mould. Leave to rise for 30 mins. before baking at 450° F. Therm. 8 for 30–35 mins. Cover with unglazed paper if the brioches brown too much. To test if cooked, insert a needle; if it comes out dry, the brioche is cooked.

BROWN BREAD (STEAMED)
Ingredients
1 tsp. bicarb. soda
1½ pt. sour milk
¾ cup treacle
1 tsp. salt
¾ lb. wholemeal

Method
Mix together the bicarb. soda and sour milk and add treacle, salt and wholemeal flour (or ½ lb. wholemeal and ¼ lb. bran or rye meal). Put into a greased tin and steam for 4 hrs. Bread can be steamed successfully according to directions given for steamed puddings; that is, water should be only halfway up the tin. For this purpose the water must boil. The tins in this case must be greased instead of floured to prevent the dough sticking. A firm crust is formed all over the loaf, and, if preferred browned, it can be put into a sharp oven (400° F. Therm. 6) for a few minutes when cooked. Steamed bread is lighter than baked bread.

CARAWAY BREAD
Ingredients
½ pt. milk
4 oz. butter
4 oz. sugar
Pinch of salt
½ oz. yeast
Lukewarm water
2 tbsp. caraway seeds
1 lb. rye flour

Method
Boil together the milk, butter, sugar and salt. When lukewarm, add the yeast dissolved in ¼ cup lukewarm water, caraway seeds and rye flour and knead together for about 30 mins. Place in a warm place to rise, and when risen to twice its bulk, shape into a long roll and bake at 350° F. Therm. 4. Plain flour can be used if necessary to help the kneading. Add a little extra liquid if necessary.

DOUGH CAKES
Ingredients
½ oz. yeast
Warm water
1 lb. flour
4–6 oz. sugar
½ lb. beef dripping or lard
2 oz. currants

Method
Make a plain bread dough and leave to rise, and when the dough has doubled its size, turn on to a floured board and roll into a long strip. Divide the dripping and sugar into 3 portions and spread one portion over the strip of dough, then fold this into three. Roll again and fold using two other portions of dripping. Fold the fruit in with the last addition. Roll the dough to fit a well-greased square tin and leave in a warm place to prove (rise again), for about 30 mins. Glaze the top with a little sugar and water. Bake at 400° F. Therm. 6 for 30–40 mins.

FRENCH BREAD
Ingredients
4 lb. flour
3 oz. salt
½ pt. yeast
2 egg yolks
3 egg whites
1 pt. milk

Method
Stir into the flour and salt sifted together the ½ pt. yeast, the yolks and whites of egg beaten separately, and the milk slightly warmed. Stir all till well mixed to a thin dough, and allow to rise for a few minutes. Make the dough into loaves of the size required, and bake at 400° F. Therm. 6 for ¾–1 hr.

FRUIT BREAD
Ingredients
1 lb. dough
2 oz. currants
1 oz. sugar

Method
To each pound of proved dough (as recipe above) knead in 1 oz. sugar and 2 oz. currants. Put in well-greased tins and leave in a warm place to rise to double its size. Bake at 400° F. Therm. 6 for first 10 mins., then reduce the heat to 300° F. Therm. 2. Allow the bread to cook through, which takes about 45–50 mins.

GARLIC BREAD. See TOASTED LOAF below.

LARDY CAKE
Ingredients
1 lb. bread dough
4 oz. dripping or fat
2 eggs
4 oz. fruit
2 oz. sugar
Nutmeg
Candied peel

Method
Take 1 lb. bread dough and place in a mixing bowl. Add the melted dripping or cooking fat, stir in with a palette knife and add the beaten eggs and 3 or 4 oz. currants or sultanas, or cooked chopped prunes, the sugar, a grating of nutmeg and a chopping of candied peel. Stir just sufficiently to mix in the ingredients and put the dough into two well-greased tins. Leave in a warm place and allow the

LARDY CAKE (*continued*)

dough to rise to double its size. Bake at 400° F. Therm. 6 for 45 mins.

MUFFINS

Ingredients
2 gills milk
4 oz. butter
2½ tbsp. sugar
Pinch salt
½ oz. yeast
¾ lb. flour

Method
Warm milk and add butter, sugar, and salt, and stir till dissolved. When this mixture is lukewarm, add yeast, dissolved in a little warm water, and enough flour to make a dough that will drop from a spoon. Leave for 12 hrs. before using and bake in small muffin tins.

PLAIN ROLLS

Ingredients
½ pt. milk
1 oz. sugar
½ tsp. salt
3 oz. fat
¾–1 oz. yeast
1¼ lb. flour

Method
Scald the milk and pour over the sugar, salt and fat; stand aside to cool. When lukewarm add yeast, and stir in the flour. Mix thoroughly, turn into greased pan and allow to double in bulk. Knead and shape and put to rise. Bake for 15–20 mins. at 425° F. Therm. 7. It will take some time to rise and will yield 25 rolls.

VARIATIONS

Clover leaf. Form bits of dough into small balls about 1 inch in diameter. Place 3 balls in each greased medium-sized muffin cup. Brush with melted butter. For *Twin rolls*, use only 2 balls in each cup.

Dinner rolls. Roll dough into cylindrical shapes with tapered ends on lightly greased baking sheet.

Crescents (Croissants). Roll dough into oblong, 6″ wide and less than ¼″ thick. Cut into long narrow triangles, stretch the wider end of triangle a little and roll up so the longer point winds up on the outside. Then stretch each roll out by pulling 2 ends and place on tin in a curved shape to form the crescent.

N.B.—*For all the following shapes, roll out the dough into long oblong shapes a little less than ¼″ thick, spread with very soft or melted butter. Fold half the dough over the other half. Trim edges to square corners. Cut into strips ¼″ wide and 6″ long. Use strips to make the following:*

Figure 8's. Hold one end of strip firmly in one hand and twist the other end stretching it slightly until the two ends when brought together will naturally form a figure 8. Seal ends well.

Knots. Twist and tie strip into knot, press ends down on greased baking sheet.

Twists. Same as figure 8 but given an additional twist just before placing on greased baking sheet.

SODA LOAF

Ingredients
1 lb. flour
1 tsp. salt
1 tsp. bicarb. soda
1 tsp. cream of tartar
Milk

Method
Sift the flour into a bowl with salt. Add the bicarb. soda and cream of tartar, moisten with the milk and mix well, but do not knead the dough. Place in a bread tin or on a warm, greased and floured oven shelf, and bake for about 40–45 mins. at 350° F. Therm. 4.

[84]

TEA BREAD

Ingredients

- 8 oz. flour
- Pinch of salt
- 1 tsp. baking powder
- 3 oz. butter
- 4 oz. sugar
- 2 eggs
- 1 oz. currants
- Spice
- Milk

Method

Sift together the flour, salt and baking powder. Cream together the butter or margarine and sugar, add the well-beaten eggs, the currants and spice, if desired, mix together, add flour mixture and a little milk to make a stiff dough. Place in a well-greased and floured tin and bake at 350° F. Therm. 4 for 1 hr.

TEA CAKES

Ingredients

- 1 lb. flour
- Butter
- 1 dsp. sugar
- 1 tsp. salt
- ½ oz. yeast
- ½ pt. tepid milk (2 parts boiling liquid to 1 part cold)
- 1 tsp. sugar
- 1 egg
- 2 oz. sultanas, chopped raisins or currants
- ½ tsp. spice

Method

Sift the flour into a bowl and rub in the butter. Add the salt and 1 dsp. sugar. Mix the yeast with the warm milk, 1 tsp. sugar and the beaten egg. Next add the fruit, and a small pinch of mixed spice if desired. Mix to a light dough, knead well and leave to prove. Re-knead, divide into three and shape into round cakes. Place in a warmed, greased tin. Put in a warm place and cover with a clean cloth; allow to prove for about 10 mins. Bake at 400° F. Therm. 6 for 10–15 mins. and when cooked, brush over with a little butter or margarine.

TOASTED LOAF. Slice a small loaf, cutting only halfway through. Separate the pieces and pour a little melted butter between each slice. Cover with greaseproof paper, tie with string and place in a moderate oven (350° F. Therm. 4) so that the loaf is slightly browned. For Garlic Bread, flavour the butter with garlic.

TREACLE BREAD

Ingredients

- 1 lb. flour
- 2 oz. sugar
- Pinch of salt
- 1 small tsp. bicarb. soda
- ½ tsp. ground ginger
- 3 oz. butter
- 2 tbsp. treacle
- Buttermilk

Method

Sift the dry ingredients. Cut and rub in the butter, add the treacle and buttermilk to make a fairly dry dough. Knead, roll out, make as soda bread or cut into rounds or scones. Bake at 350° F. Therm. 4 until cooked. Best eaten fresh.

UNFERMENTED BREAD

Ingredients

- 2 tsp. baking powder
- 1 lb. flour
- Water

Method

Sift the flour and baking powder into a bowl, and mix with sufficient water to make a dough. Make into small loaves quickly and bake at 400° F. Therm. 6 for 30 mins.

Bread and Butter Pudding
Ingredients
1 pt. custard
Butter
Sugar
Currants
Chopped lemon peel
Grated nutmeg

Method
Spread the butter on the slices of bread, and fill a fireproof dish with layers of buttered bread, currants mixed with sugar, and chopped candied lemon peel sprinkled between and grated nutmeg on top. Pour the custard over gradually, allowing the bread to become saturated, and stand aside for 1 hr. Bake at 350° F. Therm. 4 for 30 mins.

Bread and Jam Fritters
Ingredients
12 slices of bread
Butter
Jam
Batter
Lard

Method
Take the bread slices, remove crust, and spread with butter and then jam. Make a cover with another slice, press tightly together, and cut them into any desired shape. Make a batter, as for apple fritters (see **FRITTER** p. 226), dip them in and fry in boiling lard for about 10 mins. Drain on kitchen paper and serve hot sprinkled with sugar.

Bread and Parsley Fritters
Ingredients
6 oz. crustless bread
4 eggs
1 oz. chopped parsley
Pepper and salt

Method
Pour boiling water over the bread, cover and allow to stand for an hour. Beat with a fork until quite smooth, then add the parsley, pepper and salt, and eggs. Beat thoroughly, form into fritters and fry a nice brown. Serve with Brown sauce.

Breadcrumb Batter
Ingredients
3 tbsp. breadcrumbs
3 tbsp. flour
Pinch of salt
1 egg
¼ pt. milk

Method
Mix together the breadcrumbs, flour and salt; add the egg, mix in gradually the milk and beat to a creamy consistency. Allow to stand ½ hr. Use for coating cooked vegetables before frying.

Bread Pudding, Boiled
Ingredients
½ pt. breadcrumbs
1 pt. milk
3 eggs
2 oz. currants
Sugar
Grated nutmeg

Method
Soak the breadcrumbs in the milk as it boils, and when the milk has cooled, add the well-beaten eggs, currants, sugar to taste and a little grated nutmeg. Mix altogether and place in a buttered basin, cover with cloth securely tied over top and boil for 1¼ hrs.

Bread Pudding with Onions

Ingredients
- 8 oz. breadcrumbs
- 2 oz. chopped onions
- Salt and pepper
- 1 tsp. sage
- ¾ pt. milk
- 2 eggs

Method

Mix the ingredients thoroughly and bake at 400° F. Therm. 6 for 30 mins.

Bread Sauce. See SAUCES.

Bread Tipsy. Cut a French roll into thin slices and cut off the crusts, leaving round shapes. Spread each slice with raspberry, strawberry or currant jam and pile one on the other in a glass dish. Pour over them as much sherry as the bread will absorb. Ornament with blanched almonds cut into very fine strips, pour custard round and serve.

BREAM (Fr. *brème*). There are two sorts of this fish known to cooks. The sea bream, and the freshwater bream, the latter being rarely considered worthy of special treatment. Of sea bream there are many varieties, but of these the Black or Old Wife and the Gilshead are considered the choicest. Black bream is the name given to a number of different specimens of the *Sparus* family in Australia. Bream can be served baked, broiled, grilled, roast or soused.

Bream, Broiled

Ingredients
- 1 large sea bream
- 1 bay leaf
- Few cloves
- Salt
- Onions
- Thyme
- Pepper
- Olive oil

Method

Put the bream into a deep dish and cover with marinade of sliced onions, bay leaf, thyme, cloves, pepper, salt and olive oil. Leave for 2–3 hrs. Baste well during this time, then cover with oiled paper and bake at 350° F. Therm. 4 for about 30 mins. or until the fish is done (this is dependent upon its size).

BRET. See BRILL.

BRETT or TURBET. A small turbot.

BRICKBAR CHEESE. So called from its shape, which resembles a brick. It is made in Wiltshire of new milk and cream.

BRIE. A soft creamy glutinous cheese made at La Brie, which is a few miles east of Paris. The best Brie comes from Seine-et-Marne. This cheese is made in round cakes and should be well ripened, strong in flavour and creamy. If kept in a refrigerator, remove and keep at room temperature for 1 or 2 hrs. before serving.

BRILL (Fr. *barbue*). Known in Scotland as *Bonnet Fleur* and in Devonshire and Cornwall as Kite and Bret. A species of flat-fish, between a turbot and a sole, and from a culinary point of view inferior to both. It most resembles a turbot from which it can be distinguished by the absence of bony tubercles with which all turbot eaters are familiar, by the small, almost smooth scales, and by the reddish-brown spots on the upper side. It is not so firm in flesh as the turbot, and is in season from September to May. Brill may be cooked in various ways.

Brill, Baked

Ingredients
- A good-sized brill
- 1 teacup gravy or brown sauce

Method

Clean the fish, and open the back with a knife as far as the backbone will allow. Place in a buttered baking-dish and spread

Brill, Baked (*continued*)

1 teacup each chopped onions or shallots and mushrooms

1 wineglass Madeira

Breadcrumbs

¼ lb. butter

Lemon

Parsley

over the shallots, mushrooms, gravy and Madeira. Sprinkle on some breadcrumbs and pour over a little melted butter. Bake at 350° F. Therm. 4 for 30 mins., basting frequently. Serve garnished with slices of lemon and parsley.

BRINE (Fr. *marinade*). Used for pickling and preservation of meat and fish, to impart certain flavouring. See individual headings.

BRISKET (Fr. *brisquet*). The half breastbone with part of the ribs attached to one side, consisting of alternate layers of lean flesh and fat. This term is usually applied to beef.

BRIT, BRET or **BURT.** A small turbot, in England. In the United States, a small herring.

BROAD BEANS. See **BEANS, BROAD.**

BROCCOLI (Fr. *brocoli*). This member of the cabbage tribe is botanically identical with the cauliflower but it is a hardier strain. As its name indicates it is of Italian origin, and is known in that country as *broccolo*. Broccoli are seasonable all through the winter, and the earliest spring crop follows so closely upon the winter growth that no cessation takes place in supply. There is also the purple and white sprouting broccoli.

TO PREPARE. Remove the outer leaves and wash the flowers well in salt and water.

TO BOIL. Place the washed flowers in a saucepan of boiling water with a lump of salt, but do not put the lid on. Boil for 10–15 mins. according to size. When done, drain at once or they will go a bad colour. Serve with melted butter. Broccoli is sometimes served with white sauce enriched with an egg yolk and a flavouring of lemon juice.

TO PICKLE. The broccoli should be not quite ripe, but should be large, white and very close. Cut off all the outside pieces and green leaves, then partially boil in salt water to which a little white vinegar has been added to keep the flower white. When cooked strain and separate the branches into convenient pieces and place in a jar. Pour over it pickling vinegar made as follows: Bring to boil 1 pt. white vinegar, 1 oz. white ginger, 1 tbsp. salt, 1 tbsp. peppercorns, and allow to cook for a few minutes, then remove from heat to cool. When cold pour over the broccoli. The amount of vinegar required depends on the size of the broccoli.

Broccoli with Parmesan Cheese. Wash and trim the broccoli and boil in salted water for about 10 mins., but do not overcook. When the stem is soft place on a hair sieve to drain. Then break up into rough pieces and arrange on a flat dish, sprinkle with pepper, salt and a little nutmeg. Cover with well-grated parmesan cheese, then cover with breadcrumbs and pour over a little warm melted butter. Bake in a quick oven 375–400° F. Therm. 4 for 15–20 mins. and serve immediately.

BROCHAN. Scottish for "porridge". See **OATMEAL.**

BROILING. See **COOKING TERMS,** also **GRIDIRON** and **POT ROASTING.**

BROOM, YELLOW. The buds when preserved in vinegar may be used as a substitute for capers.

BROSE. A Scottish dish made by pouring boiling pot liquor (or boiling water) on oatmeal or barley meal mixed with small pieces of fat meat.

BROTH (Fr. *bouillon, consommé*). Beef stock. An unclarified gravy soup, with or without garnish. See **SOUPS.**

BROWN BETTY. This is the English cousin of the Continental Charlotte, says Kettner, bread and butter and apples being largely concerned in the production of each.

BROWN BETTY (*continued*)

Ingredients	*Method*
6 large green apples	Peel and slice apples; put a layer in a dish, sprinkle thickly with sugar into which nutmeg and cinnamon have been mixed. Sprinkle over a layer of breadcrumbs and a little orange and lemon peel. Add a few dots of butter. Put the lemon juice in water and pour a little over each layer of apples. Repeat till the dish is almost full. The last layer should be breadcrumbs. Add maraschino. Bake at 350° F. Therm. 4 for ¾ hr.
6–8 oz. sugar	
⅛ tsp. ground nutmeg	
½ tsp. cinnamon	
2 cups brown breadcrumbs	
Grated lemon peel	
Grated orange peel	
½ tsp. lemon juice	
¼ pt. water	
2 tbsp. butter	
Few drops maraschino (if desired)	

BROWN SAUCE. See SAUCES.

BROWN VEGETABLE SOUP. See SOUPS.

BROWNING. A preparation used to colour gravies and sauces. When made properly it can add flavour to soups and to other dishes. Among the brownings is **BLACK JACK** (q.v.).

METHOD I

Ingredients	*Method*
4 oz. brown sugar	Melt the sugar and butter in a frying-pan, add the water and cook till the whole has turned a deep brown. Remove pan from the stove, reduce heat, add port gradually and keep the mixture stirred until the roasted sugar is entirely dissolved. Then place in a bottle, add shallots and other seasonings and ketchup. Shake the bottle daily for a week, and then pour off the clear liquid, and if desired add a wine-glass of brandy after bottling. This helps to keep it.
1 oz. butter	
1 tbsp. water	
1 pt. port wine, beer or water (brandy if desired)	
5–6 shallots diced	
½ oz. bruised pimento	
A little mace	
¼ pt. mushroom ketchup	
½ oz. black pepper	
Finely grated lemon peel	

METHOD II

Ingredients	*Method*
2 oz. sugar	Place the sugar in a saucepan over a low heat and stir frequently to prevent burning. Very slowly add the water; when all the sugar is dissolved, put into bottles.
1 cup water	

BRUSSELS SPROUTS (Fr. *choux de Bruxelles*). These little vegetables are a sub-variety of the Savoy cabbage and grow with an elongated stem, from which sprout out small green heads like miniature cabbages. The usual mode of cooking them is boiling. They make an excellent garnish, and may be used either hot or cold for this purpose. They may also be served as a purée.

TO PREPARE. Remove the outside leaves of the sprouts and cut across the stalk. Leave to soak in cold salted water.

TO BOIL. I. Place the sprouts in plenty of boiling salted water and cook fast uncovered till tender. This will take 10–20 mins. Drain well in a colander and arrange neatly in a hot vegetable dish.

II. Wash and boil as in I. When the brussels sprouts are tender, drain and dry

BRUSSELS SPROUTS (*continued*)

them in a clean cloth. Put into a large saucepan 2 oz. butter and a little salt and pepper and toss the sprouts in this till they are quite hot again, *but do not let them fry*. Sometimes they are served on a quartered round of buttered toast.

III. Wash and boil as in I. When half-done, strain off water, add 1 tsp. butter, toss them gently, but do not stir them. Make a sauce with ¼ pt. beef gravy and bring it to the boil, then mix 1 tsp. flour or arrowroot in a little cold water, work till smooth, add ¼ pt. Brown or Tomato sauce, stir in with the gravy and boil up. Pour this into the pan with the sprouts, keep closely covered and when dishing up add a squeeze of lemon juice over them.

Omelet with Brussels Sprouts

Ingredients	Method
6 eggs 2 doz. boiled brussels sprouts 1 tbsp. butter Pepper and salt ¼ pt. Brown sauce	Beat up the eggs and mix with the brussels sprouts cut up lengthwise into four pieces or more if preferred, according to the size of the sprouts. Melt the butter in a large pan and when hot pour in the mixture, sprinkle with pepper and salt, and fry to a nice brown. Serve quickly with Brown sauce, sharpened with lemon juice. This quantity is sufficient for 5 or 6 persons.

BUBBLE AND SQUEAK. A well-known English dish, made with slices of cold meats and vegetables variously compounded according to the materials at hand. The fancy name, frequently perverted to Bubblum Squeak, arises probably from the hissing noise made by the meat and vegetables as they are warmed up. The meat is often omitted in this dish.

Ingredients	Method
Some slices of cold meat 2-3 oz. butter Any cold vegetables chopped up (potatoes, cabbage, onions, etc.) Pepper and salt	Put the meat and butter in a frying-pan and fry them to a light brown. When done remove them and fry up the chopped vegetables and seasoning. Dish up the meat and garnish with the vegetables.

BUCK. A male deer from which the finest venison is obtained.

BUCK HORN. See WHITING.

BUCK RAREBIT. A Welsh rarebit with a poached egg placed on the top.

BUGLE-WEED. The whole Carpet Bugle-weed is used medicinally for tonic tea.

BUGLOSS. There are four members of the *borage* family, Dyer's Bugloss or Real Alkanet, Common Alkanet, Italian Bugloss, and Viper's Bugloss or Blue Weed. Used medicinally.

BUGNE. A kind of pancake fried in oil, specially esteemed and commonly made in Lyons. The term gives origin to our "bun".

BULLACE. Supposed to be a corruption of the word "bull-sloe", a sort of wild plum of the *prunus* tribe, greenish yellow, and the size of a cherry. Sometimes made into pies or puddings, but best made into cheese.

Bullace Cheese

Ingredients	Method
Bullaces Loaf sugar	Place fruit in a jar and bake at 375° F. Therm. 5 until the fruit is soft, then pass

Bullace Cheese (*continued*)

through a hair sieve and to 1 lb. of pulp add 8 oz. loaf sugar crushed small. Place pulp and sugar into saucepan and boil over a low heat for 4½ hrs., stirring frequently. Pour into hot jars and seal. Sloe cheese is also made in this way.

BULLOCK. An old Saxon term for "ox", but more often used in the shambles than the kitchen.

Bullock's Heart Roasted

Ingredients

1 bullock's heart
Gravy
Some veal stuffing (double quantity given on p. 488)

Method

Wash the heart thoroughly in salt and water. Take care that it is perfectly clean and free from blood. Wipe it quite dry. Cut off the flaps, and fill the cavities with the stuffing. Grease a piece of paper with dripping, and tie it securely over the top of the heart, to keep in the forcemeat. Roast it according to the rules for roasting meat. It will take from 1½ to 2 hrs. to cook. Serve with a little gravy round it, and the rest in a boat. Redcurrant jelly may be handed with it. Some people boil the heart for ¾ hr. before roasting. When this is done it will take less time to roast.

FOR THE GRAVY

Ingredients

1 pt. stock
Trimmings from the heart
1 onion stuck with 2 cloves
1 oz. butter
1 oz. flour
Little catsup
Little colouring, if necessary
Pepper and salt

Method

Put the trimmings into a saucepan with the onion and stock, and simmer gently while the heart is cooking. Then melt the butter in a stewpan. Mix the flour smoothly and add the stock strained. Stir and boil for 3 mins. Then add the sauce, pepper and salt, and colouring.

BULL'S EYES. A very old sweetmeat made of boiled sugar, flavoured with peppermint, and moulded into irregular pieces.

BUNS. Small sweet cakes that are not cakes, having an individuality of their own, as may be seen by the numerous recipes that are given for their preparation.

BUN DOUGH

Ingredients

½ lb. flour
⅛ tsp. salt
1½ oz. butter
1 egg
½ oz. yeast
⅛ pt. lukewarm water
1 oz. sugar

Method

Sift salt and flour; cut and rub in fat; make a well in the centre and add the egg. Add yeast, sugar, and water; knead well, then put to rise. When risen to twice the original bulk, use as desired.

Bath Buns

Ingredients

Basic mixture above
1 oz. currants
1 oz. sultanas
1½ oz. peel
1 oz. sugar
½ tsp. spice
Broken sugar for top

Method

Turn on to floured board, knead in the fruit and sugar, and spice (if desired), very lightly but evenly through the mixture. Tear the dough apart into eight even-sized portions to look rough, like rock cakes. Place a little broken sugar on the top of each and put to prove. When twice the original bulk, bake at 450° F. Therm. 8 for 5 mins., then reduce heat to 375° F. Therm. 5 for a further 5 mins. Immediately the buns leave the oven, wash them over with glaze thus: Dissolve 1 tbsp. sugar in a little water, add to ½ pt. milk, bring mixture to boil and boil rapidly for 3 mins., then cool and use as desired.

Chelsea Buns

Ingredients

Basic mixture as above
1 oz. melted butter
1 oz. caster sugar
1 oz. currants
1 oz. chopped peel

Method

Turn dough on to floured board. Roll out into a large square, brush with melted butter, sprinkle with caster sugar, spread currants and chopped peel all over the surface evenly. Roll up like a Swiss roll. Cut into slices across the roll about 1½″ apart. Place them sides up on a greased tray, a little apart so there is sufficient room for them to prove. Leave to prove about 10–15 mins. Bake at 450° F. Therm. 8 for 5 mins. Reduce heat and cook a further 5–10 mins. Glaze immediately the buns are removed from the oven.

Cream Buns

Ingredients

Choux pastry (p. 370)
FOR FILLING:
½ tsp. vanilla essence
1 gill cream
1 tsp. caster sugar
Icing sugar

Method

Take the choux pastry and put it in a deep moistened and drained tin in six spoonfuls. Invert another tin exactly the same size on the top and join the edges of the tins together with a paste of flour and water. Bake at 400° F. Therm. 6 for about 35 mins. till the luting is dark brown but not burnt. Remove the buns at once to a pastry rack, split them to allow steam to escape and leave to cool. When cold fill with the sweetened flavoured whipped cream.

[92]

Currant Buns

Ingredients	*Method*
Basic mixture	Turn dough on to floured board; knead
2 oz. currants	in fruit, sugar and spice (if desired), very
1 oz. sugar	lightly but evenly through the mixture.
½ tsp. spice	Divide the mixture into eight pieces.
	Shape into buns. Flour the hands and
	press the dough down very firmly.
	Release weight and work with a circular
	movement, cup the dough with the hands
	to form a ball. Place on greased tray and
	allow to prove for about 10 mins. Bake as
	Bath Buns.

BURBOT (Fr. *lotte*). Also called Eel-pout. A European freshwater fish. The American burbot is found in the northern waters of New England, the Salt Lakes and farther north.

BURDOCK. Any of the genus *arctium* of coarse biennial asteraceous plants which have burr-like involucres. The roots are used to make ale.

Burdock Ale. Boil together 5 oz. each burdock, camomile and ginger in 5 gall. water. Add 2 oz. burnt sugar and pour through a strainer. Add 2½ lb. sugar and 35 grammes saccharine 550. Stir well until dissolved, then add the other 5 gall. water and 2 oz. crumbled yeast. Allow to work for 12 hrs. at 65–70° F. Skim and bottle for use.

Burdock and Dandelion Ale. Boil together 2½ oz. each burdock and dandelion leaves and boil juice in 5 gall. water for 15 mins. Add 2 oz. burnt sugar and pour through a strainer on to 2½ lb. sugar, 35 grammes saccharine 550. Stir until dissolved, then add the remainder of the water and 2 oz. yeast. Allow to work for 12 hrs. at a temperature of 65–70° F. Skim off yeast and bottle for use.

BURGUNDY (Fr. *bourgogne*). Wine with an acid astringent taste and fine full grape flavour, of considerable value for both culinary and table purposes.

BURNET. Lesser burnet, Salad burnet, Garden burnet. A sweet herb used in salads and sauces, resembling cucumber in flavour. It is also used to flavour vinegars. Tarragon, burnet, chives and chervil are used to make a ravigote.

BUSH BASIL. This is a low bushy plant which seldom grows more than 6″ high, and is more compact than Sweet basil. It flowers in July and August, and the leafy tops are used in the same manner as Sweet basil, i.e. in salads and for seasoning.

BUTTER (Fr. *beurre*). Butter is described as "an oily unctuous substance obtained from milk by churning". It consists of milk fat, with other constituents of milk, brought together into a mass, the oil globules of the cream with their albuminous surroundings having been broken up by agitation. The Hebrews were the first to use butter as a food. The early Greeks and Romans used it as a medicine or ointment.

TO MAKE. In a dairy everything must be kept scrupulously clean and the utensils required for butter-making should be got ready beforehand. They must be well rinsed with cold water, then scalded with boiling water, then carefully rubbed with coarse salt and lastly rinsed with cold water. Though the butter is not handled at any stage the butter-maker's hands must be kept scrupulously clean, and should a butter-worker be used the roller must be kept wrapped in damp butter muslin until required for use.

Separating. After milking, the milk is taken to the dairy to be strained through a sieve (this is a special one, specially manufactured by dairy appliance makers), and the quantity recorded. The cream is then separated by pouring into the feed tin of a centrifugal mechanical separator or else put at once into low pans, which are about 4–6″ deep and then kept at a temperature off between 46 and 50° F. It

BUTTER (*continued*)

takes from 24–36 hrs. to ripen, according to the season, a longer time in the cold weather. When ripe, the cream is skimmed off with a flat perforated skimmer. Sometimes a second skimming takes place after 12 hrs. The cream is put into a large deep earthenware crock, large enough to hold all the cream used for a single churning. When more cream is added it is all stirred together mechanically; separated milk can be used at once, as long as it is cool before churning, but it is best to leave it to ripen. Cream is usually just slightly soured before churning; when butter is made from unripened cream it lacks flavour. This is due to the chemical change through exposure to the air which causes the oxygen to unite with the soft fats. The oxygen helps to produce the lactic acid and milk fats. When "ripening" is assisted by stirring and the correct temperature there is about 0·5% lactic acid present. It is possible to ripen cream by gradual heating to 64° F. in the cool weather and to 60° F. in the warmer weather, and a very small amount of sour milk or cream is added—or buttermilk may be used instead—about 12 hrs. before churning.

Should cream be ripened by a "starter" or artificially ripened cream, the fresh milk is heated, taking about 20 mins. to raise the temperature to 150° F., then gradually cooled to 70° F., and then added in proportion according to the time available for ripening before churning. During the summer months the starter will be renewed daily but in the winter about 3 times a week should suffice. The special ferments are apt to develop bitterness which will taint the butter, unless the starter is renewed frequently. When the cream from successive milkings is added to the bulk of the cream awaiting churning, see it is thoroughly well stirred after each addition and allowed to stand 12 hrs. so that it can ripen.

Cream must not be kept too long (2 days in summer, 4 days in winter) or it becomes sour. It is essential that it should stand in pure air.

To Scald Cream. Sometimes during the winter months when the winter feeding is affected by turnips or some other cause, the cream is better scalded, by standing it in the pan in boiling water. As soon as a crinkle is seen on the thin skin the pan must be removed from the boiling water and cooled at a temperature of 50° F. It is best not to raise cream above 150° F.

To Strain Cream. Cream is strained through muslin before churning, and if necessary to get the even consistency a little cold water can be used to thin it down, but never more than 10% to the bulk of cream.

Churning. Always use a thermometer to test the temperature as this varies from day to day and it is essential to have the correct heat and churning temperature to produce good butter. The dairy temperature is important too, and the "starting" temperature for churning, if a few degrees out, will spoil the whole churning. The temperature varies according to the season and the cream temperature can be altered by standing the vessel in water. The cream must be kept below 80° F. Cream is usually tested 3 hrs. before churning so that should it be necessary to adjust the temperature this can be done evenly throughout. The cream should be well stirred and tested with a caged thermometer.

Temperature of Cream	Dairy Temperature
60° F.	48° F.
56° F.	56° F.
48° F.	60° F.

To Churn Butter. The cream should be strained through butter muslin as it is poured into the churn, and churned slowly to begin with, gradually increasing the speed for 5–10 mins. until it is at about 45 turns per minute, or as the makers direct. The churn must be well ventilated at frequent intervals to allow the gases to escape. This is continued until there is no rush of air when the vent is opened. Butter takes anything from 20–40 mins. to "break" according to the thickness of the cream, the ripeness and the temperature; also during the lactation period of cows the quality of the cream varies. When the butter has "come", there is a partial clearing of the glass window.

If cream goes "sleepy" (sticks to the sides of the churn) it may be sufficient to reverse the churn or to jerk it while reversing it, but sometimes it may be necessary

[94]

BUTTER (*continued*)

to adjust the temperature of the cream by the addition of water. In the warm weather this should be added cold. In the cold weather the water must be heated to 5° or 10° F. higher than the temperature of the churned cream, and through this the bulk temperature is adjusted. Should both these methods fail, it will then be necessary to scald the cream and cool it, and start churning again. When the butter has "broken" the water added should be 2° F. below churning temperature. Allow 1 qt. water to each gall. of cream (take the original quantity for this calculation). Never drain, but churn rather slowly until the grains are about the size of mustard seeds. Let the grains settle and strain off buttermilk. It is essential to drain all this away.

To Wash Butter. The next step is to wash the newly made butter in the churn. Plenty of cold water is added and the churn is then turned for a few times, the water drained away and more cold water added. This is repeated until the water is absolutely clear, but over-washing must not take place or the flavour of the butter is apt to be spoilt. If the grains are too hard, the temperature of the water may be raised a little, but only a few degrees. The greatest care must be taken not to churn the butter into lumps.

To Colour Butter. When the cows are grass-fed the butter is usually a good colour, and no extra colouring is needed, but when the cows are fed on hay a little pure annatto is added to give the butter a rich colour. If this is diluted with water when added, the butter may be streaky.

Faults in Butter-Making. Frothiness during churning may be caused by the cream being too thin or not properly ripened, or the wrong temperature. When the cream develops too high a percentage of acid before churning, sourness is apt to occur and if the temperature of the cream is kept too low while ripening, bitterness may result. Streaky butter is also due to over-churning, the salt being improperly mixed, or impure or insufficient washing. Should the cream be over-ripe mottled butter will result.

TO CLARIFY. Melt the butter in a clean saucepan, remove scum, etc., which rises to the top, and allow to stand by the side of the fire for all impurities to sink to the bottom again. Strain carefully through a sieve, leaving the sediment at the bottom of the pan; butter should always be clarified before it is used to cover potted meats, etc. It may be used hot instead of olive oil in salads.

TO CREAM. To reduce butter to cream beat it in a bowl with the hand or a wooden spoon in an anti-clockwise direction. Any water or milk must be thrown off. This will take about 20 mins.

TO DESALT. Pour boiling water over the butter, leave in pan till melted. Cool, strain off liquid and leave to set.

TO DOUBLE. See **CORNFLOUR.**

TO PICKLE. Pour 1 pt. boiling water on to 1 lb. salt, 2 oz. loaf sugar and ½ oz. saltpetre. Allow to stand till quite cold. Put the butter into a jar and keep well covered with this pickle.

TO POT. Beat out all superfluous milk and place the butter in layers with salt. Seal tightly. Desalt before use.

TO SWEETEN RANCID BUTTER. Pour boiling water over the butter and bring to the boil, skim and add a few pieces of toast to absorb rancid flavour and odour. Leave to cool, drain off liquid, scald as for desalting, wash and knead with new milk and beat in lime water.

BUTTERCUP. Used to garnish salads or make jam.

BUTTERMILK (Fr. *babeurre*). This is the fluid which remains in the churn after the butter has been removed from the cream; when used as a drink, fresh buttermilk is excellent, and it is used for making cakes and scones. In some parts of the country the buttermilk is put into a linen bag and after the whey has been drained through the remaining curds are served with cream and caster sugar.

BUTTER MUSLIN. Used for straining liquids and also in cheese-making.

BUTTER NUT or SWAIN NUT. Sometimes known as the "white walnut", the nut is 2–3″ long, has a hard thick shell covered with viscid matter when growing, and an oily almost flavourless kernel.

[95]

BUTTERS

Butter	To Make	Use
Anchovy	Fillet some anchovies and add equal weight in butter. Add pepper and cayenne to season. Pass through a hair sieve.	For savouries and sandwiches
Brown I	Melt 6 oz. butter in stewpan over low heat till browned. Allow to cool. Then in another saucepan put a cupful of vinegar, season with pepper and stir well. Warm over a low heat. When butter is cold, add vinegar and stir.	For fish, especially served with skate
Brown II	Put the desired quantity of butter in a saucepan; melt and, when it is browned, dip into this whatever is to be served in brown butter.	For fillets of fish
Brandy	Beat to a cream equal parts butter and caster sugar; add brandy to taste. Chill before serving.	For Christmas pudding
Burnt Sauce	Brown 2 oz. butter in a frying-pan, stir until it is a good colour, then add 1 tsp. salt, a very little cayenne and 2 tbsp. hot vinegar.	Good to serve with poached eggs or fish
Caper	Chop 2 tbsp. capers finely and pass through a sieve with a wooden spoon. Season with salt and pepper and blend with 1 oz. butter.	Serve with grilled fish or in sandwiches or savoury snacks
Capsicum	See CAPSICUM.	
Cheese	Add 1 part finely grated cheese to 2 parts butter, with pepper, cayenne and a little mustard to season.	For sandwiches or snacks and with fish
Chives	Take 1 dsp. chopped chives, add a squeeze of lemon juice, sprinkle with salt and pepper and mix with 2 oz. butter.	For grilled meat or fish or in cream cheese sandwiches
Drawn	Dissolve 4 oz. butter over low heat, sprinkle in 1 tbsp. flour, then ½ pt. boiling water and pinch of salt. Stir well and boil up for a few mins. Next add teacupful cold water, and for pudding sauce add a glass of white wine and grated nutmeg, stirring well all the time.	For vegetables (savoury) and puddings (sweet)

BUTTERS (*continued*)

BUTTER	TO MAKE	USE
Fairy	Blanch and pound 1 oz. sweet almonds, adding a little orange-flower water. Wash 8 oz. butter and beat to paste with 3 hard-boiled egg yolks. Add a little grated lemon peel and caster sugar.	Serve on biscuits soaked in wine
Filbert	Shell and pound the filberts to paste. Add finely chopped chives or parsley. Knead well together.	For sandwiches or with fish
For cold dishes	Pound together the following: 1 clove garlic, 3 hard-boiled egg yolks, 1 tsp. capers, seasoning of mace and allspice. Moisten with a little tarragon vinegar and wineglass of olive oil. Add 8 oz. butter and colour green with spinach juice. Pound until smooth. Set to cool.	Used for decoration of meat, fish, salads, etc.
Golden	Pound 2 hard-boiled egg yolks with 4 oz. butter; add a squeeze of lemon juice, pepper and salt and pass through sieve.	For fish
Green Herb	Scald few sprigs parsley, tarragon, chives, chervil. Drain and pound well. Work with 2 oz. butter, season with pepper and salt.	For fish and meat
Herb	Use any freshly chopped green herbs and blend with melted butter and a squeeze of lemon juice.	With fish or in sandwiches
Honey	Melt 1 oz. honey and add to 4 oz. butter.	Use on steamed or boiled puddings or in sandwiches
Lobster Coral	Pound lobster coral with double its weight in butter. Season with pepper, cayenne and pass through a sieve.	With fish or in sandwiches
Maître d'Hôtel	4 oz. butter, 1 tbsp. finely chopped parsley, strained juice of ½ lemon, pepper and salt. Blend well together.	Use with fish or meat, etc.
Melted I	Mix a little flour with 4 oz. butter, add wineglass water, place in saucepan, stir one way till melted and when thick and only just boiled, it is ready for use. If desired, cream may be substituted for the flour, but do not boil.	Use with fish or meat

BUTTERS (*continued*)

BUTTER	TO MAKE	USE
Melted II	Put into a saucepan some butter with salt and pepper and lemon juice. Simmer all gently, continually stirring the butter with a wooden spoon until half melted. Remove from heat and stir until butter becomes liquid.	Use with fish or meat
For Melted Butter Sauce, see SAUCES.		
Melted French	Rub 1 tbsp. flour into 4 oz. good fresh butter, put into a stewpan with a little salt, ½ tbsp. white vinegar, wineglass of water and a little grated nutmeg.	For grilled or fried fish
Montpelier	Equal quantities of tarragon, chervil, burnet, chives, making 4 oz. altogether. Add 1 hard-boiled egg yolk, 2 anchovies, 1 dsp. capers, 2 gherkins and 1 tsp. tarragon vinegar, 1 tbsp. salad oil, pepper and salt. Colour with spinach juice and keep in a cold place.	Use over meat or fish
Mustard	Take ½ tsp. French mustard, blend with 1 tsp. each chutney and English mustard and 1½ oz. butter. Add 1 tsp. vinegar.	Use with fish or meat, and cold ham sandwiches
Nasturtium	Take finely chopped nasturtium leaves or flowers or seeds and pound with equal quantities of butter.	With fish or grilled meat
Onion	Put 2 oz. butter into a saucepan, add 1 tsp. grated onion and brown together. Season with salt and paprika.	Serve with fish or meat
Prawn	Pound prawns with double their weight in butter. Add pepper to season and pass through a sieve.	With fish
Ravigote	To make ¼ lb. in all, use equal quantities of tarragon, chervil, burnet, chives, and parsley, yolks of 2 eggs, hard-boiled, 8 oz. butter, 1 tsp. tarragon vinegar, 3 tbsp. salad oil. Pound together.	With grilled meat or fish
Rum.	See RUM.	
Shrimp	Mix together pounded shrimps and a grating of nutmeg and cayenne pepper. Add half the weight in butter, mix well and pass through sieve.	With fish or in sandwiches

BUTTERS (*continued*)

BUTTER	TO MAKE	USE
Tarragon	Make as Maître d'Hôtel butter, using tarragon instead of parsley.	With meat or fish
Tomato	Blend together blanched, skinned and seeded tomato, sugar and paprika. Add to half its weight in butter. Blend again before use.	With fish, grilled meat or ham, in sandwiches
Truffle	Dissolve 4 oz. butter, add seasoning, pounded mace, nutmeg and cayenne and some small thick slices of truffle.	With fowl, turkey, poultry, veal or tongue
Watercress	Chop finely watercress leaves, season with sprinkle of salt and blend with half their weight in butter.	For grilled meat or fish or in sandwiches

BUTTER SAUCE. See SAUCES (p. 445).

C

CABBAGE (Fr. *chou*). This term is applied to a very extensive variety of esculent vegetables, which includes white and red pickling cabbages, Savoy cabbages, brussels sprouts, broccoli, cauliflower and kales (or kaels). These are classified as one botanical tribe, but differ from each other in conformation and in their culinary uses. For instance, in the white and red cabbage and Savoy, the terminal leaf bud alone forms the part selected for cooking. In brussels sprouts, all the leaf buds form a series of small heads. In broccoli and cauliflowers the flower of the plant is eaten.

The term "greens" is sometimes given to cabbage. Cabbage is too often spoilt by bad cooking; always use the freshest cabbage you can procure and cook with care. The finely shredded heart of cabbage makes a useful garnish, raw or cooked.

TO PREPARE. Remove all the dead and bruised leaves. Cut the cabbage into halves or quarters, according to size; trim off the stalk neatly. Put the cabbage head downwards into strongly salted water and leave for 15 mins. to get rid of any insects or caterpillars, but do not soak it.

TO BLANCH. Plunge the cabbage into boiling salted water for 5 mins. to blanch, then drain, and cool in cold water, the moisture being pressed out.

TO BOIL—I. Plunge into fresh boiling salted water, allowing 1 tbsp. salt to each 2 qt. water. Add a small pinch of sugar to bring out the flavour. Cook the cabbage in a large pan uncovered, for about 20 mins., and drain as soon as the cabbage is cooked. After draining out all the moisture from the cabbage, serve it in neat quarters without chopping. Greens should be patted with two spoons into an oblong shape, out of which neat squares should be cut; pats of Maître d'Hôtel butter may be laid on the quarters or squares.

TO BOIL—II. Break off root stalk, remove any bruised or discoloured leaves. Shred cabbage finely and place in saucepan, allowing to each 1 lb. cabbage, 4 tbsp. boiling water and a small walnut of margarine; cover securely. Cook quickly until tender. This takes a very short time, so watch it carefully.

TO DRESS. There are various methods of dressing cabbage after draining. Two of the most useful are:

I. Turn on to board, chop up and return to stewpan over a low heat with a little melted butter and a coffee-cup of good broth. This makes a good base for poached eggs or filling for an omelet.

II. Cut up as above, and add equal bulk of mashed potato; put into saucepan, moisten with butter and milk. Season with salt and pepper and grated nutmeg. This is good to serve with cutlets.

Cabbage Leaves, Stuffed. Parboiled white cabbage leaves may be stuffed with any savoury filling, rolled up, tied with thin string or cotton and simmered in gravy until tender. The string should be removed before serving.

Cabbage with Apple. Put parcooked cabbage with peeled sliced apple in equal proportions into a stewpan. Add a knob of butter and ½ pt. broth or water. Season with salt, pepper and sugar, and stew gently until tender. When cooked, turn the cabbage on to a hot dish and serve.

Cabbage with Rice (Fr. *chou au riz*). Blanch, drain and parboil a cabbage; shred it and put with half its bulk of half-boiled rice into a stewpan with broth to cover. Season well with seasoning, and simmer until tender. Serve with grated cheese. Diced onion and tomato may be added to this recipe if desired.

Cabbage with Sour Cream. See SALADS.

Cabbage, Boiled Red. Clean the cabbage thoroughly, cut into slices, place in boiling water for 15 mins., then boil until tender. Drain and serve with either White or Brown sauce, sharpened with lemon juice or vinegar.

Cabbage, Casserole of Red. Put shredded red cabbage and sliced apple in alternate layers into a casserole; add pinch sugar and grated nutmeg and ¼ pt. milk. Cover and bake at 350° F. Therm. 4 for about 2 hrs.

Cabbage, Pickled Red. Trim and remove hard stalks and slice the cabbage thinly. Lay on a dish, cover with salt and leave for 12 hrs., then wash the salt off the cabbage and dry well. Put into stone jar, mixing it with thyme, mint, parsley and peppercorns. Pour in sufficient strong white vinegar to cover. Leave 3–4 wks. A little brown sugar may be added if desired.

Cabbage, Slaw. Chop up a small cabbage that has been boiled and then allowed to get cold. Place in a saucepan and dissolve 1 oz. sugar in ¼ pt. vinegar; add 1 tsp. salt, a little pepper, 1 oz. butter. Pour this over the cabbage when cold. See also COLE SLAW.

Cabbage, Stewed. Take 1 lb. cabbage, trim, blanch, parcook, and drain. Mince ¼ lb. Spanish onion, take 1 tbsp. each diced celery and parsley, season with pinch sugar and salt. Turn into a saucepan with 4 oz. melted butter or dripping. Set over a moderate heat, and when softened add cabbage quartered. Turn mixture about for a minute or two, then add sufficient stock or milk to cover. Cover the pan (see lid is tight-fitting). Allow just to boil, then reduce heat and simmer gently for 20 mins. Lift out cabbage quarters, drain; place on hot dish, cover and keep hot. Strain the broth, skim, thicken with flour and butter and pour over cabbage.

CACAO. See COCOA.

CAERPHILLY. This semi-hard whole-milk Welsh cheese is now also made in Somerset, Devon and Dorset.

CAFFEINE. A bitter substance and stimulant found in coffee.

CAKE (Fr. *gateau*). Generally flour, with butter, eggs and baking powder used to make it light, and sugar to sweeten. Variations are made by the addition of dried fruits or flavourings and with fillings and icings.

CAKES, GENERAL NOTES ON MAKING. Cakes can be made quite simply at home, and it is not always necessary to use the most expensive recipe to get good results. Remember the following hints:

1. Make sure that there is air in the mixture. This is essential because the flour is sent from the mill in a sack and comes to you flattened in a bag. Always sieve flour before use (if you do not possess a sifter a strainer will do) or shake it lightly in your bowl before adding other ingredients.
2. Small cakes need a hotter oven than large ones.
3. The heat of the oven should be reduced for large cakes after the cakes have set, so that they can cook through without burning.
4. Open and close the oven door gently lest, through banging, the cake should end by being sad.
5. Never move a cake from one shelf to another, or even on the same shelf, until it is set.
6. To test whether a cake is cooked through, pierce the cake with a clean skewer or darning or knitting needle. If the skewer remains clean, the cake is cooked through.
7. Lard is better than margarine for greasing cake tins. Always see that the tins are well greased, and for a large cake line the tin.
8. If a cake sticks and refuses to leave the tin, place the tin on a damp cloth for a few minutes and the cake will soon be eased. Never cool a cake in a draught; it is apt to make it sad and heavy.
9. Dried eggs may be used to replace shell eggs, unless egg white is necessary. Allow a pinch of baking powder to each egg.
10. Margarine may be substituted for butter.

It is not the ingredients alone nor the manipulations which make a good cake, but a combination of the two. Most cakes belong to one of two families: the sponge cakes or the butter cakes. A sponge cake is made light by beating whole

CAKES, GENERAL NOTES ON MAKING (*continued*)

eggs or the yolks and whites separately. It has a delicate flavour and smooth texture. A butter cake (with butter creamed or rubbed in) is made light by the use of creamed fat and the addition of eggs, and some baking powder or raising agent. There is a very small family of warmed mix cakes where the fat and syrup are melted together in a saucepan and the hot mixture added to the other ingredients. These basic cake mixtures are very simple to master and there are many varieties of them which belong to the main groups, but have a slight change of flavour, consistency, filling or icing, without changing the basic butter.

To ensure success the following simple rules should be observed:
1. Read the recipe through to the end carefully.
2. Prepare the cake tins or baking sheets.
3. Assemble all the utensils required.
4. Prepare the oven and preheat to the stated temperature.
5. Assemble all the ingredients required, always choosing the best.
6. Measure the ingredients.
7. Never stop work once you have started mixing.

It is the sugar and fat content which determines the difference between a rich or plain cake. Both may have fruit. When making plain cakes the fat is rubbed into the mixture after being cut with a knife as in pastry. The other ingredients are then added and the mixture placed in the oven to cook quickly. If fruit is added to a plain cake the mixture should not be too moist or the fruit will sink to the bottom of the cake.

Oven heats for cakes depend upon the size, ingredients, thickness of tin, etc., as well as upon whether the mixture is sponge, plain or rich.

Rich cakes contain more air in the mix owing to the beating of the eggs and the creaming of the fat and sugar, so they require less raising agent. The eggs should be added slowly, otherwise they will curdle the mixture and the fat will separate and the air will not be held so well. A stiffer consistency is needed than in plain cakes, since rich cakes contain more fat, eggs and sugar which turn to liquid when heated. A slower oven is the general rule.

Sponge cakes need plenty of air and the eggs must therefore be well beaten, with the sugar and the flour folded in afterwards. Any fat added should be warmed. These cakes are baked in a slow oven so that the air bubbles can expand and raise the cake. It is possible to divide a sponge-cake mixture and make a two-colour cake.

TO CHOOSE YOUR CAKE. One determining factor in the choice of a cake is the time the cake must be kept. A rich one must be made if the cake is not going to be eaten fairly soon, and it should be wrapped in greaseproof paper and kept in an airtight tin. When small cakes are iced they retain their moisture longer.

TO PREPARE THE TIN OR BAKING SHEET

Round tin. Always use the best quality paper for lining the tins. Press the paper to the bottom of the tin, mark the circumference with the edge of a knife and then cut the paper just under $\frac{1}{2}''$ larger. Snip from the edge to the crease slantwise all round, then fit the paper into place with the fingertips. The paper should be greased (if necessary) after it is fitted into the tin. Cut a band of paper long enough to overlap 2″ and to stand up 2″ above the rim of the tin, but no deeper, or the heat will be prevented from getting to the top of the cake. This band of paper is greased before fitting into the tin.

Oblong tin. When lining a flat tin, cut the paper so that it extends for about 2″ beyond the edge of the tin on all sides, then cut it diagonally for about 2″ from the corner of the paper to the corner where the paper fits the tin. Fold one cut edge behind the other so that there are no creases.

Oiling and greasing tins. Use a small brush to dab on the oil or melted fat evenly so that it is flaked on. For sponge cakes mix together an even quantity of caster sugar and fine dried flour; shake this all over the surface to coat it everywhere, then tap the rim of the tin to remove any surplus.

There is a modern school of thought which advocates the use of the tin without grease or lining; the tin is heated in the oven while the cake is being made and the mixture is turned into the hot tin and immediately placed in the oven.

CAKES, GENERAL NOTES ON MAKING (*continued*)

TO MIX. When creaming fat and sugar, if the shortening is very hard, put into a dry mixing bowl that has been thoroughly well warmed with hot water. Never melt the fat. Add the sugar, gradually drawing the fat from the sides of the bowl till the mixture is lighter in colour. Add flavouring, first the eggs, either as yolks or whole eggs, as the recipe directs, then the sifted flour and salt; any liquid should be added alternately with the flour. Egg white should never be added until it is stiff enough to remain in the bowl when inverted. It should be folded in with a metal spoon in an "over and over" movement. The mixture is then placed in the tin, making it a little higher at the edges and corners (if any) to ensure even rising, and it should be placed in the oven immediately.

In a *rubbed-in mix*, which is used for cakes, pastry and scones, the fat is cut into the flour with a knife, then rubbed in with the fingertips until the mixture is crumbly and looks like one substance. The other ingredients and liquid are then added.

In a *sponge-cake mix*, or *whisked mix*, usually there is no shortening. A different method of combining ingredients is used. Sometimes the egg yolks and sugar are beaten together until they are very light, the flavouring is added, the sifted flour and salt are gently folded in and then the stiffly whisked egg whites are folded in with a metal spoon. If whole eggs are used they are beaten with the sugar. The first method gives a lighter cake, but in the second method the cakes will dry out more quickly.

In *warmed mixes* the fat and syrup are melted together over a low heat to ensure even distribution.

Texture. For a close texture add the flour and eggs alternately. For a spongy mixture add the eggs and flavouring, etc., and mix lightly together, folding the flour in last.

Flour. Use plain flour when eggs are added to a mix because air is incorporated by beating and it is easy to adjust the amount of raising agent. If self-raising flour is specifically stated it is best to use it. Always sift the flour before use; it is apt to settle both in bag and bin. Weigh it, add salt and raising agents and re-sift. If the flour is damp, spread in a tin and bake at 350° F. Therm. 4 for a few minutes with the door open.

The lightness of a mixture is produced:
(1) By the air that is introduced into the mix by sieving the flour.
(2) By incorporating air into the mix by beating.
(3) By beating eggs.
(4) By release of carbon dioxide.

Baking powder. This is usually purchased ready for use, though it can be made at home. It must be kept with a close, tight-fitting lid, and any mixture with this in it should be baked as soon as possible after moistening, as the carbon dioxide is liberated during effervescence. Allow 2–2⅓ level tsp. to each 1 lb. flour.

Cream of tartar and *bicarbonate of soda* are frequently used for eggless cakes and scones. They are sifted with the flour or dissolved in a little milk. Allow 2 level tsp. cream of tartar, 1 level tsp. bicarb. soda to each 1 lb. flour. If sour milk is used, only half portions of cream of tartar are necessary.

Sour milk and vinegar are used in plain eggless cakes in the following proportions:
1 tbsp. vinegar, ½ tsp. bicarb. soda to each 1 lb. flour.

Yeast. There are three varieties of yeast: excess of warmth will kill the cells, while too cold an atmosphere tends to retard the growth:
(*a*) Compressed yeast, which when fresh will cream easily with a little sugar.
(*b*) Brewer's yeast, which is known as "barm".
(*c*) Dried yeast, which takes longer for the cells to grow.

When yeast is kept in a cool, dry place till required for use the cells are inactive, but when it is placed in the warmth and crumbled with sugar and lukewarm liquid is added. the cells grow and multiply rapidly. When the creamed yeast is added to the flour with liquid the carbon dioxide spreads through the dough, raising it. Time is required for raising to allow for the growth of the mix. See **BREAD.**

CAKES, GENERAL NOTES ON MAKING (*continued*)

Shortening. Butter should be used whenever possible, especially if the cake is to be stored for any length of time. It helps to keep the mixture moist. Margarine may be used, but the cakes do not keep quite so long.

Lard or cooking fat may be used for plain cakes, and it is frequently used in conjunction with butter, margarine or clarified dripping. It is best for greasing tins as it is a light fat. Dripping may be used in some plain cake mixtures if clarified. Put it into a basin with an equal quantity of hot water, stir and leave to set, when any sediment may be scraped off the underside of the fat. Reheat till it no longer bubbles and pour into an enamelled bowl.

Flavouring. This important ingredient is often over-used. Always use a good flavouring extract as only a little is needed and a delicate flavour is imparted to the cake. Don't just use lemon, almond and vanilla. If fruit or dates are in the cake, lemon or orange peel, finely grated, enhances the flavour. With nuts, almond, vanilla or orange are best. With chocolate, cinnamon or vanilla. In a spiced cake a blend of mixed spices should be added.

Sugar. Fine, granulated sugar is best, as powdered sugar is apt to dry the mixture out too quickly. Brown sugar is used in some recipes; it gives a darker coloured cake which keeps longer.

Eggs. Always break each egg separately into a cup. One that is "off" can so easily spoil a cake if broken straight into the mix. Alway beat a mix after adding an egg.

Liquid. This is usually dependent upon the number of eggs in a mixture or if melted syrup is in it. Milk or tea is often added to cake mixtures.

Fruit. Fruit is cleaned by rubbing on a wire sieve or in a clean teacloth when dredged with flour. It is then picked over and all the stalks and stems removed. If fruit is washed, it must be well drained by spreading on wire trays or dishes and then allowed to dry thoroughly in a warm place, frequently turned over and never dried rapidly or in great heat as this hardens the fruit and spoils the flavour. It should be thoroughly dried before storing. Raisins should be stoned with a sharp knife, and it is best to remove the sugar from candied peel before use. This sugar is inclined to make a mixture heavy as it does not blend properly, but it may be used to sweeten fruit, etc. Use a sharp knife for chopping and turn the chopped peel round on the board and slice it through. In dates, figs and prunes the stones or seeds should be removed and figs cut into even-sized pieces. Glacé cherries should be cut as they are heavy if left whole and fall in the mixture.

Nuts. Almonds should be blanched; walnuts and brazils should be bought and shelled at home. Do not keep too large a supply of nuts as they are apt to go rancid.

TO BAKE A CAKE. Always preheat the oven. Ovens vary and cooks must get to know their own, but the average electric oven takes approximately 15–20 mins. and a gas oven about 10 mins. to heat. Most cakes are best when baked in the top half of the oven as this reaches the thermostatic or registered temperature. The lower half of the oven is frequently a little lower in temperature.

Filling the oven. Always leave a 3″ clearance at each side of a baking sheet or the heat will be thrown down.

Cooking time. This is dependent upon the thickness of the cake and also the richness of the mixture. The richer the cake, the cooler the oven, as it will take longer to bake.

When adjusting the size of a cake, the cooking time must be adjusted, but the oven temperature remains the same as given.

For $\frac{1}{2}$-*sized cake.* When $\frac{1}{2}$ quantities used, bake for $\frac{3}{4}$ of the original time.

For $\frac{3}{4}$-*sized cake.* When using $\frac{3}{4}$ quantities of all ingredients—bake for $\frac{5}{6}$ of original time.

For *larger cakes* the baking time is increased with the increased size of the cake.

6″ × 3″ tin to	7″ × 3″ tin.	Add 30 mins. extra.	
7″ × 3″ ,,	8″ × 3″	,, 45 ,, ,,	
8″ × 3″ ,,	9″ × 3″	,, 1 hr. extra.	
9″ × 3″ ,,	10″ × 3″	,, 1 hr. 10 mins. extra.	
10″ × 3″ ,,	11″ × 3¾″	,, 1 hr. 20 mins. extra.	
11″ × 3¾″ ,,	12″ × 3¾″	,, 1½ hr. extra.	

CAKES, GENERAL NOTES ON MAKING (*continued*)

Oven doors. Never open the oven door for 5 mins. after putting in small cakes, or for 20 mins. after putting in a large cake. Never move a cake while baking until it is quite set.

To test if a cake is cooked. The centre of a small cake should feel firm and an easy test is to pierce it with a darning needle, fine knitting needle or skewer. If this comes out cleanly the cake is cooked. If in doubt leave the cake in the oven a little longer with the heat turned off. A cake should smell cooked and feel firm and if you listen and the cake is still singing with a slight hissing sound it is not quite done. This should have ceased when the cake is baked.

TO COOL A CAKE. Place it on a cake sieve or cake rack or on a folded clean teacloth. Cool slowly. Never cool a cake in a draught, or it will be sad.

TO STORE CAKES. Never store a cake until it is absolutely cold and then place it in an airtight tin. Rich mixtures should also be wrapped in greaseproof paper.

TO FINISH A CAKE. Just before putting a cake into the oven, finely grated nuts or coconut may be sprinkled over it; or a little candied peel or crystallised fruit may be gently pressed on to the top of the cake batter when it is set during cooking. After baking, a loaf or cake may be dusted generously with icing sugar and a criss-cross effect is obtained if a wire cake-tray is laid over the cake lightly and sugar sifted over the surface. Whipped cream, plain or sweetened or coloured, may be used and for topping purposes is best when lightly stiffened with gelatine. Icing or frosting of any type may be used if desired. Larger cakes may be put together with fillings, e.g. jam, jelly, sweetened fruit or specially cooked fillings such as lemon curd, chocolate, cream, etc.

TO DECORATE A CAKE. Iced cakes may be enhanced by adding crystallised fruit, cherries, a border of chopped nuts, or dessicated coconut, plain or toasted, and for a birthday cake, tiny candles made of paste in special holders on the cake, and daisies of toasted almonds with centres of yellow candy and stalks of angelica and leaves of citron. Crystallised cherries may be cut into flower petals, and acorns may be made by dipping the ends of almonds with chocolate. For a special children's cake, top the cake with any coloured icing as desired, then using a toothpick or small brush, dip it into melted chocolate and paint animals or draw faces on the cake.

CAUSES OF FAILURE

If rich cakes have a close, heavy texture there is often insufficient raising agent (i.e. self-raising flour, baking powder, cream of tartar, bicarbonate of soda or beaten egg); there will not be enough gas given off to make the mixture open and spongy. If the mixture is placed in too cold an oven, the cake will expand too slowly and the elastic substance of the flour known as "gluten" will not stretch to its full capacity.

Sometimes caused by insufficient beating of the fat and sugar. This should be almost white and fluffy, and to reach this texture air must be incorporated into the mixture. The less butter and sugar are creamed and beaten, the less air they contain.

If the mixture curdles when eggs are added, a close texture will result, so that when you add eggs to the mixture add them very slowly, and if the mixture looks as though it is beginning to break and curdle, stir in just a little flour and then carry on adding your eggs as before, beating in each egg separately.

If sponge cakes have a close, heavy texture. This may be caused by insufficient beating of eggs and sugar. During the beating process, air is incorporated and the light texture of a sponge depends mainly on this. You should avoid beating or stirring after the adding of flour. Too much flour also will make the mixture close and heavy.

If the cake falls in the centre, the three chief reasons for this are:

(1) Too much raising agent in the mixture.
(2) Too hot an oven (and this fault occurs generally in gingerbreads, rich cakes and sponge cakes).
(3) Slamming the oven door before the cake is set or cooked.

CAKES, GENERAL NOTES ON MAKING (*continued*)

If the fruit sinks to the bottom of the cake. The fruit mixture may fall to the bottom of a cake if it has been added to the creamed butter and sugar before any flour has been stirred in. Cherries are far more inclined to go to the bottom than any other fruits because they are large and heavy, and it is for this reason that they are usually cut into smaller pieces before adding them to a cake mixture. The piece of candied peel on top of a Madeira cake is not put on the top until the cake is partly cooked, otherwise it may sink right through and be found in the centre of the cake after cooking. See also when you are cleaning your fruit that it is quite dry before it is added to the mixture; fruit should be carefully measured, because too much fruit will make the cake heavy and wet. Fruit sinking also may be due to too much raising agent.

If a plain cake has a close and heavy texture, the fat may have become oiled when it was rubbed into the flour. If this happens, then the fat is incapable of holding air and it does not mix evenly with other ingredients.

Almond Cakes

Ingredients

1¾ lb. flour
Pinch of salt
8 oz. butter
8 oz. caster sugar
4 oz. ground almonds
Milk
Egg and sugar to glaze

Method

Sift the flour and salt and rub in the butter, knead in caster sugar and ground almonds. Add a little milk if necessary and form into flat cakes. Brush with egg and sprinkle on sugar to glaze. Place on tin and bake at 350° F. Therm. 4 till brown.

Almond Pound Cake. See ALMOND.

American Fudge Cake

Ingredients

8 oz. flour
1 level tsp. salt
1 level tsp. baking powder
½ level tsp. bicarb. soda
2 oz. chocolate
2 tbsp. water
4 oz. butter
6 oz. caster sugar
1 egg
1 gill sour milk
Few drops vanilla essence
American frosting (half quantity, see p. 284)
Glacé cherries and half-walnuts to garnish

Method

Sift the flour, salt, baking powder and bicarb. soda. Line an oblong tin 9″ × 6″ with greased paper. Scrape the chocolate with a knife, melt in the water and boil until creamy. Then cool. Cream the butter, add the sugar and cream again thoroughly. Beat in the egg by degrees, beating well between each addition. Mix in the flour and chocolate last, alternately with the milk; add vanilla essence, mix well and turn into the prepared tin, spreading the mixture into the corners. Bake at 350° F. Therm. 4 for about 1 hr. When cold, spread with frosting and when set cut into twelve even-sized squares. Place half a cherry on top of half the squares, and walnut on the remainder.

Angel Cake

Ingredients

3 oz. flour
¼ tsp. salt
8 egg whites
1 level tsp. cream of tartar
oz. caster sugar

Method

Sift flour and salt together four times. Beat the egg whites until frothy, add the cream of tartar and continue beating until the whites are stiff. Add sugar gradually and then fold in sifted flour.

Angel Cake (*continued*)
    ¼ tsp. vanilla essence

Add the vanilla essence. Turn the mixture into an *ungreased* angel cake tin. Bake for about 45–50 mins. at 325° F. Therm. 3. After the cake has risen and begins to brown, cover with greaseproof paper. When the cake is cooked leave it in the tin inverted over a wire tray until it falls out.

Basic Plain Cake
Ingredients
    8 oz. flour
    Pinch of salt
    1 tsp. baking powder
    3–4 oz. butter or margarine
    5 oz. sugar
    1 or 2 eggs
    ½ gill milk
    Flavouring if desired

Method
Sift the flour, salt and baking powder, cut and rub in the fat, add sugar, then eggs beaten with the milk and mix to a fairly stiff consistency. Turn mixture into a well-greased 6″ tin and bake at 375° F. Therm. 5 for 1½ hr., reducing heat to 350° F. Therm. 4 when the cake rises (after being in the oven about 30 mins.).

The following recipes are variations on the above mixture:

LUNCH CAKE. Add 2 oz. each currants, sultanas and chopped candied peel and ¼ tsp. each cinnamon, ginger and nutmeg. For a plainer cake, use 6 oz. flour and 2 oz. ground rice, instead of all flour, and omit spice.

ROCK CAKES. Use self-raising flour, omit baking powder, add 2 oz. fruit, 1 oz. chopped peel, a good pinch of spice, 1 egg and mix to a very stiff consistency. Pile in rough, rocky heaps on a greased baking tin, and bake at 400–425° F. Therm. 7 for about 20 mins.

COCONUT BUNS. Use self-raising flour, omit baking powder, add 2 oz. dessicated coconut and a grating of orange or lemon rind. Mix and bake as for rock cakes.

Bermuda Witches
Ingredients
    Jam
    Coconut
    Sponge or rice cake (see p. 117)

Method
Spread strawberry, raspberry or any kind of jam without stones over slices of the cake, which has been cut very thin. Over this spread a thickish layer of desiccated or finely grated coconut. Place another piece of cake on top and press. Cut the cake into any desired shapes (squares are most suitable).

Bride's Cake
Ingredients
    2 lb. currants
    1 lb. sultanas
    ½ lb. seeded muscatel raisins
    ½ lb. glacé cherries
    ½ lb. each blanched and chopped almonds, citron and mixed peel
    1 lb. butter

Method
Line two tins with double greaseproof paper. Prepare the fruit, and mix together with almonds in a basin. Soften the butter, add the sugar and spice. Cream all together till light and fluffy then add the eggs one by one, beating after each addition until the mixture is smooth. Add flavourings and beat, then sift in the flour

[107]

Bride's Cake (*continued*)

1 lb. soft brown sugar
4 tsp. mixed spice
10 small or 9 large eggs
Few drops each almond, vanilla, ratafia essences
Grated rind of ½ lemon
1 lb. flour
1 saltspoon salt
1 tbsp. treacle
½ gill brandy

and salt, beat till smooth, but do not overbeat or the texture of the cooked cake will be too close. Add treacle and finally mix in the fruit. Weigh the cake and allow for each 1 lb., 1 hr. cooking time. Bake at 300° F. Therm. 2. When cooking time is up, test with a skewer or knitting needle. If done, remove from the oven and pour over the brandy immediately. When the cake is cooled, remove paper and store. If desired, add the almond paste (see p. 14) and Royal icing (see p. 285) just before required for use.

Butter Cake

Ingredients

10 oz. butter
½ lb. caster sugar
4 large eggs
2 tsp. caraway seeds or 4–8 oz. currants
2 tbsp. rum or sherry (or milk)
10 oz. flour
1 tsp. baking powder
1 level tsp. powdered cinnamon
¼ tsp. grated nutmeg

Method

Cream the butter, add sugar and cream again very thoroughly. Add the eggs by degrees, beating after each addition. Add the caraway seeds (or currants), and rum or sherry (or milk). Add flour and baking powder sieved together with spices, about a third at a time, and turn into an 8″ greased tin, lined with ungreased grease-proof paper. Bake at 350° F. Therm. 4 for 2½–3 hrs.

Cheese Cakes. Also called Maids of Honour.

Ingredients

Short pastry
¼ lb. butter or margarine
½ lb. sugar
2 eggs
½ tsp. baking powder
1 lb. curds
Nutmeg
Currants

Method

Line patty tins with pastry and fill with a mixture made by melting together margarine and sugar, and adding eggs, baking powder, curds, a grating of nutmeg, and currants if desired. Bake at 360° F. Therm. 4.

Cheese Cakes (Lemon)

Ingredients

2 oz. butter
2 oz. caster sugar
Pinch of salt
2 egg yolks
1 lemon
½ spongecake
1 egg white
Some remains of puff paste

Method

Cream the butter in a basin. Add to it the caster sugar and salt. Beat well together, adding one by one the yolks of the eggs. Then mix in the grated lemon peel, and the lemon juice, also the spongecake, rubbed through a wire sieve. Lastly, stir in lightly half the white of the egg, beaten to a stiff froth. Roll out the pastry. Stamp

Cheese Cakes (Lemon) (*continued*)

into rounds with a fluted cutter. Lay the rounds in patty-pans and put a little dummy of dough or bread in the middle of each. Bake at 400° F. Therm. 6. When nearly cooked, remove the dummies and fill their places with the cheese mixture. Return them to the oven until the pastry is cooked and the cheesecake mixture has taken on a pale colour.

Cherry Cake
Ingredients

4 oz. butter or margarine
Grated rind of ½ lemon
4 oz. sugar
2 eggs
7 oz. flour
Small pinch of salt
¾ tsp. baking powder
2–3 tbsp. milk to mix
2 oz. sliced glacé cherries

Method

Line a 6″ tin with greaseproof paper. Cream the butter, add the finely grated lemon rind, add sugar and cream again. Add well-beaten eggs, beating between each addition. Then fold in lightly with a metal spoon a third of the flour sifted together with salt and baking powder, add the cherries and remaining flour alternately with milk, turn into tin and bake at 360° F. Therm. 4 for 1½ hr.

Chocolate Cake
Ingredients

6 oz. flour
Pinch of salt
1 oz. ground rice
½ tsp. baking powder
½ tsp. cinnamon
1 level tbsp. cocoa
2 oz. chocolate
3 tbsp. milk
4 oz. butter
3 oz. sugar
3 eggs
½ tsp. each vanilla and coffee
  essences

Method

Sift the flour, salt, ground rice, baking powder, cinnamon and cocoa together. Grate the chocolate and dissolve in the milk over a low heat and then allow to cool. Cream the butter, add the sugar, cream again, add the yolks of eggs, one at a time, beating well. Mix in the sifted flour, lightly alternating with the chocolate and milk, add the essence and fold in the stiffly whisked whites of eggs with a metal spoon. Turn into a 6″ lined tin, and bake at 350° F. Therm. 4 for 1 hr. Next day cut the cake through and sandwich together with Buttercream or Chocolate icing (see under **ICING**). Decorate the top with chocolate cream icing: Scrape 2 oz. chocolate with a knife and melt with 3–4 tbsp. water in a saucepan over a gentle heat. Bring to the boil and cook till the consistency of a smooth batter. Remove from heat and cool, then add a few drops of vanilla essence. Cover the top, making rough design with a fork.

Chocolate Sponge

Ingredients

- 6 oz. flour
- $\frac{1}{4}$ lb. sugar
- 2 eggs
- $\frac{1}{2}$ oz. butter, melted
- $\frac{1}{2}$ tsp. cream of tartar
- $\frac{1}{2}$ tsp. bicarb. soda
- Vanilla essence
- 1 tbsp. chocolate

Method

Take flour, sugar, eggs, melted butter, cream of tartar, bicarb. soda, and a few drops of vanilla essence; beat all together, then add melted chocolate and bake at 350° F. Therm. 4 for 25–30 mins.

Christmas Cake

Ingredients

- $\frac{3}{4}$ lb. butter
- $\frac{3}{4}$ lb. sugar
- 4 eggs
- 2 tsp. baking powder
- 1 tsp. mixed spice
- $\frac{1}{2}$ tsp. ground mace
- $\frac{1}{2}$ lb. mixed peel
- $1\frac{1}{2}$ lb. mixed currants, sultanas and raisins
- 1 lb. flour
- Almond essence
- Rum

Method

Cream together butter and sugar, add eggs and beat well. Add baking powder, mixed spice and ground mace; then, alternately, mixed peel, currants, sultanas and raisins; add the flour. Beat well between each addition. Add if desired a glass of rum and a few drops of almond essence, beat well again. A little milk may be add if the consistency is stiff. Put in a well-greased and lined tin. Bake at 350° F. Therm. 4 for 2–2$\frac{1}{2}$ hrs.

Coconut Shortbread

Ingredients

- 2 oz. butter or margarine
- 2 oz. sugar
- 2 oz. shredded coconut
- 4 oz. plain flour
- $\frac{1}{2}$ tsp. baking powder
- Small pinch of salt
- 1 egg yolk
- Milk if necessary

Method

Cream butter and sugar and add coconut gradually. Add sifted flour, salt and baking powder and mix well. Add egg yolk and knead. If the mixture is not quite moist enough add very little milk, but do not make it soft or your shortcake will not be crisp. Turn on to a floured board and knead continually until the dough is pliable and can be rolled out without breaking. Cut into shape and pinch the edges with the thumb and first finger. Prick the centre so that the mixture does not rise. Dust lightly with sugar and bake at 350° F. Therm. 4 for 20 mins.

Coffee Cake

Ingredients

- 4 oz. butter
- 4 oz. demerara sugar
- $\frac{1}{2}$ cup treacle
- $\frac{1}{2}$ tsp. bicarb. soda
- $\frac{1}{2}$ cup strong black coffee

Method

Cream together the butter and demerara sugar, add alternately treacle and bicarb. soda dissolved in the coffee. Then add flour sifted with ginger, cinnamon and salt. Beat well, put in a greased tin

Coffee Cake (*continued*)
12 oz. flour
1 tsp. ginger
Sprinkle of cinnamon
Pinch of salt

and bake at 400° F. Therm. 6 for about 30 mins.

Cornflour Cakes
Ingredients
4 oz. butter
2 eggs
3 oz. sugar
3 oz. cornflour
1 tsp. baking powder
2 drops vanilla essence

Method
Cream the butter and add the yolks of eggs, sugar, cornflour, vanilla essence and baking powder. Mix together and fold in the stiffly whisked egg whites. Bake in small, well-greased tins for about 20 mins. at 350° F. Therm. 4.

Curd Cheese Cakes
Ingredients
8 oz. butter
3 egg yolks
6 oz. sugar
6 crushed macaroons
Currants (if desired)
Pinch of salt
Little grated lemon peel
Puff paste

Method
Warm butter thoroughly, add beaten egg and sugar gradually; also macaroons. (Currants may be added to the curd, if desired.) Pound well in mortar. Add salt and lemon peel. Line some tartlet pans with puff paste, fill with the mixture. Bake at 400° F. Therm. 6 for about 20 mins.

Date and Walnut Loaf
Ingredients
8 oz. flour
2 tsp. baking powder
Pinch of salt
Pinch of mixed spice
1½ oz. butter or margarine
1 oz. lard or cooking fat
3 oz. caster sugar
2 oz. chopped walnuts
2 oz. stoned chopped dates
1 egg
1½ gills milk

Method
Sift flour, baking powder, salt and spice together. Cut and rub in butter and lard; add sugar; add nuts and dates, then egg and milk, beaten together. Beat well, turn into greased bread tin and bake at 350° F. Therm. 4 for ¾ hr.

Dripping Cake
Ingredients
5 oz. dripping
¾ lb. flour
3 tbsp. caster sugar
¼ lb. sultanas
1 tsp. baking powder
1 saltspoon salt
1 egg
Sour milk

Method
Rub the dripping into the flour. When smooth, add sugar, sultanas, baking powder and salt. Work these up with the beaten egg; add sufficient sour milk to form a light dough. Turn into a greased cake tin and bake at 350° F. Therm. 4 for about 1 hr.

Dundee Cake

Ingredients

2 oz. Valencia almonds (blanched)
2 oz. ground almonds
¼ lb. sultanas
¼ lb. each currants and raisins
2 oz. shredded peel
8 oz. butter or margarine
Grated rind of lemon
8 oz. caster sugar
3 large eggs
9 oz. flour
Small pinch of salt
1 tbsp. sherry, brandy or rum

Method

Line an 8″ tin with ungreased double greaseproof paper. Slice the almonds and (reserving some for decoration) mix together with the ground almonds, peel and prepared fruit. Cream the butter, add the lemon rind and sugar, and cream until light and fluffy. Add the eggs unbeaten, one at a time, beating well after each. Add a third of the sifted flour and salt. Add the mixed fruit and then the sherry. Fold in remaining flour with a metal spoon, a little at a time. Turn the mixture into the tin. Sprinkle with sliced almonds on top. Bake for about 3 hrs. at 350° F. Therm. 4.

Eggless Cake

Ingredients

1 tsp. bicarb. soda
1 cup milk
1 lb. flour
¼ lb. margarine
¼ lb. raisins or currants
2 tbsp. vinegar
1 tsp. mixed spice

Method

Dissolve bicarb. soda in ½ cup milk. Rub the margarine into the flour and add raisins or currants, vinegar and mixed spice. Moisten to a stiff consistency with the milk, adding a little extra milk if necessary. Mix well and place in a well-greased tin. Bake at 250° F. Therm. ½ for 1½ hrs.

Fairy Cakes

Ingredients

4 oz. butter
4 oz. sugar
2 eggs
4 oz. flour
Vanilla or lemon essence

Method

For this mixture, take the weight of the eggs in butter, sugar and flour. Cream the butter and sugar, add the eggs and gradually add the flour. Beat thoroughly and add a few drops of lemon or vanilla essence. Pour into small, well-greased and floured tins and bake at 400° F. Therm. 6 until golden brown.

Fruit Cake, Eggless

Ingredients

12 oz. self-raising flour
Pinch of salt
½ tsp. mixed spice
6 oz. margarine
8 oz. currants
2 oz. mixed peel
2 tbsp. golden syrup or 4 oz. sugar

Method

Brush a cake tin with melted margarine and dust with a little flour. Sieve the flour, salt and spice into a basin. Rub in the margarine. Clean the currants in a little flour and chop the candied peel. Add both to the mixture and stir. Add the golden syrup or sugar. Then stir in first the vinegar, then the sour milk, making a

Fruit Cake, Eggless (*continued*)

2 tbsp. vinegar
¼ pt. sour milk

fairly stiff mixture. Put the dough into a prepared tin and bake for 1 hr. at 350° F. Therm. 4.

Fruit Cake, Rich

Ingredients

½ lb. flour
1 tsp. mixed spice
½ lb butter
½ lb. sugar
4–5 eggs
½ lb. currants and sultanas
¼ lb. raisins
½ lb. mixed peel
¼ lb. glacé cherries
2 oz. almonds
¼ pt. rum or brandy
Milk

Method

Sieve the flour and spice together. Cream fat and sugar, add the eggs one by one, beating after each addition. Clean the fruit; add this and stir well in. Add almonds, and rum or brandy (if desired). Fold in the flour lightly, do not beat the cake again. Add, if necessary, a little milk to make a dropping consistency. Turn into a well-greased and lined cake tin. Bake at 300° F. Therm. 2 for 1½–2 hrs., testing with a darning needle.

Genoese Cake (Sponge)

Ingredients

3 oz. flour
3 oz. fresh butter
4 eggs
4 oz. caster sugar

Method

Dry and sift the flour on to a piece of paper. Melt the butter gently but do not overheat. Fill a saucepan half full of boiling water and place a mixing bowl on to the pan so that it will rest inside it but not touch the water. Whisk the eggs in the mixing bowl, add the sugar and whisk again for at least 5 mins. in all. Remove pan from heat, and whisk, frequently turning the basin until the mixture looks thick and "ropey", also increased in bulk, and lighter in colour. (If too much heat is applied the exact opposite of this condition will occur.) Remove basin from pan and whisk continuously until the mixture cools. Fold in half the melted butter lightly, then half the flour; continue until all the butter and flour is in but do not overstir. Pour into a 7″ greased cake tin which has a disc of greaseproof paper cut to fit the bottom. Bake until set and golden brown for 40–45 mins. at 375° F. Therm. 5. If preferred pour on to a swiss-roll tin lined with paper, and bake for 25 mins. at 400° F. Therm. 6. If this mixture is overbaked it becomes tough or shrinks.

[113]

Madeira Cake

Ingredients
6 oz. butter or margarine
8 oz. flour
3 eggs
6 oz. caster sugar
1 tsp. baking powder
Pinch of salt
Little milk if necessary
Rind and juice of 1 lemon

Method
Cream butter and sugar to a froth, add beaten eggs alternately with the flour, sifted with the salt and baking powder. Add flavouring and milk if necessary to get mixture to dropping consistency. Put in greased lined tin and cook in moderate oven for 1–1½ hr. at 350° F. Therm. 4. After 20 mins. put two pieces of citron peel on top of cake.

Madeleines

Ingredients
4 oz. sugar
3 oz. margarine
3 eggs
4 oz. flour
Grated rind of ½ lemon
Apricot jam
Water icing
Glacé cherries or angelica

Method
Cream together in a mixing bowl sugar and margarine. Add eggs, then sifted flour and lemon rind. Beat well. Take some dariole moulds, about 12 for a mixture of this size. Brush the moulds well inside with melted fat and half fill them with mixture. Bake for about 20–25 mins. at 350° F. Therm. 4, but do not allow them to become too deep in colour. When they are cooked remove them from the mould, set to cool. When cool, cut a piece out of one end of each, insert a little apricot jam and turn them over, pour some water icing over them, and decorate with cherries and angelica.

Maids of Honour. See Cheese Cakes (p. 108).

Parkin

Ingredients
½ lb. butter or dripping
1 lb. brown treacle or golden syrup
8 oz. flour
2 tsp. ground ginger
1 tsp. ground caraway seeds
1 tsp. bicarb. soda
1 lb. fine or medium oatmeal
½ lb. demerara sugar
2 oz. candied peel finely chopped
½ gill milk

Method
Heat the fat together with treacle. Sift the flour, spices and bicarb. soda. Add to this the oatmeal, sugar, peel; mix well together in a bowl. Add the warmed mixture, mix well together and add a little milk. Pour into an oblong tin, lined with greaseproof paper. Bake at 350° F. Therm. 4 for about 1½ hr., according to the depth of the mixture. When the cake is cold, wrap in greaseproof paper and store in an airtight tin for a few days before cutting.

Plum Cake

Ingredients
1¼ lb. flour
Pinch of salt
1 tbsp. baking powder

Method
Sift together flour, salt, baking powder and mixed spice. Rub in dripping, add raisins and sugar and moisten with milk. Beat well for 10 mins., then put into a

Plum Cake (*continued*)

Mixed spice
6 oz. dripping
¼ lb. raisins
¼ lb. sugar
½ pt. milk

well-greased tin. Cover the top with greaseproof paper and bake at 350° F. Therm. 4 for 1½ hr. See also **PLUM.**

Poppy Seed Cake

Ingredients

¾ lb. flour
1 tsp. baking powder
6 oz. butter
Pinch of salt
½ oz. poppy seeds
Milk to mix
Sugar and poppy seeds to decorate

Method

Sift flour with baking powder. Rub in butter, add salt and poppy seeds. Moisten with milk to make a soft dough. Fold and roll as for puff pastry. Cut into rounds, brush with milk and sprinkle with poppy seeds and•sugar. Bake at 400° F. Therm. 6.

Queen Cakes

Ingredients

4½ oz. flour
Pinch of salt
Just under ½ tsp. baking powder
3 oz. butter
Grated rind of ½ lemon
3 oz. sugar
2 eggs
2 oz. currants

Method

Sift flour, salt and baking powder. Cream the butter, add lemon rind and sugar and cream again. Add the well-beaten eggs slowly, then currants, and mix the flour lightly in. Fill the mixture into 18 queen cake tins. Bake at 400° F. Therm. 6 for 15–20 mins.

Raisin Cake, Eggless

Ingredients

1 cup milk
1 tsp. bicarb. soda
1 lb. flour
Pinch of salt
1 tsp. mixed spice
¼ lb. butter
¼ lb. raisins
2 tbsp. vinegar

Method

Dissolve bicarb. soda in half the milk, add to remaining milk. Sift flour, salt and spice. Cut and rub in butter. Add fruit; add vinegar and milk mixing to a stiff consistency. Turn into a well-greased tin and bake at 350° F. Therm. 4 for about 1 hr.

Sand Cake

Ingredients

¼ lb. cornflour
½ oz. ground rice
Pinch of salt
¼ tsp. baking powder
¼ lb. butter or margarine
Grated rind of 1 lemon
½ lb. caster sugar
2 eggs

Method

Sieve the cornflour, ground rice, salt and baking powder. Cream the butter, add lemon rind and sugar and cream until light in colour. Beat the eggs and add gradually, beating well. Add the sieved cornflour, folding it in lightly a little at a time. Turn into a greased and floured tin. Bake at 350° F. Therm. 4 for just about 1 hr. When the cake is cold dust with sieved icing sugar.

Seed Cake

Ingredients

1 lb. flour
Pinch of salt
2 tsp. baking powder
4 oz. sugar
1½ oz. caraway or dill seeds
2 eggs
⅛ pt. milk
2 tbsp. golden syrup

Method

Sift flour into a basin with salt and baking powder. Add sugar and caraway or dill seeds, and mix together. Add eggs beaten with a little milk; add golden syrup. Mix well and add enough milk to give a fairly stiff consistency. Put into a well-greased tin and bake at 350° F. Therm. 4 for about 1¾ hr.

Shrewsbury Cakes. See BISCUITS.

Simnel Cake. In Lancashire the Simnel cake is a round flat cake made with ground almonds, butter, rum and eggs. The Bury Simnel cake is a yeast mixture, sandwiched together with a layer of almond paste. It is the traditional cake for Simnel or Mothering Sunday (4th Sunday in Lent), but it is also suitable for Easter Sunday.

Ingredients

4 oz. butter
Grated rinds of ½ orange and ½ lemon
4 oz. sugar
3 eggs
6 oz. flour
3 oz. each candied peel and sultanas
10 oz. currants
½ tsp. mixed spice
Small tbsp. rum
⅛ pt. milk

Method

Cream butter and orange and lemon rinds. Add sugar, and cream again. Beat in the well-whisked eggs. Caramelise a little sugar, dissolve in milk and add to make the cake a good colour. Add a third of the flour, then the fruit, and remaining flour and spice sifted together. Turn the mixture into a 6½" tin previously lined with double paper. Bake at 350° F. Therm. 4 for about 2 hrs. Next day cut the cake transversely and cut off one-third of the almond icing. Roll the rest into a round the size of the cake and place it between the two portions of the cake. Form the icing cut off into a ring round the top of the cake. Mark with a fork and brush with beaten egg. Brown gently under a hot grill or bake at 400° F. Therm. 6. When cold, dry off the centre with icing sugar, or, if preferred, put a layer of glacé icing in the centre hollow; decorate as desired, with small coloured eggs, etc.

FOR THE ALMOND ICING

Ingredients

½ lb. ground almonds
½ lb. caster sugar
1 egg
2 or 3 drops almond essence
1 tsp. lemon juice
Small tbsp. sherry

Method

Pound together the almonds and sugar. Add essence, egg, lemon juice and sherry. Whisk well together.

Snow Cake

Ingredients

½ lb. flour
½ tsp. cream of tartar

Method

Sift together flour, cream of tartar, bicarb. soda and salt. Cream butter and

Snow Cake (*continued*)
¼ tsp. bicarb. soda
Pinch of salt
1 oz. butter
3 egg whites
¼ pt. milk

Sponge Cake
Ingredients
3 eggs
6 oz. sugar
3 oz. flour
Lemon essence

Sponge Fingers
Ingredients
2 oz. flour
Pinch of salt
2 eggs
1¾ oz. sugar

Sponge Sandwich
Ingredients
4 oz. butter
3 oz. caster sugar
2 eggs
6 oz. flour
1½ tsp. cream of tartar
¼ tsp. bicarb. soda
½ gill milk
Flavouring (if desired)

add it to the flour mixture. Mix well together and add the well-whisked egg whites and milk. Put the dough into a well-greased tin and bake at 400° F. Therm. 6 for about 35–40 mins. Then brush the top of the cake with white of egg, sprinkle on caster sugar and return to the oven for 5 mins.

Method
Break eggs and separate the yolks from the whites. Put the yolks into a basin and beat well, add sugar and place the basin in another containing boiling water and beat until the mixture is warm. Sift in flour, add a drop of lemon essence and mix well. Fold in the stiffly whisked whites of the eggs with a metal spoon. Turn into a tin, well-greased and floured, then sprinkle with sugar (this gives a crisp crust to the cake), and bake at 350° F. Therm. 4 for 45 mins.

Method
Sift flour and salt. Separate the yolks from the whites of eggs and cream the yolks with the sugar till light and fluffy. Add the flour lightly and fold in the stiffly whisked egg whites. Put the mixture into a bag fitted with ½″ plain biscuit pipe, then pipe in finger lengths on to a greased floured tin. Dredge lightly with caster sugar. Shake off any surplus. Bake at 400° F. Therm. 6 until golden brown.

Method
Prepare two 8″ sandwich tins by brushing well with melted butter and dusting with flour. Beat the butter and sugar together for a few minutes until creamy. Beat the eggs and add very gradually. Sieve the flour, cream of tartar and bicarb. soda together and fold in. Add the milk and then the flavouring chosen (if any). Spread half the mixture smoothly in each tin and bake at 350° F. Therm. 4 for 20 mins. Fill cake as desired.

[117]

Swiss Roll (Chocolate)

Ingredients
- 2 oz. flour
- 1½ oz. grated chocolate
- 3 eggs
- 3 oz. caster sugar
- 1 oz. melted butter
- ½ tsp. vanilla essence

Method

Sieve together flour and grated chocolate. Whisk eggs in a basin with caster sugar until they are thick, and then add melted butter, vanilla essence and the flavoured flour. Stir lightly with a metal spoon and pour the mixture on to a lined baking sheet. Bake at 400° F. Therm. 6 for 6 or 7 mins., then turn on to a board which has been sprinkled with flour and roll up lightly. When the roll is cool, unroll and spread with whipped cream or butter icing and roll up again. Sprinkle the roll with a little icing sugar.

Swiss Roll (Plain)

Ingredients
- 3 eggs
- 4 oz. sugar
- 4 oz. flour
- 1 dsp. boiling water

Method

Break eggs into a basin, add sugar and whisk until thick, which usually takes about 10 mins. Sift in flour and stir the mixture lightly. Add boiling water and stir, then pour on to a baking tin. Bake at 400° F. Therm. 6 for about 8 mins. Sprinkle a sheet of greaseproof paper with sugar, turn out the cooked cake on to this, spread with warm jam and roll up. To warm the jam, leave the jar standing for a few minutes in a pan of warm water.

Treacle Cake

Ingredients
- ¼ lb. butter
- ¼ lb. sugar
- ½ lb. treacle
- 1 egg
- ½ cup sour milk
- 1 tsp. bicarb. soda
- ½ lb. flour
- 1 lb. mixed fruit

Method

Put together in a warmed bowl, butter, sugar, treacle, egg and sour milk and beat. Add bicarb. soda sifted with the flour. Beat well again and add mixed fruit; stir and turn into a well-greased tin. Bake at 350° F. Therm. 4 until well browned (about 1½–2 hrs.).

Victoria Sandwich

Ingredients
- 3 small eggs, their weight in caster sugar, butter and flour
- ½ tsp. baking powder
- Small pinch salt

Method

Sift flour, baking powder and salt, cream the butter or margarine, add sugar and cream again. Add the well-whisked eggs by degrees, beating. Add sifted flour about one-third at a time, and spread the mixture in two prepared sandwich tins, or in a deep Swiss roll tin 10″ × 9″.

Victoria Sandwich (*continued*)

Spread it well to the corners and leave a little hollow in the centre. Bake at 350° F. Therm. 4 for about 40 mins. Leave to stand 24 hrs. before icing. This sandwich mixture can be used for small iced cakes or for cream sandwich.

FOR THE GLACÉ ICING
Ingredients
3 tbsp. warm water
9–10 oz. icing sugar
Few drops flavouring
Colouring (if desired)

Method
Put the water into a small pan over a low heat and add the finely sieved icing sugar very slowly. Add flavouring and colouring and mix smoothly. The saucepan must never be hotter than when one can press the palm of the hand against it in comfort. Make the icing a coating consistency (test this on the back of a wooden spoon) and should the icing be too thick add a little more water. If too thin, add a little more sugar. If preferred, the cakes may be split and filled with buttercream icing, and the top brushed over with white of an egg, or a little warm apricot jam, then sprinkled with coconut, plain or toasted, or a few finely chopped nuts.

Walnut Cake, Iced
Ingredients
5 oz. flour
Pinch of salt
1 tsp. baking powder
2½ oz. butter or margarine
3 oz. caster sugar
2 eggs
1 oz. chopped walnuts
½ tsp. vanilla essence
Spoonful of milk if necessary
Few halved walnuts for decoration

Method
Line a 6″ tin, sift the flour, salt and baking powder. Cream the butter or margarine, add sugar and cream till fluffy. Add eggs separately and gradually; beat well. Add the chopped walnuts and vanilla essence and fold in flour and milk (if necessary). Turn the mixture into the prepared tin. Bake at 350° F. Therm. 4 for about 1 hr. When the cake is cold, cut through the middle crosswise; sandwich with vanilla butter icing, coat with frosting and decorate with halved walnuts.

FOR FROSTING
Ingredients
½ lb. granulated sugar
¾ gill water
2 egg whites

Method
Put sugar and water into a saucepan and brush down any crystals found just above the liquid level, using a pastry brush and warm water. When the sugar is quite dissolved, place the lid of the pan on and boil to 240° F. If the sugar is under-boiled the icing will not set; if it is over-boiled,

FOR FROSTING (*continued*)

it will be too hard, so care should be taken to boil to the correct degree. Put the egg whites into a deep earthenware bowl, and whisk the whites until stiff. Pour the syrup in a slender line into the bowl holding the saucepan at a good height to cool the sugar slightly while pouring (if this is too hot it will curdle the egg white), whisking briskly the whole time the syrup is added and continuing to whisk until the mixture loses its shiny appearance, and begins to look dull like cotton wool. Spread the icing on the cake at once, sweeping it over in quick strokes. Decorate with walnuts.

FOR VANILLA BUTTER ICING FILLING

Ingredients	*Method*
1½ tsp. cornflour	Blend and boil the cornflour with the
½ teacup milk	milk. Leave to cool. Add flavouring.
Vanilla flavouring	Cream the butter and sugar and beat in
1½ oz. butter or margarine	the thickened cornflour until the mixture
3 dsp. icing sugar	is creamy. Add the finely chopped wal-
A few walnuts	nuts. Use for filling.

Wedding Cake. See Bride's Cake.

CALABRESE. This vegetable is a variety of broccoli, producing a central head, somewhat like a green cauliflower, only rather smaller, the average size being about 6″–8″ across. When this is cut, the plant produces side shoots in continuous profusion which are cut with stems 6″ long; these stems have the flavouring of asparagus. Calabrese should be cooked without too much flavouring, so as to preserve its own delicate flavour. The central head is cooked like cauliflower, the cooking time for a medium head being about 15 mins.; the side shoots are tied into bundles and cooked like asparagus, or steamed and served on buttered toast.

Calabrese, Baked. Parcook the central head, then cut into small pieces, place in a buttered pie-dish, and cover with white sauce and grated cheese. Sprinkle with breadcrumbs and add a few dots of butter. Bake at 400° F. Therm. 6 for about 15 mins.

Calabrese Salad. The cooked central head or side shoots can be mixed with tomato pulp and a little cream and served on lettuce leaves, and garnished with finely chopped parsley.

CALAMINT. Alpine Calamint. The leaves are used for cordial tea and also medicinally.

CALCIUM. See FOOD VALUES. Calcium can be extracted from bones in stock-making by adding a little vinegar to the liquid before simmering.

CALENDULA or **POT MARIGOLD.** The petals of the flower are used to flavour and colour cheeses and for soups, stews and puddings.

CALF (Fr. *veau*). The meat of the calf, called veal, from the Norman *veau*, was a luxury of the gourmet's table, even as Anglo-saxon *cealf*. See VEAL.

CALF'S BRAINS (Fr. *cervelles de veau*). Very little difference exists in the brain tissue of the various meat animals, but there is a decided leaning in culinary quarters towards the brains of the calf, as being more marrow-like and mellow. The brains must be well soaked to cleanse away any blood that may be diffused

CALF'S BRAINS (continued)

through them, and then dipped into scalding water containing a little vinegar and salt, and boiled up for a few minutes so as to slightly harden them. The membranes can be stripped off easily, and the brains drained and dried, when they are ready to be treated in various ways.

Calf's Brains, Boiled

Ingredients	Method
3 blanched and prepared calf's brains	Put the brains in a stewpan, cover with water, add salt, vinegar, thyme and bay leaf, carrot and peppers. Boil for 5 mins., drain well. Cut each brain into halves, arrange on a dish and serve with very hot Brown butter. See p. 96. Sufficient for 3 or 4 persons.
Water	
Pinch of salt	
½ cup vinegar	
Sprig of thyme	
1 bay leaf	
1 medium-sized carrot	
6 whole peppers	
1 gill hot brown butter	

CALF'S CHITTERLINGS. These are the calf's entrails, known to some cooks as the chaudron of the calf. They are always ripped open and thoroughly cleansed, parcooked, dipped into a seasoning made with grated nutmeg, pounded cloves, mace, salt, pepper, finely minced onion, chopped parsley, and tarragon, and after being well coated with this, they are fried and served with Tartare or other sauce.

CALF'S EARS (Fr. *orielles de veau*). The ears are cut with a wide base, scalded, scraped and blanched, then boiled and served with a white sauce to which chervil has been added. Sometimes they are marinaded, and then fried and served with Tomato sauce.

CALF'S FEET (Fr. *pieds de veau*). Calf's or any other animal's feet are chiefly valued by cooks for the jelly obtained from them after boiling: this is not only nourishing, but bright and beautiful when skilfully prepared.

TO PREPARE. Break the foot across several times, split between the toes, remove the piece of fat between the toes, and all the marrow from the bones. Well wash the foot, put into a saucepan, and cover with cold water. Bring to boil, take out foot, plunge into a basin of cold water and scrape thoroughly.

TO BOIL. Split each foot into halves, remove large bones and soak in water for an hour. Wash thoroughly and drain. Place in saucepan with 2 tbsp. flour, 3 qt. water, 1 gill vinegar, a handful of salt, and a bouquet garni. Cook for 1½ hr. Drain and serve with any kind of sauce.

Calf's Foot Jelly

Ingredients	Method
4 dressed calf's feet	Put the feet in a pan and add water. Simmer over a low heat until reduced to 2 qt., then strain and leave overnight. Remove all fat and sediment; melt stock; add the juice and peel of the lemons, the wine, the egg whites, cinnamon and sugar to taste. Boil for 10 mins., skim out spices and lemon peel and strain.
3 qt. water	
3 lemons	
1 pt. wine	
4 egg whites	
3 stalks cinnamon	
Sugar	

CALF'S HEAD (Fr. *tête de veau*)

TO PREPARE. The calf's head requires considerable attention on the part of the butcher before the cook can deal with it. The head is soaked and scalded so that the hair can be removed, the bones are cut down and the eyes removed. The cook can then remove the brains and tongue. The brains are blanched and the tongue soaked in salted water until the blood is disgorged. The head is plunged into scalding water containing salt and vinegar. After a few minutes in this it can be taken out, again put into cold water, or dried with a cloth and left until wanted.

C.C.D.—5

Calf's Head, Boiled

Ingredients

Half or a whole head
Water
Salt
Vegetables, herbs and peppercorns
Bacon
Lemon
Parsley
Parsley sauce

Method

Take the soaked head, place in a saucepan with sufficient water to cover. When it boils, add salt and remove scum as it rises. Add vegetables, herbs and peppercorns, and simmer gently for 2–3 hrs. until tender. The brains must be removed, tied in muslin and boiled. Take out head, remove all bones and tongue. Place the head on a hot dish, coat well with Parsley sauce, garnish with the skinned sliced tongue, chopped brains, fried bacon, quarters of lemon and parsley. Sufficient for 7 or 8 persons. For *carving*, see under this heading.

CALF'S HEART (Fr. *cœur de veau*). The flesh of the calf's heart is hard and juiceless, and the fat, oily and rich, but when cooked nicely and stuffed, or roast or baked right through it is thought to be good eating. The heart must be blanched and soaked, then well washed and the hard tubers cut away to their roots. It is then plunged into scalding water and cooked over a low heat for 20 mins. or more, then plunged into cold water for a minute, after which it is ready to cook. It can be stuffed and roast and served with a good gravy.

CALF'S KIDNEYS (Fr. *rognons de veau*). These are generally styled veal kidneys; this is because frequently they are cooked or served with the loin, whereas sheep's kidneys are usually cooked separately or made into special dishes.

Calf's Kidneys à la Maître d'Hôtel. Cut kidneys into half lengthwise, and beat lightly. Dust with pepper and salt, dip each piece into melted butter and broil under grill for 5 mins. on each side. Put 2 oz. butter into a basin, season with chopped parsley, pepper and salt, squeeze in a little lemon juice and work near warmth until soft but not oiled. Put the Maître d'Hôtel butter (see p. 97) on a dish, place on the kidneys and serve.

Calf's Kidneys Stewed in Wine

Ingredients

Calf's kidneys
½ lb. butter
Pepper and salt
2 tbsp. shallots diced
12 mushrooms
1 tbsp. chopped parsley
Clove of garlic
½ pt. white wine
½ pt. gravy

Method

Cut the halved kidneys into slices after removing the sinewy part. Put half the butter in a frying-pan and melt it. Put in the slices of kidney, season with salt and pepper, and fry them until the moisture has evaporated. Then add shallot. Put remaining butter into a saucepan; fry without browning, the mushrooms, parsley and garlic. Add wine and gravy and reduce to half quantity, then strain, return to pan and add kidney, but do not boil, just reheat. Serve garnished with sippets of toast.

CALF'S LIVER (Fr. *foie de veau*). The liver should be thoroughly washed, dried and floured before use. As the flesh is close and dry when cooked it requires some bacon served with it.

Calf's Liver Broiled with Onions

Ingredients	Method
1½ lb. liver 1 tsp. salt 1 tsp. pepper 1 tbsp. sweet oil 1 tbsp. flour	Trim the liver and cut into 6 even-sized slices after removing the hard pieces. Mix the flour, salt, pepper and oil together, and well season the liver with this mixture. Grill for a few minutes on each side. Arrange the slices on a hot dish and decorate with a few crisply fried slices of bacon and crisply fried onions, or a little Maître d'Hôtel butter (see p. 97). Sufficient for 5 or 6 persons.

Calf's Liver Salad. Put the liver into a baking tin with a little butter to baste it with and bake at 350° F. Therm. 4. When cooked, and cold, cut into small pieces 1″ square. Serve with shredded cabbage heart.

CALF'S PLUCK. The pluck of an animal, in butcher's parlance, consists of liver, lights and heart. These are usually soaked and blanched before use, then boiled with lemon, nutmeg, onion, cloves and a little vinegar added to the water.

CALF'S SWEETBREAD (Fr. *ris de veau*). See **SWEETBREAD**.

CALF'S TONGUE (Fr. *langue de veau*). This has an inferior flavour to ox or neat's tongue, and therefore it is usual to serve it with a tasty sauce.
Calf's Tongue with Tomato Sauce. Trim and wash well a tongue, put into a saucepan with boiling water and scald it. Then drain and lard it. Place in a saucepan with 2 carrots, 2 onions, and 3 cloves, a bunch of sweet herbs, and sufficient rich stock to moisten. Simmer very gently for 4 hrs. Remove tongue when done, cut it into halves and remove skin. Place pieces on a dish and serve with Tomato sauce.

CALF'S UDDER. This is sometimes used in forcemeat. It is boiled, then pounded in a mortar and passed through a sieve before use.

CALIPASH. The green fat or portion of gelatinous matter which is found adhering to the upper shell of the turtle.

CALIPEE. The yellow fat or gelatinous matter found on the inside of a turtle's under-shell.

CALORIE. A dietetic term to measure the heat- and energy-producing qualities of food. One calorie will warm a litre (1,000 c.c. or 1¾ pt.) of water, through 1° C. (1⅘° F.). A calorie will raise 1 lb. water 4° F., and 4 lb. of water 1° F.

CAMBRIDGE CHEESE. A soft cheese made near and around Ely.

CAMBRIDGE MILK PUNCH

Ingredients	Method
2 qt. milk 1 doz. bruised bitter almonds Peel of 2 lemons ½ lb. loaf sugar 3 egg whites ¼ pt. rum ¼ pt. brandy	Boil the milk, almonds, lemon peel and sugar. When well flavoured, strain and keep warm. Stir in the well-whisked white of eggs (previously mixed with a little milk). Add, stirring, the rum and brandy. Mix to a froth. Serve at once in glasses.

CAMEMBERT. A rich soft cheese named after the French village where it is chiefly made. It is made of cow's milk which is inoculated with a white fungus. When a Camembert is ripe and beginning to go soft it is at its best. When too soft the gases which are accumulated give an advanced cheese and a violent smell.

CAMOMILE. An aromatic bitter plant with daisy-like blooms, which, when dried, are used to make a tisane with mild tonic properties.

Camomile Tea. Put a few dried flower-heads into a porcelain or glass container, cover with water and infuse for 10–15 mins. For a decoction, boil for 15 mins. Strain into a warm teacup and sweeten with honey.

CANAPÉ. Canapés are dainty savoury morsels which are served hot or cold as cocktail snacks or appetisers, hors d'œuvres, or savouries at the end of a meal. Both flavour and texture are important and a wonderful assortment of canapés is easily made. Sometimes small biscuits are used as the base for the highly seasoned canapé mixtures, but more usually slices of the crumb of bread cut about $\frac{1}{4}''$ thick are cut into fancy shapes and fried in oil or butter, or grilled until lightly browned. Only ryebread, pumpernickel and salty ryebread can be used plain and these should be well buttered. Some assorted recipes for canapés are given below. See also **APPETISERS.**

Bread browned in butter, spread with anchovy paste, and garnished with watercress.

Toasted bread, spread with anchovy paste, then with slice of tomato, $\frac{1}{4}$ tsp. mayonnaise, and garnished with egg yolk.

Toasted bread with bacon, olive, mayonnaise, and garnished with parsley.

Bread, toasted on one side only, or fried in butter, with caviare, garnished with design of red and green peppers.

Diamonds of bread, toasted both sides, with crabmeat, ring of onion lightly fried, salt, and garnished with red pepper.

Bread spread with grated cheese, salt and dash cayenne, toasted and served hot, garnished with little paprika.

Bread toasted on both sides, spread with cheese and butter creamed, and garnished with chopped stuffed olives.

Diamond of toasted bread, spread with American cheese, mayonnaise, and garnished with parsley.

Round of bread, browned in butter, spread with chicken or ham finely chopped and mixed with butter and chutney, and garnished with design of beetroot.

Squares of toasted bread, with flaked smoked haddock mixed and cooked with onions, flour, salt, cayenne and mushrooms, and garnished with grated cheese.

Round of toasted bread, spread with minced lobster mixed with melted butter, salt and cayenne, and garnished with egg.

Diamonds of bread, browned in butter, spread with pâté de foie gras, and garnished with ring of hard-boiled egg mashed with butter, with chopped parsley in centre.

Rectangles of bread fried in deep fat, with smoked salmon (thin slices) laid on top of anchovy butter, and garnished with ring of anchovy butter and sprinkle of lemon juice.

Squares of bread toasted on both sides, spread with mixture of sardines, butter and dash of Worcester sauce, and garnished with border of finely chopped hard-boiled egg, and ring of stuffed olive in centre.

See also **Cheese Balls** (p. 140) and **Tomato Canapés** (p. 498).

CANDIED FRUITS. The procedure for the making of candied fruits entails a considerable amount of labour and a large quantity of sugar. See **FRUIT.**

CANDIED PEEL. This consists of the outer rind of lemon, orange, citron or lime, encrusted with sugar, and is used as an ingredient of mincemeat, in cakes, etc.

CANDLING EGGS. See EGGS.

CANDY. This term has only one definition in cookery, that is boiled sugar, with more or less flavouring. See **SUGAR.** The process must not be confused with crystallising sugar, although it frequently is. A candy in America is any kind of sweetmeat.

CANNELONS. Made by rolling out nouille paste very thinly, cutting it into strips $2'' \times 3''$ and rolling these round small pieces of wood which are removed after baking. They may be filled with whipped cream or fruit jelly.

CANNING. A mode of preserving meats, fruits and vegetables. See also entries under FRUIT.

CANS, SIZES OF

Size						
Size 8 oz.	=	8 oz. weight	=	1 cup
,, No. 1	=	11 ,,	,,	=	1½ ,,
,, No. 1½	=	16 ,,	,,	=	2 ,,
,, No. 2	=	20 ,,	,,	=	2½ ,,
,, No. 2½	=	28 ,,	,,	=	3 ,,
,, No. 3	=	33 ,,	,,	=	3½ ,,
,, No. 10	=	106 ,,	,,	=	13 ,,

CANVAS BACK DUCK. A delicious water fowl.

CAPE GOOSEBERRY. Ground or Winter Cherry, Red Winter Cherry, Peruvian Cape Gooseberry. An edible berry, enclosed in an inflated calyx, which is used in this country for decoration and called Chinese Lanterns.

CAPER (Fr. *capre*). The plant is cultivated in Spain, Italy, the South of France, and Barbary, from which countries chiefly capers are imported into Britain. Capers are unopened flower-buds. Nasturtiums are sometimes used as a substitute for capers. Capers are only used for garnishing, in mayonnaise or for Caper sauce. **Caper Butter.** See BUTTERS (p. 96).
Caper Sauce. See SAUCES (p. 437), also **Anchovy and Caper Sauce** (p. 16).

CAPERCAILZIE. This bird, sometimes called the Wood Grouse or Cock-o'-the-Wood, is not often met with, though it is occasionally shot on the Scottish Moors and Highlands. The male is handsomely plumed and it is treated and dressed like a turkey.

CAPLIN. A small fish of delicate flavour resembling the smelt.

CAPON (Fr. *chapon*). These are young male fowls which have been castrated, secluded and fattened in order to improve the delicacy and flavour of their flesh. For *trussing*, etc., see CHICKEN.

CAPSICUM. These are perhaps better known as chillies, or sweet peppers, green and red, all of which belong to the same family (*Capsicum*), though they differ somewhat in shape and colouring. Cayenne pepper is made from the *capsicum annunum*, when the moisture has been dried out of the large withered dark red pods. There are several varieties: Cherry Pepper (*capsicum cerasiform*) bears cherry-shaped fruit, Bell Pepper (*capsicum grossum*) bears fruit shaped something like a conical bell; Bird Pepper (*capsicum boccatum*) yields very small fruit.

Capsicum Butter. Put 1 oz. cayenne pepper in a mortar and pound it, mixing in gradually ½ lb. butter; continue pounding until cayenne is well incorporated with butter. This is generally used in sandwiches.
Capsicum Syrup. Make 2 pt. strong syrup (2 lb. sugar to 1 pt. water); whilst hot, pour into 1 oz. tincture of capsicum.
Green Peppers, Stuffed—I

Ingredients	*Method*
4 green peppers	Cut the tops off the peppers and remove all the seeds and pulp. Put them into a saucepan and cover with cold water. Let them come slowly to the boil; cook for about 2 mins., remove the peppers from the water and leave to cool for a few minutes. Put the butter or margarine into a frying-pan. Peel and slice the onion and fry to a light brown in the butter or margarine. Add tomatoes, Worcester sauce, seasoning, and rice. Simmer for 2 to 3 mins.
2 tbsp. butter or margarine	
1 large onion	
½ lb. tomatoes	
Pepper and salt	
1 cup cooked rice	
1 tsp. Worcester sauce	
6 oz. grated cheese	

Green Peppers, Stuffed—I (*continued*)

Add two-thirds cheese just before removing from heat. Fill the peppers, sprinkle the remaining cheese on top of peppers and bake at 375° F. Therm. 5 until brown. Serve with Tomato sauce.

Green Peppers, Stuffed—II. Slice top off green pepper and remove seeds. Boil 2 mins. Plunge into cold water. Stuff with cooked macaroni, cheese, tomato and onion, seasoned with small pinch basil or mixed herbs, salt and pepper. Place in oven dish with small amount of water, and bake at 350° F. Therm. 4 for 30–35 mins.

Green Peppers, Stuffed—III. Wash half a dozen green peppers. Place in boiling water and boil for 5 mins. Remove from the water and rub off skins with a wet cloth. Cut off stem ends, remove seeds with a small spoon, and stuff the peppers with any kind of minced meat, mixed with an equal quantity of stale bread softened in cold water, or if preferred, use boiled rice, and season with salt and pepper. Replace stems and set the peppers in a deep earthenware plate or dish and pour over as much gravy as the dish will hold. Bake at 350° F. Therm. 4 for ½ hr. If preferred, cheese may be mixed with the soaked bread: then the peppers are fried, not baked.

Capsicums, Pickled. Put some capsicums into a jar, cover with boiling vinegar. Add for each pint liquor, ¼ oz. powdered mace, 1 saltspoon salt. When cold, tie down and leave for 6 wks. before use.

Cayenne Cheese. Put 3 oz. each grated Parmesan cheese, flour and butter into a basin and mix well. Sprinkle with sufficient cayenne pepper to taste; work into a paste, roll out very thin, cut into shapes and bake at 350° F. Therm. 4 for about 15 mins.

Chilli Sauce. Chop six green peppers and four large onions very finely and put them into a saucepan with 2 doz. peeled tomatoes, 8 tbsp. sugar, 3 tbsp. salt and 1½ pt. vinegar. Set the saucepan only over a low heat and boil very gently for 1 hr. Let the mixture cool, pour it into jars and cover. Use as desired.

CARAMEL (Fr.). Name of a favourite sweetmeat. Liquid colouring matter made by browning sugar to nearly burning-point; commonly known as "Black Jack". Also used for coating moulds for a kind of custard pudding, in which case the sugar is cooked to amber colour. The darker brown substance is obtained by heating sugar to 400° F. or 210–220° C. For how to caramelise, see **SUGAR** (p. 490).

TO MAKE. Put into a lined saucepan 1 teacup brown sugar, and ½ teacup water. Stew over a hot fire until it burns a little. If too thick, make to the consistency of thin molasses by adding a little more boiling water. Bottle and cork for use.

Caramel Bonbons. Boil some syrup to "crack" (see **SUGAR**) and flavour with either liqueurs, essences, or a strong extract of coffee. Place in a saucepan over a low heat so as to cook very slowly for about 2 mins.; in this way it will acquire flavour but little or no additional colour. Oil a slab, pour the caramel on to it and when it has cooled a little mark it with the back of a knife in the shape of small squares or lozenges. When quite cold, snap them asunder.

Caramel Custard. See **CUSTARD** (p. 188).

CARAWAY. This plant, which produces caraway seeds, grows wild in Southern Europe and some parts of Asia, but it is usually cultivated in extensive fields for the sale of its prolific crop. The under-leaves are occasionally used in soups, and at one time the spindle-shaped roots were eagerly sought after as a delicious vegetable, greatly superior to parsnips. The familiar Caraway Comfit and Seed-cake owe the favour in which they are held to this delicate aromatic.

Caraway Biscuits

Ingredients	*Method*
¼ lb. butter or margarine	Warm the butter and beat to a creamy
¼ lb. caster sugar	consistency with caster sugar, then add

Caraway Biscuits (*continued*)

2 eggs
Flour
Caraway seeds

the well-beaten eggs and sufficient flour to make a stiff paste; sprinkle some caraway seeds in it. Dust some flour on to a baking board, turn paste on to it, and roll out thin. Cut the paste into rounds with a cutter, arrange on baking sheet, bake at 250° F. Therm. ½ for 10 mins. When lightly coloured, take the biscuits off the tin and leave to cool.

Caraway Bread. See BREAD.
Caraway Cake. See CAKES, Seed Cake.

CARBOHYDRATES. This group includes starches, sugars, cellulose, etc. Carbohydrates are composed of carbon, hydrogen and oxygen.

CARDAMOM. The spicy, bitter seeds of a plant of the ginger family. Known to the brewers as Grains of Paradise, they are much used by cooks and confectioners, for their peculiarly agreeable, but pungent, aromatic flavour. In curry powder they are essential. The dark-coloured seeds are similar in size to mustard seeds, and to preserve their flavour should be bought in the pod.

CARDINAL. This name is given to dishes and sauces (see **Cardinal Sauce**, p. 439), coloured bright red, or carmine as the robes of a cardinal. The name also applies to drinks which rise from Bishop to Cardinal and thence to Pope.

CARDINAL FISH. A European sea-fish, also known as King of the Mullets. Frequently red, but not always.

CARDINATE. Keel-shaped as opposed to ratite.

CARDOON. A garden plant resembling the artichoke in flavour; the stalks are blanched, cooked and eaten like celery; the main root is used as a vegetable stewed and also in soups and salads.

CAROTENE. The orange colouring matter of the carrot. It also occurs in all green vegetables, though its colouring is masked by the green of chlorophyll.

CARP (Fr. *carpe*). A soft-finned freshwater fish, found in ponds and sluggish waters of Europe. Included in the Carp family are Tench, Barbel, Gudgeon, Bream, Chub, Roach, Dace, Minnow and Bleak. Carp has sometimes a muddy brown flavour; it should be well soaked before cooking in running water, then weak vinegar and salted water.

CARP'S ROES, FRIED. Clean the fresh carp's roes. Place in a bowl of water and leave to soak for several hours, changing water frequently. Remove and place in a saucepan with a little boiling water and vinegar, sprinkle with salt to taste, then boil for a few minutes. Drain, dip into batter, then plunge into a frying-pan of boiling fat; fry to a good brown. Drain and serve garnished with fried parsley.

CARP'S SOFT ROES, BOILED. Remove the roes from the fish and cleanse well of all blood, then steep in cold water until they are quite white. Drain and put in a stewpan with cold salted water and a little vinegar, and boil until they are done. Drain and put into some fish consommé.

Carp with Red Wine

Ingredients	*Method*
A 3 lb. carp	Cut the prepared fish into portions.
1 pt. burgundy, claret or chianti	Wipe with a damp cloth and rub each portion gently with salt. Place in deep
½ onion grated	saucepan, add wine, onion and pepper.
⅛ tsp. pepper	Bring to boil over low heat, cover and
3 tbsp. butter	simmer for 20 mins. or until fish flakes

[127]

Carp with Red Wine (*continued*)
- ¼ lb. mushrooms finely chopped
- ¼ tsp. salt
- 2 tbsp. flour
- 2 tbsp. chopped parsley

when tested with a fork. Place 1 tbsp. butter in saucepan, add mushrooms, season lightly with salt. Simmer for 15 mins. When fish is cooked, strain wine through a sieve. Mix with flour till smooth, add 2 oz. butter and mushrooms; cook sauce gently for 10 mins. over medium heat. Add fish and cook a further 5 mins. Serve piping hot garnished with finely chopped parsley.

CARRAGEEN. An edible seaweed or Irish Moss. It is cartilaginous, flexible and dark purple in colour.

Carrageen Jelly

Ingredients
- ½ oz. moss
- 2 pt. milk
- Small piece of lemon rind
- Sugar

Method

Wash well the freshly gathered moss, then place in a saucepan of water, boil up and strain before use. Place in a saucepan with milk and lemon rind. Bring slowly to the boil, strain into a moistened mould, add a little sugar to sweeten. Leave to cool and set, turn out and serve with stewed fruit.

CARROT (Fr. *carotte*). The carrot was introduced into Great Britain during the reign of Queen Elizabeth. It is available for most of the year and is rich in Vitamin A.

TO PREPARE. Use a sharp knife when scraping carrots. For young carrots plunge into boiling water for a minute or two, then strip off the skins.

CARROTS, BOILED. Put into boiling salted water, and boil until tender. Cut into ½" squares and put into a saucepan with 1 tbsp. butter and flour, and stir until the mixture boils, then stir into it 1 pt. boiling milk. Add seasoning, salt, pepper and a grating of nutmeg; reboil, and add some finely chopped parsley. An egg yolk may be added to the sauce if desired, but do not boil the mixture after this addition. *Cold Boiled Carrots* are good reheated by frying in butter; serve garnished with finely chopped parsley or chives.

CARROTS IN SALAD. Raw carrots should always be freshly grated a few minutes before being added to salads and served as soon as possible. Cooked carrots may be used in some salads and should be cut into even-sized pieces (see **VEGETABLE SALAD**).

Carrot Casserole

Ingredients
- 6 or 7 medium carrots peeled and cut into pieces
- 2 tbsp. butter
- Salt and pepper
- 1 egg
- 1 teacup cheese grated or cut in pieces
- 1 medium onion chopped

Method

Cover carrots with enough water to cook them. Season with the butter, salt and pepper. When cooked tender and boiled down a little, pour off juice and save it; mash carrots with potato masher; add egg, cheese, onion and mix well. Put in a casserole and pour a little of the juice over mixture adding a little extra cheese if desired. Bake at 350° F. Therm. 4 till browned a little and the onion has had time to cook.

[128]

Carrot Ring

Ingredients	Method
1 tbsp. onions chopped	Boil finely chopped onions, pepper and parsley in salted water for 3 mins.; add to mashed carrots, then add crumbs, unbeaten egg yolks and white sauce. Mix well. Beat egg whites till frothy, add baking powder and beat till stiff and creamy. Fold into carrot mixture. Sprinkle crumbs in bottom of greased baking ring. Bake at 300° F. Therm. 2 for 1¼ hr. Unmould on serving plate and fill centre with beans or peas.

Ingredients

1 tbsp. onions chopped
2 tbsp. green pepper chopped
4 tbsp. parsley chopped
Salt to taste
2 cups cooked carrots mashed
1 cup soft breadcrumbs
2 egg yolks
½ pt. thick white sauce
2 egg whites
1 tsp. baking powder
Seasoned cooked French or runner beans or peas

Carrot Soup. See **SOUPS**, Crecy Soup.

CARVING. Carving is not really difficult; with some easily acquired knowledge and a little practice, the average person can become an expert carver. No matter how well the joint has been cooked, if it is not properly carved a great deal of it is wasted. An expert understands how to combine the best cuts of the meat with the less choice portions and so divide these evenly among the diners.

A good and very sharp knife is necessary and also a two-pronged fork with a guard to prevent accidents should the knife slip. The dish on which the joint is served should be large enough to allow the joint to be carved with ease, and to be turned if necessary. Gravy should not be served on the dish with the joint, but should be handed separately in a sauceboat. Secateurs with specially long cutting edges are used for disjointing poultry and game.

Knowledge of the exact position of the bones in the various joints or birds is necessary.

Ask the butcher to joint the bones in the loin or neck of any animal so that the carver has only to cut the meat between them. The flat bone that lies almost along the surface of a leg of mutton should also be removed, as it is then much easier to carve the joint.

FISH. For carving fish, a silver fish knife, or slice, and fork are required as steel impairs the flavour. Fish such as pilchards, smelts, etc., that is the smaller fish, are served whole; some other small fish may sometimes be cut into two, according to the method of preparation and cooking.

COD OR SALMON. If whole, either of these fish should be placed on a dish, the underside being nearest to the carver; remove the skin from the upperside, then make an incision the entire length of the fish, nearer the underside, then carve thick slices from the top of the fish to this line, right through to the centre of the backbone. Remove the bone when the top part is finished and the lower portion is carved in the same way.

MACKEREL AND HERRINGS. These are always served head to tail and the meat is divided from the bone by cutting down the back lengthways.

5*

Salmon

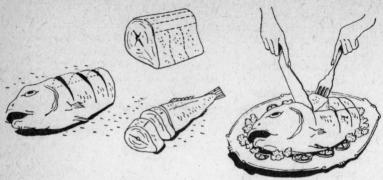

Dividing cod or salmon into portions

PLAICE. Large plaice are curved like turbot and small plaice like sole.

SOLE. Make three incisions, one right down the backbone and the other two down the fins on either side; raise a fillet from each side. After removing the bone, cut the bottom portion of the fish into two fillets. Sole is sometimes divided into 3 or 4 pieces widthways, the backbone being cut right through.

Turbot

Removing bone from sole

TURBOT AND BRILL. With a silver slice, make an incision down the backbone, and then cut flat pieces from the backbone to the fins, first on one side of the fish and then on the other.

GAME. Pheasants, grouse and large game are carved in the same way as fowls (see POULTRY below).

Partridges and small game birds are carved like pigeons, or cut into three as follows:

[130]

CARVING (*continued*)

From each side cut the leg and wing, together with a small portion of breast, then divide the breast from the carcase and serve it as a third portion; any trimmings from the back may be added to it.

Quails, wheatears, snipe, larks, ortolans and other small birds are usually served whole or, when only small portions are needed, they may be cut into two. PIGEONS. These are usually cut right through the middle making two equal parts. If too large, they may be divided into quarters.

POULTRY. To carve poultry really well, it is necessary to have a thorough knowledge of all the joints of the birds. Roast or boiled fowl should be sent to

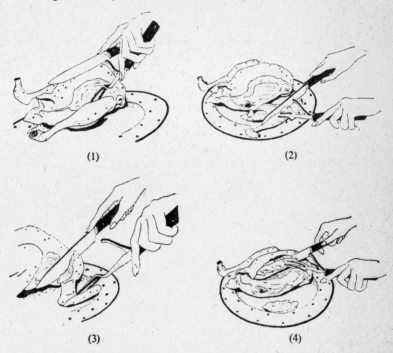

(1)   (2)

(3)   (4)

table with the legs towards the carver; (1) insert the fork into the lower part of the leg, then put the knife between the leg and the side, steadying the bird with the knife and prising the leg back with the fork. (2) The joint will then come apart and the leg only requires cutting through. (3) The wing portion is removed by cutting right through from the breast to the joint of the wing, pressing it back as with the leg, then separating the joint. Now make an incision just above the merry-thought (wishbone), turn this back on to the dish, cutting through. (4) Meat from the breast should be cut in thin slices the whole length of the bird. Turn the carcase over and remove the oyster, the small dark portion which lies in the centre near the side of the bone. If the bird contains stuffing, this should be sliced from the front of the breast as far as possible, and the rest scooped out with a spoon.

MEAT.

BEEF, RIBS. These are carved in a similar way to the uppercut of the sirloin, beginning at the thick end and cutting slices parallel with the bone, down to the thin end. Loosen the meat by running the point of the knife along the rib bone. If the ribs are boned and rolled they are carved in slices as in a round of beef.

CARVING (continued)

BEEF, ROUND AND SALT SILVERSIDE. Thin slices should be carved right across the surface of the joint. A small piece of fat, cut as thinly as possible, should also be served. The aitchbone is carved in the same way.

BEEF, SIRLOIN. The undercut must be carved first across the bone, not parallel with it. The joint must be turned before carving as the sirloin is generally served with the undercut turned downwards. The uppercut should be carved in thin, long slices from the backbone to the flap, parallel with the bone, and it is usual to serve a little fat with each portion. The meat should be loosened from the bone with a long-pointed knife.

CALF'S HEAD. Cut from one end of the cheek, right through to the bone, making long slices. A small piece of throat sweetbread should also be served with the meat, this being found at the fleshy part of the neck end. Remove the eye by cutting right round it with the point of a knife: by some people this is considered a great delicacy. Next remove the lower jaw which contains finely flavoured lean. A portion of the palate should also be offered and this is found under the head.

Round of Beef   Sirloin of Beef

HAM. This should be sent to table with the knuckle end nearest the carver. About 5″ or 6″ away from the knuckle end, cut through to the bone with slanting slices as thinly as possible.

HARE AND RABBIT, ROAST. Cut slices across the back from the head towards the tail. If young, the back of the hare can be cut across through the backbone into neat thick pieces, but the shoulders and legs must be removed first. It is not practicable to cook a full grown hare unless it is boned first. Remove the shoulders and legs by placing a knife between them and turning them back with the joint. The joints are then seen and can be easily separated. Lastly remove the head. Divide it from the neck, remove the lower jaw, cut through to the division from the nose to the top of the skull and cut it open. Serve a small piece of stuffing with each portion.

KID. This is served like venison if kept until the age at which lambs are killed. If killed at 3 or 5 months, it is served whole and carved in the kitchen.

LAMB QUARTERS. This is cut like mutton. Small lamb is usually cut into quarters, the forequarters and the hindquarters. Shoulder, ribs and breast are the forequarters and to carve, insert the fork near the knuckle end and cut out the shoulder in a deep circle right round the foreleg starting where the foreleg joins the joint. By lifting the joint with the knife at the same time, the shoulder is obtained, and this should be placed on a separate dish. Separate the neck from the ribs and cut slices from the breast or neck, according to preference.

MUTTON OR LAMB, LEG. About 3″ or 4″ from the knuckle end, insert a knife and cut right down to the bone in fairly thick rather slanting slices. Continue cutting up to the thick end of the joint, then turn it over and cut the under part in the same manner.

CARVING (continued)

MUTTON OR LAMB, LOIN. If small, this joint should be carved in chops, beginning with the outer chop. If large, slices should be cut the whole length of the joint. Be careful to see that all bones have been jointed before it is sent to the table.

MUTTON OR LAMB, NECK. All bones should be properly jointed and the whole carved in chops, beginning with the outer chop. Before serving the joint, remove the chine bone and scrag.

MUTTON OR LAMB, SADDLE. This is the two loins undivided. Carve into slices lengthways from the neck to the tail; thin slices of fat may be cut from the bottom

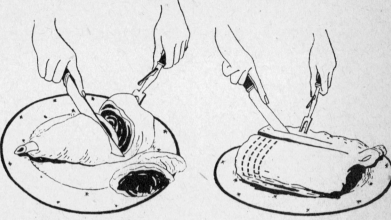

Leg of mutton or lamb   Saddle of mutton or lamb

part of the joint. Lines may be cut down the centre of the joint on each side of the vertebrae and then crossways lines carved towards the thin end of the joint. A slice of kidney should also be served.

MUTTON OR LAMB, SHOULDER. This joint is difficult to carve. It should be dished with the skin side uppermost with the knuckle end to the left of the dish. Raise the joint slightly by inserting a fork near the knuckle end, then cut as many fairly thin slices as possible from the top of the joint, near the foreleg, down to the bone, thus making wedge-shaped pieces. Good pieces may then be taken from the blade bone, cutting right across the joint from the foreleg to the other end in thin slices. Crisp fat is cut in circular slices from the bottom of the joint. Many prefer to cut the underside of the joint first as this is where the best portions of the shoul-

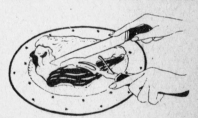

Shoulder of mutton or lamb

der lie, in which case, having turned the joint over, carve wedge-shaped slices vertically through to the bone from the meat nearest to the foreleg. Then take more slices horizontally from the blade bone end.

MUTTON, HAUNCH. This is carved like haunch of venison.

PORK, LEG. This is carved in a similar way to leg of mutton, care being taken to serve some of the crisp fat or crackling and stuffing to each person.

PORK, LOIN. This is carved in a similar way to loin of mutton, separating the cutlets. The bones should be jointed before sending it to table.

CARVING (continued)

RABBIT, BOILED. First remove the legs and shoulders, divide the back into two parts and cut each part into joints or slices. Add a little liver to each portion.

RABBIT, ROAST. See HARE AND RABBIT, ROAST.

SUCKING PIG. Before serving, divide into two down the middle of the back; the head is removed, cut in half and served on each side of the body. First cut away the front and back legs from the carcase and then separate the ribs into chops or cutlets. If stuffed, serve a small piece of stuffing with each portion.

TONGUE. Start by cutting fairly thick slices from the middle of the tongue, cutting from each side alternately. Do not cut right through to the bottom of the tongue but loosen the slices from it with a sharp knife. Serve a little fat from the root with each portion. When rolled, the tongue must be cut horizontally across the top and carved in thin slices as in a round of beef.

VEAL, BREAST. The ribs are separated from the brisket and a line cut horizontally right across the joint about two or three inches from the bottom. Divide the ribs,

Breast of Veal

which should have been previously jointed, from the top to this line. The smaller bones on the bottom of the line are also cut into joints. It is usual to serve small portions from the small bones of the larger ribs with one of the long ribs, as some people consider this the sweetest part of the joint. This joint is usually stuffed and rolled when it is quite easy to cut into thin slices.

VEAL, FILLET. Thin slices are carved right across the upper part, as in a round of beef. Each portion should contain a little stuffing and a small piece of fat.

VEAL, KNUCKLE. When sending this joint to table place the underpart uppermost. Carve it like a shoulder of mutton, beginning at the knuckle end.

VEAL, LOIN. First of all turn the joint over and cut out the kidney and fat. Turn it back into its proper position with the thin end towards the carver and cut in slices like a sirloin of beef, from the backbone towards the end, parallel with the bone. If small, the loin may be cut into chops as with mutton or lamb, but normally a veal chop would be too large to serve to each person.

VEAL, NECK. See MUTTON OR LAMB, NECK.

VENISON, HAUNCH. This joint is the leg and loin undivided. First of all cut lengthways down to the bone, turn the dish with the knuckle end away from you and cut slices sufficiently near the knuckle to prevent any gravy escaping from the centre of either side of the first cut made. Make the cut slanting and fairly thin and serve plenty of gravy with each portion.

Always serve venison on a hot-water dish as the fat chills very quickly and is most unpleasant if served cold. Serve a little fat with each portion of meat.

VENISON, SADDLE. See MUTTON OR LAMB, SADDLE.

CASHEW. The cashew tree is grown in the East and West Indies. From the end of a pear-shaped fruit hangs a kidney-shaped bean, the kernel of which is the cashew nut, used in cooking, in the making of chocolate, and sometimes in Madeira wine to improve the mellowness of its flavour. Roasted and salted it is served with cocktails and for dessert. The pear-shaped fruit is also edible and the juice from it is fermented into wine. The stem of the cashew tree yields a gum with somewhat the same qualities as gum arabic.

CASSAVA. The bitter and the sweet cassava are grown in the West Indies, Brazil and other parts of the world with a similar climate. From the meal into which the roots of the bitter cassava are ground, tapioca is obtained. The juice from the roots, called Cassareep, is used in sauces, and fermented with molasses into an intoxicating liquor.

CASSEROLE. A copper stewpan. Also a fireproof earthenware pan or pipkin. Casserole cookery is the slow cooking of food in the oven in a covered fireproof dish. When used in menus the term sometimes indicates a shape of rice or baked paste crust, filled with minced meat, game purée, etc.

CASSIA. An aromatic bark from the East which is difficult to distinguish from cinnamon. It is coarser and less expensive, but may be used in the same way.

CATFISH. The name given to a large group of fish, mostly freshwater, which have feelers about the mouth. One of the marine members is the Wolf-fish.

CATMINT. The name by which catnep is commonly known. Used mainly for infusing tea.

CAUDLE. Oatmeal or any other gruel sweetened and enriched by the addition of eggs, spices and wine, brandy or whisky.

TO MAKE. Rub 3 or 4 lumps of sugar over the rind of a lemon, and dissolve these in 1 tbsp. hot water. Beat up an egg and whisk this in with it adding, a little at a time, 1 wineglass port, madeira or sherry. Stir in ½ tsp. ground ginger and a good dusting of grated nutmeg. Have ready ¾ pt. fine oatmeal gruel and just before serving stir the mixture into it.

CAUL. A membrane, in the shape of a net, covering the lower portion of an animal's intestines, used for wrapping up minced meat, sausages, salpicon, etc. Pork caul is considered to be the best.

CAULIFLOWER (Fr. *chou-fleur*). There is so little difference between broccoli and cauliflower that a large specimen of the former might be easily mistaken for the latter. The head of the cauliflower should be close, foamlike, white and freshly cut, and it should be soaked in strongly salted water, which will rid it of any insects which may have taken refuge in the sprays.

CAULIFLOWER, BOILED. Cut the stalk so that the cauliflower can sit up as it were, the flower in the centre and a few leaves round it. Trim the leaves and parboil the cauliflower in water, then place in a saucepan and simmer gently in the following sauce: Heat 4 tbsp. butter well rolled in flour. As the butter melts, add ½ pt. milk and water gradually. Simmer the cauliflower till tender, then remove on to a hot dish, add a well-beaten egg yolk and a squeeze of lemon juice to the sauce; reheat, but do not boil, and pour over.

CAULIFLOWER, BAKED. Boil the cauliflower and when almost done, drain and arrange in oven-proof dish; pour over a good thick cream sauce, flavoured with a grating of nutmeg and the yolk of an egg stirred in smoothly. Dust all over with grated cheese and bake at 350° F. Therm. 4 for about ½ hr.

CAULIFLOWER, PICKLED. Divide two cauliflowers into sections and soak in salted water for 12 hrs.; afterwards boil in salted water for about 4 mins. Place on a sieve and leave to cool, then boil again in milk and water for 4 mins., drain, and put the pieces into bottles or jars. Pour boiling vinegar seasoned with mace and white peppercorns over and cover securely. In a few days the pickle will be ready for use.

Cauliflower and Mayonnaise. Break cold boiled cauliflower into flowerets and season with pepper, salt and a little vinegar, then heap on to a dish. Surround with cooked carrots, turnips and green vegetables. Pour over plenty of mayonnaise and serve.

Cauliflower and Peas with Shrimp Sauce

Ingredients	*Method*
1 boiled cauliflower ½ lb. cooked green peas ½ pt. shrimp sauce 1 tbsp. chopped parsley	Put the cauliflower into the middle of the dish, arrange the peas in a border round it and pour the Shrimp sauce over both; garnish with a sprinkling of finely chopped parsley.

[135]

Cauliflower Purée. See SOUPS.

Cauliflower Salad. See SALADS.

Cauliflower Vinaigrette. See SALADS.

CAVIARE (Fr. *caviare*). Salted sturgeon's roe. The best caviare still comes from Russia. For *Caviare Canapés* see CANAPÉ.

CAYENNE. See CAPSICUM.

CECILS. These are described as savoury balls of minced meat, served garnished with fried parsley, and accompanied by a sauceboat of clear beef gravy.

CEDRAT. See CITRON.

CELERIAC (Fr. *céleriache*). This is a variety of celery having a root shaped like a turnip; it is boiled and eaten when cold dressed with oil and vinegar. Celeriac also makes a good cream soup. Take some celeriac, remove the peel from the roots, and cut them into slices or quarters. Put into boiling water or meagre broth. Keep boiling until tender, drain and serve with melted butter.

CELERY (Fr. *céleri*). An aromatic plant of the same family as parsley, cultivated from wild smallage and now extensively grown; it is in season in England from September to April. Celery may be sent to the table raw to be eaten with cheese or salad, boiled or braised as a vegetable, or made into an excellent soup.

Curling Celery

TO PREPARE FOR SERVING RAW. Well wash 2 or 3 heads of celery, pare off the green stalks and trim, taking care to save the clean white hearts. Cut each head lengthwise into quarters. Rinse these in cold water and let them stand in clean cold water with a piece of ice until wanted. Arrange in a celery glass or on a china dish with a piece of ice in the centre and serve. Alternatively, slit the individual stalks closely with a small knife, taking care that the slits all end at an even line, then place in ice water to curl.

CELERY, BOILED. Cut off all the outside pieces and trim the roots. Cut into 6″ lengths. Wash well and tie together. Cover with boiling water in a saucepan. Add 3 peppercorns, a piece of mace, a little onion and some salt, boil until just tender, drain, and serve with melted butter or any sauce.

CELERY IN SALAD.
(I) Dice the celery, mix with grated carrot, apple, beetroot and dress with French dressing or mayonnaise.
(II) Dice the celery and season with salt and pepper. Dress with French dressing. See also SALADS.

Celery Sauce. See SAUCES.

Celery Soup. See SOUPS.

CÈPE. A member of the mushroom family (apparently a native of France). It sometimes grows exceedingly large, and has an unusual texture and flavour. It is tinned in brine and used for hors d'œuvres, entrées, vegetables and for garnishing. It has an agreeable nutty flavour.

CEREAL. A grass yielding grain used for food.

CEREAL COOKING TIMES
(Also see under own headings)

CEREAL	METHOD	TIME	PRESSURE COOKING TIME
Barley	Boiled in water or soup In pudding	1¼–1½ hr. 2 hrs.	20 mins.
Cornmeal	Boiled in double pan	2–3 hrs.	
Hominy	Boiled in double pan	1 hr.	
Oatmeal: 　Coarse 　Medium 　Fine	Boiled in double pan In soup In soup	3 hrs. 15–20 mins. 40–60 mins.	10–15 mins. 20 mins.
Pearl Barley	Boiled in double pan	40–60 mins.	30 mins.
Rice, Ground	Boiled	8–10 mins.	
Rice, Whole	Boiled in double pan in milk Simmered Fried 　then stand	40–60 mins. 10–15 mins. 5–10 mins. (10–15 mins.)	5–7 mins. 　in milk 1½ min. 　in water
Rolled Oats	Boiled in double pan	25–30 mins.	2½–3 mins.
Sago, Large	Boiled in milk pudding Boiled in water 　then baked	40 mins. 10 mins. 30 mins.	
Semolina	Boiled in water 　then baked	10 mins. 30 mins.	
Tapioca: 　Large 　Seed	Boiled 　then baked Boiled Boiled 　then baked	10 mins. 30 mins. 15 mins. 5 mins. 20 mins.	

See also **MILK PUDDINGS** for cooking times of cereal puddings.

CHABLIS. A famous French white burgundy wine, grown in and near Chablis in the Burgundy District.
Chablis Cup. Put 6 lumps of sugar into 1 pt. boiling water with a little lemon peel added. When the liquor is cold, add 1 wineglass dry sherry, 1 lb. ice and a bottle of chablis. If desired, a liqueur glass of chartreuse, maraschino or noyau may be added too.
CHAFING DISH. A dish or vessel used on the table for cooking and for keeping food warm.
CHAMOMILE. See CAMOMILE.

CHAMPAGNE. Sparkling wine of the champagne district which includes Rheims, Épernay and Châlons-sur-Marne. The wines differ in every vineyard and most champagnes are composed of skilful blends of more than one kind of wine. The renown of champagne as a sparkling wine only dates from the 17th century. The term *fine champagne* is also applied to old cognac or brandy of fine quality produced in the Charente district.

Champagne Cup. Pour a large bottle of champagne into a bowl, stir in 1 wineglass of brandy or curaçao, 2 tbsp. caster sugar, 2 large bottles soda water well iced. Put a few lumps of ice to float about and a sprig of green borage.

Champagne Ice. Rub off the zest of 4 lemons with pieces of loaf sugar, then put into a basin with the strained juice of the lemons. Pour in 1 pt. champagne, add sufficient syrup to sweeten. When well mixed, put to freeze.

Champagne Jelly. Dissolve 2 oz. gelatine in 1 qt. cold water. Put into saucepan; add the juice of 2 lemons, 3 oranges, the whites of 2 eggs and their shells, 12 oz. sugar. Mix well, then pour in another pint of water. Set over a low heat, and keep hot but not boiling for a further 15 mins. Then pour through a jelly bag. Add 1 pt. champagne, pour into moulds and leave to set. Turn out and serve.

Champagne Sauce. See **SAUCES**.

CHAMPIGNON. Mushroom or fungus. *Champignon de prairie*. Field mushroom. Among the numerous edible fungi with which France abounds, those known commonly as the Fairy Ring mushrooms or Champignons, cream in colour, still possess the most valuable flavouring qualities, but they must not be mixed up with the poisonous champignon, the gills of which are dark.

Champignons (Mock). Make a meringue (see **MERINGUES**). Set on paper in shape of a half ball. Sprinkle well with powdered chocolate. Place in the oven and bake at 200° F. Therm. ¼. Make the stems on paper in shape of pyramid and bake as the half balls; then when the meringue forms a dry crust, and is able to be lifted from the paper, press the bottom gently with the finger and place on the stem. Leave to dry, and use to decorate gateaux, sweets, etc.

CHANTARELLES. There are several species of mushrooms known by this name, only one of which is recognised as edible.

CHANTILLY (BASKETS AND CUPS). These baskets and cups are made in all shapes and sizes from marzipan, sugar, orange peel and other materials; originally they were made of savoury cake scooped out.

CHAR. The trout of the Alps found in some English, Welsh and Scottish lakes, also in the Lake of Geneva, where it is styled *Ombre Chevalier*, Cardhui or Red-black Loch Leven trout. It is cooked as trout. Potted char is considered a great delicacy.

CHARD. A variety of white beet producing large succulent leaves which are blanched and used for the table. Cooked like spinach.

CHARD SALAD. Cut the leaves off the chard without cutting the mid-ribs; cut the mid-ribs into even-sized pieces, tie these in small bundles and boil for 15 mins. When cooked, drain the bundles and leave till cold. Then remove strings, place in a salad bowl and cover with French dressing.

CHARLOTTE. A pudding of fruit and breadcrumbs, baked. Or it may be encased in sponge-cake or biscuits. A variety is Charlotte Russe, below. See **Apple Charlotte** (p. 23).

Charlotte Russe. Russian charlotte. A cream centre encrusted with thin biscuits or cake.

TO MAKE. Soak 1 oz. gelatine in cold water till soft. Make a syrup with ½ lb. sugar, ¼ pt. lemon juice, 1 pt. orange juice. When boiling pour syrup into the beaten yolks of 4 eggs and cook in a double boiler till it thickens, then add the soaked gelatine, stir till dissolved and strain at once on to tin pan placed on ice. Beat occasionally till cold but not hard. Beat the whites of eggs to a stiff froth, and then beat altogether till the mixture thickens. When almost stiff drop at once into mould or moulds lined with lady's fingers or slices of sponge cake. Keep on ice and serve with whipped cream. See also **Apricot Charlotte Russe** (p. 28).

CHEDDAR CHEESE. This hard, pale-coloured, whole-milk cheese came originally from Somerset. The name covers a multitude of cheeses, which undergo the "cheddaring process" (milling, salting and pressing).

CHEESE (Fr. *fromage*). Cheese consists of the essential food nutrients of milk coagulated by natural souring or the use of rennet into a curd which is separated from the whey and then pressed. It contains some of the fat, casein, calcium, Vitamin A and some of the sugars and salts of the milk from which it is made. Most cheese is cured or ripened by the action of moulds or bacteria which also develop its characteristic flavours. Among the cheeses made are the following types: soft unripened cheeses, soft ripened cheeses, semi-hard ripened cheeses, very hard cheeses with gas holes and processed cheeses which do not ripen beyond a certain stage and are packed in tinfoil to keep them.

Among well-known cheeses made in the British Isles, see **BLUE VINNEY, CAERPHILLY, CHEDDAR, CHESHIRE, COTHERSTONE (cream cheese), DUNLOP, DOUBLE GLOUCESTER, LANCASHIRE, LEICESTER, SLIPCOAT, STILTON, TRUCKLES, WENSLEYDALE.**

Among the better-known continental cheeses are:

Aettekes, a Belgian winter cheese.
Bel Paese, an Italian rich, mild-flavoured cheese.
Bondes or Bondon, a small loaf-shaped soft cheese made of whole milk.
Bra, an Italian soft creamy small mild cheese.
Brie. At its best in the autumn. From November to May it is known as Gras; in the spring and summer Bries are not so good and are known as Migras and Maigre.
Brie de Coulommiers, a Brie made from October to May.
Bruxelles, Fromage de, a Belgian soft fermented skim-milk cheese.
Camembert. See under that heading,
Cantal, a hard and shiny cheese made in France.
Coulommiers. See under that heading.
Danish Blue Cheese, the imitation of Roquefort made in Denmark. See under individual heading.
Demi-Sel, a whole-milk soft cheese made in France.
Double Crème, a soft cream cheese made in France.
Edam, a Dutch cheese with a bright red outside. See under individual heading.
Emmenthal, a Swiss hard cheese.
Étuve and **Demi-Étuve,** full size and half-sized Dutch cheeses.
Gammelöst, a Norwegian cheese.
Gorgonzola, a semi-hard, blue-veined cheese made in Cremona, Milan and Pavia.
Gouda, Goudsche, Kaas, a Dutch cheese similar to **Edam** (made in two grades) and known as "little Dutch".
Gruyère, a cooked, hard cheese with large holes in it, and pale yellow in colour.
Hushallsöst, the Swedish household cheese.
Mainauer, a German semi-hard full cream cheese, red outside and yellow inside.
Mesöst, a sweet cheese made in Sweden.
Parmesan, an Italian cheese, the hardest known; it is good for grating.
Pommel, a French unsalted double-cream cheese.
Pont L'Évêque, a semi-hard French fermented cheese.
Port-du-Salut, a French semi-hard whole-milk pressed cheese.
Pultöst, an all-the-year Norwegian cheese.
Roquefort, a French cheese made with ewe's milk.
Tilsiter, a semi-hard cheese made in Germany all the year round.

Cheese Aigrettes

Ingredients	*Method*
1 oz. butter	Put the butter and water into a saucepan
¼ pt. water	and bring to the boil. Shake the flour
3 oz. sifted flour	quickly into the water when boiling.
3 egg yolks	Stir and cook thoroughly, remove from

Cheese Aigrettes (*continued*)

Pepper, salt and cayenne
2 oz. grated parmesan cheese
2 egg whites

heat, then add the egg yolks, beating them in one by one. Add seasoning and cheese, then fold in the stiffly whisked whites of eggs. Drop the mixture by teaspoonfuls into hot fat, and fry till golden brown. They will take about 10 mins. to cook. When the mixture is in the pan draw it to the side of the heat otherwise the aigrettes will colour before they are cooked. Drain on paper and serve at once.

Cheese Balls

Ingredients

½ cup grated cheese
1 tsp. flour
Cayenne pepper
3 egg whites

Method

Mix cheese, flour and pepper well. Add beaten egg whites. Roll in cracker crumbs and fry in deep fat. These may be made before needed and placed in the refrigerator, but must be cooked at the last minute. Stick with a toothpick when serving as a canapé.

Cheese Butter. See BUTTERS.
Cheese Cakes and Cheese Cakes (Lemon). See CAKES.
Cheese D'Artois

Ingredients

1 oz. butter
1 whole egg
1 egg yolk
2 oz. grated parmesan cheese
Cayenne, pepper, pinch of salt
Remains of puff paste or some flaky crust

Method

Cream the butter in a basin. Beat in the eggs and add the grated cheese. Season with pepper, salt and cayenne. Divide the pastry into two portions and roll them out as thinly as possible. Lay one piece on a greased baking sheet, spread it over with the cheese mixture and lay the other on top. Mark into strips with the back of the knife, 1″ long × 3″ wide. Brush with beaten egg and bake at 400° F. Therm. 6: then, when the paste is cooked, cut into strips and serve with grated cheese.

Cheese Fondue

Ingredients

1 oz. butter
½ oz. flour
¼ pt. milk
Little pepper, salt and cayenne
2 eggs
3 oz. grated parmesan cheese

Method

Prepare a tin as for a steamed soufflé. Melt the butter in a saucepan. Mix the flour in smoothly, then add milk and cook well, stirring all the time. Add seasoning, beat in the yolks of 2 eggs, then add the grated cheese. Fold in the stiffly whisked whites of eggs. Put the mixture at once into the tin and bake for 25 mins. at 400° F. Therm. 6. When cooked it will be firm in the middle. Serve in tin with folded napkin round it.

Cheese, Potted. Take ½ lb. grated Cheshire cheese and place in a mortar with
3 oz. butter; add 1 tbsp. caster sugar and ½ tsp. mace. Pour over 2 wineglasses
sherry. Pound well and leave 2 or 3 mins. Work to paste. Put in jar and pour
clarified butter on the top.

Cheese Ramekins. Make the mixture as for cheese fondue, partly fill the little
ramekin cases with it and bake at 400° F. Therm. 6 for a few minutes.

Cheese Sandwiches

Ingredients

Yolks of 3 hard-boiled eggs
1 oz. butter
¼ lb. grated cheese
Little pepper, salt and
 cayenne
4 slices buttered bread

Method

Beat the yolks well with the butter. Add
the cheese and seasoning. Spread the
mixture on two of the slices of buttered
bread, and place others over.

Cheese Soufflé (Hot)

Ingredients

3 oz. butter
3 tbsp. flour
½ pt. milk
½ tsp. salt
Cayenne
Pinch of mustard
6 oz. grated cheese
3 eggs

Method

Melt butter, add flour, blending well;
gradually add milk and cook, stirring
constantly, till smooth and thickened.
Add salt, a few grains of cayenne, mustard and grated cheese. Stir over a low
heat until cheese is melted, then remove
from heat and add the beaten yolks of
eggs. Set aside to cool. About ½ hr. before
cooking, beat whites of eggs until stiff but
not dry; fold into cheese mixture with
metal spoon. If cheese mixture seems too
stiff, beat lightly before folding in egg
whites. Pour gently into well-greased
casserole and bake at 300° F. Therm. 2
for 1½ hr. If necessary, this soufflé can
wait another 10–15 mins. before serving.
The soufflé can be baked at 425° F.
Therm. 7 for 25 mins., but it must then
be served at once or the mixture will drop.

Cheese Soufflé (Cold)

Ingredients

1 gill cream or evaporated
 milk
½ tsp. made mustard
1 oz. grated parmesan
 cheese
Salt and cayenne
½ tsp. chopped chives (if
 desired)
½ gill aspic jelly
Sprigs of watercress or cress
 to garnish

Method

Prepare the soufflé case by fastening a
stiff band of paper securely round it. Put
the cream into a basin, add mustard,
cheese and seasonings, slightly whisk the
aspic and pour into the other ingredients,
stirring lightly with a fork. When almost
set pour into soufflé case. When firm,
remove paper and garnish.

Cheese Soup

Ingredients

1 small onion finely minced
1 oz. butter
1½ pt. milk
½ oz. cornflour (or flour)
Pinch of mustard
3 oz. grated cheese
Salt and pepper
Grating of nutmeg
Parsley or watercress to garnish.

Method

Fry onion in butter, bring milk to the boil, add onion; blend cornflour and mustard with a little cold water, add to hot liquid, stirring the whole time. Re-boil, stirring till the mixture thickens, reduce heat, cook for 15 mins., add cheese, pepper, salt, nutmeg; serve garnished with finely chopped parsley or watercress.

Cheese Straws

Ingredients

2 oz. butter
3 oz. flour
2 oz. grated parmesan cheese
Cayenne, pepper and salt
1 egg yolk

Method

Rub the butter lightly into the flour, add the grated cheese and seasoning and mix with yolk of egg. If necessary, add another yolk, but *no* water. Roll out, cut into fingers about ¼″ wide and 2″ long. Lay on a greased baking sheet. Stamp out with a cutter the size of an egg-cup some rounds, then make into rings by stamping out the middle with a smaller cutter. Lay on a greased baking sheet and bake till they are all pale fawn in colour at 350° F. Therm. 4. Serve them with a bundle of straws in each ring.

Cheese, Toasted

Ingredients

Slices of cheese
Slices of very hot toast
Made mustard
Pepper and salt

Method

Toast the cheese nicely and lay it quickly on the hot toast. Spread a little mustard thinly over it, season with pepper and salt and serve very hot.

Golden Buck. Make three slices toast and remove crusts. Cut up ¼ lb. cheese, place in a saucepan with ¼ tumblerful of ale, and sprinkle with pepper. Stir over a low heat until melted. Pour over slices of toast and place a poached egg on top of each. Garnish with sprigs of fried parsley.

Mock Crab. Rub 1 oz. grated cheese and 1 oz. butter together. When well mixed, add 1 saltspoon dry mustard, ½ saltspoon cayenne pepper, few drops of anchovy essence, 1 tsp. vinegar and a little salt. Work into a smooth paste and spread on to slices of dry toast.

Welsh Rarebit

Ingredients

Slices of bread about ½″ thick
Slices of cheese
Little butter

Method

Toast the bread and keep hot. Cut cheese or grate and place in saucepan with butter, mustard, pepper and salt to taste, and stir until the cheese melts. Mix in the

[142]

Welsh Rarebit (*continued*)

Cayenne, pepper, salt and pinch of mustard

1 egg yolk

2 or 3 tbsp. beer (if desired)

egg yolk and beer and stir well. Spread on the toast and brown under grill or bake at 400° F. Therm. 6.

CHERRY (Fr. *cerise*). The cherry belongs to the plum tribe. The stones or pits of the fruit are usually rounded instead of flattened. The French divide the cherries into three groups: *griottes*, tender-fleshed; *bigarreaux*, hard-fleshed; and *gingues*, small fruit. Among the eating cherries the large sweet White Heart and Black Heart are favoured. For cooking the Morello Cherry is good.

CHERRIES, BRANDIED. See FRUIT (p. 328).

CHERRIES, TO PICKLE. Put some cherries with stems removed into a thick layer on the bottom of a stone jar. Sprinkle about a teacup of sugar over them and put in a few cloves and pieces of broken cinnamon; fill jar up in layers like this, and then fill up with some cold vinegar. Tie securely and leave in a warm temperature for a few days, then put in store cupboard till required for use.

Cherry Cake. See **CAKES**.

Cherry Jam

Ingredients

4 lb. cherries

1½ pt. water

4 lb. sugar

Method

Stone cherries carefully to reserve juice. Place sugar and water in preserving pan and bring to boiling point. Allow to boil for 10 mins., then add cherries and let the whole boil for about ½ hr. Test for setting, then bottle and seal when cool.

Cherry Jelly

Ingredients

6 lb. cherries

Sugar

Method

This jelly will be better if not quite ripe cherries are used. Place them in a pan over a very low heat or bake at 200° F. Therm. ¼ until all the juice is extracted. Strain through muslin, then boil juice till it is reduced by one-third. Measure and allow 1 lb. sugar to each pint of juice. Heat the sugar in slow oven, then add to jelly and boil for 20 mins. until jelly sets. Bottle and cover when cool.

Cherry Salad

Ingredients

1 lb. pitted cherries

1 dsp. caster sugar

Pinch of salt

1 tbsp. strained lemon juice

1 cabbage lettuce

Mayonnaise

Method

Put cherries in a basin and sprinkle caster sugar over them, cover the basin and leave in a cool place for 30 mins. Wash the lettuce, drain and dry the leaves and place them on individual plates. Use the heart leaves placed together to form cups. Pile into the centre of each a few cherries and 1 dsp. mayonnaise alternately, topping with mayonnaise. See also **SALADS**.

Cherry (Black) Salad

Ingredients	Method
1 cherry jelly	Dissolve the cherry jelly in hot water.
¾ pt. water	Add ½ pt. juice from the black cherries
1 tsp. vinegar	and the vinegar. Chill until slightly
1 tin black cherries	thickened, then fold in black cherries
½ cup blanched almonds	halved, and the almonds halved. Chill
	until firm, cut into squares and serve on
	lettuce with mayonnaise.

Cherry Wine. Measure the cherries and bruise them, allowing to each 4 lb. cherries, 1 qt. boiling water. Leave 24 hrs., stirring occasionally, then strain off the liquid and put in a jar; to each gallon add 2 lb. sugar, stop tightly and allow to stand for 2–3 mths. before use.

CHERVIL. The leaf is used in sorrel and spinach soup to give added flavour, also in egg dishes, fish, French dressing, salads and sauces (Béarnaise, Ravigote sauce and butter for chicken, and also with wine and melted butter for fish).

Chervil is fit for drying in May, June and July. Its leaves are tender and delicious, combining the flavour of parsley and fennel, though more aromatic than either. Chervil improves the flavour of any herb with which it is mixed and is therefore invaluable in a salad or for soups and stews. The root can be boiled and eaten in vinegar.

CHESHIRE CHEESE. This hard, whole-milk cheese is of a rather crumbly texture, white in colour or with a reddish tinge. It is the oldest English cheese. There is also a Blue Cheshire, a red cheese which develops blue veins.

CHESTNUTS. It is the Sweet or Spanish chestnuts which are used in cooking. In France they are known as *marrons* and they are adapted to use with some dishes, or candied, or used in sauces and stuffings. For **Marrons Glacés**, see FRUIT (p. 237).

CHESTNUTS, BOILED. Wash well 2 lb. chestnuts, and cut through the stem end of shells with 2 cuts crossing each other so that the shells can be easily stripped off. Tie the nuts in a napkin and boil till tender in boiling salted water. Take them out; turn them into a fresh napkin and serve hot with fresh butter and salt: Bordeaux wine should accompany them.

CHESTNUTS, ROASTED. Split the skins on one side of some large chestnuts; put them on a pan with a perforated bottom, stand over a moderate fire. When done, wrap in a cloth for about 10 mins. Serve with salt and butter.

Chestnut Cream. Peel the dark skins from 20 chestnuts and parboil them. Rub the light skins off, then pound them in a mortar and pass them through a sieve. Dilute 1½ oz. gelatine in ½ pt. milk, and put in a stewpan with 6 blanched and bruised sweet almonds with thinly cut rind of ½ lemon and a little sugar. When milk comes to the boil move from one side to the other until cool, then strain and mix with the chestnut purée. When worked to a smooth paste, add a wineglass of dry curaçao, ½ pt. whipped cream, pour into a mould and stand on ice. Whip some more cream and sugar to a froth and when the chestnut cream is set, turn out and serve the whipped cream round it.

Chestnut Forcemeat and Stuffing

Ingredients	Method
1 lb. boiled riced chestnuts, or equal parts chestnuts and chopped, cooked (lightly sautéed in butter) oysters	Put the chestnuts through a hair sieve. Combine them with the other ingredients. Use for stuffing 3½–4 lb. dressed chicken. For a turkey of about 12 lb. dressed, make double quantities. This forcemeat
4 oz. melted butter	may be used in fish if desired.
¼ cup cream	

CHESHIRE

LEICESTER

LANCASHIRE

ENGLISH CHEDDAR

STILTON

DOUBLE GLOUCESTER

WENSLEYDALE

Chestnut Forcemeat and Stuffing (*continued*)
1 cup dry, white bread-
  crumbs
1 tsp. salt
⅛ tsp. pepper
2 tbsp. chopped parsley
1 tbsp. grated onion (if
  desired)

Chestnut Mousse. Mix together ¼ lb. chestnut purée with 6 oz. sugar flavoured with vanilla. Beat well with a spoon until quite smooth, then add 3 wineglasses sweetened whipped cream. Pour into a dome-shaped mould and chill. When set, turn out.

Chestnut Purée. Peel off the brown skins and immerse the chestnuts in boiling water until the underskin can be removed, then put into a saucepan with some chicken consommé and leave to simmer for 20 mins. When done add half the quantity of Spanish sauce, reduce, then pass through sieve. Finish by adding a little butter, a sprinkle of caster sugar and a few spoonfuls of cream. See also SOUPS.

Chestnut Sauce. Peel and blanch ¼ lb. large chestnuts. Put them into a stewpan with a breakfast cupful good gravy and a couple of strips of lemon peel. Simmer till soft, then rub through a fine hair sieve. Return to saucepan, add ¼ pt. cream and a little pepper and salt to taste; simmer for 5 mins. longer before serving.

CHICKEN (Fr. *poulet* or *volaille*). Chick or Squab chicken (Fr. *poussin*).
Chickens are sold as:
Fresh-killed poultry, which have been killed and chilled not very long before going to market.
Cold packed or chilled poultry, which have been kept in cold storage and, if kept too long once out, are apt to lose their flavour.
Quick-frozen birds, which are disjointed and frozen ready dressed for the table and may be cooked either thawed or frozen. One point which must be remembered is: *Never re-freeze a bird after thawing.*
A fowl is a mature hen and has probably more flavour than all other chickens, although it requires slow cooking which can be either braising or fricasséeing. In boiling (which would be more correctly called "poaching") these birds range from 3–8 lb. and are usually quite fat. A fowl is either prepared whole or cut into convenient-sized serving pieces.
Capons are unsexed male birds; they are at their best from 6–12 mths. old. They lead a very inactive life, and develop into large and delicately flavoured birds sometimes weighing as much as 8–9 lb. They are good for roasting, braising or serving cold.

APPROXIMATE COOKING TIMES

Chicken 6 mths.	320° F. Therm. 3.	Roast about 30 mins. in all.
„ 12 „		Boil about 1½ hrs.
Capon 12 „	320° F. Therm. 3.	Roast about 30 mins. per lb.

TO CHOOSE
For Grilling. The best chickens for grilling are from 7–12 wks. old. They usually weigh from 1–2 lb.; the smaller ones weighing about 1 lb. are often served whole, one to each person. The larger ones are usually split or quartered.
For Frying and for Sautés. The birds may be anything from 14–20 wks. old and their weight ranges from 1–3½ lb. Those with full plump breast, compact structure and a little fat are the best; they may be split, cut or disjointed before cooking.
For Roasting. The best chickens are from 5–10 months old, and a roasting chicken should have a soft, pliable breastbone, in addition to the structural qualities of grillers and fryers.
For Casseroles. Fricasséeing, boiling or roasting chickens, are sometimes used for these dishes, although a fowl is better flavoured for long, slow methods of cooking.

CHICKEN *continued*)

TO PLUCK. Dip the bird into water which is about 130° F. Remove the feathers and re-dip if the feathers do not come out easily.

TO STUB AND SINGE. Also remove the pen feathers and singe the bird with a taper or lighted piece of paper.

TO DRAW. Cut off the head and neck close to the body; do not cut the skin when removing the neck but leave loose. Remove the windpipe and crop through this opening, carefully cutting the skin joining the crop. Cut off the legs 2″ below joint, bend and break off; (1) then take out the tendons, eight in each leg, pulling them over a skewer held firmly, one at a time (if they are not pulled out they might make the meat tough). (2) Cut an opening between the vent and tail. Then

(1)   (2)

insert the two first fingers and loosen the internal parts from the frame. Take care not to damage the gall bladder. Pull gently and the whole inside will come out. Put on to boil, covered with salted water. Wash the fowl well under running cold water. Dry well with clean cloth. Separate the liver and heart, wash well in cold water.

TO DISJOINT. Use a sharp knife and cut the skin around the thigh. Cut through the joint which joins the thigh to the body and remove leg and thigh. If desired, separate the leg from the thigh at the knee joint. Cut through the base of the wing and either remove the wing completely by cutting it away from the breast at the joint, or tear off the long strip of white meat from the breastbone. Use your knife to help to do this. This is the proper way to prepare a chicken if you are to sauté it. Remove the other leg, thigh and wing and split the chicken in two with a sharp knife, separating the breast from the back and ribs. The breast then is easily cut into two pieces and the back separated from the ribs, then disjointed into two pieces. Always use a sharp, heavy kitchen knife for this purpose.

TO TRUSS. This art cannot be properly taught by book unless there are clear explanations or illustrations; whenever possible get a few practical instructions from a poulterer, or other skilled person. These will be found of infinitely more value than any printed directions can possibly be. Particular instructions are, however, given for the trussing of a fowl for roasting or boiling, as on these methods most of the others are based, and where the trussing of other birds differs, general directions for these will be found under their individual headings.

For Roasting. The fowl should first be plucked. If necessary, scald the pinions to get them quite free from any stumps of feathers. Turn the fowl on its breast and cut 1″ long slit in the skin at the back of the neck, 3″ below the head. Loosen the skin round the neck with the fingers, put a sharp knife under the skin and cut off neck quite close to the body, then cut the skin, leaving a piece fully 2″ long for folding over the back. Remove crop and with the fingers loosen the liver and other parts at breast end of the bird. Place fowl on its back and cut a small opening at the vent. (3) With the hand draw out all the interior of the fowl, taking care not to break the gall bladder, which is attached to the liver. Wipe the inside of the fowl with a damp cloth, and, with a lighted taper, singe off all the hairs. Cut off claws, scald the legs in boiling water, and peel off outside skin. Then place the fowl on its breast, pull the piece of skin closely over the back, and cross the

TO TRUSS POULTRY (*continued*)

ends of the wings over the back of the neck. Take hold of the legs and press the thighs well into the sides of the fowl to give it a nice plump shape; pass a trussing-needle and string through the bottom of one thigh, through the body, and out through the other thigh. (4) Then turn the fowl on its breast, and pass the needle through the middle of the pinion, fastening with it the skin to the back, and bringing the string out through the other pinion; pull ends of the twine tightly

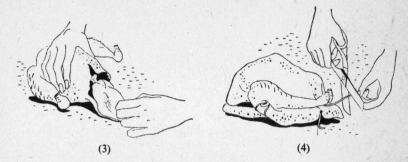

(3)   (4)

and tie firmly together at the side. Turn fowl on its back again, pass the needle and thread through the skin, over the bottom of the breastbone, over one leg, then through back of fowl, and finally tie it firmly over the legs at the other side. It is not usual now to place the liver and gizzard in the wings; this is a pity, because they were considered delicacies. When they are used, wash the liver and cut away the gall bladder without breaking it. Empty gizzard, and simmer in a little stock or water for an hour to make it tender. When stuffing a fowl the vent may be held together with two tooth-picks, and a little strong thread laced across to hold them together.

Trussed for Roasting

Trussed for Boiling

For Boiling. When a fowl is trussed for boiling, proceed according to the fore-going directions, with the exception that the legs are cut off at the knee-joint. In doing this, cut the skin round the leg and pull it off, bringing with it the sinews. Put fingers through the hole made for drawing, and loosen all the outside skin from the thighs, so that the joints of the legs can be pushed right inside. Then commence trussing as for a roast fowl. Pull the skin well over the breastbone and tuck the ends of the leg well in, pass the trussing needle through the skin, and then through underneath at the back, tying the string securely. Choose fowls with black legs for roasting and white for boiling.

TO BONE A FOWL. Pluck and singe, but do not draw. Make a slit in the back of the neck, and, with a sharp knife, cut the neck off close to the body, leaving a piece of skin two inches long to fold over; then with the knife, divide the joints between the pinions and carcass, and remove the merrythought. Having done

TO BONE A FOWL (*continued*)

this, cut off the legs at the knee joint, removing the sinews, then begin carefully to work the flesh off the bones, either with the fingers or with a small sharp knife —turning the bird, in fact, completely inside out. The wings are not boned, but are left on to give the bird a more natural appearance. Care must be taken to remove the flesh cleanly from the bones, the latter being removed entire, and the inside of the bird not being allowed to break through. When the boning is accomplished, the fowl should be replaced in shape, the leg part being left inside. All small birds may be boned in the same manner.

TO LARD. Larding, although very easy, is required to be seen to be properly understood. Very hard bacon is necessary, as soft bacon breaks on being passed through the meat. The bacon should be cut into small blocks, and then again cut into even strips, called lardoons. In larding, strips of bacon are put through the meat, with the ends showing; this should be done in even rows, taking care to keep the larding as neat as possible. Larding improves the flavour of birds and meat which, not having much fat, would have a tendency to get dry when cooked. When time cannot be spared for larding, a piece of sliced bacon is sometimes placed over the meat instead, but the result i; not so satisfactory.

TO CARVE. **See CARVING.**

CHICKEN, BOILED. Take a 5 lb. fowl trussed for boiling. If stuffed, sew up vent; if not, place a bay leaf and a small onion inside the bird. Place the fowl in a deep kettle, cover with boiling water and add onions, 2 cloves, celery, carrots, salt, bay leaf, thyme, parsley, peppercorns. Cover with tight-fitting cover. Add $\frac{1}{2}$ tsp. salt for each 1 lb. chicken *after cooking for $\frac{1}{2}$ hr.* Cover the pan and leave to simmer, but *do not boil*, till tender. Remove chicken and reduce liquid if too thin. Serve with steamed rice or macaroni. For the sauce: To each 1 pt. hot broth add $\frac{1}{2}$ pt. cream or evaporated milk and 2 egg yolks. Stir constantly until the liquid has a thick creamy texture. Season with salt and pepper and add plenty of finely chopped parsley.

CHICKEN, FRIED. Cut a spring chicken into serving portions and steam until tender. Just before frying sift together 4 oz. flour, $\frac{1}{4}$ oz. baking powder and a little pepper and salt. Add 1 egg and 6 oz. milk. Dip each piece of seasoned chicken into the batter and fry in deep fat at 375° F. until golden brown.

CHICKEN, GRILLED. Split the prepared chicken down the back with a sharp knife and remove the entire spinal column and neck; then remove some of the breastbone so that the chicken will lie flat in the pan or on the grill tray. Clean the bird, singe and leave at room temperature for an hour before cooking. Preheat the grill and rub the outside of the chicken well with oil or butter. Sprinkle with salt and pepper and then place the chicken on the broiling rack with the skin side down (this means that the bony side will be about 3″ from the flame), and allow the chicken to cook for 10–20 mins. (according to size) before turning. Turn the skin side up, brush well with melted butter or oil, sprinkle with salt and pepper and a little paprika and cook till done.

Test by cutting into the thigh; if there is still some red juice running, cook a little longer. White meat always cooks quicker than dark meat so always test the dark meat, but do not overcook this. It should have just the slightest pink tinge otherwise the white flesh will be too dry.

CHICKEN, ROAST

Ingredients	*Method*
14 lb. chicken	Take the bird, trussed for roasting, and
Veal forcemeat (see **Force-**	stuff with forcemeat, pull the skin over
meat)	the opening and secure with skewer or
Bacon rashers	stitch with thread. Squeeze a little lemon
Lemon	juice over the bird and rub the breast over
	with the lemon, then place the rashers
	over the breast and cover with grease-
	proof paper. Bake at 325° F. Therm. 3

CHICKEN, ROAST (*continued*)

and allow 25 mins. per lb.—approximately 1¾ hrs. for this weight chicken. Serve garnished with bacon rolls and watercress accompanied by thick gravy and Bread sauce (see **SAUCES**).

CHICKEN, SAUTÉ. Joint the chicken into convenient-sized pieces for serving. Melt some butter or olive oil or bacon fat in the frying-pan and brown the chicken quickly on both sides. Reduce the heat when the chicken is browned, cover the pan, continue cooking. This is to ensure that the chicken becomes tender quickly, taking about 25 to 30 mins. Test with a fork to see that it is done, then add peeled shallots, peeled mushrooms, tomato sauce and a sprinkling of mixed herbs—chervil, chives, tarragon, thyme, parsley.

CHICKEN, SAUTÉ (WITH WINE). Proceed as above and when the chicken is browned, add ¼ pt. dry white wine and continue to cook for about 10 mins. Add 3 chopped shallots, 2 tsp. paprika; cover and continue cooking for 5 mins. When cooked remove from pan and place on hot dish. Add ½ pt. cream or evaporated milk to liquid in pan and blend well; season as desired and pour over chicken. Serve the chicken on a very hot dish with the juice from pan and a little butter. Sprinkle with a little chopped parsley and serve with crisp potatoes (or small new potatoes browned in butter), peas, tiny onions, or halved grilled tomatoes and mushrooms.

Chicken à la King

Ingredients	Method
1 pt. white sauce	Prepare the sauce with ½ pt. milk and ½ pt. chicken stock, add cream and bring to the boil. Peel and sauté the mushrooms and green peppers in butter for about 10 mins., stirring frequently. Add pimiento, chicken, sherry and lemon juice to sauce. Season to taste with pepper and salt then simmer for about 5 mins. Stir in egg yolks and cook for about a minute, stirring constantly. Serve in vol-au-vent cases or on toast, and garnish with chopped almonds.
½ pt. cream	
¼ lb. sliced mushrooms	
1 green pepper minced	
3 oz. butter	
1 pimiento thinly sliced	
1 lb. diced cooked chicken	
1 wineglass sherry	
1 tsp. lemon juice	
Salt and pepper	
2 egg yolks slightly beaten	
Buttered toast	
¼ cupful chopped almonds	

Chicken à l'Italien. Prepare and sauté the jointed chicken. Heat ⅛ pt. olive oil in a large pan and brown the chicken on both sides in the hot oil. Reduce flame and continue to cook for about 10 mins. Add 1 clove garlic finely minced, 3 tbsp. chopped parsley, and ¼ lb. finely shredded ham or bacon. Mix well with the chicken. Add ¼ pt. red wine and cook for 5 mins. Add ½ pt. tomato purée, 1 tsp. dried basil and a few fresh basil leaves. Turn the chicken joints so that they are thoroughly coated with sauce and continue cooking until tender. Remove the chicken to a hot plate and add another ¼ pt. red wine to the sauce. Reheat, but do not boil, and pour over the chicken; garnish with parsley and serve.

Chicken Broth. See SOUPS.

Chicken, Bonnes Bouches of

Ingredients	Method
1 chicken	Bone the chicken and boil until tender. Remove the meat from the skin, chop up fine; next chop the truffles finely and place in a saucepan with white sauce and
4 large truffles	
½ pt. white sauce	
Little chicken glaze	

Chicken, Bonnes Bouches of (*continued*)

6 egg yolks
Cayenne pepper
Salt
Stale bread
Chopped parsley

chicken glaze; bring to the boil, add the egg yolks, season with cayenne and salt, boil again and pour on to a flat dish to set. Rub the stale bread through a sieve. Cut the "bonne bouches" mixture into pieces about ½″ thick, 1″ wide and 1½″ long; roll in breadcrumbs, pat into shape, dip into well-beaten eggs, dip in crumbs again and fry in hot lard until they are a golden colour. Garnish with fried parsley and serve.

Chicken, Creamed. Combine ½ lb. diced cold chicken with ½ pt. Béchamel sauce (see p. 438), and heat through; add seasoning of pepper and salt and serve on toasted bread, a rice ring or rolled in thin pancakes. Garnish with finely chopped parsley.

VARIATIONS

1. Combine equal portions of chicken and mushrooms and flavour with sherry or madeira.
2. Combine equal portions of chicken and ham.
3. Combine oysters and chicken.
4. Combine sliced mushrooms, finely cut green peppers, with diced chicken, flavour with sherry.

Any of the above variations may be garnished with chopped parsley or sprigs of watercress.

Chicken, Curried

Ingredients

4 lb. roasting chicken (or a steamed boiler)
4 oz. flour
1 tsp. salt
½ oz. pepper
¼ oz. butter or margarine
2 tbsp. salad oil
1 medium onion
4 tbsp. chopped celery
½ pt. stock or milk
1 tsp. curry powder
2 tbsp. chutney or plum jam
1 apple peeled and diced
Rice, boiled and strained
24 stuffed olives (if desired)
Few mushrooms

Method

Cut the chicken into joints and dredge with flour seasoned with pepper and salt. Fry brown in butter (this will take about 20 mins.) and place in casserole. While the chicken is frying in another pan heat the oil, sauté the onion, add celery, stock or milk, curry powder, chutney or plum jam, apple and cook together for a few minutes. Then pour over the chicken, cover with lid and cook at 350° F. Therm. 4. Serve with boiled rice. Garnish with olives and sauté mushrooms.

Chicken Fricassée (Brown)

Ingredients

3–4 lb. chicken
12 small carrots
18 small onions
12 small mushrooms
6 tbsp. butter

Method

Disjoint the prepared chicken. Clean and prepare vegetables and mushrooms and brown in 3 tbsp. butter over a low heat. Sift flour on to paper and dredge the chicken pieces in the flour, then season

[150]

Chicken Fricassée (Brown) (*continued*)

½ lb. flour
Salt and pepper
Chicken stock
½ cup chopped parsley
¼ pt. heavy cream
Rice boiled and strained

each piece with salt and pepper. Melt the remaining butter in deep pan and brown the chicken pieces on each side till golden brown. Reduce heat, and add sufficient hot stock to cover the chicken. Cover the pan and simmer about 15 mins. Add vegetables and continue cooking for 35 mins. Add mushrooms and cook for a further 5 mins. Remove chicken pieces to hot casserole. Add the parsley and vegetables, and leave to cook for 3 or 4 mins. Add the cream and blend with sauce. Add more seasoning if necessary and pour sauce over chicken. Serve with boiled rice.

Chicken, Fried (Maryland). Cut a spring chicken into serving portions, then roll in seasoned flour, dip into beaten egg and finally into breadcrumbs. Season with pepper and salt. Melt 3 oz. butter or margarine in a frying-pan, add the chicken and fry till golden brown, but be careful not to burn it. It will take about 10 mins. for a young chicken. When cooked, put on to a platter with cream sauce, and serve garnished with corn fritters and potato croquettes and a few rashers of fried bacon.

Chicken, Grilled Devilled. When the chicken is cooked, roll in well-buttered crisp crumbs pressing these into the flesh. Return to the grill for a few minutes and serve with a hot "devil" sauce.

Chicken Mayonnaise

Ingredients

1 egg yolk
½ pt. olive oil
1 tbsp. wine vinegar
1 tsp. salt
1 tsp. dry mustard
¼ cup chopped parsley
Tarragon
Lettuce leaves or endive
Chicory
Chicken pieces
2 cupfuls diced cold chicken
2 hard-boiled eggs
Pimiento strips
Capers

Method

Make a mayonnaise of the egg yolk and olive oil (beating with a fork), flavour with vinegar, salt and dry mustard. Add chopped parsley and few freshly cut tarragon leaves. Arrange the chicken pieces on the chicory and lettuce leaves together with diced chicken, cover with mayonnaise garnished with sliced hard-boiled egg, capers, pimento and chopped parsley. Sliced cucumber and blanched sliced tomato may also be used if desired. Serves 4 persons.

Chicken Provençale

Ingredients

1–2 lb. chicken, jointed
⅛ pt. olive oil
¼ pt. dry white wine
1 clove garlic
3 tomatoes blanched and seeded

Method

Heat the oil and sauté the chicken, brown well; reduce heat and add half the white wine; continue cooking. After about 10 mins. add 1 clove garlic finely chopped and cook again for about 5 mins., then add the peeled sliced mushrooms and the

[151]

Chicken Provençale (*continued*)

8 mushrooms
Salt and pepper
1 tbsp. chopped parsley

tomatoes diced. Turn the chicken and mix with mushrooms and tomatoes. Continue cooking until the chicken is tender, then remove to a hot plate; add remaining wine and blend well with sauce. Taste and season if necessary. Add 1 tbsp. chopped parsley and then pour the sauce over the chicken and serve. Sufficient for 4 persons.

Chicken Pudding. See **Beef Steak Pudding** (p. 59).
Chicken Salad. See SALADS.

CHICK PEAS. These small leguminous vegetables do not become soft and pulpy in consistency when boiled; therefore they are frequently sprinkled singly or used as a garnish only for certain viands, and they are sometimes made into soup.

CHICORY. The roots are used blanched for salads and sometimes sold under the name of Witloof. Also, roasted and ground, they are added to coffee to give a bitter taste. Chicory is also used medicinally. The leaves may be used raw in salads or braised as celery.

Chicory as Salad. Quarter or halve the heads or cut into $\frac{1}{2}''$ slices; cover with French dressing or mayonnaise. Add if desired to any other salad vegetables.

Chicory and Cheese Pie. Parboil the chicory and place in well-greased casserole. Cover with cheese sauce, sprinkle on breadcrumbs and dot with butter. Bake at 350° F. Therm. 4 for 25–35 mins.

CHIFFONADE SALAD. See SALADS.

CHILLI. See CAPSICUM.

Chilli Con Carne. (A Mexican Stew)

Ingredients	*Method*
2 lb. steak	Cut the meat into small cubes and add the suet and salt. Cook the onion in the oil and when brown add meat, stirring occasionally till the meat browns. Add the boiling water, chilli powder and garlic. Cover and simmer for $2\frac{1}{2}$ hrs. Serve with kidney beans.
2 oz. chopped suet	
2 tsp. salt	
2 chopped onions	
2 tbsp. olive oil	
$\frac{3}{4}$ pt. boiling water	
2 tbsp. chilli powder	
1 clove garlic chopped finely	
Kidney beans	

Chilli Sauce. See CAPSICUM.

CHINE. This is to sever the ribs from the backbone (Fr. *échine*) in a joint of meat such as loin or neck of lamb, mutton, veal or pork. The ribs are sawn through close to the backbone and it is then easier to carve the meat into chops or cutlets.

CHINESE ARTICHOKE. See ARTICHOKE.

CHINOIS. The name of a small fruit rather like a tangerine orange usually sold crystallised. In French, the term means a pointed strainer with fine holes used for straining soups and gravies.

CHIPOLATA. A small, Italian, highly seasoned game sausage which is used for dressing other dishes of game, or served on sticks with cocktails. Some cooks have introduced chestnuts into chipolata stuffing for turkey and caused some confusion in the significance of the term.

CHITTERLINGS. Correctly speaking these are the small intestines of any animal, and the small tripe. Those of the pig are chiefly used as skins for small sausages. The name is also applied to sausages.

CHIVE. A small green perennial onion. The leaves are used finely chopped in omelets, soups, salads, canapés and vegetables, including mashed potatoes.
Chives Butter. See BUTTERS.

CHOCOLATE (Fr. *chocolat*). The beans of the *Theobroma Cacao* tree, which are universally made into cake form, paste and powder. This tree is a native of the West Indies and South America. Chocolate has been known as a favourite beverage for more than 400 years and was introduced into England in 1520 from Mexico; it was first sold in the London coffee-houses in 1650. Sometimes vanilla, cinnamon, cloves and anise are added to enhance the flavour.
Chocolate Cake. See CAKES.
Chocolate, Drinking. Boil 1 qt. equal quantities of milk and water in a small saucepan, then scrape down 1 oz. chocolate and throw into the boiling liquid; beat with a wire egg-whisk for about a minute or until all the chocolate is dissolved. Serve in cups and sweeten if desired. To keep hot, set it where it will not reboil. A little rum may be added if desired.
Chocolate Ice. See ICE CREAM.
Chocolate Mousse. A very good chocolate mousse can easily be made without using any cream at all. Whip white of egg to a stiff froth, fold in gradually a little caster sugar, mixing with a metal spoon, and add to taste a little melted chocolate. (This mousse can be made with other flavourings such as lemon or coffee.)
Chocolate Pudding

Ingredients
4 oz. butter
1 gill milk
4 oz. grated chocolate
4 oz. cake crumbs
3 oz. sugar
1 tsp. vanilla essence
3 eggs

Method
Bring the butter to the boil in the milk, and add chocolate and cake crumbs. Stir until the mixture thickens and leaves the sides of the pan. Allow to cool, then stir in the sugar, vanilla essence and the well-beaten yolks of eggs, one at a time. Whisk the whites of egg till stiff then fold lightly into the mixture. Turn into a buttered mould and steam for 2 hrs. or bake at 375° F. Therm. 5 for 1 hr. Serve with this sauce: $\frac{1}{2}$ gill liqueur syrup, 2 oz. lump sugar, lemon rind. Put the syrup into a pan with the lump sugar, rubbed on the lemon rind. Then stand this in another pan three parts full of boiling water and whip the mixture over a low heat until it becomes a light and frothy mass. Do not overheat or it will curdle.

Chocolate Sauce. See SAUCES.
Chocolate Soufflé

Ingredients
2 tbsp. butter
2 tbsp. flour
Pinch of salt
$\frac{3}{4}$ cup milk
2 squares bitter chocolate
6 tbsp. sugar
$\frac{1}{2}$ tsp. vanilla extract
2 or 3 drops coffee essence

Method
Melt butter, add flour and salt, stir well, add warmed milk and stir well till thoroughly blended. Melt chocolate in a double saucepan, add sugar, vanilla and coffee essence in water, mix well and combine the two mixtures. Separate the yolks from white of eggs, add yolks beating in stiffly, whisk whites of eggs,

C.C.D.—6

Chocolate Soufflé (*continued*)

2 tbsp. water
3 eggs

and fold into the mixture with a metal spoon; turn into a buttered mould and bake in moderately hot oven at 350° F. Therm. 4 for about 20 mins., the mould standing in a pan of hot water. Garnish the top with powdered sugar, and serve with whipped cream, or ice cream.

Chocolate Soufflé (Cold)

Ingredients

2 oz. chocolate
¼ oz. gelatine
3 tbsp. water
3 eggs
2 oz. sugar
Few drops vanilla essence
1 tbsp. brandy (if desired)
1½ gills cream or evaporated milk

FOR DECORATION:

½ gill cream or evaporated milk
½ oz. each grated chocolate and chopped nuts

Method

Prepare the soufflé case. Melt the chocolate and gelatine in water very gently. Whisk the yolks of eggs and sugar until thick and creamy; add vanilla, and brandy if desired, then stir in the dissolved chocolate and gelatine. Half-whip cream and fold in, then fold in stiffly whisked whites of eggs. Pour into a soufflé case and leave to set. Remove band of paper with a knife dipped in hot water. Decorate with whipped cream, chocolate and nuts.

Chocolate Sponge. See CAKES.

CHOPS. There is no other word in any other language that can be called the direct representative of "chop". It means just what it says, a piece chopped off; the orthodox chops are of lamb, mutton or pork, being cut to include a rib or from the chump or tail end of the loin. Broiling or grilling are the correct ways of cooking chops.

CHOW CHOW. A kind of pickle, consisting of mixed vegetables in a mustard sauce which is seasoned with strongly flavoured aromatic spices.

CHOWDER (Fr. *chaudière*). A dish of American origin of fish or meat, sliced with fried onions and mashed potatoes, placed in a stewpan in alternate layers and seasoned with spices, herbs, claret and ketchup. Often made with clams (see CLAM), and shrimps.

CHRISTMAS PUDDING, see **PLUM PUDDING**

CHUB. A freshwater fish, handsome in appearance but tasteless in flavour. The flesh resembles that of the carp and is therefore cooked in much the same way; it is best stuffed and roasted, baked or broiled. The flesh when cooked is apt to turn yellow even when lemon juice has been used or other precautions taken.

CHUTNEY. A condiment of Indian origin made of a variety of fruits, sugar, spices and vinegar. The fruit mostly found in chutney is apple, but there are other delicious varieties to be found under **ELDERBERRY, GOOSEBERRY, TOMATO,** etc.

Chutney, Apple—I

Ingredients

2 lb. green apples
1½ pt. vinegar
1 oz. each chillies and garlics
2 oz. shallots

Method

Peel, core and chop the apples. Place in a saucepan with vinegar and boil to a pulp. Turn into a basin when cold and add the other ingredients. Stir well. Put into

[154]

Chutney, Apple—I (*continued*)

1 oz. ground ginger

2 oz. salt

4 oz. each mustard seed and
tamarinds

12 oz. stoned chopped raisins

1 lb. moist sugar

bottles and cork up. Keep in a cool place
until required for use.

Chutney, Apple—II. Core, peel and quarter 2 lb. apples, place them in a saucepan
with 2 cups vinegar and boil to pulp, then remove the saucepan from the fire and
let the pulp cool. Stone ¼ lb. raisins, pound them in a mortar and mix with ½ lb.
moist sugar and 2 oz. each garlic, ginger, and mustard seed also pounded. Add 1
oz. cayenne pepper, and mix well together. Then put the mixture into an earthenware jar and keep in the warmth till next day, when it may be put into small pots
and tied down ready for use.

CICELY (SWEET). Sweet Chervil. For culinary purposes the root is boiled and
eaten with an oil and vinegar dressing in salads; industrially, the oil is used in
Chartreuse.

CIDER. The juice of the apple, fermented, and containing between 3 and 8 per cent.
alcohol.

Cider, Home-made. Select ½ lb. tart apples, grate them and put equal portions
into 2 qt. champagne bottles. Add 1 tsp. sugar to each bottle and spring water
until the bottles are full; cork and tie down, then set in a warm place and the cider
wine will be ready for use in about 3 days' time. A slice of quince in each bottle is a
great improvement.

Cider Jelly. Soak 2 oz. gelatine in cold water, then put 2½ pt. cider into a pan and
when it boils, pour it on to the gelatine. Stir in two cups caster sugar, and mix well.
Strain through a tammy into moistened mould and leave to set. Turn out and
serve garnished with whipped cream, or, if preferred, set in individual glasses and
top off with cream.

Cider, Mulled. Take 3 eggs and whisk them well. Add sufficient sugar to 1 qt. cider
to tone down the acidity, then boil and pour over the lightly beaten eggs. Stir
briskly, return to the pan and stir until the mixture boils again. Serve hot in glasses.

CINNAMON. The inner bark of a tropical tree imported from Ceylon. It is
golden yellow in colour with a hot aromatic flavour. Cinnamon, being a costly
spice, often has the harsher-flavoured cassia substituted for it.

Cinnamon Toast. Take a slice of buttered hot toast and sprinkle with cinnamon
and sugar.

CISCO. The lake herring, a white fish found in the Great Lakes of Canada and the
United States.

CITRIC ACID. Commonly known as "acid of lemons" it derives its name from the
citron tribe to which the lemon belongs. Although first obtained from the juice of
lemons it is also found in and frequently obtained from acid fruits generally, such
as citrons, lemons, oranges, quinces, gooseberries, currants, etc. Citric acid is
chiefly used in confectionery, aerated water and liqueurs. It is also used in jam-
making, allowing 1 level tsp. dissolved in a little water to each 4 lb. fruit. Imita-
tions of lemon and lime juices are made by dissolving citric acid in water and
flavouring with soluble essences of lemon or lime.

CITRON. The fruit of the citron tree is well known in medicine, possessing antiscorbutic properties as also do other fruits of the citrus tribe, such as lemons,
limes and oranges. The peel is candied for use in cookery. It is sometimes known
as Cedrat.

CLAM (Fr. *lucerne*). A large, bivalvular shellfish much prized in the United States.
Technically this familiar name applies to a very large assortment of bivalves,
varying in size, shape and colour. The clam graciously submits to every form of
cooking that can be devised for shellfish; the young specimens called Little Necks
are usually eaten raw like oysters.

Clam Chowder

Ingredients	Method
2 oz. butter	Fry the bacon in butter; add leeks, onions,
4 oz. streaky bacon diced	celery, potatoes, pepper and tomatoes.
2 leeks	Fry together for a few minutes, add thyme.
4 oz. each onions, celery and potatoes diced	Poach the clams in another saucepan, strain the liquor and keep back "nuts";
1 sweet pepper chopped	moisten the vegetables with this liquor
2 tomatoes skinned and sliced	and simmer gently for 1 hr. Just before serving add the bearded clams and a few
Pinch of thyme	broken-up water biscuits. Season and
3 doz. clams and their liquor	serve.

CLARET (Fr. *clairet*). The English name for red Bordeaux wines.

Claret Cup. Pour into a jug ½ pt. claret and ¼ pt. filtered water; add 1 tsp. caster sugar, 2 tsp. brandy and 2 or 3 slices of orange; mix thoroughly. Stand the jug on ice for ½ hr., strain and decant.

CLARY. A pot-herb of the sage family not much used.

CLEAR SOUP (Fr. *consommé*). Clarified stock, being a strong broth which is obtained by boiling meat bones and vegetables. For recipes, see SOUPS.

CLOD. The upper part of a bullock's shoulder.

CLOUDBERRY. A raspberry of the north temperate regions bearing large white flowers and edible amber-coloured fruit.

CLOVE. An aromatic spice, the dried, unexpanded flower-bud of an evergreen shrub or small tree of the myrtle family and a native of the Molucca or Spice Islands. Cloves are used in culinary preparations, in confectionery and in the making of liqueurs.

CLOVER, RED. These honey-flavoured flowers can be used to garnish or as flavouring.

COALFISH. This fish of the cod family has a black back from which it derives its name, and ranges from the Arctic Regions to the Mediterranean. In the Orkneys, the year-old fish caught with rod and line is called a Sillock; at two years it is fished for from boats and called Cooth; as it gets old it is known as Sethe. In Edinburgh the young fish are called Pooleys. The coalfish is cooked as cod.

COBBLER. A fruit pie of a deep layer of fruit covered with pastry or scone dough. Also a cooling drink of fruit and wine.

COBNUTS. Hazelnuts or filberts.

COCHINEAL. Colouring matter obtained from the dried bodies of the females of an insect which infests the cacti of Mexico, Brazil and Guatemala. The insects are brushed from the plants into bags and then dried under heat. There are two kinds of cochineal: silver which shows a purplish-grey and black which gives a red or purple-black colour.

COCK-A-LEEKIE. A soup made of leeks and fowls; a favourite dish in Scotland.

COCKLE (Fr. *coque* or *palourde*). The name for this very delicious little bivalve shellfish is undoubtedly derived from the French *coquilles*, shells. Cockles may be classed among the scallops. When cooked and removed from their shells they are prettily diversified in colour, yellow and red predominating. As their usual habitat is the sand of the sea-shore they are gritty even after cooking unless extraordinary precautions are taken for cleaning by soaking them in numerous renewals of cold salted water before putting them in the pot to boil. The largest cockles come from the North Devonshire Coast, Scilly Isles and the Hebrides.

COCKLE (*continued*)

TO PREPARE. After washing in several waters as many cockles as may be required (leave them to soak at least 1 hr. in each water), put them into a final bath with a piece of salt in, cover the bowl with a cloth and leave overnight; by morning they will probably have discharged all the sand and be ready for cooking.

TO COOK. Put the cockles into a large saucepan with very little water at the bottom, then set over a low heat and shake up now and again as the cockles warm up. When the shells open they are done; do not cook them any longer or they will be hard and unpalatable. The liquor at the bottom of the saucepan may be strained through a cloth and used for sauce. Pick the cockles out of the shells with a fork.

Cockle Ketchup. Pound two cups boiled cockles to a pulp and put into a lined saucepan with 1 pt. very strong ale or sherry. Season with 1 oz. salt, ¼ oz. mace, 1 dr. pepper, put the saucepan on a low heat and simmer gently for 10 mins. Pass the ketchup through a strainer or cloth. Bottle when cool and add a little brandy to each bottle. Cork up securely and store in a cool place till required.

Cockle Soup

Ingredients	*Method*
To each pint of cockles allow:	Boil and trim as many cockles as you require, keep the liquor, and place them in a soup tureen. Melt the butter, add flour, stir till blended and leave to cool. Add white stock, milk and the strained cockle liquor and trimmings. Stir over a low heat until the liquid boils. Add anchovy essence, mace and seasonings and boil a further 10 mins. Add the cream and then strain over the cockles in tureen. Serve hot.
¼ lb. butter	
¼ lb. flour	
2 qt. white stock	
1 qt. milk	
1 dsp. anchovy essence	
2 saltspoons salt	
6 peppercorns	
1 blade mace	
¼ pt. cream	

COCK'S COMBS (Fr. *crêtes de coq*). Used for garnishing rich ragoûts.

COCK'S KERNELS. The hard secretions found in the flesh of the cock; esteemed a great delicacy.

COCKTAIL. An alcoholic beverage or non-alcoholic drink, prepared with ice, sweetening and flavouring in various ways. Mixtures of spirits and liqueurs or wines with water.

When making cocktails, use a shaker or mixing glass slightly larger than is actually required. Put the ice cubes in the shaker. Add ingredients. Shake well. Be sure that the drink is served as soon as it is mixed, and a cocktail without ice is no cocktail but a mere mixed drink. See that it is as cold as possible. Be sure that you shake till a frost has been formed on the outside of the shaker.

COCKTAIL	INGREDIENTS
Absinthe	½ absinthe, ½ water, 1 dash syrup, 1 dash angostura bitters
Appetiser	½ gin, ½ Dubonnet, juice of half an orange
Apricot	¼ lemon juice, ¼ orange juice, ½ apricot brandy, 1 dash gin
Bacardi	¼ lemon or lime juice, ¼ grenadine, ½ Bacardi rum

COCKTAIL (*continued*)

COCKTAIL	INGREDIENTS
Bacardi Rum Sweet	1 tsp. sugar, ½ Bacardi rum, ¼ orange juice, ¼ lemon juice
Bacardi Sidecar	One third each lemon juice, Bacardi rum and cointreau
Brandy	⅛ curaçao, ⅞ brandy
Bronx	¼ orange juice, ¼ French vermouth, ¼ Martini, ¼ gin. *Stir well*
Brut	3 dashes orange bitters, 3 dashes acid phosphate, 1 glass Martini vermouth. *Stir well*
Cinzano	2 dashes angostura bitters, 2 dashes orange bitters, 1 glass vermouth. Serve with a piece of orange peel
Clover	3 dashes grenadine, ½ gin, ¼ French vermouth, ¼ Dubonnet. Serve with a cherry
Clover Club	Juice of a lime, ⅓ grenadine, ⅔ gin, white of an egg
Clover Leaf	Same as Clover Club, but a sprig of mint is added to the top before serving
Dubonnet	½ Dubonnet, ½ gin
Grapefruit Blossom	⅔ Bacardi rum, ⅓ grapefruit juice, 1 dash grenadine
Grenadine	⅔ Bacardi rum, ⅓ lime juice, ½ tsp. grenadine
Jockey Club	½ rye whiskey, ½ Martini vermouth, 3 dashes maraschino
Manhattan	2 dashes maraschino, ½ rye whiskey, ½ mixed vermouth, 1 dash absinthe. Stir well and serve with quarter slice lemon
Martini	3 dashes orange bitters, ⅔ gin, ⅓ Martini vermouth. Stir well and serve with a piece of lemon peel
Passion	½ passion fruit juice, ½ gin, 1 dash absinthe
Pink Lady	White of an egg, 1 tbsp. grenadine, 1 glass gin. Serve in medium-sized glass
Planters	1 dash lemon juice, ½ orange juice, ½ rum
Rum	½ rum, ¼ cointreau, ¼ fresh lime juice, pinch aromatic pepper

COCKTAIL (*continued*)

Cocktail	Ingredients
Rye Sour	$\frac{3}{5}$ rye whiskey, $\frac{1}{5}$ lemon juice, $\frac{1}{5}$ cream, 1 dash syrup. Serve with a cherry
Sidecar	$\frac{1}{4}$ lime juice, $\frac{1}{4}$ cointreau, $\frac{1}{2}$ brandy
Vermouth	1 glass Martini vermouth, 4 dashes orange bitters. Stir well
Whiskey Old-fashioned	Put a lump of sugar in a glass and just enough hot water to cover it. Crush and add some ice, 2 dashes bitters, 1 glass rye whiskey and 1 piece lemon peel. Serve with a small spoon
White Lady	$\frac{1}{4}$ lemon juice, $\frac{1}{4}$ cointreau, $\frac{1}{2}$ gin

COCKTAILS, FRUIT. See **FRUIT.**

COCKTAILS, SAVOURY. These are generally made of shellfish or cold flaked fish and should properly be served in cocktail glasses which in their turn are embedded in cracked ice. Soup plates or glass plates can be used for this. Garnish with a little parsley. A green hollowed-out tomato or green pepper may be used instead of the glass. A good cocktail sauce to serve with the fish can be made as follows:

Ingredients
½ pt. tomato catsup
6 tbsp. lemon juice
⅛ tsp. salt
½ tsp. celery salt
3 drops Tabasco sauce or ½ tsp. Worcester sauce
1 tbsp. finely grated horse-radish or ½ tbsp. finely minced onion
1 tbsp. finely chopped celery (if desired)
(Chopped green pepper or chopped stuffed olives may be substituted for the horse-radish if preferred)

Method
Blend all the ingredients together in a small bowl. Chill for at least 30 mins. Use with any shellfish or cold, flaked fish. Sufficient for 4 fish cocktails.

Cocktail	Ingredients
Clam	Allow 6 Little Neck clams per head; combine with cocktail sauce
Crabmeat, Lobster, Shrimp	Allow ⅓ cup diced crab, lobster meat or shrimps; combine with cocktail sauce
Oyster	Allow 6 raw oysters per head; combine with cocktail sauce
Sea Food	2 scallops, 2 oysters or clams per person; combine with cocktail sauce

COCOA. A beverage which is prepared from the seeds of the *Theobroma Cacao* tree (see **CHOCOLATE**). Cocoa is a peculiar English corruption of "cacao".

METHOD I. Mix 3 tbsp. cocoa powder with 1 pt. water, and 1 pt. milk, and boil for 20 mins., whipping the whole time with an egg whisk. Sweeten when served.

METHOD II. Put 1½ tsp. cocoa into a cup. Pour in a little milk, and stir to a paste, then fill up the cup with more boiling milk. Sweeten to taste and serve. If preferred, the cup may be filled ¾ full of water and then filled up with milk.

COCONUT. The fruit of the tall, straight coconut palm which flourishes in Eastern Asia, and the Islands of the Indian Seas whence its products are imported into all parts of Europe. The nuts are found clustering under the plume of leaves and frequently number as many as a hundred on one palm. Many commercial products come from the coconut palm. For culinary purposes the nut is the most valuable. The pulp can be blended with a little lime juice and madeira for use in confectionery, or it can be rasped and dried or desiccated for flavouring and decorating cakes and puddings: in this state it will keep for several years. The coconut "milk" can be used in coffee or for flavouring certain dishes. A little vanilla flavouring is an improvement to the milk as a beverage.

Coconut Biscuits

Ingredients

2 whites of eggs
4 oz. caster sugar
2 oz. desiccated coconut

Method

Beat the whites of eggs to a stiff froth, add slowly the sugar and coconut. With teaspoon put the mixture on sheets of white paper spread on a baking-sheet and bake at 250° F. Therm. ½ for about ½ hr. Take them out, remove the paper by damping and use the biscuits when cold.

Coconut Buns. See CAKES (p. 107).

Coconut Candy

Ingredients

1 lb. sugar
Water
½ lb. grated coconut

Method

Put the sugar and a little water into a saucepan over a low heat; bring to the boil and stir for 5 mins. or until the syrup hangs in threads from the spoon. Then add ½ lb. grated coconut. Drop the candy in tablespoonfuls on to a buttered baking-sheet. When cold, take them off the tin by slipping a knife underneath.

Coconut Ice

Ingredients

½ lb. granulated sugar
¼ pt. milk
Pinch of cream of tartar
3 tbsp. desiccated or freshly grated coconut
Few drops cochineal

Method

Place the sugar, milk and cream of tartar in a saucepan, stirring frequently to prevent it sticking to the pan. Boil to 240° F. or until it forms a soft ball when tested by dropping a little of the mixture from a spoon into cold water. Remove the pan from heat and place it in a bowl of cold water to cool for a minute or two. Add the coconut, stirring briskly, and beat until the mixture is white and thick.

[160]

Coconut Ice (*continued*)

Turn half into a small well-lined (with waxed paper) tin, add a few drops of pink colour to remainder, spread on top of white. When cold, cut and store in a tin (if it isn't eaten as soon as it is made!).

Coconut Pudding

Ingredients

6 glacé cherries
4 oz. grated coconut
¾ pt. milk
2 oz. butter
2 oz. sugar
2 oz. breadcrumbs
2 oz. stale sponge cake
    crumbs
3 egg yolks
2 egg whites
1 tsp. vanilla essence

Method

Butter a mould, sprinkle with sugar and decorate the bottom and sides with halved glacé cherries. Put the coconut and milk into a saucepan, bring gradually to the boil and allow to boil for 5 mins. Beat the butter and sugar together, add the breadcrumbs and cake crumbs. Pour over the boiling milk, stirring well, then add the beaten egg yolks, stir well. Fold in the stiffly beaten whites of egg and vanilla essence. Turn into the mould, cover and steam 1½ hr., then turn out and serve with a wine sauce.

Coconut Shortbread. See CAKES.

COD (Fr. *cabillaud*). This fish is soft-finned. It inhabits Northern latitudes and is caught in large quantities along the coast of Newfoundland.

TO CHOOSE. When the fish is fresh, the eye will be found rising from the head and surrounded by a transparent and red substance. The gills should also be bright red, not brown nor turning so, and the flesh should be firm and transparently white. A thick neck and well-marked yellow spots indicate good quality. Imported cod is already beheaded, split open, gutted and salted.

TO CLEAN. Remove the gills by cutting through their connection with the rest of the head and shoulders, and pulling them out. Then lay the fish on its back, open the belly by a straight cut down the centre, and remove the inside carefully, preserving the liver and roe and leaving the sounds uninjured. If the fish is to be cooked whole it should be "scored" to the bone transversely at intervals of 2″, but if it is to be cooked in pieces, cut it into slices 3″ thick and soak the fish in water for 15 mins.

Cod, Crimped. Cut a crimped cod, which should be quite fresh, into rather thick slices and lay these for about 3 hrs. in salted water with a little vinegar. Three parts fill a fish kettle, put in a large handful of salt, and let it boil quickly; then put in the cod and keep it boiling for 10 mins. Remove slices of fish with care, lay on a dish and garnish with sprigs of parsley and sliced lemon. Serve with Shrimp or Oyster sauce (see SAUCES).

Cod Fish Cakes

Ingredients

1 lb. cod
1 lb. peeled potatoes
1 egg
1 oz. butter or margarine
1 tsp. each grated parsley
    and grated onion
Pepper and salt

Method

Boil the potatoes and cod together with very little water. When cooked, mix well together, add egg, butter, parsley, onion and seasoning; beat till light, then drop by spoonfuls into deep fat, brown and place on paper to drain. Serve garnished with sliced lemon and watercress.

Cod (Salt) Salad. Soak some small square pieces of salted cod in cold water, changing the water occasionally. After soaking for 10–12 hrs., drain and dry the pieces of fish on a cloth; brush them over with warmed butter and broil over a clear fire. Peel and boil 5 potatoes; when cooked, drain and slice while hot. Place in a salad bowl, put in the pieces of fish and pour in 1 wineglass Rhine wine. Place a plate over the bowl and leave the salad till cold. Pick and wash a quantity of endive, add to the salad bowl and add 2 or 3 skinned and filleted anchovies and 2 tbsp. finely chopped parsley. Mix together in equal quantities vinegar and oil, season with pepper, salt and sugar, and pour over the salad. Stir lightly with fork and serve.

Cod Stewed with Milk

Ingredients	*Method*
1 lb. cod fillets	Wipe fillets over with damp cloth, sprinkle
1 qt. milk	each side lightly with salt; place in well-
1 bay leaf	greased top half of double saucepan and
1 onion sliced	steam over boiling water for 10 mins.
$\frac{1}{8}$ tsp. pepper	Remove fish, using a fork, and flake well.
$\frac{1}{2}$ tsp. salt	Put the milk into a deep saucepan, add
$\frac{1}{4}$ tsp. paprika	bay leaf, onion, pepper, salt, paprika and
1 pt. oysters	heat well, but do not boil. Add both cod
Chopped parsley or chives	and oysters, and when the edges of the
	oysters begin to curl (this will take about
	3 mins.), serve piping hot in soup bowls.
	Garnish with chives or parsley.

Vol-au-Vent of Cod (with Cream Sauce). Remove the skin and bones of some cold cooked cod (use any remains up), and divide the flesh into flakes with a fork. Put 1 teacupful Béchamel sauce in a stewpan with 2 oz. butter and work it over the fire until the butter has dissolved, then put in the fish, season to taste with salt and pepper and warm up again. Make vol-au-vent (see p. 374). When baked, stand on a folded napkin or ornamental dish paper. Turn fish into it. Serve quickly.

CODLING. A small codfish.

COD'S LIVER. This is very delicious when used in a forcemeat, combined with breadcrumbs, egg yolk, salt, pepper and finely chopped parsley.

COD'S ROES. Dried and smoked, they can be preserved for a length of time. When fresh, they can be boiled in water with a little vinegar added for 15 mins., then drained and served with Hollandaise sauce.

COD'S SOUNDS. These are the gelatinous fringes that run along each side of the backbone on the inside of the belly. Soak them in water before cooking in milk and water until tender, then remove, drain and place them on a folded napkin or dish-paper spread, and serve with Egg sauce.

COD'S TONGUES. Although these tiny organs are not often noticed in the mouth of the fish they can be brought to the boil in water, flavoured with cloves, pepper-corns, onion, bouquet garni, sliced lemon and they are then ready for use.

COFFEE (Fr. *café*). The coffee-plant is a native of Arabia, and the better kinds are generally known as "Mocha", now cultivated in all tropical countries. Fine varieties come from Brazil, Jamaica, Java and Mysore. The stone of the fruit consists of two half beans encased in a husk which is dried; the husk is then removed and the beans roasted.
TO ROAST. Coffee can be roasted at home by placing the beans in an oven tin and baking them at 400° F. Therm. 6 until they look well roasted. When cool, grind and store in jar or tin with tightly fitting lid.

TO MAKE. Heat the coffee-pot with boiling water, then when thoroughly hot, empty out the water and put into the pot 1 tbsp. coffee. Stand the pot in a warm place and add ½ pt. freshly boiled water. Leave to infuse for about 10 mins., strain, and serve hot. Serve with hot milk (in a separate jug). Sometimes a pinch of salt or a sprinkle of mustard is added to inspire the flavour.

To ensure good coffee:

1. Always use coffee as fresh as possible.

2. Keep the roasted and ground coffee airtight in a screwtop jar so that the very volatile oil of the coffee will not deteriorate.

3. Scour the coffee boiler daily.

4. Measure coffee carefully.

5. Be sure the water boils before adding to coffee.

6. Do not let coffee boil, except to make very black.

7. Remove grounds from coffee as soon as made.

8. Serve as soon as possible after making.

9. Serve piping hot.

10. Use grounds only once.

COFFEE, BLACK (Fr. *café noir*). Pour 1 qt. boiling water on a breakfastcup of coffee. Stir well and let it stand in a warm place for about 15 mins. For very black coffee boil for 5 mins. To make black coffee clearer, add a tablespoonful of cold water.

COFFEE SUBSTITUTE. See **ACORN COFFEE.**

Coffee Cake. See **CAKES.**

Coffee Cream

Ingredients	*Method*
1½ pt. milk 1 pt. very strong coffee 4 oz. sugar 8 egg yolks 2 drops vanilla essence	Boil milk, add coffee and sugar; add this gradually to the beaten yolks of eggs, stirring the whole time. Add vanilla essence. Pour through a sieve into saucepan and place over a low heat, stirring the whole time, watching carefully, especially when the mixture begins to thicken. *Do not allow to boil* or reach curdling point. When about the consistency of cream remove from heat, pour into serving dish and stir occasionally till cool. Serve with macaroons.

COGNAC. The name is usually applied in France to brandy of various qualities. The term originated from a locality famous for its brandy.

COLBERT SAUCE. See SAUCES.

COLCANNON. This is sometimes spelt Kolcannon. Boil separately some cabbages and potatoes in equal quantities: when cooked, drain, mix them together in a saucepan and put in a lump of dripping; season with pepper and salt and mash them over the fire. Turn the mixture out on to a hot dish and serve. If desired, boiled onions can be mixed in too.

COLD WATER CRUST. See PASTE AND PASTRY.

COLE. An undeveloped cabbage. See **KALE.**

Cole Slaw

Ingredients	*Method*
½ head finely shredded cabbage ½ grated carrot	Toss the vegetables together, add seasoning, sour cream and mayonnaise and garnish with chopped parsley.

[163]

Cole Slaw (*continued*)
½ sliced apple
½ tsp. each salt and pepper
¼ pt. each sour cream or milk
  and mayonnaise mixed
  together
1 tbsp. chopped parsley

COLEWORT COLLARD. This is a species of cabbage which does not produce a firm head. In cooking these names are used to describe young cabbages which have not yet developed a head.

COLLARED MEAT. The strict meaning of collaring as applied to meat, is to roll up tightly and bind with string. It may be pickled, rolled, boiled and served cold.

COLLATION. Cold collation signifies a collection of cold food.

COLLOP. The origin of this word is doubtful but it is probably from the French *escalope*. The meaning of it in kitchen parlance is understood to be a small slice of meat. Rub the bottom of a saucepan with butter or margarine, then lay in some thin slices of meat, season with pepper and salt and add an onion and an apple, both finely chopped. Cover securely and cook over a low heat until tender. Serve very hot.

COLOURING. In some confectionery and cooking the success of the dish is dependent in a great measure upon the free use of bright colours and their artistic blending. Colouring can be vegetable or artificial. See GARNISHES.

COLTSFOOT. Sometimes called Son-before-Father. Used for wines and medicinally.
Coltsfoot Wine. Take 2 qt. freshly picked and dried coltsfoot (spreading it on trays to dry). When quite dry put into a pan and pour over 1 gall. boiling water. Leave for 3 days, stirring 3 times daily, then strain off liquor and add 3 lb. sugar and boil well for ½ hr. When cool, add to the liquid a little piece of yeast on some toast, and allow to ferment. Next day remove toast, pour liquor into a cask. Add 1 teacup raisins, 3 sliced Seville oranges and 2 lemons to each 4 gall. liquid. Leave for 3 mths. and then bottle.

COMFITS. This word, formerly spelt Confit or Confite, is derived from the old French *confit* (meaning confected or prepared). Comfits are small sweetmeats, but the word is sometimes applied to preserves.

COMFREY. A pot herb which is used in both soups and stews, and sometimes made into wine.

COMPOTE. Fruit stewed with sugar; also a stew of small birds.

CONDIMENTS. Commonly known as "seasoning", the term embracing all those materials that are added to foods to give flavour or improve their digestive qualities. Some are served at the table but most are incorporated and mixed in the cooking. Those most familiar to us are: salt, peppers, mustard, vinegar, spices, aromatic herbs and preparations of them in sauces and pickles. Lemon juice is often used as a condiment in place of vinegar. See also individual entries.

CONFITS. See COMFITS.

CONGER EEL or SEA-EEL (Fr. *congre*). The conger lives in the seas, and does not enter the freshwater streams like some other eels. It often grows to a length of about eight feet and its flesh is less oily than that of the smaller eels.

CONSISTENCY. See COOKING TERMS.

CONSOMMÉ (Fr.). Clear Soup. This is a clarified liquor in which meat or poultry has been boiled or the liquor from the stock pot clarified with, or without, meat and soup vegetables. See SOUPS.

COOKING. The chief reasons for cooking food are:

1. To render it more digestible, e.g. by cooking, starchy foods and those containing cellulose are made easier to masticate. Foods containing much protein and albumen are the chief exceptions, because these substances harden at a high temperature, e.g. white of egg, meat. Also, fatty foods, butter, cream, dripping, etc., develop irritating fatty acids at a high temperature.

2. To render it more palatable. Frequently the cooked food is more palatable than the raw food, e.g. meats, because they develop both flavour and odours while cooking. Exceptions to this are butter, cream, citrus fruits and salads.

3. Food may be rendered more wholesome by cooking for a few minutes at 212° F., or at 160–180° F. for a longer time. This last temperature is high enough to destroy many germs and parasites which may be in the food. This is especially important in the hot weather when rapid changes can be brought about in food by those germs of putrefaction. Among the foods which deteriorate rapidly in hot weather are fish, meat and milk. They should be kept very cool or used as soon as possible after purchase.

4. Food when cooked can be more varied.

COOKING TERMS

Au Gratin. Baked or roasted dishes which are prepared with breadcrumbs and sometimes cheese sprinkled over the top. Cheese is not an essential ingredient in an "au gratin".

Bake. Cooking by dry heat in an oven. This term is used in conjunction with roasting when applied to meat cookery. Sometimes the term is applied to cooking on griddles, hot plates, etc.

Barbecue. Originally this meant an entire carcass at an open fire, but this term now denotes any type of outdoor cooking of meat, and some dishes which are cooked indoors, but served with the pungent sauce which is customary in barbecue dishes.

Bardé (Fr.). Larded, covered with salt pork or slices of bacon or meat. *Une poulet bardé de lard* is a pullet larded with bacon.

Barding. This term is sometimes confused with "larding". A thin sheet of bacon fat is sliced off, trimmed square to fit, and tied over the breast of the bird with two or three pieces of thread. (See Lard below.)

Baste. To moisten roast meat, fowl, game or other foods while baking, with juices from pan. This prevents scorching and diminishes evaporation of the meat. It gives added flavour and succulence to the meat, especially towards the end of the cooking, to pour the melted fat or gravy over it at intervals.

Batter. A blended mixture essentially of flour and liquid, but often egg and other ingredients are added.

Beard. To remove the beard of shellfish (small black speck, as in oysters).

Beat. To force air into a mixture by a rotary motion. This may be done by hand or with a rotary or electric beater. Never stir a mixture after beating as this will break the air bubbles. Meat is sometimes beaten with a mallet or rolling pin to tenderise it.

Beurre (Fr.). Butter. *Au buerre noir*, with Butter sauce browned in the pan.

Beurré (Fr.). Buttered.

Bind. To add sufficient liquid, water, milk or eggs to make a mixture hold together.

Blanch. To pour boiling water over foods, e.g. rice, macaroni, etc., then drain and rinse in cold water. Fruit, tomatoes, nuts, etc., are blanched by leaving them in boiling water for a minute or two until the skins slip, then rinsing in cold water. Vegetables are sometimes blanched in boiling water to preserve colour and remove strong taste. The water is thrown away and fresh water added for cooking.

Blaze. To ignite with brandy or other spirit which is poured over the food.

Blend. To thoroughly mix two or more ingredients.

Boiling Point. No solid can boil unless it is changed into liquid and this cannot happen until it is at its own melting point (e.g. fats). Liquid is boiling when it reaches the temperature at which it is converted into steam. The boiling point of

BOILING POINT (*continued*)

water is 212° F. This means that bubbles rise all over the surface and is fast boiling. Boiling points vary: salt water boils at 224° F., milk at 196° F. and sugar has the highest boiling point. The boiling point of all liquids varies according to altitude. When we talk of boiling foods, we mean cooking food in liquid at boiling or simmering temperature. 205–20° F. is *simmering point*, when a few bubbles rise on the surface. 180–190° F. is *slow simmering*, when only one or two bubbles rise occasionally, creeping up the side of the pan. *Tepid water* is approximately 80° F.

BONE. To remove the bone, as in fish, meat and poultry.

BRAISE. To brown meat or vegetables in a very small amount of fat, then cover with meat stock, juices, water, milk or cream, and cook slowly at 250° F. Therm. ½ or over a low heat.

BREADCRUMB. To roll or coat with breadcrumbs before cooking, or to dip fish or other foods into an egg or milk mixture and then into fine breadcrumbs.

BREAD DOWN. In bread-making, to knead down the risen dough.

BREAK. When the butter begins to appear in churning.

BRIDER (Fr.). To truss.

BROIL. To expose food to direct heat. Food to be broiled is placed over, or under, or in front of, a flame or heating unit. (See GRILL below.) For broiling, a utensil called a "gridiron" is required. This must be kept dry, clean and well-greased. It is usually wiped clean with paper to remove any pieces, then rubbed clean with butter paper before putting away.

BROWN. To place under the grill or in the oven till the dish is a light brown colour. A good colour can be achieved by sprinkling with grated cheese or fine raspings of brown breadcrumbs, or by brushing with egg or milk in the case of buns, cakes or pastry.

BRULÉE (Fr.). Burnt. Often applied to caramel dishes.

BRUSH. To spread with butter, oil, etc., using a brush or a small piece of cloth or paper.

BUTTER. To brush the insides of moulds, pie dishes, etc., with melted fat or oil.

CANDY. To cook in sugar or syrup.

CARAMELISE. To melt sugar in a heavy pan over a low heat, stirring constantly until it is deep brown in colour and the characteristic flavour develops.

CASSEROLE COOKING. The slow cooking of food in either an earthenware, glass or metal vessel, which has a close-fitting lid. Due to the long, slow cooking, old fowl, game or tough meat are rendered more tender.

CHILL. To place in a cool larder or refrigerator to become thoroughly cold or to stand a small vessel in a larger basin with cold water to come three-quarters of the way up the side.

CHOP. To cut into small pieces. Pieces of meat, usually from the loin or ribs, chopped off.

CLARIFY. To remove the odour or impurities of fats or foodstuffs. To clear a liquid such as soup by adding slightly beaten egg white and the egg shells. These coagulate the liquid and it is then strained. To melt fat with water and bring to the boil, leave to cool, remove fat and scrape off any sediment.

CLEAN. To free dried fruit of dust and stalks before use in cakes (see **CAKES**). Also, to gut fish.

CLEAR. To remove scum from jam (see **JAMS**). To remove scum from soups by skimming and adding egg shells (see **SOUPS**). To move cloudiness from coffee (see **COFFEE**).

COAT. To cover a fillet, cutlet or other food by dipping into thick sauce or a gelatine mix (see **ASPIC** and MASK below).

COCADE. A fan-shaped decoration; applied to sugar or paste ornaments.

CODDLE. A method of soft-boiling eggs (see **EGGS**).

COLOUR. To tint with vegetable or artificial colouring.

COMBINE. To mix ingredients together.

CONSISTENCY. This term is used to denote the texture of a mixture, batter or dough.

[166]

CONSISTENCY (*continued*)

Pouring Consistency is a batter that is stiff enough to drop from a spoon with a plop.

Soft Dough is a mix just stiff enough to knead.

Stiff Dough is a mix which is sufficiently stiff to roll out.

COOL. This means to leave the food to cool, but the process can be hurried by standing the dish in cold water or putting the food, e.g. rice, macaroni, vegetables when par-cooked or cooked, under running cold water.

CORE. To insert a long thin-bladed knife, or corer, into the centre of an apple and to cut out the core with a quick twisting movement. Also to remove hard centre of pears.

CREAM. To rub until soft, smooth and creamy with a heavy spoon or firm spatula. To embody poultry, vegetables and other foods in a white sauce.

CREE. To simmer.

CRIMP. To slash a large fish at intervals; this ensures that the whole is evenly cooked and crisp.

CRUMB. To sprinkle with dry breadcrumbs or to dip into breadcrumbs.

CRYSTALLISE. To cook fruits in hot syrup. (See GLAZE below.)

CUBE. To cut out even-sized cube-shaped piece. These are generally small.

CURDLE. To change into curd, coagulate, thicken, congeal.

CURE. To dry or smoke previously salted meat or fish.

CUT. To divide foods with a knife or scissors.

CUT IN. To incorporate and distribute shortening (butter, margarine or fat) evenly through the dry ingredients with little blending so that the fat remains in small particles. Literally, it is to cut in with two knives or pastry blenders.

DAUB. To put strips of pork through a punched hole in meat.

DECANT. To pour wine or liquid which has a sediment from the original bottle to the decanter without transferring the sediment.

DÉSOSSER (Fr.). To bone.

DEVILLED. Grilled or fried, sometimes in crumbs, and served with a hot sauce.

DICE. To cut into tiny cubes.

DIGEST. To soak until the flavour is extracted.

DISJOINT. To cut a fowl into cooking or serving pieces by dividing at the joints.

DISSOLVE. To melt or to liquefy a solid food.

DOT. To place small bits of a substance on a surface.

DOUGH. A thick mixture of uncooked flour and liquid, sometimes with other ingredients.

DRAIN. To get rid of surplus liquid by the use of a sieve or colander. To place fish or fried foods on paper so that the fat is absorbed.

DRAW. To remove the entrails of poultry, game, etc.

DREDGE. To sprinkle food evenly with flour, oatmeal, sugar, so that it is completely covered. It is easier to use a dredger or sifter.

DRESS. To prepare food for cooking or serving. Generally to pare, clean, trim, etc., and dish up in good shape. Some foods must be dressed in a special way, such as crab, lobster and poultry. Dressed vegetables are cooked in rich style and neatly garnished.

DRESSÉ or GARNI (Fr.). Dressed or garnished.

DRIPPING. The fat and dripping from roasted meat.

DRIPPINGS. The drippings of game into the roasting tin.

DUST. To sprinkle lightly with dry substance, such as flour, seasoning, sugar and spices.

DRY INGREDIENTS. These ingredients in a mix can be sifted together when necessary: flour, salt, baking powder, etc.

EGG AND CRUMB. To dredge the food with fine crumbs, then dip into diluted, slightly beaten egg and milk, or water, then dredge with crumbs. This treatment is used for fried foods and forms a surface which is easily browned and so prevents fat soaking into the food.

EXTRACT. To simmer with very little liquid, to obtain the natural juices.

[167]

FARCE (Fr. *farci*). Stuffed. To make a forcemeat and stuff poultry, game, tomatoes, etc.

FAT. Butter, margarine, lard, dripping.

FILLET. To remove flesh of fish, poultry or meat from the bone. This term also refers to the undercut of a loin of beef. A *filet mignon* is a steak cut from the smaller end of a fillet of beef. It is usually rather thick.

FILTER. To strain liquid through a filter, a cloth, e.g. fine linen or muslin.

FINE. A term used in wine-making meaning to clear by adding isinglass or egg white.

FLAKE. To break up into shavings like flakes.

FLAMBER (Fr.). To light spirit poured over food, e.g. brandy on Christmas Pudding. To singe.

FLOUR. To dredge flour over the surface of food to dry it for frying and prevent it sticking, or over a pastry board, rolling pin, baking sheet or one's hand to prevent sticking. Always remove any surplus flour.

FOLD. To add to a mixture a delicate ingredient without allowing the air already beaten in to escape. The mixing spoon (usually metal) cuts vertically through the mixture, continues across the bottom of the bowl, and turns upwards, folding under part of the surface.

FONCER (Fr.). To line the bottom of a casserole or baking dish with bacon, etc.

FRAPPÉ (Fr.). Iced food or cold soufflé. Beaten ice. Applied to a water ice, frozen to a mush, which may be drunk, instead of eaten with a spoon.

FRICANDELL. A small round cake or ball of mincemeat mixed with breadcrumbs, eggs, seasoning and simmered in liquid or fried.

FRICASSÉE. A combination method of cooking. Usually lightly fried and then stewed game, poultry or meat. The food so cooked is then served in sauce (see CHICKEN).

FRIZZLE. To fry in a minimum amount of fat so that the food is crisp.

FROST. To decorate with icing, etc., or to cover with stiffly whisked whites of eggs, dredge with sugar and place in a cool oven to set and lightly brown.

FROTHING. To dredge the surface of roast joints, or roasts in general, with flour, then briskly heat to a brown colour with a salamander.

FRY. To cook food in hot fat. When the food is cooked in a small amount of fat it is called *sautéing*, in deep fat it is called *deep fat frying*.

FRY OUT. To place fat or meat with fat interdispersed in the pan over a gentle heat and to fry till the fat is separated from the membrane.

GARNISH. To add watercress, parsley, etc., to foods to decorate, add colour and to make the dish more appetising.

GLACÉ (Fr.). Iced, frozen. Applied to glazed, frosted, crystallised or candied fruits, which have been dipped into hot syrup cooked to hard crack stage. Also refers to a concentrated less-thickened mixture which is used to coat certain rolls and pastries.

GLAZE. To give a glossy surface to a dish by the addition of a jellied sauce, or to cover with a thin transparent film of sugar syrup; buns and pastry are glazed by brushing with egg and milk and sometimes sprinkling with sugar.

GOULASH. Hungarian stew.

GRATE. To reduce to small particles against a grater.

GREASE. See BUTTER.

GRILL. To cook by direct heat, placing the food on the grill tray under a heated grill, or on a gridiron over a clear fire.

GRIND. To put food into a mincer or grinder, to chop the food.

GUT. To remove the insides of fish.

HANG. To place game, venison or other meat in any airy place to ripen and so improve both flavour and texture.

HEAT. To place over a low heat and so warm up without bringing to the boil.

ICE. To cover with icing or to decorate a cake, buns, etc., with sugar glaze. (See GLAZE.)

INFUSE. To extract flavour from tea, coffee, herbs, etc., into a liquid.

JUG. To stew and serve a hare, or rabbit, in a thick rich sauce to which port wine is added.

JULIENNE. To cut vegetables into match-like strips.

KIPPER. A method of preserving fish, usually herrings, which are split, salted and smoked.

KNEAD. To work the dough by manipulating it with a pressing motion.

KNOCK DOWN. To break the dough by kneading when making bread.

KOSHER. A term applied to foods prepared with special precautions to fulfil the requirements of the Jewish law.

LACE. To add a dash of spirits or sugar to a beverage.

LARD. To insert lardoons (small strips of fat) into or on top of uncooked lean meat or fish to give an added flavour and to prevent dryness.

LIAISON. The thickening element in sauces, such as flour (most common), egg yolk, arrowroot, cornflour, crumbs, potatoes, rice flour.

LIFT. To turn a mixture over and over from below and so mix gently.

LINE. To cover the bottoms and sides of pie-dishes or pudding basins with pastry; to coat the insides of moulds with gelatine liquid; or to cut greaseproof paper to fit the insides of cake or soufflé tins.

LUTE. To seal joints with flour and water paste.

MACEDOINE. A mixture of vegetables or fruits cut into even-shaped pieces. Vegetables used for this purpose are usually confined to the size of peas or beans with which the other foods are mixed.

MACERATE. To immerse fruit in blood-heat liquid and leave for some time.

MARINADE. A mixture of oil and seasonings, or vinegar and seasonings, or other specially prepared liquids, in which food is placed and left for a given time. This helps to soften the fibres of meat and to make foods more succulent and palatable. In some instances, marinading meat or fish in brine or pickle keeps it fresh.

MARINATE. To treat with a marinade.

MASH. To reduce to pulp.

MASK. To cover completely with sauce, jelly or mayonnaise.

MELT. To reduce to liquid by heating.

MINCE. To chop up finely by putting through a mincing machine.

MIX. To combine two or more ingredients together.

MOISTEN. To add just sufficient liquid to damp meat and vegetables after tossing in fat. This term is also used in pastry-making when covering a pie-dish.

MOULD. To form into a shape or to set in a jelly.

MOULIER (Fr.). To moisten.

MULL. To warm, spice and sweeten wine or ale.

OIL. To melt butter; to brush tins with melted butter or oil.

PANADA. A thick coating or binding sauce.

PANBROIL. To cook food in a hot pan pouring away the surplus fat as it accumulates.

PANFRY. To cook in a small amount of fat.

PANÉ (Fr.). Covered with breadcrumbs.

PARBOIL. To cook in boiling water until partly cooked.

PARCH. To apply dry heat and brown.

PARE. To remove only irregular parts and trim.

PASTEURISE. To kill bacteria by exposing to a high degree of heat.

PAUNCH. To remove inside of hare and rabbits.

PEEL. To remove the outer coverings with a sharp knife, or to blanch it off.

PICKLE. To preserve by the addition of vinegar, salt or sugar.

PIPE. To decorate with icing using a forcing bag: sometimes this is fitted with a special ribbon, rose, star, plain or fluted nozzle to produce a design. Mashed potatoes or other vegetable purée are passed through the forcing bag.

PIT. To stone dates, olives, or other fruit.

PLANK. To cook or serve a food, usually a fish or steak, on a wooden plank or board specially made for the purpose. To remove the outer covering by the aid of heat or a mechanical device; to remove and strip off the outer covering or rind.

PLOAT. To pull off the feathers, hair, etc., as to pluck a fowl.

PLUCK. To pull out the feathers of game and poultry (see **POULTRY**).

POACH. To cook in hot liquid, retaining the original shape of the food.

POT. To preserve fish, fowl, game or meat by cooking and then sealing the pot or jar with melted butter or fat.

POT ROAST. To cook meat or poultry in a saucepan with closely fitting lid, in a very little stock or liquid as well as fat.

POUND. To pulverise by beating in a pestle and mortar. Also a measure of weight: 16 oz. avoirdupois and 12 oz. troy.

PRE-COOK. To cook before further cooking.

PROVE. To rise in bread-making.

PURÉE (Fr.). To press the fruit or vegetables through a sieve or ricer; also a soup made with food put through a sieve or ricer and then thinned with cream, milk or stock.

RACK. To draw off the wine from the lees. To store in special racks in the wine cellar.

RARE. A term used to signify underdone or nearly raw meat, such as rare beef or mutton.

RASP. To make fine breadcrumbs by grating the crusts of stale bread on a fine grater. Brown breadcrumbs are sometimes known as raspings.

RECHAUFFER (Fr.). To reheat.

REDUCE. To evaporate liquid and moisture by fast boiling and to increase flavour.

REFRESH. To put the blanched vegetables in cold water; to reheat bottled fruit before serving and so increase flavour.

RENDER. To free fat from the connective tissues by heating slowly until the fat melts and can be drained off.

REQUER (Fr.). To lard.

RICE. To rub cooked floury potatoes through a sieve or to push hard-boiled egg through a sieve.

RISE. The rising up of dough, due to the reaction of yeast, and of cakes, due to the expansion of air in mixtures under heat (see **BREAD**).

RISSOLÉ (Fr.). Browned.

RISSOLER (Fr.). To roast until the food is golden brown.

ROAST. To bake. This term is commonly applied to meat.

ROLL. To place on a board and roll out with a rolling-pin.

ROUX. A thickening for soups, stews and sauces made with fat and flour and cooked without colouring when white sauce is required, cooked till it is brown when brown sauce is being made.

RUB. To rub breadcrumbs or other foods through a sieve; to work fat that has been cut into flour by mixing with the fingertips until the consistency is of fine breadcrumbs.

SALT. To cover with dry salt as in pickling.

SAURÉ. Fried or cured in smoke.

SAUTER. To fry in a small amount of fat to bring out the flavour.

SCALD. To pour water which is scalding hot over food to remove rank odour, or to cleanse and loosen hair or skin. Always bring milk almost to boiling point to prevent it turning sour.

SCALLOP. The food is usually cut into pieces, covered with liquor or sauce and crumbs, and baked in scallop shells or fireproof individual dishes; sometimes browned before serving.

SCORE. To cut narrow grooves or gashes, usually in parallel lines.

SCRAMBLE. To stir beaten eggs while cooking.

SEAR. To brown the surface of meat by the application of intense heat for a short time. This process usually develops the flavour and also improves the appearance.

SEASON. To add pepper and salt and other condiments to bring out the flavour.

SEASON OR PROVE A PAN. See **OMELET**.

SEETHE. To simmer.

SEPARATE. To remove cream from milk; to separate the white of egg from yolk.

SET. To leave a liquid to become firm. This is usually applied to gelatine mixes.

SEW. To bring two edges together with a needle and thread as when stuffing poultry, fish, etc.

SHELL. To remove shells from nuts, or from peas or broad beans.

SHIRR. To bake eggs in the oven and serve in the dishes in which they are cooked.

SHORTENING. See FAT above.

SHRED. To cut into very thin strips or slices.

SIEVE. To pass food through a fine hair or wire sieve to reduce to pulp.

SIFT. To well mix flour and dry substances and then shake through a sieve or sifter.

SIMMER. See BOILING POINT above.

SINGE. To pass a lighted taper or flame over game or poultry to remove any feathers or down still left after plucking.

SKEWER. To fasten fish, fowl and meat, etc. with a metal or wooden pin to hold in shape, or to close openings in it. A long metal skewer when used for grilling small pieces of meat, fish or vegetables, is called cooking *en brochette.*

SKIM. To remove scum or fat from the surface; or cream from milk.

SKIN. To peel after blanching; or to remove the skin from fish, poultry or meat.

SLIVER. To shred or cut finely into lengths.

SMOKE. To cure by smoking as in Finnan haddocks or bacon.

SOAK. To immerse in a liquid for a certain time.

SOFTEN. To parcook vegetables or fruit until they lose their firmness.

SOUSE. To immerse in vinegar or spices. Usually applied to herrings.

SPONGE. To set the yeast, liquid and flour together to begin the rising process.

SPRINKLE. To scatter grated cheese, breadcrumbs, etc., on the surface of a dish.

STEAM. To cook the food in steam with or without pressure. Steam may be applied directly to food as in a steamer, or to the vessel as in a double boiler.

STEEP. To extract the flavour and colour and other qualities by adding boiling water and allowing mixture to stand.

STERILISE. To kill bacteria by applying a high degree of heat.

STEW. To cook in a small amount of liquid which is always kept below boiling point.

STIR. To mix food materials with a circular motion, so blending them or bringing them to a uniform consistency; to keep liquid in motion by using a spoon or fork as in sauce-making.

STONE. To split fruit and remove stone with knitting needle or skewers.

STOVE. To heat, or to bake in the oven.

STRAIN. To pass liquid through fine muslin or a strainer.

STUFF. To fill poultry and certain cuts of meat with forcemeat or to make a seasoned mixture to fill vegetables or tomatoes.

STUB. To remove the pen feathers from fowls.

SWEAT. To heat gently to extract flavour.

SWIRL. To whirl or move the mixture with an eddying motion.

TAMMY. To put into a cloth, twist the ends opposite ways and so squeeze.

TEMPER. To prepare a pan before use by heating.

TEMPERATURE. The degrees of heat in cooking. Temperature is generally measured in degrees Fahrenheit.

TEPID. The temperature obtained when mixing two parts of cold water to one part of boiling water, 80° F.

THICKEN. To give body to soups, sauces and some gravies by adding flour or cornflour.

TOAST. To apply direct heat to the surface of bread or other food to brown.

TOSS. Vegetables are tossed in melted butter; a pancake is turned by tossing.

TRIM. To use a knife or scissors and trim off loose edges from fish or meat; to remove breadcrusts; or to remove loose edges in pastry-making.

TRITURATE. To grind to a fine powder. Not often used.

TRUSS. To tie a fowl or other meat so that it retains its shape.

TRY OUT. To heat slowly until the fat is liquid and melts away from membranes. This term is usually applied to bacon.

TURN. To turn over cutlets of meat when grilling, with tongs or other blunt utensils.

TURN OUT. To remove cream, jellies, etc., from the mould in which they have been cooked or set. The edge may be gently released with the fingers or it may be necessary to insert the mould into hot water for a second or two.

WHIP. To beat rapidly and so increase volume by the incorporation of air.

WORK. To keep a mixture pliable.

ZEST. The outer skins of lemons or oranges. This is the only part used for flavouring. (The white pith underneath is very bitter.)

COOT. When trussed this bird is best soaked for 24 hrs. in several waters before cooking. Stuff with goose stuffing before roasting.

COQUILLES. Literally shells. Any meat, fish or vegetable preparation served in scallop shells.

CORAL (Fr. *corail*). The soft, greenish matter, the ovaries of the hen lobster, which turns red in cooking.

CORIANDER (Fr. *coriande*). This dried fruit is much used by confectioners and cordial makers for the sake of its aromatic flavour. It is also an important ingredient in Eastern cookery and is frequently powdered and put unto curry powder. A native of Southern Europe and Asia, the plant grows now in many other parts and is found wild in Essex and in the locality of Ipswich. The seeds are about the same size as white peppercorns, and of a yellowish-brown colour.

CORNCRAKE. Sometimes known as Corn-birds and also called Land Rail. These birds are migratory and to be seen here only from the end of April to the end of September. They are frequently found in the long grass of meadowland near rivers, in fields of green corn or clover and beds of osiers, where they can be recognised by the harsh grating noise they make in the night. They should be roasted with frequent basting and brought to table with a rich brown gravy and fried breadcrumbs or Bread sauce, if preferred.

CORNED MEAT. These meats (usually beef) are well salted before being cooked. The salt used is of coarse grains, or corns, hence the term "corned meat".

CORNET. Shell of paper screwed into a conical shape used by confectioners for a variety of purposes. The point of the cornet is cut off to leave as large an opening as may be required. The cornet is nearly filled with icing or other soft material, and the top carefully folded over so that upon pressure the contents ooze through as required by the operator.

CORNFLOUR. Sometimes known as Cornmeal or Indian Meal, this fine flour is made by grinding the kernels of Indian Corn. It is used for thickening purposes and in conjunction with flour in some cake mixes. (See **Melting Moments** under **CAKES.**) Sometimes a little cornflour is beaten with butter to make it go further for spreading in sandwiches, etc.

Cornflour Blancmange

Ingredients	Method
1½ oz. cornflour	Blend the cornflour with a little cold milk.
1¼ pt. milk	Add pinch of salt. Boil the remaining

Cornflour Blancmange (*continued*)

Pinch of salt
Sugar
Flavouring as desired

milk with the sugar, pour slowly on to the cornflour stirring continually. Return to the pan, reboil for about 5 mins. stirring the whole time, then pour into a a well-moistened mould.

FOR A RICHER MOULD blend an egg yolk with cornflour and milk. Add the stiffly beaten white, folding in with a metal spoon just before turning into a dish or moistened mould.

FOR FLAVOURING. The finely grated peel and juice of an orange or lemon added to blended paste; a few drops vanilla, lemon or almond essence to taste; a bay leaf simmered in the milk while boiling to give an almond flavour.

Cornflour Cake

Ingredients

2 oz. butter
¼ lb. caster sugar
2 eggs
¼ lb. cornflour
1 tsp. baking powder
Pinch of salt

Method

Beat the butter to a cream. Then add sugar, beat again till light and creamy. Add the eggs, and beat all well together. Lastly, stir in the cornflour, and add baking powder and salt. Turn the mixture into a cake tin lined with paper. Bake for about ¾ hr. at 350° F. Therm. 4. See also CAKES.

Cornflour Pudding

Ingredients

2 tbsp. cornflour
2 tbsp. caster sugar
1 pt. milk
1 egg (if desired)

Method

Put the cornflour into a pie-dish with the sugar. Mix smoothly with a little cold milk. Put rest of milk on to boil; pour boiling milk over cornflour, stirring quickly until it thickens. Add the egg, well-beaten, and a little flavouring essence. Bake in the pie-dish for about 30 mins. at 350° F. Therm. 4.

CORNISH PASTY. The Cornish pasty is a baked torpedo shape of pastry filled with finely chopped meat, kidney, onions, bacon, parsley, etc., moistened with a little gravy. It makes a palatable lunch or supper dish.

CORN ON COB. See INDIAN CORN.

CORN SALAD. An annual herb sometimes used in salad, and known also as Lamb's Lettuce. It has a slightly bitter taste and although it can be used by itself it is better as an addition to lettuce salads. In France it is known as *doucette*.

COS LETTUCE. See LETTUCE and SALADS.

COSTARD. The name of a cooking apple.

COSTMARY. Bibleleaf, Sweet Mary, Alecost. This mint-flavoured plant has been cultivated in British gardens ever since its introduction in the 16th century. At one time it was largely used to flavour ale, hence its name Alecost. It is added to negus.

COTHERSTONE. A double cream cheese made in Yorkshire, in the Tees Valley.

COTTONSEED OIL. An oil, both colourless and tasteless, which is sometimes used as a salad oil.

COULOMMIERS. A whole-milk cheese made in the Brie district of Seine-et-Marne and similar to Brie though inferior.

COURGETTE. A vegetable not unlike baby marrow. Can be eaten sliced and unpeeled, lightly sautéed in butter.

COURT BOUILLON. A highly seasoned stock used to boil freshwater fish, thereby redeeming something of its general tastelessness.

TO MAKE. Slice up a large carrot and a full-sized onion and put these into a 4-qt. saucepan, together with a bunch of well washed parsley, a sprig of thyme, 1 tsp. peppercorns, 1 tsp. salt, a pat of butter, and 2 or 3 bay leaves or a blade of mace. Cook together gently then add gradually 2 qt. water and ½ pt. white vinegar. Bring to the boil, simmer gently for 1½ hr., then strain and set aside for use. Wine is frequently added to this during cooking.

COWBERRY. The berries of one of several shrubs which grow in the pastures, e.g. the Partridge Berry, the Mountain Cranberry.

COWHEEL. In Scotland these are more generally known as Ox-feet.

COWHEEL, BOILED. Thoroughly wash the heel, if not already dressed, and scald it with boiling water; scrape off all the hairs, and remove all the fat from between the claws. Put it into cold water and bring to the boil. Throw the water away, well wash the heel and cut into four pieces. Put these into a saucepan with an onion and a few sprigs of parsley, a little pepper and salt, and cover with cold water. Simmer for four hours or more until tender. Place on a hot dish and serve with Piquant, Tomato or Parsley sauce. See **SAUCES**. If the latter, use the liquor from the heel for making it. If no vegetables are used in cooking the heel, the stock may be clarified for a jelly.

COWHEEL JELLY. Get an unskinned cowheel, cut the foot through the joints, and chop the long bone; remove the fat and wash it well. Put in a saucepan and cover with cold water. Boil for 10 mins. then strain off the water and wash it again. Put it in an enamelled saucepan, cover it with cold water and stew gently for 6 hrs., skimming continually. When done, strain the stock into a basin. Let it get cold and skim off fat. In using the jelly be careful not to mix the sediment with it.

COWSLIP. This spring primula can be gathered in April and May. The leaves are sometimes used as herbs for the pot.

Cowslip Wine. To each gallon of cowslip flowers allow 3 lb. sugar and peel of 2 lemons. Boil the water and sugar together and, when cooled to bloodheat, pour over the cowslips and lemon peel. Spread a small piece of toast with yeast and add. Allow 1 tbsp. to each 3 gall. liquid. Leave 10 days, stirring once a day at least. Then strain and bottle.

CRAB (Fr. *crabe*). Crabs are usually sold ready boiled. The best crabs are always heavy for their bulk, the claws and legs should all be on and the eyes should be bright. The male crab has larger claws than the female, but less body in proportion, therefore the selection should depend upon whether one's taste is for the white meat of the claws, or for the mellow liver and creamy fat of the body. The liver is the soft yellow substance which nearly fills the body. Crabs are in season from April to October.

CRAB, HARD-SHELLED

TO BOIL. Hard-shelled crabs should always be alive when plunged into boiling liquid: 2 qt. water, ½ cup vinegar, 2 tbsp. salt, 1 tsp. cayenne pepper. Boil rapidly for 5 mins. then simmer for 15 mins. When cool enough to handle, remove from shells.

TO CLEAN.
Break off claws, legs; crack and remove meat. (1)
Break off the apron which folds under the body at rear. (2)
Use a strong knife and force shell open by wedging between opening at apron.
Insert thumbs at opening between the shell halves, and pull upper shell away from lower shell, or hold crab in left hand, with the back towards you. (3)
Then slip the fingers under top shell, and pull downwards so as to release it.
Remove the spongy digestive tract while under running water. (4)

TO CLEAN (*continued*)

Hold crab's body in left hand and cut with a sharp knife the covering round outer rim.

Remove meat with pick.

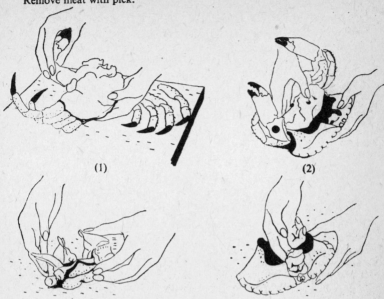

(1)   (2)

(3)   To Clean Hand-shelled Crabs   (4)

CRABS, SOFT-SHELLED. When cooked (see HARD-SHELLED CRABS), the whole body is eaten.

TO CLEAN

Use a sharp knife to cut off apron.

Turn crab and cut off face at the point behind the eyes.

Lift each point at sides with fingers.

Clean out gills.

Wash the crab thoroughly in salted water.

Dry on absorbent paper.

Crabmeat, Baked

Ingredients	*Method*
2 tbsp. butter or margarine 1 tbsp. flour ½ pt. milk 2 hard-boiled eggs chopped Salt, pepper and dash of cayenne 1 teacup crabmeat 1 tsp. chopped olives (or gherkins) Buttered breadcrumbs Sliced lemon and parsley or watercress to garnish	Melt the butter, stir in flour, and cook until the flour just bubbles. Add milk, gradually stirring the whole time. Cook about 8 mins., then add eggs, seasoning, crabmeat, olives or gherkins. Divide mixture into shells and sprinkle with buttered crumbs. Bake at 350° F. Therm. 4 for about 15 mins. until well heated. Serve garnished with slices of lemon, parsley or watercress.

Crabmeat Canapé (or Sandwich). Use flaked crabmeat, seasoned with pepper, salt and a spoonful or two of cream or mayonnaise for filling or spreading.

Crabmeat, Devilled

Ingredients

1 egg yolk beaten
¾ cup hot thick white sauce
3 teacups flaked crabmeat
½ tsp. parsley
2 tsp. Worcester sauce
¼ tsp. minced mace
¾ cup buttered crumbs

Method

Stir egg yolk into white sauce, and add crabmeat, parsley, Worcester sauce and mace. Fill shells, rounding full, cover with crumbs and bake at 350° F. Therm. 4 for about 10 mins. until brown.

Crabmeat, Maryland

Ingredients

2 tbsp. butter
1 tbsp. flour
2 hard-boiled eggs chopped
Salt and pepper
1 tsp. chopped chives
1 lb. fresh crabmeat
2 tbsp. wine or Worcester sauce
4 slices buttered toast
Watercress

Method

Place the butter in the top of a double saucepan, over low heat (the bottom half filled with water), and add flour; blend till creamy and stir till mixture thickens. Add the chopped eggs, seasoning, chives and crabmeat; stir for 5 mins. Add the Worcester sauce (or wine). Place in generous portions on slices of buttered toast. Serve each garnished with watercress or freshly chopped herbs.

Crab Mousseline. Mix together 1 cup crabmeat, ½ tsp. paprika, ¼ pt. white sauce and ½ tsp. salt. Fold in the stiffly whisked white of an egg and 2 tsp. mayonnaise or cream. Serve on lettuce leaves and garnish with sliced tomatoes.

Crab Patties

Ingredients

1 lb. flaked crabmeat
2 eggs
4 tbsp. melted butter
¼ lb. mushrooms cooked and chopped
6 stuffed olives
½ tsp. salt
⅛ tsp. pepper
Pinch of cayenne
2 tsp. water
1 cup breadcrumbs
½ pt. vegetable oil

Method

Chop the crab flakes into small pieces; break the eggs into a bowl and beat with a fork. Melt the butter, add crabmeat and chopped mushrooms, olives if desired. Season with salt, pepper and cayenne. Add sufficient egg to bind, then mould into small flat patties. Add water to remaining eggs to moisten the patties, before rolling in crumbs. Heat the vegetable oil in deep pan, put the patties into the frying basket, and fry quickly for 3 mins. or until light golden brown. Drain and serve very hot with any chosen sauce.

Crab Puff Canapés

Ingredients

1 cup water
½ cup butter
1 cup sifted flour
4 eggs
  FILLING:
1 cup white sauce

Method

Let water and butter come to the boil. Then add the flour all at once and stir briskly. Remove from heat and let mixture cool. Beat eggs until very thick, combine with beaten paste mixture and mix thoroughly. Drop on greased pan in

[176]

Crab Puff Canapés (*continued*)
Small tin of crabmeat
Dash of cayenne

Crab Salad, Jellied
Ingredients
2 tbsp. gelatine
¾ tin evaporated milk
1 tin tomato soup
½ cup boiling water
1 tin crabmeat
½ tsp. salt
1 tsp. chopped parsley

Crab Suprême in Rice Ring
Ingredients
3 tbsp. butter
3 tbsp. flour
1 cup chicken stock
½ cup cream
2 oz. cheese diced
4 oz. mushrooms
8 oz. chopped pimento
3 tbsp. sherry
Pinch of salt and pepper
Paprika to taste
2 cups crabmeat

½ tsp. and bake at 450° F. Therm. 8 for 10–15 mins. Split each puff down side with a sharp knife and fill with a mixture of white sauce, crabmeat and cayenne. Serve at once. Makes about 15 puffs.

Method
Soak gelatine in cold water. Heat soup and milk separately then combine. Pour boiling water on to gelatine. Add milk and soup mixture, chill; add crab and salt and turn into a moistened mould, sprinkled with parsley. Leave to set. Serve on lettuce leaves.

Method
Melt butter over direct heat; stir in flour; add stock and cream and cook, stirring all the time until mixture is thickened. Set over hot water, add cheese, mushrooms, pimento, sherry, seasonings and crabmeat. Serve in centre of rice ring. Shrimp or lobster can replace crab.

CRAB APPLE. See APPLE.

CRAB, OYSTER. These are best known in America. They are the tiny baby crabs found on the coast of New England, not too plentiful in supply, good when fried or stewed in cream with a little madeira added at the time of serving. They are eaten whole, shell and all.

CRACKER. A plain dry biscuit, often hard or crisp. When soaked it is used for puddings. This term is used generally for biscuits in U.S.A.

CRACKER NUTS. This term is popularly applied to the Common Spanish or Barcelona nuts, also to some delicious cakes and wafers.

CRACKLING. There are two or three dishes of confectionery known by this term, e.g. almond crackling, etc., but the word commonly used means the scored and browned skin of roast pork.

CRACKNELS. Biscuits made of paste which is boiled before it is baked. After boiling they are put into cold water to harden, then dried and finally baked, when they curl up.

CRADLE SPIT. This was used for roasting poultry, small birds, game, etc., or small pieces of meat not suitable for the ordinary spit.

CRANBERRY (Fr. *airelle*). There are two plants which bear this fruit, the one a fine tree, the High cranberry, and the other a very small shrub, the Low or Marsh cranberry. The berries are very sour.

Cranberry Jam
Ingredients
 2 qt. cranberries
 4 cups water
 1 tsp. bicarb. soda
 Sugar

Method
Stalk the fruit, place in preserving pan with the water and simmer for 1 hr. Remove from heat, add bicarb. soda, and stir and skim until the fruit is reduced to a pulp, soft enough to pass through a sieve. Allowing 1 lb. sugar to each 1 lb. pulp, place in pan and simmer for 30 mins. Bottle and cover when cool.

Cranberry Jelly
Ingredients
 1 qt. cranberries
 1½ cups water
 Sugar

Method
Stalk the fruit, place in preserving pan with water and simmer for 1 hr. until fruit is tender. Strain through muslin, measure juice and add 1 lb. sugar to each 1 pt. juice. Boil juice and sugar for 10 mins., then bottle and cover when cool.

Cranberry Pie
Ingredients
 1 qt. cranberries
 4 oz. caster sugar
 Juice of ½ lemon
 Wineglass white wine
 Pastry

Method
Plunge the cranberries into a pan of cold salted water, and leave for 12 hrs., then wash well in several waters to remove salty flavour. Remove them, drain and put on a cloth to dry. Pick them over carefully and place in a basin with sugar and lemon juice and mix well. Add wine and fill up a pie dish with fruit. Cover the top with a light paste and put pie in the oven. Bake at 350° F. Therm. 4 for about 30 mins. Dredge with caster sugar and serve hot or cold.

Cranberry Sauce
Ingredients
 2 cups cranberries
 ½ pt. water
 1 teacup moist sugar

Method
Put together into a saucepan and cook 30 mins. Then mash the berries with a spoon. Remove pan from heat. Stir well and use as desired. See also **SAUCES** (p. 441).

CRAPAUDINE (Fr.). This word is derived from Fr. *crapaud*, a toad. It denotes the preparation of partridges, quails and pigeons for broiling in which the birds have the legs and wings arranged in a toad-like manner.

CRAQUELOTS. The French name given to half-bloatered herrings.

CRAWFISH. Langouste, also known as Rock Lobster. A saltwater crustacean somewhat like the lobster but much larger. Is used in many lobster recipes and is much cheaper.

CRAYFISH (Fr. *écrevisse*). This fish lives entirely in fresh water and is like a miniature lobster. It is considered a great delicacy and was much esteemed by the Ancient Greeks and Romans. Frequently used for garnishing. Prepare by washing well, removing intestinal tract from under tail with pointed knife, and then boiling in salted water or court bouillon for 10 mins.

Crayfish à la Bordelaise. Chop a faggot of mirepoix fine, and mix it in a little butter; add a tumblerful of white wine. Boil it up, put the crayfish into it and toss them for at least 20 mins. When done, put them on to a dish, take the sauce and finish it with a little fresh butter. These crayfish are eaten entire, with the fingers, and finger bowls should therefore be provided with this dish.

Crayfish Cardinal

Ingredients

2 crayfish
4 oz. butter
2 tbsp. cognac
2 tsp. freshly chopped chives
½ pt. Hollandaise sauce

Method

Take the boiled crayfish, cut in half lengthwise, remove meat and cut into cubes. Melt butter in a saucepan over a low heat, add crayfish, chives and cognac. Mix gently. Pour steaming hot Hollandaise sauce (see p. 443) over crayfish, stirring gently. Serve very hot in preheated shells.

Crayfish with Mushrooms

Ingredients

2 crayfish
3 oz. butter
4 oz. mushrooms
3 tbsp. flour
¼ tsp. dry mustard
1 cup cream
2 hard-boiled eggs chopped
4 tbsp. sherry
1 tsp. Worcester sauce
½ tsp. salt
⅛ tsp. pepper
¼ tsp. lemon juice
Paprika
Watercress

Method

Cut the crayfish into cubes. Melt 1 oz. butter in a saucepan, add mushrooms and sauté for about 15 mins. Melt the remaining butter in a saucepan, add flour and mustard, stirring the whole time over a low heat. When smooth, add cream, stirring until mixture thickens. Add the eggs chopped, sherry, Worcester sauce, salt, pepper and stir well. Then add fish and lemon juice, stirring gently. Fill into buttered shells or individual dishes and bake at 350° F. Therm. 4 for 15 mins. Remove from oven, serve garnished with paprika and watercress. This recipe may also be used for lobster, prawns, shrimps, etc.

CREAM (Fr. *crème*). Cream is the thick oleaginous fluid which rises to the top of the milk after standing, and from which butter and cheese are made. When milk is allowed to stand 12 hrs. the cream thus obtained is single cream, when it is allowed to stand twice as long it is double cream. Creaming, or separating, as it is technically called, is brought about in either of two ways: by setting the milk in a large earthenware pan in a dairy at an even temperature and taking the cream off with a skimmer as it rises and accumulates on the surface, or by the use of a machine called a "separator". Separators are used with new milk just after milking. The milk is put into a cylinder which spins rapidly so that the centrifugal force separates the cream which trickles out of one pipe whilst the "separated" milk pours out from the other.

Cream setting pans are made in various sizes and styles and a cream spoon is useful for collecting the cream as it forms, but it is not so frequently used as a skimmer. See **BUTTER, CUSTARD, MAYONNAISE, SAUCES (Béchamel and Velouté).**

FOOD VALUE OF CREAM

	Proteins	Fats	Carbo-hydrates	Calories
Cream 20% 8 oz.–1 lb.	6	42	10	440
40% 8 oz.–1 lb.	5	91	7	864

CREAM, MOCK—I

Ingredients	Method
1 oz. butter or margarine	Cream the fat and sugar. Add the boiling
1 oz. caster sugar	water gradually, beating well, then add
1 tbsp. boiling water	cow's milk drop by drop. Use as desired.
1 tbsp. cow's milk	

CREAM, MOCK—II. To make cream with an emulsifier or cream machine, use the following proportions:

For thick cream allow 3 oz. unsalted butter or margarine to ¼ pt. milk.
For medium cream allow 2½ oz. unsalted butter or margarine to ¼ pt. milk.
For thin cream allow 2 oz. unsalted butter or margarine to ¼ pt. milk.

Make according to the directions supplied with the cream-making machine. Heat the milk and margarine together, cool to blood heat and pass it quickly through the cream machine. Vanilla flavouring and sugar should be added to taste. To get fluffy cream, add 1 tsp. gelatine to ¼ pt. milk and 2 oz. butter. After emulsifying, whip as desired.

CREAM, MOCK—III

Ingredients	Method
1 egg white	Whisk the egg white, boil the golden
1 tbsp. golden syrup	syrup, pour over the egg white and add
3 drops vanilla essence	salt and vanilla essence. Whisk the mix
Pinch of salt	until cold. Make just before use.

CREAM, CLOTTED (*a favourite West of England recipe*). Put the milk into a bell-shaped metal vessel, and let it remain for 24 hrs., then put it over a wood fire (or low even heat) so that it will be thoroughly heated. When it has been heated for about 1½ hr. and is about to simmer, strike the vessel with the knuckles and when it ceases to ring or at the appearance of the first bubble, it must be removed (because the great secret is not allowing it to do more than simmer). Take it off the fire and let it stand for 24 hrs. longer, when the cream will have risen thick enough to cut with a knife. It must then be skimmed off and put into jars for use.

CREAM, CONFECTIONER'S (Fr. *crème pâtissière*). Put 1 pt. cold milk into a saucepan and place over a low heat. Mix in a basin 2 oz. caster sugar, 1 oz. wheat flour, ½ oz. cornflour; break in 2 whole eggs and beat well together with the whisk for 2 mins. When the milk is boiling add to it the preparation and stir well. Put it into another saucepan, and place it over a low heat. Beat till it comes to the boil then remove from the heat, add immediately 1 tsp. vanilla essence. Mix again for a minute. Pour into a bowl and leave to get cold. (This cream is used for many confectioner's purposes.)

CREAM FLAVOURED WITH LEMON. Put 1 pt. milk and the thinly pared yellow rind of a small lemon into a saucepan, place it over a slow fire and boil for 5 mins. Put 5 tbsp. caster sugar into a basin with the yolks of 4 eggs and beat well. Stir gradually into the milk, from which the lemon peel has been removed. Put the cream into small cups and stand them in a flat stewpan with boiling water to half their height and simmer gently at the side of a low heat. Leave till cold then turn out on to a dish and serve.

CREAM, WHIPPED. This is made from cream skimmed off day-old milk. Put it into a large basin and set on ice to keep cool while it is whipped with a whisk. By taking off, with a spoon, the froth as it forms and putting it on to a coarse hair sieve, the free cream runs through leaving froth only. The liquid cream may be put back to the other cream being whipped. (A little white of egg added before whipping will make the cream stand better.)

CREAM, MOCK WHIPPED

Ingredients	Method
4 oz. unsalted margarine	Cream together the margarine with sugar.
2 tbsp. sugar	Add cream of tartar and lemon or

CREAM, MOCK WHIPPED (*continued*)

Pinch of cream of tartar
Vanilla or lemon essence
1 tsp. gelatine
3 tbsp. hot water

vanilla essence to flavour; then add gelatine dissolved in hot water. Whip for 15 mins. till the mixture is creamy.

Cream Buns. See BUNS.

Cream Horns. See PASTE AND PASTRY (p. 377).

Cream Meringues. See MERINGUE.

Cream Pastry. See PASTE AND PASTRY (p. 371).

Cream Puffs. Put 1 pt. water into a saucepan with 7 oz. butter and 3 oz. caster sugar and boil them. Then add 10 oz. flour and stir till it becomes a thick paste. Remove from the fire and stir in 4 eggs, one at a time, beating with a spoon against the side of the pan. As the last egg is added, add 2 tsp. vanilla extract. The more the paste is beaten, the lighter the puffs will be. Take some baking sheets, wipe them clean, and grease them. Put the paste on the sheet in pieces the size of a walnut, giving plenty of room between them and shape with a knife and spoon. Bake at 350° F. Therm. 4 for 20 mins. Fill the hollow centres of the puffs with some Crème Pâtissière (see above) and, if desired, some fruit jelly.

Cream Sauce. Put into a saucepan 2 oz. butter and 1 oz. flour. Place on a low heat and stir lightly with a spatula for 2 mins., adding 2 oz. caster sugar, 1 wineglass madeira wine, and 1 teacup cream. Stir well again for 2 mins. to avoid mixture coming to the boil. Take it from the fire and immediately add 1 wineglass of rum, stirring lightly again. Serve at once.

Crème Brûlée (Burnt Cream)

Ingredients

1 pt. heavy cream
4 egg yolks
1 tbsp. caster sugar
Little brown sugar

Method

Heat the cream slowly in a double saucepan, then pour over the beaten egg yolks, add caster sugar, return to double saucepan and stir well together for about 5 mins. over gentle heat. Put into a well-greased baking dish, and bake for an hour at 250° F. Therm. ½. Keep the dish in a shallow tin of water about ¼–½" thick. Put the dish in the shallow tin again, filling the sides with water and crushed ice. Sprinkle the top of the pudding with brown sugar and put under hot grill for a few minutes to brown. Take care not to burn sugar.

Crème Caramel

Ingredients

FOR THE CARAMEL:
2–3 oz. caster sugar
FOR THE CREAM:
2 whole eggs
2 egg yolks
1½–2 tbsp. sugar
1 tsp. water
Few drops vanilla
1 pt. milk

Method

Put the caster sugar and water into a very small saucepan and leave to melt slowly, unstirred. When the colour begins to turn, stir carefully until a good brown. Pour into a warm soufflé or oven dish, running the caramel all over the bottom and round the sides till well coated. Put the eggs in a basin, add sugar and vanilla and beat lightly with a fork. Bring the milk to scalding point and pour on to the egg

[181]

Crème Caramel (*continued*)

mixture; stir gently and pour into the mould. Stand in a baking tin half full of water, cover with a piece of greaseproof paper and set tin to bake at 350° F. Therm. 4 until the custard is set. Remove from oven and place to cool. When quite cold turn out.

CREAM OF TARTAR. In a general sense this is purified tartar or argol, a crystalline substance found in the interior of wine bottles and known as "crust". Chemically it is better known as potassium bitartrate, or acid potassium tartrate. Cream of tartar is used as a raising agent in cookery and is an ingredient of baking powder and self-raising flour. When cream of tartar is used in conjunction with bicarbonate of soda, to each 1 lb. flour allow 2 tsp. cream of tartar and 1 tsp. bicarb. soda.

CRECY SOUP. See SOUPS.

CREOLE SAUCE. See SAUCES.

CRESCENTS. The name given from their shape to almond- or vanilla-flavoured biscuits or small cakes. They are generally iced over before serving. Also crescent-shaped rolls (croissants).

CRESSES (Fr. *cressons*). There is a variety of plants included under this general denomination—all of which are used in salads. The *Garden Cress* or Pepper Grass, commonly eaten with the young leaves of the mustard, is a native of Persia and the island of Cyprus, and was introduced into England in the 16th century. It germinates rapidly so that during the greater part of the year a constant supply may be obtained by sowing every week and if moderate heat be artificially applied, the supply can be kept up in the same way during the winter. The *Watercress* (*cresson de fontain*) is a creeping amphibious perennial putting out rootlets at the joints of the stems. When the plant grows in a rapid current, the rootlets from the young shoots do not easily take root, then a considerable portion of the plant rises above the surface of the water causing a change in the shape of leaves. While the plant keeps close to the surface of the water the leaves are broad but as it elevates they grow longer and narrower. Care should be taken when gathering wild watercress as it may in the altered shape of its leaves easily be confused with the water parsnip, a poisonous plant very commonly found growing amongst watercress. Watercress appears to have been cultivated in Germany about the middle of the 16th century and in England later, about the 17th century. It makes a useful garnish.

Indian Cress is more commonly known as Nasturtium. The leaves have an agreeable pungent flavour and are therefore sometimes used in mixed salads and the seeds if gathered while green make a nice addition to mixed pickles.

Cress Vinegar. Pound ¼ oz. garden cress seeds and put in a clean dry bottle, pour over 1 pt. best vinegar and cork the bottle tightly. Let this stand for 10 days, shaking the bottle daily, and when strained off, the vinegar will be ready for use.
Watercress Butter. See BUTTERS.
Watercress Salad. Clean and pare off the stalks, wash the leaves and dry in a clean cloth. Place in a salad bowl and season with pinch of salt and a little pepper. Add 2 or 3 tbsp. vinegar or lemon juice. Watercress does not need any oil.

CRISPS (or CRESPS). An old-fashioned term for pancakes. In America, a thin crisp biscuit is known by this name.

CROISSANTS. Crescent-shaped rolls made from a special yeast dough. See **BREAD** (p. 84).

CROMESKIES. A kind of fritter, made of fish, fowl or any cooked meat, the preference being given to oysters wrapped in paste.

CROQUES. A kind of crisp, rather hard confection made of fruit pastes well coated with sugar. They derive their name from the French word *croquer*, to crunch.

CROQUETTES. Diced or minced fish, meat, poultry or vegetables, moulded with two tablespoons or by hand, egged and crumbed and deep fried.

CROWBERRY (Fr. *camarine*). Small blackberry-like fruit, also called Crakeberry. Sometimes boiled with fish.

CROWDY. A thick gruel of oatmeal and milk and water. A food of the porridge kind.

CRULL. The word is a corruption of the word "curls" which exactly describes the article it is used to denote. Potato crulls, or krulls, are potatoes cut into curls and fried in fat.

CRULLERS. A kind of sweetcake cut in strips and curled and twisted, from which peculiarity they derive their name (sometimes spelt Krullers or Curlers). They are then fried crisp in boiling fat.

CRUMBS. Crumbs or small particles of bread are used in cookery for many purposes. They form an important ingredient in various puddings and are very useful in forming, together with beaten egg, a covering or envelope for cutlets and different kinds of meat or fish, intended for frying, or for rissoles and many other foods.

To prepare breadcrumbs, see **BREAD** (p. 81).

CRUMPET. The name of a teacake, in the North sometimes known as a pikelet. Crumpets are rarely made at home.

CRUST. Outer part of loaf on baked dish; sediment in wine.

CRYSTALLISING. This is one of the simplest and most useful processes known to confectioners. The first thing to procure is a crystallising tin, a tin box filled with wire grating or trays so arranged that they can be let into the box at even stages one above the other. The articles to be crystallised are carefully arranged upon these trays with room between them. When the box is filled and packed, the next step is to prepare a strong crystallising syrup made by boiling 2 lb. sugar to 1 pt. water until the syrup reaches 220° F. See **SUGAR** (p. 491). It should then be removed from the heat and stood in a cool place until blood heat. Pour the syrup over the articles to be crystallised and fill tin to well above the top layer. Set in a cool pantry for several hours until a thick strong hard crust is formed on the surface. This will indicate that crystallisation has taken place and that the articles on the trays are also crystallised. Pull out the plug and drain off the syrup. Leave the articles a bit longer to dry and set, then use as desired. Flowers and liqueur bon-bons need no preparation, but fruit should be previously lightly boiled in syrup.

CUCUMBER (Fr. *concombre*). Cucumber is most commonly eaten raw in salad, but it may be dressed in a variety of ways. Originally the cucumber plant was cultivated in Egypt and other Eastern countries. Its growth in England dates back to the reign of Edward III, though it was not generally cultivated until Henry VIII's time.

CUCUMBER FOR SERVING WITH SALMON. Peel the cucumber and slice thinly. Place in a small dish, season with pepper and salt and cover with vinegar.

Cucumber Salad. See SALADS.

Cucumber Sauce (for fish)

Ingredients	*Method*
½ pt. heavy cream	Beat cream, add seasoning and then cucumber.
¼ tsp. salt	
3 tbsp. vinegar	
Few grains of cayenne	
1 peeled and diced cucumber	

Cucumber Soup. See SOUPS.

[183]

CULINARY HERBS. See **HERBS** and individual entries.

CULINARY UTENSILS. See **KITCHENS.**

CUMBERLAND. An English nobleman to whom was dedicated Cumberland sauce, prepared with red currant jelly, orange and lemon, mustard, and served with game. See **SAUCES.**

CUMMIN. Sometimes spelt Cumin. Aromatic seeds resembling caraway seeds, sometimes used in curries. In Germany they are used in breadmaking, in Holland to flavour cheese and in Turkey in ragoût.

CUPS. To be "in one's cups" is exceedingly significant, although perhaps not correctly defined. At one time the word "cup" was habitually used to indicate a sense of joviality and good fellowship and, in some instances, the fashion of loving, grace and parting cups and other excuses for quaffing have been handed down to posterity. The following recipes are given as illustrations of these three, but numerous other cups will be found under special headings, e.g. **LOVING CUPS.**

LOVING CUP. Rub the thin rind of a lemon with lumps of sugar and put them into a jar with 2 lemons rinded and sliced, also the thin rind of one of them, 4 oz. loaf sugar and ½ pt. brandy. Stir well until thoroughly mixed. Pour in 1 qt. cold filtered water, 1 pt. Madeira wine and a bottle of cider. Grate in a nutmeg and sweeten to taste using sugar or capillaire. In summer add a small handful of freshly gathered balm and borage in flower, stalks downwards and put the liquor jar into an ice tub for an hour before use. In winter, ale may be substituted for cider and the cup should be drunk warm, *not* hot.

OXFORD GRACE CUP. Rub the rind of a lemon with lumps of sugar so as to obtain the zest. Put them back into a bowl with the remainder of the lemon cut into thin slices. Pour over 3 breakfast cups strong but not bitter beer and 1 pt. sherry. Add more sugar to sweeten and a little grated nutmeg. Stir till the whole of the sugar is dissolved. On the surface float 4 or 5 browned slices of toasted bread. Let it remain for 2 hrs., strain it and it is then ready for use.

PARTING CUP. This should be made only a few minutes before serving. Well brown three slices of bread by toasting, put them into a bowl for serving, grate over nutmeg to taste; pour over a little more than ½ bottle sherry and 1 qt. mild ale, stir well. Add sufficient simple syrup to sweeten and when upon point of serving add a bottle of soda water. Clove or cinnamon for flavouring may be added if desired.

CURAÇAO. A liqueur made of the zest of the rind of the bitter orange cultivated in the island of Curaçao in the Dutch West Indies and originally made there. There are two kinds, white and brown, which is believed differ only in respect of colour, the brown being due to burnt sugar. It is used also for flavouring.

CURD. This term refers to the parts of milk which coagulate when a vegetable or mineral acid is added to it and heat applied. Other substances produce the same effect, e.g. rennet. Technically, curd is described as casein, the basis of cheese, charged with the oil globules of milk which it has involved in its formation. The remaining liquor is called whey.

Curds are principally used for making cheese but are also served fresh-made with or without the whey and generally eaten with sugar or preserved fruit of some kind or sweetened and covered with rich cream. See **CHEESE** and **JUNKET.**

TO PREPARE. Put 1 qt. milk into a perfectly clean saucepan, and place over a moderate heat until it begins to bubble. Then turn into a basin. When cool, put 1 tbsp. old curd into the milk and stir it well with the handle of a wooden spoon. Stand the basin in a warm cupboard, cover with a thick piece of blanket or flannel, and leave 12 hrs. At the end of that time the curd should be well set, and the top covered with a thick layer of cream. It can be served in cups or glasses for breakfast or luncheon.

Curd Cheese Cakes. See **CAKES** (p. 111).

CURE. Curing in culinary language means the drying or smoking of previously salted meat or fish.

CURLY CRESS. The common name for Garden Cress. Sometimes also known as Pepper Grass. The curly leaves make an excellent garnish or salad.

CURRANTS. There are two distinct kinds of fruit known by this name. The first is a group of sweet berries of the Ribes family—black, red and white currants, the second the dried fruit of the Corinth grape, better known as "grocer's currants". The name is derived from the fact that they were originally imported from Corinth. The small seedless grapes from which they are made are originally red or blue. They are the principal articles of export from Greece, where a very sweet kind of wine is also made from them.

Currants, Black. These are black, strong-flavoured, aperient and tonic. In cookery they hold an important position due in great measure to their richness of juice and colour.

Currants, Red. The fruit of the *ribes rubrum*, a very hardy shrub which grows freely in any part of the British Isles and some parts of the Continent.

Currant (Black) Cheese

Ingredients	*Method*
Blackcurrants Equal weight of sugar	See that the currants are ripe and dry. Pick over carefully, removing the stalks and tops. Place in a preserving pan with the sugar and place over a low flame until the sugar has dissolved. Then increase the heat and bring gently to the boil. Simmer for 1 hr., stirring gently and skimming. If desired, pass through a hair sieve before using.

Currant (Black) Geneva Liqueur. Place some blackcurrants in a stone jar with a small mouth, add 1 lb. candy sugar to each quart of fruit. To this add 2 or 3 cloves and 1½ pt. gin. Cork the jar tightly and shake it frequently for 6 wks. The liquid should be quite clear when poured off.

Currant (Black) Jam—I

Ingredients	*Method*
6 lb. blackcurrants 2 cups water 6 lb. sugar	Remove stalks from the fruit, place in preserving pan with water and boil until the fruit is tender. Add the sugar (previously warmed in a slow oven) and stir frequently whilst the jam is boiling for 15 mins. Skim and pour into warmed jars. Cover when cool.

Currant (Black) Jam—II

Ingredients	*Method*
6 lb. sugar 8 lb. blackcurrants	Remove stalks from blackcurrants and place in a bowl with the sugar. Crush together thoroughly. Then place in preserving pan and boil for 30 mins., stirring frequently and skimming. Pour into warmed jars and cover.

Currant (Black) Jelly

Ingredients	*Method*
6 lb. blackcurrants ½ cup water Sugar	Place fruit in preserving pan with water. Simmer gently for 15 mins. Mash a little, then strain through muslin. Boil juice a

C.C.D.—7

[185]

Currant (Black) Jelly (*continued*)

further 10 mins., then measure and to every pint of juice allow 1 lb. sugar. Place together in preserving pan and boil for 10 mins. Pour into warmed jars and cover when cold.

Currant (Black) Lozenges
Ingredients
2 oz. brown sugar
½ pt. blackcurrant juice
1 tsp. isinglass

Method
Mix the sugar into the juice, place in an enamelled saucepan and add the isinglass dissolved in a little warm water. Allow to simmer gently for ¾ hr. Pour over small plates in layers about ⅛″ thick. Keep in warm place until the mixture is hard and dry. Store in a tin, interlayered with sheets of paper. Stamp and cut as required.

Currant (Black) Preserve
Ingredients
1 lb. blackcurrants
½ pt. redcurrant juice
1½ lb. sugar

Method
Cut off the heads and stalks of the currants. Place them in a preserving pan with the redcurrant juice and the sugar. Boil gently, shaking the pan to prevent damaging the fruit, and skim. Allow to boil for 15 mins. Pour into warmed jars and cover when cool. Especially suitable for tarts or served with cream.

Currant (Black) Pudding. See Fruit Pudding (p. 229).

Currant (Black) Syrup. First heat the fruit in a basin over a pan of boiling water until the juice begins to run freely from it, then crush it with a wooden spoon. Strain through a jelly bag or press out the juice in a cloth or hand press. Filter through double muslin then put into cask or earthenware jar to ferment. When bubbles of gas are forming at the surface, fermentation has progressed far enough. Strain, press and filter as before. Now mix the clear juice with sugar to stabilise flavour and colour, and add ¾ lb. sugar to each pint of juice. Bottle the syrup; cork and wire the bottles and sterilise in water. The temperature of the water should be raised from cold to 170° F. in 1 hr. and maintained at that temperature for 20–30 mins. When bottles are cold, invert them and dip the necks in melted paraffin wax to form an airtight seal. The syrup in a bottle should all be used within 2 or 3 days of opening. After that time the contents will ferment.

Currant (Black) Wine. Choose ripe blackcurrants and to each pint of juice allow 1 pt. cold water, 1 lb. preserving sugar and 1 glass brandy. Stalk the currants and place in an earthenware bowl. Using a wooden spoon, bruise well to release juice. Drain off and measure. Add water to the bruised berries, leave to infuse for 4 hrs. then strain and add sugar in proportion to the juice and leave to dissolve. Turn into a small cask and when fermentation ceases add brandy. Bung closely. Leave for 12 mths. in a warm place, then drain off the wine into dry bottles and store in a moderately warm place.

Currant (Red) Jam
Ingredients
4 lb. redcurrants
4 lb. sugar

Method
Pick over fruit, place in preserving pan and add sugar. Simmer until sugar is well dissolved, then test for setting. Pour into warm jars and cover when cool.

[186]

Currant (Red) Jelly

Ingredients

6 lb. redcurrants
Sugar

Method

Place currants in preserving pan and whilst they are coming to boil, mash against sides of pan to expel juice. After boiling for 1 min. strain through flannel until juice is quite clear. Measure and allow an equal amount of sugar to juice. Boil sugar for 3 mins. then add juice and boil for 10 mins. Skim well, pour into heated jars, and cover when cool.

Currant (Red) Sauce. Boil a handful of redcurrants (or ¼ lb. redcurrant jelly) or 1 oz. redcurrants dried, for a few minutes. Add 1 oz. butter, 4 cloves, 3 tbsp. sifted breadcrumbs, and 1 wineglass port wine. Stir till it boils and serve very hot.

Currant (Red) Jelly Sauce. Make ½ pt. Brown sauce (see SAUCES), strain well and add 1 teacup warmed redcurrant jelly. Sir together until the jelly is quite hot and serve at once.

Currants (White) Sugared. Take a few dozen freshly gathered bunches of white currants and dip each one separately into well-whisked white of an egg with 1 tsp. each of maraschino and water, mixed together. Warm 1 lb. caster sugar. After dipping the currants into the egg and allowing them to drain, dip them into sugar and well cover them. Place on strainer until the sugar is set, then serve.

CURRY (Fr. *kari*). An Indian condiment; a stew of meat, fish or fowl in a sharp spiced sauce. See SAUCES (p. 442), also CHICKEN.

ACCOMPANIMENTS TO SERVE WITH CURRY. Salted almonds, peeled sliced bananas, Bombay duck, marinated cubed cucumber in coconut milk, sliced hard-boiled egg, chutney, chives, fillets of anchovy, peeled and chopped onions, diced pineapple, vegetables and tinned fish.

Curry Kubab

Ingredients

Tender mutton, veal or other suitable meat
Bacon, Onions, Green Ginger
Curry sauce (see p. 442)

Method

Cut the meat into pieces 1″ square and ¼″ thick. Cut the bacon into pieces 1″ square but of the thickness of a rasher. Parboil the onions, and cut them the same size and thickness as the bacon, and cut the ginger also the same size. Thread these alternately on skewers, and then cook in curry sauce until tender.

CUSHION. That part of the leg of an animal which is adjacent to, and partly covered by, the udder.

CUSK, TUSK or TORSK. A large sea fish about the size of a cod. It frequents the northern coasts of Europe and America and is known in this country. The flesh is firm and white and is cooked as cod. In U.S.A. it is served with a cream sauce.

CUSTARD. A composition of milk and eggs mainly sweetened and flavoured, parboiled or baked. All custards must be cooked slowly well below boiling point to ensure smooth texture. Too great a heat will cause the albumen to harden and shrink and it may curdle.

CUSTARD, BAKED

Ingredients

Plain. 2 eggs

Method

Beat the eggs with sugar, add milk and flavouring. Pour into greased pie-dish and

CUSTARD, BAKED (*continued*)
　　　　1 oz. sugar
　　　　1 pt. milk

Rich. 3 eggs or 2 whole and
　　　　1 yolk
　　　　1 oz. sugar
　　　　1 pt. milk
　　　　Grated nutmeg or
　　　　vanilla flavouring

CUSTARD, BOILED
Ingredients
Plain. 1 egg
　　　　½ pt. milk
　　　　½ oz. sugar

Rich. 1 egg and 1 yolk
　　　　½ pt. milk
　　　　½ oz. sugar

CUSTARD, STEAMED
Ingredients
Plain. 2 eggs
　　　　½ oz. sugar
　　　　½ pt. milk

Rich. 3 egg yolks
　　　　½ oz. sugar
　　　　½ pt. milk

Caramel Custard
FOR CARAMEL:
Ingredients
　　10 lumps sugar
　　2 tbsp. water

FOR CUSTARD:
Ingredients
　　½ pt. milk
　　2 whole eggs
　　2 yolks
　　1 oz. caster sugar
　　Vanilla essence

Custard Sauces. See SAUCES.

bake at 250° F. Therm. ½ for 45 mins. If the dish is put into a tin half-filled with water this will ensure cooking slowly.

Method
Beat the egg(s) with a little of the milk. Pour remaining milk into the pan and heat. Then pour it gently on to the eggs and stir well. Rinse pan and pour in the mixture. Return to a gentle heat and stir till the mixture thickens and coats the back of the spoon. Add sugar.

Method
Beat the eggs and sugar together. Add milk. Pour into a well-buttered mould or basin. Cover with greaseproof paper. Stand the mould on a wooden rack or folded dishcloth in a saucepan. Add sufficient water to cover about halfway up the mould. Place over a low heat and simmer the water only. Steam 30–40 mins. Stand for a few minutes before turning out. If individual custards are made, steam 15–20 mins.

Method
Boil together until dark golden brown. Shake but do not stir. Pour into a suitable cake tin or individual dariole mould and move the tin gently until the bottom and sides are evenly coated. Leave to set.

Method
Mix the custard as basic recipes above. Pour into prepared tin and steam as above (large mould 30–40 mins., individual ones 15–20 mins.).

CUSTARD APPLE (Fr. *pomme cannelle*). A native of the West Indies, the inner pulp is yellow and the consistency of custard. In outward appearance, it is netted all over and dark brown in colouring.

CUSTARD MARROW. A variety of vegetable marrow.

CUTLETS (Fr. *côtelettes*). Chops are cut from the best end of mutton, lamb, veal or pork. These are literally small ribs, being a corruption of the French word *côtelettes*. The term is often applied by cooks to slices of meat, especially of lamb, mutton or veal, which are neatly trimmed or otherwise tastily prepared for cooking.

CYGNETS. Young swans, deriving their name from the French *cygne*, a swan. When quite young the flesh is very tasty and tender. Swans are, of course, protected birds.

CYMLINGS. A variety of the genus *Cucurbita*, the family to which belong also all other varieties of pumpkins, melons. In America popularly called "squashes".

D

DAB (Fr. *limande*). This small dark-brown flat-fish is a species of flounder, called "dab" because of the rapidity with which it dabs or dives under the sand. It is commonly caught along the shores of the English Channel and in the tidal stretches of rivers, and is good fried or cooked as flounders. The American dab is called Sand or Rusty dab.

DABCHICK. A species of small water fowl, so called on account of its dexterity in diving. It is known variously in different parts of the country as Dabchick, Dopchick, Dipchick, Dobben, Devil-diver, Hell-diver and Pied-billed Grebe. The flesh is tasty, but unless the bird is young, it is apt to be hard and stringy when cooked.

DACE (Fr. *vandoise*). This pretty little silvery river fish, sometimes called Dar or Dart, is common in almost all rivers. It is in season the whole year except in March and April, and is sometimes dipped in batter and fried. The American dace is somewhat different, and is known as Black-nosed or Striped dace.

DACE, STEWED. Scale the dace, cut off their gills and wash them well in plenty of water; dry on a cloth, flour them and fry lightly in boiling butter. Put ½ pt. claret in a stewpan with a small quantity of sliced ginger, ½ blade of mace, two or three cloves, ½ saltspoon of grated nutmeg, a little salt and one sliced orange. When this boils place the fish in the stewpan, put on the lid and set it over a quick fire. The fish should be turned occasionally while stewing. When cooked, place the fish on a hot dish, put a lump of butter into the liquor in which the fish was cooked, stir till dissolved and then pour over the fish. Sprinkle over grated breadcrumbs fried in butter, and serve with slices of orange or lemon.

DAMSON (Fr. *prune de damas*). The fruit of the *prunus domesticus*, a small oval plum of a blue colour, known as the Damask plum. It is not a suitable dessert fruit and should be cooked or preserved with sugar or syrup.

Damson Cheese

Ingredients

    5 lb. damsons
    Sugar

Method

Wash damsons and place in large bowl; cover with paper and stand in slow oven (250° F. Therm. ½) until fruit is soft and juice running. Pass through a sieve. Measure pulp and allow ¾ lb. sugar to each pound of pulp. Return pulp to preserving pan, add sugar and boil till jam thickens. Break damson stones, remove kernels and add to jam if desired. Pour into warmed jars and cover.

Damson Jam

Ingredients

    5 lb. damsons
    5 lb. sugar

Method

Wash the damsons, cut in half and remove stones. Place in preserving pan with water to cover, and simmer till fruit is soft. Add sugar, previously warmed, and boil until jam thickens and sets. Pour into warmed jars and cover when cool.

[190]

Damson Jelly

Ingredients

8 lb. damsons

Sugar

Method

Wash damsons well, place in preserving pan with water to cover and simmer for 30 mins. Strain through muslin and measure juice. Allow 1lb. sugar to 1 pint. Add sugar to juice and boil for 15 mins. Pour into warmed jars and cover when cold.

Damson Sauce. See SAUCES.

DANDELION (Fr. *dent de lion* or *pissenlit*). "Lion's tooth" is the popular name for this plant on account of its deeply notched leaves. The roots are used for medicinal purposes, for making dandelion tea and are sometimes roasted and ground and used as a coffee substitute. The young leaves are best for making salads as they are sweeter than those that have been exposed or matured.

DANISH BLUE CHEESE. A name given in England to the Danish imitation of Roquefort.

DARIOLE. A small entrée paté composed of a compound of forcemeat, or mince, baked or steamed in a small mould.

DATE (Fr. *datte*). The fruit of the date palm. There are three varieties, the soft and juicy, the hard, and the fibrous (which do not keep well). The best dates come from Tunis. The so-called date-wine which is made in North Africa of dates and water has a certain analogy with madeira. Dates pitted are sometimes used alone or with other fruit in cakes or suet puddings.

DATES FOR DESSERT. Ornament a fancy dessert dish with lace-edged paper and cut some pieces of green angelica in shapes like leaves. Build some dates on the paper in conical form, sticking the pieces of green angelica among them.

Date and Banana Preserve

Ingredients

1 lb. dates

4 bananas

1 lb. sugar

Method

Stone dates and slice them lengthways. Peel bananas and slice them very thinly. Place both in preserving pan, add sugar simmer gently for 20 mins., stirring frequently. Boil till jam thickens, skim, and pour into warmed jars. Cover when cool.

Date and Walnut Loaf. See CAKES.

Date Jam

Ingredients

5 lb. stoned dates

3 pt. water

2 lb. sugar

Method

Place fruit and water in preserving pan and cook until fruit is tender. Add sugar and boil for 5 mins., stirring frequently. Pour into heated jars and cover. If desired, chopped blanched walnuts (up to 1 lb.) may be added after boiling.

DATE-PLUM. This fruit is common in China and known there as Kaki. It is about the size of a small apple, of a reddish colour and with a very luscious tawny, semi-transparent juicy pulp. It is usually dried with sugar like plums. See also **PERSIMMON.**

DEER. See VENISON.

DEHYDRATED. Deprived or freed of water. This method of preservation is applied to eggs, milk, herbs, vegetables and some fruits.

TO USE DEHYDRATED EGGS AND MILK. Always sift dehydrated eggs or milk before adding any liquid; use given proportions and mix as directions.

If, when you mix the *milk*, you find it is a little gritty because it has not been very well blended, it is quite simple to pour it through a strainer before use. Always moisten your pan by rinsing it round with cold water before pouring in the milk, and when using the milk in a sauce, stir the liquid occasionally while it is boiling up and the mixture thickens so that the sides of the pan do not catch and spoil the sauce by a slightly burnt flavour.

To reconstitute one *egg* allow 1 level tbsp. egg powder, pinch of baking powder and 2 level tbsp. water. Blend the egg and water together, beat well and allow the powder to absorb the moisture. Use a wooden spoon to mix and then a fork to whisk to lighten the mixture. Use immediately after mixing. Remember that the eggs alone will not raise a cake; it is wise to add ½ tsp. baking powder for each egg.

When using the egg in cakes and batters it may be mixed dry with the other ingredients, but remember to allow an additional 2 tbsp. water for each dried egg used, when adding the liquid. Keep the egg powder in a cool, dry place and store it in a jar or tin with a tightly fitting lid. Dried egg may be used as a substitute for shell eggs in any of the recipes in this book except those in which egg white is specially mentioned.

DEMI-GLACE. Half-glaze. See SAUCES.

DEMI-SEL. A soft, whole milk cheese made in many parts of France and Normandy.

DEMOISELLES DE CAEN, or **DEMOISELLES DE CHERBOURG.** The French culinary term for very small lobsters.

DENTEX. A marine fish of the perch tribe commonly caught off the shores of Italy. The flesh when cooked is beautifully white, firm and savoury. It may be boiled in court bouillon with or without wine, or it may be cooked *au gratin* or grilled if preferred, accompanied by Shrimp sauce.

DEVILLED. See COOKING TERMS.

DEWBERRY. The creeping blackberry or bramble as opposed to the bush blackberry.

DEXTROSE. Grape sugar.

DIGBY CHICK. A kind of pilchard or small herring called by the fishermen who catch them Nova Scotia Sprats. They are named after Digby, a seaport in Nova Scotia.

DIGESTER. An iron cooking-pot, the lid of which fits so tightly that steam can only escape through a valve at the top.

DILL. A hardy biennial plant, possessing powerful flavouring properties. The leaf of this herb is used in cream cheese to give added flavour, also in fish sauce, potato salad, cream sauces, tomato soup. The seed is used in pickles, vinegar, and pastry.

DIP. A Yorkshire term for sauce or gravy served at table with a spoon.

DIPPER. A sort of ladle used for baling out liquor from the stock-pot, made in various sizes.

DOGFISH. This name is given to several species of the smaller sharks.

DORSE, DORSCH. Common names for a variety of cod found in the Baltic. Dorse are cooked like cod.

DOTTEREL. European bird of the plover family. It is in season in October, November and December and cooked like ordinary plover.

DOUBLE CREAM. See CREAM.

DOUBLE CRÊME. A soft cream cheese made in many parts of France when cream is plentiful during the summer months.

DOUBLE GLOUCESTER (GLOSTER) CHEESE. A hard whole-milk cheese made in Gloucestershire.

DOUGHNUTS

Ingredients

1 lb. flour
1½ tsp. baking powder
4 oz. sugar
¼ tsp. salt
½ tsp. grated nutmeg
½ egg
1 tbsp. melted butter or shortening
½ pt. milk
¼ tsp. vanilla extract

Method

Sift dry ingredients together; beat egg, add to milk, melted shortening and vanilla. Pour these into the dry mixture and work to a light dough. Roll out ½″ thick on a floured board. Cut with doughnut cutter and drop gently into hot fat (350° F.). As soon as the doughnuts rise to the top, turn them over with a fork. Cook about 3 mins. and drain. Dust with sugar if desired.

Doughnuts, American. These differ from the English doughnuts in that they always have a small hole in the centre, and they are frequently raised with baking powder or bicarbonate of soda and cream of tartar, but sometimes yeast is used to raise them.

Ingredients

¾ lb. flour
1½ oz. butter
2 oz. caster sugar
1 level tsp. each cream of tartar and bicarb. soda
½ tsp. salt
¼ tsp. each ground cinnamon and grated nutmeg
1 egg
About ½ gill milk (sour)

Method

Sift the flour, salt, spices, bicarb. soda, and cream of tartar together. Beat in egg, butter and sufficient milk to make a soft dough. Turn on to a floured board and roll out to ¼″ thickness. Stamp out into rounds about 2″ in diameter, using a small round cutter; remove the centres of each. Fry in deep fat which is just beginning to smoke. The doughnuts will sink to the bottom of the fat when they are first put into it, but they will soon rise. When they are brown on one side, turn them to the other. See the fat is sufficiently hot to cook them, otherwise it will be absorbed by the doughnuts. Should the fat be too hot the doughnuts will brown before they have risen. Drain and allow to cool, then roll in caster sugar.

DOVES. Among the doves, the Wood Pigeon or Ring Dove can be used in the kitchen, broiled or in soups.

DOWITCHER. The name for the Red-breasted Snipe; also called Red-breasted Sandpiper. See **SNIPE.**

DRAWN BUTTER. See **BUTTERS.**

DRESS. See **COOKING TERMS.**

DRIPPING. 100% fat which drips from roasting meat; as it takes other flavours and can absorb other matter it is necessary to clarify it.

TO CLARIFY. Put some dripping into a saucepan, boil it over a slow fire for a few minutes, then skim well and leave to cool a little. Put a small quantity of cold

TO CLARIFY (*continued*)

water into a jar, tie a piece of fine muslin over it and strain the dripping through this into the jar. When cold and set, remove fat from water and put into another jar.

Dripping Cake. See CAKES.

DRUPE. Fleshy fruit containing a stone with a kernel, e.g. plum, cherry, peach.

DRYING. This method of preservation depends on warmth evaporating the water from certain foods into vapour. See HERBS, FRUIT.

DUCK (Fr. *canard*). There are many kinds of duck, most of them edible, requiring such a variety of culinary treatment that it is best to discuss them under their own headings and confine this entry to domestic duck and duckling. Aylesbury ducks, which weigh as much as 7 lb. or more, are the best for cooking. Ducks are in season all the year round, ducklings beginning as early in the year as it is possible to get them large enough to make a dish, and assuming more maturity by the middle of the year. It is generally thought that a duck more than 12 months old is too tough to make a good roast. Young birds can be chosen by the yellow colour of their feet and bills which snap easily and are free from hair. The feet should be pliable. If the feet are cut off and the beak singed, the duck may be an old one. Ducks are plucked and drawn like chicken (see CHICKEN), and trussed with the wings turned under and the legs fastened to the sides by skewers. For CARVING, see under this heading.

Duck, Roast

Ingredients	*Method*
A duck	Stuff the duck with the forcemeat and truss it nicely. Roast it at 325° F. Therm. 4 for ¾–1 hr. Make the gravy by simmering the giblets in the water with the beef, the onion and apple sliced, and pepper and salt for 3 hrs. Strain and thicken with the flour. Colour if necessary, and if liked, add a glass of port wine. Pour a little gravy round the duck and serve remainder in a boat. Hand Apple or Tomato sauce. Serve with potatoes and green peas.
Sage and onion stuffing	
1 oz. flour	
1 onion	
1 apple	
¼ lb. gravy beef	
Rather more than 1 pt. water	

Duck, Stewed. Melt 1 oz. margarine in a pan and add a sliced onion. Dredge in slowly 1 oz. flour, stir all together and cook for 3 mins. Then add 1 pt. vegetable stock, 2 cloves and a small onion and bring to the boil. Add the duck and simmer very gently for about 30–35 mins. Add pepper and salt to season, a bouquet garni and 6 young turnips and simmer together for 30 mins. more. Serve the duck with the turnip round it and garnish with watercress.

DUCKLING. Cooked and served like duck, but without any stuffing.
Duckling à la Presse. Take a roast duckling and carve (see CARVING) into neat slices. Keep these hot. Chop up the carcass and put it into a press to extract all the juices. Add to these a glass each of red wine and brandy, together with the finely minced liver. Pour this liquor over the fillets and serve very hot, but do not boil.

DULSE. A seaweed of a reddish-brown colour which in some parts of Scotland is a savoury food. Pepper dulse is a very aromatic variety.

DUMPLING (Fr. *quenelle*). In culinary parlance this term may be considered to be strictly British and a diminutive of "dump", a thick, ill-shapen piece. The Germans under the name of *klösse* surpass our efforts in variety. Dumplings are very satisfying.

Dumplings for Broth. Sift 1 tsp. baking powder with ½ lb. flour, add a pinch of salt and mix to a smooth dough with water. Drop small quantities of this from a spoon into the broth, where they should float, and put on the lid. When they are three parts done remove the lid and put the saucepan in the oven to brown the tops of the dumplings, basting them once with the liquor.

Dumplings for Stew. Dissolve 1 tsp. cream of tartar and ½ tsp. each bicarb. soda and salt in a teacup of milk and mix in 1 lb. flour, adding as much more milk as will be required to make the dough soft enough to be easily handled. Divide the dough into small pieces, round them with the hands and drop them into the boiling stew; the dumplings require cooking for 10 mins. The dough may be made quite soft to drop from a spoon.

Dumplings, Norfolk. Divide about 1 lb. light bread dough into small pieces. Mould these with the hands into balls and drop them into a saucepan of boiling water; boil quickly for ¼ hr. without taking the lid off the pan. Take them out, drain, put them on a hot dish and serve hot with wine sauce, sweetened butter sauce or butter.

DUMPODE. Probably a corruption of the Persian words *dam purht*, signifying slowly cooked or stewed.

DUNDEE CAKE. See CAKES.

DUNELM. A dish of braised mutton or veal originating in Durham, of which Dunelm is the abbreviated Latin name.

DUNKING BOWL. A scooped-out cabbage heart filled with cheese fondue, into which potato crisps are dipped. In America, bowls of coffee or other beverage into which doughnuts are dipped.

DUNLOP CHEESE. A Scottish whole-milk cheese of flat shape. The taste is not unlike cheddar but more moist and of a closer texture. It was originally made at Dunlop in Ayrshire.

DUTCH CHEESE. See EDAM.

DUTCH OVEN. A roasting or toasting utensil provided with hooks to be attached to the bars of a grate.

DUTCH SAUCE. See SAUCES (Hollandaise).

E

EARS. To all culinary intents and purposes the ears of any animal would appear to offer little temptation. As a matter of fact they are neither digestible nor nutritious, but with careful cooking they can become soft and can be made into an appetising dish. See under individual headings.

EASTER EGGS. Painted or coloured eggs given at Eastertide. To colour eggs, wash them well and put into a saucepan of water with a little carmine or cochineal; boil for 10 mins. When done leave in the coloured fluid for 5 mins. longer, then take them out, wipe dry and rub them over with an oiled cloth. Other colours may be used such as spinach for green, saffron for yellow, or, by tying the eggs up in outside skins of onions, a very pretty maize may be obtained. To write a name or make a design on an egg, use a piece of candle as a pencil, before boiling.

ÉCLAIR. A French pastry filled with cream; to make éclairs, see **PASTE AND PASTRY** (p. 377).

EDAM. A Dutch cheese, ball-shaped, with a red outside and yellow or orange inside. It is unmilled, but pressed into moulds.

EDAMEC. The Yugoslavian imitation of the Edam cheese.

EEL (Fr. *anguille*). There is no other kind of fish found as universally as the eel. It is found in all countries and all climates, and seems to be equally at home in the sea, river or pond; when in need of food it will wander about the fields by night in search of snails or other prey.

TO PREPARE. Eels must be killed by piercing the backbone with a sharp-pointed skewer where the neck joins the head, or it may be killed by knocking its head hard on a wooden block or stone. The next step is to skin it, which is generally accomplished by putting a cloth over its head and holding it in one hand whilst with the other you cut round the neck and turn the skin down an inch or so. By holding the head in one hand and the skin in the other and pulling steadily, the skin strips off. Chop off the head and tail of the skinned eel, open the throat with the point of a knife and make an incision at the navel, then with the assistance of a larding needle push the gut from the small hole in the navel through the opening at the throat; wash and dry eel before cooking.

Eel Broth

Ingredients

1 lb. eels
Sprigs of parsley
1 onion
1 carrot
8 peppercorns
2 cloves
1 bay leaf
Salt
Pepper
Chopped chives
Chopped parsley

Method

Have the eels skinned and cleaned and cut into even-sized 2″ pieces. Put the water into a deep pan, add all the ingredients, cover and bring to boiling point. Reduce heat, and simmer gently for about 1½ hr., reducing liquid by half. Remove scum as it rises, and strain through hair sieve or muslin. Leave overnight to cool and remove fat from top. Reheat with croûtons and garnish with chopped chives and parsley.

[196]

Eel Pie

Ingredients
6 oz. flaky pastry
1 eel
1 gill milk and water
Salt and pepper

Method
Cut the skinned eel into small lengths, season with pepper and salt and place in a greased pie-dish. Cover with a little milk and a pastry crust. Bake at 350° F. Therm. 4 until well browned, about 45 mins.

Eel with Sage

Ingredients
2 lb. thick eel
6 tbsp. olive oil
Pinch of paprika
8 sage leaves
Salt and pepper
Watercress or parsley

Method
Have the eels skinned and cleaned and cut into 4″ pieces. With a damp cloth wipe all over. Blend oil, paprika and sage leaves. Dip eels in; add salt and pepper to season. Grill under hot grill 10 mins. on each side. Serve piping hot, garnished with parsley or watercress.

EELPOUT (Fr. *barbotte*). This remarkable fish has something of the character of an eel. The flesh is hard and coarse and it is not a favourite of the cook. It may be better known as the Burbot, Greenbone, Guffer, Bard, Maroona, Eel-lote, etc. Eelpout can be boiled, stewed, used in pies or soups.

EGGS (Fr. *oeufs*). Though this term is applied to the unhatched young of all kinds of life whether birds, fish, reptiles or insects, and especially turtles, in cookery the eggs of birds are principally used, and reference is here made exclusively to their eggs in general use, whether fowl's, duck's, turkey's or, more rarely, those of geese. Special eggs or those requiring special treatment, such as guinea fowl's, plover's, etc., are treated under separate headings. Eggs are considered a valuable food and are of great importance in the diet. For guidance, the weight of eggs is as follows:

Eggs	Approximate Weights	Dehydrated Weight
6–8 whole eggs	1 lb.	$\frac{1}{6}$ lb.
12 egg whites	,,	,,
6 egg yolks	$5\frac{1}{2}$ oz.	,,

TO TEST FOR FRESHNESS. Eggs must be fresh when used (unless preserved).
1. The shells are generally slightly rough.
2. When held towards the light they should be semi-transparent with no black specks appearing.
3. Put the egg into a solution of 1 oz. salt and 1 pt. water.
　　(a) If the egg sinks to the bottom it is quite fresh.
　　(b) If it is suspended it is not so fresh.
　　(c) If it floats it is stale.
Egg albumen can be mixed with cold liquids, but when heat is applied it begins to coagulate.
　　TO BREAK. Hold the egg in the left hand and tap it gently with a knife to crack shell. Then put the thumbs into the crack, pull shell apart and slip the egg on to a saucer. Always break eggs one at a time to ensure that no mix is spoilt, then slip into a basin or pan as required.
　　TO SEPARATE. Crack the egg; hold one half of the shell firmly in each hand, tip the yolk gently from one to the other, letting the white run out between the two halves of the shell into the basin below.

TO WHISK EGG WHITE. Whisking incorporates air into the white of egg; the greater the amount of air trapped and the cooler the temperature, the greater the expansion when heated. By adding a tiny pinch of salt the temperature is lowered. Whisk the egg in a cool place using a deep bowl if whisking with a rotary beater, or a wide bowl if using a wire egg whisk. When using only one or two egg whites, beat with a table fork or knife on a flat plate. Always begin to beat slowly, gathering speed gradually; this helps to keep the mixture cold. Continue to whisk until the white of egg is stiff. Use a metal spoon to fold into a mixture to avoid expelling air. Cook immediately to coagulate the egg and so prevent the air from escaping. Eggs whip best when they are twenty-four hours old or over.

EGGS, TO BOIL. Eggs are best left at room temperature for a short time before boiling. (If cooked immediately on removal from a refrigerator their shells are apt to crack.) When heat is applied the egg becomes firm and opaque, the longer it is cooked and the greater the heat, the tougher the egg. Always lower the egg carefully into the saucepan to prevent it cracking: a little vinegar added to the water also helps to prevent this.

TO SOFT-BOIL. *Method I.* Place in sufficient cold water to cover the egg so that it can cook evenly; bring slowly to the boil and remove immediately the water boils. *Method II.* Put into boiling water, boil for 3 mins., or to taste.

TO HARD-BOIL. Put the eggs into boiling water, cook for 10 mins. If cold water is used, the yolks are apt to be on one side when cooked.

EGGS, TO CODDLE. Boil the water and place the eggs in the pan (or, if preferred, break into cup and place in saucepan), cover the pan and reduce heat so that the water does not boil.

For soft-cooked eggs leave 4 mins.
 „   medium „   „   6–7 „
 „   hard   „   „   15–20 „

EGGS, TO PICKLE. See PICKLE.

EGGS, TO POACH. Half fill a frying-pan with water, bring to the boil. Add two drops of lemon juice or vinegar. Break the egg into a saucer, then lower carefully into the water, using a spoon draw the white carefully together; baste the top with water. Cook gently for 2–3 mins. or until the white becomes opaque and the egg sets. Lift out with a fish slice, drain and serve on hot buttered toast. If desired, eggs may be poached in either gravy or sauce in the same way.

EGGS, TO PRESERVE.

WATERGLASS. The prepared solution is bought at the chemist or grocer. It should be mixed in the proportions as stated on the packet, and poured over the eggs in a bucket or large crock. A cloth should be put over the top to keep out the dust and help to prevent evaporation. The eggs should be new laid so that the pores will be sealed and the bacteria and air will not pass through the shells.

WAX AND OILS. This wax is a commercial preparation which is rubbed over the shell of the eggs. The eggs are then stored in boxes. Some country folk have been known to preserve eggs by rubbing them or dipping them in melted butter or coating them with boracic ointment. There is also a liquid preparation into which the eggs are dipped so that they become evenly coated in a few seconds and can then be stored without difficulty.

EGGS, TO SCRAMBLE. To each fresh egg allow ½ oz. butter or margarine, 1 tbsp. cream or milk, ¼ tsp. salt and pinch of pepper, a round of hot buttered toast and watercress or parsley to garnish. *For variation*, add one or more of the following: a small blanched sliced tomato, 1 tsp. chopped parsley, ¼ tsp. mixed herbs, 1 dsp. finely minced ham, bacon, or grated cheese. Beat the eggs; add seasonings. Put the fat into the saucepan and add milk. When this is heated, add egg and stir lightly over a *gentle* heat. Remove from the heat as soon as the egg begins to set. Serve on hot toast and garnish.

Egg and Bacon Pie. Line a shallow dish with pastry; beat up 2 or 3 eggs, add pepper and salt to season and 1 teacup milk. Then add ¼ lb. minced fat boiled

Egg and Bacon Pie (*continued*)

bacon or diced rashers, pour gently into the pie-dish, cover with pastry and pinch the edges. Bake at 350° F. Therm. 4 for about 30 mins. If cooked in a hot oven the pastry cooks before the custard sets. Do not make a hole in top of pastry or the filling will run out when the mixture boils. Blanched, sliced tomatoes or parcooked thinly sliced onion may be added if desired.

Eggs, Baked

Ingredients

¼ lb. minced ham or corned beef
½ pt. white sauce
4 eggs
Breadcrumbs
Small nut butter

Method

Mix the ham or corned beef with sauce, turn into greased baking dish. Break the eggs separately and place on top. Cover with breadcrumbs and dot with butter. Bake at 400° F. Therm. 6 for 15–20 mins. (The whites of the eggs should be cooked but the yolks soft.) Serve garnished with finely chopped parsley. Eggs may similarly be baked in nests of spaghetti, rice, cheese, potato, etc.

Eggs, Breakfast. Grease an individual dish with butter, add a pinch of herb mixture, break the egg into the dish and stir carefully (to distribute the herbs). Place the dish in a pan over a low heat with hot water 3 parts of the way up side of it, and leave to set.

Eggs, Buttered

Ingredients

4 eggs
Pepper and salt
2 oz. butter

Method

Beat the eggs well and season with pepper and salt. Melt the butter in a sauté- or stew-pan and pour in the eggs, stirring the mixture quickly until it is a soft yellow mass; take care it does not get hard. Spread quickly on hot buttered toast, and serve at once. Well-cooked green peas, asparagus, mushrooms or ripe tomatoes diced may be mixed with the buttered eggs, if liked. A more savoury dish is made by spreading anchovy paste on the toast before putting on the eggs.

Egg Nog. An invalid's drink made with 1 egg beaten in 1 pt. milk; sometimes whisky, brandy or sherry are added.

Egg Omelet. See OMELET.

Egg Salad

Ingredients

6 hard-boiled eggs
7 small sweet gherkins
1 small tin pimentoes or sliced tomatoes
Salt
Paprika and red pepper
½ lb. grated cheese

Method

Chop all the ingredients rather fine, season, add grated cheese and mix. Mould with hands quickly and let set overnight. Cut 1½″ thick and serve on lettuce with asparagus tips, mayonnaise and French dressing.

Egg Sauce. See SAUCES.

Egg Soufflé. See SOUFFLÉ.

Eggs, Stuffed

Ingredients

2 hard-boiled eggs
1 oz. butter
1 tsp. chopped parsley or other flavouring
Pepper and salt

Method

Halve the egg either with a straight or crinkly cut. Cut off a small piece of the bottom so that the egg will stand easily. Have ready small rounds of buttered toast. Put the yolks into a basin and pound with seasoning or flavouring. Fill the halves with the mixture, decorate and serve.

FLAVOURINGS

Anchovy	1½–2 anchovies, pinch of cayenne pepper, ½ tsp. anchovy essence
Cheese	½ oz. grated cheese, pinch of mustard
Chutney	1 dsp. each chutney and parsley, squeeze of lemon juice
Curry	1 dsp. curry paste; decorate with chopped capers
Sardine	1 tsp. sardine (mashed), 2 drops lemon juice or vinegar, pinch of cayenne; garnish with cress or watercress
Shrimp	1 tbsp. diced shrimp; garnish with cress

EGG-PLANT. See AUBERGINE.

EGG PLUM. Also known as *magnum bonum*. There are two kinds, one red, the other white and yellow. The flesh of the fruit is firm and though not juicy is of good flavour.

ELDER. This very common tree may be found growing wild in almost all parts of Europe, the flowers being used in various medicinal preparations. They afford a pleasing aroma and flavour to wines and liqueurs and the juice of the elderberry, either plain or fermented, is much used for doctoring wines. When elder flowers are dried they are sometimes added to tea to make a mock China tea. The elder flowers are also used with any sweet herb for vinegar. For culinary purposes the berries which grow in large spreading clusters are most used, although the shoots of the tree are sometimes pickled. See **ENGLISH BAMBOO.**

Elderberry Jam

Ingredients

4 lb. elderberries
4 lb. sugar
Juice of 3 lemons
Grated lemon rind

Method

Pick over elderberries carefully, removing all stalks. Place in preserving pan and bring to boil, stirring frequently and bruising a little. Add a third of the sugar and boil until the berries are soft. Pass through sieve, but do not allow any seeds to get through. Return pulp to preserving pan, add lemon juice, a little grated lemon rind and the remaining sugar and allow to boil for 30 mins., stirring and skimming all the time. Test for setting, then pour into warmed jars and cover when cold.

[200]

Elderberry Jelly

Ingredients

1 qt. elderberries
2 pt. water
1 qt. crab apples
Sugar

Method

Pick over elderberries, removing stalks. Place in pan with 1 pt. water and simmer till fruit is soft. Strain through muslin and set aside juice. Quarter the crab apples, but do not peel. Place in pan with 1 pt. water and simmer till soft. Strain off juice, add this to elderberry juice and measure. Allow 1 lb. sugar to every 1 pt. juice. Bring juice to boil, add sugar and boil for 10–15 mins. Test for setting; pour into heated jars and cover when cold.

Elderberry Ketchup

Ingredients

1 qt. ripe elderberries
Vinegar
Few shallots
Blade of mace
Few cloves and peppercorns
½ lb. sugar

Method

Place the berries in a stone jar, cover with vinegar and bake at 200° F. Therm. ¼ for about 3 hrs. Strain off liquor, add the shallots, mace, peppercorns, sugar and cloves. Simmer together over a low heat for about 1 hr. until thickened; strain and cork securely.

Elderberry Wine. Put 3 gall. elderberries into a vessel with 3½ gall. water, 2 oz. allspice, 1 oz. ginger and a few cloves. Boil for ½ hr. Press the berries through a sieve and add 3½ lb. moist sugar for each gallon. Boil together till the liquor becomes clear, removing any scum as it rises. Pour the liquor into a small cask and leave it until lukewarm, then put in a small piece of toast thickly spread with yeast. When fermentation ceases bung the cask tightly down. In three months' time the wine will be fit for drinking. If fermentation does not commence the day following that on which the wine is poured into the cask, take a little of the wine out, boil it and pour it back again. If that does not have the desired effect, put in a piece more toast spread with yeast.

ELECAMPANE. House leek. The root is used for candy and puddings, also for flavouring absinthe, vermouth and herbal tobacco.

ELVERS. Young European eels, which reach English shores in late spring after a year's journeying.

EMMENTHAL. A Swiss cheese, of the Gruyère type. A similar cheese to Emmenthal is made in France and Italy and Emmenthalia is the Yugoslavian imitation.

EMULSION. A combination of oil and water. Unconsciously the cook frequently prepares emulsion, e.g. salad dressing.

ENDIVE (Fr. *chicoree*). Some continental cooks use very large quantities of this plant in their salads to give lettuce and other things with which it may be mixed a pungency of flavour that is exceedingly palatable. There are three kinds, the Broad-leaved or Batavian (known in France as *escarole*), the Curly-leaved, and the Wild. Endive is sometimes cooked and served with poultry as a vegetable.
Endive Salad. Pare off the green leaves from two heads of white endive and cut away the roots. Wash thoroughly and drain well on a napkin. Place them in a salad bowl. Season with salt and pepper. Dress with 2 tbsp. vinegar and 1½ tbsp. sweet oil mixed well together.
Endive Salad au Chapon. Prepare as above, but add a garlic flavouring.

Endive, Stewed (French Style). Clean and pick over 6 heads of endive, and blanch them by first putting them into hot water and then into cold. Chop finely and put into a stewpan with sufficient broth to cover; stew till the endive is tender and the broth all boiled away, leaving the vegetable quite dry. Then add 4 oz. butter, a little grated nutmeg and salt and pepper to taste. Mix well and send quite hot to the table.

ENGLISH BAMBOO. The name given to a pickle which is made from the young shoots of the elder tree which are salted and dried, and a pickle vinegar poured over them.

ENTRÉES. Served as a course between fish and main meat course at very formal dinners or as the main course at informal luncheons, dinners and suppers.

Entrées may be either hot or cold, light or heavy. (See under individual headings for recipes.) Fish may only be served during Lent. Sauces are very important to entrées.

Light entrées. Bouchées, vol-au-vents, cassolettes, croustades, cannelons, crepinettes, scallops, croquettes or sweetbreads.

Heavier entrées. Made-up dishes of poultry or game, cutlet fillets, tournedos, small steaks.

Cold entrées are usually elaborately decorated and garnished.

ENTREMETS. Dishes of vegetables served as an accompaniment to a main dish: side dishes.

EQUIVALENTS. When no scales are available, it is usual to measure quantities by equivalents. Thus, in liquid measure, ½ pt. may roughly be described as a breakfast-cupful; a gill is a teacupful. A similar scale is used with dry measures.

Table of Weights and Approximate Equivalents in Measure

Food	Weight	Equivalent Measure
Almonds: blanched	1 lb.	4 cups
in shell	1 lb.	2 cups
Apples: sliced	1 lb.	2½–3 cups
„	½ lb.	1 pt.
diced	1 lb.	4½ cups
sauce	1 lb.	2 cups
Apricots: dried	1 lb.	3 cups
steeped, cooked and no juice	1 lb.	5 cups
fresh	1 lb.	8 apricots
canned, halved without syrup	1 lb.	2 cups (20 halves)
Asparagus: fresh	1 lb.	20 stalks
canned tips	1 lb.	About 19 stalks
Aubergine: drained	1 lb.	4 slices 1″ × 1½″
Avocado	1 lb.	2 medium sized
Bacon: raw	1 lb.	According to cut— 15–20 slices
cooked	1 lb.	85–95 slices
Baking powder	1 oz.	2½ tbsp.

Table of Weights and Approximate Equivalents in Measure (*continued*)

FOOD	WEIGHT	EQUIVALENT MEASURE
Bananas: whole	1 lb.	3 medium sized
sliced	1 lb.	2½ cups
Barley flour	1 lb.	4 cups
Barley, Pearl	1 lb.	2 cups
Beans: baked	1 lb.	1 pt.
dried	1 lb.	2⅓ cups
Kidney beans	1 lb.	2⅔ cups
„ „ (after cooking)	1 lb.	7 cups
Runner beans (cut and cooked without liquid)	1 lb.	3½ cups
Beef: minced	1 lb.	2 cups
Beetroot: whole	1 lb.	2–3 medium sized
cooked and diced	1 lb.	2¼ cups
cooked and sliced	¾ lb.	1 pt.
Blackberries	1½ lb.	1 pt.
Bread:	2 lb. loaf	24 ½″ slices
sandwich loaf		36–38 ¼″ slices
Breadcrumbs: dried	6 oz.	2 cups
soft	4 oz.	2 cups
Brussels sprouts	1 lb.	1 qt.
Butter	½ lb.	1 cup
Cabbage: cooked	½ lb.	1¼ cups
shredded	6 oz.	1 pt.
Carrots: whole	1 lb.	About 6 small carrots
raw, grated	1 lb.	3½ cups
diced and cooked	1 lb.	3 cups
Cake crumbs	5 oz.	1 pt.
Cheese: cream	1 lb.	2¼ cups
grated	½ lb.	1 pt.
cubed	8½ oz.	1 pt.
Cherries: glacé	1 lb.	About 95 cherries
Chocolate: grated	½ lb.	2 very full cups
melted	½ lb.	Scant cupful
Citron: dried and chopped	3 oz.	About 1 cup
Cloves: whole	3 oz.	About 1 cup
Cocoa	½ lb.	1¼ cups

Table of Weights and Approximate Equivalents in Measure (*continued*)

Food	Weight	Equivalent Measure
Coconut: desiccated	½ lb.	About 3½ cups
Coffee: coarsely ground	½ lb.	2½ very full cups
Corn: canned	1 lb.	About 1¾ cups
Cornflakes	1 lb.	4 qt.
Cornflour	1 lb.	3½ cups
Crabmeat: flaked	1 lb.	6 cups
Cranberries: raw cooked sauce	1 lb. 1 lb. ½ lb.	4 cups 1 qt. 1 cup
Cream of Tartar	1 oz.	3 tbsp.
Cucumber: whole diced	10 oz. ½ lb.	1 about 9″ long About 1½ cups
Currants	1 lb.	3 cups
Curry powder	½ oz.	2 tbsp.
Dates: whole pitted	½ lb. ½ lb.	1¼ cups 3 cups
Eggs: whole broken whites yolks hard-boiled and chopped	1 lb. 1 lb. 1 lb. 1 lb. ¾ lb.	8 eggs 2 cups (10–11 eggs) 2 cups (12–14 eggs) 2 cups (18–20 eggs) 1 pt.
Figs: dried	1 lb.	2¾ cups. 43–44 figs
Flour: white, unsifted ,, sifted wholemeal, sifted	1 lb. 1 lb. 1 lb.	3¼ scant cupfuls 4 cups 4 cups
Gelatine: granulated	1 oz.	4 tbsp.
Ginger	1 lb. 1 oz.	4¾ cups 1 piece sbout 2″ × 2″ × ½″ deep
Grapefruit	1 lb.	1 fruit
Grapes: cut and seeded in bunches	1 lb. 1 lb.	2¾ cups 1 qt.
Green peppers: whole sliced	1 lb. ½ lb.	7 medium sized 1¼ cups
Ham: cooked, diced uncooked	1 lb. 1 lb.	3 very full cups 1 cup cooked
Hominy: raw	½ lb.	1½ cups

Table of Weights and Approximate Equivalents in Measure (*continued*)

Food	Weight	Equivalent Measure
Honey	10 oz.	1 cup
Ice cream	½ lb.	1¼ cups cream
Jam: raspberry	1 lb.	1⅓ cups
Jelly: blackberry	1 lb.	1½ cups
Lard	½ lb.	1 cup
Lemons	1 lb.	Approx. 4 lemons
Lemon juice	8 oz.	1 cup or 4–5 lemons
Lettuce: whole shredded leaves	9–10 oz. ½ lb. 1 lb.	1 average head 4 cups 30–35 salad garnishes
Macaroni: uncooked	1 lb. ½ lb.	4½ cups 2½ lb. or 1⅙ qt. (cooked)
Marshmallow	½ lb.	2¼ cups
Mayonnaise	½ lb.	1 cup
Meat: cooked, chopped	½ lb.	1 cup
Milk: condensed, sweetened evaporated powdered	11 oz. ½ lb. ½ lb.	1 cup 1 cup 1¼ cups
Mincemeat	½ lb.	1 cup
Molasses	1 lb.	1½ cups
Mushrooms: sliced, unstemmed sliced and fried canned	 1 lb. 1 lb. ½ lb.	 About 7 cups 1½ cups 1 cup
Mustard: dry	½ lb.	2½ cups
Noodles: raw and dried	½ lb.	4¼ cups
Rolled oats: uncooked cooked	1 lb. ½ lb.	About 4¾ cups 1¾ cups
Olives: green ripe	100 approx. 60–70 ,,	1 pt. 1 pt.
Onions: whole chopped	½ lb. ½ lb.	2½ medium sized 1–1½ cups
Oranges	½ lb.	1 fair sized fruit

Table of Weights and Approximate Equivalents in Measure (*continued*)

FOOD	WEIGHT	EQUIVALENT MEASURE
Oysters	1 pt.	20–30 small oysters
Parsnips	1 lb.	2 medium sized
Peanuts: whole	½ lb. ½ lb.	1 pt. 5 oz. 1 cup (shelled)
Peanut butter	1 lb.	1 pt.
Peaches: whole, fresh canned, sliced and drained	½ lb. ½ lb.	2 medium fruits 1 cup
Peas: fresh canned and drained split and dried dried	2½ lb. ¾ lb. 1 lb. 1 lb.	1 lb. (shelled) 1 cup 2⅓ cups 2½ lb. 5½ cups (cooked)
Pears: fresh canned, drained and diced	1 lb. ½ lb.	3 good-sized fruits 1¼ cups
Pickles	½ lb.	1½ cups
Pineapple	2 lb.	1 fruit
Potatoes: whole cooked and mashed chips	1 lb. 2 lb. ½ lb. ½ lb. 1 oz.	4 potatoes 1 qt. 1 cup 2½ qt. 1 serving
Prunes: whole after cooking pitted	1 lb. 1 lb. 1 lb.	2 cups 3–4 cups 3¾ cups
Raisins	1 lb.	3 cups
Rhubarb: cut up, uncooked cooked	1 lb. 1 lb.	4 cups 2½ cups
Rice	1 lb.	2 cups
Salad oil	1 lb.	2⅛ cups
Salmon: tinned	½ lb.	1 cup
Salt	1 oz.	1½ tbsp.
Sardines: canned	1 lb.	Approx. 24 in tin
Sausages: small	½ lb.	Approx. 8 sausages
Shrimps	1 lb.	3¼ cups

Table of Weights and Approximate Equivalents in Measure (*continued*)

Food	Weight	Equivalent Measure
Spaghetti	1 lb.	Approx. 3 lb. 14 oz. or 2⅓ qt. (cooked)
Spinach: raw canned	1 lb. ½ lb.	13 oz. (cooked) 2¾ cups
Strawberries	1 lb.	2¼ cups
Sugar: brown granulated loaf powdered, sifted	½ lb. 1 lb. ½ lb. 1 lb.	1½ cups 2⅛ cups 43 lumps 3½ cups
Tea	½ lb.	2 cups
Tomatoes: canned fresh fresh and sliced	½ lb. 1 lb. 1 lb.	1 cup About 4 medium tomatoes 2¼ cups
Turnip	½ lb.	1–1½ cups
Vanilla	1 oz.	1 tbsp.
Walnuts: in shell after shelling	1 lb. 1 lb.	Approx. 52 small nuts 2 cups
Watercress	½ lb.	2½ bunches
White sauce (medium)	9 oz.	1 cup
Yeast	1 lb.	Approx. 32 cakes

Approximate Substitute Equivalents

½ tsp. baking powder ½ tsp. bicarb. soda	= =	1 egg white 2 tsp. baking powder	Raising Agent
1 cup or ½ lb. butter 1 cup or ½ lb. butter 2 cups or 1 lb. butter	= = = = = = =	5 cups or 2½ pt. 20% cream 2½ cups or 1¼ pt. 40% cream ⅘ lb. lard 2 cups or 1 lb. margarine ⅘ lb. oil ⅘ lb. hydrogenated shortening ⅞ lb. chicken fat	Fat
1 cup or ½ pt. coffee cream 1 cup or ½ pt. heavy cream	= =	⅘ cup milk + ⅕ cup fat ⅗ cup milk + ⅖ cup fat	Cream
1 oz. chocolate	=	3 tbsp. cocoa + 1 tsp. fat	
1 oz. flour	=	¾ oz. breadcrumbs	
3½ whole eggs	=	7 egg yolks	Thickening

ERYNGO. A plant commonly known along the coasts as Sea Eryngo or Sea Holly. It has short and rigid leaves and stems and thistle-like blue flowers. The roots are fleshy and cylindrical and used for preparing a sweetmeat called candied eryngo or eryngo candy. The leaves when quite young are sometimes pickled in vinegar and used to garnish salads. The eryngo of the United States is said to be fetid and unfit for food.

ESCALLOP. See SCALLOP or SCOLLOP.

ESCALOPE. A thin slice of meat, usually veal, egged and crumbed and then fried.

ESCAROLE. Broad-leaved Endive. Chicory.

ESSENCE. A virtue which is extracted from any substance.

EXTRACTS. There is little difference, practically speaking, between extracts and essences. The former should signify that the active principal has been extracted and the latter that it has been produced in a high state of concentration.

F

FADGES. These are not now very generally known in England, although at one time they were great favourites. In Ireland they are still made.

TO MAKE. Pour ½ pt. new milk into a saucepan and place over a low heat; add 3 oz. butter and melt it, shaking the pan continually so that it does not burn. Sift 1 lb. flour with a little pinch of salt into a bowl. Make a well in the centre, pour in the milk and stir to a paste. Put on to a floured board and roll out to about ¼" thickness. Cut into cakes and lay them on a griddle or hot plate and cook them, turning them frequently to prevent burning.

FAGGOTS. Faggots are a savoury preparation of pig's liver, pork, onions, bread-crumbs, herbs, etc., covered with caul and slowly baked in a tin. The mixture is usually divided into squares before cooking.

Faggot of Mirepoix. Chop together finely 2 each carrots, onions and shallots, bay leaves, a sprig of thyme, a clove of garlic, ½ lb. fat bacon, ½ lb. ham. Toss in butter for a few minutes, sprinkle over with salt and pepper.

Faggot of Parsley. Tie together 2 or 3 sprigs of parsley and 6 spring onions. This faggot is used to flavour a variety of dishes.

Faggot of Pot Herbs. This is mixture of vegetables and sweet herbs which usually consists of 2 each carrots, onions, cloves and a faggot of sweet herbs. All are mixed together with ½ lb. beef fat, melted over a low heat and moistened with broth, seasoned slightly with salt and rendered piquant by the addition of the juice of a lemon. This differs from mirepoix in that it has less onion flavour and that beef fat is used instead of grated bacon.

Faggot Ravigôte. A bunch consisting of equal parts of tarragon, chervil, burnet and chives, tied together. Parsley is sometimes added, but not recommended.

Faggot D'Uxelles. (Fine herbs.) This consists of equal weights of mushrooms, parsley and shallots, minced and fried for about 5 mins. with rasped bacon and pepper. Sometimes truffles are added.

FAIRY BUTTER. See BUTTERS.

FAIRY CAKES. See CAKES.

FAIRY RING. An edible fungi with a cap sized 1–2"; bell-shaped, pale buff or deep cream coloured. It has distinctive scent, and thin, tough stem.

FANCHETTES. Delicate little pieces of French pastry, baked, filled with cream, and then decorated with a meringue top and piped with coloured sugar or candied fruits. The flavourings of the cream may be varied, coffee, chocolate or almond, and the meringue may be flavoured with noyau.

FANCHONNETTE. Small custard tartlet covered with meringue froth.

FARCE. Although this term is still maintained upon the Continent, it finds little favour in this country: the British cook prefers to speak of stuffing and forcemeat, the latter being a corruption of "farce meat". See FORCEMEAT.

FARL. Scottish oatmeal cake.

FAT. Fat is described as an oily substance found in the adipose tissue of animals, or vegetable oil which is widely distributed in the seeds of vegetables. Animal fats used for frying, for which purposes beef fat and lard are best, are rendered or tried out. Lamb and mutton fats are not good for frying, as they are too hard in texture. See also BUTTER, DRIPPING, LARD, MARGARINE and COOKING TERMS (CLARIFY and TRY OUT).

TO RENDER. Remove all lean meat from the fat, also any fibrous skin; cut into pieces, then place in a large low pan. Cover with plenty of water, cook rapidly, uncovered until the water has evaporated; by then the liquid in the pan will be opaque and milky-looking. When all the water is gone and only the fat remains, the liquid will look clear; then cover the pan and cook over a very low heat until all fat is extracted from the cellular tissues. Cool slightly and strain through muslin.

FAWN. The young deer does not often find its way to the kitchen. It must be skinned and dressed as venison and should not be kept longer than is absolutely necessary, as the flesh deteriorates very quickly.

FEATHERFOIL, FEATHERFEW. See FEVERFEW.

FECULA (Fr. *fécule*). The technical name for the sediment, especially starch, left in cold water by certain bruised or rasped vegetable substances. Continental and American cooks apply this term occasionally to potato flour, a very fine flour used for binding soups and sauces.

FEET. Animal's feet are much prized for the large proportion of gelatine which they contain. See CALF'S FEET, COW HEEL, LAMB'S FEET and PIG'S FEET.

FENNEL. Also called Carosella. A herb used chiefly with fish; its refreshing anise flavour is a good appetiser. Sometimes it is served as a vegetable and known as Italian celery or *finocchio*.
Root. The bulbous base of the finocchio leaf is used for culinary purposes either raw or boiled. Served also as sauce based on meat stock, and used to flavour wine.
Stem. The stems of carosella are cut and eaten like celery. The leaf is used as a flavouring for fish sauce and soft cheese, and as a garnish in soups and salads.
Seeds. Wild or garden, used in puddings, soups, spiced mixtures and sauces. Also in confectionery and medicinally. The pungent black seeds with aromatic odour and spicy taste are like nutmeg. Used like dill and poppy seeds for bread, cakes and flavouring wines.

Fennel Sauce

Ingredients	*Method*
1 bunch fennel ½ pt. boiling water 1 tbsp. flour 3 oz. butter	Put the bunch of fennel into boiling salted water and leave to boil for 2–3 mins. Remove and squeeze out as much water as possible. Remove stalks and chop leaves finely. Knead the flour into the butter, stir into boiling water, simmer for 10 mins., then add chopped fennel. See also SAUCES.

Fennel and Gooseberry Sauce. Make ½ pt. green gooseberry sauce (see GOOSE-BERRY), boiling a few sprigs of fennel with the gooseberries. Put the whole through a hair sieve. Add a nut of butter before serving.

FENUGREEK. Also called Bird's Foot, Greek Hayseed. The elongated seed pods resemble those of string beans. Used to give maple flavour to confectionery, also in curry and medicinally.

FERMENTS. The bodies, e.g. bacteria, yeast, which induce the process of fermentation in certain substances and liquids.

FERNS. The uncurled fronds of young ferns are sometimes eaten as salad.

FEVERFEW. Featherfew, Featherfoil. A herb used medicinally to make an infusion said to reduce fever.

FIBRIN (Fr. *fibrine*). A protein which occurs in freshly drawn blood and helps it to coagulate. It is eminently nutritious.

FIDELINE. A kind of straight vermicelli paste.

FIG (Fr. *figue*). The fruit of the fig-tree. The flowers are borne on the inside of a hollow receptacle which matures into a pear-shaped multiple fruit. Figs are easily dried by exposure to the hot sun; they contain a vast quantity of sugar and as this oozes and is dried on the surface it is possible to say they are preserved in their own syrup. The term *green figs* signifies fresh figs.

Fig Compôte. Put the required quantity of green figs in a basin with the juice and peel of 1 or 2 lemons. Add sufficient boiling water to cover them and leave until cold. For each 2 lb. fruit, put in ½ lb. crushed sugar or golden syrup and 1 pt. water. Boil until the sugar is dissolved, then drain the figs, put them in the syrup with one thinly sliced lemon, and simmer gently till tender. Leave the figs in the syrup until cold, then group them in the centre of a glass dish and strain the syrup over them. For *Green Figs in Syrup*, see **FRUIT** (p. 235).

Fig Jam

Ingredients
3 lb. figs
Juice of 3 lemons
3 tsp. lemon rind
3 lb. sugar

Method
Use dried cooking figs. Scald them in very hot but not boiling water, drain and slice in half, removing stems. Place in preserving pan with lemon juice and rind and simmer until soft and clear. If necessary a little water may be added. Add sugar and cook over low flame until the jam sets. Pour into heated jars and cover.

Fig, Green, Jam

Ingredients
1 lb. figs
2 lb. sugar
Juice of ½ lemon

Method
Place figs in double boiler and heat through. Add sugar and lemon juice and boil till thick, stirring frequently. Remove from heat and pass through coarse sieve. Return to flame and reheat. Pour into warmed jars and cover.

FILBERTS (Fr. *avelines*). There is no record of how the cultivated hazel-nuts became called Filberts. It is suggested they were so-called after St. Philibert whose day (22nd August) fell about the commencement of the nutting season. For **Filbert Butter** see **BUTTERS**.

FILET MIGNON. The dainty steak cut from the smaller end of a fillet of beef.

FILLET (Fr. *filet*). The undercut of the sirloin of beef, a thick slice of mutton, pork, veal, also boned breasts of poultry and game birds and the boned slices of fish. These are all described under their special headings.

FINE CRUST. See **PASTE AND PASTRY.**(p. 371).

FINE HERBS (Fr. *fines herbes*). A combination of finely chopped fresh herbs mostly used in omelets, salads and sauces.

UNCOOKED. Chop separately half an onion, 2 shallots, 2 sprigs parsley, 4 spikes chives and an equal quantity of chervil: mix before serving.

COOKED. Put 2 oz. finely chopped shallot into a saucepan with ½ oz. butter, and salt and pepper to taste. Stir gently over the fire, then add 4 oz. each chopped mushrooms and finely chopped, well washed and dried parsley. Cook for 5 mins. then turn the whole into a basin; cover securely till required for use.

Fine Herb Sauce. Put a chopped onion and 2 peeled and chopped shallots into a saucepan. Brown in 1 oz. butter, then add double the quantity of finely minced mushrooms and a grain of garlic, season with ½ tsp. salt and finish with 1 tbsp. chopped parsley. Cook 10 mins. longer and pour in 1 pt. white sauce. Stir well and serve.

FINNAN HADDIES. See **HADDOCK FINDON.**

FINOCCHIO. See **FENNEL.**

FIRKIN. This is a rather indefinite measure signifying 9 galls. of beer, or the fourth part of any barrel. A firkin of butter or lard signifies 56 lb. or a small barrel.

FIRMITY. See **FRUMENTY.**

FISH (Fr. *poisson*). Fish cannot be too fresh, and should be properly cleaned before use. It should also be soaked for a few minutes in salted water, or water to which a small proportion of vinegar has been added. *Saltwater fish* are those caught in the sea; *freshwater fish* are those caught in rivers, lakes and streams. *Frozen fish* is available most of the year. It is prepared in the same manner as fresh fish but it is best to allow additional cooking time unless the fish is thoroughly thawed immediately prior to cooking. Frozen fish must be kept frozen until required for use and should never be re-frozen. Fish may be grouped under two distinct headings, oily or fat fish, and lean fish. The former have oil running through the flesh, and are best for broiling or grilling. In the lean fish the flesh is drier and good for deep frying and chowders. When serving fish, remember to enhance the dish by a succulent sauce or garnish. *Canned, smoked or salted fish* may be used in place of fresh fish in many of the following recipes and in fish cakes, soufflés, puddings, vol-au-vents, etc. (see individual entries). The energy value of fish is slight, but the high protein content of all fish and the fat content of some varieties, make this food a very useful addition to the menu.

TO CHOOSE. The eyes must be bright and the flesh firm to the touch, plump but not flabby. The scales should be plentiful and gills red, except in herrings, as in this case it means stale fish.

TO PURCHASE. Appetites vary, but the usual portions per head of uncooked fish are (for one serving):

      $\frac{1}{3}$–$\frac{1}{2}$ lb. fish (allowing for bone weight), e.g. steaks, fillets, chunks, etc.
      $\frac{1}{4}$ lb. dressed fish.
      1 lb. whole or round fish.

Both fresh and frozen fish may be purchased in different forms, depending on their size. *Small fish* are usually sold whole or round, cleaned, or dressed, while other varieties of fish are sold in single or butterfly fillets. *Large fish* are sold as steaks or large fillets, and in some instances as whole fish.

TO KEEP. Always keep fish cold. Fish must be clean and all blood removed before storing.

TO CLEAN AND DRESS. Wash the fish in plenty of cold salted water, allowing 1 tsp. salt to 1 qt. water. Lay the fish on a wooden table or wooden board and hold the head firmly with one hand. With a sharp knife, holding the blade almost

Skinning fillets of fish   Removing entrails

vertical to the fish, scrape from tail towards head and remove scales. Remove the entrails by cutting the whole length of the belly from vent to head. Cut around the pelvic fins (which are near the head) and remove them; then, cutting above the collar-bone and through the backbone, remove both the head and the pectoral fin. If the backbone is very large it may be necessary to cut down to it at each

TO CLEAN AND DRESS (*continued*)

side of the head, and then break it by snapping over the edge of the table. Cut off any flesh which holds the head to the body.

TO SKIN. Put the fish on to a board; with a sharp knife, starting at the tail end, cut through the flesh. Keep the knife in a slanting position with the blade on the skin and with a sawing movement ease the flesh from the skin rolling the flesh away from you.

TO FILLET FLAT FISH. Cut down the centre of the back from head to tail, using a sharp knife carefully remove the flesh from either side of the backbone so that

Filleting Flat Fish

it is left clean. Proceed to work to the outer edge. Turn the fish over and repeat so that *four fillets* result.

TO FILLET ROUND FISH. Using a sharp knife cut down the centre to the backbone, starting from the bone to remove flesh all the way round. *Two fillets* only are obtained from this type of fish. Then cut off the tail; the back fin is removed by cutting flesh along each side of the fin and giving a quick pull towards the head, which will remove the fin with root bones. Remove the other fin in this way. *Fins must never be cut off with scissors.* Put the fish quickly into cold, salted water to remove blood and any remaining membranes. The fish is now ready for use.

FISH BAKED. Any size of fish either fresh or salt (after soaking to remove salt) may be baked. If the fish is marinated in herbs, wine vinegar or a little French dressing before baking, it will have extra flavour. Instead of always basting with butter, try for a change a little cider, white wine or fish stock. Always get the fish cleaned and dressed for baking. If it requires to be washed, dip it very quickly into cold, salted water then wipe dry with a clean, damp cloth. Season fillets with salt and pepper and a squeeze of lemon juice. Always weigh the fish, with or without the head, before you bake it. When the head is left on it seals the juices; if desired the head may be removed before serving. When stuffing fish, never fill the cavity more than two-thirds full; close the cavity with skewers or sew it up with needle and thread, lacing it together to keep the stuffing inside.

Put the fish in a shallow tin or oven-proof dish and cover with a layer of greaseproof paper. Remember to preheat the oven before putting in the fish; bake it at

Stuffed Fish

350° F. Therm. 4, but *never over-bake* or the flavour and juices will dry out. Serve at once as fish that stands is apt to become soggy. Small fish fillets take about 2 mins. per oz. cooking time; whole fish 10–16 mins. per lb. and 10–16 mins. over, according to fish.

FISH BOILED. *Remember a fish boiled is a fish spoiled: to "boil" fish means to simmer gently, not boil.* Use a fish-kettle or pan with a drainer, or stand an enamel

FISH BOILED (*continued*)

plate on the bottom of the pan; tie the fish in a piece of muslin, the corners of which should be held in place by the lid or by tying to the handles. Put the fish into warm water, adding to each 1 pt. water 1 tsp. each salt and vinegar. (Fish may be cooked in court bouillon or fish stock instead of water.) Season the fish with a few drops of lemon juice and tie it in the muslin. Bring the liquid to the boil slowly and simmer gently over a low heat. The time for cooking varies according to the size and thickness of the fish; some pieces take only 10 mins. while others require 20 mins. To test the fish, pass a skewer through the thickest part; it will pass through easily if the fish is cooked. Always serve a boiled fish with a succulent sauce, garnish with fresh parsley and serve plain boiled potatoes.

FISH BRAISED. This mode of cooking large fish requires the same preparatory processes as frying or boiling. The fish is lightly fried and then placed in a casserole or vegetable dish with liquid, sauce or stock to which a little wine is sometimes added. Add seasoning and herbs, cover with the lid and gently cook till the flesh is tender.

FISH BROILED OR GRILLED. Serve with Anchovy or Parsley butter.

FOR FILLETS OR SMALL WHOLE FISH. Wash fish quickly in cold, salted water. Split a whole fish. Dredge lightly with flour. Brush over with melted butter and season. Place on grill rack, at required distance from grill, preheated to red. Never turn fillets or split fish during grilling time. Baste well, and season again before serving.

FOR STEAKS of cod, halibut, salmon, etc. Prepare as above. Grill on one side, then turn and cook on the second side. Baste after turning and season before serving. The broiling or grilling time for steaks will vary according to thickness from 3–5 mins. each side, allowing in this for one or two bastings.

FISH FRIED (SHALLOW). For plaice, sole, herrings, smelts, mackerel. Wash and dry the fish; dip into seasoned oatmeal, flour, or egg and breadcrumbs. Toss very gently to remove any surplus coating. Heat a very small amount of butter, margarine or oil until a blue haze appears (allowing sufficient fat to cover the base of the pan). Reduce heat and place fish in pan, turning over when well browned to allow fish to cook through.

FISH FRIED (DEEP). Filleted fish or small whole fish are best for deep frying and, when the fat or oil is not allowed to smoke, the process is odourless. Always wipe the fish with a damp cloth. Dip into milk, and then into crumbs or batter; put the fish in one layer only into wire frying basket, and heat fat or oil to 350–385° F. Fry to golden brown, approximately 3–5 mins. Serve garnished with fried parsley and cut lemon, accompanied by Anchovy, Tartare or other suitable sauce if desired.

FISH PICKLED OR SOUSED. See **HERRING.**

FISH PLANKED. When possible use a well-seasoned wooden plank (oak or ash) approximately 1½″ thick. If this is not available use an oven-glass dish. Grease well with butter or oil. Place in cold oven and preheat for 10 mins. to 400° F. Therm. 6. Then reduce heat to 350° F. Therm. 4. When fat is melting, place prepared fish in centre adding parboiled vegetables. Garnish fish, and bake at the lower temperature above. Serve very hot.

FISH POTTED. The cooked flaked fish is seasoned with salt and pepper (spices if desired), pounded with butter, then pressed into a pot, covered with melted butter and sealed.

FISH SAUTÉED. The fish may be in fillets, steaks or cut into cubes. Wipe with damp cloth. Melt plenty of butter in saucepan over a medium heat. Add sparingly herbs and seasoning and liquid (a little fish stock and red or white wine), and simmer very gently over a low heat. Serve very hot in the liquid in which the fish was cooked.

FISH STEAMED. Steamed fish never dries up or shrivels and retains its juice and flavour, if the pan has a tight well-fitting lid. Wipe fish with a damp cloth. Tie carefully in butter muslin (so that it may be easily lifted out in one piece). Use deep pan with tight-fitting cover, and add only 2″ water, no more. Heat water until it boils rapidly; place fish on rack, or in wire basket which does not touch water,

FISH STEAMED (*continued*)

cover pan tightly. Allow for fish less than 2″ thick, 1 min. per oz. steaming time. Do not salt or season the fish until after it has cooked: sometimes herbs, wine, garlic, onion, celery, parsley, etc., are added to the water to impart flavour to the fish. Garnish with fresh parsley and serve with plain boiled potatoes.

ADJUNCTS TO SERVE WITH FISH

COD, BOILED. Serve Oyster, Egg, Shrimp or Parsley sauce.

COD, FRIED. Serve Anchovy or White sauce, and sometime Tartare sauce.

HERRINGS, GRILLED. Serve Mustard sauce.

MACKEREL, BOILED. Serve Fennel or Parsley sauce.

RED MULLETS, GRILLED OR BOILED. Serve Parsley, Butter, Tomato, or a sharp Brown sauce.

SALMON, BOILED. Serve Hollandaise, Lobster or Shrimp sauce; garnish with sliced cucumber, plain or dressed as for salad.

SALMON, GRILLED. Serve Maître d'Hôtel, Anchovy or Lobster butter.

SALMON, COLD. Serve Mayonnaise or Tartare sauce and cucumber salad.

SALMON, SMOKED. Serve with brown bread and butter and lemon.

SKATE, BOILED. Serve Black butter or Parsley sauce.

SMELTS, FRIED. Garnish with cut lemon, fresh or fried parsley.

SOLE, FRIED. Garnish with cut lemon, and serve Anchovy or White sauce if desired.

TURBOT, BOILED. Serve Anchovy, Béchamel, Hollandaise, Lobster or Shrimp sauce or Parsley butter.

TROUT, GRILLED OR BOILED. Serve Hollandaise sauce or oiled butter.

WHITING, FRIED. Garnish with cut lemon and serve Anchovy or plain White sauce.

WHOLE, LARGE FISH. Garnish with oysters, mussels, crayfish tails and mushrooms. For *Wines to Serve with Fish* see WINE.

Fish, Aiguillettes. Cut a slice of any fish to little more than $\frac{1}{2}$″ thick. Remove skin, and divide the slice into two, having removed the bone. Cut the slices into very thin strips (forming aiguillettes), salt them, dip into oil, roll in flour and plunge into hot fat to fry. As soon as the flesh is firm, remove with a skimmer, drain and season. Serve garnished with fried parsley.

Fish Broth

Ingredients	*Method*
2 lb. fish tails	Choose fresh fish tails. Leave them whole
3 pt. water	and wash well. Pour water into a deep
3 stalks celery	pan, add all ingredients except vinegar.
1 bay leaf	Bring to the boil, cover, simmer gently
1 large onion sliced	about 30 mins. or until the fish will flake
1 carrot	when tested with a fork. Remove fish
8 peppercorns	and flake, strain liquid through muslin
$\frac{1}{2}$ tsp. thyme	or hair sieve, add vinegar, heating
2 tbsp. butter	thoroughly. Just before serving add
Salt and pepper	flaked fish. Serve very hot.
Chopped parsley	
2 tbsp. vinegar	

Fish Cakes

Ingredients	*Method*
5 oz. potatoes	Sieve potatoes, add the flaked fish,
$\frac{1}{2}$ lb. chopped flaked fish	seasoning and chopped parsley. Mix
Pepper and salt	together. Bind with a little beaten egg.
Chopped parsley	Form into round or oval cakes. To
1 egg	firm up, reshape, dip each cake into the
Egg and breadcrumbs to coat	beaten egg, toss in breadcrumbs, shake

Fish Cakes (*continued*)

Deep fat for frying

off any surplus and fry in deep fat until golden brown. Drain on paper, garnish with parsley and serve at once.

Fish Cocktails. See COCKTAILS, SAVOURY.

Fish, Creamed Salt. Remove the bones and skin from some cooked salt fish. Break the flesh small, put it into a saucepan and cover with white sauce. Leave to heat through near heat or in a Bain Marie. Butter sufficient slices of toast to hold the fish. Put them on a dish; pour over the fish and serve with lemon and parsley for garnish. Alternatively, make a nest of mashed potatoes in a pie-dish, turn in the fish, brown under the grill or in the oven before serving.

Fish Forcemeat. Remove the skin and bones of about $\frac{3}{4}$ lb. white raw fish; pound the flesh and put it into a saucepan with $\frac{1}{2}$ lb. breadcrumbs, 1 tbsp. finely chopped parsley, $\frac{1}{4}$ lb. butter or margarine, 2 or 3 egg yolks, 2 tbsp. milk, juice of $\frac{1}{2}$ lemon, a little grated nutmeg and pepper and salt to season. Beat till smooth over a low heat, then use as desired.

Fish Fritters. Take any cold boiled fish (pick it free from all bones and skin) and pound it in a mortar. Peel a small onion, cut it into thin slices and pound it with the fish. Season to taste with salt and pepper and add an equal bulk of mashed potatoes. Mix well together and make into a paste with a beaten egg. Spread on a board, cut into small pieces of about 3″ either round or square, drop them into boiling fat and fry to a light brown. Fold a napkin on a hot dish, pile the fritters on it, garnish with parsley and serve with any fish sauce.

Fish Kedgeree

Ingredients

2$\frac{1}{2}$ oz. rice
$\frac{3}{4}$ lb. flaked fish
1 or 2 hard-boiled eggs
1 egg
Seasoning
Chopped parsley

Method

Wash the rice in cold water and boil until tender, then turn on to a sieve and let cold water run freely through. Drain well. Flake the fish and mix with one chopped egg and boiled rice. Add seasoning, also beaten egg to bind the mixture. Reheat in a double saucepan. Decorate with the second egg white cut into rings and the yolk sieved over the top. Add a sprinkling of parsley. Serve hot or cold. Sufficient for 4 persons.

Fish Omelet aux Fines Herbes

Ingredients

$\frac{3}{4}$ lb. white fillet of fish
5 eggs
Milk
Salt and pepper
$\frac{1}{8}$ tsp. basil
1 tbsp. chopped parsley
$\frac{1}{2}$ tbsp. flour
$\frac{1}{4}$ tsp. baking powder
2 oz. butter

Method

Wipe fillets with damp cloth. Put some water into a saucepan and boil. Then put fish in a wire basket, but do not let it touch the water. Steam for 10 mins. till the fish flakes easily when tested with a fork. Make the omelet mixture. Break the eggs into a bowl, beat lightly with a fork, add milk, salt and pepper, basil and parsley. Stir well. Sift in flour and baking powder, when smooth add fish. Heat butter in a frying-pan until very hot (but not smoking) and pour in the mixture. Cook over a low flame very carefully for 5 mins. till the underside is golden

Fish Omelet aux Fines Herbes (*continued*)

brown. Tip up the omelet with a palette knife so the uncooked mixture flows to the bottom of the pan and browns. When the mixture is set, serve immediately on a preheated dish or plate, garnished with sprigs of parsley.

Fish Pie

Ingredients

1 lb. cooked fish
1 pt. white sauce (see p. 436)
Seasoning
Breadcrumbs
Grated cheese and grated nutmeg (if desired)

Method

Flake fish and remove bones and any skin. Prepare the sauce; add seasoning and nutmeg (if desired); add fish. Turn into a well-greased dish, sprinkle with breadcrumbs and dot with butter. Sprinkle with grated cheese if desired. Bake at 400° F. Therm. 6 to reheat or lightly brown. Sufficient for 4 persons. If preferred this mixture may be divided into individual dishes.

Fish Pudding

Ingredients

2 lb. cod fillets
1 tsp. salt
⅛ tsp. pepper
⅛ tsp. each nutmeg and cayenne pepper
4 egg whites
Cream

Method

Wipe fillets with a damp cloth and put the fish through mincer. Place in large bowl. Add salt, pepper, cayenne, nutmeg; fold in egg whites stiffly whisked. Force this mixture through a hair sieve into another mixing bowl; place the bowl standing on ice (or in cold water). Add the cream and turn into a well-buttered pudding mould. Stand in a baking tin of boiling water and bake very slowly for 12 mins. in preheated oven at 300° F. Therm. 2. Unmould into hot dish. Garnish with watercress and serve with Cheese or D'Uxelles sauce (see SAUCES) or, if preferred, served direct from mould.

Fish Ring Jellied

Ingredients

1 dsp. gelatine
1 pt. hot water
¼ pt. tomato juice
1 tsp. onion
1 tbsp. horseradish
½ tsp. salt
⅛ tsp. pepper
Vinegar and lemon juice

Method

Soak gelatine in cold water, then dissolve in hot water. Add tomato juice, onion, horseradish, salt, pepper, vinegar and lemon juice. Place to chill till slightly thickened (about 1 hr.), then fold in celery and fish; turn into premoistened salad ring. When set, remove ring and turn on to a dish. Serve garnished with

C.C.D.—8

Fish Ring Jellied (*continued*)

1 lb. cooked white fillets
Diced celery raw
3 hard-boiled eggs
6 tsp. mayonnaise
Lettuce leaves

lettuce leaves, hard-boiled eggs and mayonnaise.

Fish Salad

Ingredients

12 crisp lettuce leaves
8 sprigs watercress
Mayonnaise
1 tbsp. lemon juice
8 radishes sliced
½ green pepper diced
½ beetroot chopped
⅛ tsp. chopped dill
Cooked fish
French dressing
2 tomatoes blanched
1 hard-boiled egg
6 sliced spring onions (if desired)

Method

Wash the lettuce and cress and dry. Blend mayonnaise and lemon juice. Place the radishes, green pepper, beetroot, watercress and dill in bowl. Add fish and mix well. Place to chill. Pour over mayonnaise and French dressing and toss lightly. Add the tomatoes sliced. Arrange the lettuce leaves on individual dishes, place salad in centre. Garnish with hard-boiled egg sliced and spring onions.

Fish Sandwiches. May be served hot using freshly toasted rounds of bread sandwiched together with fish filling; or spread the fish mixture on rounds of toast to eat cold; or between slices of buttered brown or white bread. Garnish with sprigs of parsley, watercress or lettuce leaves, or fresh celery tops; freshly grated carrot may also be used if grated and added just before serving. Cucumber sliced, eggs scrambled or hard-boiled and then diced, freshly sliced tomatoes blanched and skinned, green peppers, gherkins, herbs, horseradish cream, pickles or walnuts may be used to give added flavour, and make an appetising sandwich. If beetroot is used, add as a garnish whole small ones, skinned just before serving, or they will bleed and colour the sandwich.

Fish Soufflé

Ingredients

3 lb. white fish
2 tbsp. butter
2 level tbsp. flour
1 pt. milk
4 eggs
Salt and pepper
⅛ tsp. thyme
½ tsp. butter extra
2 tbsp. breadcrumbs

Method

Wipe the dressed fish with a clean cloth and place in a wire steaming basket. Pour water into saucepan, bring quickly to boil; do not allow fish to touch the water, cover and steam 10 mins. Remove skin and bones and chop fish small. Melt butter in saucepan over a medium heat. Stir in the flour gradually, heat 2 mins., stirring the whole time. Add milk slowly and blend together until smooth. Cook 5 mins. Separate the yolks of eggs from whites. Beat each well, the whites to a stiff froth. Add egg yolks and chopped fish to the mixture in saucepan. Season with salt and pepper and thyme. Carefully fold in the whites of egg (with a metal

Fish Soufflé (*continued*)

spoon so as not to break the air bubbles). Grease the casserole with the extra butter, and sprinkle the bottom with breadcrumbs. Pour the fish mixture into the casserole, place in a shallow tin of boiling water, and bake at 350° F. Therm. 4 for 30 mins. Serve piping hot with plenty of Melted Butter sauce (see p. 445).

Fish Steaks in Wine Aspic
Ingredients
2 lb. fish steaks
1 clove
1 bay leaf
1 sliced onion
Sauterne
2 sprigs parsley
Salt and pepper
FOR ASPIC
Ingredients
¾ oz. gelatine
¼ cup cold water
1 wineglass white wine
Pinch of salt
FOR GARNISH
Ingredients
3 hard-boiled eggs
12 stuffed olives
6 tbsp. mayonnaise
6 sprigs watercress

Method
Wipe fish steaks with damp cloth. Tie in muslin; put with wine and seasoning into saucepan of water and simmer for 12 mins., but do not overcook. Remove fish from muslin, taking care not to break it.

Method
Soften gelatine. Bring water and wine to boil. Remove from heat and dissolve gelatine in heated liquid. Leave to cool.

Method
Line a moistened mould with a little of the gelatine liquid. Place to set. Arrange the cold fish in centre of mould. Surround with hard-boiled eggs (halved) and olives. Pour over balance of cold gelatine and place carefully to chill. When set, un-mould and serve garnished with mayonnaise and watercress.

Fish Stock
Ingredients
2 lb. fish trimmings
2 qt. water
1 bay leaf
1 tbsp. salt

Fish Stock and Vegetable Fumet
Ingredients
1½ lb. fish trimmings
2 qt. water
1 bay leaf
1 onion sliced
Sauterne
1 carrot sliced
2 stalks celery
2 tbsp. chopped parsley
Salt and pepper

Method
Put all ingredients into large pan and bring to boil quickly. Simmer for 30 mins. and then strain. *For spiced stock* add 6 peppercorns, parsley, ½ tsp. mace.

Method
Put into large saucepan and bring to boil. Cover and simmer gently for 30 mins. When liquor is reduced to half, strain through hair sieve.

FISH ROES. There are two kinds of roe, classified as hard (Fr. *oeufs de poisson*) and soft (Fr. *laitance*). Hard roe is the eggs of the female fish, soft roe the milt of the male. Roe is taken from many different species of fish and is now available nearly all the year round. Cod, herring, mackerel, mullet, salmon roes are all available in fresh, frozen or tinned forms. The roe of the sturgeon is scarce because it is widely used for preparing caviare. The white herring milt is considered a great delicacy creamed or served on toast.

TO COOK AND SERVE. Place the roe in a saucepan, cover with boiling water and simmer gently for 15 mins. Drain and use as desired. Can be gently fried in a little butter and served on slices of hot buttered toast or placed in a casserole and cooked slowly with a little white wine, a few peppercorns, 2 cloves, a sprig of parsley, a bay leaf, a squeeze of lemon juice and rind, half a shallot or onion grated, and a little white sauce. Bake for 20 mins. at 350° F. Therm. 4. *Tinned Roe* may be wiped, dipped into beaten egg and, if desired, breadcrumbs, and fried in butter.

FLAG. *Sweet flag.* The rhizome is infused for fevers, and also cut up, boiled in syrup and cooled for confection to flavour custards, puddings, rice, etc. Sometimes used as a substitute for cinnamon or nutmeg and the oil of the root is used to improve flavour of gin, bitters, Benedictine and Chartreuse. *White flag.* Used as a sweetener, also to disguise the smell of garlic, liquor, etc.

FLAGEOLETS. The beans of the Kidney Beans (*haricots verts*)—French Beans, Scarlet Runners and Dwarf Beans—when shelled green and served in various ways are known abroad as "flageolets". The young beans when about three parts grown are delicious if cooked like peas, omitting the mint. See **BEANS**.

FLAKE. Dogfish is sold in England under this name.

FLAKY PASTRY. See **PASTE AND PASTRY** (p. 371).

FLAN. A French custard tart or an open fruit tart.

FLANK. The side below the ribs of a beef carcass. It is sold by the butcher under the names thick flank and mid-flank.

FLAP JACK (Fr. *tôt-fait*). A kind of hasty pancake.

FLAVOURINGS. These ingredients consist principally of spices, herbs, essences, which are added to food to make it more palatable. See **SEASONINGS** and **HERBS**.

FLAWNS. Flat pies or tarts generally made by lining broad shallow rings with paste and filling the interior with custard or fruits. See individual headings, also **PASTE AND PASTRY** (p. 369).

FLESH. Cooks use this term as applying to the muscles or the lean principally of any animal. Also, in culinary parlance, the meaning is extended to the flesh of some fruits, e.g. plum, pumpkin.

FLET MILK. An old name for skimmed milk.

FLIP. A drink which consists of eggs beaten up with milk and some spirit, beer or wine, and sugar. A favourite drink in cold weather.

FLITCH. A side of pork, salted or cured.

FLOUNDER (Fr. *carrelet* or *flet*). Flat fish of which many kinds are caught off the coasts of this country. The best is the Common English Flounder. There are many ways of serving these fish, e.g. baked, fried, cooked and in salads.

Flounders Cooked in Wine

Ingredients	Method
8 mushrooms	Sauté the mushrooms in 1 oz. butter and
4 oz. butter	keep hot. Wipe fillets with damp cloth
4 flounder fillets	and place in shallow dish. Add wine to
Dry sauterne wine	½ lemon juice. Pour liquid over fillets,

FLOUNDERS COOKED IN WINE (*continued*)

Juice of 1 lemon
Salt and pepper
1 oz. flour
2 egg yolks beaten
Cream

season with salt and pepper and bake at 350° F. Therm. 4 for 10 mins. Remove, drain sauce into double pan; add flour and remaining 3 oz. butter, egg yolks and cream. Beat till thick. Serve fillets garnished with mushrooms, squeezed lemon juice and sauce.

FLOUR (Fr. *farine*). Flour consists of crushed or decorticated grain reduced to powder. Wheaten flour is made from wheat; cornflour from maize or Indian corn; rice flour from rice; both barley and maize are deficient in gluten and cannot therefore be used to make upright loaves.

Seasoned Flour is flour which has been sifted with salt and pepper. It is frequently used for thickening gravies and soups or as a coating for fish.

When making a flour mix, always read the recipe through completely before beginning to work. Weigh or measure all the ingredients accurately and whenever possible use the best of ingredients.

Always use plain flour, adding the required raising agent, unless self-raising flour (sometimes it is necessary to add a little extra raising agent) is given in the recipe. Always sift flour, adding the smallest pinch of salt. Preheat the oven, and collect all ingredients and utensils required before beginning to mix with liquid.

The *final weight of a flour mix equals the weight of the raw flour* unless it is a fruit cake in which the weight of the fruit is added. When making pastry, if a recipe says ½ lb. pastry make your recipe in the required proportions of ½ lb. raw flour, plus fat, liquid, etc. See individual headings.

FLOWERS IN COOKING. See ANCHUSA, BEDSTRAW, BORAGE, BROOM, BUTTERCUP, CALENDULA, CAMOMILE, CAPER, CATMINT, CLOVER, COLTSFOOT, ELDER, FUMITORY, JESSAMINE, LILIES OF THE VALLEY, LOVAGE, MARIGOLD, MELILOT, NASTURTIUM, OREGANO, PASQUE FLOWER, PRIMROSE, SAFFRON, VEGETABLE MARROW, FLOWERS, VIOLETS.

FLUKE. Another name for Witch Flounder.

FLUMMERY. This term is of Welsh origin and derived from the word *llymrig* meaning harsh, raw, crude. It is a cold sweet dish made mainly of cereals (originally oatmeal), set in a mould, and usually served in a special large round bowl.
Dutch Flummery. Made from gelatine or isinglass, egg yolks and flavourings.
Spanish Flummery. Made from rice, cream, cinnamon and sugar.

FLUTE. A flute or finger-shaped roll.

FOIE GRAS. Fat goose's liver. See under that heading.

FONDANTS. This term is used for kinds of soft sweets that "melt" in the mouth.

FOOD VALUES. Food, which is a necessity for life, has three chief functions:
To produce heat and energy by combustion in the body; such foods are known as fuel foods. Among them are fats, carbohydrates and proteins.
To build and repair tissues. These foods are known as body-builders; among them are proteins with mineral salts and water.
To regulate the body processes and to prevent disease. These foods are known as protective foods; among them are milk, eggs, fruit and vegetables and other foods rich in vitamins and minerals.

FOOD VALUES (*continued*)

Foods are classified according to the tables which follow:

PROXIMAL CONSTITUENTS OF FOOD	IMPORTANCE	FOUND IN
PROTEINS	Essential for growth and repair of wear and tear	Nearly all foods, but especially in cheese, eggs, fish, meat, and milk. Also, of second quality in pulses and cereals
FATS	Useful as fuel material and carrier of some vitamins	Lard, suet, fat of meat, butter, margarine, salad oils
CARBOHYDRATES Sugar and starches	Useful as fuel material	Sugar, honey, jam, golden syrup, treacle, dried fruits, cereals, bread, biscuits, pulses
MINERAL ELEMENTS Calcium	Essential for building bones and teeth and for muscular contraction	Cheese, whitebait, most oily fish and shellfish, milk, and to smaller extent green cabbage and watercress
Copper	Essential for manufacturing blood	Most foods, but particularly liver
Iodine	Essential in regulating the rate the body burns its fuel	All sea fish
Iron	Essential for manufacturing blood	Liver, egg yolk, all green vegetables save spinach (the iron in spinach is not available to the human body)
Magnesium	Essential for muscle contraction	All green vegetables
Potassium	An essential ingredient of all cells of the body	All plant foods, meat, fish
Silicon	Of doubtful importance	
Sodium	Essential for making gastric juice, for carriage of oxygen in the blood, and for muscle contraction	Usually added as a condiment (salt) in excess of that needed
Zinc	An ingredient of insulin, the anti-diabetic hormone made in the pancreas	Most foods have a little
VITAMINS A (Anti-xerophthalmic)	Essential for night vision, keeps external and internal coverings of the body healthy	Fish liver oils, all livers, all animal fats (except lard), milk and foods made from milk, e.g. butter and cheese, green and yellow vegetables

FOOD VALUES (*continued*)

PROXIMAL CONSTITUENTS OF FOOD	IMPORTANCE	FOUND IN
VITAMINS (*contd.*) B (Anti-neuritic)	Essential for activity of the nervous system	Liver, sweetbreads, heart, kidney, pig-meat, germs and bran of cereals. Most foods have a little
Riboflavin	Keeps the cornea and skin round the mouth healthy	Milk, butter, cheese, liver. Most foods have some
Nicotinamide	Keeps the tongue, the skin and the nervous system healthy	Meat, fish
B.12	Essential in the manufacture of blood	Liver
C (Anti-scorbutic)	Essential for keeping the blood capillaries healthy	Citrous fruits, summer fruits except cherries, green plants, radishes, swedes, turnips and watercress
D (Anti-rachitic)	Essential for correct building of bones and teeth	Fish livers and fish liver oils
E	Doubly essential for human beings	
K	Essential for clotting of blood	Most fruits have some
P	Keeps the blood capillaries impermeable to blood	Most fruits have some
EXTRACTIVES	Give flavour to foods	
WATER	Replaces water lost by evaporation from the skin, by excretion and by breathing. Essential for life	Drinks and most foods save sugar, lard and dripping

ROUGHAGE. Foods without nutritive value are included in the diet because they are useful to stimulate the muscular action of our intestines, to assist secretion of the digestive juices, and to prevent constipation. The cellulose in fruit and vegetables and the husks in wholemeal bran and oatmeal both act as roughage.

HOW TO CALCULATE THE CALORIFIC VALUE OF FOODS

Proteins	yield 4·1 calories per gram or	116 calories per oz.
Carbohydrates ,,	4·1 ,, ,,	116 ,, ,,
Fats ,,	9·3 ,, ,,	263 ,, ,,

Hence, if the percentage composition of a food is known, its calorific value can be calculated, as in the following example. To calculate its calorific value to the first decimal point:

$$\text{Fat} \quad 11\cdot6 \times 263 \div 100 = 30\cdot5$$
$$\text{Protein} \quad 13\cdot5 \times 116 \div 100 = 15\cdot7$$

WHY FOOD IS COOKED. In most instances food is rendered more digestible by cooking: this is especially so with starchy foods: foods which contain cellulose are softened and therefore more easily masticated. Exceptions to this rule are foods which contain much protein albumen, e.g. white of egg and the fatty foods, such as butter, cream, dripping, etc. These are not improved as irritating fatty acids are apt to develop in them when they are exposed to a high temperature.

By cooking, food is also rendered more palatable; this is especially true of animal foods, in which both appetising flavours and odours are developed through exposure to heat. Some exceptions among raw foods are butter and cream, some fruits and vegetables and salads.

Some food is rendered more wholesome by cooking at a sufficiently high temperature (by boiling in water at 212° F. or by cooking for a longer time at the rather lower temperature of 160–180° F., as in pasteurization, to destroy many of the germs and parasites and so to help keep the food). This is essential in hot weather, when food changes are rapid and the germs of putrefaction develop, e.g. in some animal foods, milk, fish, etc.

By cooking, both texture and taste of food can be varied, and also different combinations of ingredients help to give variety to the menu.

HEAT AND ITS EFFECT ON FOOD. There are two methods of cooking: by "moist heat" as in boiling, simmering, steaming, stewing, braising or poaching, and by "dry heat", as in baking, broiling, frying, grilling, roasting and toasting. Some foods are well basted with hot fat to prevent dryness, others are "coated".

ANIMAL FOODS. The albumen which is present in most animal foods, e.g. fish, eggs, milk, meat, etc., is hardened. The connecting tissue (gristle) can be softened by long, slow simmering into a soft, soluble and gelatinous substance which is easily digested.

Muscular tissue (flesh). By long, slow cooking fibres are softened and are therefore more easily digested and masticated.

Fats. These are melted at low temperature, dissolve, and the fat when free is easier to digest. Fat melted at a high temperature burns, decomposes and develops fatty acids and irritants which make it indigestible.

Extractives are the portions of the animal foods which give the characteristic flavour and through exposure to heat develop aromatic flavours and odours. This makes the digestive juices flow more freely, so aiding the digestion.

VEGETABLE FOODS

Starch. By adding moist heat to the starchy foods, e.g. flour, cornflour, etc., the starch is turned into a thick, glutinous and semi-transparent paste. When the starch grains swell, their outer envelopes burst and free the starch, which mixes with hot liquid and so "thickens" it; but unless cereals are blended with water or liquid and mixed to a creamy paste before the boiling liquid is added the thickening is uneven, because the heat does not reach all the starch grains simultaneously and so they clog into lumps. It is therefore essential to blend carefully and stir constantly to obtain a smooth and creamy consistency.

Dry heat turns starch to dextrin, which is a substance between starch and sugar; it also browns it, but it burns and puffs up when left too long in the heat, then blackens and carbonises. The dry heat also causes the brown crusts on cakes, scones and toast. Starch is much more digestible when cooked than when raw.

Gluten. When exposed to heat, this vegetable protein, contained in wheat, first becomes sticky and glutinous and then hard: it thus helps to hold the air in a mix and to keep its shape.

Cellulose. This is the cell-wall tissue of fruits and vegetables which is rendered softer by cooking and so becomes more easily masticated and swallowed.

Sugar. The sugar used in cooking is known as sucrose. This includes both cane and beet sugar. Glucose is used for special invalid cookery (e.g. diabetic) and in some confectionery. When sugar is melted and gains heat it goes through various stages. See **SUGAR** (p. 489).

Mineral Salts. These are soluble, frequently altered by heat and extracted by long, slow simmering in liquid.

Vitamins. These elements which are present in most fresh animal and vegetable foods are rendered less potent on exposure to heat, and, in some cases, destroyed.

FOOL. This dish is made by crushing stewed fruit, especially gooseberries, and mixing it with milk, cream, or custard. See **GOOSEBERRY.**

FORCEMEAT (Fr. *farce*). Pounded or finely minced meat which is used for stuffing birds or meat. This word is applied also to other ingredients combined together, e.g. suet, parsley, breadcrumbs, herbs, chestnuts, etc. See also **STUFFINGS.**

Veal or Forcemeat Stuffing

Ingredients

4 tbsp. breadcrumbs
1 tbsp. chopped suet
2 tsp. chopped parsley.
Grated rind of ½ lemon
½ tsp. mixed herbs (fresh preferably)
¼ tsp. salt
Pinch pepper
Egg or milk to bind

Method

Mix the dry ingredients together. Add egg or milk to make a firm mix. Use for fish, meat or poultry.

Forcemeat Balls or Quenelles. For garnish. The forcemeat is formed into balls, rolled in flour, fried to a light golden brown in butter and used to garnish poultry, etc. See also **QUENELLES.**

Making a Forcing Bag

FORCING BAGS. Forcing bags made of strong calico can often be bought, but if these are unobtainable, it is possible to make one from greaseproof paper by twisting the paper up to form a cone-shaped bag and cutting the pointed end to make a nozzle. Metal pipers may easily be fitted to the calico bags, the different-shaped fittings giving a variety of designs to the icing. Among the nozzles available are:

Leaf. For leaves, ribbon and ribbon borders.
Rose. For rosettes and borders.
Shell. For borders and shells.
Star. For stars, ribbons and borders.

Eclairs and cream buns are forced through the larger pipers, which are also used to force vegetable purée and mashed potato into garnishes and borders for casseroles. Large-sized bags are also useful for forcing cake mixture into small tins, since it is easier to fill the tins evenly and quickly when using a forcing bag.

FOWL. As a culinary term, domestic birds used for food. See under individual headings. As a general term, chiefly used to refer to wild and water fowl.

FOXGLOVE. Gloves of Our Lady. Thimble flowers. The leaves are used medicinally.

FRANGIPANE. A substitute for custard made of eggs, milk and some flour, with lemon rind, brandy and vanilla, etc. Used as a confectioner's custard. Also a pastry filled with cream, almonds and sugar.

8*   [225]

FRAXINELLA. Bastard Dittany, Gas Plant, Burning Bush. The leaf is used infused in water to make a refreshing tea and the root is used medicinally.

FREEZE. The subjecting of food to a temperature below freezing point (32° F. or 0° C.) at which the liquid particles become solid. This process produces some of the luxuries of the table.

FRENCH BEANS. See **BEANS.**

FRENCH DRESSING. See **SALAD DRESSINGS.**

FRENCH ROLL. This bread is superior to ordinary household mix because the dough should contain both milk and butter. The rolls are baked and made up in various shapes.

FRENCH SALAD. See **SALADS.**

FRIAR'S OMELET. A baked omelet prepared with apples stewed to a pulp.

FRITTER (Fr. *beignet*). Anything dipped in batter and fried.

FRITTER BATTER

Ingredients	*Method*
½ lb. flour	Sift together the flour, baking powder,
1 tsp. baking powder	sugar and salt. Beat the eggs slightly, add
3 tsp. sugar	milk and butter. Stir in flour mixture
Pinch salt	gradually with a wooden spoon and
2 eggs	combine thoroughly.
¼ pt. milk	NOTE. When this batter is used for dishes
2 tbsp. melted butter	other than sweet ones, omit sugar.

Fritters, Batter. See **BATTER.**

Fritters, Cheese

Ingredients	*Method*
¼ pt. milk	Scald the milk and add butter to it.
1 tbsp. butter	Remove from the fire. Make a paste of
¼ lb. flour	the flour with a little cold water and stir
2 eggs	it into the milk until it is smooth. Add
¼ lb. grated cheese	the eggs well beaten, then the cheese and
Paprika	seasoning. Drop by spoonfuls into deep
Salt	fat, and fry to a light brown. Serve very
	hot.

Fritters, Corn. See **INDIAN CORN.**

Fritters, Fruit. Any desired fruit may be used for fritters, e.g. cherries, or large fruits cut into small slices. When cooked, drain on absorbent paper, sprinkle with sugar and serve very hot with a fruit or custard sauce, or cream.

Apple. Peel, slice, sprinkle with sugar and lemon juice and let stand for an hour.

Apricot. Use halves; if tinned apricots are used, drain well.

Banana. Peel and split the bananas lengthwise; sprinkle with lemon juice and sugar. Leave half an hour before dipping into batter.

Peaches. Use halves; cut into two before dipping into batter.

Pineapple. Cut into cubes or thin slices, or small diagonal-shaped pieces. If quick-frozen pineapple is used it should be drained of all syrup.

Raisins. Use ¼ lb. seedless raisins. The fruit may be flavoured with a little Kirsch or Triple Sec Brandy if desired, and should be drained well before dipping into batter.

Fritters, Yeast. See **YEAST.**

FROG (Fr. *grenouille*). Although each continental country has its own popular name for the frog, it usually appears in the kitchen under its French name. The edible frog in Europe is the Green or Gibbons Frog. It is considered a great delicacy and is in season in Lent. Sometimes it is served in a rizotto.

Frog's Legs Fried

Ingredients	*Method*
8 frog's legs 2 oz. butter Pepper and salt	Wipe the legs with a damp cloth and join two legs together by passing joint of one leg through the muscle of the other. Melt the butter in a saucepan and season lightly with salt and pepper. Dip legs in this, arrange on grill tray, then place under hot grill for 5 mins.

FROSTING. A culinary term which means to make certain dishes appear like frost. It consists of the whipped whites of egg spread roughly over the dish, then dredged with caster sugar and baked at 250° F. Therm. 1. In U.S.A. the term "frosting" is used for icing.

FRUCTOSE. A sugar found in fruit.

FRUIT (Fr. *fruit*). The distinction which the cook draws between "fruit" and "vegetables" is not made according to the botanist: rhubarb, not being a seed-bearer, is only a "fruit" in the kitchen, while cucumbers and vegetable marrows, botanically fruits, are vegetables to the cook. The distinction is drawn from their culinary uses. Fruits are very much used as food either raw or cooked. Whether familiar or "luxury" they are of exquisite beauty, entrancing to the eye, and their perfumes and flavours are a great addition to our menus. Fruits can be divided into two groups: those which are grown in the open air in Great Britain; and hot-house and imported fruits. Almost all fruits can be preserved either by bottling or canning, drying, boiling with sugar, or soaking in spirits or vinegar: today, frozen fruits are available all the year round.

Always gather fruit on warm, dry days, when the midday sun is on it, because it will then hold the maximum amount of sugar and any dew or moisture will have evaporated. Never leave ripe fruit on a tree unless it is to be dried, and gather fruit carefully, placing it in a basket so that no bloom, which is an essential beauty, will be lost. Always discard damaged fruit. Lay the fruit on a board and see that no fruits are touching each other. Keep in a dark cupboard where a current of air will blow upon them. Every few days the fruit should be sorted out and those removed which show signs of decay. All fruit should be cleaned very carefully before serving or cooking. It should be unbroken, not over-ripe and as fresh as possible. Soft fruits must be very carefully looked through as they are liable to harbour grubs. Put them in a colander and immerse them in a bowl of cold water; then drain and very carefully pick them, removing any bruised or unsound fruit. Currants can be easily picked with a fork. Gooseberries must be topped and tailed (scissors are useful for this purpose.)

FRUIT BAKED. Fruits are sometimes baked whole, e.g. apples, grapefruit. They are placed in a buttered dish with 1 or 2 tbsp. water or syrup. Sugar and a knob of butter is also added.

FRUIT COCKTAILS. These are served as appetisers, so they must be served in small quantities and not too sweet. When making these cocktails, one fruit should be fresh and firm; if all fresh fruit is served, add extra fruit juice, or make a little light syrup. When using bottled or tinned fruits in syrup, the fresh fruit is mixed in this syrup. Sometimes an extra squeeze of lemon juice is added. These cocktails must always be served well chilled. It is never wise to serve more than 2 tbsp. fruit in the stem cocktail glasses. Here are some combinations of different fruits. Mix pineapple pieces, grapefruit segments and avocado cubes, cover with pineapple juice, honey and lemon juice.

Slice bananas into $\frac{1}{4}''$ slices. Place in glasses and cover with iced pineapple, crushed. Place cherry on top.

Cover grapefruit sections with cranberry juice.

Mix diced orange sections, shredded coconut and pineapple.

Mix chilled pineapple pieces and seedless grapes, cover with pineapple juice.

FRUIT COCKTAILS (*continued*)

Serve pineapple cubes and diced pear with mint ice.

Cut ripe water melon into little round balls, cover with ginger ale and leave for 30 mins. Drain and cover with fresh ginger ale.

Sprinkle orange sections with fine sugar, cover with mixture of pineapple and lemon juice, and garnish with mint leaf.

Cut fresh pineapple into cubes, and combine with fresh strawberries.

Serve fresh raspberries with raspberry ice or syrup.

Place pieces of cooked rhubarb in glasses, combine with strawberries and chill.

Add cherries to crushed pineapple and diced banana and cover with orange juice.

Serve strawberry ice on syrup over fresh ripe strawberries.

Serve small white grapes in cocktail dishes, covered with chilled orange juice and use cherry garnish.

Fruit salads which should, when possible, be served in glass bowls, may be made with any of the above fruits and cocktails, cups or salads may be given added flavour by the addition of little Kirsch or sherry.

FRUIT FOR DESSERT. Always choose the choicest unblemished fruits for this purpose.

Apples, Bananas, Oranges, Pears. Clean the fruit and polish the apples with a soft cloth until they shine; arrange the different fruits on separate plates or make a mixed bowl of apples, bananas, grapes, oranges and pears.

Dates. Tastefully arrange on a dessert plate or else serve in the box, this being placed on a plate.

Gooseberries. Top and tail and arrange on a dish.

Grapes. The bunch of grapes is either arranged with the other fruit in a bowl or served on a plate alone with grape scissors for cutting.

Melon. Choose a ripe melon (this can be tested by the texture at the end of the melon and the riper colour). Wash the melon, dry carefully, then wrap in grease-proof paper (to prevent everything else in the refrigerator being tainted). Before serving, cut it into sections or slices, removing the seeds, and serve with sugar or ground ginger.

Pineapple. The fruit should be cut into slices; sometimes the skin is loosened the whole way round so that the pineapple looks whole when put together again and served. It is wise to sprinkle the pineapple with sugar at least two or three hours before serving.

Raspberries, Strawberries, Currants. These are served on leaves or in a bowl, dredged with sugar, with a squeeze of lemon juice added to give extra flavour and also to enhance the colour.

FRUIT PURÉE. The fruit is stewed with very little liquid and then passed through a hair sieve to reduce it to a creamy consistency.

FRUIT, STEWED. When stewing unpeeled whole or sliced fruits and soft fruits, allow ½ pt. water to 1 pt. fruit. For freshly peeled fruits make a syrup with 4 oz. sugar to each pint water. Add the smallest pinch of salt, bring to the boil, and cook for about 2 mins.

Fruit Fritters. See FRITTERS.

Fruit Pie

Ingredients   *Method*

½ lb. short crust (see p. 375)   Wash and prepare fruit. Fill a pint pie
Fruit   dish with the fruit; add sugar to taste; add
Sugar to sweeten   water. Roll out the pastry to the shape of
2 tbsp. water   the dish and half an inch larger all round.

Cut off this ½″ edge; damp the edge of the pie dish and lay the pastry strip on to it. Moisten strip (without stretching); cover with remaining pastry; trim the edge and using the back of a knife, flake

Fruit Pie (*continued*)

all round. Decorate with a spoon into small scallops. Bake from 30 to 40 mins., according to fruit, at 400° F. Therm. 6.

Fruit Pudding

Ingredients

½ lb. suet crust (see p. 375)
1½ lb. fresh fruit
Sugar to taste
1 tbsp. water

Method

Grease a pudding basin. Roll out the pastry into a circle sufficiently large to line the basin's base and sides. Cut out a section for top. Ease the larger circle of pastry into the basin and press against top rim with the fingertips. Fill dish with prepared fruit and sugar in alternate layers. Finish off with fruit, add water. Damp the edges of the pastry, fit on the lid, press together. Cover with greased paper and steam for 2–2½ hrs.

Fruit Tart. See PASTE AND PASTRY (p. 369).

FRUIT PRESERVATION

EQUIPMENT BOTTLED FRUIT

Corer for apples or pears. (Sometimes a teaspoon is used to remove the core of a halved pear.

Peelers can be used for apples, pears, plums and beans. There is less waste to the skins, and the work is quickly and easily done.

Bottle Brush. Useful for cleaning thoroughly the interiors of the jars.

Bottle Tongs. These rubber-covered wire grips are useful for lifting bottles out of the steriliser. They lift either horizontally or vertically and can also be used to hold fruit and tomatoes in hot water before peeling.

Cherry Stoner. Useful when stoneless cherries are to be packed.

Funnels. Those with 1½″ bottom tube and 4½″ diameter top are useful for filling small jars with raspberries, currants and peas.

Juice Extractor. Useful to extract lemon, orange or grapefruit juice.

Labels. All bottled fruits and jams should be labelled and dated before storing.

Muslin. Used for immersing vegetables in boiling water.

Packing Spoon. If no long-handled, small-bowled wooden spoon is available a foot-long piece of wood, not more than 1″ wide × ¼″ thick, smooth, with a pointed end, can be used. This is also useful for "paddling" out air bubbles after the fruit is packed.

Screw Band Remover. A small appliance for removing bands will be found most useful. It will loosen the tightest screw band.

Seals.

1. Synthetic skins; use as directed on the package.
2. Mutton fat or paraffin wax melted down and run on to the hot liquid, which when cool forms an air-tight seal.
3. Greaseproof paper; use three thicknesses of greaseproof paper, with a well-cooked home-made flour paste. Cover the fruit while it is piping hot, pasting down each thickness of paper immediately.

To test seals, when the bottles are quite cold (after 24–28 hrs.), test the lids to see whether they are loose. If they come off, drain off the liquid and boil it, put the jars in an oven on an asbestos mat, heat through, cover with the boiling liquid and re-seal immediately.

Vegetable Strainers. These are used for immersing vegetables in boiling water before packing into bottles (see *Muslin* above).

[229]

GENERAL NOTES ON BOTTLING. If the fruit has to be kept overnight, remember to spread soft fruits out thinly on sheets of greaseproof or thick brown paper in a cold room. Always pick through the fruit and discard soft, mouldy or squashed specimens. Over-ripe fruit should not be used, because although the full flavour will be there, the shape may be lost when heated, and a squashy bottle of fruit will result. It is best to pick the fruit on a dry day and not to bottle unripe fruit, with the exception of gooseberries which should be bottled unripe. Always grade the size of the fruit and choose unblemished and uncut skins. Fruit can be washed if desired. Wash large fruit and dry with a clean cloth. For small fruit, e.g. raspberries and currants, wash in a jar, then invert and drain the water through the fingers. Repeat the washing three times. The skin of peaches, plums and tomatoes are best removed. This can easily be done by putting the fruit into a butter muslin bag and holding the bag in boiling water for about $\frac{1}{2}$–1 min. The skins will then be slipped off easily by the fingers or they can be removed with a knife. Always peel both apples and pears before they are cored and cut into quarters or halves; green gooseberries are topped and tailed and currants stripped; plums and cherries may be stoned, if desired; raspberries and loganberries need careful packing as the fruit is liable to sink. All bottles and jars should be of clear white glass and must be uncracked and scrupulously clean, as must be the fastenings; use a detergent if necessary to dissolve any grease. After cleansing, the bottles must be rinsed in clean, hot water and left to drain (they can be packed wet). All caps must fit perfectly and the rubber bands must be fully elastic and well fitting. They should be steeped in warm water before use. If a spring clip is used this must be effective and strong. If a brass screw band is used this must effect a perfect closure. The fruit must be carefully packed and all available space used in the oven method of sterilisation, but $\frac{1}{2}''$ should be left at the top of the jars to allow for the liquid. After the fruit is packed, knock it down by tapping the jar gently on the table or with a wooden stick. Tap also as the liquid is added, and when the bottles are full, to release any bubbles. Sterilised water, either hot or cold, is used; or if sugar is available the fruit may be bottled in syrup (see following entry).

Hot liquid is added when the fruit is sterilised in an oven (dry pack method) but is not poured over the fruit until after the fruit has been heated.

Cold liquid is added when the water-bath method of sterilisation is used, and in oven wet-pack method. In both these cases the bottles are filled before heating, but do not screw up the jars tightly before sterilising. Cold solution is also added when preserving tablets are used. If bottling fruit with preserving tablets, the instructions on the packet must be followed exactly, and when the fruit is revived for use, it must be boiled hard to clear it of the chemical or it will be uneatable.

Reviving Bottled Fruits. When using any method except the tablet process, bottled fruits should be restored to their fresh flavour by straining the liquid from the jar, putting it in a pan and bringing it to the boil, then adding the fruit, covering the pan tightly and removing from the heat. When it is cool the fruit is ready for use.

Methods of Sterilising. If a steriliser or copper boiler or bath is used, place a piece of folded sacking at the bottom of the vessel and stand the bottles packed with the fruit on this, padding between the bottles if necessary with newspaper, to stop the bottles vibrating and cracking. Put only enough cold water into the steriliser for it to come to the necks of the jars. Bring slowly to simmering point and when the fruit shrinks and begins to crack it is well sterilised. Remove the jars, put them on a wooden table and place on the rubber washers. Fill the jars with boiling syrup (see below) or water, to the brim (almost over-flowing) and cover immediately. Tighten up the rings.

If the bottles are filled with syrup before they are sterilised, fill them only to the necks of the bottles, with a loose lid or cover on the jars.

If sterilised by the oven method, place the jars, packed with the fruit, on an asbestos mat or a piece of wood in the oven, which should be at 230° F. Therm. $\frac{1}{2}$. Leave the fruit till it is shrunk, then pour over boiling water or syrup and seal immediately.

FRUIT STERILISATION TABLES

FRUIT	OVEN METHOD	TEMPERATURE TO BE REACHED IN 1 HOUR °F.	TIME TO BE MAINTAINED
Apples	1 hr.	175	10 mins.
Apricots	1 hr.	175	10 mins.
Blackberries	50 mins.	175	10 mins.
Blackcurrants (washed well and drained)	50 mins.	185	15 mins.
Bullaces	45 mins.	165	10 mins.
Cherries (washed and stalks removed)	30 mins.	190	10 mins.
Cranberries	50 mins.	180	15 mins.
Damsons	35 mins.	165	10 mins.
Figs		Boiling Point	75 mins.
Gooseberries (Topped and tailed and washed)	30 mins.	165	10 mins.
Grapes	30 mins.	165	10 mins.
Loganberries	50 mins.	165	10 mins.
Mulberries	50 mins.	165	10 mins.
Nectarines	About 1 hr.	165	10 mins.
Peaches	1 hr.	165	10 mins.
Pears	45 mins.	190	10 mins.
Pineapple	45 mins.	190	20 mins.
Plums	45 mins.	165	10 mins.
Quinces	45 mins.	190	20 mins.
Raspberries	About 50 mins.	165	10 mins.
Redcurrants	50 mins.	185	15 mins.
Rhubarb	About 50 mins.	165	10 mins.
Strawberries	35 mins.	165	10 mins.
Tomatoes	1 hr.	190	30 mins.

[231]

VEGETABLES
(BLANCHING CHART)

When blanching vegetables prior to bottling, use no more water than is absolutely necessary to cover the vegetables when they are packed in the bottles or cans.

VEGETABLE	BLANCHING TIME
Artichokes—Globe	5 mins.
Asparagus	3 mins.
Beans—Broad Dwarf and Runner	3 mins. 5 mins. (steaming)
Beetroot	15 mins. (steaming)
Broccoli	5 mins.
Brussels Sprouts	5 mins.
Carrots	10 mins.
Cauliflower	5 mins.
Celery	5 mins.
Leeks	3 mins.
Macedoine of Vegetables	Each vegetable is blanched separately
Mushrooms	Generally stewed in casserole
Parsnips	3 mins.
Peas	5 mins.
Pumpkins	Steamed till just tender
Spinach	3 mins.
Turnips—whole diced	10 mins. 2 mins.
Vegetable marrow	2 mins.

VEGETABLE STERILISING

If a larger bottle than the 2 lb. size is used, the time in each instance should be increased by 5 mins. to ensure adequate heating in the centre of the bottle.

VEGETABLE	TIME OF STERILISING AT 10 LB. PRESSURE (240° F.)
Artichokes—Globe	35 mins.
Asparagus	30 mins.

VEGETABLE	TIME OF STERILISING AT 10 LB. PRESSURE (240° F.)
Beans—Broad, French and Runner	35 mins.
Beetroot	35 mins.
Broccoli	35 mins.
Brussels Sprouts	40 mins.
Carrots	35 mins.
Cauliflower	35 mins.
Celery	30 mins.
Leeks	30 mins.
Macedoine of Vegetables	40 mins.
Mushrooms	30 mins.
Parsnips	35 mins.
Peas	40 mins.
Pumpkins	35 mins.
Spinach	50 mins. (15 mins. at 15 lb.—250° F.)
Turnips	35 mins.
Vegetable Marrow	35 mins.
Vegetable Pulp	50 mins. (15 lb. pressure)

Fruit Butters. Fruit butters require very little sugar—they are practically simple fruit pulp boiled until thick, slightly flavoured and sweetened. When apples are cooked for "butter", cider is sometimes added, and in other butters, a little cinnamon or spice is used for flavouring.

Fruit Cheese. Boil down any fruit until it can be passed through a sieve, the skins and stones being so removed; weigh the pulp, then boil again to get it as dry as possible. Sugar is then added, ¾ lb. sugar to each 1 lb. pulp, and the paste is boiled again till it is quite stiff. It is then tightly pressed into pots or put to dry on flat dishes. (The test for cooking is that the solid mass should come away from the side of the pan.)

Fruit Pulp. Pick the fruit carefully over and remove any diseased fruits and all stems and leaves. Place in a saucepan with just enough water to prevent its burning and bring to the boil. Cook thoroughly through and, while still boiling, pour immediately into very hot, clean jars. Seal at once with hot lids. (Sugar may be added, if desired, to sweeten the pulp before boiling.) Then immerse the bottles in pans of hot water, bring to the boil and keep boiling for 5 minutes. Seal immediately. Lids should not be screwed down tightly until the bottles have been removed from the steriliser, or the jars may burst.

FRUITS, BOTTLED WHOLE IN SYRUP OR SUGAR. This is a very delicious method of preserving fruit; usually it requires a good deal of sugar and the fruit is either whole or halved. The same syrup can be used for different batches of fruit, till they have all been cooked in it. Stone fruit is probably best for this purpose. It must in any case be perfectly sound, and of a good quality. Never use windfalls for this method. The fruit should be of an even size. It can be peeled, cored, stalked or stoned according to the species. There are several methods:

METHOD I. Place uncooked fruit in bottles. Pour the syrup over the fruit, cork the bottles then stand them, up to their necks, in a large vessel of boiling water until the fruit reaches boiling point (inside the bottles); then leave the bottles to cool in the water.

METHOD II. Cook the fruit very carefully so as not to break it or spoil its shape (the smaller stone fruits should be pricked with a darning needle) in water brought from cold to boiling point; remove fruit then rinse in cold water and drain on a sieve. Then boil up in a syrup to "thread" 216–218° F. See SUGAR (p. 490). The syrup is boiled up again the day after and re-added to the fruit. This is a tedious process because it may continue for anything from 3 to 6 days. On the last day, however, the fruit is again boiled up in the syrup and bottled and corked at once.

METHOD III. Pour the boiling syrup of "thread degree" over the uncooked fruit, which is arranged in the bottles. This method is only really suitable for soft fruits, e.g. raspberries, strawberries. It is thought by some people that cold syrup should be used for these all-red fruits because it preserves their colour better. To make the cold syrup let the sugar dissolve in cold water instead of by boiling up. Allow to each 1 pt. water 2 lb. sugar. It is a heavier syrup than a "boiled" syrup and takes much longer to prepare.

METHOD IV. For *acid fruits* allow 1 lb. sugar to each qt. water. For *sweeter fruits* allow only ¾ lb. sugar to each 1 qt. water. Put the fruit in the jars into pans containing 2″ boiling water (the tops of the jars are on but *no* rubbers), then put the jars into the oven at 350° F. Therm. 4) for ¼ hr.; remove, one by one, fill up with the boiling syrup, put the rubber ring on and cover tightly.

METHOD V. Pack small soft fruits in jars in layers with powdered sugar. Allow about 4 oz. to each 1 lb. fruit and see that all the spaces are filled up evenly till the jars are filled. The smaller jars (1 lb. size) are best for this. The fruits must be of uniform size and arranged in circles or layers in the bottles, being compactly and evenly packed.

METHOD VI. This is an old-fashioned way of bottling fruit in syrup: Choose sound ripe fruit of uniform size; wipe with a dry cloth and place carefully so as not to bruise in wide-mouthed jars. These should be well-filled. Tap gently on the table or with a wooden stick to make the fruit settle down firmly. Place the bottles, with space between each, in a cool oven (200° F. Therm. ¼) till the fruits begin to crack, then remove the bottles from the oven. Fill with boiling syrup (¼ lb. sugar to each 1 qt. water).

Apples or Pears, preserved whole. Take a dozen choice, well-flavoured apples or pears. Peel and core them neatly (but do not remove the pear stalks), or, if preferred, slice them. Place in salted water (1 oz. salt to each 1 qt. water.) Leave them for 24 hrs., then remove, wash them well and leave for some hours in cold water. Then drain and dry them. Make a syrup with 1 lb. sugar, ½ pt. water and the juice of a lemon; when thick, add the fruit carefully, seeing it is spread in a single layer in the preserving pan, then simmer until quite clear and opaque. Bottle, adding hot syrup, or, if preferred, dry them on sieves.

Grapes, preserved whole. Choose just ripe grapes and wash them and cut them off the bunch. Do this carefully and leave a little stem on each. Have ready a syrup made with 1 lb. sugar to each 1 qt. water; put the grapes in jars (pre-heat these) in a large pan of cold water, then allow them to heat very gradually. When the water boils, pour the boiling syrup into the jars till they are almost full. Let the water boil 10 mins. longer, then fill up the jars with the syrup and cover immediately.

Green Figs, preserved whole. Take green figs, weigh them, and cut a small slit across the top of each. Place them in strong brine for 8 days then drain and put them into a preserving pan with sufficient water to cover. Boil till tender and then drain again. Return to pan and cover with cold water. Leave for 3 days, changing the water each day. On the 3rd day make a syrup, allowing to 1 lb. figs, 1 lb. sugar, and ¼ pt. water. Bring this to the boil; put the figs in and boil for 10 mins. Pour all off into a bowl and repeat this for 3 consecutive days or until the figs are quite green and tender. Then put them into jars, fill up with syrup and cover securely. Keep in a dry place.

Raspberries, preserved whole. Make a strong syrup (and see SUGAR, p. 493) and when it is quite thick, put the raspberries into it. Boil them for 5 mins., skimming off any scum that may rise. Remove from the heat and add a little caster sugar, process should be repeated three or four times, then let the pots stand for two days before securely sealing. Pour on top a thin layer of mutton fat or salad oil. Tie with a greaseproof covering or, if preferred, use screw top jars.

Fruits, Candied. These are cooked in syrup for the most part, making the syrup stronger for each coating. Subsequently they are sprinkled very thickly with icing sugar.

Candied Cherries. For each 1 lb. stoned cherries, allow 1 lb. sugar and ¼ pt. water. Let this simmer in a preserving pan till it is all melted. When the syrup boils add the cherries, simmer them very slowly till they are quite clear. Pour off the syrup then place the cherries on a flat dish. Let them dry in a slow oven 250° F. Therm. ¼. This may take about 10 hrs. When thoroughly dry, dust with sugar and place them in a papered box or tin.

Candied Oranges or Tangerines. Peel the oranges or tangerines. Remove as much of the white pith as possible, then divide into sections (removing any pips with as little damage as possible). Boil in strong syrup (see SUGAR, p. 493) for 30 mins., then remove from heat and allow to stand till cold. Repeat this process 3 or 4 times until the syrup is very thick, then remove the oranges or tangerines and powder them with fine sugar. Place them in the oven to dry at 200° F. Therm. ¼.

Candied Pineapple. Choose just ripe pineapples. Peel them and slice thickly. Remove eyes and cores and halve the slices so that each is crescent-shaped. Weigh, and for each 1 lb. pineapple add ¼ pt. water and simmer slowly until the pineapple is clear and tender. Remove fruit from the water and add 1 lb. pre-heated sugar for each 1 lb. fruit. Let this syrup boil till reduced by ⅓. Replace the fruit and allow to boil until it becomes transparent. Remove with a skimmer and put on to flat dishes to dry. Boil the syrup till it candies and pour over the fruit. Leave till completely dry then pack in large jars or tin boxes in powdered sugar. Keep very tightly covered.

Fruits, Canned. It is possible to can either fruit or vegetables at home. After the original outlay on the machine, the advantages of canning over fruit bottling are: the product can be cooked quicker in a can; after sterilising the can is unbreakable and cannot crack; the process is quicker; no thermometer is necessary as there are no temperatures to take; the cans can be sealed before sterilisation, and so ensure the full flavour of the fruit; the cans are easier to handle when heating as they weigh less than bottles and they also pack more easily and are cheaper.

Method. Never use a can with a scratched lacquer inside. Always rinse in cold water and then drain, never dry with a cloth. Choose fruit as for bottling. Pack the cans tightly to within ¼" of the top only. Pour the boiling water or syrup (preferably) to within ¼" of the top, *never more.* Seal each can at once to prevent evaporation. Put the sealed cans into boiling water and re-boil the water as quickly as possible. Leave them for the given time (see Table). Always remove the cans from the steriliser with tongs and cool them in several changes of, or under running, water. Remove them when at blood heat; this can be tested by holding the hot can in the hand for half a minute. There is no need to dry the cans, they dry themselves as they cool. Test for sealing (note the concave drawn-in appearance) both ends; see there is no leaking liquid and that the cans when tapped have a clear ring. Label at once. Store in a cool, dry place. For sizes of cans, see CANS. For *Sterilisation Table for Fruit,* see FRUIT, BOTTLED.

STERILISATION TABLES FOR FISH, MEAT, GAME AND POULTRY
(for 2½ size cans)

This pack requires exhausting 10 minutes in boiling water.

FOOD TO BE STERILISED	TEMPERATURE	TIME TO BE MAINTAINED
Fish—dry packed		- 80 mins.
Game—if partly deboned whole game		75 ,, 65 ,,
Hares—with bones deboned		80 ,, 50 ,,
Minced Meat	250° F. 15 lb.	55 ,,
Pigeons—with bones de-boned		80 ,, 50 ,,
Poultry—roast or boiled whole small chicken		60 ,, 65 ,,
Rabbits—with bones de-boned		80 ,, 50 ,,
This pack requires to be exhausted 5 mins. in boiling water. Shrimps—wet packed 240° F. 10 lb.		30 mins.

VEGETABLE STERILISING CHART FOR CANS IN A PRESSURE COOKER

It is best, when possible, to use silver resisting cans (S.R.) but plain cans (P) of course can be used in some instances. The fruit lacquer (F.R.) or silver resisting cans must be used in certain cases as shown in this list.

VEGETABLE	TEMPERATURE	TIME TO BE MAINTAINED	TYPE OF CAN
Artichokes—Globe		30 mins.	F.R.
Asparagus		25 ,,	S.R.
Beans—Broad, Dwarf or Runner		30 ,,	S.R. or P.
Beetroot		30 ,,	F.R.
Brussels Sprouts	240° F. 10 lb.	35 ,,	S.R. or P.
Carrots		30 ,,	S.R. or P.
Cauliflower		30 ,,	S.R.
Celery		25 ,,	F.R.
Leeks		25 ,,	S.R.

VEGETABLE	TEMPERATURE	TIME TO BE MAINTAINED	TYPE OF CAN
Mushrooms		25 ,,	S.R.
Parsnips		30 ,,	P.
Peas	240° F. 10 lb.	35 ,,	S.R. or P.
Potatoes		35 ,,	S.R.
Pumpkins		30 ,,	S.R. or P.
Spinach	250° F. 15 lb.	45 ,,	S.R. or F.R.
Turnips	240° F. 10 lb.	30 ,,	S.R. or P.
Vegetable Marrow	,,	30 ,,	S.R. or P.
Vegetable Pulp	250° F. 15 lb.	45 ,,	S.R.

FRUITS, CRYSTALLISED OR GLACÉ

NOTE. This process cannot be used for all fruits, only for those which are comparatively dry. The juicy moisture of some fruits ruin this process. Those fruits and nuts which can be crystallised are: almonds, cherries, chestnuts, figs, filberts, grapefruit peel, lemon, orange, prunes, peanuts, walnuts. The fruit must be sound, firm and ripe, rather under- than over-ripe. Remove skin, stalks and stones, if any.

METHOD I. Make a syrup using 2 parts sugar to 1 part water. Stir well and when the sugar is dissolved, add a small level saltspoon of cream of tartar. Then do not touch again until it boils to "crack" 290° F. See SUGAR (p. 490). Dip each fruit or nut into the syrup, very carefully, so that it is completely coated over. Then place on a buttered tin and slab to dry. Leave in a cool place and when they are quite hard store in a paper-lined and tightly closed tin box. Fruits and nuts may both be redipped if they fail the first time.

METHOD II. Mix together 1 lb. caster sugar and 1 saltspoon each bicarb. soda and cream of tartar. Roll the fruit in this, coating each fruit separately with a thick covering of sugar, then lay them on a large, flat dish. Place in a hot oven 400° F. Therm. 6 and when the fruits are cooked and quite tender, remove the dish and set it in a cool place. When the fruits are *cool*, roll them again in the sugar, and then place on a coarse sieve for 24 hrs. Store in a papered tin and put layers of greaseproof paper between each layer.

Chestnuts: Marrons Glacés. Boil together 1 lb. sugar and ¼ pt. water to 28° F. It is ready when it becomes white and graining as it is rubbed on the sides of pan with a wooden spoon. Peel, blanch and boil 2½ lb. chestnuts over a low heat. Test for tenderness. Remove the brown skins and drop the peeled chestnuts into lemon juice and water (this keeps them white). Drain and pour all the syrup and add to it extra sugar so that the saccharometer will register 22. Pour this over on alternate days and on the tenth day the syrup must have a density of 28. Finally pour over the nuts and place them in bottles.

TO GLACÉ. Remove the required number of chestnuts. Prepare syrup to 25 (on saccharometer) seeing that it grains, and stir the syrup very gently till opaque. Dip the chestnuts in on a dipping fork, drain and place in small paper cases. When cold place in paper-lined tin.

FRUITS, DRIED. For the best flavour, the sun-drying method is the best to use, but it is not always possible in this climate.

For good colour, choose the oven method, where the fruit can be dried by a very slow process in cool ovens on shallow trays, or sliced and strung, e.g. apples.

[237]

METHOD I.—WITHOUT SUGAR. Prepare the fruit, peeling and coring if necessary, and lay it on trays in the oven to dry at a temperature of 120–150° F. Heat very gently or the fruit will be hard on the outside. It will take about 4–6 hrs. to dry and should be left at least 12 hrs. in a cool room temperature to cool before packing in paper bags, boxes or jars for storing. Apples, after being peeled and sliced or cut into rings, should be placed in a little salt and water to prevent discolouration; if cut into rings they can be strung across the room or oven to dry.

METHOD II.—WITH SUGAR. To each 1 lb. prepared fruit allow 1 lb. crushed or powdered sugar. Place the fruit on large shallow dishes, sprinkle with sufficient sugar to cover it. Then place the remaining sugar in a very small quantity of syrup (only sufficient to dissolve it slowly). Next day boil up the sugar, then add the fruit. Boil for 10 mins., then remove the fruit and continue to boil the syrup until it thickens; return the fruit to the syrup, simmering slowly over a very low heat, for 30 mins. then skim out the fruit. Place on buttered dishes, and leave in the sun to dry.

TO PREPARE DRIED FRUIT FOR USE. Soak the dried fruit well for 24–48 hrs. and then bring it slowly to the boil; add sugar to sweeten just before serving.

FRUITS, FROZEN. These are available all the year round. They can be used in many different recipes and fruit salads.

FRUITS, SPICED. These fruits are a cross between preserved fruits and pickles. The vinegar and sugar are first boiled up together until the syrup is a little thick, then the spices (whole spices tied in a little bag) are put into it; the fruit is added to this and simmered for 2–3 hrs., then removed. The syrup is then reboiled and poured over the fruit.

Spiced Peaches. Choose peaches that are just ripe. Peel them, halve them and stone them if desired. Place them in an earthenware crock. Put into a pan 3 lb. sugar, 1 pt. vinegar, $\frac{1}{2}$ oz. each ground cloves and allspice, 2 oz. powdered cinnamon. Bring just to the boil and then pour over the peaches. Leave 24 hrs., then drain off the liquid. Reboil it and pour over the peaches. Leave overnight. On the third day, place the whole in a preserving pan, bring to the boil and simmer gently till the peaches are tender (but not broken). Remove fruit and pack into large jars. Reboil the syrup till reduced and thickened. Fill up the jars and cover at once.

FRUITS IN SPIRITS OR LIQUEURS. This is a more expensive method of preserving. There are three methods:
1. To bottle the cooked fruit in syrup and add brandy liqueur to taste.
2. To bottle the fruit dry and uncooked with layers of sugar and then add sufficient brandy to fill it up.
3. To prepare and bottle the fruit with brandy. Cork up and leave for a month. Then strain off the brandy and to each 1 pt. brandy add $\frac{1}{4}$ lb. sugar candy, which must be dissolved in the brandy and then the liquor strained through a jelly bag and returned to the bottled fruit.

The second method above does not keep so well as the other two.

Brandied Cherries. Take white heart cherries and place them in a deep jar; cover with brandy, leave 48 hrs. Then prepare a thick syrup (see SUGAR BOILING). Strain off the brandy from the fruit, and measure it, then add an equal quantity of syrup and strain over the cherries. Leave overnight, having corked the bottles, then if the syrup has shrunk, fill up with the rest of the syrup.

Brandied Figs. Take 5 lb. green figs and cut off half the stems. Place them in a glass jar with 1 lb. sugar sprinkled between them. Fill up with brandy, cork tightly. Shake well. Do not use for a month.

Brandied Peaches. Take 5 lb. sound, ripe peaches. Peel, halve, remove the stones and place the fruit in a glass jar. Break the stones and add the kernels to the peaches. Add 1 lb. crushed lump sugar. Fill up with brandy, cork tightly and shake well. Leave a month before use.

FRUMENTY. This is a favourite dish in some parts of the British Isles. It is made of wheat or barley, boiled and eaten with honey, sugar, milk or treacle. It was once a Lord Mayor's dish and a staple food.

FRY, TO. To cook food in hot butter, fat or oil. There are two methods, *deep fat frying* and *shallow fat frying*: for both the fat should be smoking (i.e. with a blue haze over it at 350° F.) before food is added. To test heat of fat when no thermometer is available, drop a piece of bread into it and if it browns lightly in $\frac{1}{2}$ min. the temperature is 375° F.; in 1 min. 350° F.; in $1\frac{1}{2}$ mins. 325° F.; in 2 mins. 285° F. See table below for cooking times of various foods. Wire frying baskets with handles, in a deep, heavy saucepan, are used for deep frying so that the food can easily be lifted out of the boiling fat and drained before serving. The temperatures and cooking times vary according to the type of food and method of preparation.

When the fat is cooling it must be kept active, otherwise it is apt to change colour and texture. Remove the fat from the heat and drop a slice of raw potato into it to absorb the surplus heat and clarify the fat.

DEEP FAT FRYING TEMPERATURES

Definitions of Methods A, B and C.
  A Dipped into seasoned flour and then milk and egg.
  B Dipped into milk, drained, then dipped into flour.
  C Seasoned with salt and pepper, dipped into breadcrumbs, egg and breadcrumbs again.

	METHOD	PREPARATION	TEMPERATURES		TIME
			° F.	° C.	
Asparagus	A		375	191	2–3 mins.
Aubergine	A	Peel, slice and soak in salt water for 2 hrs.	370	188	5–8 mins.
Bananas	A	Peel, scrape, cut into pieces, sprinkle with lemon juice and caster sugar and leave 30 mins.	375	191	2–3 mins.
Cauliflower	A	Cold cooked	375	191	2 mins.
Cheese Balls		See CHEESE	350	177	3 mins.
Cucumbers	C	Wash and peel, slice lengthwise into $7\frac{1}{2}$" slices	390	199	4–5 mins.
Cutlets			360–400	182–204	6–8 mins.
Doughnuts			375	191	4–5 mins.

Fish fillets
  ,, ,, in
    batter
	C		370
			368–375
				188
				186–191
					About 5 mins.

Fritters			370–380	188–193	3–5 mins.
Onions	B	Peel, slice into rings, pre-soak in milk for about 1 hr.	370	188	About 2–3 mins.
Oysters	C	Shells removed and bearded	375	191	4–5 mins.

	METHOD	PREPARATION	TEMPERATURES		TIME
			° F.	° C.	
Potatoes: Chips	A	Peel and slice very thin	325	163	About 4–6 mins.
French fried	A	Peel, then cut into ⅛″ lengthwise	365–375	185–191	About 5–10 mins.
Matches	A	Peel thin, then cut into strips	325–335	163–168	About 4–10 mins.
Rissoles			375–390	191–199	3–5 mins.
Scallops	C	Wash and dry	360	182	About 5 mins.
Shrimps	C		375	191	4–5 mins.
Whitebait			400	104	1–2 mins.

Fats and oil begin to burn if they are raised above the following temperatures:

	° F.
Beef Fats	356
Butter, Clarified	270
Butter, Unclarified	378
Lard	292
Olive Oil	554
Vegetable Oils	482–518

FUMITORY. Earth smoke. The flower is infused in water and used as a tonic and the whole herb is used medicinally.

FUNGI. Among the edible fungi are Beefsteak, Blewitt, Fairy Ring, Shaggy Cap, etc. See also individual headings and **MUSHROOM**.

G

GALACTOSE. Lactose. The sugar and milk must be broken before digestion, in the monosaccarides—these are glucose and sucrose. A sweet crystaline glucose obtained from milk-sugar by treatment with dilute acid.

GALANTINE. A French term used to denote a dish of white meat, rolled, pressed, glazed, and served cold. A fowl, or breast of veal, boned and stuffed with force-meat, i.e. farce, tongue, truffle, etc.

GALL. The taste of this bitter fluid, which is very pungent, is impossible to get rid of from the flesh of a fowl or any other creature possessing a liver if the gall bladder happens to be broken. Use the knife unsparingly to cut away all the liver that is stained by proximity to the gall bladder.

GALLON. A measure of capacity, equalling 4 qt. See WEIGHTS AND MEASURES.

GAME (Fr. *gibier*). This term covers pheasants, partridge, grouse, black cock, heath fowl, moor fowl, bustards, hares, etc., snipe, quail and landrails, etc.

It is an offence by the Chief Statutory Laws, also the Local County Laws to take or to kill wild birds during the nesting season. There are special dates given when particular game may be shot or killed in most countries. (For seasons see table p. 242). Roast game is usually reserved as the "rôti" course which follows the remove.

TO CHOOSE. *Young birds* will have soft quills, rounded spurs; *year-old birds* will have short, blunt pointed spurs; *old birds* will have long, coarse bills, sharp, long spurs and the sinews of the legs will be stiff. The vent should be firm and not flabby and discoloured. If the birds are old and seem tough after plucking and drawing, steep them in milk just before cooking: this will help to make them more tender.

TO HANG. Game birds should be hung from the neck *unplucked* and *undrawn* in a cool place in a current of air. An old-time custom was to place a clove of garlic and a dusting of pepper in the place where the bird was shot and to put a few peppercorns in the mouth. Birds which are wet, through accident or shattered by shot should be cooked first. If the eyes are well sunk, the bird has been shot for some days. *If the bird is sufficiently hung, a tail feather or a feather from the back can be pulled out without resistance. If when blowing up the breast feathers the flesh has a distinctly greenish tinge, the sooner the bird is cooked, the better.*

TO PLUCK. Pluck carefully, reserving some of the tail feathers for garnishing the roast. Remove head and neck and clean as for a fowl. Do not remove sinews from legs. Remove claws and scald, and skin the legs. Place a box between your feet so that the feathers may fall into it. Put an apron over your knees so that it falls into the box. Put the bird on your knee on its back with the head hanging down between the knees (so that the blood will continue to drain); grip the skin round the root of feathers with the fingers of the left hand while you pluck them with your right hand. Always pluck in the direction in which feathers lie. Remove the quill feathers first, then tail and flight. Pluck breast on both sides of wings and then finally the back (the skin is apt to rub if this is plucked first). Leave the collar feathers round the neck. Care should be taken round the region of shoulders and down back (these parts are tender). Cut off the wings at the first joint. Wipe with a damp cloth, but do not wash. If the flesh is rather dry, place a piece of butter or a piece of rump steak inside.

TO STUB AND SINGE. Use an old blunt knife to pass underneath the short quill (stub), grip with the thumb and pull backwards. Singe with taper or over a gas-ring, and take care not to discolour or darken the flesh.

TO DRAW. Work if possible on a smooth-surfaced table (scrubbed or enamel), have a 10″ needle and some string or skewers and a sharp-pointed knife with a 5″ blade which is well embedded into the handle, a slightly damp cloth and a dry cloth, and a saucer for the giblets.

Make an incision round the hock halfway down, and pull out sinews. Trim wings (by cutting off thum and underskin) flap either end, then put the bird (with its head away from you) on its breast. Lift the skin at the back of the neck, cut downwards towards the shoulders so that there is a strip of skin about 1″ wide by 3″ long. Insert the knife at the junction of neck and shoulders and cut off neck here; remove it and the gullet by scraping up front of neck skin and cutting off front skin the same length as back skin. Using your fingers, remove crop, cutting out attachments as low as possible, then hold the bird in your left hand, insert your middle finger, and along the backbone loosen the lungs and membranes attached to them. Make sure the tissues are loosened all round between the backbone and breastbone. Stand the bird on its shoulders, holding the knife perpendicularly, and taking the vent between the finger and thumb of the left hand make a circular incision round the vent. Put the bird on its back and insert the long middle finger of the right hand, work loose membranes round bowels and gizzard; after removing any fatty tissue take hold of gizzard with thumb and first finger of the right hand and pull firmly. The intestines, gizzard, and bladder should come out with one movement. Wipe the bird inside with a clean dry cloth (never wet a bird inside as it keeps better if not wetted) unless the bird is high, then wipe with vinegar and cold water. Season inside with sprinkling of salt and add walnut of butter or margarine. A shallot may also be added if the bird is very high. Roll back the skin down to between shoulders and stuff the neck through the vent. Turn back wings and turn over front of neck. Truss as for roast chicken (see page 146).

TO ROAST. Bard the breast or lard if preferred, or wrap bird in a thin rasher of bacon. Baste frequently during roasting. Five minutes before dishing dredge the breast well with flour and baste. Return to the oven to froth the breast. Serve on game toast with suitable garnishes and accompaniments (see below). For times of roasting and seasons of game see table following.

NAME	AT BEST	IN SEASON	ROASTING TIME	OVEN TEMP.	THERM.
Black Cock	Sept.–Oct.	20th Aug.–20th Dec.	25–45 mins.	325° F.	3
Black Game		20th Aug.–20th Dec.	,, ,,	,,	,,
Capercailzie		20th Aug.–20th Dec.	,, ,,	,,	,,
Coot			30–35 mins.		
Cormorant	Aug.–Dec.	12th Aug.–31st Jan.			
Corncrake	Oct.–Nov.	12th Aug.–31st Jan.			
Curlew	Oct.–Jan.	1st Sept.–1st Mar.			
Grey Hen		20th Aug.–20th Dec.	25–45 mins.	325° F.	3
Grouse	Sept.	12th Aug.–10th Dec.	30–40 mins.	,,	,,
Hare	Oct.–Feb.	1st Aug.–End Feb.			
Landrail	Oct.–Nov.	12th Aug.–31st Jan.			

TO ROAST (*continued*)

NAME	AT BEST	IN SEASON	ROASTING TIME	OVEN TEMP.	THERM.
Lapwing	Oct.–Jan.	1st Sept.–End Feb.			
Moor Cock		12th Aug.–10th Dec.	25–45 mins.	325° F.	3
Moor Hen			30–40 mins.		
Partridge	Oct.–Nov.	1st Sept.–31st Jan.	25–35 mins.	400–425° F.	6–7
Pheasant	Nov.–Dec.	1st Oct.–31st Jan.	40–45 mins.	375–425° F.	5–7
Pintail	Oct.–Nov.	12th Aug.–31st Jan.	20–25 mins.		
Plover	Oct.–Jan.	1st Sept.–1st Mar.	15–20 mins.	325° F.	3
Ptarmigan	Sept.–Oct.	20th Aug.–20th Dec.	25–45 mins.	325° F.	3
Quails	May–Sept.	All year round	25–30 mins.	350° F.	5
Rail	Sept.–Nov.	12th Aug.–31st Jan.			
Snipe	Oct.–Nov.	12th Aug.–31st Jan.	15–20 mins.	425° F. 450° F.	7–8
Teal	Oct.–Jan.	12th Aug.–31st Jan.	About 20 mins.	450° F.	8
Venison (Hind)		Oct. to end Dec.			
Venison (Stag)		End of June to end of December			
Widgeon	Oct.–Nov.	12th Aug.–31st Jan.	15–20 mins.	450° F.	8
Wild Duck	Oct.–Dec.	12th Aug.–31st Jan.			
Wild Geese		1st Aug.–15th Mar.	15 mins. per lb.	300° F.	1
Woodcock	Oct.–Nov.	12th Aug.–31st Jan.		425–450° F.	7–8
Wood Pigeons		All year round	Approx. 30 mins.	425° F.	7

Fig Bird Hazel Hen Ortolan } Now imported.	Ruffs Reeves Wheatears } Now protected all the year.

ACCOMPANIMENTS TO SERVE WITH GAME

BREAD SAUCE. Remove the crusts from 2 slices of white bread, rub this through a wire sieve. Soak the crumbs in milk for 1 hr., add 1 onion stick with 2 or 3 cloves, season with pepper and salt to taste and walnut-sized knob of butter. Heat well, remove cloves and onion and thin down with a little cream just before serving.

BROWNED CRUMBS

Ingredients

1 cup soft white crumbs
1 oz. butter

Method

Place crumbs and butter together in pan over a low heat, stir well and leave until golden brown. Place on sieve to drain, season with salt and pepper and serve very hot.

FORCEMEAT

Ingredients

4 oz. diced lean ham or bacon
1 oz. each chopped liver, suet or butter
4 oz. fine breadcrumbs
1 oz. fat bacon
$\frac{1}{4}$ oz. each lemon peel (grated), thyme, parsley, shallot (chopped)
Grating of nutmeg, pepper and salt to season
Beaten egg to bind

Method

Form into small rounds and place in a tin to cook.

GAME CHIPS. Choose even-sized smallish potatoes. Wash well, peel and with a very sharp knife cut very thin slices across the width of the potato. Place in a clean dry cloth, dry thoroughly, then place in a frying basket. Immerse the basket in smoking hot fat; when chips are crisp and pale brown, remove from fat. Place basket on dish to drain, reheat fat and, when smoking, replace potatoes, shake well and cook to a golden brown. Drain on soft paper, keeping well heated. Sprinkle with salt and serve very hot.

GRAVY FOR GAME. Place the trimmings and giblets in a saucepan with seasoning and a bouquet garni, an onion and a carrot, cover with cold water and allow to boil. Remove fat from this, strain lightly and reduce, add salt and pepper to season; pour into dripping tin (after straining off the clear fat, just leaving the sediment) and boil up. Strain and serve in a well-heated sauceboat.

GAME SALAD. Make a salad with lettuce, endive, watercress and a thinly sliced apple. Arrange on a dish, add dressing and put some mustard and cress on top; squeeze over the juice of an orange, then place some neatly cut pieces of cold pheasant or other game on top, garnish with a little minced shallot and parsley mixed together, sliced hard-boiled egg and beetroot.

GAME TOAST. Prepare rounds of bread of medium thickness (removing crust), toast well on both sides, hold in steam for a second (this prevents hardening), butter well, add a squeeze of lemon juice to flavour, place in tin under birds while cooking, to soak up the drippings. Then serve the birds on the toast.

GARNISHES

Lemon. Slice thinly or cut into halves or quarters.

Watercress. Pick through the watercress, removing faded leaves, and wash well. Drain and dry in clean cloth. Choose nice sprigs gathered together in a loose bunch, and place at the side of the dish.

Bouchées with Sauce. See PASTE AND PASTRY (p. 376).

Chartreuse de Faisan

Ingredients

1 pheasant
$\frac{1}{4}$ lb. sausage meat
1 hard-boiled egg

Method

Make a gelatine of ingredients as above and slice when cold. Make savoury jelly by boiling up bones in about 1 qt. water

[244]

Chartreuse de Faisan (*continued*)
¼ lb. sliced tongue
Few pistachios
FOR SAVOURY JELLY
  Pheasant bones
  Carrot
  Turnip
  Onion
  1 oz. gelatine
  2 egg whites and shells

with vegetables. Reduce, strain and skim; there should be one pint. Clear as for jelly. Set a little of the savoury jelly in the bottom of a mould and decorate. Set slices of galantine and jelly in layers, finishing with jelly. Garnish with peas and truffles.

Chartreuse de Gibier

Ingredients

Cooked pheasant or other game (about 1 lb. meat)
1 tsp. chopped mushrooms
Pepper
Salt
1 egg yolk
2 tbsp. brown sauce
2 oz. flour
1 oz. butter
¼ pt. stock
2 eggs
FOR SAUCE
  Game bones
  1 oz. butter
  Bay leaf
  Thyme
  Shallot
  1 pt. stock
  1 oz. flour
  1 tomato
  Mushroom stalks
  ¼ pt. sherry
  ½ tsp. lemon juice

Method

Cut breast of pheasant into dice. Add chopped mushrooms, salt, pepper, and egg yolks and brown sauce. Make a panada with flour, butter and stock. Cook well and cool. Mince remainder of pheasant and pound with panada, 2 eggs, pepper and salt. Press through a wire sieve. Grease a charlotte tin and dust with flour. Fill with ¾ mixture, leaving a well in the centre. Fill this with diced breast, etc., and cover with rest of mixture. Cover with buttered paper, and steam *gently* one hour. Make sauce. Fry bones in butter with herbs. Add flour and brown. Add stock, tomato and mushroom stalks. Cook well until reduced to ½ pt. Add sherry and lemon juice. Strain over chartreuse. Garnish with mushrooms.

Fumet of Game. Peel and cut into slices 1 carrot and ½ onion. Put them with ½ sprig of thyme, 1 bay leaf, a little chopped raw lean ham and the carcass of any kind of raw game in a covered saucepan. Let them brown; add 1 wineglass of madeira and boil. Then moisten with 1 qt. of white broth or consommé. Add a pinch of salt and 12 whole peppers. Cook well for 40 mins. then strain.

Game Pie—I

Ingredients

Brace of partridge or pheasant
1 oz. butter
Onion
Rashers of bacon
Stock
½ lb. veal or steak (if desired)

Method

Using partridge or pheasant, pluck, singe, wash and joint the birds and fry for a few mins. in butter with a chopping of onion. Place in a pie dish, add a few curled rashers of bacon and just enough stock to cover. Add also, if desired, a little steak or veal, and simmer all together

[245]

Game Pie—I (continued)

Rosemary
Thyme
3 hard-boiled eggs
Pepper and salt
Mushrooms or oysters
8 oz. pastry (rough puff or short crust)

until tender. Remove from the heat and allow to cool. Add a sprig of rosemary, a little thyme, 2 or 3 hard-boiled eggs and pepper and salt to season. Mushrooms or oysters may be added to this pie if desired. Cover with pastry crust and bake at 350° F. Therm. 4 till well browned.

Game Pie—II

Ingredients

Hot water pastry (see p. 372)
A partridge or a pigeon
½ lb. fillet of veal
1 sausage
2 oz. bacon
1 tsp. each chopped parsley, chopped mushroom, chopped truffle
1 tbsp. stock
Seasoning
¼ pt. seasoned veal stock

Method

Make pastry. Grease a raised pie tin and line with three-quarters of the pastry. Line pastry with minced veal and bacon mixed with sausage meat, seasoning and herbs. Fill pie with joints of pigeon and cover with remainder of pastry. Decorate top and brush with egg. Tie a band of buttered paper round and insert a cone of paper in centre hole. Bake at 350° F. Therm. 4 for 1½ hr. When nearly cold fill up with good seasoned veal stock. When set, brush all over with glaze and decorate with aspic jelly. Game of all kinds may be used for this pie. If desired the feet may be glazed and inserted in centre hole after cooking.

Game Pudding

Ingredients

6–8 oz. suet crust (see p. 375)
Partridges
Bacon
½ lb. veal or steak
Herbs
Oysters

Method

Prepare the birds as for game pie, above, and cook them in a pan for about 20 mins. in very little water. Then place in a pudding basin lined with suet crust. Add oysters and mushrooms, cover with suet crust and steam 4–6 hrs.

GAMMON. A term applied to the thigh of a hog when pickled or dried and smoked. Particularly good for grilling and frying or baking with a piquant sauce.

GAPER. A bivalve which lives buried in sand or mud in an upright position near the low water mark at the mouth of rivers and estuaries. Boiled and eaten like cockles.

GARFISH. Also called Gar Pike. *Gar* was the Anglo-Saxon for spear, to which it may be supposed this fish bears some resemblance. It has also been styled Gar, Gerrick, Greenback, Greenbone, Gorebill, Hornfish, Long Nose, Sea Pike. It requires little cleaning and is generally boiled and served with anchovy-flavoured Butter sauce.

GARLIC (Fr. *ail*). There is no other article used in cookery that is so valuable and yet so much despised. Garlic is a bulb with a pungent flavour which, amidst several membraneous sheaths, is divided into what are termed "cloves", the French call these cloves of garlic *gousses* (pods) *d'ail*. The great art of using garlic

GARLIC (*continued*)

is to apply it to the dish so that it cannot be individually detected even though supplying the basis of the special flavour desired. When used with discretion in some dishes and salads it greatly enhances them and garlic is also used medicinally.

GARLIC, EXTRACT OF. Peel and chop 1 tsp. clove of garlic; put into a bottle, pour in ½ pt. spirits of wine and cork tightly. Shake the bottle occasionally for 8 days, then use as desired in very small quantities for flavouring.

GARLIC FLAVOURING FOR A SALAD (*chapon*). Cut a thin crust 2″ by 1″ from a loaf, sprinkle over it a little salt. Rub a peeled clove of garlic over both sides of the crust. Lay it at the bottom of the salad bowl, place the salad over, and stir it about.

Garlic Butter. See AYOLI.

Garlic Bread. See BREAD (p. 85).

Garlic Pickle. Put 4 oz. ginger into a bowl with strong brine, leave it to soak for 5 days, then cut it into slices and dry it in the sun. Put it into a stone or earthenware jar and pour over 1 gall. white vinegar. Remove the peel from 1 lb. garlic. Cover with salt, leave for 3 days. Wipe on a cloth, dry (also in the sun), and add it to the ginger together with ¼ lb. long pepper, previously soaked in salted water and dried, ¼ lb. turmeric seed and 1 lb. crushed or bruised mustard seed. Cover the jar, give it a shake, and leave it for a year before using. Any dried herbs in season may be added.

Garlic Sauce. Remove the peel from some garlic, separate into cloves. Put these into a saucepan of water and boil for 5 mins. Change the water 3 times, boiling for 5 mins. each time. Strain off the water, add white sauce to the cloves, boil up and serve. The strength of the flavour is determined by the length of boiling: the longer it boils, the weaker it will be. If garlic is properly cooked, it will have an almond flavour.

Garlic Vinegar. Peel and chop 3–4 oz. garlic, pound 3 cloves, and grate half a nutmeg. Put them all into a bottle. Pour over 1 pt. vinegar and cork the bottle. Shake daily for a week, strain, put into small bottles, cork securely. It is then ready for use.

GARNISHES. Sometimes when food is set upon a dish it may be very good to eat yet possess little attraction to the eye. Garnishes are for ornamentation, to enhance the general appearance of the dish and so whet the appetite. Some are used because their flavours blend happily with that of the main dish but others are used for colour and appearance only and need not even be served out to each guest.

Numerous garnishes and modes of applying them suitable for special foods and dishes will be found throughout this dictionary: the following are a few to which special names have been given, and under these names they are generally recognised. In the first list are savoury garnishes, in the second, French garnishes, and in the third, garnishes for sweet dishes.

Savoury Garnishes

Asparagus	Scrape the asparagus lightly, cut the green part into pieces the size of peas or a little larger if desired. Boil until tender; drain well, toss over heat in a sauté pan with a little butter, pepper and salt
Beetroot	Cook and slice the beetroot, stamp it into rounds or fancy shapes with cutters, or dice
Brunoise	Take vegetables mentioned in recipe for Julienne and cut into small dice. Cook separately until tender, finish as for Julienne
Brussels Sprouts	Take cooked brussels sprouts and use them hot or cold

Savoury Garnishes (*continued*)

Button onions	Blanch and cook in strong stock which should afterwards be reduced to glaze them. When onions are required for a white garnish, merely blanch them and cook in white stock or milk
Carrots and Turnips	Cut into round or fancy shapes, cook until tender in light stock or use raw, freshly grated on salads
Carrots and Turnips Glazed	Slice them, cut into round or fancy shapes, and cook in strong stock which should be reduced afterwards and used to glaze the vegetables
Cauliflower	Divide the flower into flowerets and boil gently until cooked, taking care no scum settles on them
Chervil	The leaves of chervil are very delicate, and they make an effective, quick finish for a chaudfroid of white meat. They may also be chopped like parsley or shredded and blanched for soups or salads
Chives	Use chopped chives to garnish soups, salads, vegetables, etc.
Cocks' Combs	Place combs in cold water, cook until skin begins to rise, then immediately pour in cold water; remove the combs and the skin. If they are allowed to cook after the skin rises they will not whiten. Trim and put into water with a little salt for eight hours. Then put into fresh cold water, changing frequently until they are quite white. Place in saucepan, cover with water, add a little butter, lemon juice, pepper and salt and boil gently until tender
Croûtons of Bread	Cut the bread into crescents, heart-shapes, squares, etc., as desired; fry in clarified butter or margarine until a golden brown colour. Drain on kitchen paper
Cucumber	1. When used for a hot entrée, slightly peel the cucumber, *not* removing *all* the green skin. Cut into pieces about 1″ long and ¾″ wide and cook until tender in water with a little salt and butter in it
	2. For a cold garnish, cut the pieces double the length but the same width, or notch the cucumber down the sides with a knife or the prongs of a fork. Then slice it thinly and curl it
Custard (Savoury)	Beat 2 whole eggs, 2 yolks and 1 gill of clear soup together. Season with pepper and salt, cover with buttered paper and steam carefully (see CUSTARD). Allow to cool before turning out. Cut into slices and stamp these into fancy shapes or cut into dice or diamonds
Eggs	Boil steadily for 10 mins. Peel and rub the yolks through a wire sieve and chop the white finely. Sometimes the whole egg is rubbed through a sieve, or sliced or diced for garnishing canapés. Cut the hard-boiled eggs into slices or quarters for salads

Savoury Garnishes (*continued*)

Egg Balls	Pound yolk of 6 hard-boiled eggs in a mortar with a little pepper and salt, moisten with the raw yolks of 2 eggs. Slightly flour the hands and make the mixture into balls the size of marbles. Drop into boiling water and poach gently for 2 mins
Eggs for Boiled or Roast Fowls, etc.	Cut some hard-boiled eggs in halves and remove yolks. Cut the round end of each so that they will stand and fill the eggs alternately with green peas, the cooked liver of the fowls, and the yolks rubbed through a wire sieve
Endive	Wash and break into neat pieces
Financière Ragout	Mix equal quantities of prepared mushrooms, small quenelles, scallops of sweetbread, cocks' combs and truffles in sufficient Financière sauce to moisten nicely
French beans	Cut into small diamond shapes and cook according to directions given
Gherkins	Cut the gherkins into small round or oval shapes or dice them
Green peas	(See directions under individual heading)
Julienne	Take the red part of 2 large carrots, 2 turnips, the white of half a head of celery and 6 leeks, and cut them into shreds. Cook separately until tender, taking care not to over-cook them. Shredded lettuce may be cooked and added to the other vegetables when possible. When cooked, drain well. They may then be tossed in a little warm butter
Lobster Coral	Wash and dry the lobster coral and rub through a wire sieve, or dry it in a slow oven (250° F.) and pound it
Lobster Spawn	Put live spawn into warm water, simmer to remove any salt, drain and dry in a slow oven (250° F.). Then pound in a mortar. When coral cannot be procured, this makes an excellent substitute
Macaroni	Cook according to directions given under main heading **CHEESE**, using cheese with it or not according to the purpose for which it is required
Macedoine	Cut some carrots and turnips into small pieces with a round cutter the size of a small funnel (not more than ¼″ in length), using the red part only of the carrots. Cook them separately; the turnips will take from 5–10 mins., the carrots from 15–20 mins. Mix with French beans and green peas prepared as for garnish
Macedoine à la Russe	Mix the macedoine, when prepared, with a little thick Mayonnaise sauce just before using
Mushrooms	Prepare some button mushrooms for cooking, and sauté in butter until tender

Savoury Garnishes (*continued*)

Olives	Remove the stone by paring the olive round it with a small, sharp knife. This is called "turning", and should be so skilfully done that when the stone is removed, the olive can be replaced in shape. Olives which are very salty should be allowed to soak in cold water before use. There are two kinds of olives, French and Spanish; the French are small and dark green in colour. Ripe olives are rarely used for garnish
Olives Farcies	Stoned olives, in the centre of which are placed small pieces of fillets of anchovies. These olives can be bought in bottles ready for use
Parsley, chopped	Wash parsley thoroughly, pick off stalks and scald in boiling water to remove the acrid flavour. Wring in a cloth and then chop very finely. Put in a cloth and wring again. To make an effective garnish, the parsley should be very small and quite dry. Coarsely chopped wet parsley is more of a disfigurement than a decoration
Parsley, fried	Wash and dry the parsley and pick off stalks. Fry in hot deep fat until crisp, then remove instantly. Drain on kitchen paper and sprinkle with a little salt. Care should be taken not to use parsley which has been frosted, as it will blacken in frying
Potato Chips, Croquettes, Ribbons, etc.	See **POTATO**
Potato Olives	These are potatoes cut into small, cone-like shapes and sautéed in butter
Quenelles	Use for this veal or chicken quenelle meat, shaping it in a teaspoon. Poach according to the directions given under **QUENELLES**
Rice cooked for Curry	See **RICE**
Spinach	Use spinach purée
Sweetbreads	Braise the sweetbreads, cut into scallops and glaze
Tarragon	This may be blanched, shredded or chopped, according to the purpose for which it is required
Tomatoes	See **Tomato farcies** (p. 500). Cherry tomatoes should be carefully baked in the oven. Blanch tomatoes before slicing, or cut as illustration when used whole.
Truffles	Simmer in rich stock until tender. Wine may be added to stock if desired. The truffles may be cut in round or olive shapes
Watercress	Wash thoroughly and dry the watercress, then season with a little oil, pepper and salt

Savoury Garnishes, French

ADMIRAL GARNISH (À L'AMIRAL). A fish garnish made up of boiled crayfish tails, prawns and mussels, mashed with white sauce, covered with breadcrumbs, fried in fat and parsley and placed in groups round the dish.

BORDEAUX GARNISH (À LA BORDELAISE). Shallot with Spanish sauce, ox marrow and wine. Finely chop the peeled shallot and put it in a sauté pan with $\frac{1}{2}$ wineglass of red wine; cook for 5 mins. Then add $\frac{1}{2}$ pt. Spanish sauce and a small quantity of cayenne, and cook for 5 mins. longer. Serve with beef steaks or fillets. Place over 6 slices of ox marrow, previously boiled.

Halving a Tomato for a garnish

CHIPOLATA GARNISH (À LA CHIPOLATA). Chestnuts, onions, mushrooms and chipolata sausages, prepared as follows: Blanch and cook the chestnuts in some rich broth, glaze a few onions, and cook some mushrooms in onion and lemon juice. Arrange with sausages round the dish and mask with Madeira sauce (see p. 444).

D'UXELLES GARNISH (À LA D'UXELLES). Fine herbs and Madeira sauce, prepared as follows: reduce 1 breakfastcup cooked fine herbs with a teacupful of Madeira sauce (see p. 444) in a saucepan over a moderate heat for about 10 mins., or until it thickens.

FERMIÈRE GARNISH (À LA FERMIÈRE). Small rounds of potatoes, fried in butter or margarine, glazed carrots, very small cabbages and lettuces, braised and arranged in groups round the dish.

FINANCIÈRE GARNISH (À LA FINANCIÈRE). Cock's combs, sweetbreads, forcemeat, quenelles, artichoke bottoms, mushrooms and truffles, prepared as follows: Blanch the cock's combs by steeping them in boiling water, dry and rub off the skin, soak them in cold water for several hours. Dry them and stew them in butter, lemon juice and a little salt. Moisten with a small quantity of stock. When boiling add 3 lamb's sweetbreads, 6 forcemeat quenelles, 5 artichoke bottoms, 6 mushrooms and 6 truffles, sliced. The garnish is then ready for use.

FLAMANDE GARNISH (À LA FLAMANDE). Cooked knuckle of ham, boiled bacon, sausages, German sausage, boiled carrots and turnips and glazed onions. The larger part of the garnish is made up of well-boiled white cabbages which have been well dried after cooking in the saucepan. Brussels sprouts may be used if desired. This garnish is specially good for rump steak or baked ham.

GARNISH FOR GAME. Calf's kidney, ham, parsley, tarragon and seasoning. Prepare by scalding half a kidney and 2 small slices of ham and cutting into small pieces. Put 3 oz. butter into a frying-pan, and when hot, lay in the meat; add a little chopped parsley and tarragon, salt and pepper to taste, and 3 thin slices of lemon. Fry gently until the kidney is of a light colour and a little gravy has run from it.

MARINIÈRE GARNISH (À LA MARINIÈRE). Blanch some mussels and trim them. Boil some truffles and crayfish, removing their tails and keeping them whole. Prepare some fish quenelles, highly seasoned with cayenne. Put some Velouté sauce (see p. 448) into a frying pan with a little of the liquor in which the mussels were blanched. Leave over a low heat and allow to thicken, then add the mussels, etc., and stir until hot.

MÂTELOTE GARNISH (À LA MÂTELOTE). Boil some soft roes of carp, and separately some mussels; cook also some crayfish and take out the meat from the tails, keeping them whole. Glaze some truffles, mushrooms and small onions. Should the garnish be required to be dished in heaps, Mâtelote sauce must be served in a sauceboat. But if it is to be served otherwise, all the ingredients should be put into a sauté pan with some Mâtelote sauce and stirred over a low heat for a few mins. until the sauce thickens.

MILANESE GARNISH (À LA MILANAISE). Cut 2 truffles, 6 mushrooms and equal quantity of cooked smoked ox-tongue into pieces. Put them into a saucepan with 2 breakfastcups boiled rice, $\frac{1}{2}$ pt. each Tomato (see p. 448) and Madeira (see p. 444) sauces, 1 tsp. salt, a little pepper and 3 tbsp. grated cheese (Parmesan or Gruyère), cook for 10 mins. and use as desired.

PARISIAN GARNISH (À LA PARISIENNE). Put $\frac{1}{2}$ wineglass of madeira into a saucepan, add 6 sliced mushrooms and 3 sliced truffles and cook for 4 mins., then add 1 cup Madeira sauce (see p. 444). Cook for 5 mins. longer and use as required.

PAYSANNE GARNISH (À LA PAYSANNE). Peel some large carrots, cut them into slices about $\frac{1}{2}$″ thick, blanch and braise them. Have ready some small broiled sausages, cooked stuffed cucumbers, all cut into thickish slices. Arrange the slices alternately, overlapping one another round the dish.

PROVENÇALE GARNISH (À LA PROVENÇALE). Cooked mushrooms and stuffed tomatoes arranged round the dish in alternate groups. This garnish can be served with almost any entrée and should be accompanied by Madeira sauce (see p. 444).

REFORM GARNISH (À LA REFORME). Shredded cooked ham, boiled carrots in slices, truffles and white of hard-boiled egg.

SCARLET GARNISH (À L'ÉCARLATE). Pour 1 cup each of Spanish sauce (see p. 442) and Tomato sauce (see p. 448) into a saucepan, adding a little finely chopped, cooked smoked ox-tongue. Cook for about 6 mins. and use as required.

SOUBISE GARNISH (À LA SOUBISE). Cut up 3 onions and put them in a saucepan with 1 oz. butter, $\frac{1}{2}$ cup white broth, 1 tsp. salt and 1 level saltspoon white pepper. Cover the saucepan and simmer over a low heat for 20 mins., stirring frequently. Add 2 cups Béchamel sauce (see p. 438) and boil for 5 mins. longer. Strain through a cloth, return to the saucepan, add a little more seasoning if necessary. Also add a little grated nutmeg, and thin with a little warm milk if the sauce is too thick. Re-warm and use as required.

Garnishes, Sweet

ALMONDS BLANCHED.	Put the almonds in water and bring to the boil. Drain, rub off the skins and throw them into cold water to keep them white. Dry them.
ALMONDS COLOURED.	Chop or shred the almonds. Pour a little cochineal on a plate and roll the almonds in it. Allow to dry before using. Almonds may be coloured brown in the oven.
ANGELICA.	Cut into neat strips or leaves.
CHERRIES.	Glacé cherries.
COCONUT, SHREDDED OR DESICCATED.	Coconut may be used; and sometimes it is lightly browned in the oven.
NUTS.	Finely chopped toasted nuts.

GAS. A combustible gaseous mixture used for fuel. See **KITCHENS**, COOKING BY GAS. See also **OVEN TEMPERATURES** for COMPARATIVE OVEN HEATS table.

GÂTEAU. This French term denotes a round, square or oval-shaped flat cake, generally decorated. Essentially a rich cake made of well-beaten butter, eggs, sugar, dough, etc., and, with few exceptions, these cakes are usually iced over with Butter, Fondant, or Royal icing and decorated. See **CAKES**.

Gâteau Mille Feuilles

Ingredients	Method
$\frac{1}{2}$ lb. puff pastry (see p. 373)	Divide the pastry into three, and roll out
$\frac{3}{4}$ pt. confectioner's cream (see p. 180)	each piece into a strip no more than 4″ wide. Place on a moistened baking sheet
Raspberry or strawberry jam	and bake until brown and well risen.
Apricot marmalade	When cool, trim the edges and spread a
Icing sugar	layer of jam on one strip, then place
Rum or vanilla flavouring	another piece of pastry on top. Cover with cream. Spread again with jam and

[252]

Gâteau Mille Feuilles (*continued*)

spread with cream This is sufficient for 6 large servings, 8 smaller. Cover with the third piece of pastry, putting the smooth side outside. Press together, then ice with 1 oz. icing sugar, rum or vanilla to flavour, and sufficient water to cream. Warm and coat top of pastry. If desired, crush the pastry trimmings and use to decorate the edges. Place on long wooden board and cut into slices.

Gâteau Pithiviers. This is a puff paste tartlet or tart filled with almond filling (see p. 13).

Gâteau Russe. Three or four distinctly coloured Genoese cakes which are sandwiched together with layers of apricot marmalade, rolled in almond paste and then sliced.

Gâteau St. Honoré. Puff paste or short crust foundation with a border of baked choux-paste balls, dipped in sugar glazing: the centre is filled with a rich confectioner's custard with a decoration of whipped cream on top.

GAUFFRE or GAUFER. See WAFFLE. The term is from Fr. *gaufrer*, to goffer, or print a pattern.

GELATINE. Jelly obtained from animal tissues (tendons, bones and ligaments) by prolonged boiling. Glue and size are the coarse kinds of gelatine, obtained from skin, hoofs, etc. Isinglass is obtained from the bladder of fish, especially sturgeon, sometimes from fish skins and bones. Gelatine is sold in thin cakes, or "leaves" or in granulated form. It is used in the preparation of both savoury and sweet dishes.

TO USE

Gelatine mixtures may be divided into three groups.
1. Clear jellies, which sometimes have fruit, vegetables, fish, etc., added, and suspended in them when the mix is set.
2. Mixtures containing eggs.
3. Mixtures which contain cream and are known as cream.
Always use the correct proportions: 1 oz. to each 1 pt. liquid (stout, milk, water, etc.). ¾ oz. to each 1 pt. liquid if either egg or cream is added (because both of these help to thicken and to set the mixture).

PROCEED AS FOLLOWS

1. Dissolve in a little hot water before adding to the mixture. If you bring the mixture to the boil without first dissolving the gelatine in water or softening it, if it is sheet gelatine it may become stringy.
2. Never let the mixture boil (except when clearing jellies; then the mixture sometimes boils for one minute to bring it to a head and remove scum).
3. When adding gelatine to milk, e.g. milk jelly, take great care that the milk is not too hot or the mixture will curdle.
4. When cream is added do not whip it too stiffly, and the gelatine must not be too hot when it is stirred with the cream or curdling may result.
5. Rinse the mould with cold water, and place the gelatine mixture into wet moulds to set.
6. To turn out dip mould for a second or two into hot water, ease round the inner rim of the mould; shake down in the hand to be sure that it is free in the mould, then slip on to the centre of the dish.

GÉNOESE. The name of a sponge cake (see **CAKES**) and a rich brown sauce.

GENTIAN. The dried root is sometimes used in the manufacture of bitters (see **BITTERS**).

GERANIUM. The oil of this plant is sometimes used in flavouring confectionery. It resembles attar of roses, for which it has been substituted. It is believed by some authorities to be the spikenard mentioned in the Scriptures as "very precious". Geranium leaves can be used as a garnish for salads and sweets, also they are used for jam (see **Rose Petal Jam**, p. 424).

GERMAN SAUCE. See SAUCES, SAVOURY **(Allemande).**

GERMANDER. Wall Germander. This whole herb is used medicinally.

GHEE. A clarified butter much used in India.

GHERKINS. These are a kind of small prickly cucumber, much in demand for pickling. Small undergrown cucumbers are sometimes used for this purpose.

GHERKINS, PICKLED. Put some gherkins into a stone jar and cover them with strong brine, adding a small piece of alum to prevent loss of colour. When they have been soaking for 7–8 days take them out, put them into fresh water and leave for 2–3 days in that. Boil some malt vinegar in a saucepan and leave to get nearly cold. Take the gherkins out of the water and put them into a jar, pour the cold vinegar over them and they are then ready for use. Cloves, allspice, cinnamon, mustard may be added to the vinegar before boiling, if desired. For a sweet pickle, add sugar to taste, as desired.

Gherkin Sauce. See SAUCES.

GIBLETS. The inmeats, or edible viscera of birds, together with the feet, joints of pinions, head and neck. Before cooking they must be thoroughly cleansed in plenty of water. The head should be chopped off the neck, the neck skinned and the pipe drawn away, the pinions thoroughly plucked, and the feet skinned by scalding and wiping with a rough cloth. The toe nails must also be chopped off, the heart well squeezed, the gall bladder carefully removed from the liver and all stained parts cut away. The gizzard has to be cut open and turned inside out so that the gritty contents can be washed off, and the thick lining membrane torn away. Giblets can be used for many tasty dishes.

Giblet Pie

Ingredients

3 or 4 sets of giblets, meat from the neck and pinions
Few slices of boiled bacon
Little gravy
Celery
Sweet herbs
Few mushrooms
Pepper and salt
Pastry to cover

Method

Prepare and stew the giblets and when they are done place in a dish with the meat from the neck and pinions. Arrange in layers with slices of cold boiled bacon between. Pour a little gravy over the dish and cover with a good pie crust. Bake at 350° F. Therm. 4 for about ¾ hr. Mashed potatoes may be put on top instead of paste, if desired.

GIETOST or GJETOST. The national cheese of Norway, made from goat's milk; it is made all the year round.

GIGOT. This term is commonly used in Scotland, and is French for "a leg of mutton". It is probably derived from the Old French *gigue*, a fiddle, in allusion to its shape. Sometimes the word is spelled "giggets", signifying small sups or slices of any kind of flesh.

GIMBLETTE. Very tasty French biscuit made in the shape of a ring and similar to *croque en bouche*.

GINGER. This is the dried rhizome or underground stem of the ginger plant. The Black or East Indian ginger is the unscraped rhizome prepared by scalding. White or Jamaican ginger is the scraped rhizome dried in the sun, and there is also the "unbleached" Jamaican ginger which is an uncoated variety occurring in fleshy, pale-coloured pieces. The inferior varieties occur in smaller pieces and are dark-coloured, flinty and shrivelled.

Ginger Beer

Ingredients

3 oz. pounded ginger
3 gall. boiling water
5 lb. loaf sugar
½ pt. yeast
2½ oz. cream of tartar

Method

Steep the ginger in the boiling water. When cold, strain through flannel. Dissolve the loaf sugar in the liquor; add the yeast and cream of tartar. If the weather is cold, stand the cask in a warm place to help the fermentation. As soon as this subsides, rack off the clear liquid, wash the cask and return the liquor to it. Allow to work for 2–3 days. Drain it off and bottle it. Cork tightly, fixing the cork down with wire or string.

Gingerbread. This is a household favourite which was probably introduced into England during the reign of Henry the Fourth. Shortly after this treacle came to be used instead of honey in making it. Gingerbread, made in the shape of men, animals, etc., was commonly sold at fairs up to the 19th century, covered with gilt paper: hence "to take the gilt off the gingerbread".

Ingredients

8 oz. flour
3 oz. fat (margarine or cooking fat)
2 oz. golden syrup
3 oz. sugar
½ tsp. salt
¼ tsp. mixed spice
1 tsp. ground ginger
1 level tsp. bicarb. soda
1 egg
Milk to mix

Method

Melt the fat, syrup and sugar together in a saucepan over a low heat. Sift the flour, salt, spice, ginger and bicarb. of soda together. Pour the syrup mixture gradually on to the flour, etc. Add beaten egg and sufficient milk to make a soft consistency. Turn into a greased Yorkshire pudding tin. Bake for ¾–1 hr. at 325° F. Therm. 3.

NOTE. For dark gingerbread, use treacle instead of golden syrup. If you want a dry, spongy type of gingerbread, store in an airtight tin. If a soggy gingerbread is required, store the cake wrapped in a moist cloth inside the tin. (It will not keep too long.)

Ginger Marmalade

Ingredients

2 lb. crystallised ginger
4 lb. sugar
3 pt. water
1 tsp. ground ginger

Method

Cut the ginger into very small pieces. Boil sugar and water to syrup, add chopped ginger and ground ginger and boil until it will set when tested on a saucer. Pour into warmed jars and cover.

Ginger Pudding

Ingredients

3 oz. flour
3 oz. breadcrumbs
3 oz. brown sugar
3 oz. shredded suet
½ tsp. bicarb. soda

Method

Mix all the dry ingredients together in a basin; add the beaten egg and sufficient milk to mix to a stiff consistency. Pour into a greased pudding basin and cover with a cloth. Boil for 2 hrs. and serve

Ginger Pudding (*continued*)
1 dsp. golden syrup
1 tsp. ground ginger
Pinch of salt
1 egg
½ pt. milk

with Custard (see p. 449) or Treacle (see p. 452) sauce.

GLOBE ARTICHOKE. See ARTICHOKE.

GLUCOSE. Commercially, a variable mixture of carbohydrates resulting from the hydrolysis of starch. It is produced by the action of dilute acids or ferments, e.g. yeast, upon starch and is used in sweets, confectionery and jams.

GLUTEN. A sticky albuminous substance obtained from the flour of wheat by washing in water, in which it is insoluble. Gluten flour is chiefly used for diabetic recipes.

GLYCERINE. A viscid, sweet, colourless liquid obtained from animal and vegetable fats and oils.

GNOCCHI. Light savoury dumplings boiled and served with grated Parmesan cheese. Also applied to *pâté à choux* which, after being passed through a forcer, is cut into short lengths and poached, then served in white sauce.

GOAT. Goat's milk is considered to be very nutritious. Both the milk and goat's milk cheese assume a musky smell and taste.

GOBY. The family name of a large number of sea fishes and a few spiny-finned fishes, which are distinguished by the broad depressed head. Gobys are used for Bouillabaisse.

GOLDEN BUCK. See BUCK RAREBIT.

GOLDEN THISTLE. This decorative vegetable has prickly foliage and the flowers are golden-coloured; the roots are long and thin and the flavour is good, but it is troublesome to slip the outer part of the roots off the centre tough part. No matter how long these roots are cooked, the centres remain tough. The flavour resembles salsify.

GOOD KING HENRY. Also called Fat Hen. The whole herb is used as a pot-herb, like spinach, and medicinally as a cooling infusion and laxative.

GOOSE (Fr. *oie*). The goose is a water-bird which has long been domesticated in all parts of the world. The age of the goose is easily tested by breaking the upper bill with finger and thumb and the feet, too, give strong indication of age, being coarse and worn in the old goose and comparatively smooth in the young one. For *Plucking* and *Trussing*, see **CHICKEN**.

GOOSE, ROAST—I. Take the prepared goose and stuff it with apple, chestnut, sage and onion, or other stuffing. Prick with a needle the skin into the fat layer which is situated near the legs and wings. Truss the goose. Place in a large meat tin; cover with piece of buttered greaseproof paper. If desired, place an onion or shallot, clove of garlic and celery leaves round the goose in the tin. Cook for 25 mins. per lb. plus 20 mins., roasting uncovered at 350° F. Therm. 4 and basting the goose every 15 to 20 mins. When the goose is half-cooked remove paper, season well with salt and pepper. When cooked, skim off fat, thicken the drippings with flour, add stock, reboil to thicken, and serve with Apple sauce, Chestnut purée (optional) and gravy.

GOOSE, ROAST—II

Ingredients
A goose
Sage and onion stuffing
½ lb. gravy beef

Method
Draw the goose and let it hang for several days. Truss and stuff the breast with forcemeat. Roast 1½–2 hrs. according to

[256]

GOOSE, ROAST—II (*continued*)

1 qt. water
1 onion or clove of garlic
1 apple
3 sage leaves
1½ oz. flour

size. To make the gravy, simmer the giblets in water with the beef cut small, onion, and sliced apple, sage leaves and a little pepper and salt for 3 hrs. Thicken with flour and, if necessary, colour the gravy. If desired a glass of port wine may be added. Pour a little gravy round the goose and serve the rest in a tureen. In the West of England the gravy is sometimes made with boiling cider.

GOOSE, GREEN is a bird of 3–4 mths. Cook like geese, but without stuffing them. Serve Gooseberry sauce (see p. 258) with them or, if preferred, dish *au cresson* (see **WATERCRESS**).

GOOSE'S FAT LIVER (Fr. *foie gras*). The celebrated Strasburg Goose's Fat Liver pies (*pâtés de foies gras*) are well known. Geese are specially fed for this purpose. Pâtés de foies gras are imported in terraines for keeping purposes: the livers are also preserved in tins so that cooks can make their own pâtés. The pâtés, which are imported fresh in October–November, are generally admitted to be best imitation pâtés de foies gras.

GOOSEBERRY (Fr. *groseille*). The fruit or berry of a prickly shrub indigenous to Great Britain, the English term being a corruption of "groseberry"; the Scottish name Grossart or Groset is derived from the French name. The gooseberry has been a favourite in this country since the time of Henry VIII. Gooseberries are divided into classes distinguished from each other by the colour of the fruits and the absence or presence of hairs on the skins. The smaller fruits have the best flavour, while the larger ones are fit for cooking early in the season. The red-skinned ones are less acid and are used for dessert at the end of the season. The amber and yellow varieties which are very tender in the skin, and mostly early ripening, are the best flavoured. Gooseberries are topped and tailed before use. (This is quickly done when scissors are used for this purpose.)

GOOSEBERRIES, TO BOTTLE. See **FRUIT**.

GOOSEBERRIES, STEWED. Put the topped and tailed gooseberries into a light syrup (made with sugar to taste and water). Simmer gently until tender. Allow to cool and serve.

Gooseberry Chutney

Ingredients	*Method*
1 qt. gooseberries	Top and tail the gooseberries. Add to
1 pt. vinegar	vinegar. Chop raisins, peel and slice
1 lb. seedless raisins	onions, and add to fruit together with
1 lb. onions	salt, sugar and ginger; the cloves and
½ tsp. salt	peppercorns should be added tied in
6 oz. sugar (brown if	muslin bag and removed when mixture is
possible)	cooked. Cool till tender. Pot and seal
½ tsp. ground ginger	securely.
Few cloves and peppercorns	

Gooseberry Fool. Pick and wash 2 qt. gooseberries and place them in a saucepan with ¼ lb. caster sugar. Cook over a low heat till quite tender, then pass through a sieve. Warm 1 qt. milk, 2 egg yolks lightly beaten and 1 teacup cream and simmer gently until thick, but do not boil. Leave to cool. Mix more sugar with the gooseberries if desired. Stir them into the milk, pour on to a fancy dish and serve. A little nutmeg may be grated over the top. Served with sponge fingers or sweet biscuits if desired.

9*

Gooseberry Jam

Ingredients
- 6 lb. gooseberries
- 1 cup water
- 6 lb. sugar

Method

Top and tail gooseberries and wash thoroughly. Place in preserving pan with water and boil for 7 mins. Add sugar and stir well until it is dissolved. Then boil for 30 mins., stirring frequently. Skim, pour into warmed jars and cover when cool.

Gooseberry Jam, Green

Ingredients
- 4 lb. sugar
- 2 pt. water
- 5 lb. green gooseberries

Method

Place sugar in preserving pan with water, and boil gently until it is syrup. Top and tail and wash gooseberries, put into syrup, and allow to simmer slowly until mixture thickens and sets. Pour into heated jars and cover.

Gooseberry Jelly

Ingredients
- 6 lb. ripe gooseberries
- Sugar

Method

Place fruit in preserving pan and heat slowly, pressing the fruit with a spoon against sides of pan to expel juice. When fruit is soft and tender, strain through muslin, measure juice and allow 1 lb. sugar to each pint of juice. Return to pan and boil gently until the jelly sets, in approximately 10–15 mins. Pour into heated jars and cover when cool.

Gooseberry Pie. See PASTE AND PASTRY (p. 368).

Gooseberry Sauce (for fish)

Ingredients
- Unripe gooseberries
- Sugar
- Melted butter
- Green colouring

Method

Top, tail and wash the gooseberries. Place in saucepan with ½" water at bottom of pan. Stew gently over low flame for 15 mins. until tender. Measure amount of pulp and add same amount of melted butter and sugar to taste. Add colouring. Serve piping hot with any white fish, usually grilled mackerel.

Gooseberry and White Currant Jam

Ingredients
- 4 lb. gooseberries
- 4 lb. white currants
- 8 lb. sugar

Method

Top and tail the gooseberries, wash and place in preserving pan. Stalk the currants and add to gooseberries. Simmer slowly, mashing gooseberries a little with wooden spoon. Add sugar, boil for 50 mins. until jam is thick. Pour into warmed jars and cover when cool.

[258]

GORGONZOLA. A semi-hard, blue-veined cheese made in Lombardy, also in the provinces of Pavia, Milan and Cremona. There is also a white Gorgonzola which is seldom found outside Italy.

GOSLING (Fr. *oison*). A young goose.

GOUDA, GOUDSCHE KASS. A Dutch cheese similar to Edam but of a different shape and larger; the diminutive gouda is known as Little Dutch.

GOULASH, GULYAS. A meat stew made in Austria and Hungary.

GOURDS. A name given to a very extensive tribe of fruit which numbers in its ranks some of the most delicious, largest and most useful natural growths in existence—cucumber, melon, pumpkin and vegetable marrow are all gourds and when emptied of their seeds, pulp and scraped dry, form cups, bowls, spoons and other useful vessels. The growing tops of gourds form a vegetable when boiled and pressed and served with lemon juice and butter.

GOURMANDS AND GOURMETS. These words are, in a sense, antitheses and yet both are concerned with the love of eating and drinking. Gourmands are literally gormandisers or gluttons, while on the other hand, gourmets are epicures, refined judges of good eating and drinking.

GRAINING. A term used in sugar boiling (see **SUGAR**).

GRAINING. Another name used for the dace.

GRAINS OF PARADISE. These are also known as Guinea Grains, Malaguetta Pepper, and by other names. They are the seeds of an African plant of the ginger family, are hot, acid and aromatic and in properties somewhat similar to other peppers. In some parts of the world they are used as a condiment, but chiefly used in this country to give fictitious taste of alcoholic strength to wine, beer and vinegar.

GRANITO. The name given to an iced drink composed of fruit juices mixed with syrup, and also to various kinds of punch. Coffee granito is a favourite, also orangeade and lemonade.

GRAPE (Fr. *raisin*). The grape is not much used in cookery save in the form of raisins, wine vinegar, wine and verjuice. See also **CURRANTS, RAISINS, WINE.** For *crystallised grapes*, see **FRUIT.**

Grape Jam

Ingredients

4 qt. green grapes
1 pt. water
Sugar

Method

Stem the fruit, wash well and drain. Simmer in preserving pan until fruit is soft. Press through a sieve and measure. Allow an equal amount of sugar. Place in a preserving pan and boil fast for 20–25 mins., stirring frequently to prevent jam from burning. Pour into heated jars and cover.

Grape Jelly

Ingredients

3 lb. Muscatel grapes
Sugar

Method

Stem the fruit, place in preserving pan and heat gently till grapes burst and juice runs freely. Strain juice through muslin, but do not press. Return to preserving pan and boil fast for 15–20 mins. Remove from heat, weigh it, add 14 oz. sugar to each 1 lb. juice. Return to heat and stir frequently until sugar dissolves. Boil for 15 mins., stir and

[259]

Grape Jelly (*continued*)

skim. Pour into heated jars and cover when cool.

GRAPEFRUIT. A citrous fruit, usually larger than an orange and with a yellow skin. Originally grown in the East it has now spread to many countries with hot

climates. The acid juice of the grapefruit makes it a good appetiser and it can be used with advantage mixed with other citrous fruit in marmalade.

GRAPEFRUIT, SERVED COLD. Cut in half, horizontally; remove seeds. With a knife cut round rim and loosen each section of pulp. Sprinkle with sugar, add a cherry to garnish. Grapefruit rind can be used as a jelly mould by serrating as illustration. Heat the grapefruit slightly in the oven to give it added flavour and juicyness. See also **FRUIT (COCKTAILS)** and **HORS D'ŒUVRES**.

Halving a Grapefruit

GRAPEFRUIT, BROILED. Sprinkle the grapefruit halves with brown sugar, or coat the top with honey and dot with butter. Add a tbsp. of madeira or sherry and place under preheated grill.

Grapefruit Marmalade

Ingredients

4 grapefruit
6 oranges
Juice of 6 lemons
2 qt. water
Sugar

Method

Place grapefruit in pan with just enough water to cover. Place oranges in another pan in a similar way, and cook until fruits are tender. Turn into separate bowls, water and all, and allow to stand overnight. Next day cut grapefruit in halves, remove pulp and rub through sieve: shred the rinds very finely. Slice the oranges whole and add to grapefruit. Retain all juice possible by slicing over a basin. Add the strained water to fruit, measure in pts., then place in preserving pan to heat through whilst the sugar— $1\frac{1}{2}$ lb. to each pint of fruit—is heating in cool oven (200° F. Therm. $\frac{1}{4}$). When heated through, add sugar and lemon juice and simmer gently until marmalade thickens. Pour into warmed jars, but allow to stand 24 hrs. before covering.

GRASS LAMB. A lamb which is born after Lady Day.

GRATIN. The literal significance of this French word is scraping of a dish or saucepan and therefore the culinary term is applied to certain dishes which are cooked in shallow dishes, which admit of tasty morsels being scraped from the dish. Baked with an encrusted or browned surface (Fr. *gratiner*, to brown the surface of the contents of the dish). *Au Gratin* usually means cooked with breadcrumbs. Sometimes grated cheese is added before dish is browned.

GRAVY. The sediment which drains from cooked meat. The juice of the meat being heavier than the hot fat, sinks to the bottom, just as greaves, which word has the same origin, sinks to the bottom when tallow is melted for manufacturing

GRAVY (*continued*)

purposes. The French term for gravy is *jus* so that meat served *au jus* is served with its own gravy, not with a made sauce. When roasting meat, the dripping pan catches the juice and fat exuded during the process, and when the meat is cooked, the fat is poured very carefully from the dripping, leaving the juice. To this, pepper and salt are added, and then hot water or stock, without impoverishing the gravy too much. The tin is placed over the heat until the gravy is boiling hot; stir with a fork until the juice is taken up in the water. This is poured over the meat through a gravy strainer or served in a sauceboat. Some meats yield very little juice, or juice of a very light colour only; it is then usual to add to the gravy a little burnt sugar or colouring. Sometimes garlic, onion or shallot are added. A few drops of anchovy essence greatly improve the gravy for beef.

TO MAKE COLOURING

1. Put a little burnt Spanish onion into a basin, pour some boiling water over it and work with a spoon. Put into the gravy and boil up.
2. Put an old iron spoon over the heat until it is very hot, then drop a little caster sugar into it; this gives a caramel that only requires to be mixed with the gravy to give the latter any depth of colour desired.
3. Baked raspings from bread thicken and brown all kinds of gravies, but they will not colour without thickening also.
4. A little flour baked until it is quite brown in a tin dish, is a colouring that can always be kept ready for use, but it does not colour without thickening.
5. Put ½ lb. sugar into a frying-pan. Place over a low heat until dissolved. Care should be taken to see that the mixture does not boil over. Then add ¾ pt. water; mix well, boil up. Remove from heat, put into a bottle, cork. A few drops only will be sufficient for colouring.

GRAVIES WITHOUT MEAT (*au maigre*). These are vegetarian gravies and they are of first importance. They are used as flavourings where it is difficult to get gravy stock, and there is no yield from meat.

1. Dice a few carrots, turnips, onions and a little celery. Put them into a frying-pan with some butter, and brown them. Pour in sufficient liquid to moisten them, season with salt and pepper and boil until the vegetables are tender. Pass the whole through a fine sieve and use as desired.
2. Slice a large onion, dust with flour and put into a frying-pan with a little butter or lard, and brown. Turn into a saucepan with ½ pt. water and a little grated lemon peel. Sprinkle over with salt and pepper to taste. Cover over the saucepan and simmer slowly for about 20 mins. Pass through a sieve into a basin. Allow to cool. Remove fat or scum and use as desired.

GRAVIES, THICK (*jus lie*). Thick gravies are thought sometimes to destroy, or swamp, the natural flavours of the meat.

GRAVIES FOR SPECIAL PURPOSES. Although a compound gravy may be considered good enough for a dish, some cooks prefer to prepare special gravies for certain dishes, but these, with few exceptions, partake so decidedly of the character of sauces, that many of them will be found under that heading.

Gravy, Thick, with Anchovies (*jus lie aux anchois*). Put 1½ teacups brown sauce with 1 teacup each broth and gravy into a saucepan over a low heat and, when they boil, stir in 2 oz. Anchovy butter. The liquor should not boil after the butter is added. This gravy sauce should be served at once.

Gravy, Thick, with Fine Herbs (*jus lie aux fines herbes*). Chop finely a large onion, put it into a saucepan with a pat of butter. Stir over a low heat until lightly coloured, then add 1 pt. half-glaze and ½ pt. broth. Boil until reduced by one third, then skim it well, stir in 1 tbsp. chopped mushroom, 1 tbsp. parsley, pinch of sugar and a little cayenne, and boil for five mins. When about to serve, squeeze in the strained juice of half a lemon.

GRAYLING (Fr. *ombre*). This favourite fish is allied to trout; it has a broad dorsal fin and is found in cold mountain streams. The grayling is sometimes known as "umber" and has a fine flavour with lemon. Cook like trout, bake or broil and serve with lemon. The smallest fish are considered best.

GREEN FIGS. See FIG.

GREEN FISH. See POLLOCK. Also referred to as Fresh Ling. This was a popular Lenten dish in Elizabethan days.

GREENGAGE (Fr. *reine claude*). A variety of plum, possibly more highly esteemed than any other for firm flesh, delicate flavour and sweetness. The term gage was given to this fruit by a family named "Gage" who lived near Bury St. Edmunds, and who obtained cuttings from France about the end of the eighteenth century. In France and other continental countries it is known as "*reine claude*" after the Queen of Francois I. Bluegage, Frostgage, Goldengage are possibly sub-varieties of the greengage.

GREENGAGES, To BOTTLE. See **FRUIT** (p. 231).

Greengage Jam

Ingredients	Method
8 lb. greengages 8 lb. sugar 1 cup water	Wipe fruit with damp cloth, remove stalks and stones and place in preserving pan with cup of water. Heat very slowly and, when boiling, continue to boil fast for 10 mins. Crack some stones and after blanching kernels, add to fruit. Next add sugar, previously warmed, and stir until it dissolves. Then boil the whole fast for 20 mins., skim, pour into warmed jars and cover.

GREEN GOSE. A common term for a gosling in the spring.

GREENING. A vegetable colouring matter made by expressing the juice of spinach; occasionally used in confectionery and for other purposes.

GREEN PEA. See PEA, GREEN.

GREEN PEA PURÉE. See SOUPS.

GREEN PEPPER. See CAPSICUM.

GREEN SAUCE. See SAUCES.

GREEN TURTLE. See TURTLE.

GREENS. This term is commonly applied to all kinds of cabbages.

GREY MULLET. See MULLET.

GREY PLOVERS. See PLOVER.

GRIDDLE. This is an iron plate or pan used for cooking cakes and scones. It is sometimes mentioned in the lowland districts of Scotland as a "girdle", but this is a corruption of "griddle".

GRIDIRON or GRILL. A grating (a row of thin steel bars fastened in an iron frame), placed before or over the fire. A grill is used for broiling or grilling. A *mixed grill* consists of a selection of bacon, cutlets, kidney, tomatoes, sausages and sometimes mushrooms, all grilled and served on a dish with mashed potato.

GRIG. A small freshwater eel.

GRILLADE. The French term for anything grilled, such as broiled ham.

GRILSE. A young salmon in its second year, after its first return from the sea, not being much used except for potting.

GRISKIN (of pork). The spine, chine or backbone of a pig, which is cut away when preparing sides of bacon, and considered by some to be a titbit when baked or grilled. In the small pig the griskin and spare rib are not separated.

GRISTLE. Cartilage.

GROATS. Dried grain, such as oats or wheat, milled and coarsely broken or crushed. Sometimes known as "grits" or "grouts".

GROG. A mixture of spirits, hot water and sugar. Usually rum is used for this hot beverage.

GROUND RICE. See RICE.

GROUSE. Though there are many varieties of grouse, the Ptarmigan or White grouse of Norway is sometimes substituted for the Scotch Red grouse or Hazel grouse. The Scotch grouse is shot on the North British Moors from the middle of August (12th) to the end of January. Whether young or old, the bird has a very fine flavour. See also GAME for instructions on preparing and serving grouse.

GROUSE, TO ROAST. Put the prepared birds in a baking tin and cover the breasts with bacon or dripping. Place in a hot oven, 400° F. Therm. 6, and bake for 25–35 mins. Put some toast with crusts removed into the dripping and then place on hot dish. Serve the grouse on this with brown gravy and breadcrumbs and garnish with watercress.

Grouse, Braised

Ingredients

Brace of grouse
4 rashers streaky bacon
3 pieces of celery
1 onion stuck with 6 cloves
Bunch of parsley
Few sprigs sweet herbs
Few slices carrot
12 peppercorns
1 beetroot
1 onion
2 oz. butter
½ pt. broth
1 tsp. brandy
½ pt. brown sauce
1 tbsp. red wine

Method

Prepare and truss the grouse then put in a casserole on a layer of bacon. Pack them round with celery and the onion stuck with cloves; add parsley and some sprigs of sweet herbs. Add the carrot and peppercorns. Peel and slice beetroot and onion and put them into the frying-pan; add a little butter and fry. When brown, stir in the broth and pour into the casserole; add brandy and cover the birds with greaseproof paper. Place over a low heat and simmer for 2 hrs., then remove grouse and place on a hot dish. Keep hot. Strain off liquor from vegetables into another pan, skim off the fat and reduce it to half-glaze. Add brown sauce and red wine, boil for 7 mins., then strain over birds. Cut the bacon into small pieces and garnish the dish with it. Chopped boiled carrots can also be used as a garnish.

Grouse, Hashed. Take the remains of grouse, cut into neat joints putting the skin, bones and trimmings into a saucepan with 2 sliced shallots. Add 2 oz. butter or margarine rolled thickly in flour. Shake the pan over the fire until the butter is melted and slightly browned. Add ½ pt. stock (or milk and water), 1 tsp. salt, ¼ tsp. pepper and ½ blade of mace, pounded. Cover the saucepan closely and simmer gently for 1 hr. Strain the gravy and return to saucepan; add a glass of claret and reboil. Then add pieces of grouse, leave to heat through thoroughly and serve with toasted sippets round the dish. The gravy *must not* boil after the grouse is added.

Grouse Soufflé. Take the breasts of two cooked grouse, pound them in a mortar with 2 oz. fresh butter, and ½ tsp. onion. When you have rubbed this through a sieve fold in the yolks of 4 eggs, and the whites, which must be whipped up to a stiff froth. Season lightly with salt and a little cayenne pepper. Bake at 450° F. Therm. 8 for about 20 mins. Serve immediately.

GRUEL. This name is of French origin and is given to a sort of thin porridge or paste made of almost any kind of fine or coarse meal, oatmeal, barley or other farinaceous food.

GRUYÈRE. A cooked hard cheese, pale yellow in colour, which is honeycombed with age. It comes from the canton of Emmenthal in Switzerland; now also made in parts of France and Italy.

GUAVA. The tree upon which this fruit grows is found wild in the tropical part of America and the West Indies, and has become naturalised in India and other Eastern countries. There are two kinds of guava, commonly known as bearing delicious fruit; one bears an apple-shaped guava, and the other a pear-shaped fruit. Guavas are described as having a thin, bright yellow rind with a yellowish or reddish pulpy flesh which has a pleasantly acid-sweet flavour, not unlike a combination of raspberries and strawberries.

Guava Jelly

Ingredients	Method
1½ lb. ripe guavas 1½ lb. under-ripe guavas Juice of 1 lemon Sugar	Slice the fruit and place in preserving pan with enough water to cover bottom of pan. Simmer until fruit is soft, strain without pressure through muslin, and return to pan and boil for 20 mins. with lemon juice. Measure carefully and add cup for cup, an equal amount of sugar. Boil together for 20 mins. until it sets. Pour into warmed jars and cover when cool.

Guava Preserve

Ingredients	Method
3 lb. guavas 3 lb. sugar 2 pt. water	Peel, halve and remove seeds from fruit. Place the sugar and water in preserving pan and boil until it will candy in cold water. Add fruit until it is clear and tender but unbroken. Pour into heated jars and cover when cool.

GUDGEON (Fr. *goujon*). There are two or three kinds of gudgeon, but the white or silver is thought to be the best. They are caught either by rod and line or in hauls on the West coast of England at all seasons of the year. Usually fried and served with fried parsley, like smelts.

GUINEA-FOWL (Fr. *pintade*). The guinea-fowl is a bird of the turkey species, and the flesh is of a kind between a fowl and a pheasant. It is in season when game is not.

TO ROAST. Tie slices of slitted fat bacon over the breasts and cook like roast fowl or turkey. Serve Bread sauce and gravy. If desired, dish *au cresson* (with watercress).

GUINEA-PIGS (Fr. *cochons d'Inde*). These prolific little animals are better known in this country as pets than subjects for the kitchen, though they are edible.

GUINETTE. The old name for Guinea-fowl.

GUMBO. Also called Okra, an annual pod of a tree of the hibiscus family. These nutritious green pods are much used in the West Indies, etc., for soups and pickles.

GURNARD or GURNET (Fr. *goujon rouget*). A very small river fish. The varieties are the Red, the Piper, the Streaked, the Grey and the Little gurnard. The Red gurnet or gurnard is caught in hauls off the west coast of England at all seasons of the year. It is about a foot long and also caught with rod and line. They may be fried.

GWYNIAD. The white fish, freshwater herring, found in Bala Lake, North Wales.

H

HADDOCK (Fr. *aigrefin*). Along the northern coasts of both Europe and America these fish are very plentiful, but those of the best quality are caught along the coast of Devonshire or Cornwall, and in Dublin Bay. These fish are allied to cod, being marked with a similar lateral line, but differing in that they show a dark spot on each side of the body just behind the gills. Scotland is famous for the drying and smoking of haddocks (see **HADDOCK, FINDON**). Fresh haddocks cannot be cooked too soon after catching; due to the gummy character of the flesh and skin, decomposition quickly sets in. The haddock should be gutted and thoroughly cleansed, its fins and tail cut close with a pair of sharp scissors, and the interior should then be dusted over or rubbed with salt. Small haddocks are frequently skinned and trussed like whiting, with their tails in their mouths. The haddock is coarser and darker in colour than the whiting. The Norway haddock is known as Rodfish. In Denmark it is the gastronomically prized Red haddock.

Haddock au Gratin

Ingredients

1 lb. haddock fillet
2 oz. butter or margarine
½ tsp. salt
⅛ tsp. pepper
½ onion minced
½ green pepper, minced
2 tbsp. flour
Milk
½ tsp. Worcester sauce
2 oz. dry breadcrumbs
1 oz. grated cheese

Method

Wipe the fillets with damp cloth and cut into cubes. Melt butter in saucepan, add salt and pepper to taste and onion and green peppers. Sauté gently over a low flame for 10 mins., add flour blended with milk, reheat until sauce thickens. Add Worcester sauce and the fish cubes. Turn into greased fireproof dish, sprinkle with combined crumbs and cheese. Bake at 310° F. Therm. 2 for 10 mins. until golden brown. Garnish with parsley or chives.

Haddock Stewed with Tomatoes. Cod, hake, halibut or whiting may be used alternatively.

Ingredients

¼ pt. olive oil
¼ tsp. marjoram
⅛ tsp. basil
Salt
⅛ tsp. pepper
1 lb. tomatoes (or a tin)
2 cloves garlic
3 stalks celery
2 lb. haddock fillet
4 sprigs parsley
4 rounds buttered toast

Method

Put the oil in deep saucepan. Add marjoram, basil, salt, pepper, garlic, celery and tomatoes. Cover and simmer for 20 mins. Wipe the fillets with a damp cloth, sprinkle with salt on each side and place in a steamer. Steam over boiling water for 10 mins. or till fish will flake with a fork. Remove and place in pre-heated dish. Pour over sauce, garnish with sprigs of parsley and toast squares.

HADDOCK, FINDON (or Dried Haddock). Haddock salted, dried and smoked. The "Scotch Rizzared" haddock is merely salted inside and out and left overnight

HADDOCK FINDON (*continued*)

before hanging in the air, preferably in the window or the sun, but the Finnan haddock or Findon haddock, after salting and drying, also undergoes a process of smoking which gives it a strong flavour.

Haddock, Boiled, Dried

Ingredients	Method
About 1 lb. dried haddock ¼ pt. milk ¾ pt. water 1 oz. butter	Put the fish in a deep frying-pan. Pour in the milk and water, place over a low heat and bring to the boil slowly, then simmer gently for about 10 mins. Put the fish on-to a hot dish, dot with butter and serve immediately. If desired, garnish with poached eggs and a little finely chopped parsley. (If preferred, cook the haddock in water.)

Haddock Soufflé

Ingredients	Method
6 oz. cooked flaked Finnan haddock 1 gill cream or top of milk 2 oz. butter or margarine 2 level tbsp. flour ¾ cup of milk Cayenne, pepper and salt 1 dsp. lemon juice Few drops anchovy essence 2 eggs	Pound fish in a mortar or basin with cream. Melt the butter in a saucepan, stir in the flour gradually until quite smooth, add milk by degrees, stirring the whole time over a gentle heat, boil for 2 mins., remove from heat and leave to cool. Season with cayenne, salt and a little pepper, add anchovy and lemon juice; add to, and mix with the sauce. Stir in the beaten egg-yolks and fold in the stiffly whisked white of egg (with a metal spoon). Turn into a well-buttered soufflé case, which has a piece of folded, double, buttered greaseproof paper tied round it (standing above the rim about 2″). Bake at 400° F. Therm. 6 for 25–30 mins.

HAGGIS. This is a famous Scottish national dish. Haggis, when boiled for 2 hrs., may be kept for a week or two. When cold it gets so firm that haggis is often sent from Scotland to distant countries. It is essential that it should be very dry and covered with oatmeal. Haggis does not keep so well when onion is added. It is made with the stomach or pluck of a calf, lamb, or (most frequently) sheep. Haggis is usually boiled in the stomach-bag, and care should be taken that no thin parts are left unrepaired or it may burst in boiling water, then the haggis will be spoilt.

Ingredients	Method
1 calf's udder 1 calf's kidney 1 calf's pluck 1 bay leaf Dozen sprigs of parsley Few young green onions Few shallots	Blanch the udder; split both kidney and pluck. Boil in water for 25 mins. with bay leaf. Blanch and chop parsley; peel and chop onions, shallots and mushrooms. Toss all together in butter. Add madeira and salt and pepper to season. Mince the veal fat and the meat (having removed

HAGGIS (*continued*)
Few mushrooms
Little butter
Wineglass madeira
Salt and pepper
Web of veal fat
2 tbsp. gravy
2 eggs yolks
2 tbsp. breadcrumbs

bay leaf) and mix all together. Add beaten egg-yolks, gravy and breadcrumbs. Fill the bag and prick round to prevent bursting. Tie up and boil about 3 hrs.

HAKE (Fr. *merluche*). This fish is thought to be superior to haddock or plaice in flavour, digestibility and nutrition. The word "hake" is a derivation from "hook" in allusion to the peculiar hook-like fin just behind the neck, which is always cut away by the fishmonger when he desires to make hake look like cod. A sharp eye would soon know a cod from a hake by the cut root of the fin, that is if the part bearing it is left.

Hake and Potato Soufflé

Ingredients
1 lb. hake fillet
2 oz. butter
2 stalks celery diced
1 small onion minced
½ chopped green pepper
4 parsley sprigs
Mashed potato
1 tbsp. lemon
Salt and pepper
3 eggs

Method
Wipe fillets with damp cloth and place in wire basket. When saucepan of water is boiling, put in the basket but do not allow fish to touch water. Steam for 10 mins. then remove skin and flake with fork. Melt butter in a pan, add celery, onion, green pepper, and parsley, and simmer for 15 mins. until tender. Put the mashed potatoes into a large mixing bowl, add fish and lemon juice, salt and pepper to taste; beat the egg yolks, add, and mix well. Separate the whites of eggs, beat to a stiff froth. Fold into mixture (with a metal spoon) and turn into a greased casserole. Place this in shallow tin of hot water, and bake in a preheated moderate oven (350° F. Therm. 4) for 30 mins. or until golden brown. Serve immediately with a chosen sauce.

HALBRAN or HALEBRAN. See ALBRAN.

HALF-FISH. A common name for a salmon when half-grown.

HALF-GLAZE. See SAUCES, SAVOURY.

HALIBUT (Fr. *fletan*). Halibut is one of the largest of the flat-fish tribe and one can weigh from 75–100 lb. The Chicken halibut, which only weighs 3 lb. or less, is considered the best.

Halibut Steak, Curried

Ingredients
2 lb. halibut steak
1 bay leaf
2 oz. butter
1 small onion minced
½ green pepper chopped

Method
Wipe steak with damp cloth. Place in a shallow saucepan, cover with cold water, add bay leaf, cover and bring to boil. Reduce heat and simmer for 10 mins., drain fish and keep hot; keep the fish

HALIBUT (continued)

1 stalk celery diced
3 tbsp. flour
¼ tsp. curry powder
Wineglass sauterne
2 drops tabasco
Salt and pepper

Halibut with Sauterne

Ingredients

1½ lb. halibut fillet
Juice of half lemon
Salt and pepper
1 small carrot
3 medium potatoes
Olive oil
2 medium-sized onions sliced
1 sprig parsley
2 cloves garlic
1 stick celery diced
Tomato purée
Wineglass sauterne

stock. Melt butter in saucepan, add onion, green pepper and celery. Sauté over low flame for 10 mins. Blend flour and curry powder with a cupful cooled fish stock. Add sauterne, tabasco and salt and pepper to taste and bring to boil; remove skin and centre bone of fish, arrange on a hot plate, pour over sauce and garnish with finely chopped parsley.

Method

Wipe fillets with a damp cloth, cut into portions and sprinkle with lemon juice. Season to taste with salt and pepper. Pour water into saucepan, parboil diced carrot and potatoes for 10 mins. Put the olive oil into frying-pan over medium heat. Sauté onions until light brown. Remove from oil. Put the potatoes, onions, carrots in casserole, add parsley, garlic and celery; next the fish, with more potato and onion. Add mixed together the tomato purée and sauterne. Cover and bake at 340° F. Therm. 3 for 45 mins.

HAM (Fr. *jambon*). Ham is the hind legs of pork, salted and cured and sometimes smoked, frequently cured together with the side of bacon. Hence it follows that localities famous for bacon are also famous for ham, the quality depending largely on the superiority of the meat, and in a measure also on the method adopted for curing. Wiltshire and Hampshire and parts of Yorkshire are celebrated for home-cured ham. York ham is large, round and plump, of pink meat with delicate white fat which has a slightly pinky tinge. Westphalian ham resembles York ham. The small hams which are cured in Ireland make good breakfast and lunch dishes. Canadian hams are small, long and generally quite as well cured as any, but the fat is not so white or marrowy as in the large hams.

TO BOIL. Soak the ham overnight, then put it in a saucepan and cover with hot water. Simmer gently for 5 hrs. and then move the saucepan to one side and let the ham remain in the water a further hour or two longer. When nearly cold, take it out and skin it. Sprinkle over baked breadcrumbs and about 3 tbsp. moist sugar. If preferred, after skinning, finish off by sticking a few cloves in the fat, sprinkle with bread crumbs and coarse brown sugar, and bake at 350° F. Therm. 4 for about 1 hr.

TO CURE AND SMOKE. See **BACON**.

BOILED SLICES OF HAM. Melt 3 tbsp. redcurrant jelly in a saucepan; mix with 1 tsp. melted butter. Add some thin slices of ham seasoned with a little pepper, then turn on to a hot dish and serve.

HAM AND EGGS. Broil some thin slices of ham and poach as many eggs as there are slices of ham. Put the ham on a hot dish with an egg on each slice. Serve hot.

Ham Omelet. Beat up 3 eggs and mix them with 1 tbsp. finely chopped ham, a little chopped parsley and shallot. Season with salt and pepper to taste. Put some butter into an omelet pan, when melted pour in the mixture. When set, serve on a hot dish, garnished with finely chopped parsley.

HAMBURGER. A flat cake of minced beef very popular in America. Basically the same mixture as rissoles, but many variations of ingredients can be used.

HAND OF PORK. This joint is the foreleg, usually salted and boiled and served hot or cold.

HARD BAKE. This is a sweetmeat made by boiling coarse sugar or molasses with almonds, and orange or lemon flavouring. See **ALMOND** (p. 12).

HARD SAUCE. See **SAUCES (SWEET).**

HARE (Fr. *lièvre*). Hare flesh is dark, thus differing from the white flesh of the rabbit; if kept long enough it assumes a game flavour. Hares come into season in August, and they are prime quality until March.

TO CHOOSE AND KEEP HARES. Choose those with the cleft in the lip narrow, sharp claws and with ears that will tear easily. Old hares are only fit for jugging or soup. When fresh, the body will be stiff. To develop their game flavour, the insides should not be removed for a few days after killing, and they should be hung by their forelegs so that they may not lose their juices from the wound that caused their death. After 4 or 5 days it is advisable to open them and remove all the paunch, reserving the heart and liver for sauce or stuffing. Let these be scalded, and wipe the insides every day with dry cloths, rubbing the lining with a mixture of ground pepper and ginger. The older the hare the longer it should be hung, and it will require slower cooking in order to reduce toughness of the flesh. It can be hung for 10 days in cold weather, but in muggy weather the time will be shorter.

TO SKIN. Cut off the paws at joints, then pushing the hind legs through the skin, gently ease up the back, otherwise as the skin is pulled off it will tear the flesh. Pull the front legs through the skin then pull it over the head. If the head is not needed, cut it off at this stage. If it is to be left on, run a skewer between the skin and head and pull off the ears in the skin. Cut nose and lips.

Hare, Jugged (Fr. *civet de lièvre*)

Ingredients

1 hare
2 oz. flour
3 oz. butter
1½ pt. beef stock
1 onion stuck with 6 cloves
Rind of 1 lemon
Pepper and salt
2 wineglasses port
Veal forcemeat (see **FORCE-MEAT**)

Method

Dry the hare well and cut into neat pieces, then flour and fry in butter. Pour in stock or gravy and stir until boiling, then put the gravy into an earthenware jar with the hare, onion, rind of lemon, pepper and salt and one glass of port. Cover closely, put jar into the oven (350° F. Therm. 4) and let the contents simmer gently from 3 to 4 hrs. until the hare is tender. Make some balls of veal forcemeat, to which the chopped liver of the hare has been added, and either fry or bake them. When the hare is cooked, place on a hot entrée dish, add the other glass of port to the gravy and strain it over the hare. Garnish with forcemeat balls and serve red currant jelly with it.

Hare Pie

Ingredients

1 well-hung hare
2 oz. flour
2 oz. butter or dripping
¾ lb. veal
½ lb. bacon

Method

Cut the hare into neat joints and bone them; flour and fry them in butter. Set them on one side to get cold. Mince the veal and bacon; season with pepper and salt, add chopped parsley. Line a mould

[269]

Hare Pie (*continued*)

Pepper and salt
2 tbsp. parsley
Hot water crust (see **PASTE AND PASTRY**)
Veal forcemeat balls (see **FORCEMEAT**)

with the pastry, and put a layer of veal and bacon at the bottom. Season each piece of hare with pepper and salt and place them in the mould alternately with veal and bacon, add parsley and some forcemeat balls. Pour in a good gravy made from the bones of the hare which will jelly when cold. Cover with paste, decorate with paste leaves, and bake at 350° F. Therm. 4. When nearly cooked, after about 3 hrs., glaze with beaten egg. Care must be taken to see that the crust does not take too dark a colour. If served cold, serve with a garnish of chopped parsley and aspic.

Hare Soup. See **SOUP**.

HARICOT BEAN. See **BEANS, HARICOT**.

HARSLET. The inside organs of a pig, also their best parts, liver, sweetbread, etc., which are prepared and spiced, enclosed in caul, then roasted and served with sauce.

HARTSHORN. The shavings of a stag's horn which are said to yield a very nutritious jelly.

HASH. Hashed meat, re-dressed meat.

HAUNCH. This word is taken from the French *hanche* which probably originated from the German *hancke*, signifying in each case the loin and leg taken together in one piece. See **MUTTON** and **VENISON**.

HAZEL HEN (Fr. *gelinotte*). In season from December to June. The roasting time varies according to size, heat and taste, but approximately 20 mins. is the time taken. Cook as grouse.

HAZEL NUTS. These are plentiful in some parts and possess a mild farinaceous taste. They are used for flavouring biscuits or cakes.

HEADS (Fr. *têtes*). These are described under **BOAR, CALF, LAMB, OX** and **SHEEP**, and will be found to include Tongue and Brains.

HEARTS (Fr. *cœurs*). All birds, beasts, fishes and reptiles endowed with a system of circulating blood are possessed of hearts. Directions for using those which are edible will be found under individual headings, **CALF, BULLOCK, SHEEP**, etc.

HEATH COCK. See **BLACK COCK**.

HECTOGRAM; HECTOLITRE. See **WEIGHTS AND MEASURES** (page 519).

HEDGEHOGS (Fr. *herisson*). Amongst the eccentricities of gastronomy, the hedgehog may be classed. Although it is strong-flavoured, the flesh when stewed is both savoury and tender. The gypsies are said to cook them by rolling them in soft clay and then leaving them in the ashes of a camp fire until wanted. By breaking open the clay shell when they are baked sufficiently, the skin peels off, leaving the steaming hot flesh.

HENWARE. See **SEAWEED**.

HERBS. Culinary herbs may be treated as additional seasonings to the usual ones of salt, pepper, mustard and vinegar. Always use a small amount, a pinch (which is less than ¼ tsp.) until you are familiar with the various flavours. The seasoning

HERBS (*continued*)

should help to bring out the flavour of the food but should not be recognisable itself. The flavour of each herb is held in its oil, and it should be remembered that the longer the herb remains in the food the more oil will be released, and that heat acts upon it more quickly than cold. Never add more herbs than a recipe states; if you put too much of a herb into the mixture or infuse too long the dish will have a bitter taste.

Herbs should be added to soups and stews about ¾ hr. before the end of cooking. To cold foods, soft cheese, vegetables and cocktails add the herbs several hours before serving, or overnight. When adding savoury seeds, these should be crushed and soaked in the liquid stated in the recipe at least an hour before the making of the recipe.

When adding foliage herbs to salads, chop and sprinkle over the salad. When adding fresh herbs to some recipes, even though the food is only to be cooked a short time, they do not need to be soaked, but added directly to the fish or meat mixtures, or sprinkled over the roasts, because the oils are readily released. For jellies and moulds the herb is bruised before boiling in the mixture.

Fresh herbs always contain more oil than dried ones, but it is immaterial whether fresh or dried are used. Dried herbs should always be kept in glass bottles or jars with tightly fitting lids, as they do not retain their oils for much more than a year. Leaves are left whole when they are to be used for teas, but they are pounded for cooking.

TO DRY LEAVES AND STEMS. Gather the herbs on a sunny day before they flower. Be sure to see that they are free from dust. If necessary, wash them, and then dry thoroughly with a dry cloth. Herbs can be dried in the sun or hung in an attic or room with cross-ventilation and a little sun. Tie the leafy stems into small bunches and stretch them across a line or wire; put a sheet on the floor to catch any leaves that fall. Remove the bunches as soon as they dry, otherwise the fragrant oils will be lost. Never store dried leaves in a paper bag as they are apt to get damp. Dry, also, by laying the leaves on a baking sheet and placing them in a low oven, 250° F. Therm. ½, with door open. Mint, marjoram, savory and thyme usually take about 1 hr.; parsley and sage about 1½ hr.

An old-fashioned method of drying dill, fennel, mint and parsley is to strip the foliage from the stems and dip the leaves into boiling salted water just long enough to wilt them; then lift them out with a strainer, shake off the water and spread the leaves on a fine wire-mesh sieve. Lay on a baking sheet and put into an oven at 350° F. Therm. 4 for about 5–10 mins.; then rub the crisp dry leaves through a sieve to powder them; store in glass jars, closely corked; watch, and if they show any signs of moisture, pour out and dry for 3 or 4 days, depending upon the weather, and when the leaves are crackling, return to jars and cover tightly. Never store herbs on a sunny shelf as the sun's rays may fade their colour.

TO DRY ROOTS. If the roots of herbs are to be dried, e.g. angelica, lovage and Florentine iris (orris root), dig them up in the autumn when the growing season is over, or in the early spring when they are dormant, otherwise they will shrivel greatly. After digging up, wash the roots thoroughly and scrape them if necessary to remove any dirt. Split or slice large roots and spread the slices in layers on wire screens so that the air can pass over or under them. Turn the slices 3 or 4 times a week so that the air can get through them. Put out of doors on a suitable day or, if preferred, dry in a very low oven at 200° F. Therm. ¼. The drying may take up to 6 wks. The best test for dryness is for the root slice to break with a snap when it is bent. Store in airtight containers.

TO KEEP SEEDS. When the seeds are brown and stalks dry, cut off seed heads, spread a paper in a basket and cut the seed pods or umbels directly into the basket. Then lay them on a layer of thick cloth or butter muslin spread over a drying screen or sieve; keep in a warm, well-ventilated room for about 5 days. Always remove the seeds from the pods carefully, as they bruise easily, and put the pods or umbels between the palms of the hands and rub very gently. Then put the seeds on a sieve fine enough to hold them but coarse enough to let the fine particles of the stems pass through. Next place the seeds on a butter-muslin-covered

HERBS (*continued*)

wire tray or sieve, and let them dry for 7–10 days longer. Put the seeds into glass jars and watch for any signs of moisture.

TO KEEP FLOWERS. Camomile flowers are gathered when in full bloom. When the flowers are well dried they may be rubbed through a sieve until the green part or calyx shows. The orange calendula and saffron flowerets are spread on a screen so that they do not touch, and dried in the shade to preserve their colour, then stored in closely capped jars (care should be taken to watch for moisture).

HERBS AND THEIR USES (*see also under individual headings*)

HERB	USE
Agrimony	Tea
Angelica	Tea. Decorations on Cakes and Desserts
Anise	Breads, Cakes, Desserts, Fish, Pastries, Salads, Tea (seeds)
Balm (lemon)	Cold beverages, Garnishes, Salads, Tea
Basil	Cheese, Cocktail (tomato), Beetroot, Egg dishes, Potatoes, Salads, Sauces, Soups and Stews, Tomatoes, Vinegar
Bay Leaves	Sauces, Soups and Stews
Bergamot	Tea
Boneset	Tea
Borage	Cold beverages, Confectionery, Pot herb, Salads
Burnet	Beverages, Salads and Vinegar
Calamint	Tea
Calendula (Marigold)	Green Salads (flower petals)
Camomile	Tea
Caraway	Beetroot, Breads, Cabbage, Cakes, Cheese dishes, Confectionery, Desserts, Pastry, Salads (leaves), Tea (seeds)
Cardoon	Pot herb, Salads. Also cooked as a vegetable
Catnip	Tea
Chervil	Egg dishes, Fish, Garnishes, Meat and Poultry Sauces, Salad, Salad dressing, Soups and Stews
Chicory	Pot herb and Salad
Chives	Cheese dishes, Egg dishes, Fish, Pork, Potatoes, Salad, Soups and Stews
Cicely (Sweet)	Pot herb (leaves)
Coriander	Beetroot, Bread, Cakes, Confectionery and Pastry

HERBS (*continued*)

HERB	USE
Costmary	Tea
Cumin	Breads, Cakes and Pastry
Dill	Lamb, Salad, Salad dressing, Sauce for meat and fish, Vinegar
Fennel	Beetroot, Cabbage, Pickles, Salads, Tea (seeds)
Fenugreek	Confectionery, Curry powder
Feverfew	Tea
Glasswort	Pot herb (shoots are pickled)
Ground Ivy	Tea
Hops	Pot herb (young shoots)
Horehound	Tea
Houseleek	Salad (leaves)
Hyssop	Tisanes
Lovage	Pot herbs (leaves), Salads, Tea
Marjoram (Sweet)	Beef, Cocktail (tomato), Desserts, Egg dishes, Garnishes, Hot cheese dishes, Lamb, Pork, Poultry, Meat Sauces, Soups, Stews, String beans, Tomatoes, Vinegar
Mint	Cabbages, Confectionery, Desserts, Fruit cup, Jams, Jellies, Peas, Potatoes, Salads, Sauces for meat and poultry, Soups and Stews, Spinach and Vinegar
Mustard	Pot herb and Salads (seedlings)
Nasturtium	Salads (leaves, petals and pickled seeds)
Orach	Pot herb
Parsley	Broad beans, Carrots, Fish, Potatoes, Salads, Sauce for fish, Soups and Stews
Pennyroyal	Tea
Pokeweed	Pot herb
Rampion	Pot herb and Salads
Rose: petals hips	Salads Jams, Syrups
Rosemary	Beef, Beverages, Garnishes, Jams, Jellies, Lamb, Peas, Pickles, Pork, Tea and Veal

HERBS (*continued*)

HERB	USE
Rue	Cocktails, Salads, Stews
Saffron	Tea (Stigmas)
Sage	Cheese, Fish, Pickles, Pork, Poultry, String beans, Tea, Tomatoes
Samphire	Pot herbs (shoots are pickled), Salads
Savory (Summer)	Beef, Beetroot, Carrots, Cocktail (tomato), Garnishes, Lamb, Peas, Poultry, Salads, Soups, Stews, String beans, Veal
Sesame	Bread, Cakes and Confectionery
Skirret	Pot herbs
Sorrel	Pot herb, Salads
Speedwell	Tea
Tarragon	Cocktail (tomato), Egg dishes, Hot cheese dishes, Onions, Pickles, Poultry, Salad, Sauces for meat, poultry and fish, Soups and Stews, Vinegar
Thyme	Beef, Beverages, Carrots, Cocktail (tomato), Fish, Garnishes, Hot cheese dishes, Onions, Pickles, Poultry, Salad, Salad dressing, Savoury Sauce, Soups, Stews, Tisane
Verbena (lemon)	Jams, Jellies, Tea
Violet (Sweet)	Salads (flower petals)
Wintergreen	Tea
Yarrow	Tea

HERB MIXTURES

FOR BEEF STEWS. 1 tsp. each basil, celery leaves, lovage, parsley, savory, sweet basil and sweet marjoram.

FOR COCKTAILS (VEGETABLE). 1 pt. liquid, $\frac{1}{2}$ tsp. basil, chopped chives, tarragon, thyme, summer savory and sweet marjoram.

FOR EGGS. 1 tsp. each basil, chervil, chives, summer savory and tarragon.

FOR FISH SAUCE. To 1 pt. sauce add $\frac{1}{4}$ tsp. each basil, fennel seeds (crushed), thyme, sage and sweet marjoram.

FOR LAMB. 1 tsp. each rosemary, summer savory and sweet marjoram.

FOR POULTRY. Sauce as for Eggs.

FOR POULTRY STUFFING. 1 tsp. each basil, celery, parsley, summer savory, sweet marjoram, sage and finely grated lemon peel.

FOR SOUPS. To 1 qt. liquid add $\frac{1}{2}$ tsp. each basil, chervil (or parsley), celery, thyme, sweet marjoram, rosemary and grated lemon peel.

HERB SEASONING. See **SEASONING.**

Herb Soup

Ingredients	Method
Small lettuce shredded	Cook lettuce, cress, herbs and butter together for a few mins. Add chicken stock and simmer for 30 mins. Remove from heat, add cream and egg yolk. Season and stir. Serve without straining accompanied by croutons.
Bunch of cress	
Bunch of sorrel	
Few sprigs chervil	
3 tbsp. melted butter	
1 qt. chicken stock	
½ pt. cream (or evaporated milk)	
1 egg yolk	
Salt and pepper	

Herb Tea—I. Take equal parts of aniseed, fennel, caraway, coriander. Infuse by pouring on boiling water. Leave till cool, strain and drink either hot or cold.

Herb Tea—II

Ingredients	Method
5 oz. dried rose-leaves	Mix well together and use as required. Add 1 tsp. to each ½ pt. boiling water. Infuse for a few mins. and drink with sugar and milk.
2 oz. balm	
1 oz. rosemary	

HERB O'GRACE. See RUE.

HERRING (Fr. *hareng*). The common herring is a smooth, well-formed fish of a silvery colour averaging from 8–12″ long. There are several varieties and these differ in their habits of life so that it is possible to keep up a constant supply for the whole year round, with the exception of the spring. The common herring which travels in shoals, comes to our shores in April or May and spawns at the end of October or the beginning of November. The kind which is heavy with roe in January spawns in February. Then there are the glorious Scotch Loch Fyne herrings which are in season during only a very short time of the year.

The flesh of the herring is very delicate when fresh; after a little keeping it becomes oily, but preserves well if dried and salted, and better still if smoked. In Holland and Germany herrings are usually salted and dried. Smoking is much resorted to and this gives the herring a red metallic lustre from which has come the name "red herring". Those which are only slightly salted and smoked are known as *Bloaters* (see under that heading). These have brought repute to Great Yarmouth. *Kippered herrings* vary from all others in their preliminary preparation. They are cut open before salting, then after drying, smoked, whereas bloaters and red herrings are cured whole. *Salted herrings*, generally called "Dutch" herrings, are eaten raw, the flesh being nearly transparent.

HERRINGS (FRESH) TO BROIL. Scrape, clean and wash the herrings. Dredge with salt and flour lightly and put them into a frying-pan with very little oil and broil over a low heat, turning them when one side is done. They will take 7–8 mins. to cook. Then arrange them on a hot dish and serve with melted Butter sauce (see p. 445) with a little mustard mixed in.

HERRINGS (RED), DRESSED. Cut the red herrings open. Boil some beer and pour it over them. Let them steep for 30 mins. Drain dry, warm them in an oven. Rub a little fresh butter over them and serve with Egg sauce (see p. 442) and mashed potatoes.

HERRINGS (SALT), TO PICKLE

Ingredients	Method
2 large salt herrings	Clean the fish, remove heads. Soak overnight in cold water. Drain dry on absorbent paper. Cut crosswise in ½″ slices.
¼ tsp. allspice crushed	
1½ whole ginger	

[275]

HERRINGS (SALT), TO PICKLE (*continued*)

½ tsp. mustard seed
1 piece horseradish
2 shallots sliced
½ carrot
½ pt. white vinegar
¼ pt. water
¼ lb. sugar

Place together with dry ingredients in large jar. Mix vinegar, water and sugar, bring to boiling point, leave to cool. Pour over herrings, stand overnight and serve from jar.

HERRINGS (SALT), FOR SALAD. Wash the required quantity of freshly salted herrings, and let them soak in milk for 3 hrs. Cut off their heads and tails and split the body to remove the bones. Arrange on a dish, garnish with mixed onions and thin slices of pickled gherkins. Sprinkle a few whole capers round, pour a little oil and vinegar over the fish and serve.

Herrings and Apples

Ingredients

4 herrings
Fish stock
2 tart apples
2 tbsp. grated horseradish
1 tsp. granulated sugar

Method

Wipe the cleaned herrings and place in saucepan. Add fish stock, cover and boil gently for 12 mins., or until the fish flakes. Leave 10 mins. over a low flame. Put grated apple and horseradish and sugar into mixture, boil, and mix well. Lift out fish onto a hot dish and spread with apple mixture.

Herring Roes (Fresh) on Toast. Take out the soft roes and wash and drain them. Put a small lump of butter in a saucepan, warm it, add a few mushrooms, onions, shallots and a little parsley, all finely minced. Warm them slowly over a low heat, add the roes and simmer all together for a few minutes. Serve on buttered hot toast.

HET (Hot) PINT. This is a Scottish drink made with ale, eggs, whisky, and a grating of nutmeg, at the time of the Hogmanay Festival.

HICKORY NUT. The fruit of a tree that grows very profusely in America. There are many varieties known by such names as Shag-bank, Hickory, Bitter-nut, Pecan and Hognut.

HIPS. The fresh fruits of the dog-rose. They should be used as soon as they are ripe, and are made into rosehip syrup and rosehip jam.

HOG. The male pig. See BOAR, also BACON.

HOGSHEAD. See WEIGHTS AND MEASURES.

HOLLANDAISE. This French term signifies "Dutch Style", also the name of a rich, white fish sauce. See SAUCES and SOUPS.

HONEY (Fr. *miel*). Honey is used for all purposes of sweetening. It forms also the basis of fermented liquors known to the Anglo-Saxons as mead and megethlin (see MEAD). Honey is a sweet substance which is obtained by the bee from the nectariferous glands of flowers, elaborated in the body of the bee, and ultimately deposited in the honeycomb. It is a natural form of invert sugar with distinctive scent and flavour. Honey should never be removed from the hives until it is ripe, and the combs are thoroughly sealed by the bees.

Strained Honey is liquid honey which has been pressed from the combs, and then strained through cloth. Always seal the containers when storing honey. (Biscuit tins are excellent for this purpose.) Store in a cool even temperature. When honey becomes granular, remove cap, place jar in water, within an inch of the top, heat slowly to 120° F. until dissolved. The flavour is sometimes less delicate and heavier after heating honey in this way.

HONEY (*continued*)

The four main types of honey are:

(*i*) *English Honey.* Produced by bees which have mainly collected it from clover, furze, heather and broom flowers. The type of flower affects the flavour and colour of the honey.

(*ii*) *Narbonne Honey: Continental and other honeys* are gathered chiefly from rosemary, and other highly-scented flowers.

(*iii*) *The bizonde Honey* is slightly intoxicating when eaten.

(*iv*) *Kwno Honey.* Is used for liqueurs and medicine. It comes from the lime forests of Lithuania.

Honey Crisps

Ingredients	*Method*
½ lb. shelled walnuts, hazel nuts or brazil nuts 1 pt. honey	Chop the walnuts (or other nuts) into small pieces, spread them all over a well-oiled (use salad oil) baking tin. Put the honey into a saucepan, place it over a low heat and bring it to the boil. When it reaches boiling point, boil for 5 mins.; stir it occasionally (to prevent it catching and burning), then pour the boiling honey over the nuts, set it aside to harden, and when ready for use, crack into small pieces. If chocolate-covered crisps are required, melt some dipping chocolate, mark the crisp into squares when almost cold, and when cooled break at the marked line. Drop each square individually into the melted chocolate, remove each one with a fork, and place to dry on a waxed paper, or on an oiled slab.

Honey Dressing (for any fruit salad). Heat ¼ pt. honey over hot water until very thin. Pour ⅛ pt. sherry or dry white wine. Stir till blended, then pour over the prepared fruit. Chill well before serving.

Honey Salad Dressing. ¼ pt. thin honey, ¼ pt. strained lemon juice, 1 tsp. chopped mint, chives or parsley. Beat the honey and lemon together. Add mint or chives, and use as desired.

HONEYWARE. See SEAWEED.

HOPS. The catkins of the female plant of the common hop are commercially known as "hops". They are not frequently used for culinary purposes, although the tops or shoots of the young plants are much prized by epicures when prepared and cooked as vegetables, or used in salads.

HOREHOUND. The leafy top is used medicinally for infusions, lozenges and candy. It grows wild in almost all parts of the British Isles.

Horehound Tea. Infuse 1 oz. herb with 1 pt. boiling water; let stand for 1 hr. By that time it will be ready for use. It can be taken sweetened with sugar if desired.

HORS D'ŒUVRES. When serving a meal, it is never necessary to add a large number of staple foods to the menu, but to enhance with savoury tit-bits the usual number of courses for specially festive occasions. Hors d'œuvres should tempt the appetite, but not impair the meal; they are eaten either hot or cold, and do not form any substantial part of the meal, being served as an "extra". Some come as a first course; others form a relish and are served between the different courses.

HORS D'ŒUVRES (*continued*)

Cocktails. The appearance of this "food" is half its attraction because beautifully arranged dishes can be a perfect picture. Oyster, lobster, crabmeat, or fruit cocktails (see **FRUIT**). These may be served either for luncheon, dinner or supper according to the season. Savoury cocktails (cocktail sauce with any fresh, frozen or tinned fish) are usually garnished with parsley, watercress or the heart of lettuce leaves, while fruit cocktails can be topped off with crême de menthe or maraschino cherries, whole strawberries, or a section of the fruit itself.

Relishes. These are also classed as hors d'œuvres and consist of olives (ripe, green, or pitted), stuffed small pickled gherkins, radishes cut into roses, plain small pieces of celery, stuffed celery, salted nuts, pickled peaches or pears.

When serving these relishes, a dish with compartments is both convenient and practical. Each relish is arranged in its own section: the dish may be divided into 2, 4 or more compartments.

Canapés. These must be neatly made, and the mixture must be smoothly spread. The garnish is decided by the canapé mixture. Some of the most useful are: the smallest slices of lemon with finely chopped parsley sprinkled over the top in flower designs, piping of stiff mayonnaise or cream cheese, petals of flowers cut out of the thinnest slices of pickles; cheese, vegetable and slices of tomato all call for the savoury garnish of sprigs of parsley or watercress, olives halved, or sliced capers and the smallest sprig of a chosen fresh herb. Remember that hot canapés cannot be garnished with anything that will melt. For ideas see **CANAPÉS** and **APPETISERS.**

FOODS WHICH MAY BE USED FOR HORS D'ŒUVRES.

FRUIT

Fruit Appetisers. Plain orange juice; a mixture of orange and lemon juice, sweetened to taste; strawberry pulp with a squeeze of lemon juice; pineapple pulp or canned pineapple.

Cantaloup Melon. A water melon. Scoop out the pulp and put to chill well. Serve with ground ginger and sugar.

Grapefruit. Wash well and dry and cut into halves crosswise with a sharp knife or curved grapefruit knife. Loosen pulp at edges with scissors or sharp knife. Cut out centre and membranes of the connecting sections, add a little sugar and a little sherry, if desired, and garnish with a cherry. (Crême de menthe or Maraschino cherries.) Serve in a grapefruit glass or on a plate.

Whole Fruit. Serve plain, peaches, apples, pears, plums, etc.

FISH. Smoked eel, smoked cod, smoked salmon, smoked sturgeon, smoked trout, tuna fish, anchovy fillets, roll mops (all these are flaked or in small fillets), also shrimps or lobster meat. Serve smoked fish with sliced lemon and brown bread and butter, and oyster likewise, but on crushed ice, allowing 6 or more per person.

MEAT. Slices of meat loaf, home-made pâté, the thinnest slices of smoked ham, smoked tongue. See also **GOOSE'S FAT LIVER.**

SAUSAGES

Blood Sausages. Many ' arieties are available. Serve thinly sliced.

Bologna Sausage. A large smoked sausage made of bacon, veal and pork suet at Bologna, Italy.

Cervelat. A rather dry, well-seasoned sausage which is available everywhere.

Chipolata. A very small spiced sausage.

Liver Sausage. Liver sausage is often called *pâté de maison.*

Mortadella. An Italian sausage of fine flavour and coarse texture.

Salami. The Italian style and the Kosher Salami. Some are highly flavoured with garlic, some are coarse-grained and some are fine-grained.

VEGETABLES. Sliced beetroot, potato salad, Russian salad, sliced tomatoes, dressed with French dressing; green beans in mayonnaise, artichoke bottoms, beans. sweet corn, small onions, sliced onion and diced beetroot, green peppers in slices, carrot in strips, radish, macedoine of vegetables.

HORSE MACKEREL. This name is applied to so many fish in different parts of the world that it is difficult to define it. It is not a mackerel, nor is it a good fish.

HORSE MACKEREL (*continued*)

It is mostly seen near the European coasts. Sometimes the young fish are tinned and sold as sardines; they are very inferior.

HORSE MUSHROOMS. Usually larger than the field mushroom. The flesh turns a browny colour when bruised.

HORSERADISH (Fr. *raifort*). This plant grows wild throughout the British Isles and in almost every climate. It is also extensively cultivated. The root stock is the part which is used for culinary purposes on account of its hot, pungent flavour, approaching that of mustard. Taken as a condiment, it provokes the appetite and assists digestion. The sticks of fresh root are scraped and used as a garnish for roast beef; they may be scraped and dried, or if preferred made into a sauce. This is good when served with beef, and often helps to cheer up a dull fish dish.
Horseradish Sauce. See SAUCES.
Horseradish Vinegar. Scrape a stick of horseradish and steep it in a pint of vinegar for a fortnight; a little sliced shallot may be added if desired. Shake occasionally.

HOT CROSS BUNS. See BUNS.

HOT WATER CRUST. See PASTE AND PASTRY.

HOTCH-POTCH or HOTCH POT (Fr. *Hochepot*). A soup or stew generally made from neck of mutton with peas, barley and vegetables cut up into dices. A favourite dish in Scotland.

HOUSE LEEK. Sometimes known as Hen-and-Chickens. The bruised leaves are used medicinally as a cooling application and the juice is said to cure warts. See also **ELECAMPANE.**

HUCKLEBERRY. See BILBERRY.

HUMBLES (or UMBLES). The internal organs of the deer.

HUNG BEEF. Beef hung until tender, salted and rolled tightly in a cloth, then hung for about 21 days until it becomes dry. If smoked, it will keep quite a time.

HYDROMEL. A drink made by dissolving honey in boiling water and cooling in ice.

HYSSOP. The leafy top is used medicinally to induce perspiration and also in Chartreuse.
Hyssop Tea

Ingredients
¼ oz. dried hyssop flowers
1 pt. boiling water
1 tsp. honey

Method
Place the hyssop flowers into a basin and pour over the boiling water. Cover and leave 15 mins. Then pass the liquor through a strainer and mix with honey.

I

ICE (Fr. *glace*). This can be of great service to a cook, helping her to serve up many foods in the most appetising way.

ICED BEVERAGES. The following ice cube may be served instead of the plain one: set a maraschino cherry in each ice-cube section before adding the water and putting to freeze, so that the cherry, with ice around it, can be served in a cocktail after shaking.

ICE CREAM and WATER ICES. Frozen desserts are easily made from the simplest mixture to the elaborate-moulded "bombe". Ice creams are not only delicious but nutritious, and can add protein to a meal. Both texture, flavour and ingredients can be varied. Some ices take their name from the shape into which they are moulded. When served from a large-sized glass bowl, a large spoon is used for serving. A moulded ice is served from a plate, being cut with a knife or spoon. Ices may also be served in individual glasses. If a sauce accompanies an ice as a garnish, it is served with the ice cream in the glasses (parfaits, etc.). When an accompaniment to a moulded ice, served at the table, it should be in a special bowl and poured on to each serving before it is passed to the guests. For a true ice cream both cream and eggs should be included amongst the ingredients. Today, these are not always obtainable; however, quite creamy ices can be made from a tested reliable recipe without these ingredients. Always see your mix is absolutely cold before turning it into the freezing tray. Turn the thermostatic knob to its coldest to freeze the mix rapidly. It takes from ½–2 hrs. according to the type of mix.

Tinned milk (sweetened or unsweetened) may be used instead of fresh milk. If sweetened milk is used, add less sugar to the mix. If no cream is available, add, instead, undiluted evaporated milk, previously scalded, cooled and whipped.

If too much sugar is used in making the ices, they will not freeze to the right consistency; too little, on the other hand, will make them hard and rough, like snow.

Do not overfreeze. Should the ice cream be ready before it is required for use, turn down the thermostatic control knob to normal.

Sorbets are half-frozen water ices, generally lemon-water, flavoured with rum or spirit. These are served before roasts. When ices are moulded as puddings, they should be only half-frozen when they are put into the moulds. If they are frozen too dry they will not take the shape. After putting them in their moulds well butter the joints (unless a cave is used), and pack in ice and salt until required. Any cream ices may be made into puddings. A mixture of fresh or preserved fruits may, if desired, be added to them before they are moulded. The moulds may be decorated with fruits, and the pudding attractively coloured. *Water ices* set in fancy shapes and placed round the puddings make an excellent finish. Turn the ice pudding out like a jelly or cream, the essential difference being that it should be dipped into cold, not hot, water. Place it on a silver or fancy dish with an attractive dessert paper under it.

ICE CREAM (INEXPENSIVE)

Ingredients	*Method*
1 pt. milk	Blend the cornflour and a little of the cold
1 oz. cornflour	milk. Boil the remainder of the milk and
3 oz. sugar	pour over the blended mixture, stirring
1 egg	continuously to mix well. Return to the
Flavouring (vanilla, lemon,	saucepan, add sugar, and boil for about

[280]

ICE CREAM (INEXPENSIVE) (*continued*)

almond or pineapple)   3 mins., stirring continuously. Beat the egg in a large bowl and pour over the hot mixture. Whisk well. Flavour as desired. Allow to become quite cold before freezing.

ICE CREAM (RICH)

Ingredients

1 pt. milk
1 oz. cornflour
3 oz. sugar
2 fresh eggs
Flavouring as desired
¼ pt. thick cream

Method

Blend the cornflour with a little milk. Heat the remaining milk in a double saucepan with the sugar. Add the blended cornflour. Stir over the heat until the mixture thickens, then cook for 10 mins. Remove the mixture from the heat and allow to cool slightly. Beat up the eggs in a basin, pour the thickened mixture gradually over them, stirring the whole time. When blended, flavour as desired, strain the mix and add the cream or evaporated milk. Allow to cool before freezing. When the mixture is frozen round the edges it is firm enough. Remove from tray. Turn into a well-chilled bowl, whisk it well and return to the freezing tray. Stir occasionally during the remaining freezing time.

CREAM ICES VARIOUSLY FLAVOURED

Apricot Cream Ice	½ lb. apricot jam Juice of a lemon 1 pt. cream (or evaporated milk)	Rub the apricot jam through a hair sieve; add a few drops of strained lemon juice. Beat the cream stiffly, mix with the apricot purée and freeze
Banana Cream Ice	See **BANANA**	
Chocolate Cream Ice	½ pt. milk 1 whole egg 1 egg yolk 3 oz. chocolate 3 oz. sugar Vanilla ½ pt. cream (or evaporated milk)	Dissolve broken chocolate in milk. Make a custard in the usual way with vanilla flavouring: when cold add whipped cream
Coffee Cream Ice	8 egg yolks 1 pt. cream ¼ lb. mocha coffee beans (roasted but not ground) 6 oz. caster sugar	Make the eggs and cream into a custard (see **CUSTARD**). Add to it the coffee berries, and let it stand until they have well flavoured it. Then strain it, add the sugar, and when the custard is quite cold, freeze

CREAM ICES VARIOUSLY FLAVOURED (*continued*)

Maraschino Cream Ice	1 pt. double cream 2 oz. caster sugar 2 wine glasses maraschino	Beat the cream stiffly; add the caster sugar and maraschino and freeze. Noyau or any other liqueur may be substituted for the maraschino
Neapolitan Cream Ice	For this a proper mould is necessary. Lay three ices, differently flavoured and coloured, in it in three layers. Choose flavours that will go well together. Freeze for an hour	
Pineapple Cream Ice	1 lb. pineapple 6 oz. caster sugar Juice of ½ lemon 1 pt. double cream	Cut up the pineapple. Pound it in a mortar, and rub through a hair sieve. Add the pulp, sugar and lemon juice to the cream, and freeze
Raspberry Cream Ice	¾ lb. raspberries 8 oz. caster sugar 1 pt. double cream or custard Juice of ½ lemon Little cochineal	Take the stalks from the raspberries and rub them with the sugar sprinkled over them through a hair sieve. Add the raspberry purée to the custard when cool, with the lemon juice and a little cochineal, and freeze
Vanilla Cream Ice	1 whole egg 5 egg yolks 1 pt. milk 4 tbsp. caster sugar Vanilla ½ pt. double cream	Make the eggs and milk into a custard, add sugar and vanilla. Beat the cream stiffly. When cold, partly freeze the custard and then mix in cream and continue to freeze until the right consistency. This mixture may be used for an ice pudding

WATER ICES

Apple	2 lb. apples Juice of 2 lemons Rind of ½ lemon Syrup of sugar and water	Wash and cut up the apples. Place in an enamelled saucepan with a little water and the lemon juice and rind and stew until soft. Then rub through a hair sieve. Mix the purée with an equal quantity of syrup made as for lemon water ice, and freeze. If desired, a little noyau may be added
Apricot, Banana and Peach		Make like *Strawberry Water Ice*
Cherry	1 lb. Morello cherries 1 liqueur glass of noyau	Stone and pound cherries, and rub through sieve. Add an equal quantity of syrup, made as for lemon water ice, and a glass of noyau, and freeze

WATER ICES (*continued*)

Lemon	1 pt. water ½ lb. lump sugar Thin rind of 3 lemons 1 pt. lemon juice 2 egg whites	Put water and sugar into a saucepan and boil for 10 mins. Strain lemon juice. Pour syrup of sugar and water on to lemon peel and let it get cold. Add lemon juice and freeze. When half-frozen, add whites of eggs, whipped stiffly
Orange	Make like *Lemon Water Ice*	
Pineapple	Make like *Strawberry Water Ice*, chopping and pounding the pineapple before passing through a sieve	
Raspberry	Make like *Strawberry Water Ice*	
Strawberry	Make a syrup of sugar and water, as directed in the recipe for *Lemon Water Ice*. Rub sufficient strawberries through a sieve to make 1 pt. purée. Add a little lemon juice and freeze	

Bombe aux Bananes. Line the bombe mould with orange water ice. Fill the centre with banana cream ice. Freeze for 4 hrs. To turn it out, dip it into cold water. Different varieties of this pudding may be prepared. Always put the water ice outside.

Ice Pudding

Ingredients	*Method*
1 pt. milk 4 eggs 2 oz. caster sugar 1 glass maraschino ½ glass brandy ½ pt. whipped cream ¼ lb. candied or glacé fruits	Make the eggs and milk into a custard. Add sugar, strain it and let it boil. Add the brandy and maraschino, then half-freeze; add the fruits and whipped cream. Finish freezing, then put into a pudding mould and pack in ice until required. The fruits must be cut into pieces and soaked in a little brandy before use.

Iceland Moss. One of the lichen tribe found between the Arctic Regions and North Temperate Zone. It is used as a food for invalids. Scald, then soak in cold water to extract its bitterness. It can then be boiled and the liquor strained off to form a jelly.

ICING. Icings are made with a fine powdered white sugar, prepared specially for confectionery. Large surfaces of cakes are spread with icing by means of a

Covering the top of cake with
Almond Paste

Levelling the sides

ICING (*continued*)

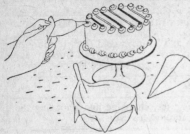

Piping Royal icing

confectioner's spatula and are placed on stands, rather smaller than the base of the cake so that the icing may be easily spread over the surface. Any ornaments are added after the coating has set. Designs are sometimes piped on the surface, before setting, from forcing bags (see under that heading). Some icing, e.g. feather icing or frosting, require a sugar thermometer. Royal icing can be used for large cakes, glacé or butter icing for small cakes. When icing cakes, always brush off loose crumbs and, with a large cake, place on an inverted plate on a sieve so that it is well raised, if no stand is available. Never put icing on top of almond paste until this is well set.

Butter Icing

Ingredients

   3 oz. butter
   6 oz. icing sugar
   2 tsp. boiling water
   Flavouring

Method

Beat the butter, sugar and boiling water together until quite soft, white and fluffy. Add flavouring and spread over cake. Decorate as desired.

   For CHOCOLATE BUTTER ICING. Add 1 heaped tsp. grated chocolate or cocoa and a drop of vanilla essence.

Feather or American Icing

Ingredients

   1 lb. loaf sugar
   1 gill water
   2 egg whites
   Flavouring and colouring

Method

Put the sugar and water into a thick or lined saucepan. Dissolve sugar and then boil to a temperature of 240° F. Pour the syrup gradually onto the stiffly whisked whites of egg. Add colouring and flavouring, beat until set and pour over cake. For transparent glaze to use over Royal icing, make as above without whites of egg.

Glacé Icing

Ingredients

   ¼ lb. sifted icing sugar
   4–5 tsp. water (or 2 tsp. lemon or orange juice and 2–3 tsp. water)

Method

Put the ingredients together in a small saucepan but do not boil (if boiled, the icing is dull when set); remove pan from heat and beat icing with a wooden spoon until it will thickly coat back of spoon. Pour over cake and spread quickly with a warm spoon (have a jug of boiling water handy and dip the knife into this). Add any decorations such as nuts and fruit before the icing sets, to prevent cracking, but any piped decorations should be added after setting.

Glacé Icing (continued)

For CHOCOLATE GLACÉ ICING. Use ¼ lb. icing sugar, a few drops of vanilla essence, 1 heaped tsp. grated chocolate or cocoa and 6 tsp. water. Heat the water and chocolate or cocoa together, allow to boil, then cool slightly. Add sugar and beat icing.

For COFFEE GLACÉ ICING. Substitute 1 tsp. coffee essence for chocolate or cocoa and add 5 tsp. water.

Meringue Icing

Ingredients

1 egg white
½ lb. icing sugar
1 tsp. gelatine
¼ pt. hot water
Colouring and flavouring if desired

Method

Dissolve the gelatine in hot water. Leave to cool and then add a few drops of lemon or vanilla flavouring. Add the stiffly beaten white of an egg and the icing sugar and whisk steadily until the consistency is thick. Add colouring, if desired, and use between the layers of cake and to cover the top. Garnish with chopped nuts or cherries.

FOR COFFEE MERINGUE ICING. Use the recipe for Meringue Icing, but dissolve the gelatine in ¼ tsp. strong hot coffee and add a few drops of vanilla essence and chopped nuts. Use chopped nuts also for the garnish. If nuts are not available, fine oatmeal may be browned in the oven and used in their place for a garnish.

FOR ITALIAN MERINGUE ICING

Ingredients

4 oz. sugar
3 egg whites
Water

Method

Put the sugar in a saucepan, cover with water and bring to the boil. Whisk the whites of egg until stiff. Meanwhile allow the sugar to boil to 270° F. (small crack) then add gradually the stiff whites of egg and continue to beat until stiff.

Royal Icing

Ingredients

1 lb. icing sugar
Strained juice of 1 lemon
Whites of 2 large eggs (or 3 small ones)

Method

Pound the sugar and sift until smooth and free from lumps. Whip the whites of egg to a froth (but not stiff) and work well into the icing sugar with a wooden spoon, adding lemon juice. Beat thoroughly and cover with a damp cloth until ready for use.

IMPERIAL. This name is given to a refreshing medicinal or summer drink prepared by putting ½ oz. cream of tartar, 2 lumps sugar and a slice of lemon into a large jar, pounding over 1 qt. boiling water, and leaving til lcold. It may be cooled with ice or in refrigerator.

INDIAN CORN (Fr. *mais*). This corn grows to perfection in America; there it is commonly known as corn, popcorn or sweet corn, whereas in other countries it takes its name "maize" from the botanical one, *Zea Mays*. It is sold in many prepared forms, i.e. cornflour, cornstarch, hominy, maizena, polenta. When young, the corn is eaten off the cob.

CORN ON COB, BOILED. Corn, if kept in a refrigerator for two or three hours, seems to regain its freshness. Remove the husk, and the silk from the ears, cut off the stem end and the undeveloped tip. Put into cold water, and bring just to the boil, or plunge the ears into rapidly boiling water and cook for 3–6 mins.

CORN ON COB, BOILED (*continued*)

(without salt). A little sugar, no more than a teaspoonful, helps to improve the flavour. Serve wrapped in a linen napkin with plenty of butter and salt and freshly ground pepper.

CORN ON COB, ROAST. Strip husks back, but do not remove from stem. Remove all silk and replace husks. Dip into cold water and then bake at 400° F. Therm. 6 or place under a hot grill, turning occasionally, for 10–15 mins. Remove husks and serve.

CORN ON COB, SAUTÉ. With a sharp knife remove the kernels from 8 or 9 ears of corn. Sauté very gently in 4 tbsp. butter for about 5 mins., stirring to prevent the corn sticking. Season with salt and pepper, and add if you wish $\frac{1}{4}$ pt. cream and a sprinkle of paprika.

Corn Créole
Ingredients

2 tbsp. chopped onions
4 tbsp. butter
4 tbsp. flour
1½ cups tinned or bottled tomatoes
1 tin whole kernel corn
1 tsp. parsley
2 green peppers (chopped)
2 egg yolks

Method

Brown onions in butter. Add flour and mix until smooth. Add tomatoes, corn and seasonings and cook 10 mins. Pour over beaten egg yolks and cook 3 mins. longer. Serve very hot.

Corn Pudding
Ingredients

1 tin whole corn
1 tbsp. each butter and sugar
Pinch of salt
1 tbsp. flour
1 pt. milk
2 or 3 eggs

Method

Mix butter, sugar, salt and flour in with corn. Add milk, and then well beaten eggs. Turn into greased oven dish and bake for $\frac{3}{4}$ hr. at 350° F. Therm. 4.

Corn Soufflé
Ingredients

1 tbsp. butter
½ green pepper (if desired)
2 oz. flour
$\frac{3}{4}$ pt. milk
1 cup grated cheese
1 tin creamed corn
½ tsp. each salt and paprika
3 eggs

Method

Put butter and green pepper into a saucepan and cook until pepper is tender; add flour mixed with milk and stir into the pepper. Add cheese, corn and seasoning and cook for 10 mins., then add the yolks of eggs well beaten. Cook for 2 mins. longer. Remove from heat and fold in the stiffly whisked whites of egg. Pour into a deep buttered baking dish set in water. Bake at 350° F. Therm. 4 for ½ hr.

Corn and Tomato Salad
Ingredients

3 ears corn
Tomatoes
Mayonnaise
Lettuce

Method

Cook the ears of corn in boiling water for 5–8 mins. then remove corn from cob (or use canned corn). Blanch the tomatoes, remove skins, cut off tops and remove a little pulp. Make a mayonnaise and add

Corn and Tomato Salad (*continued*)

to corn. Fill the cavities of the tomatoes with the mixture. Place lettuce leaves on individual plates, pile a little corn in the centre and stand filled tomatoes on top of that.

IRISH MOSS. See CARRAGEEN.

IRISH STEW. A national Irish dish.

Ingredients

2 lb. potatoes
2 lb. mutton
4 large onions
About ½ pt. water

Method

Prepare and cut meat: prepare and slice the vegetables. Put alternate layers of meat, onions and potatoes in stewpan finishing with a layer of onions. Add water to half cover and simmer about 2 hrs. stirring occasionally. Serve potatoes to form a border with meat and gravy in centre.

ISINGLASS. This is a very refined form of gelatine prepared from the dried bladders of certain fish, especially sturgeon. The bladders are dried just as they are removed from the fish and to the shapes assumed by them in drying do they owe their classification as purse, pipe, lump, leaf, honeycomb, stable or book isinglass. Both isinglass and gelatine are used to give firmness to liquids; use approximately 1 tbsp. per 1 pt. liquid. See also **BLANCMANGE.**

ITALIAN MERINGUE. See ICING and MERINGUES.

ITALIAN PASTES. See MACARONI.

ITALIAN SAUCE. See SAUCES.

J

JACK. See **PIKE** for the fish; **ROASTING** for the spit and **SNIPE** for the game bird.

JACOBINS. Quenelles custard, which were fashionable during the Revolution, and renamed "Royals" after the Restoration.

JALOUSIES. Small puff paste cakes.

JAM (Fr. *confiture*). A confection or conserve of fruit made by boiling fruit with sugar to a certain consistency.

GENERAL RULES FOR JAM-MAKING. Pick over fruit very carefully discarding any that is unsound. Wash and wipe the fruit and place in pan. Allow ¾ lb. preserving sugar to each lb. fruit (unless otherwise stated). Bring very slowly to the boil, and never allow the juice to boil until all the sugar is melted. Boil rapidly for 20 mins. or until the mixture will set upon cooling. Pour into dry, warm jars, filling right up to the top. Tie down, label and store in a dry, airy place. See individual headings. Add wax paper.

Pectin may be added to fruit in making jams when the fruit is itself deficient in pectin. The average proportions of extra pectin to 4 lb. fruit are as follows:

As lemon juice:	2 tbsp.
As red currant or gooseberry juice	¼ pt.
As citric or tartaric acid	1 level small tsp.

Commercially prepared pectins are also available and they should be used as directed on the packets. Pectin must be added with care; if too much is added the flavour will be spoilt.

TO MAKE PECTIN STOCK. Prepare the fruit, allowing 3 lb. fruit to 1 pt. water. Simmer the fruit and water till the fruit is soft, then put the pulp into a jelly bag and strain. Return the pulp to the pan with just enough water to make it mushy, and simmer for a further 1–1½ hrs. Strain as before and mix the two extracts of juice together. To sterilise the pectin for keeping, reboil the juice and place it in hot jars. Seal and sterilise as with bottled fruit.

Jam Fritters. Cut some small sponge cakes into halves and spread with jam. Moisten the edges and stick them firmly together. Make a batter using white wine instead of milk. Dip the cakes into it and fry in boiling butter. When well browned, drain the fritters, dredge over with icing sugar and then glaze in a hot oven (400° F. Therm. 6) for a few mins. Arrange on folded napkin or lace-edged paper on a hot dish and serve.

Jam Puffs

Ingredients	*Method*
Flaky or puff pastry (see pp. 371–373) Jam	Roll the pastry and cut into squares. Put a little jam on each. Damp the edges and fold diagonally. Brush over lightly with beaten egg or with milk and sprinkle well with sugar. Bake at 450° F. Therm. 8 for 20 mins.

Jam Roly-Poly

Ingredients	*Method*
½ suet crust (See p. 375) 2–3 tbsp. jam	Roll suet crust into an oblong piece. Spread with jam to within ½″ of the edge. Damp the edges and roll up the strip.

Jam Roly-Poly (*continued*)

Fasten the edges securely. Place in a prepared cloth. Tie at both ends, and secure with a safety-pin if necessary. Boil for 2 hrs. Jam Roly-Poly may be made with shortcrust and baked in a moderately hot oven (375° F. Therm. 5).

Jam Sauce. See SAUCES.

Jam Tart

Ingredients	*Method*
6 oz. short crust (see p. 375)	Roll the pastry a little larger than a
Jam	dinner plate, and cut off a strip about 1″ wide for edge of the plate. Damp edges of pastry and cover plate. Decorate the edge. Fill the centre with jam, decorate with strips of pastry. Bake at 450° F. Therm. 8 for about 20 mins.

For *Small Tarts*, make in the same way, but omit band of pastry round the edge.

JAMAICA PEPPER. See ALLSPICE.

JEDCOCK. See SNIPE.

JELLY. Inspissated juice of fruits or meats; concentrated essence of any kind of food having gelatinous substance. It is obtained by boiling to a glutinous consistency.

TO CLEAR. Choose a large saucepan, and see that it is perfectly clean. Put into it all the ingredients for the jelly, and both the whites of two eggs, which are used to clear the jelly, and the shells which form a filter through which to strain it. Whisk all together over a quick heat until the jelly begins to simmer; then immediately leave off stirring and let it well boil up. The heat of the boiling jelly hardens the egg which rises to the surface in a thick scum, bringing all impurities with it. Stirring during the boiling would prevent the scum rising properly, and the jelly would not clear. When the jelly has well boiled up, remove away from the heat and let it stand for a few minutes till a crust is formed. A jelly bag may be used, or a chair turned upside down with a cloth tied firmly to its four legs. Any cloth which is clean and not too closely woven will answer the purpose. Put a basin under the cloth and pour some boiling water through it. This is to heat it. Change the basin for a clean dry one, pour the whole contents of the saucepan onto the cloth. The first runnings of the jelly will be cloudy, because the filter which the eggs make will not have settled in the cloth. As soon as the jelly runs slowly, and looks clear, place a clean basin under the cloth, and put the first runnings through it again *very gently* that they may not disturb the filter of egg and crushed shell. Strain the jelly in a warm place out of draughts. Two eggs are usually sufficient to clarify a quart of jelly, but if the eggs are small it is advisable to use a third. When the weather is so hot that it is necessary to use more gelatine, more eggs will be required, for if there is not sufficient white of egg the jelly will not clear. The jelly should be allowed to get nearly cold before it is put into the moulds. When put hot into metal moulds it may become cloudy.

TO TURN A JELLY OUT OF ITS MOULD. Take a basin of hot water, as hot as the hand can bear; draw the mould quickly through it, letting the water quite cover it for a second. Wipe off all moisture quickly with a cloth. Shake the mould gently to make sure that the contents are free. Lay the dish on the open side of the mould, quickly reverse it, and draw the mould carefully away.

Aspic Jelly

Ingredients

2½ oz. gelatine
1 qt. nicely flavoured stock
¼ pt. tarragon or plain vinegar
½ pt. sherry
1 piece each carrot, turnip and onion
2 bay leaves
1 sprig each parsley, thyme, and marjoram
5 cloves
12 peppercorns
2 sticks celery
1 blade mace
Whites and shells of 3 eggs
Salt

Method

Put all the ingredients into a large saucepan; add the whites beaten slightly; clarify and strain (see above).

Aspic of Lobster

Ingredients

Aspic jelly
Lobster
Cucumber
Lettuce for garnish

Method

Pour into a border or plain, moistened mould, aspic to the depth of ¼″. When this is firm, add cucumber and lobster pieces. Add a few drops of jelly. When set, cover with aspic and leave to get firm. Proceed in this way until the mould is full. When a border mould is used, place a lobster salad in the centre. If preferred, use individual moulds, and garnish with lettuce.

Aspic of Prawns. Skin the prawns and proceed as for Aspic of Lobster, putting the prawns in the mould so that they will have a good appearance when turned out.

Decorating a mould

Bananas in Jelly

Ingredients

Bananas
Sweet jelly
Pistachios

Method

Pour melted sweet jelly to the depth of ¼″ into a plain charlotte mould. Peel the bananas and cut them in slices across. Place them on the jelly when it is firm, arranging them in a circle, one resting on the other. Make a small circle in the middle of the mould. Drop on each piece of banana a little melted but cold jelly, to keep them in position. When they are set, cover with jelly, and when that is firm put in more banana and proceed, using

Bananas in Jelly (*continued*)

some blanched and shredded pistachio kernels with the banana, or the jelly may be slightly coloured pink.

Calf's Foot Stock and Jelly
Ingredients
    2 calf's feet
    4 pt. water

Method

Cut each foot into four pieces. Blanch them by putting them in cold water and bringing to the boil. Throw the water away, and well wash the feet. Put them into a saucepan with the water and boil gently for 5 hrs. Strain the stock from the bones and set it aside until the next day. The layer of fat must then be carefully removed, or the stock will not clear. To turn this into calf's foot jelly, add: ½ pt. white wine, rind of 3 and juice of 5 lemons, ¾ lb. lump sugar, whites and shells of 4 eggs. Clarify and strain (see above). See also under **CALF'S FEET**.

Claret Jelly
Ingredients
    1 oz. gelatine or leaf gelatine
    ½ pt. water
    ½ lb. lump sugar
    1½ pt. claret
    Few drops cochineal

Method

Soak the gelatine in the water; add the sugar, and stir over heat until dissolved. Pour in the wine, colour with cochineal and strain into a wetted mould. When firm, dip into hot water for a second and turn on to a glass dish. This jelly is not clarified. Cake is usually served with claret jelly.

Macedoine of Fruit
Ingredients
    1 qt. sweet jelly
    Various fresh fruits

Method

Line a wetted ornamental mould with sweet cool jelly. When firm arrange some

Preparing a jelly mould

Macedoine of Fruit (*continued*)

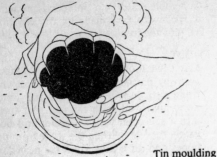

Tin moulding

of the fruit on it. Drop on each piece of fruit a little jelly. When the fruit adheres to the layers of jelly in the mould, pour in gently sufficient cool sweet jelly to cover it. When that is firm, place in more fruit and proceed to set it in the same manner. Continue in this way until the mould is full. When quite set, turn on to a glass or silver dish. For setting fruit, etc., in jelly, be careful the jelly used is quite cool but not at all set. It is well to put the mould on ice or to stand it in cold water so that the jelly may set quickly. Remember that the fruit, etc., put into a jelly will be reversed in position when the jelly is turned out, and arrange it accordingly. Macedoine of Fruit may also be set in a border mould.

Orange Jellies. Nearly half fill little fluted darioles with Maraschino jelly (Wine jelly). When set, place in each a little tangerine orange quite freed from skin and pith. Drop a few drops of jelly on it, and when set, fill up the mould.

Pineapple Jelly

Ingredients
1 pineapple
1½ oz. gelatine
1 qt. water
½ lb. lump sugar
Rind of 1 and juice of 3 lemons
Whites and shells of 3 large eggs

Method
First put the gelatine in the water. Cut up the pineapple and bruise it in a mortar. Add it and all the other ingredients to the gelatine, then clarify.

Savoury Jelly without Acid. Prepare some stock as directed for First Stock for Clear Soup. To every qt. add, when ready and quite free from fat, 2 oz. finest French leaf gelatine, the beaten whites of 2 eggs and, if liked, a wineglassful of sherry. Clarify and strain (see above).

Savoury Jelly without Acid (*continued*)

In making either the aspic or savoury jelly, care must always be taken to have nicely flavoured stock. The colour of the aspic can be varied to taste by using light or dark stock, or it may be artificially coloured.

Wine Jelly

Ingredients	Method
Thin rind of 2 and juice of 5 lemons 1 qt. water 2 oz. leaf gelatine 10 oz. lump sugar 6 cloves Whites and shells of 3 eggs 2 wineglasses sherry	Soak the thin lemon rind in 1 pt. cold water for ½ hr., add the gelatine, strained juice of lemons, sugar, cloves, the whites and shells of eggs, sherry and the remainder of the water (which may be hot). Put all these ingredients into a large saucepan, clarify and strain. This jelly may be varied by using liqueurs, brandy, rum, etc., in place of the wine. For Maraschino, use no lemon rind.

JELLY BAGS. These bags are made of flannel and are used for straining: the liquid is poured into the bag and drips slowly through into a basin below.

JERKED BEEF. Beef cut into thin slices and dried in the sun.

JERUSALEM ARTICHOKES. See ARTICHOKES.

JERUSALEM OAK. Ambrosia, feather geranium. The whole herb is used medicinally.

JESSAMINE. An essence is made from the flowers of this plant and used to give flavour to some confections. Place a pressed quart measureful of fresh petals of jessamine into a jar with 2 oz. coriander seeds and steep them in 2 qt. rectified spirit and 1 qt. distilled water. Let this remain for 3 wks.; drain off through filter and bottle.

Jessamine Water Ice. Mix the juice of 7 lemons and the zest of 3 in a pan with 3 gills syrup and a few drops of essence of jessamine, 1 wineglass brandy and a little water. Pass it through a fine sieve into the freezer. Put into moulds and serve.

JEWISH TRADITIONAL RECIPES. The Jewish dietary laws ordain that Kosher meat needs special preparation, so the housewife prepares her food in accordance with the methods described in orthodox Jewish cookery. Eash festival requires special dishes, and in the following alphabetically arranged recipes you will find a selection from which to choose food according to the calendar.

TO KOSHER LIVER. When koshering liver, wash well and cover freely with salt. Place on greaseproof paper and heat at a low heat till well browned and the blood is congealed. Wash well and fry. For chopped liver, it is advisable to boil it first to make it tender.

TO KOSHER MEAT. Take a bowl that is used for no other purpose and put into it a little cold water. Put into this the meat and soak for ½ hr. Have ready a perforated draining-board, lift out the meat and thoroughly salt it on both sides. Leave the meat to drain for ½ hr. and then wash three times in cold running water. It is essential to have the board slanting so that the blood may drain out.

TO KOSHER POULTRY. Completely remove the whole of the inside lights and lungs, then proceed as for meat.

Almond Milk. Put 4 oz. ground almonds into a saucepan with 1 pt. water and simmer together for about ¾ hr., stirring occasionally; then strain through muslin.

Almond Pudding. Beat 4 eggs together for 10 mins., add 4 oz. caster sugar and beat for a further 10 mins.; add 2 oz. ground almonds and beat for 30 mins. Grease a pie dish well with olive oil and turn in the mixture. Bake for ¾–1 hr. at 350° F. Therm. 4, and when the pudding begins to shrink from the sides of the dish remove from the oven. Allow to cool, then turn out of the dish, sprinkle with fine sugar and serve.

Almonds, Salted. Blanch ½ pt. almonds and place on a tin in a cool oven 200° F. Therm ¼; increase heat to 350° F. Therm. 4 and in 15 mins. the almonds should be

Almonds, Salted (*continued*)

dry. Remove from the oven and sprinkle them with olive oil. Mix them round and replace in the oven to cook till golden brown, stirring occasionally to ensure even browning. Remove and sprinkle with salt and allow to cool on greaseproof paper. Store in airtight jars.

Apple Meringue. Peel, core and slice 2 lb. apples, place in a pan with 4 oz. brown sugar, the rind and juice of 1 lemon and 2 tbsp. water. Cook until tender and then rub through a sieve. Add 4 oz. finely chopped figs and ¼ tsp. cloves; separate the whites and yolks of 3 eggs. Add the beaten yolks to the pulp. Turn into a well-greased pie dish. Whisk the whites of the eggs stiffly, then add 1 oz. caster sugar and beat again. Fold in 2 oz. caster sugar and pile the mixture on to the apple pulp. Bake at 200° F. Therm. ¼ for 1¾ hrs.

Apple Pudding. Soak 6 oz. bread in a little cold water and when soft, drain and beat up with a fork. Peel, core and slice very finely 2 lb. cooking apples, mix together with 2 oz. stoned raisins, 3 oz. sugar, ½ tsp. cinnamon, 1 oz. ground almonds, 4 oz. suet. Add the bread and mix well. Separate the whites and yolks of 3 eggs, beat separately, mix the yolks with the bread and fruit and mix well. Fold in stiffly beaten egg whites. Turn the mixture into a well-greased pudding-dish and bake for about 1 hr.

Apple Strudel. Warm 8 oz. flour and mix together with ¼ oz. yeast, 1 tsp. sugar and ¼ pt. warm water. Pour this into the middle of the flour and leave for 10 mins. Mix this together to a dough, knead thoroughly and leave to rise for 1 hr. Re-knead very lightly, then roll out as thinly as possible. Take the dough, put it on to a cloth and pull it out so that it spreads to the thinness of a wafer. Take 1½ lb. chopped apples, 3 oz. stoned raisins and 3 oz. currants, and mix with a sprinkling of cinnamon. Add sufficient oil to make a paste that will spread easily over the dough; holding the cloth by one end, roll up the dough and tip it on to a well-greased baking tin. Bake for about ¼ hr. at 400° F. Therm. 6, basting occasionally with oil.

Beolas. Take 2 eggs and break them into a bowl and beat together until they are light and frothy. Add sufficient fine motza meal to make a medium batter; beat well together and drop the mixture, a tbsp. at a time into smoking hot fat. Fry the beolas to a pale brown, then lift out and place on paper to drain. Serve cold with a syrup made by boiling ½ pt. water with 3 oz. sugar and ½ tsp. cinnamon.

Biscuits, Noyau. Warm 8 oz. butter to soften. Add 4 oz. caster sugar, 1 beaten egg and 1 tsp. noyau; beat well together, sifting in 8 oz. flour. Work together and turn onto a floured board. Roll out very thinly and cut into shapes; place on a floured tin, brush with egg white and sprinkle with a little caster sugar. Put a small piece of citron peel in the centre of each biscuit. Bake at 250°–300° F. Therm. ½ for 15 mins.

Biscuits, Vanilla. Beat 1 egg till it is frothy with 8 oz. caster sugar, add ¾ lb. ground sweet almonds, mix well; add vanilla essence to flavour and 1 oz. cornflour. Knead to a smooth paste, roll out about ¼″ thickness and cut into 3″ strips. Place on rice paper and cook for 20 mins. When the biscuits are almost cooked, brush over with beaten egg and sprinkle chopped blanched almonds on to the biscuit.

Bitki. Mince 1 lb. blade beef. Soak in a little water 4 oz. bread, beat together and add salt, pepper and celery salt. Mix all together with 1 beaten egg. Mould into an oval shape and place in a casserole with a small onion. Cover with lid and cook gently for 2 hrs.

Bola. Take 1 lb. dough and rub into it 8 oz. butter; add 1 oz. brown sugar to sweeten and roll out thinly. Cut off a strip of dough and line a well-greased tin. Mix together on the remaining piece of dough, ½ oz. cinnamon, 8 oz. brown sugar, 8 oz. shredded candied peel and 1 egg. Roll out the dough, re-roll like a roly-poly pudding and cut into 4 pieces; place on the tin, cut end upwards. Bake for ¼ hr. at 400–500° F. Therm. 6–7, then 1¼ hr. at 350° F. Therm. 4. When nearly baked, make holes in the dough and pour on syrup sugar.

Bread, Sabbath Twist Challas. Mix together in a large basin, 2 lb. sifted flour and 1 tsp. salt. Place in a saucepan 1 oz. kosher margarine, ¾ pt. water, and warm to blood heat. Beat together 2 eggs and add the water and melted margarine. Mix 1 oz. yeast, 1 tsp. fine sugar and add to the water. Make a hole in the centre of

Bread, Sabbath Twist Challas (*continued*)

the flour and pour in the liquid, work together to form a light dough, sprinkle a little flour on the top and leave in a warm place to rise for 3½ hrs. Turn on to a well-floured board and work lightly; cut off 2 large pieces and shape for the lower portion of the twists and brush with beaten egg. Take the remainder of the dough and divide into 6 pieces, knead and shape into a long strand and make two plaits and place one on the top of each twist. Brush with beaten egg and then sprinkle with poppy seeds. Allow to rise for about 20 mins., then bake at oven 350° F. Therm. 4 for 30 mins.

Bread, Unfermented. Sift together into a mixing bowl ½ lb. flour, 1 tsp. baking powder and a good pinch of salt. Add sufficient water to make a stiff dough, knead for 5 mins. and then place on tin and bake for 15 mins. at 400° F. Therm. 6.

Cakes, Hanucah. Sift 8 oz. flour into a mixing bowl and rub in 4 oz. butter, then add 4 oz. brown sugar and 1 well-beaten egg. Mix together and roll out ¼″ thick, cut into rings and brush over with egg. Toss in 4 oz. crushed loaf sugar and bake on a well-greased tin at 400° F. Therm. 6 for ½ hr.

Cake, La Koch Honey. Sift together into a mixing bowl, 8 oz. flour, 1 level tsp. bicarbonate soda, adding 2 oz. sugar and 1 tsp. ground ginger. Cream together in another bowl 4 tbsp. warm golden syrup, 2 oz. butter, and 1 well-beaten egg and mix all together, adding about ¼ pt. warm milk. Pour into a well-greased cake tin and sprinkle with chopped almonds. Bake for 1 hr. 20 mins. at 200–250° F. Therm. ¼.

Cake, Palestinian Honey. Mix together ¾ lb. flour, pinch of salt, 1 tsp. mixed spice and ½ tsp. bicarb. soda. Separate the white and yolk of 1 egg and beat up the yolk with 2 whole eggs; add to the flour. Then add 3 tbsp. honey and the juice and half peel (grated) of a lemon. Mix all together. Turn the dough on to a well-floured board, roll out to ¼″ thickness and cut into fancy shapes. Brush with white of egg and sprinkle with chopped almonds. Bake for about 10 to 12 mins. at 400° F. Therm. 6.

Cake, Poppy Seed. Mix together in a bowl 8 oz. flour, 1 tbsp. sugar, ⅛ pt. olive oil and 4 eggs. Knead well together and roll out, cutting into squares. Prick to prevent blistering and bake at 350° F. Therm. 4 for 20 mins. Put 1 lb. honey into a pan and bring it to the boil; drop in the squares of cake and boil for a few mins. Remove and sprinkle the cakes with poppy seeds and leave them to brown, then place separately on a dish and sprinkle with a little cold water.

Capon Roast. Take a trussed capon and stuff with ½ lb. parboiled onions, chopped and mixed with 2 tbsp. breadcrumbs, the grated rind of 1 lemon, and salt and pepper to season. Smear the capon well with clarified fat and place in a meat tin with a piece of greaseproof paper over it. Roast for 1¼–1½ hrs. at 400° F. Therm. 6. TO MAKE THE GRAVY. Pour out nearly all the fat, add just enough flour to soak up the remainder, stir over a low heat till brown, add water slowly, stirring the whole time. Continue stirring, adding pepper and salt to taste and boiling for a few mins.

Chanucah Plum Cake. Beat together to a cream 6 oz. butter, 6 oz. demerara sugar, add separately 3 eggs, beating after each. Sift in ½ lb. flour and beat well. Add 1 tbsp. golden syrup, stir all together. Add 4 oz. chopped candied peel, 8 oz. currants, 4 oz. sultanas, 2 oz. shelled almonds (chopped), ½ tsp. mixed spice. Warm ¼ pt. milk, dissolve ¼ tsp. bicarb. soda in this and stir into the mixture. Pour into a lined cake tin and bake for 3 hrs. at 200° F. Therm. ¼. If desired, when the cake is cooked, it may be iced.

Chicken Broth with Kreplech. Place a boiling fowl in a casserole and fill with water, add (diced or sliced) 1 turnip, 1 onion, and 2 sticks of celery, 2 tbsp. pearl barley, salt and pepper to season. Cover and cook for 2½–3 hrs. Remove the chicken and add kreplech. Add after a further 15 mins. the beaten yolk of 2 eggs, and stir to prevent curdling. Do not allow the soup to boil. Serve immediately.

Chocolate Mousse. Dissolve ¼ lb. plain block chocolate in almost ½ pt. water. Soak 4 oz. isinglass with the remaining ½ pt. water; cool, but do not allow to set. Separate the yolks from the whites of 3 eggs. Beat up the yolks, add to the hot chocolate, stirring the whole time. Cook gently, without allowing the mixture to boil, for 5 mins.; add 1 oz. sugar and allow to cool, then add the isinglass, stirring

Chocolate Mousse (*continued*)
it at the same time. Add the stiffly whisked egg whites, folding carefully in, then turn into a moistened mould to set. Plunge the mould into hot water a moment ot two before turning out.

Chrine. Grate 1 horseradish and half a beetroot finely. Mix together with a pinch of salt and a little sugar. Add just sufficient white vinegar to cover, and serve with any hot or cold dishes as a relish.

Cucumbers, Salted. Soak some small, fine cucumbers for 12 hrs. in cold water. Arrange these in a small barrel in layers with vine and cherry leaves, bay leaves and peppercorns; pour on boiled water, allowing 1 tsp. salt to each pint. Leave in the garden, turning the barrel daily, for 2½ wks.

Einaulf. Mix together to a smooth paste, 1 egg, pinch of salt, 3 tbsp. flour and ¼ cup of water. Drop into the soup slowly from the end of a fork and cook for 3 mins.

Fish, Curried. Take 1 lb. cold, cooked fish, flake it and remove the skin and bones. Peel and cut up 1 apple, 1 stick rhubarb, 2 onions and fry till brown in 2 oz. butter. Add 1 tbsp. curry powder and 1 tbsp. flour, salt and pepper to season, 1 tbsp. lemon juice or vinegar, and 1 pt. water. Stir and bring to the boil gradually; simmer for ½ hr. Strain, return to the saucepan, add the fish and heat. Serve with bowl of boiled rice.

Fish Fillets with Wine. Take the required number of fillets and place in a casserole; sprinkle with pepper and salt and a chopped shallot. Add sufficient White wine to cover the fish and cook for 25 mins. Pour out the liquid into a small saucepan and add the yolks of 2 eggs, juice of a lemon and 2 oz. kosher margarine, stirring briskly the whole time. Pour this sauce onto the fish and serve immediately.

Fish, Fried. Wash and scale the fish; put the oil in a deep frying-pan and heat till there is a blue haze. Cut the fish into slices and dry in a clean cloth. Put a little sifted flour on to a plate and on a second plate beat up an egg with a pinch of salt. Dip the fish into flour and then into the egg and fry till crisp and brown.

Fish, Gefillte. Take a large haddock and cut it into thick slices, scoop out a hole, removing the backbone. Chop finely the remaining fish with a little parsley and onion, then mix with 1 tbsp. breadcrumbs, pepper and salt. Add 2 eggs, well-beaten, and fill the hole cut in the fish with the mixture. Put the fish into a casserole and cover with cold water. Add 5 small onions, a little chopped parsley and a carrot. Cook for 45–50 mins. Mix to a batter 1 tbsp. flour and ¼ pt. milk and blend with a little of the fish liquid. Return to the casserole and cook for 10 mins. before serving.

Fish Roe, Herring. Take soft herring roes and place them in an ovenware dish with four laurel leaves. Boil together in 3 tbsp. vinegar, ½ pt. water and 6 peppercorns. Strain and pour over the roes. Cover with oil-paper and bake for about 10–15 mins. at 350° F. Therm. 4. When cold, serve on rounds of toast with a garnishing of chopped cucumbers, capers and salad oil mixed together.

Fish, Salt Herring. Soak the herring in cold water and drain, then cut into strips ½″ wide. Serve before the first course of a meal.

Fish Stew, Brown. Peel and slice 3 onions and simmer gently with 2 pt. water in a casserole. Add 3 lb. salmon, trout or mackerel. Add pepper and salt to season, cook for 20 mins. Melt 6 oz. treacle, add 2 small gingerbreads and ¾ cup vinegar, and pour over the fish. Leave to marinate for 15 mins. Serve cold with a garnishing of sliced lemon and chopped parsley.

Fritters, Purim. Remove the crust from a small continental loaf and cut the crumb into slices ½″ thick; soak carefully in ½ pt. boiling milk. Beat together 3 eggs and pour on to a plate; dip the soaked bread into the egg and then fry in boiling salad oil. Remove from the oil, redip in milk and eggs and refry to a golden brown. Drain on greaseproof paper and place on a dish; pour on hot syrup sugar and serve cold, after decorating with hundreds and thousands. The fritters may also be baked at 375–400° F. Therm. 5–6 till crisp and when half-done glazed with white of egg and sugar.

Fritters, Swiss. Cut the crumb of a French roll into squares ½″ thick. Beat up 1 egg, add a pinch of nutmeg, a pinch of cinnamon and a little sugar. Dip the slices in the mixture, then fry in hot oil till they are golden brown. Drain and serve with jam or clarified sugar.

Gefillte Milt (Spleen). Pare off the thin outside skin of the milt and remove all the fat. Remove the centre vein with all its spearings and cut through the centre, but take care not to pierce the lower skin. Scrape out all the flesh without piercing the milt. Soak 2 oz. bread in cold water, squeeze it dry and put it into a greased saucepan, add 1 small onion chopped finely, and fry together. Shake and do not let it burn. Mix the flesh, 2 eggs, salt and pepper and a pinch of ground ginger, fill the milt and sew it up. Prick with a fork, place in a pan of boiling soup and cook till it is tender. Remove from the soup, place in a well-greased tin and bake at 375–400° F. Therm. 5–6 till a crust is formed and the milt is cooked through.

Grimlich's. Soak 2 motzas until they are soft, and then squeeze dry, adding ¼ lb. motza meal and 1 egg to make a crust. Work this into an oval shape in the hand and fill the inside with a mixture made as follows: 2 oz. ground almonds, 2 oz. stoned raisins, 2 oz. sultanas, ¼ lb. brown sugar and 2 eggs. Cover the top with a piece of the crust and shape carefully. Sprinkle with motza meal and fry in hot oil or fat. Serve with clarified sugar.

Haman's Ears (Hamantaschen). Sift into a bowl ½ lb. flour; heat 1 tbsp. oil, beat up 2 eggs in the oil and add to the flour to make a paste. Roll out very thinly, cut into rounds, then cut each round into four and drop into hot frying oil a few at a time. Whilst frying, draw them up with two forks into the shape of ears. When light brown, drain on paper and serve piled high on a dish and sprinkle with caster sugar.

Kreplech. Mix together to a stiff dough 1 egg lightly beaten, a little flour and a pinch of salt. Knead well for 10 mins., adding a little extra flour if necessary. Roll out the dough very thinly and leave to dry before cutting into squares about 3″ in diameter. Fill these with mincemeat and fold into three-cornered shapes, taking care to seal the edges well.

Krimlech. Mix together to form a batter, 1 tsp. soaked motzas, strained dry, 1 oz. chopped almonds, ½ tsp. motza meal, 1 tsp. cinnamon and the grated rind of ¼ lemon, 4 oz. brown sugar, a pinch of ginger and 2 eggs. Drop by spoonfuls into hot fat and fry. Serve as fritters.

Kugel. Make a pudding with ¼ lb. shredded suet, ½ lb. flour, ¼ lb. brown sugar, ¼ lb. currants, ¼ lb. raisins or sultanas, and 2 oz. candied peel, spiced to taste. Mix well together; add 2 eggs well beaten and place in a pudding basin; tie a cloth over the top and place in the bottom of a large earthernware pan. Put a plate on top of the basin and put on 2 lb. clod. Put in a pan 1 pt. dried peas, 1 qt. haricot beans (previously soaked), 1 large onion stuffed with cloves, pepper and salt, 1 tbsp. flour, and cover with water. Put a piece of brown paper over the top of the pan. Place in the oven when all the cooking is finished on Friday and dish up when required on Saturday, serving soup, meat and pudding each as a separate course.

Motza Appetiser. Rub the motzas lightly with raw onion, then sprinkle with salt and put into a hot oven for a few mins. Spread with dripping and serve very hot.

Motzas, Baked. Soak the motzas in cold water and squeeze dry, add ½ lb. dried fruit, 2 oz. dripping, 2 tbsp. motza meal, 2 oz. brown sugar and spice to taste, then add 2 well-beaten eggs and pour into a well-greased pie dish, bake for about 30 mins. at 350° F. Therm. 4. Serve with syrup sugar.

Motza, Boiled Pudding. Use 2 oz. suet instead of dripping as for Baked Motza and put the mixture into a well-greased pudding basin and boil or steam for 1½ hr.

Motza Kleis. Soak 4 motzas in cold water and squeeze them very dry. Beat very lightly, adding 6 oz. chopped suet, a little chopped parsley, a sprinkle of ginger, pepper and salt. Brown 3 sliced onions in a little fat, add to them 3 well-beaten eggs, then add to the other ingredients. Mix to a stiff consistency with a little motza meal, then form into balls, drop into soup and cook for 25–30 mins.

Noodles (Passover). Beat up 2 eggs and mix with potato flour to make a thin batter; put a little fat or dripping into the frying-pan and heat. Pour in the batter, shake gently and then when it is cooked, lift out and leave on a board to cool. Cut into thin strips and heat by dropping into the soup a minute or two before serving.

Pancakes (Purim). Make a very smooth batter with 1 egg, ½ tsp. salt, ½ pt. water and ¼ lb. flour. Heat a frying-pan and pour in a little oil; then pour out most of the oil and pour in a little batter. Let this run level, fry on one side only, and remove from the pan. Reheat the fat and make pancakes till the batter is all used. Spread on the uncooked side of the pancake the following filling: Mince ½ lb. apples, add 1 oz. sugar, 1 oz. ground almonds, pinch of cinnamon and juice of ½ lemon. Fold over the dough three-cornerwise and seal the edge. Fry in hot oil, serve dredged with sugar.

Pfarvel. Make a dough with egg and do not let it rise; put on to a board, roll out into long strips and cut into pieces the size of coarse barley. Heat 2 tbsp. kosher margarine. Peel and chop an onion and fry until golden brown, mix with the egg dough and turn into a pie dish. Cover with hot water and bake at 200° F. Therm. ¼ for ¾ hr. Serve as a vegetable.

Potatoes, Browned. Wash, peel and cut each potato into 3 pieces, place in a pan with a little hot water and cook gently for a few mins. Drain off the water and place potatoes in the oven in a tin with a little hot dripping. Baste well and bake at 350° F. Therm. 4 for about ¾ hr.

Potatoes, Manaska. Peel and boil 6 potatoes, drain off the water and mash them with a level dsp. parsley and a beaten egg. Add pepper and salt to season, make into small balls and place on a greased tin, but do not let them touch each other. Bake for 25–30 mins. at 350° F. Therm. 4.

Prelato Pudding (Milk). Put 6 prelatos into a dish. Beat up the yolks of 3 eggs, add ½ pt. milk, 1 oz. ground almonds and 2 oz. caster sugar. Pour over the prelatos. Bake for 30 mins. slowly at 200–250° F. Therm. ½. Beat the egg whites stiffly, stir in 3–4 oz. caster sugar and spread over the top of the cooked pudding. Return the pudding to the oven for the meringue to set lightly. This will take about 10 mins. Serve hot.

Raisin Wine. Put 6 lb. raisins with 8 pt. water into a wine jar. Stand this in a Passover vessel containing water. Kosher the hotplate and leave the vessel on for 7 days. The water should be just warm, and it is not necessary to leave heat on the whole time. Add sugar and cinnamon to taste on the 6th day and strain on the 7th day through a fine mesh.

Rinderboraten. Take 2 lb. brisket, a few peppercorns, 1 chopped onion, and pepper and salt, and stew with a little water in an earthenware casserole covered with the lid, cooking slowly for 3 hrs. Make a stiff dough. Roll out on a well-floured board and cut into four. Roll out each piece thinly and leave to dry. Fold into four and cut into thin slices; drop into boiling stock and cook for 20 mins.

Rodgrod. Stew 1 lb. raspberries and 1 lb. red currants together for ¼ hr. Soak 8 oz. sago in ½ pt. water, add the fruit, a little grated lemon peel, a few almonds and sugar to taste, and cook until the sago is clear, stirring to prevent burning. Pour into a well-moistened mould and serve when thoroughly chilled.

Salad, Bean. Take a salad bowl and place in it ½ lb. cold boiled fresh beans or ½ lb. cold boiled haricot beans and mix with 1 tbsp. salad oil, 2 tbsp. vinegar and ¼ tsp. ground ginger, adding pepper and salt to taste. Mix well together.

Salad, Cabbage or Cauliflower. Red or white cabbage and cauliflower may both be used as above.

Salad, Celeriac. Wash the celeriac, boil it and, when cold, peel and cut into slices. Pour on ½ gill white vinegar and add pepper and salt to taste.

Salad, Tomato. Take a salad bowl, finely slice 6 tomatoes and add a little chopped onion. Sift on a little caster sugar and add, mixed together, 1 tbsp. olive oil, 2 tbsp. vinegar; garnish with olives.

Salad, Tomato (Whole). Blanch and slice the tomatoes and serve separately from the main dish on a lettuce leaf or with cress; add a sprinkle of salt and pepper. Dress with the following mixture: 1 tbsp. salad oil, 2 tbsp. vinegar, ¼ tsp. ground ginger and a pinch of pepper and salt. Garnish with grated horseradish.

Salmagundy. Wash a Dutch herring (see **HERRING**) and remove the bone. Place the boned fish on a small dish, put on a sliced onion, add a dusting of pepper. Boil together ½ pt. vinegar and a little allspice and ginger. When cold, pour over the herring.

Sassafras. Tie up together liquorice and aniseed in a muslin bag; put the bag into a jug with sassafras and pour boiling water over it.

Sauce, Piquant. Melt in a saucepan 1 oz. dripping; add 1 chopped shallot and 1 garlic and fry till brown, then add ½ gill vinegar and boil. Blend together ¼ oz. flour and ½ pt. white stock; cook for 3 mins. After the liquid boils, add pepper and salt to season and serve.

Soup, Liver. Take a qt. liquor and place in a saucepan. Cut into small pieces 6 oz. liver. Place in another pan 2 oz. flour and 2 oz. dripping, and brown together to a good rich colour. Add the liver and half a crumbled small roll, break in an egg, and brown all together. Season with salt and pepper. Place all together in the saucepan and simmer about 1 hr.

Soup, Shabbas. Wash ½ pt. haricot beans, ½ pt. coarse barley, and place in a large casserole; add a little fat meat and a marrow bone. Add 5 pt. water and pepper and salt; cover tightly and cook gently at 350° F. Therm. 4.

Syrup Sugar. Put ¼ lb. lump sugar into a saucepan, add 1 gill water and 2 egg-shells. Place over gentle heat, stir frequently until the sugar is dissolved and a thick syrup is formed. Strain well and reboil.

Triflech. Make a batter with 2 tbsp. flour, pinch of salt, 1 egg, and ¼ pt. water; from a teaspoon drop into the soup 10 mins before serving.

Tsimess. Take a fat piece of brisket, about 3½-4 lb. in weight, and put it into a large casserole. Add a little ground nutmeg, pepper and salt to season, ½ lb. Demerara sugar and 2 lb. carrots; cover with 1½ pt. water. Cover with a well-fitting lid and simmer gently for 3½-4 hrs. Just before serving add a little flour and water mixed to a smooth paste and cook until the gravy has thickened. Serve very hot.

JOHN DORY. This fish is caught along the south coast from Beachy Head to Land's End in this country, and elsewhere in Europe. The name is an evident corruption of *jaune doré* (yellow and gold) from the golden colour of the skin. There are few fish so exceedingly ugly, but the flesh is of a delicate flavour. It is best eaten filleted and cooked as sole.

JOINTS. The name is given to those pieces of meat into which it is usual to cut up the whole animal. They are specifically described under the animals to which they belong, and recipes are given thereunder for the cooking of them. In this country the joint is usually served after the entrée, while on the Continent it is served after the fish, the *gros-pièce* or *pièce de résistance* of a dinner.

JOLERIE. A freshwater fish similar to perch.

JORDAN ALMOND. See ALMOND.

JORUM. An old-fashioned earthenware jar holding a large quantity of liquor.

JUDCOCK. See SNIPE.

JULEP. An ancient Arabian name for a cooling drink containing mucilage and opium. This term is now a common name in America for drinks composed of sugar and spirit in an aromatic water flavoured with fresh mint and chilled with broken ice.

JULIENNE. The name of a vegetable clear soup which was first made in 1785 by a well-known French chef, Jean Julien. This name is also given to the vegetable roots cut into fine shreds.

JUMBLES. See Brandy Snaps (p. 76) for the description of difference between these and Jumbles.

JUNIPER. This is the name given to a shrub which bears blue berries, used to flavour gin. They have a warm pungent taste and can also be used for juniper-berry ice.

JUNKET. The old English name for cream cheese, made in a rush basket. Devonshire junket is milk turned with rennet, double cream and sugar, ground cinnamon or other flavouring. Usually served with fruit. TO MAKE from fresh milk. Take ½ pt.

JUNKET (*continued*)

milk, rennet as stated on container, 1 level tbsp. sugar. Place milk in a saucepan and heat to blood heat. (Test with thermometer or dip in little finger to test heat.) Add rennet in proportion stated. If the rennet is fresh, this should be a large or standard teaspoon; if in tablet form, use as directed. Add sugar if desired, stir well, pour into bowl to set. Serve as desired with fruit or cream.

VARIATIONS. Do not add sugar, add grated nutmeg, or place a vanilla pod in pan while heating milk, or make junkets with coffee-flavoured milk; add chocolate flavouring; add fruit flavouring essence or syrup. Colour pink for children.

K

KABOB. As in the case of other Hindustani words, when converted into English, the spelling of this one is varied. Hence we find Cabob, Kebob, Kebah, Kibab, Kespa. It is a word signifying a roast with sundry modifications. The modern acceptance of the term is a piece of meat roasted on a skewer or small spit, also small pieces of meat grilled on skewer with herbs and onions, whereas the original kabob was a leg of mutton or sometimes a whole sheep boned and then stuffed with herbs and herrings. See also **AIGUILLETTES.**

KALE (Fr. *chou frise*). This is known more commonly as Scotch Kale or Kail; either way of spelling is accepted. The word itself is of Gaelic origin, and signifies broadly a cole or undeveloped cabbage. Kale is of the cabbage family but it never forms a head. Kales are very hardy and well adapted for winter use.

TO BOIL. Wash in cold water, tie in small bundles, put into boiling water and boil for 20 mins. Drain in a colander and serve while hot with lumps of melted butter and seasoning of salt and pepper.

KEBOBS. See **KABOB.**

KEDGEREE. An Indian dish, *kishri, kitchri,* of fish and rice curried (see **FISH**). Also a mixture of rice and lentils cooked with butter.

KELKEL. A slice of sole dried and salted.

KERN MILK. The Scottish term for buttermilk.

KESLOPS. The dried vells used for curdling in making Wensleydale cheese.

KETCHUP. A piquant sauce of Japanese origin (also called catsup) usually with one predominant flavour, although anchovies, barberries, cockles, cucumbers, elderberries, mussels, oysters, peppers, tomatoes, walnuts and wine are all in their turn used to make it, as will be seen from the recipes.

KID (Fr. *chevreau*). A young goat killed between six weeks and four months old, and considered a great delicacy. In the time of our forefathers, the flesh was esteemed as much as lamb. The meat is very sweet and tender. Usually cooked whole like a sucking pig, larded, and sometimes marinaded.

KIDNEY (Fr. *rognon*). The kidneys of many animals are eaten but most usually sheep's, lamb's or pig's. When a kidney is specially named it will be found under the name of the animal to which it belongs. A favourite breakfast or luncheon dish, they are best grilled or sautéed.

Kidneys à la Tartare. Grill the kidneys and serve Tartare sauce (see p. 448) in a boat.

Kidneys Grilled. Well wipe the kidneys, split lengthwise, put the smallest piece of butter on each, season with salt and pepper, and grill them. Serve on toast with a little Maître d'Hôtel butter (see **BUTTERS**) on the top of each kidney.

Kidneys Sautéed

Ingredients	*Method*
Kidneys	Skin the kidneys. Cut them into slices
Clarified butter	and then into dice. Gently sauté them in
Toasted bread	a little butter. Serve very hot on toast. Sprinkle them with a little pepper and salt.

Kidney Soup. See **SOUPS.**

KIDNEY BEANS. See **BEANS.**

KILDERKIN. See WEIGHTS AND MEASURES.

KILKIS. Norwegian anchovies.

KILOGRAM, KILOMETRE. See WEIGHTS AND MEASURES.

KIMMEL. See KUMMEL.

KIPPER. The literal meaning of the word is taken from the Dutch "to hatch" or "to spawn", and is used in zoology to describe salmon after spawning. When they were caught in this condition in Scotland they were split open and smoked, hence the term which now has been extended to herrings and other fish.

TO COOK. Plunge the kipper into hot water for a minute or two (this helps to soften it). Then drain carefully and place on a grill tray. Add a knob of butter or margarine, season with a dusting of pepper, and place under a hot grill for a few mins. till cooked through.

Another method is to plunge the kipper into a jug of boiling water and leave for five or more minutes to cook; drain and serve as above.

KIRSCHENWASSER, KIRSCHWASSER, or KIRSCH. This valuable liqueur is made from cherries crushed with their stones and kernels and fermented. It can be made with almost any kind of cherry, wild or cultivated, but the Girotte, Morello or Black cherry is chiefly employed in making the best qualities.

KISSING CRUST. That portion of the crust of a loaf that has been touching another loaf during baking.

KITCHEN PEPPER. A mixture of finely powdered ginger, cinnamon, black pepper, nutmeg, jamaica pepper, cloves and salt. This must be kept in small bottles, closely stoppered.

KITCHENS. Today kitchens have their modern appliances and utensils, and in some instances the kitchen is also used as the dining-room. It may be small, but it should be well lighted and scrupulously clean and bright, as should be every utensil.

The kitchen can be termed the heart of the house, as the woman, the heart of a home. It is through her orderly, systematic, time-saving methods that law, order and leisure appear. Her well-equipped, clean and orderly, well-planned kitchen, her "workshop" arranged for the short cuts to work, with her sink and table at the right height to ensure that she does not suffer from backache, her cooker, table and sink conveniently placed to save walking about, her time-savers, can shorten considerably the daily work. Here are one or two simple rules:

1. Always wipe out greasy utensils with paper.
2. Drain, rather than dry, the dishes.
3. Fill the used cooking dishes with cold water and allow them to steep before washing.
4. Drain everything into the sink through a strainer. Scald strainer after use and empty after every meal.

A secret of success. Clear up, and be tidy while working. You will soon find that this becomes a habit. It is much easier to work in a tidy atmosphere than in a muddle, and very much less tiring than having to clear everything up at the last minute.

It is essential to consider in detail the equipment and utensils which are necessary for cooking. Through the years the methods of heating, and appliances, have greatly improved. It is not the kitchen that is cluttered up with every new gadget that is the best "workshop". Therefore, when planning and equipping a kitchen, consider in great detail your requirements.

COOKING BY ELECTRICITY. Electric cookers can offer flexibility for top-stove cookery, especially when sheathed radiant elements are used. When a saucepan is placed on these glowing red-hot elements, which take any flat firm-based saucepan, there is immediate contact and quick response. The hob usually has two to three circular boiling-plates and grill-boiler. These can be of radiant or solid type. For the latter, machine-ground based pans are essential for even distribution of heat. Most modern electric ovens are swiftly preheated, often within 15 mins. of

KITCHENS (*continued*)

switching on. Thermostatic control guards against overheating and current wastage. Instructions are given by the makers with all cookers for their use.

All boiling-plates can be adjusted to required heats, and simmer controls (infinitely variable controls) are fitted on most cookers. With the griller-boiler solid plate a highly polished deflector is fitted to direct the heat upward when it is used alone.

Electric cookers are easily and quickly cleaned after use. The main switch should be at OFF when cooking is completed, and before cleaning begins. (See cleaning instructions issued with the cooker).

Small quantities of water can be heated quickly and economically using an electric kettle, but the element must be covered with water before switching on. Always remove the plug after use.

This chart of oven packing is suitable for most Electric cookers:

FOOD	TEMPERATURE		POSITION
	PREHEAT TO	REDUCE TO	
Bread	450–550°	450°	Lowest runner
Cakes:			
Fruit	300°	Very moderate	Lowest runner
Christmas	300°	,,	,, ,,
Plain	325°	Moderate oven	,, ,,
Sandwich	375°	,,	Second runner from top
Scones	500°	475°	,, ,,
Small cakes	500°	475°	,, ,,
Joints:			
Alone	325°	moderate	Floor of oven
With potatoes			Meat surrounded by potatoes on floor of oven
Yorkshire pudding and pie	450°	hot	Yorkshire pudding and pie on shelf above
Milk Puddings	300°	slow	Centre
Puff Pastry	450°	hot	According to recipe
Short Pastry	400°		According to recipe

COOKING BY GAS. The chief advantages for gas cooking lie in the speed and flexibility attainable. It is possible, because of the design and variety of sizes of hotplate burners on modern gas cookers, to generate heat from burning gas in such quantities and so quickly that, for instance, three pints of water can be raised from cold to boiling in as little as seven minutes. With no other fuel can the heat be so readily and quickly regulated. For example, on a hotplate burner anything can be attained from rapid boiling at full-on to a gentle simmer on the lowest possible flame.

In the majority of gas ovens regulation is carried out automatically by the thermostat. This can be likened to a flexible universally-regulating gas tap, which controls the gas consumption in accordance with the heat conditions required in the oven, and, moreover, compensates for changes in gas pressure during use. As a result, oven cooking is stripped of one of its old bugbears—uncertainty of cooking conditions. By a simple dial setting, the desired heating can be repeated time and again with certainty.

KITCHENS (*continued*)

The dial should be set at the required mark and the oven tap left full on during cooking. Arrange the oven shelves before lighting the gas and allow the oven to heat up before inserting the food. Most gas-cooker manufacturers supply a chart which gives minimum times for heating the oven. When an oven thermostat is fitted there should be no need to alter the gas or open the door until the end of the cooking time is reached.

The upper part of the oven is hotter than the lower, so it is possible to cook several dishes requiring different temperatures at the same time. In such cases the thermostat setting to be used is that needed for the dish requiring the highest temperature, and this dish is put in the upper part of the oven. Food requiring a lower temperature is then placed lower down.

The spacing of oven shelves is important. It is seldom necessary to use the top runner of the oven. This is intended for hanging meat and takes the place of a centre hook. When two or more shelves are used, leave two or three runner spaces between them.

Lastly, a word about the *cleaning of the modern gas cooker*. On enamelled surfaces, wipe up all accidental spillages immediately. Clean all soiled surfaces each time you have used the cooker by first wiping with a cloth rinsed in hot, soapy water, then with the cloth rinsed in clean water. Occasionally clean the underside of the hot plate so that spilled food will not become charred when the grill is used. If you have neglected your cooker you may use very fine steel wool, moistened and liberally coated with soap. Avoid coarse abrasives which damage the gloss of the enamel. Alternatively, if the deposit is of long standing you may use one of the semi-liquid or soft jelly-like caustic cleaners, and thoroughly wash afterwards.

Wipe oven shelves over with a dry rag or newspaper immediately after use. Do not be afraid to leave a little grease on the shelves, because this helps to preserve them. No abrasives should be used.

Over plated parts a wipe with a damp cloth is usually sufficient. When the surface has become tarnished it can easily be cleaned by rubbing with a soapy cloth and afterwards drying. A thin coating of petroleum jelly helps to protect the plate's parts. Abrasives should never be used.

Clean hotplate burners by rubbing with a pad of paper, then with a cloth wrung out in hot soapy water. Finish off with a cloth rinsed in clear water and dry thoroughly.

GENERAL NOTES ON PACKING AN OVEN. It is essential to preheat the oven to the given setting so that it is at this temperature before the food is inserted.

The general method of packing an oven will be usually suggested by the makers, because this depends upon the position of the heating element.

If you are using an electric oven, as there are no burners inside the whole space can be filled with food, but the oven must not be overcrowded so that the distribution of heat is interfered with.

When using a gas oven the oven grid shelves should always be pushed back as far as they will go. This ensures the correct circulation of hot gas rising from the burners.

Poultry should be arranged for roasting with no part of the bird projecting beyond the back of the grid. As a general rule, trays and tins should be centrally placed on the working area of the oven grid, so leaving space at front, back and sides. It is best that the baking tray should be placed towards the front of the grid rather than at the back against the stop.

The topmost runner is provided for convenience of hanging meat for roasting if this method is used. Under no circumstances should it be used for any other cooking operation. The highest runner position normally used is the second from the top. A single tray of biscuits, scones or cakes is usually cooked on this runner. Items such as sponge sandwiches, pies, etc., are cooked on the third runner. Large cakes, bread, etc., are cooked on the third or fourth or fifth runners from the top. If two trays of biscuits or small cakes are to be cooked simultaneously, leave at least two runner spaces between the shelves. The top tray will be cooked first and the second tray should then be moved to the top position. Casseroles and stews

KITCHENS (*continued*)

go on the middle shelf because they require long, slow cooking, and milk puddings go on the base plate.

The oven door should never be banged, it should always be carefully closed.

When a variety of foods are being cooked together, always have the pastry at the top of the oven, the meat and any other foods which require a moderate temperature on the middle shelf, and place puddings in the cool zone on the base plate.

PRESSURE COOKERS. The rules for the principle of cooking by the pressure method are given with each cooker. It is a method of cooking in controlled steam heat, and the rules are governed by the capacity of the cooker. It must always be remembered *never to fill the pressure cooker more than two-thirds full and for soups or stocks only half-full.* It is essential always to be accurate in both measurements and cooking time and never forget that the cooker must be taken off at the right time. *You must also remember that the pressure must be reduced before the cooker is opened.* Each cooker has its own directions in the recipes and although pressure is reduced at once, while the food remains in the cooker, even though there is no heat underneath it, it will continue to cook.

When cooking vegetables, it is essential that they should be the same size, otherwise the smaller pieces will be overcooked by the time the larger pieces are ready. The cooking time for frozen vegetables in pressure cookers are approximately 1 min., with the exception of peas and cauliflower which only take $\frac{1}{2}$ min. Only 1 gill of water is added, as the vegetables will thaw during cooking and provide extra moisture. The cooking time is the time from when the required pressure is reached; the following table gives a general guide:

FISH	Fillets	5–6 mins. according to size
	Whole Fish	6 mins. per lb.
	Steaks	6 mins. per lb.
FRUITS	Apples and pears	4–6 mins.
	Cranberries	$1\frac{1}{2}$–2 mins.
	Plums	,,
	Other fruits	Just bring to pressure
	Dried fruits	4–10 mins.
MEAT	Beef	10–12 mins. per lb.
	Chicken	5 mins. per lb.
	Guinea-fowl	5 mins. per lb.
	Lamb, mutton, pork or veal	12–14 mins. per lb.
	Pigeon	10 mins. per lb.
	Rabbit	6 mins. per lb.
	Stewing	20 mins. per lb.
SOUP		Not more than 30 mins.
VEGETABLES	See tables under individual headings	
VEGETABLES, DRIED	Butter beans	30 mins.
	Haricot beans	30–35 mins.
	Lentils	15 mins.

STORED HEAT COOKING. The full instructions for the use of cookers which cook by stored heat (where there are no naked flames) will be given by the makers when the cooker is installed. These cookers need rest periods to store fresh heat. Various designs are available with two or more ovens and surface hot plates. In

KITCHENS (*continued*)

some cookers there are facilities for heating water. Utensils with thick flat bases are essential and the insulating point covers must be kept closed when the cooker is not in use. The cookers are easily cleaned, and it is essential to keep the plates brushed and free from spilled food and wiped with a damp cloth before the lids are shut down.

COOKING BY OIL. Very successful cooking can be done with oil stoves, and once the art of this type of cookery is mastered, it ensures the best results. Full directions will be given with the stove by the makers.

KITCHEN UTENSILS. Whether the kitchen be the tiniest flat kitchen or the largest country house or London kitchen, only those who are to work with the utensils can decide what their minimum or maximum list should contain. Most cooks have found that the majority of their so-called kitchen gadgets lie in a drawer untouched. The favourite wooden spoon, the short two-pronged fork, the little kitchen knife, mixing bowl and pudding basin, two or three saucepans and an omelet pan may be found in daily use. Great care and thought are necessary when furnishing a kitchen. Always remember to what extent the utensils or gadgets will be used before they are purchased.

1 large refrigerator
1 white enamel-topped table
  chairs
1 kettle
1 small double boiler
1 large double boiler
2 small saucepans
2 large saucepans
1 fish kettle
1 small frying-pan
1 large frying-pan
1 omelet pan
1 coffee percolator
1 colander
4 strainers of different sizes
1 apple corer
3 large metal spoons
1 iron fork
1 set wooden spoons
1 corkscrew
1 tin-opener
4–6 earthenware bowls of different
  sizes
6 store jars
1 salt-dredger
1 pepper-dredger
1 ice-pick
1 large iron frying-pan
1 deep frying-pan
1 frying basket
1 small roasting-tin
1 medium roasting-tin
1 large roasting-tin
1 egg beater
1 egg poacher
1 wire whisk
2 small jugs
2 large jugs
6 soup plates
2 wire forks
3 knives of different sizes

1 spatula
1 ladle
1 pastry-bag
1 vegetable-cutter
1 pastry-brush
1 lemon-squeezer
1 nutmeg-grater
1 grater
3 moulds of different sizes
1 layer-cake tin
1 éclair tin
1 set patty tins
2 ramekins
2 pastry-cutters (1 large, 1 small)
3 biscuit-cutters of different sizes
2 bread tins
1 bread board
1 rolling-pin
1 flour-sifter
2 baking-sheets
1 meat mincer
6 egg cups
1 teapot
1 coffee pot
12 glasses
2 salts
2 peppers
1 ricer
1 knife sharpener
3 pie-cans of different sizes
1 measuring cup
6 skewers
Scales
1 wooden chopping board
1 meat chopper
1 chopping knife
1 dishpan
1 dish-mop
1 metal-mop
6 dish-cloths
1 soap-dish

KITCHEN UTENSILS (*continued*)

1 soap-shaker	1 toasting fork
1 sink-brush	Pie frills in all sizes
1 sink saver	1 forcing bag and nozzles for icing and
1 potato cutter	vegetable piping
½ set dinner ware	1 potato masher
6–12 dish towels	1 funnel
4–6 glass cloths	1 casserole
2 mops	1 ball poultry-twine
1 mop-handle	1 roll brown paper
1 good broom	6 rolls greaseproof and kitchen paper
Cornet moulds	1 large dustbin
1 perforated spoon	1 scrubbing brush
1 wire cake tray	3–6 roller towels

Thermometers: Oven Thermometer (if no thermostatic control on oven)
                        Candy Thermometer
                        Frying Thermometer
                        Sugar Thermometer (for measuring densities)
Pressure Cooker

KLIP- or CLIP-FISH. A common name for dried cod imported from Norway.

KNEADING. The process by which the ingredients of dough are thoroughly blended (see BREAD).

KNOT, KNUTE or KNOUT. This is the name given to a kind of sand-piper, a small bird, which, when cooked, can scarcely be distinguished from the quail. It is said to have been a favourite of King Canute.

KNOTTED MARJORAM. See MARJORAM.

KNUCKLE. This refers to the part of a leg of veal below the knee joint. It is mostly used for stews and stock.

KOHL RABI (Fr. *chou rave*). There are three varieties, white, green and purple. The name is derived from the German and means "cabbage-turnip".
    TO BOIL. Peel in the same way as turnips. Cut into quarters, place in a saucepan with boiling water and a lump of salt. Simmer gently for 20 mins. until tender. When cooked, drain them and cut into slices. Serve with Melted Butter sauce (see p. 445), and a seasoning of pepper, salt and grated nutmeg.

KOSHER. This term is used in Jewish cookery. Foods marked Kosher have undergone special examination and been stamped with the Rabbi's seal. The meaning of the word is "pure". See JEWISH TRADITIONAL RECIPES.

KRONA PEPPER. A mild red pepper seasoning free from pungency, of excellent flavour, for both kitchen and table use.

KUMMEL. The name of a famous Russian and German liqueur, sometimes spelled Kimmel, made from aromatic seeds.

KUMQUAT. A Japanese fruit of the citron tribe. It is very pleasingly sweet and yet slightly acid with a strong orange flavour and odour.

L

LACTEAL, LACTEAN. Pertaining to milk and milky lactic acid; the acid of sour milk.

LACTOMETER. A glass tube which is used for estimating the richness of milk.

LACTOSE. A hard crystalline sugar $C_{12}H_{22}O_{11}$ which is present in milk. It is also called sugar of milk, or milk sugar.

LAKE HERRING. See CISCO.

LAMB (Fr. *agneau*). Young sheep. A house lamb is one born in the middle of winter which is reared under shelter and fed in great measure upon milk: it is considered a great delicacy. A grass lamb is one brought up out of doors upon grass: it comes into season at Easter.

Like all young animals the lamb must be thoroughly cooked, or it is most unwholesome. The joint should not be removed from the oven until the gravy drops from it.

JOINTS OF LAMB. Lamb is usually cut into quarters.

The *forequarter*, which consists of (1) the shoulder, (2) the breast, (3) the neck, is considered the best. It must be cooked when fresh and its quality can be tested

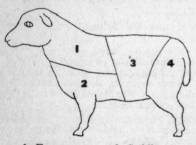

1. Forequarter
2. Loin
3. Saddle
4. Hindquarter

by the appearance of the vein at the back of the neck which should be a ruddy—or bluish colour. It is generally roasted, though a very young lamb may be boiled and served with White sauce. Before serving a forequarter of lamb, divide the shoulder from the ribs and place between them about $1\frac{1}{2}$ oz. butter and a squeeze of lemon juice and season with salt and pepper.

The breast and neck of lamb are sometimes cooked as one joint and are called a "target". When this is done they are roasted and served with the accompaniments of a hindquarter of lamb.

The *hindquarter* consists of (1) the leg and (2) the loin, which is better after hanging for 2 or 3 days. Forequarters, hindquarter, saddle and loin of lamb are all roasted or baked and served with Mint sauce and salad. The vegetables which usually accompany lamb are potatoes, green peas, spinach and others as desired. Lamb may be dished with celery or tomatoes or *au cresson*.

TO CHOOSE. The fat of lamb should be light and firm and a clear faintish white in colour. If the fat of lamb is yellow, and the lean flabby and red, it will not keep.

TO KEEP. Any taint may easily be discovered by the smell, and if the weather is unfavourable lamb will not keep for any length of time. It must be examined daily and the moisture carefully wiped from the joints, and if a peppercorn or two is placed between the loin and kidney any taint may be easily discovered.

LAMB, BOILED. The leg of lamb is placed in a saucepan with as much boiling water as will cover it and simmered slowly (over a low heat). Allow 15 mins. per lb., and 15 mins. over. The scum is removed and a good pinch of salt added when the meat is half cooked. When serving, the dish is garnished with tufts of cauliflower and carrots and sent to the table accompanied by Caper sauce with a little of this poured over the joint, and the rest sent in a sauceboat.

LAMB, ROAST. Trim the joint and place in a baking tin with a little fat. Cover with a piece of greaseproof paper and place in the oven. Cook for 20 mins. per lb. and 20 mins. over, basting frequently. Remove paper when the meat is part cooked. About 10 mins. before taking out, dredge with flour and froth (by basting). Allow to brown nicely and if the joint has a shank bone serve this with a cut paper ruffle round it and send a little of the joint's own gravy in a dish with it. Mint sauce and salad generally accompany this dish. With a hindquarter of roast lamb send a cut quarter of lemon so that the carver can place a squeeze of this over the leg when severed from the loin.

LAMB, STEWED. Joint 1 lb. neck of lamb and place it in a pan or casserole. Add ½ pt. hot water, 2 sliced onions, 6 small young turnips, 6 carrots, and pepper and salt to season, and simmer gently together for 30 mins. Add 1–1½ lb. new potatoes, 1½ lb. green peas and 1 tbsp. chopped mint. When cooked, serve in a casserole or on a dish.

Lamb Chops, Grilled. Trim the chops. Brush with melted butter or oil, place on gridiron which has been previously rubbed with melted fats. Place under a hot grill. According to thickness this will take from 5–10 mins. Turn the cutlets every few minutes and season with salt and pepper. Put a paper frill on each cutlet bone and dish them up in a circle inside a border of mashed potatoes. Serve with green peas and accompanied by gravy.

Lamb Cutlets à la Russe. Carefully cook some neck of lamb in stock or braise it. When cold, divide into small cutlets. Trim them neatly and coat with a brown chaudfroid sauce. Decorate with pretty designs cut from truffles and savoury custard (see GARNISHES). Pour some melted butter into a deep baking-tin or sauté-pan to the depth of ¼″. When set, lay the cutlets on it and cover with aspic. When firm cut out the cutlets with a border of aspic to each. Dish the cutlets in two rows, one leaning on the other, down the centre of a dish, and place Russian Salad (see p. 429) between them.

Lamb Cutlets in Aspic. Prepare and cook the cutlets as for mutton cutlets. When cold, place on a tray and mask in aspic. When this is set, cut into shape round the cutlets and serve garnished with pickled walnuts or olives.

Lamb Cutlets, Fried. Prepare the cutlets as for mutton cutlets and cook. Allow to cool and when cold, mask with White sauce, dip in breadcrumbs and egg and fry to a deep brown in boiling fat. Serve with peas or asparagus.

Epigrammes d'Agneau (with Sharp Sauce). Take two breasts of lamb near the cutlet, and braise or boil until quite tender. Remove the bones and press between two dishes. When cold, cut into neat cutlets or rounds; dip each piece into well-beaten egg, then into warm butter, then into breadcrumbs. Flatten the crumbs with the aid of a knife. Place on a well-buttered baking-sheet, and brown quickly in the oven at 400° F. Therm. 6. Serve with them a sauce made as follows: Fry in butter one large onion, and work into the same pan 1 tbsp. flour, 1 gill good brown meat gravy, 1 tbsp. brown vinegar, 1 tsp. meat extract, and 1 lump sugar. Boil all together for 20 mins., strain, add 1 tbsp. chopped gherkins and 1 tsp. capers. Serve in a sauceboat with the epigrammes.

Épaule d'Agneau Bonne Femme. Fry in butter a small shoulder of house lamb, This done, transfer it to a fireproof earthenware dish with 12 small onions browned in butter and 3 or 4 medium-sized potatoes cut into large dice and blanched. Sprinkle the whole well with melted butter and cook gently in the oven. Serve the preparation as it stands in the earthenware dish, placing the dish on a folded napkin.

LAMB'S BRAINS (Fr. *cervelles d'agneau*). These are considered a great delicacy and are very tender and suitable for invalids. They require careful cleaning. See **BRAINS.**

LAMB'S EARS (Fr. *oreilles d'agneau*). These are very crisp and tender when fried. For frying, they should be scalded after being cut off the head, and skinned by rubbing with a cloth whilst still hot.

LAMB'S FEET (Fr. *pieds d'agneau*). They are thought to be infinitely more delicate than those of the older animal, the bones being more gelatinous, and the sinews and ligaments about them more amenable to softening by boiling. They should be skinned and the hoofs torn off, after a little sharp boiling.

LAMB'S FEET (*continued*)

TO BOIL. Take the prepared feet, parboil and keep their shape as much as possible. Dust over with salt and pepper and rub in a little warmed butter. Sprinkle with some chopped parsley and leave to cool. Roll in grated breadcrumbs, lay side by side on gridiron and broil till nicely browned. Then arrange the feet on a folded napkin upon a hot dish, garnish with fried parsley, and serve with a sauce-boatful of Ravioli sauce (see SAUCES).

LAMB'S FRY OR PLUCK (Fr. *animelles*). All that can be considered edible of the lamb's internal organs may be included in this comprehensive term, although the butcher uses it for lungs, liver and heart only.

TO COOK. Wash the fry thoroughly and simmer all but the liver in stock or water for ¼ hr., then dry and slice it. Flour and fry in butter or dripping until cooked and brown. Put the fry on a hot dish, pour a little stock or water (stock is best) into the frying-pan. Stir and boil well and then strain over the fry. Garnish with fried parsley.

LAMB'S HEAD (Fr. *tête d'agneau*). Lamb's head is the best of all heads used in cookery. It must be carefully stripped of its wool, the eyes scooped out and the lip of the snout cut off. After plunging for a short time into boiling water, it can be easily cleaned and otherwise prepared for cooking.

TO BOIL. Soak the head with liver and lights in cold water, so as to disgorge the blood. Put the head into a stewpan, cover with cold water and boil gently till tender. Boil the liver and lights until 3 parts cooked, then chop them up finely. Put 1 oz. butter and 1 tbsp. flour in a saucepan. Stir over a low heat until well mixed. Strain in some of the liquid in which the lights were boiled. Put the mince into the sauce to flavour it. Season to taste and keep it simmering over a low heat. When cooked the head should be put on a hot dish and Mint sauce (see p. 335) poured over it. Garnish with parsley.

LAMB'S HEAD STEWED

Ingredients	Method
1 lamb's head Veal forcemeat ½ pt. oysters ½ pt. mushrooms Some good stock Flour Pepper and salt Blade of mace	Well cleanse the head, soaking it in salt and water. Dry and bone it and remove brains and tongue. Place the veal stuffing in the centre of the head and roll head round it. Fasten it into a neat shape with tape, and place it in a stewpan with the oysters, mushrooms and blade of mace. Simmer for about 2 hrs. until the head is cooked. Then place it on a hot dish, thicken the stock nicely with flour and pour round it, placing the oysters and mushrooms in heaps. The brains should be tied in muslin, and boiled for about 5 mins. then fried in batter and used as a garnish. The tongue should be cooked with the head and skinned and sliced for a garnish. Sheep's head may be cooked in the same way.

LAMB'S KIDNEYS (Fr. *rognons d'agneau*). When quite fresh (the fat should be white and not turning at all), these are placed first amongst kidneys. They are very digestible and good for invalids. They are cooked as other kidneys. See KIDNEY.

LAMB'S LETTUCE (Fr. *mache*). See CORN SALAD.

LAMB'S LIVER. The greatest care is required when cleaning and preparing this for cooking to ensure that the gall bladder and its appurtenance shall be cleanly

LAMB'S LIVER (*continued*)

cut away without leaving any stain or this will be bitter. The blood must be squeezed out of the liver under water, and the whole thoroughly washed. The fresher it is used the better.

TO COOK. Cut into thin slices and let these marinate in oil and chopped parsley for about ½ hr. Drain the slices and dust them over with salt and pepper. Roll them in grated breadcrumbs. Lay on a girdle and broil under a hot grill. Put 1 oz. butter into a saucepan, melt and mix with it the juice of a lemon, 1 tbsp. chopped parsley; season with salt and pepper. Put the cooked slices of liver on a hot dish, pour sauce over them and serve.

LAMB'S PLUCK. See LAMB'S FRY.

LAMB'S STONES. Certain parts of young lambs, taken from them when they are converted into wethers. It is not often that these are collected for cooking, but, if so, they are cooked like sweetbreads.

LAMB'S STOVE. A lamb stew which is slowly cooked.

LAMB'S SWEETBREADS (Fr. *coquilles d'agneau*). There are two kinds in all animals: one lying under the heart and called the heart sweetbread; the other the large gland that embraces the windpipe, called the throat sweetbread. They are both valued in cookery, although the throat sweetbread is the least familiar. For methods of cooking see **SWEETBREAD.**

LAMB'S TAILS (Fr. *gigues d'agneau*). As it is usual to leave these attached to the saddle, haunch or hindquarters, they are not often met with in sufficient quantities to make a dish.

LAMB'S TONGUES (Fr. *langues d'agneau*). These are generally cooked and served with the head, but are excellent for cooking as a dish in themselves when sufficient are available. They can be baked, broiled and glazed, etc.

LAMPERN. See LAMPREY.

LAMPREY (Fr. *lamproie*). There are two kinds of this eel-like fish known in England, which so closely resemble each other that it is difficult to tell them apart. The larger ones are known as Lampreys, the smaller, Lamperns. The lampreys visit certain rivers in the spring for spawning and then return to the sea. Both lampreys and lamperns are thought to be dangerous for food because of the two filaments they have in the back which are poisonous and which must be removed before cooking.

LANCASHIRE CHEESE. A hard cheese more like cheshire than cheddar. The best comes from the Fylde, north of the Ribble.

LANDRAIL. A bird of fine flavour, also called Corn Crake.

LANGOUSTE. The French for spiny lobster or crawfish. Any lobster recipe may be used for langouste.

LANGOUSTINES. The French for Dublin Bay prawns.

LARD. This is, or should be, the white fat of the pig melted down and purified (see **BACON**, p. 41). The fat should be cut from the pig in small pieces, washed and all the water pressed out. Put into a pot (to hold 4 gall. water) to boil with 1 gall. water. Boil quickly over a sharp heat, until the crackling begins to brown, then the heat should be reduced to ensure slow cooking, which will prevent burning. When the lard is done, the crackling will sink to the bottom. This is called "leaf lard".

TO LARD. See **COOKING TERMS.**

LARDING NEEDLE (OR PIN) (Fr. *lardoire*). Used to thread small strips of fat pork or bacon through lean meat.

LARDOONS (Fr. *lardons*). Strips of bacon fat used in larding.

LAVENDER. Spike, True or English or French are used in the household as moth preventatives; medicinally as Spirits of Lavender, also as Oil of Lavender.

LAVER. See SEAWEED.

LEAVEN. See YEAST.

LEEKS. The leek is said to be intermediary between the onion and garlic.

LEEKS, BOILED. Select young leeks, carefully wash them in cold salted water and trim away the roots and the broken tops; tie in small bunches, and place over a low heat in boiling salted water (or with 1 tbsp. vinegar). Boil for 20 mins., then drain. Place on a dish and serve White sauce, or place on slices of toast then pour the White sauce over them.

LEEKS FOR GARNISH. Cook prepared leeks of an even size in just enough salted boiling water to cover. Stew gently until done, then drain and chop into even-sized lengths. Place in a pan with a knob of butter rolled in flour. Add pepper and salt to season, add just sufficient stock to moisten, stew gently until thickened. Add a little cream and the yolk of an egg beaten in a little milk.

Leeks with Cheese Sauce. Cook the leeks and place in sauce made as above with grated cheese, a little nutmeg and a pinch of mustard added. Pour over the leeks, cover thickly with grated cheese and dot with butter. Brown at 400° F. Therm. 4 or under a hot grill.

Leek Salad. Wash and trim a few young leeks into small even-sized pieces. Mix with a large blanched and sliced tomato. Add a little mayonnaise or French dressing, pile on lettuce leaves and serve with a garnish of grated cheese.

LEEK SOUP. Make as Onion soup (see **SOUPS**), substituting leeks for onions.

LEG (Fr. *gigot*). See **LAMB** and **MUTTON.**

LEGUMES. This word properly refers to pulse or any plant which bears *legumes* (pods). In France the term is adopted to signify vegetables generally.

LEICESTER. A hard cheese made from whole milk in the shape of a millstone; made in the same way as cheddar.

LEMON (Fr. *citron*). The lemon, citrus, lime, bergamot, orange and others of this perfumed tribe have their own special culinary value. Their cultivation in Europe dates from the 15th century, but they grow in the gardens of many sub-tropical countries. The peel of the lemon contains an aromatic bitter oil of great value in flavouring, being used frequently in cooking for the same purpose as Chablis or other good wines, and possibly with a better effect. The juice partakes very slightly of the aroma; it is used in cooking for many purposes, not only on account of its acidity, being used frequently in preference to vinegar, but to bring out or intensify the flavours and whiteness of delicate white flesh, such as veal and fish.

Lemonade. Take a lemon, wipe it and cut off a few thin pieces of rind; squeeze juice from fruit and strain. Put the rind, juice and 1 dsp. sugar into a ½ pt. jug. Fill with boiling water. Cover, and strain when cold.

Lemon, Baked. Bake a lemon for 20 mins. at 350° F. Therm. 4. When baked, cut it at one end and scoop out the inside; beat with sugar or syrup as desired.

Lemon Cheese Cakes. See **CAKES.**

Lemons, Compôte of. Peel the lemons very thinly and turn them spirally. Make transverse incisions in them and cut out some fancy designs. Place them in a saucepan with just sufficient water to cover. Boil gently for about 20 mins. Drain the lemons and put them into a saucepan with some light syrup made of ½ lb. sugar to 1 pt. water, dissolved together. Simmer for a further 20 mins. When ready to serve, place in a glass dish and serve with the syrup over them.

Lemon Curd. Beat together 4 oz. butter or margarine and ½ lb. sugar. Add the juice and grated rind of 2 or 3 lemons and a well-beaten egg and simmer together in a double pan until the mixture becomes thick and creamy.

Lemon Curd (Mock). Make ½ pt. custard with custard powder and add ¼ pt. each lemon squash and water. Add golden syrup to sweeten and extra lemon essence, if desired. Use immediately to fill pastries, flans and tartlets.

Lemon Fritters. Place in a mixing bowl 2 oz. shredded suet, 1 dsp. flour, 3 oz. fine breadcrumbs, 2 tbsp. powdered sugar and lemon peel. Beat 2 eggs well, then add to dry mixture, together with 1 tbsp. milk, and 1 tbsp. strained lemon juice. Mix together until thoroughly blended. Fry in hot fat in small quantities until lightly browned on each side. Drain on kitchen paper, serve as hot as possible, sprinkled with sugar and lemon juice.

Lemon Jelly

Ingredients

12 lemons
5 qt. water
Sugar

Method

Wash the lemons, dry and cut into pieces, removing pips. Place in a jar or bowl, cover with water and allow to stand for 24 hrs. Then place in preserving pan with the water and boil for 2 hrs. Strain through muslin, measure juice and allow 1 lb. sugar to each 1 pt. juice. Return to saucepan and boil fast for 10 mins. Test for setting, pour into jars and cover when cool.

Lemon Marmalade

Ingredients

12 lemons
Their weight in sugar
Water

Method

Wash and wipe the lemons, squeeze out juice and place on one side. Place pips in a cupful of cold water and then place peel of lemons in pan with cold water and boil until very tender. Remove from heat, and cut away all pith; then slice the rinds very thinly into pieces not more than ½″ long. Place the sugar, juice and water from pips into preserving pan and boil steadily to a syrup. Add the shredded rinds and boil until the marmalade will set when tested on a saucer. Bottle and cover when cool.

Lemon and Orange Marmalade

Ingredients

4 lemons
4 sweet oranges
3 Seville oranges
Water
Sugar

Method

Wipe fruit clean, peel and place peel in a bowl of brine to soak for 12 hrs. Remove from brine, place in a preserving pan with cold water and bring to boil. When tender take out, remove pith and white lining, and shred rind very finely. Slice the pulp and boil with the juice in a separate pan. Add this to the rind and cook till the rind is clear. Weigh and allow an equal amount of sugar. Place in preserving pan together and boil gently until of right consistency. Bottle and cover when cool.

Lemon Meringue Pie

Ingredients

8 oz. short (see p. 375) or biscuit (see p. 370) crust
3 eggs
5 tbsp. cornflour
¾ pt. boiling water
½ lb. sugar
1 tbsp butter
Juice of 2½ lemons
Grated rind of ½ lemon

Method

Line a deep pie-plate with crust and bake blind (see p. 369). Blend the cornflour with ¼ pt. water, boil remainder and stir into it. Cook rapidly until the mixture thickens. Add sugar, butter, lemon juice and rind, pour into the slightly beaten egg yolks. Bake until the crust is brown (about 15 mins.) at 400° F. Therm. 5. Whisk the whites of egg and salt until stiff, then heap on to the pie, dust with sugar and return the pie to oven. Bake at 350° F. Therm. 4 for 10 mins. longer.

Lemon Peel, Candied—I. Take the peel from the fruit in neat halves and remove the white pith. Soak the peel in a solution of salt and water for 24 hrs., then wash it well and put it into a pan with equal proportions of sugar and water, and boil until it is tender. Remove the peel from the syrup and drain it. Add equal quantity of sugar to the liquid, reboil and return the peels to the pan. Boil until the sugar flakes when a spoon is dipped into it. Remove the peels and put them to dry in a warm place. When dry, pack in lined tins.

Lemon Peel, Candied—II. Peel fruit and cut into quarters. Put these into a pan with very little water. Boil until tender. Drain and measure the liquid. Allow ½ gill liquid to 8 oz. sugar and reboil. Return the peel to the liquid and boil for about 25 mins. more; dry and roll in soft sugar and leave to harden. Then put into a lined tin and store in a dry place.

Lemon Pudding

Ingredients

Suet Paste (see p. 375)
Lemons
Brown sugar

Method

Peel the lemons and slice into halves. Remove any pips. Line a well-greased pudding basin with suet crust, fill with halved lemons and sprinkle with brown sugar. Cover with suet crust; cover with greaseproof paper. Tie down securely and boil for 2 hrs. Serve with custard or sauce or golden syrup.

Lemons, Pickled. Wipe 2 doz. lemons, rub them well with salt and put in a bowl and cover with salt. Leave them for 4–5 days, turning them occasionally. Remove them and place on a sieve to dry in the sun if possible. When dry, pack them into jars, sprinkling over evenly with 2 oz. each bruised white ginger and white peppers, ¼ oz. chillies, ½ oz. each coriander and mustard seeds. Pour over sufficient white vinegar to cover and leave 3 wks., then fill up with more vinegar. Leave 6 mths. before use if possible. For a sweet pickle, add a little sugar to the vinegar. Boil up and cool before pouring into jars.

Lemon Rind Preserve. Use lemons from which the juice has been removed for another purpose. Place the squeezed lemons into a bowl of water and allow to soak for 10–14 days, changing the water every 2 days. Take the lemons, remove pith and white lining, and shred the rinds. Weigh and allow an equal amount of sugar. Place in preserving pan the rind and sugar and cook gently until thick. Pour into warmed jars and cover when cool.

Lemon Sauce for Puddings. Boil 3 oz. sugar in a saucepan with the rind and strained juice of 1 lemon and ½ pt. water. When the sugar is dissolved, the same may be served immediately, or a grating of nutmeg or a few drops of sherry added if desired. See also SAUCES.

Lemon Sponge. Warm a little water, add 1 oz. gelatine and dissolve, add water to make up to 1 pt., juice of 2 lemons and 2 tbsp. sugar. Whisk the whites of 2 eggs very stiff, fold into the liquid, whip again until well combined, turn into a well-moistened mould to set, or, if preferred, into individual sundae glasses, and serve garnished with strawberries, raspberries or any fresh fruit available.

LEMON BALM. See **BALM**.

LEMON SOLE (Fr. *limande*). A small European flat-fish which resembles a sole. It is at its best from December to March and is cooked as sole.

LENTIL (Fr. *lentille*). The fruits of a leguminous plant. It is smaller than an ordinary pea, and shaped like a double convex lens. Lentils play an important part in the diet; they are a source of second-class protein and should be used to help to build up the nutritional value of foods.

TO COOK. Presoak in boiling water. Sometimes, to tenderise, a pinch of bicarb. soda is added. After soaking for 2–3 hrs., boil slowly for about 1 hr. If unsoaked, they will take about 2½–3 hrs.

LENTILS IN SOUPS. Cook as given above and add to the purée after rubbing the lentils through a sieve; extra liquid, vegetable stock and milk may be added to give the required consistency. Garnish before serving with chopped fresh parsley or mint. Allow 2 oz. lentils to 1 pt. liquid.

LENTILS AS A SALAD. See **SALADS**.

LENTIL PURÉE. Drain the cooked lentils and pass through a sieve, add seasonings and a walnut of butter; beat well together, serve hot garnished with chopped chives.

LENTILS AS A VEGETABLE. Drain the cooked lentils, add seasonings, toss in melted margarine and serve on a piping hot dish garnished with chopped parsley.

LENTILS WITH SAUCE. Rub the cooked lentils through a sieve, or use whole. Place in a pan with a little White or Tomato sauce (see **SAUCES**) and reheat. Add seasoning and a walnut of butter, stir gently until the mixture boils. Serve very hot garnished with grated cheese or parsley.

LETTUCE (Fr. *laitre*). There are two varieties, the Cabbage lettuce with short, open leaves and the Cos lettuce (romaine), with the longer leaves which during growth are tied together to blanch.

LETTUCE, BOILED. Well wash the lettuces, remove the damaged leaves and cut off the stalks. Boil them according to the directions for cooking green vegetables, for 15 or 20 mins., according to their age and size. Drain well before serving. If liked, they may be chopped and mixed with a little White sauce.

LETTUCE FOR SALADS. The leaves must be well washed in cold water to remove grit, and it is necessary to look over all the leaves and see that any insects which may have been enfolded there have been washed away. Use as desired in various salads. The heart leaves make an attractive garnish for some foods. See entries under **SALADS**.

LETTUCE SALAD. Arrange the prepared leaves in a salad bowl, sprinkle over 1 tsp. chopped chives, ½ tsp. each chopped chervil and tarragon. Season with a pinch of salt and pepper diluted in 2 tbsp. vinegar or lemon juice and 1½ tbsp. oil. Cup up, mix well and serve.

LETTUCE AND CHEESE SALAD. Use dry rich cheese and allow 2 oz. for a head of lettuce of medium size. Wash the leaves, tear them apart, lay in a salad dish; grate the cheese or break into small pieces and scatter among the leaves. Pour over a French dressing and serve.

LEVERET, LEVERANT (Fr. *levreteau*). A young hare.

LEVULOSE. A sugar found in fruit.

LEYDEN. Also Liedsche Kaas or Kummel. A Dutch cheese made of partially skimmed milk with cummin seeds added.

LIAISON. The literal meaning of the French word is a joining, conjunction or association, and thus it has been extended to those materials which are added to sauces to give them body, known as "thickening". The use of liaisons constitutes one of the greatest of "culinary arts" and the following will answer most purposes.

LIAISON (*continued*)

Liaison of blood. Used for game mostly. The blood, having been saved, is mixed in a little of the cooked sauce and then stirred into the rest.

Liaison of butter. This is merely the addition of a certain quantity of butter at the last moment of cooking the sauce.

Liaison with butter and cream. The same liaison as butter with the addition of cream. Beat the butter and cream together with the sauce.

Liaison of eggs. Beat up the egg yolk or yolks in some of the sauce, after cooling it, and then pour this in, stirring very slowly. If the yolks were added to the hot sauce without first beating with the cooled liquor they would be almost certain to set and curdle before they were well blended in.

Liaison of flour (e.g. flour, cornflour, crumbs, rice flour, potato flour and arrowroot). Sometimes sauce is thickened by dredging into it either flour, cornflour or even arrowroot, but the better plan is to blend it until smooth with a little water, milk or broth, then pour it into the sauce through a strainer.

Liaison of roux. Put into a bright, clean frying-pan twice as much flour as butter and let them mix together as the butter melts, stirring continually with a spoon or fork until the flour turns browny red, without burning. See SAUCES (p. 436).

Other liaisons such as caramel, glaze, etc., and reduced gravies need no further explanation, details being under those headings.

LIGHTS. The lungs of an animal. They are further described under the animals to which they belong.

LILIES OF THE VALLEY. Male lily, Our Lady's Tears. The root is used medicinally, and the flower and leaf also. In Germany a wine is made from the flowers of this plant mixed with raisins.

LIMA BEANS. See BEANS.

LIMBURGER. A semi-hard, fermented, full-flavoured cheese, made in Belgium, Germany and Alsace. In Germany it is known as Allgauer-Limburger.

LIME. A citrus fruit closely allied to the lemon, but rather sweeter and smaller. The juice, for which it is chiefly cultivated, is imported into England and used for making cordials and for the manufacture of citric acid.

LIMPETS. These unattractive superabundant shell fish are very good to eat. They have only one shell and are prepared for the table like cockles and other bivalves. They can be substituted advantageously for oysters.

LING (Fr. *lingue*). A very large species of cod which frequents the seas of Northern Europe, the Orkneys, the Yorkshire coast and Cornish coast, as well as the Scilly Isles. Cooked as cod.

LINSEED. The seed of flax from which linseed oil is obtained; it is slightly aromatic and exceedingly glutinous, hence its use in invalid cookery.

Linseed Tea. Boil 3 tbsp. linseed in 1 pt. water for 10 mins. Strain into a jug, put in 2 lemons cut into slices and 1 glass port or sherry. Sweeten to taste. A good invalid drink.

LIQUEUR (Fr. *liquor*). A sweet liquid cordial such as Maraschino, Curaçao, Kummel, Chartreuse, Benedictine, etc.

LIQUORICE. This plant, which grows wild in all sub-tropical climates, is much imported from Spain or Italy. This sweet root is sometimes dried or powdered, but more generally an extract is obtained from it by slicing and boiling. After a time the liquor is strained and made to evaporate until it becomes of a proper consistency.

LITRE. A measure of capacity in the metric system; equivalent to 1·76 English pints. See WEIGHTS AND MEASURES.

LIVER (Fr. *foie*). The liver is a large abdominal vascular gland. The livers of most animals, such as the calf, bullock and pig; of fish, such as cod's liver, with nutrient oil; and of poultry, such as goose's liver fat, may be made into very tasty dishes.

[316]

LIVER AND BACON

Ingredients
- ½–1 lb. fat bacon
- 1 sheep's liver
- Some flour
- Pepper and salt
- 1 pt. hot water

Method
Remove rind from bacon. Cut the liver into slices, dip these into seasoned flour. Fry the bacon slowly in a frying-pan, then remove it and fry the liver in bacon fat, adding a little dripping if necessary. When the liver is cooked, place on a well-heated dish. Dredge the frying-pan with flour (about 1 oz.), fry until brown then pour in 1 pt. water. Reboil and serve with the liver and bacon.

LIVER FRIZZLE. Season a little flour with salt and pepper. Using a very sharp knife, slice the liver as thinly as possible (tissue paper thickness), dip into the seasoned flour and coat well. Drop into boiling fat, quickly seal and brown for 2 or 3 mins. and serve on toast.

Liver with Herbs and Wine

Ingredients
- 1 lb. liver
- 4 or 5 mushrooms
- Olive oil
- 1 onion
- Clove of garlic
- 1 bay leaf
- Pinch of salt
- Pinch each of thyme and basil
- ¼ cup each White wine, stock and hot water
- 1 oz. flour
- 1 oz. butter
- Lemon juice

Method
Cut and slice the liver into small, even-sized pieces; peel, slice and sauté the mushrooms in a little oil, add the onion and garlic minced, and the bay leaf crushed and mixed with salt, basil and thyme. Mix well. Then take a small deep saucepan, add sufficient olive oil to cover the bottom; put in a layer of liver, then a sprinkle of the mixture, in alternate layers, sprinkle on a little melted oil, start cooking over a low heat, covering the pan; leave for about 5 mins., and then add wine, stock and water and cook very gently (uncovered) for about 1 hr. Remove liver. Thicken with flour and butter. Add lemon juice and, when well blended, reboil and serve poured over the liver.

LOACH. A small fish found in rivers, cooked as smelts and other small fish. It is very sweet but very bony.

LOAF SUGAR. See SUGAR.

LOBSTER (Fr. *homard*). In lobsters, the largest pieces of white succulent meat and the sweetest are found in the huge claws and tails. When taken fresh from the sea and boiled, the lobster is juicy and very tender to eat. Lobsters must be 1 lb. in weight before they may be taken from the sea, the usual weight being about 1½–2½ lb. Their shells are black and turn red when boiled. They are best from April to October.

TO CLEAN, BOIL AND SPLIT. Pick up the lobster carefully from behind the head (live lobsters are apt to try to injure with their claws) and plunge it head first into boiling salted water (allow to each quart of water 1 tbsp. salt). If preferred, the spinal cord may be severed before putting it into the boiling water by inserting a sharp knife between the body and tail of the lobster. The time required for

TO CLEAN, BOIL AND SPLIT (*continued*)

boiling (that is counting the time as and when the water is boiling after the lobster has been plunged into it) is approximately 10 mins. per 2 lb. of lobster; the meat will be tough and stringy if overboiled. For smaller lobsters allow only 7 mins. Remove and cool at room temperature. Rub over with oil, then remove meat.

Put lobster on its back and with a sharp knife split open from end to end, beginning at the mouth. Remove the vein which runs from head to tail. Remove the small bag or sac from back of head. Both the green and coral parts are edible; do not remove. Pry the body meat loose with fork and then remove. Crack claws with mallet or hammer, remove meat and use as desired.

TO USE TINNED LOBSTER. This may be substituted for fresh lobster in some recipes. It may be used in fish cakes, fish soufflé, Lobster en Coquille and lobster cutlets, also in lobster soup.

Homard à l'Americaine

Ingredients

1 live lobster
3 tbsp. butter
1 each sliced carrot and onion
1 bouquet garni
1 small celery stalk
1 small glass good brandy
2 tbsp. meat glaze
1 tbsp. tomato purée
1 glass White wine
Salt
Red pepper
Little extra butter

Method

Cook the lobster, then cut into 4 or 5 pieces. Set aside the coral and the greenish liver. Put the butter in an earthenware saucepan, heat well. Then add the pieces of lobster (flesh side downwards). Sauté over a quick heat, shaking the pan continuously, then add the carrot, onion, bouquet garni and celery. Sauté all together for a few mins., then pour over the cognac, ignite and allow it to burn itself out. Add meat glaze, tomato purée and White wine which has been boiled until reduced to half. Season well and keep hot. In another oven-dish place 1 tbsp. butter, heat this then add the coral and green mixture, blending all this well for a moment or two. Remove and pound mixture in a mortar with a little more butter. Arrange the pieces of lobster on a hot dish, keep hot. Mix the sauce and pounded lobster together, pour over the lobster and serve sprinkled with finely chopped parsley.

[318]

Lobster à la Newburg

Ingredients
1 pt. thick cream or evaporated milk
2 tbsp. flour
2 egg yolks
1 glass sherry
3 cups lobster in pieces size of walnut
2 oz. butter or margarine
Pepper and salt

Method
Blend the flour with 1 tbsp. cream; heat the remaining cream; add egg yolks and blended flour, stirring quickly. Add 1 oz. butter. Add wine and, when mixed together, add lobster. Dot with remaining butter. Place over low heat for about 3 mins. Return mixture to the shells. Place under a hot grill to brown. Serve very hot.

Bisque of Lobster (Fr. *bisque d'homard*)

Ingredients
2 lobsters
2 qt. fish stock in which shells of lobsters have been boiled
1 oz. spawn
¼ pt. cream
4 oz. flour
Little milk
Pepper and salt
Juice of 1 lemon
1 oz. butter

Method
Boil the lobsters and cut them into pieces, using the shell to flavour the stock. Strain the stock into a saucepan, and place over a low heat; bring to the boil. Pass the spawn through a hair sieve with butter. Blend the flour with a little milk, season and stir into the soup. Add the spawn, reheat the soup for 5 mins., then add cream, lobster and lemon juice.

Lobster Boiled in Court Bouillon

Ingredients
3 qt. water
1 tbsp. salt
1 carrot
1 bay leaf
1 clove
3 peppercorns
1 small onion
Wineglass red wine
1 celery stalk
2 lobsters

Method
Put the water into the pan, add salt and carrot, bay leaf, clove, peppercorns, onion, red wine and celery, cover and bring rapidly to boiling point. Then remove to medium heat and boil a further 10 mins. Add the lobsters and when broth begins to boil, cook for a further 10 mins., (cook smaller lobsters, less than 2 lb., for 7 mins.). Remove lobsters and cool at room temperature, then place in refrigerator to chill. Split and serve with mayonnaise.

Lobster Broiled

Ingredients
2 × 2 lb. lobsters
4 oz. butter
4 oz. breadcrumbs
1 tsp. Worcester sauce
¼ tsp. salt
1 lemon cut into quarters

Method
Take the prepared lobsters. Melt 2 oz. butter in a small saucepan, add the breadcrumbs and blend with melted butter. Add Worcester sauce and salt. Fill into the small cavity where sac was, place the lobsters on the grill tray under a hot grill 3″ from flame and cook for 12 mins. See that the lobsters are not

[319]

Lobster Broiled (*continued*)

overcooked. Melt and pour the remaining butter over the lobsters. Serve garnished with sliced lemon.

Lobster Croquettes. Prepare a mixture as for lobster cutlets, form it into balls or egg shapes, egg and breadcrumb them and fry in hot deep fat. Garnish with fried parsley.

Lobster Cutlets

Ingredients

1 hen lobster
Some spawn or coral
1½ oz. butter
1 oz. flour
1 gill cold water
2 tbsp. cream
Few drops lemon juice
Pepper
Salt
Cayenne
Egg and breadcrumbs
Parsley

Method

Remove the flesh from the lobster and cut it up. Pound the coral in a mortar with ½ oz. butter and then rub through a hair sieve. If spawn is used, it need not be pounded. Melt butter in a saucepan, mix in the flour smoothly; add water, stir until it thickens. Add the coral butter, stir and cook well: add cream and allow to boil in the sauce; then the lemon juice, pepper, salt, cayenne and lobster. Spread mixture on a plate to cool. When cool, make into cutlets, egg and breadcrumb them, flattening the crumbs on with a knife and shaping them nicely. Fry in hot fat to a golden brown. Dish on a folded napkin, with a piece of the feeler stuck in each cutlet to represent a bone, and garnish with fried parsley. If desired the cutlets may be dished in a circle on a border of whiting quenelle meat or mashed potatoes, without the napkin, Cardinal sauce (see SAUCES) poured round and over them, and hot Indian pickles placed in the centre of the dish.

Lobster Salad

Ingredients

1 good-sized lobster
1 lettuce
Some mayonnaise dressing
Some aspic jelly
1 endive (if possible)
3 or 4 hard-boiled eggs

Method

Remove the flesh from the body and claws of the lobster and cut it in pieces. Well wash and dry the lettuce, cut up and mix it with lobster and mayonnaise sauce. Put a border of chopped aspic on a dish. Heap salad in the middle. Decorate the salad with pieces of endive and hard-boiled eggs cut in quarters.

Lobster Sauce. See SAUCES.

Lobster Stew with Wine

Ingredients

1 lb. lobster meat
2 tbsp. each cream and madeira

Method

Blend lobster, cream, wine and seasoning. Melt the butter in a saucepan over a low heat, add lobster, simmer for 5 mins. and

[320]

Lobster Stew with Wine (*continued*)

⅛ tsp. cayenne
Pinch pepper
Salt
2 oz. butter
4 slices toast
Lemon sliced
Watercress

serve very hot on hot buttered toast on preheated plates. Garnish with lemon and watercress.

Lobster Soup. See SOUPS.

Lobster Thermidor

Ingredients

1 cold boiled lobster
1 tbsp. butter (or margarine)
1 tbsp. flour
¾ cup cream or top of milk
1 tsp. dry mustard
¼ tsp. salt
Few grains cayenne pepper
¾ lb. finely chopped cooked mushrooms
3 tbsp. sherry
Little grated Parmesan cheese
1 tbsp. parsley finely chopped

Method

Split the lobster lengthwise, remove meat and chop finely. Make a sauce with the butter, flour, cream and allow to boil for about 2 mins. Then add the mustard, blended with a little milk, salt and cayenne. Add the chopped lobster and mushrooms and stir well; add sherry, stir again. Fill the shells liberally and sprinkle with the grated Parmesan cheese. Place under a hot grill or brown in the oven at 400° F. Therm. 6. Garnish with parsley.

LOIN (Fr. *longe*). That part of an animal which extends along the backbone, between the ribs and tail. For special loins, see **LAMB, MUTTON, PORK, VEAL** and **BEEF.**

LOGANBERRY. A hybrid fruit which was raised in America, possibly a cross between blackberry and raspberry. This fruit has a large hard core which comes away from the vines in gathering: it can be eaten raw, stewed or in fruit pies.

Loganberry Jam

Ingredients

5 lb. loganberries
5 lb. sugar

Method

Stem and pick over loganberries, place in preserving pan and crush. Place lid on pan and heat slowly for 30 mins. Add the sugar and allow to simmer for 30 mins. Test for setting, pour into heated jars and cover when cool.

Loganberry Jelly

Ingredients

5 lb. loganberries
Sugar

Method

Pick over fruit, place in preserving pan with just enough water to cover bottom of pan. Allow to heat through until fruit pulps. Strain through muslin, measure juice, and allow 1 lb. sugar to each pint of juice. Boil up juice, add sugar and continue to boil for 20 mins. Test for setting, pour into warmed jars and cover when cold.

LONG PEPPER. This spice is similar in taste and smell to the ordinary pepper and is much used in making curry powder.

LOQUAT. The fruit of the Japanese medlar. It is about the size of a small plum, grows in clusters, and each fruit contains four to five seeds.

LOTE or BURBOT (Fr. *Lotte*). The whiting of freshwaters. Rarely caught in English lakes. More often in the lakes of Savoy.

LOVAGE. Known also as Smallage or Smellage. The rhizome is used medicinally; the leaf used fresh or dried as a substitute for celery flavouring; the seed is used in confectionery and cordials. Leaf, stalk and stem are blanched and used like celery for a fragrant tea. Flowering top and leaf used industrially for flavouring and perfumery.

Lovage Cordial. Macerate 1 oz. fresh lovage roots and ¼ oz. each root of celery and fennel in 1 gall. spirits of wine. Distil before use. If desired, add a small quantity each of oil of savin and valerian root.

LOVE IN DISGUISE. An old name for a calf's heart stuffed with veal stuffing, wrapped round thickly with forcemeat, rolled in vermicelli and baked.

LOVING CUPS. I. Take two bottles each sherry and madeira, 1 bottle each port and claret, the juice of 6 lemons, 1½ lb. loaf sugar, and 1 qt. water. Mix these, then stir in 1 large tsp. liquid spice and a grated nutmeg. Keep well iced until required for use.

II. Take ¼ lb. loaf sugar and rub it over the rind of a lemon, extracting all the flavour possible. Dissolve the sugar in 1 qt. warm water and let this stand till cool. Pour into a large jug ½ pt. brandy over the peel of another lemon, cut very thin. When the brandy and lemon peel have infused together for an hour, pour on to them 1 pt. madeira, grate in a whole nutmeg, then add the sweetened water and 1 teacup capillaire. Chill well. Stir in a large bottle of champagne cider when very cold, and pour into a well-chilled loving cup. Have ready a handful of freshly gathered balm and borage. Plunge this into the cup and it will be ready to serve. If desired, ale may be substituted for cider, and in winter the cup may be served warm.

LUTING. The paste used to fasten on lids or pastry covers, as in potting game.

M

MACARONI (Fr. *macaroni*). A paste made from wheaten flour: a characteristic Italian food, though made and widely used in other European countries. Macaroni is divided into two classes, *paste lunghe* and *paste tagliate* (known in France as pâtes d'Italie). **Paste lunghe** is shaped into various lengths and thicknesses, known as vermicelli, tagliatelle, spaghetti, etc. **Paste tagliate** is macaroni made into various decorative shapes, such as rings, stars, crosses, letters of the alphabet, etc. Some of these are available in this country.

TO COOK. There is no need to wash the macaroni before cooking and it is never soaked. Throw into a pan of **boiling water** (salted) and boil for 20 mins. at least. When tender, drain and rinse in cold water under a running tap, then reheat in a colander if the macaroni is for garnish or to be served with a little melted butter, or else reheat in sauce. Can also be used in a milk pudding (see under this heading) or as a soup garnish.

VARIATIONS FOR USE. Serve cold, with raw grated carrot, cheese and celery, garnished with lettuce.

In batters, or fried as fritters with diced cheese and apple added.

In curry sauce garnished with peas or other vegetables parboiled.

With melted butter and sweet pickle.

With tomato purée and parboiled onion, all mixed together and reheated.

With White sauce and grated cheese, a sprinkle of mustard, pepper and salt. If desired, a dash of Worcester sauce also.

As a garnish in a clear soup.

With butter and grated cheese and sliced tomatoes.

With cooked diced celery and grated cheese.

With fried onion and cheese.

With Parsley sauce, garnished with tomatoes.

With grated beetroot and onion.

Cold, dressed with mayonnaise or French dressing and garlic.

All dishes should be garnished with cress or parsley.

MACAROONS (Fr. *macarons*).

Ingredients

6 oz. sugar
2 oz. icing sugar
¼ lb. almond paste or ground almonds
2 egg whites
Pinch of salt
Halved almonds

Method

Work the sugar into the almond paste; add very gradually the egg whites which have been stiffly whisked. Add the salt. Work well until perfectly smooth. Drop the mixture from the tip of a spoon or pass through a forcing bag on to a greased baking tin covered with rice paper. Place half an almond in the middle of each macaroon if desired. Damp lightly with a cloth or pastry brush before putting to bake in a slow oven (250° F. Therm. 1) for about 25 mins. until light brown. When cool, break off the surplus rice paper round the macaroons.

[323]

MACE. This spice is the irregular kind of leafy network which covers the nutmeg. It is very aromatic and forms, either whole or ground, an excellent basis for other and more delicate flavourings. The expressed oil of mace is used to form an essence for flavouring. If used too freely, it is apt to be somewhat sickly in its effect.

MACEDOINE. A medley of diced vegetables or fruit with sauce or syrup. Used generally for a garnish, or formed into shapes with jelly.

MACERATE. See COOKING TERMS.

MACKEREL (Fr. *maquereau*). Mackerel contain a larger proportion of fatty matter than any other fish and must be eaten when very fresh. These fish frequent our coasts in great shoals. They are in season from October to July, but at their prime during the months of May, June and July. After that they spawn, and the flesh is comparatively poor. By October they have generally regained both flesh and flavour. The common mackerel is marked with blue-black over the back, falling in transverse stripes down the sides towards the silver belly. The markings or bars on the back of the male are straight, whilst those on the female are wavy, a distinction it is well to be aware of, as the male is decidedly finer in flavour. When buying mackerel, always choose fish which have a glossy coat and a bright and full eye, and there should be a decided springiness about the body when handled which indicates freshness. The quality of the fish is reckoned by the time of the year, and the depth of the fish from the shoulder downwards. Mackerel that have lost their roes before the proper time—"shotten" as it is called—are not of good flavour. Horse Mackerel is fish of quite a different kind; it is not considered of any value for food, though at times it is eaten.

When cleaning mackerel it will be noticed that they have no scales, but a gelatinous skin. It is here that poisonous qualities are generated, mostly by long keeping or exposure to the sun. The skins should be thoroughly cleansed with a stiff brush. Mackerel are sometimes split open, salted, dried and smoked.

MACKEREL, GRILLED, WITH GOOSEBERRY SAUCE. Clean, gut and split mackerel, grill moistened with butter and serve with gooseberry sauce (see p. 258).

MACKEREL, GRILLED, WITH MUSTARD

Ingredients	Method
1 mackerel	Clean and split mackerel. Wipe with damp cloth. Melt half the butter in shallow saucepan. Add chopped parsley, salt and pepper. Stir well. Brush mackerel with this mixture and place on hot grill. Cook for 5 mins. In meantime melt rest of butter, add mustard, lemon juice and fennel and mix well. Pour over mackerel and cook 5 mins. Garnish with sliced lemon.
2 oz. butter	
2 tbsp. chopped parsley	
Salt and pepper	
1 tbsp. prepared mustard	
2 tbsp. lemon juice	
⅛ tsp. fennel	
1 lemon sliced	

MADEIRA (Fr. *madère*). A very fine Spanish wine, which ranges from the rich and costly, almost like a liqueur, to the light, dry and palatable. It is a wine often used in cooking, and a wineglass of madeira added to soup just before serving greatly enhances the flavour.

MADEIRA CAKE. See CAKES.

MADEIRA SAUCE. See SAUCES.

MADELEINES. See CAKES.

MADRAS. This name is usually applied to a dish which is flavoured with curry.

MAIDS OF HONOUR. See CAKES (p. 114).

MAITRE D'HOTEL, À LA. A French term applied to modes of serving that are noted for their simplicity suitable for the steward of the household.

MAÎTRE D'HÔTEL BUTTER. See **BUTTERS.**
MAÎTRE D'HÔTEL SAUCE. See **SAUCES.**

MAIZE (Fr. *mais*). Indian corn. See under this heading and also **CORNFLOUR.**

MALIC ACID. An acid that occurs in many fruits, especially in the green acid fruits.

MALLARD. See **WILD DUCK.**

MALLOW. Any of the genus of plants which bear fruits commonly known as "cheeses". These are eaten raw.

MALT. A name given to various kinds of grain, but chiefly barley, which have become sweet from the conversion of their starch into sugar during a process of controlled germination. There are various kinds of malt, such as pure malt, yellow or pale amber malt; amber malts differ in quality and character according to the temperature to which they have been exposed in drying. Good malt has an agreeable smell and taste. It is friable, and when broken discloses a floury kernel. It is used chiefly in brewing and distillation. Malt extract is frequently used in invalid foods.

MAMMEE APPLE. The fruit of a lofty tree which grows in tropical America. It is about the size of a small melon and is covered with a tough outer rind of a brownish-yellow enclosing a fine yellow flesh. It has a pleasant taste and a sweet aromatic odour, and is known as the Wild Apricot.

MANDARIN. A small kind of orange supposed to be of Chinese origin.

MANGEL WURZELS. See **MANGOLD WURZELS.**

MANGO (Fr. *mangue*). The Mango Tree is mainly found in sub-tropical Asia. The mango is the shape and size of a goose's egg, and in its early stages is a fine olive green colour. Some varieties continue green when ripe, but others assume an orange tint: the flavour is exquisite. The fruit comes to this country canned in syrup or in mango chutney.

MANGO FISH. An edible freshwater fish of India.

MANGOLD WURZEL. A large beet which can be cooked like turnip but is usually grown for cattle feed.

MANGOSTAN. This fruit, sometimes spelt Mangosteen, is about the size of an orange, and resembles that fruit in structure. The rind, which is brownish when ripe, is exceedingly thick, enclosing a juicy flesh with a flavour not unlike a mixture of grapes and strawberries. For eating, the rind is pared off all round, and the pulp consumed whole.

MANIOC. A tropical plant from which tapioca and cassava are taken.

MAPLE SYRUP AND SUGAR. The juice of the Sugar Maple Tree and the sugar obtained from it. See **SUGAR.**

MARASCHINO (Fr. *marasquin*). This white liqueur is made chiefly in Italy and Dalmatia from wild cherries. It is also made in France and Germany from either cherries or plums. The nutty flavour is obtained from the kernels of the stones and to get this flavour extra peach kernels and raspberries are sometimes added. Maraschino is famous for its beautiful flavour and is used in many dishes.

MARBLED. This term denotes the interdispersal of fat with the muscle fibres and the connective tissues in meat; it is a sign of good feeding of the animal. The marbling helps to keep the meat moist inside while cooking.

MARGARINE. Made mainly of vegetable oils emulsified with pasteurised ripened skim milk. Margarine stands up to creaming, and will give cakes a good texture and bulk, but it is not good for frying or greasing tins as it leaves a sediment when melted which causes food to stick.

MARIGOLD. A flavouring or pot herb. The flowers of the common marigold are used for culinary purposes. They are used in salads, a conserve, a wine and to give added flavour to cream cheese. See **HERBS (CALENDULA).**

MARINADE, MARINATE. See COOKING TERMS.

MARJORAM. Pot marjoram, Wild marjoram and Strong marjoram may all be used for seasoning but the Sweet or Knotted marjoram is the most fragrant. The leaf is used in cheese, dressings, egg dishes, as a garnish, in meat pies, minced meat, puddings, with pulses, roast lamb, soup, tomatoes, in White sauce and in vinegar.

MARLING. The old English name for Whiting.

MARMALADE. Special marmalades are described under their various headings, APRICOTS, LEMONS, ORANGES, etc.

Marmalade Pudding. See PUDDINGS.

Marmalade Sauce. See SAUCES.

MARROW BONE. Large hollow bones of animals which contain a fatty substance called marrow. See OX MARROW.

MARSHMALLOW

Ingredients

¼ oz. powdered gelatine
½ pt. water
4 dsp. orange-flower water
10 oz. caster sugar
1 dsp. glucose
1 egg white stiffly whisked in a little sifted icing sugar

Method

Dissolve the gelatine in a little of the cold water. Put ¼ pt. water into a saucepan, add orange-flower water and gelatine and put over a low heat. Dissolve sugar in remaining water, add the glucose and bring to the boil; boil to 260° F. Add other, now lukewarm, mix and whisk well together. Fold in the white of egg and whisk until the mixture is white and quite stiff (this may take about 15 mins.). Leave in the pan for 30 mins. Run knife round edge of pan and turn mix on to sifted icing sugar; toss well, then cut into squares with scissors, and leave to dry for about 24 hrs.

MARZIPAN. The name given to a sort of almond paste, much used by confectioners for edible ornaments.

Ingredients

½ lb. granulated sugar
¼ gill water
6 oz. ground almonds
1 egg white
1 tbsp. icing sugar

Method

Put the granulated sugar into a saucepan, add the water and stir over a gentle heat until the sugar is dissolved. Then boil to 242° F. Remove the pan from the heat, add the almonds and the egg white and stir the mixture vigorously. Return the pan to the heat, and allow the egg to cook. Pour the mixture on to a slab and work it with a spatula until it thickens and cools. Then knead in the icing sugar until the marzipan has a smooth firm texture. See also ALMONDS.

MASH, MASK. See COOKING TERMS.

MATELOTE BLANCHE. Prepare a court bouillon with half water and half wine. Add one each onion and carrot sliced and a bouquet of parsley and thyme: simmer for 15 mins. Melt a little butter in saucepan and add some button onions

MATELOTE BLANCHE (*continued*)

and sliced mushrooms. Toss lightly but do not brown. Cook a trout in the court bouillon. When the fish is done, remove and place in a fireproof dish; add the onions and mushrooms. Reduce the court bouillon by half and make the sauce with this reduction mixed with a white roux. Put through a strainer over the fish, cook a little longer and bind with an egg yolk.

MAXIXE. A Brazilian vegetable which resembles a cucumber. To make into a salad, peel the rough skin off a maxixe, and cut the vegetable crosswise into very thin slices. Peel and slice a few spring onions and place both together in a salad bowl. Mix together sugar and oil with the oil predominating, season with salt and pepper, pour it over the salad which should be lightly tossed with a fork to mix well, and serve.

MAYONNAISE. A savoury dressing essentially an emulsion of oil and egg yolks.

METHOD I

Ingredients	*Method*
2 raw egg yolks	Put the yolks into a basin with a little salt, and stir them quickly with a whisk, or wooden spoon, dropping the oil on them drop by drop, until the sauce is as thick as butter in the warm weather, then add the vinegar and remainder of seasoning. NOTE: Success in making this sauce will depend on careful mixing.
½ pt. best salad oil	
2 tbsp. tarragon, French or plain vinegar	
Pepper and salt	

METHOD II

Ingredients	*Method*
2 raw egg yolks	Place the egg yolks in a basin, add the salt, cayenne and mustard; add the oil drop by drop, stirring the whole time. This prevents curdling. When all the oil is added, add the vinegar, gradually stirring in. Add cream last. Place in a sterilised bottle and cork securely to keep airtight.
Salt and cayenne	
½ tsp. mustard	
1 gill salad oil	
1 tbsp. tarragon or French vinegar	
1 tbsp. cream (or evaporated milk)	

Mayonnaise, Aspic

Ingredients	*Method*
½ pt. liquid aspic jelly (just on the point of setting)	Put the aspic in a basin, and put it to stand on ice. Whip it with a whisk, adding, drop by drop, oil and vinegar; whiten it with lemon juice, and, before using, add the tarragon and chervil. Use this sauce for masking cold fish and other entrées. For *Red Mayonnaise*, add beetroot juice: for *Green*, add parsley or spinach juice.
Some salad oil	
Vinegar	
Lemon juice	
A little finely chopped tarragon and chervil	

MEAD. This is a liquor brewed from honeycombs after the honey has been drawn away. The ancient Sack Mead, called so most probably from the French, was a beverage from France strengthened with brandy and flavoured with spices.

MEADOWSWEET. There are several meadowsweets to be found in the garden, but only two varieties have medicinal value, and are truly herbs, Dropwort and

MEADOWSWEET (*continued*)

Queen of the Meadow. Dropwort imparts a delicate flavour to soup, and the root is used medicinally. Both the leaf and root of Queen of the Meadow are used for medicinal purposes.

MEASURING INGREDIENTS. Always sift the flour before measuring; if the size of the eggs vary, the proportions of flour and liquids may need variation. When no scales are available, for handy measures, a half-pint measuring cup divided into fourths and thirds is useful, also measuring spoons and knife: these are obtainable commercially. A cup should always be filled a little more than brimful when measuring dry materials and then a knife used to brush off all that is piled above the brim: never shake a cup to level ingredient. When measuring with spoons for a tablespoonful and teaspoonful always use the special rounded ones, filled either round or heaping full, and with the back of a knife brush off all that is heaped above the edge of the spoon. See also **WEIGHTS AND MEASURES.**

MEAT. Although this word is frequently applied to food in general, it has become usual to confine its signification to what might properly be called "flesh". See under **BEEF, LAMB, VEAL, MUTTON, PORK,** etc., and also **CARVING.**

MEDLARS. The fruit of the medlar tree is appreciated for the agreeable acidity which sets in after the purple flesh has begun to decay. The skin of the medlar is brown and the flesh firm and austere, not at all good to eat when first gathered, nor until disintegration or "bletting" as it is called, has set in. In this state the fruit will keep for some time. The medlar grows wild in many parts of Europe and Asia, but the cultivated kinds yield the best fruit. Japanese medlars are described under **LOQUATS.**

Medlar Jelly

Ingredients	Method
24 medlars	Make sure the medlars are fully ripe, peel very thinly, slice and remove pips. Place in a preserving pan with sufficient cold water to cover. Add lemon juice and rind and boil gently until the fruit is really soft. Strain through muslin, but do not apply pressure. Measure juice and allow 1 pt. to 1 lb. sugar. Place in preserving pan and, if desired, add juice of other half of lemon, but no more rind. Boil gently for 1½ hr., skim well and pour into heated jars. Cover when cool.
Juice and thinly pared rind of ½ lemon	
Water	
Sugar	

MEGETHLIN. Dissolve about 5 lb. fresh honey in 1 gall. water and stir frequently for 2 days. Then add a little yeast and ¾ oz. hops boiled in water. Allow the mixture to ferment, and when this has ceased, draw it off. Add water if required and bottle.

MEGRIM. A common flat-fish, of the flounder family: in the United States it is called Lantern Flounder.

MELBA SAUCE. See **SAUCES SWEET.**

MELILOT. A plant of the clover tribe of somewhat aromatic character, used in Switzerland to flavour sapsago (schalszieger) cheese. The stems, leaves and flowers are crushed up and mixed with the curd, for which reason the plant is known in Switzerland, where it grows wild and profusely, as *Zeigen-Kraut* or Curd Herb.

MELON (Fr. *melon*). Melons are ranked among the choicest fruits of warm countries. The colour and flesh of melons vary: the Cantaloupe, one of the musk melons, is said to be one of the first introduced into Europe: the other two most

MELON (*continued*)

commonly seen are the Honeydew and Water Melons. Melons are generally served uncooked, sliced and chilled with salt, sugar and ground ginger, and in compôtes and fruit cocktails. A squeeze of lemon juice brings out the flavour. See also **FRUIT**.

MELON BALLS. Use a ball-shaped cutter. Scoop out balls of various kinds of melon (according to season) and blend together for a fruit cup; add a little Kirsch or port.

WATER MELON WITH BRANDY. Take a large ripe melon and cut a piece in centre about 2″ square by 3″ deep. Remove the piece carefully, gradually add a little brandy. Put to chill 2 hrs. before serving.

Melon Preserve

Ingredients	*Method*
1 musk melon Sugar ½ lemon thinly sliced Water 1 tsp. ground ginger 1 saltspoon ground cloves 2 tart cooking apples	Peel, seed and cut the melon into small pieces. Weigh it and allow two-thirds of its weight in sugar. Place the sliced melon in preserving pan with lemon and enough water to cover. Boil gently until tender. Then add ginger, cloves and the cooking apples, peeled, cored and diced. Boil fast until melon becomes clear. Skim, pour into warmed jars and cover.

MELTED BUTTER (Fr. *beurre fondu*). This name stands for a plain white sauce described as an "English sauce" by the French. See **SAUCES**.

MELWEL. The old English name for Hake.

MENESTRA. A Spanish stew or potage.

MERINGUE (Fr. *meringue*). A mixture essentially of whites of eggs and caster sugar beaten to a froth and then set in an oven. For meringue covering see **LEMON** (Lemon Meringue Pie).

Meringues

Ingredients	*Method*
4 egg whites 8 oz. caster sugar Flavouring essence	Beat the whites to a very firm froth. Sift the sugar, and mix lightly and quickly with them. The flavouring essence should be put in with the sugar. Cover a meringue board (a strip of thick wood or old baking-board) with stout paper, and oil it. Put the meringue mixture on this with a spoon, or forcing-bag, in half-egg shapes. Dust them with sifted sugar. With a small bellows blow off the waste sugar, and bake the meringues at 250° F. Therm. ½ for 2–3 hrs. Do not let them take more than a pale fawn colour. Detach meringues from the paper. With a spoon scoop out all the soft inside and put them into the oven for a few minutes to dry the insides. They must be filled only just before serving, or they will become soft. The meringues may be filled with preserve

[329]

Meringues (*continued*)

or beaten cream sweetened and flavoured (CREAM, p. 180; CONFECTIONER'S CREAM, p. 180; ICE CREAM, p. 280), and must be joined together in twos with white of egg (or without) to take the shape of eggs.

Meringues, Italian

Ingredients
4 eggs
8 oz. caster sugar
3 oz. almonds
Some orange flowers

Method
Blanch the almonds and cut them into strips. Make the paste as in foregoing recipe, and mix the almonds and orange flowers with it. Bake in square cases at 200° F. Therm. ¼.

MERRYTHOUGHT. The wishbone of poultry.

MIDDLINGS. The coarser part of flour.

MIGNONETTE PEPPER. Coarsely ground white peppercorn seeds which resemble mignonette seeds.

MILK. Milk contains all the elements that are required for the growth and maintenance of the human body. It is the white, homogeneous fluid secreted by the mammary glands of animals. Cow's milk is used in this country; in Sweden and Denmark, sheep's milk; in Switzerland, goat's milk; in Lapland, reindeer milk; in Tartar, mare's milk, which also is used for Koumiss. Goat's and ass's milk are sometimes used here. In India large quantities of buffalo milk are used for both dietary purposes and for the manufacture of Ghee.

Milk has a higher boiling temperature than water, and it is best to use a double boiler or one of the patent saucepans to prevent boiling over.

The first sign of decomposition in milk is acidity.

Biestings is the first milk drawn from the cow after calving.

Condensed is milk reduced approximately two fifths in volume by extraction of water and sweetened.

Evaporated is milk reduced to half its volume by extraction of water.

APPROXIMATE FOOD VALUE OF MILK

	PROTEINS grm.	FATS grm.	C.H. grm.	CALORIES
Milk (whole) 8 oz. or 1 cup	8	10	12	169
Milk (skimmed) 8 oz. or 1 cup	8	1	13	96

TO RECONSTITUTE MILK.

Whole Cream Dried Milk To make ½ gall. (2 qt. or 4 pt.) allow 3¾ pt. water and ¼ lb. dried whole milk.
For ½ lb. liquid whole milk = 8 oz. milk, allow 7 oz. water and 1 oz. whole dried milk.

Skim Dried Milk For ½ gall. (2 qt.) allow 6 oz. skim milk powder and ½ gall. water.

Condensed Milk For ½ lb. sweetened condensed whole milk, allow 2¼ oz. dried whole milk, 3¼ oz. sugar and 2½ oz. water.

To mix, put the water into bowl of an electric mixer. Turn to lowest speed. Sprinkle the milk powder on water and mix very gradually until well combined.

MILK, TO SCALD (FOR SERVING HOT). If milk is to be served hot it must never be boiled, but heated in a double boiler or over hot water until a scum forms. This is scalding point: 186° F. If boiled, the milk is indigestible. Serve it plain or with flavouring as desired.

Put the milk into a double saucepan or oven glass basin wedged in a pan of water, or place in a small enamel jug and stand in a pan of cold water. Place over low heat, bring to the boil, allow to simmer for a few minutes.

MILK PUDDINGS. These are frequently unappetising through careless cooking, but, with very little trouble, they make an excellent and appetising addition to the diet.

Whole Grains   (A) 2 oz. grains and 1½ oz. sugar to each 1 pt. milk (without eggs).

Vanilla and grated nutmeg can be added as flavouring.

(B) 1½ oz. grains and 1½ oz. sugar to each 1 pt. milk (with 1 or 2 eggs as desired).

Powdered Grains   (C) 1½ oz. grains and 1½ oz. sugar to each 1 pt. milk (without eggs).

(D) 1 oz. grains and 1½ oz. sugar to each 1 pt. milk (with 1 or 2 eggs as desired).

Add flavouring as above.

MILK PUDDING I   Place whole grains in buttered pie-dish with milk, sugar and flavouring. Leave to stand for a short time, then cook gently at 300° F. Therm. 2 until the grain is soft and pudding creamy.

MILK PUDDING II   Rinse the saucepan with cold water (to prevent the milk burning), add milk and whole grains and cook over a gentle heat until the grain is tender (a double saucepan may be used), then turn into buttered dish. Add sugar, flavouring and egg (if used). Cook in a moderate oven (350° F. Therm. 4) until tender.

Arrowroot Pudding

Ingredients

1 tbsp. arrowroot
½ pt. milk
Rind of ½ lemon
Sugar or golden syrup
1 egg

Method

Blend the arrowroot in a little milk and pour over it the boiling milk. Return to the pan and stir well until mixture boils. Remove from the heat and add the grated lemon rind or a few drops of lemon essence, and sugar or golden syrup to sweeten. Add the yolk of an egg and fold in the stiffly whisked white. Pour into a well-greased dish and bake at 400° F. Therm. 6 until the pudding rises and becomes golden brown. Serve quickly as the pudding is apt to sink.

Ground Rice Pudding

Ingredients

Apple rings, syrup or jam
1 pt. milk

Method

Well grease a dish and spread with jam or syrup or apple rings. Put the milk in a

Ground Rice Pudding (*continued*)

2 oz. ground rice
Sugar
Vanilla or lemon essence
1 or 2 eggs

saucepan and stir in the ground rice, over the heat. Allow to boil and cook gently for 5 mins. Allow to cool, add sugar and vanilla or lemon essence to flavour, the yolks of 1 or 2 eggs and mix well. Fold in the stiffly-whisked whites of the eggs and pour the mixture into the dish. Bake for 20–25 mins. at 350° F. Therm. 4.

Macaroni Pudding

Ingredients

2 oz. macaroni
1 pt. milk
1 egg
2 oz. sugar

Method

Break up the macaroni and boil until tender in the milk. When cool, add the beaten egg and the sugar, and pour into a well-greased pudding dish. Bake for about ½ hr. at 350° F. Therm. 4.

Rice Pudding I

Ingredients

1½ oz. rice
1 dsp. sugar
1 pt. milk
Nutmeg
Margarine

Method

Well wash the rice in a little cold water and place it in a pie-dish with the sugar. Add the boiling milk, a grating of nutmeg, a knob of margarine, and bake slowly for 1 hr. at 250° F. Therm. ½.

Rice Pudding II

Ingredients

1½ oz. rice
1 dsp. sugar
1 pt. milk

Method

Simmer rice gently in a little water until almost tender, then add milk and sugar and simmer together for 2–3 mins., pour into a pie-dish and brown in the oven or under the grill.

Sago Pudding. Using sago in place of tapioca, proceed as for Tapioca Pudding (see below).

Semolina Dumplings

Ingredients

1 pt. milk
Sugar
½ cup semolina
2 oz. raisins or currants
1 oz. margarine

Method

Boil the milk, add sugar to sweeten and gradually add the semolina to make a soft paste; add raisins and currants, if desired. Allow the mixture to cool and, when almost cold, form into small balls and fry in margarine. Serve with a sprinkling of sugar.

Semolina Pudding

Ingredients

2 tbsp. semolina
1 pt. milk
Grated rind of 1 lemon
2 eggs

Method

Mix the semolina with a little milk. Place the remainder of the milk, using 1 pt. of milk altogether, into a saucepan and bring to the boil. Pour it on to the semolina paste and stir well. Return the

[332]

Semolina Pudding (*continued*)

mixture to the saucepan over a gentle heat and stir until it boils. Add sugar to sweeten, grated lemon rind, and 2 egg yolks Fold in the stiffly whipped egg whites and pour the mixture into a greased dish. Bake until well-browned at 350° F. Therm. 4. If the pudding is to be turned out of the dish before serving, the dish should be well greased and some browned breadcrumbs should be sifted into it. Currants may be added, if desired, or ginger, cinnamon and other spices; or the greased pie-dish may be spread with a little jam; or whole cooked prunes or tinned fruit may be added, in which case only half the quantity of milk should be used and fruit syrup substituted for the other half.

Tapioca Pudding (Baked)

Ingredients
  2 tbsp. tapioca
  1 pt. milk
  Sugar
  Vanilla or lemon essence
  1 egg

Method

Soak the tapioca in half the milk for about 1 hr. Then put it into a saucepan, add rest of the milk, and simmer gently until the tapioca is quite soft. Stir occasionally to prevent the mixture from sticking to the pan, and cook with the lid on the pan. Allow the mixture to cool and add sugar to sweeten, a few drops of lemon or vanilla essence and the well-beaten egg. Turn into a greased pie-dish and bake until well browned on the top at 350° F. Therm. 4. Extra eggs may be added, if desired. If the yolks are beaten and added and then the white stiffly whisked and folded in, the pudding will resemble a soufflé.

Tapioca Pudding (Steamed). Prepare as above, but place in a well-greased basin or mould. Garnish with cherries or fruit, fold in the egg whites and tie a band of greased paper round the mould or basin. Steam from 1¼ to 1½ hr. and serve with sweet fruit or Custard sauce.

MILK SUGAR. Lactose.

MILKWEED. Any of the genus of perennial herbs which abound in a warm milky juice. To make into a salad, the young shoots of milkweed should be gathered and thoroughly washed in cold water. Break off the few leaves that have appeared (or if preferred they may be cooked with shoots); tie the shoots into small bunches and boil for 20 mins. in slightly salted water. When cooked, drain the milkweed, and put it on a dish. Serve with plain salad dressing (see p. 430) or Melted Butter sauce.

MILLET. The small round seeds of this plant can be used for milk puddings.

MILT (Fr. *laitance*). The soft roe of a fish. The spleen of an animal is sometimes erroneously called milt, or melt, as it was believed to correspond with a fish's soft roe. See SOUPS.

MINCE. See COOKING TERMS.

MINCEMEAT. This word evidently takes its culinary origin from the French, *émincer* and signifies anything that is chopped up finely.

Ingredients	*Method*
1 lb. suet	Chop the suet; wash and dry the currants; stone and cut the raisins in halves; peel, core and mince the apples. Chop the candied peel. Soak ratafias in wine and brandy. Mix all the ingredients well together. Put them into a stone jar, cover closely and keep for a month.
1 lb. currants	
1 lb. raisins	
1 lb. apples	
1 lb. candied peel	
1 lb. sugar	
Grated rind and juice of 3 lemons	
1 tsp. mixed spice	
Pinch of salt	
¼ lb. ratafias	
½ pt. wine and brandy mixed	

Mince Pies

Ingredients	*Method*
Puff pastry (see p. 374)	Roll the paste out, and stamp it into rather large rounds with a fluted cutter. Lay half the rounds on patty-pans. Wet the edges of the pastry and put some mincemeat in the middle of each round. Cover with the remaining rounds, pressing the edges lightly together. To glaze, brush them with a little white of egg and dust with caster sugar. Bake at 400° F. Therm. 6 for 15–20 mins.
Mincemeat	
Caster sugar	
White of 1 egg	

MINESTRA. See MINESTRONE.

MINESTRONE. A favourite Italian stew.

TO MAKE. Chop ¼ lb. bacon and cut up a Savoy cabbage and put both into a stewpan with ½ lb. chopped raw ham and 1 cup haricot beans. Pour in 5 to 6 pt. clear broth, and place the stewpan over a low heat. Bring to the boil and simmer. After 5 mins. cooking add 1 teacup chopped celery, an equal quantity of haricot beans and about 1 teacup cabbage stalk, cut into small squares. Boil these for about 10 mins., then mix in 1 teacup each broad beans, asparagus heads, green peas, ¾ lb. unwashed rice, and two chopped smoked Milan sausages and continue to simmer very gently until the rice is tender. Grate 2 oz. Parmesan cheese into a soup tureen and, when the soup is cooked, pour it in. Serve with a plate of croûtons and fried bread, or sippets of dry toast.

MINNOW. Very tiny river fish which are often raised to the dignity of the table under the guise of whitebait, from which it is very difficult to distinguish them.

MINT. Also called Spearmint. This is one of the most powerful herbs used in cooking.

Mint Chutney. Pick the leaves from freshly gathered mint. Remove all stalks and dead leaves and chop up finely. To 2 cups mint, allow ¼ lb. caster sugar, ¾ cup vinegar, 2 small cloves minced garlic, and 4 or 5 green chillies. Mix well together, put into a bottle and cork tightly. Use after a fortnight. Only make in small quantities.

Mint Jelly

Ingredients	*Method*
1 pt. apple juice	Boil apple juice and sugar together. Test
1 lb. sugar	for setting. Add few drops of colouring
3 or 4 finely chopped mint	and the chopped mint. Boil about a min.,
leaves	pour into small hot jars and seal.
Green colouring if desired	

Mint Sauce

Ingredients	*Method*
4 tbsp. finely chopped mint	Mix together and allow to stand for a
2 tbsp. caster sugar	short time before serving. Lemon juice
$\frac{1}{2}$ pt. vinegar	may be diluted and substituted for vinegar
	if preferred.

MIREPOIX. A flavouring used for a savoury stew.

METHOD I. Take 2 carrots, 2 onions, 2 shallots, 2 bay leaves, a sprig of thyme, a clove of garlic, mince them together with $\frac{1}{2}$ lb. fat bacon and raw ham. Toss in a sauté-pan with 2 oz. butter and season with salt. Stew in $\frac{1}{2}$ pt. red or white wine. Add to stock or sauce as required.

METHOD II. Take small pieces of meat, poultry or game, and with a little diced bacon, peeled sliced carrot, grated onion, and turnip, fry them together until lightly browned. Add a bouquet garni and seasoning of salt and pepper, then add hot brown stock, simmer for about 2–3 hrs., skim well and rub through a wire sieve.

MOCK TURTLE SOUP. See SOUPS.

MOISTEN. See COOKING TERMS.

MOLASSES. A dark-coloured, thick, uncrystallisable liquid which drains off sugar in the course of its preparation and refinement. See SUGAR.

MONKEY NUTS. See PEANUT.

MOOR FOWL. The Red-legged Ptarmigan is known by this name; but more often spoken of as Moor Cock, or Moor Hen, and sometimes dignified with the name of Moor Game. It does not often find its way to the table. For roasting, truss them with their heads under their wings, and stuff with a mixture of breadcrumbs and butter. They require frequent basting to prevent the flesh becoming dry during cooking. They are also good in game pie. Allow 30–35 mins. cooking time.

MOREL (Fr. *morille*). When mushrooms and other edible fungi are scarce, the cook can always fall back upon the morel, a fungus found in woods and orchards, for flavouring soups and sauces. Morels grow in many different shapes, some conical, others strawberry shape, and others quite round, the bulbous part being deeply reticulated. When cut open they are hollow, with thick fleshy walls; they may be stewed, stuffed or served with sauce.

MORELLOS. See CHERRY.

MORTADELLA (Fr. *mortadelle*). A kind of Italian sausage manufactured in Bologna, Italy, and used in hors d'œuvre, etc.

MOUNTAIN ASH. See ROWAN BERRIES.

MOUSSE. This French term indicates froth or foam and is applied to light-textured dishes, hot or cold, sweet or savoury.

MOUSSELINE SAUCE. See SAUCES, SWEET.

MUFFIN. A light, spongy cake baked on an iron plate usually toasted and eaten for tea.

MUGWORT. Common mugwort, White mugwort and Western mugwort: the whole herb is used medicinally.

MULBERRY (Fr. *mure*). The fruit of the black mulberry. This tree is cultivated for its leaves for food for silkworms, and its fruit, which is sweetly acid in flavour, only to be eaten when quite ripe, and then it decomposes or mildews readily. Mulberries can be served for dessert very carefully arranged on a dessert dish in a pyramid.

Mulberry Jam

Ingredients

4 lb. mulberries
4 lb. sugar

Method

Place the ripe mulberries in preserving pan and allow to simmer gently until they are tender. Add sugar and boil until jam thickens. Test for setting, pour into warmed jars and cover when cool.

Mulberry Jelly

Ingredients

1 qt. ripe mulberries
1 qt. unripe mulberries
1 pt. water
Sugar

Method

Place fruit and water in preserving pan and simmer gently, mashing fruit against sides of pan until juice is expelled. Strain through muslin, measure and allow an equal amount of sugar. Return to pan with sugar and boil for 4 mins. after sugar has dissolved. Skim well, test for setting, pour into warmed jars and cover when cool.

MULL. To heat, spice and sweeten wine, sherry, claret or beer, in a muller, which may be either a single saucepan or an elaborate apparatus designed for the purpose.

MULLED WINE. The rind of ½ a lemon and ½ an orange, 6 cloves, a very small pinch of nutmeg, 6 oz. loaf sugar, ½ pt. water. These ingredients are well mixed, heated, and strained through a sieve. Just at the last add one bottle of wine, and make it as hot as possible without boiling.

MULLET. There are two kinds of mullet known to us. The Red or Sun mullet is a brilliant colour and has a sort of beard appendage. It is best between April and October. When cleaning the red mullet it is only necessary to scrape it well and pull out the gills, with which will come away all that it is necessary to remove of the inside; the liver, which is an especial delicacy, remains. Grey mullet are best cooked as soon as they are caught. They must be scraped, emptied, and thoroughly cleaned before cooking. The roe of the Grey mullet is prepared by drying, salting and forming into a sausage.

Mullet Chowder

Ingredients

3 mullet
2 tsp. salt
Water
2 sprigs parsley
2 stalks celery
2 slices bacon diced
1 small onion chopped
2 potatoes diced
4 oz. mushrooms chopped
1 oz. flour
1 tbsp. butter or margarine

Method

Remove gills and eyes; wash fish heads and fish well in salted water. Place in deep saucepan fish, salt, water, parsley and celery. Cover and simmer for 15 mins. Strain and put stock into clean pan. Put bacon in large pan and brown over a low flame for 5 mins., then add onion, potatoes, mushrooms and sauté together for 5 mins. until the onion is light brown. Turn all into pan, and boil for 10 mins. Put flour and butter previously rolled

Mullet Chowder (*continued*)

Seasoning to taste
Milk

together into small pan with seasoning. When butter melts, stir until smooth, add milk, and cook for 5 mins. stirring constantly until slightly thick. Add flaked fish flesh. Combine the two mixtures, and stir well together. Reboil and serve in heated bowl with garnish of paprika, parsley and other green herbs.

Mullet, Spiced

Ingredients

2½ lb. mullet (filleted)
Olive oil
Wine or vinegar
2 tsp. salt
¼ tsp. pepper
¼ tsp. thyme
½ tsp. tarragon
1 crushed bay leaf
1 grated onion
Juice of 1 lemon
3 tbsp. fat
Watercress

Method

Wipe fillets with damp cloth and cut into serving portions. Pour into bowl olive oil and vinegar. Add seasoning and lemon juice. Blend well and marinade the fish in this mixture for an hour. Drain and roll in flour; melt the fat in frying pan, heat but do not allow to smoke, fry fish for 10 mins. Turn carefully, fry 5 more mins. until golden brown. Serve garnished with watercress. The mullet may be baked in preheated moderate oven 350° F. Therm. 4 for 30 mins. if preferred.

MULLIGATAWNY SOUP. See SOUPS.

MUSH. A sort of porridge made with Indian corn meal in the United States.

MUSHROOM (Fr. *champignon*). A term applied to nearly all edible fungi, but in France and other parts of the Continent they have various names, such as Champignons, Chantarelles, and Cèpes, etc. We still have morels and truffles as differing essentially from mushrooms (see under individual headings).

TO DRY. Take mushrooms and wipe with a clean, dry cloth. Thread a needle with a length of strong linen thread and string the mushrooms on this. Hang in a cool oven (240° F. Therm. ¼) to dry slowly. After 24 hrs. in the warm air, pack into glass jars.

TO RECONSTITUTE DRIED MUSHROOMS. Steep in a little cold water and, when they have regained size, drain, dry and use as fresh mushrooms.

TO PICKLE. Rub button mushrooms with flannel and salt to clean them. Well wash and dry them. Place in a stewpan and sprinkle with a little salt, adding a blade or two of mace and a little pepper. Cook them at a slow heat until the liquor comes out. Shake them well and continue cooking until it is again absorbed. Just cover with vinegar, boil up once and put in glass jars. Cover when cold.

TO SALT. Place mushrooms in a crock pot in layers with salt and fill up to the brim as they sink. Steep in water for a short while before use to remove salt.

MUSHROOMS, BAKED. Peel the mushrooms, rinse them to remove any grit, and cut off the ends of the stalks. Place on a greased baking-tin with stalks upwards, and put some little pieces of butter on each mushroom, add a little pepper and salt. Cover with buttered paper and cook in a very moderate oven 300° F. Therm. 2 from 15 to 20 mins., or until tender. Serve on toast, with the liquor from the tin poured over them.

MUSHROOMS AND BACON ON TOAST. Toast or fry some bacon cut into neat pieces, and toast some squares of bread. Dip each piece of toast into the bacon fat in the pan, and place it on a hot dish. Place a piece of bacon on each, and on top a fried or baked mushroom. Dust with a little pepper and serve hot, if possible on a hot-water dish.

MUSHROOMS, STEWED. Peel and rinse mushrooms; cut off the ends of stalks, and stew gently in water, stock or milk until quite tender, adding a little pepper and salt to taste. Thicken the gravy with a little flour, cooking it well. Before serving, stir in a little butter or cream.

Mushrooms, Croûtard of

Ingredients
1 lb. small mushrooms
2 oz. butter
Pinch of pounded mace
Pepper and salt
¼ oz. flour
Little lemon juice
Some stale bread

Method
Peel, rinse and dry mushrooms. Melt the butter in a saucepan and place the mushrooms in with mace and a little pepper and salt. Fry gently without discolouring for 15 mins.; mix in flour thoroughly, add stock and simmer mushrooms until tender. Add lemon juice. While the mushrooms are cooking, cut a slice of bread 2″ thick. Cut it into a round or oval shape with a vol-au-vent cutter. Scoop out centre evenly, leaving the sides and bottom ¼″ thick. When mushrooms are ready, fry the bread case in hot fat. Drain well, fill with mushrooms and serve at once.

Mushroom Ketchup

Ingredients
8 qt. large flat mushrooms
¾ lb. salt
Black pepper and mace

Method
Cut off the ends of the stalks of mushrooms; break up and place in a saucepan and mix well with the salt. Allow to stand for three days stirring and mashing well every day. Drain off the liquor, but do not press the mushrooms. Return liquor to saucepan and boil until reduced one-half, then add to each quart ½ oz. black pepper and 1 drm. mace. When cool, pour into bottles free from any sediment, cork well and tie down.

Mushroom Pasty

Ingredients
Equal quantities of mushrooms and potatoes
Little onion
Some short or flaky crust

Method
Peel and rinse the mushrooms well and peel and slice potatoes. Cut them both into small dice, and chop the onion finely. Mix them together and add pepper and salt to season. Roll out pastry and cut into rather large rounds. Wet the edges of the paste rounds with water, and place the vegetables in the centre. Draw the edges of the pastry together and goffer them with the fingers. Place them on a slightly greased baking tin and bake for 1 hr. at 350° F. Therm. 4.

[338]

Mushroom Pie
Ingredients
2 lb. mushrooms
Salt and pepper
Little butter or dripping
2 lb. potatoes
Some flaky or other pastry

Method
Place a layer of mushrooms, when peeled and rinsed, at the bottom of a pie-dish. Sprinkle with pepper and salt and dot with butter. Cover with slices of potato, seasoning them in the same way, and continue to place the mushrooms and potatoes in layers until the dish is full. Cover with pastry, and bake at 400° F. Therm. 6 for about ¾ hr.

Mushroom Pudding
Ingredients
Suet paste (see p. 375)
Mushrooms

Method
Peel and rinse the mushrooms, and prepare the paste as for beefsteak pudding. Fill the paste-lined basin with mushrooms which should be well seasoned with salt and pepper. Pour in a little water, cover and finish off as directed for beefsteak pudding, and boil for 2 hrs.

Mushroom Rissoles
Ingredients
Pastry
Mushrooms
Egg and breadcrumbs or vermicelli

Method
Stew some mushrooms according to directions given at the top of page 338. When cooked, mince and pour them on to a plate to cool. Roll out pastry very thinly, not thicker than a shilling. Stamp into rounds with a paste-cutter, brush the edges of the paste with beaten egg, and place some of the mushrooms in the centre. Double the paste over, pressing the edges together. Brush with beaten egg and cover with breadcrumbs or crushed vermicelli. Fry in hot fat and garnish with fried parsley.

MUSK. Essence prepared from the contents of the musk bag of the musk deer which yields a powerful, pleasing scent with a warm aromatic flavour, used for sweets, etc.

MUSSEL (Fr. *moule*). The mussel is found in vast numbers along almost every coast. The very large ones are called House mussels and are also edible.

TO CLEAN AND STEAM. Mussels should be tightly closed. Never use opened mussels. Scrub the shells under running water, and place them in a large deep pot, covered with cold water, and leave for 2 hrs. Remove and discard any mussels which are floating. Then place the mussels in a large iron (if possible) pan, adding 1 tsp. salt, and cover. Steam for 3 mins. only, or until the shells open. Remove the mussels from the pot, remove mussels from shells. Cut away hairy beard and then set the mussels aside to use as desired.

Mussels au Gratin
Ingredients
4 doz. mussels
4 oz. butter or margarine

Method
Take the prepared mussels (see above). Melt 2 oz. butter in a saucepan over a

Mussels au Gratin (*continued*)

1 small grated onion
2 tbsp. flour
½ pt. mussel stock
Salt and pepper
2 tbsp. sherry
4 oz. breadcrumbs
4 oz. grated cheese
Watercress

low heat, add the onion, sauté gently until golden brown. Add flour gradually, stirring the whole time. When smooth, add the mussel broth and stir until the liquid is thick. Add salt, pepper and sherry. Add extra mussel broth if necessary to make the sauce the desired thickness. Put the mussels into a casserole or oven-glass dish, add sauce, crumbs and grated cheese and dot with the remaining 2 oz. butter. Bake at 350° F. Therm. 4 for 15 mins. until top is golden brown. Serve garnished with watercress.

Mussel Bisque

Ingredients

2 qt. mussels
1 qt. milk
1 sliced onion
4 tbsp. butter or margarine
1 tbsp. flour
1 tsp. salt
¼ tsp. pepper
1 pt. tomato purée

Method

Clean and steam mussels (see above). Remove from shells and chop finely. Place in saucepan, add milk, onion, and scald for about 2 mins Then remove onion. Melt butter in a double boiler (filling the lower pan only half full of water), add gradually the flour, milk, then the seasoning and tomato purée and stir constantly. Heat to boiling point, but do not boil. Serve immediately with croûtons.

Mussel Casserole

Ingredients

1 lb. quick macaroni or noodles
1½ lb cleaned mussels
1 tsp. dried mixed herbs
1 tin cream of mushroom soup
½ tsp. chopped parsley

Method

Cook noodles or macaroni until soft, place a layer in a greased casserole, then a layer of mussels, with a thin sprinkling of herbs. Repeat layers, the top one must not be fish. Pour soup over the whole and heat for 40 mins. in the oven at 350° F. Therm. 4. This dish must be kept moist, and if it seems to dry over-much before it is heated through, add some "top of the milk" to it. Garnish with chopped parsley.

Mussels, Fried

Ingredients

4 doz. mussels with shells
Juice of 1 lemon
1 egg beaten
Salt and pepper
Crumbs
½ pt. oil

Method

Choose and prepare fresh mussels (see above), remove the meat and sprinkle with lemon juice. Set to one side. Beat the egg until foamy, add salt and pepper to season, roll mussels in crumbs, dip in the egg and roll in crumbs again. Put the

[340]

Mussels, Fried (*continued*)
  Paprika
  Watercress
  2 lemons quartered

oil into frying pan, heat, but do not allow to smoke. Fry mussels until golden brown, about 3 mins., but do not overcook. Drain on paper. Sprinkle with paprika and garnish with watercress and lemon quarters.

Mussel Puffs
Ingredients
  1 pt. shelled mussels
  1 tbsp. minced onion
  1 small carrot minced and cooked
  1 egg well beaten
  ⅛ tsp. Worcester sauce
  Mashed potato
  Salt and pepper
  Breadcrumbs
  4 oz. butter
  Watercress and chives
  ¼ tsp. chopped gherkin

Method
Drain mussels and remove beards. Mince, add onion and carrot and blend. Then add egg, Worcester sauce, potatoes, salt and pepper. Mix well and put to chill. Remove and form into round puffs, then dip into crumbs, into egg and into crumbs again. Melt the butter in frying pan, and fry the puffs 4 mins. each side, until golden brown. Serve on heated dish piled high, garnished with watercress sprigs, chives and chopped gherkin.

Mussels, Stewed
Ingredients
  42 mussels
  ½ carrot and onion diced
  ¼ cup white wine or tarragon vinegar
  Squeeze of lemon juice
  1 bay leaf
  1 sprig of thyme
  ½ clove of garlic (if desired)
  Salt and pepper
  Drop of tabasco
  2 tbsp. butter or margarine
  2 tbsp. chopped parsley

Method
Scrub and wash the mussels and place them in a large pan (iron if possible) with the carrot, onion, wine or vinegar, lemon juice, bay leaf and thyme. Add garlic, salt, pepper, tabasco and butter. Cover the pan and place over a good heat. When the mussels are all open, remove from pan as they are cooked. Serve in soup plates removing the top shell of each. Strain over the liquid (taking care that there are no particles of shell in this) and add an extra chopping of parsley to garnish. (If the mussels are prepared at home, remove the black speck after the mussels are opened).

Mussels with Saffron
Ingredients
  4 doz. mussels in shells
  Mussel stock
  ½ tsp. saffron
  2 oz. butter
  1 tsp. flour
  1 tsp. salt
  Pepper
  4 egg yolks beaten

Method
Choose fresh mussels and prepare as on page 339. Take a little of the mussel stock, place in pan. Dissolve the saffron in just a little of the liquid, add to the saucepan, stir well, heat for 2 mins. Melt butter in separate saucepan over medium heat, add flour stirring all the time, add remainder of stock and egg yolks and

Mussels with Saffron (*continued*)

Strained juice of a lemon
Croûtons
Parsley

when smooth add saffron liquid; bring to boil stirring constantly, until the sauce thickens. Drop in lemon juice, season with pepper and salt. Arrange mussels on dish, cover with hot saffron sauce and serve in individual dishes on croûtons. Garnish with sprigs of parsley.

MUST. The juice of the grape before fermentation.

MUSTARD. The commercial product which we buy is made from the ground seeds of two varieties of mustard plant; those of the White mustard, yellow in colour and sharp in taste, and those of the Black mustard, dark brown in colour and of stronger flavour. The seeds of the Field mustard or Charlock are sometimes sold as a substitute.

MUSTARD, CASTER. I. 2 oz. mustard, 1 saltspoon sugar, add sufficient milk to mix to a smooth paste.

II. For keeping mustard, mix 4 oz. mustard with $\frac{1}{2}$ tsp. of salt; when smooth add gradually $\frac{1}{2}$ teacup horseradish vinegar and 2 tbsp. white vinegar. Put into wide-mouthed bottles and cork securely.

MUSTARD, FRENCH. Put 1 pt. brown mustard seed into a basin with 2 or 3 tbsp. each of parsley, burnet, chervil and tarragon, and about $\frac{1}{2}$ tsp. each celery seeds, clover, mace, garlic. Pour over these ingredients sufficient quantity of white wine or vinegar to cover them. Put a plate on the basin and let them steep for 24 hrs. Then pound the mixture in a mortar and pass it through a fine hair sieve. Add a little more vinegar to bring to the desired consistency. Put into wide-mouthed jars and cork tightly.

MUSTARD, PIQUANT. Peel and slice an onion, put it into a saucepan with 2 or 3 thinly sliced cloves of garlic, 2 bay leaves, 1 tsp. crushed peppercorns, a few cloves, a sprig of tarragon and 1 pt. best vinegar. Boil all together for 15 mins. Leave the vinegar until cold. Keep the lid on the saucepan and stir in sufficient mustard to make a stiff paste. Pour into jars and cork tightly.

MUSTARD, SPICED OR AROMATIC. Mix 2 tbsp. powdered mustard with 1 tsp. each of flour and sugar, and half the quantity each of salt, pepper, cloves and cinnamon. Stir them into a smooth paste with boiling vinegar. Add a little salad oil and in a few hours the mustard will be ready for use.

Mustard Sauce. Put 2 oz. butter into a saucepan and heat without browning. Mix in 2 tbsp. flour, pour in gradually 1 pt. hot stock or water and stir until the mixture thickens and is perfectly smooth. Add 2 oz. more butter pulled into small pieces. Stir well and sprinkle with salt and pepper. Mix in 3 tbsp. made mustard and a little cayenne, then use as desired, with fish, devilled turkey, etc. For **Brown Mustard Sauce** see SAUCES, SAVOURY.

MUTTON (Fr. *mouton*). The quality of mutton is dependent not only upon the breed of sheep but also upon the sex, age and pasture.

TO CHOOSE. The lean should be firm and finely grained and red in colour, although not so red as that of beef. The fat should be white and firm. The best mutton is small boned and plump. Avoid mutton with very light-coloured lean and yellowish fat, especially if moisture exudes from it on being pressed. These are sure signs that the meat is not good.

JOINTS OF MUTTON.

Leg of Mutton. To be roasted, baked or boiled. If roasted, serve redcurrant jelly with it, or Tomato, Mushroom or other piquant sauce. The vegetables which accompany it may be baked potatoes, artichokes, and any green vegetables, also haricot beans and well cooked macaroni. The latter may be served plain or as macaroni cheese. When the leg is boiled, serve Caper sauce with it, potatoes, carrots and turnips. The two latter should be cooked with the meat and then may be served plain or mashed.

JOINTS OF MUTTON (*continued*)

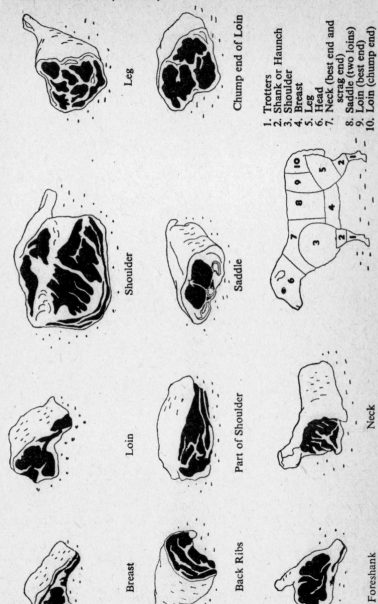

Leg

Chump end of Loin

Shoulder

Saddle

Loin

Part of Shoulder

Neck

Breast

Back Ribs

Foreshank

1. Trotters
2. Shank or Haunch
3. Shoulder
4. Breast
5. Leg
6. Head
7. Neck (best end and scrag end)
8. Saddle (two loins)
9. Loin (best end)
10. Loin (chump end)

JOINTS OF MUTTON (*continued*).

Haunch of Mutton, Loin of Mutton and Saddle of Mutton. These are always roasted or baked. Serve with the accompaniments directed for roast leg of mutton.

Shoulder of Mutton. This should be roasted or baked. Serve Soubise or Onion sauce with it, and any of the vegetables directed of roast leg of mutton.

Chine and Neck of Mutton (*Best End*). These are roasted or baked. Serve with accompaniments directed for leg of mutton.

Scrag End of Neck. This is boiled and requires long and gentle cooking to make it tender. Serve Caper sauce with it, and for vegetables, carrots, turnips or parsnips and potatoes.

MUTTON, BOILED LEG OF. For boiling, this joint should not hang so long as for roasting. Two or three days will be enough if the colour is considered of importance. This and careful skimming will prevent the necessity for a floured cloth, which some inexperienced cooks resort to. Cut off the shank-bone, and if necessary wipe the joint with a damp cloth. Put it into a large oval stewpan with as much boiling water as will cover it. When restored to its boiling state, skim the surface clean, and draw the stewpan to the side of the heat to allow the contents to simmer until done. Time, about 20 mins. to each pound. Boil very young turnips for a garnish; these will take 20 mins., but allow 1 hr. for older ones, which are to be mashed. Place the turnips, which should be of equal size, round the dish, and send the mashed ones to table separately. Melted butter, with capers added, should accompany the dish. The liquor from the boiling may be converted into good soup at a trifling expense.

MUTTON, ROAST LEG OF. Get a leg of about 8 lb., which has hung at least a week, weather allowing. During hot summer weather this joint gets quickly tainted. Rub it lightly with salt, and put it at once before a brisk, sharp fire. Place it close to the fire for the first 5 mins., then draw it further back and let it roast more slowly until done. Time, 15 mins. per lb., and 15 mins. over. Baste continually with a little good dripping until that from the joint begins to flow. When within 20 mins. of being done, dredge it with flour and baste it with butter or dripping; when the froth rises, serve on a hot dish. Make a gravy; if the dripping-pan has been floured, any essence will adhere to it and the fat may easily be thrown off. Add a little extract of meat to this, and a little boiling water, pepper and salt. Pour the gravy round the meat, not over it.

MUTTON, ROAST LOIN OF. Follow the directions given for roast leg in every particular (see above recipe), but trim off all unnecessary fat, which may be used for a common suet crust. If the fat is not turned to account there is no more expensive joint than a loin of mutton. Cover the fat with paper until within a ¼ hr. of its being done, then remove, baste, and flour slightly to get it frothed. Time: ¼ hr. per lb.

Mutton Broth. See SOUPS.

Mutton Cutlets à la Maintenon

Ingredients

Mutton cutlets cut with 2 bones to each
Pepper and salt
Mushrooms ⎫
Parsley ⎬ ¼ lb. mushrooms and parsley to 1½ oz. shallots
Shallots ⎭
Butter
Brown sauce (see p. 439)

Method

Cut the cutlets with two bones to each, then remove one bone. Flatten the cutlets with a wet cutlet bat and trim neatly and season. Cut them in two, but without dividing them at the bone. Cook the mushrooms, parsley and shallots in the butter, put some of this inside each cutlet, press the edges together and broil each cutlet for about 8 mins. Mix some of the fried vegetables with the Brown sauce, using the proportion of 2 tbsp. to each ½ pt. sauce. Dish the cutlets neatly, and pour the sauce over them.

[344]

Mutton Cutlets à la Milanaise
Ingredients

7 mutton cutlets
2 eggs
Some white breadcrumbs
3 oz. grated Parmesan cheese
Pepper and salt
2 oz. clarified butter
1 pt. Espagnole sauce (see p. 442)
Some mashed potatoes
Some well cooked macaroni

Method

Trim the cutlets neatly, brush them with egg and cover them with breadcrumbs mixed with 2 oz. of the Parmesan cheese and a little pepper and salt; flatten the crumbs on to the cutlets. Fry them from 4–5 mins. in the cutlet-pan in the clarified butter or fat skimmings. Serve with Espagnole sauce, mashed potatoes and macaroni to garnish.

Mutton Cutlets à la Soubise
Ingredients

Small mutton cutlets
Egg and breadcrumbs
Little clarified butter
Mashed potatoes
Soubise sauce (see p. 447)

Method

Trim and egg and breadcrumb the cutlets, flattening the crumbs on with a knife. Fry them in the butter, and dish on a border of mashed potatoes, in a circle. Pour the Soubise sauce round the base, using 1 pt. sauce for every 12 cutlets; if liked, glazed button onions may be put in the centre.

Mutton Stew. See IRISH STEW.

N

NAARTJE. Cape Orange about the size of a mandarin.

NASEBERRY. See SAPODILLA..

NASTURTIUM (Fr. *capucine*). Indian cress, a native of Peru, but acclimatised in Britain. The seeds, which have such a pungent taste, are used for culinary purposes in pickles, also as mock capers. Leaf and flower are both used in salads. The young shoots also make good pickles.

Nasturtium Buds, Pickled. Gather the buds on a dry day and leave them for 3 days, then put into a jar, pour spiced boiling vinegar over them and, when cold, tie cover over the jar. Leave several months before use.

Nasturtium Flower Vinegar. Pick sufficient full-blown nasturtium flowers to fill a quart bottle; add ½ clove of garlic and 1 chopped shallot. Fill up the bottle with vinegar. Leave for 2 mths., then rub the whole through a very fine sieve. Season with cayenne pepper and salt and bottle.

Nasturtium Salad. Pick the required quantity of nasturtium flowers; put them in a salad bowl and sprinkle over them 1 tbsp. finely chopped chervil and a small quantity of salt. Squeeze the juice of two lemons in 3 tbsp. salad oil, stir it until well mixed, then pour over the salad, toss it about with a wooden spoon and serve without delay.

Nasturtium Sauce. Stir 3 tbsp. pickled nasturtium seeds into a teacupful of Drawn butter (see p. 96) in a saucepan and add a little salt and pepper. Place the pan at the side of the fire and simmer gently. It is then ready for use.

Nasturtium Seeds, Pickled. Put the nasturtium seeds in a basin and pour over some strong boiling brine, straining, boiling it again and pouring it over frequently (every few days) for 3 wks. or so. Then put the seeds into some clear water, changing it repeatedly in order to extract the salt. Put them into bottles and pour over them some boiling vinegar mixed with cloves, allspice, ginger, mace and sugar, using 2½ oz. of these to each 1 pt. vinegar. When cold, tie down the bottles and put them in a cool place.

NATIVES. A popular name in England given to English oysters from the Essex and Kentish beds.

NEAT'S FEET. See COWHEEL.

NEAT'S TONGUES. See OX TONGUE.

NECK. This is the name given to that part of the animal which intervenes between the shoulders and the head, supporting the latter, and being therefore proportionately muscular and ligamentous, not considered a choice part for culinary purposes. But it can be utilised with good effect. See **MUTTON,** etc.

NECTARINE (Fr. *brugnon*). The nectarine is a smooth-skinned variety of the peach. Although allied to the almond, the covering of the stone differs entirely. Nectarines are better suited for culinary purposes than peaches, probably in consequence of the delicate flavour of the fruit. The Spanish nectarine or Cocoplum is quite distinct.

TO CANDY NECTARINES. See **FRUIT.**

Green Nectarine Pickle. Put a thin layer of salt on a dish: over this put a layer of green nectarines, then salt, then more fruit and continue this way until as much is used as is required. Cover with a thick coating of salt and leave for 4–5 days. Carefully remove fruits, wipe them dry and place in sun to dry for 3–4 days, then pack into jars and pour over, when cold, sweet pickling vinegar; cover and store for future use.

NEEDLES. These are used in both larding and trussing; the spiral, long trussing needle makes it easy to sew the bird together.

NEGUS. Mix a bottle of port or sherry with twice its bulk of hot water sweetened with ¼ lb. lump sugar. Flavour this with the juice of a lemon and a grated nutmeg. The thin peel of a lemon, 10 drops of essence of ambergris and 1 tsp. essence of vanilla greatly improve the flavour.

NEPAUL PEPPER. A species of capsicum. Yellowish pepper of the same character as cayenne and guinea pepper, pungent in flavour but less hot. Grown in Hindustan.

NEROLI. Orange flower essence.

NETTLES. These are delicious when gathered young and tender and cooked. They should not be left until the flowers appear, as they then become stringy and the leaves strong-flavoured.

NETTLES, TO BOIL. Wash well young tender nettles, then chop finely and place in a saucepan with very little water and steam until tender. Toast 2–3 slices of bread, trim crusts, and lay on a dish. Drain the nettles well and spread on dish. Dust with pepper and salt and add a little melted butter and a squeeze of lemon juice. Serve quickly.

NETTLE, DEAD. Bee Nettle, Blind Nettle. Used medicinally.

NOGGIN. A small measure equivalent to a gill.

NORFOLK DUMPLINGS. Frequently called drop dumplings, or spoon dumplings, because the batter, made of milk, flour and egg is dropped in the boiling water from a spoon. See **DUMPLINGS.**

NORMANDY PIPPINS. Apples that have been peeled, cooked and dried under pressure (see **BIFFINS**), which, when soaked, can be stewed and flavoured with moist sugar and cloves and a little lemon peel and simmered gently. Arrange in a glass dish.

NOUGAT

Ingredients	*Method*
10 oz. almonds	Blanch and dry the almonds, shred them
½ lb. pounded sugar	and put them inside the oven until a golden colour. Dissolve the sugar until it is a light golden colour, and add the almonds quite hot. Mix them well in, pour at once on to an oiled slab or dish. Press the mixture out flat, using an oiled lemon for the purpose, and then line the mould or moulds you intend to use. They should previously have been well oiled, and they should be lined as quickly as possible.

NOUILLES or NUDELS. These are virtually the same, the former being a French adaptation of the original German paste, but national tastes have served in a measure to modify the shapes and applications as will be seen by the following definitions which classify the variations into nouilles, nudels, and damf nudels. The best paste for these is made by working together eggs and flour in the proportion of 5 eggs to 1 lb. sifted flour. This is then manufactured into *nouilles* by making a stiff dough and rolling out very thinly, cutting up in thin strips and boiling. Served as a garnish or fried, also as a sweet savoury. *Nudels* are made with the same kind of paste but the peculiarity of these, according to the German idea, is that they are cut into shreds or thin strips of ½″ or ¼″ thick,

NOUILLES or NUDELS (*continued*)

and boiled in boiling salted water for about ¼ hr., then used as desired. *Damf Nudels* are made of nudel paste, to which ½ oz. yeast has been added to each 3 lb. flour and 4 eggs, and a little sugar and milk, so that in cooking they swell up, and are much lighter. For recipes, see **MACARONI** and **SPAGHETTI**.

NUT (Fr. *noisette*). Nuts may be described as the fruit of certain trees and shrubs, containing within a hard case, a kernel more or less pleasing to taste. They will be found under their own headings.

TO BLANCH. Remove shell and place in boiling water for a few mins. (see **ALMONDS, CHESTNUTS**), then into cold.

Nut Cakes. Mix together 4 tbsp. oatflakes and 1 oz. chopped nuts and bind with 1 tbsp. honey or golden syrup. Knead and form into small cakes, place in a greased tin and bake until well browned at 350° F. Therm. 4.

Nut Hash. Using any pieces of nut roast left over, chop up the pieces and mix with cold sliced potatoes. Melt 2 oz. margarine in a pan, add 1 tsp. vegetable extract and the nut hash. Turn out when well browned and serve garnished with cress.

Nut Roast—I. Cook a grated onion in ¼ pt. water until tender. Add 1 oz. margarine, pepper and salt, 1 tbsp. chopped parsley, 1 cup each chopped walnuts, grated cheese and breadcrumbs, and mix well together. Pour into a well-greased shallow fireproof dish and bake until brown at 350° F. Therm. 4. Serve garnished with watercress.

Nut Roast—II. Mix together 1 cup each nuts and breadcrumbs and put them through a mincing machine or grinder. Add 1 cup boiled rice, ¼ tsp. sago. ½ tsp. thyme, 1 grated onion, pepper and salt and 1 oz. butter. Dissolve 1 tsp. vegetable extract in a cup of boiling water and pour on the dry ingredients. Mould and place in a greased tin with a little margarine and bake at 350° F. Therm. 4, and baste well while roasting. Serve with Cheese sauce.

Nut Salad—I. Mix together 1 cup each shelled walnuts and raisins, dress with French dressing and place in the centre of a bowl. Garnish round with shredded spinach.

Nut Salad—II. Mix together 1 cup each chopped nuts and grated cheese, and a small grated onion or a good chopping of chives. Place on a bed of lettuce leaves and serve garnished with chopped parsley.

Nut Sauce. *Cold.* Use mayonnaise and add chopped nuts and a garnish of chopped chives.

Hot. Use white sauce and add chopped nuts and golden syrup.

Nut Soufflé. Melt 1 oz. butter, add 1 oz. flour and stir until blended. Gradually add ½ pt. milk and stir constantly over heat until it boils. Then add 2 oz. breadcrumbs, ½ tsp. salt, a sprinkle of pepper and celery salt, 1 tsp. grated onion, 1 cup cold chopped nut roast or 1 cup chopped nuts and the beaten yolks of 2 eggs. Mix all together and fold in the beaten whites of the eggs. Place in a well-greased soufflé dish and bake until browned at 350° F. Therm. 4. Serve with Tomato sauce.

Nut Spread. Mix together finely grated nuts, chopped parsley or chives and cream cheese, and use to spread on toast or cracker biscuits. Garnish with a little sprinkling of paprika.

NUT FATS. Obtainable in both hard and soft forms; they give good results when combined with other fats.

NUTMEG (Fr. *noix de Muscade*). The shelled seed of a tree which grows from 20–25 ft. high, with oblong aromatic leaves and fruit something like a peach, having a longitudinal groove on one side and bursting into two pieces. When the enclosed seed, covered by mace, is exposed, the seed itself has a thick hard outer shell, which may be removed when dry, and which encloses the nucleus of the seed. Grated nutmeg is used for flavouring cakes, puddings, etc.

O

OAT. Oats contain, though not in such well-balanced proportions as wheat, all the nutritional properties.

OATMEAL. Oatmeal is the grain of the oat deprived of the skin, kiln-dried, and afterwards ground in a mill. It is rich and oily or fatty, and as a flesh-former holds high rank; it is generally considered a complete food. There are three kinds of oatmeal, coarse, fine and groats, the latter being unground. The coarse or fine depend upon the grinding.

Oatmeal Biscuits or Farls. Mix 1 lb. medium oatmeal, ½ lb. flour and 1 tbsp. baking powder. Rub in ½ lb. butter; when quite smooth stir in sufficient warm milk to knead the whole into a paste. Turn on to a board and roll out very thinly. Using a round cutter of about 2″ diameter, cut the paste into rounds. Lay them on baking sheets and bake at 400° F. Therm. 6 for about 5 mins.

Oatmeal Porridge (Brochan). Use medium oatmeal, put 1 pt. water into a saucepan over a low heat, bring to the boil and add 1 tsp. oatmeal. Mix in 1 teacup cream, together with sufficient salt to taste. Boil for about 1 hr. Serve in cups or small basins with a little golden syrup, or, if preferred, thin slices of cheese. **Gruel** is thin porridge made by boiling meal in milk and water.

OCHRA or OCRA. See **OKRA.**

OCTAVE. A small cask of wine holding about 1½ galls.

OFFAL. The technical name given to those parts of a slaughtered animal that are not supposed to be used for food, such as the hide and the internal parts. But most of these are now specially dressed and make very tasty dishes. See individual entries for recipes.

OIL (Fr. *huile*). A sort of fluid grease extracted from animal, vegetable or mineral substances. The best-known oil to cooks is salad or olive oil. Some others, such as seed, etc., are used for frying.

OKA. A cheese from Canada, richly flavoured.

OKRA. The name of this plant is also spelt Ochra, or Ocra. It is a native of the West Indies, but also grows elsewhere. The pods are used to thicken soup, being exceedingly mucilaginous and aromatic. Okra is cooked like aubergine and sometimes pickled.

OKRA, BOILED. Put some young okras into a saucepan of salted water and boil them until quite tender. Take them out and drain, then place in a saucepan with a little more than 1 tbsp. butter and ½ gill cream. Place over low heat and reboil, then turn on to a dish, dust over with salt and pepper and serve very hot.

OLD MAN. See **SOUTHERNWOOD.**

OLD SQUAW. A common sea duck of the Northern Hemispheres.

OLEIC ACID. An oily acid found in the form of oleine in some fats and oils, such as olive oil, sperm oil, etc.

OLEINE. A fat substance contained in animal fat, i.e. pig fat, and to a lesser degree in that of mutton or beef. Causes fluidity.

OLIVE. The fruit of the olive tree is extensively cultivated in Italy, Spain and France. The unripe green fruit is pickled in brine, and served at table to cleanse and prepare the palate for choice wines. Olives are also served as appetisers with the sherry or cocktails. The ripe black olives yield oil which is used for culinary

OLIVE (*continued*)

purposes. Olives are oval in shape and with a smooth rind, resembling small green plums, and they grow in massive bunches on the trees. They are usually bought pickled in brine. When served at table, it is usual to place here and there a few small glass dishes of olives. However, they are also used in various other ways.

OLIVES, HOT, RIPE. Drain the ripe olives and add to the liquid 1 clove minced garlic or 2 minced shallots. Bring the liquid to the boil, add the olives and when they are well heated through, drain and serve very hot on toothpicks.

OLIVES FOR GARNISH. Remove the stones from some large olives by cutting them round and round in a spiral form so that when the stones are out the olives retain their original form. Put them into a saucepan, cover with stock and wine in equal proportions and stew very slowly until done. This garnish is frequently used for salmi of duck.

OLIVES IN SANDWICHES. Stone and chop the olives. Mix them with fresh butter and a pinch of cayenne pepper. Cut some very thin slices of bread and butter and spread them with the olive mixture. Press another slice of bread over each, cut into fingers and arrange on a folded napkin or dish paper and serve.

OLIVE, BEEF. See BEEF.

OLIVE OIL. Excellent oil of good texture and very little taste, therefore especially good for frying. There are Spanish, Italian and French olive oils. When the olives are ripe they are gathered and gently pressed, by which means the best quality of oil is obtained. A stronger pressure is applied which breaks the kernels and produces a second quality oil. After settling, the bright oil is at once put into flasks. The inferior quality is exported in casks or jars.

OMELET (Fr. *omelette*). An omelet can be described as eggs beaten up sometimes with water and milk. If possible, always use an omelet pan. If you possess no such pan use a scrupulously clean frying pan.

TO PROVE A PAN. When you use a new pan, add a sprinkling of salt to the bottom and place it over a gentle heat. Scour well, rubbing the salt round with a piece of paper, then polish with a clean, soft, dry cloth. Take a walnut-sized piece of fat, place in pan over gentle heat; let the fat melt, continue heating until the fat darkens and runs and covers the surface, so that the pan is both well greased and hot. Pour the fat away, add the butter and you are ready to make the omelet.

FAT. Whenever possible, use butter for omelets. It gives a much better flavour and also prevents the omelet sticking to the pan.

EGGS. Use the freshest of eggs and beat them well so that plenty of air is introduced into the mixture. An omelet depends on these tiny air bubbles for its lightness; their expansion is caused by the heat of the cooking medium. As eggs do not retain air as well as the gluten of flour, the mixture should not be kept long before cooking.

OMELET, PLAIN OR FRENCH (BASIC RECIPE)

Ingredients

Savoury

To each egg used add ½ oz. butter

½ tsp. finely chopped parsley

⅛ tsp. salt

Pinch of pepper

Small chopping of onion (if desired)

Sweet

For each egg used add ½ oz. butter

1 tsp. each sugar and water

Method

Break the eggs into a basin and beat well with a fork. Add flavourings and seasonings, or sugar. Add one-third butter cut into tiny pieces. Beat again. Season the pan by melting a walnut of fat in it. When it is smoking hot, pour away and rub the pan with soft paper to prevent the omelet sticking. Melt the rest of the butter and when the pan is very hot and the butter froths, pour in the egg mixture and stir lightly on the top with a fork over a very quick heat; an omelet should not

[350]

OMELET, PLAIN OR FRENCH (BASIC RECIPE) (*continued*)

Flavouring

Jam or purée

take more than 3 mins. to cook. As it begins to set, and if you are not folding in any other ingredients, tilt the pan and scrape the mixture into a half-moon shape to one side of the pan. Leave it for a moment or two to set, slightly pulling the pan away from or reducing heat. When an omelet is done, it should be quite moist in the centre. An overcooked omelet is heavy. Place the hot dish against the pan, with a very quick movement invert omelet on to it, and serve immediately. When adding other ingredients to an omelet, do not shape it but keep it round, lifting up the edges as it begins to set so that the liquid flows underneath it. When almost done, place the filling in the centre and fold over. Cook for a minute longer and serve. Omelets should be a light golden brown colour when served. Savoury omelet may be glazed, if desired, by brushing with a little melted butter just before serving. Sweet omelets, after folding, are dredged lightly with fine sugar and placed under a hot grill for a minute before serving.

SAVOURY FILLINGS AND SEASONINGS. For a 2-egg omelet—1 oz. cheese, $\frac{1}{2}$ tsp. chopped chervil, tarragon, chives, shallots or mixed herbs. These are added to egg before cooking.

1$\frac{1}{2}$ oz. bacon or ham, diced and cooked in 1 oz. butter, 1$\frac{1}{2}$ oz. mushrooms, sliced and cooked in $\frac{3}{4}$ oz. butter. These are folded into the cooked omelet just before serving.

2 small skinned sliced tomatoes, tossed and heated through in $\frac{3}{4}$ oz. butter, placed in the middle of the omelet just as it sets before serving.

Omelet with Fine Herbs. Break 2 eggs into a basin and mix in a little chopped shallot, a small pinch each of thyme, marjoram, basil, chervil and parsley. Sprinkle in a very little pepper. Melt 1 oz. butter in a pan over low heat, tossing the butter so that it goes all over the pan, but do not let it burn. When at boiling point, pour in the omelet mixture and fry until golden brown.

Omelet Soufflé

Ingredients

4 egg yolks

6 whites of egg

1 tsp. grated lemon rind or flavouring

1 dsp. caster sugar

Method

Separate the yolks from whites of egg. Beat the yolks until they are light in colour, add the sugar and lemon peel or flavouring, whisk the whites of egg to a very stiff froth, fold into the yolks, and pour mixture into a well-greased omelet pan. Bake in the oven at 400° F. Therm. 6 for about 10 mins. Invert the omelet on

[351]

Omelet Soufflé (*continued*)

to a hot dish and sprinkle with sugar before serving.

For a smaller omelet, use half quantities of ingredients and only bake 5 mins.

Omelet Soufflé, Savoury. Omit the flavouring essence and substitute pepper and salt for the sugar. Serve the omelet with a rich gravy poured over it.

ONION (Fr. *oignon*). The onion belongs to the tribe of lilies but it is readily distinguished from the sweet-scented flowers by the odour of the bulbs. There are many varieties of onions and they vary in size. The Spanish onion has a milder flavour than the English variety.

TO PEEL. Hold the onion under cold water while peeling. This reduces the risk of watering eyes. Wash the knife in cold water after peeling to remove onion flavour.

ONIONS, BAKED. 1. Prepare some onions and put them into a greased tin; cook gently in a moderate oven (350° F. Therm. 4) for about 1 hr. until tender.

2. Wash well, dry and remove root but not skins. Place in greased tin and bake at 350° F. Therm. 4 for about 1 hr. (Sometimes baked onions are stuffed with forcemeat before cooking.)

ONIONS, BOILED. Peel some onions and place in a saucepan with sufficient water to cover them and boil until tender. Place them on a dish, pour over the Butter sauce and serve. Or they may be finely chopped and stewed with milk, butter and a little salt.

ONIONS, FRIED. 1. Slice finely and fry until golden brown, drain on paper, reheat fat and put the onions in to crisp.

2. Dip the onions into seasoned flour and fry in deep fat, drain, reheat fat and fry again to crisp, then drain on paper.

3. Peel and slice 2 lb. Spanish onions and put them into a frying pan containing 2 tbsp. butter. Heat to smoking hot, season with salt and pepper and stir until tender. When done, serve as a garnish or on toast, pouring over the gravy they yield.

ONIONS, PICKLED. Take the outer peel from as many small round onions as required, dry them well and put them into a saucepan. Cover with vinegar and parboil them. Remove the onions with a skimmer and place into hot, wide-mouthed bottles in layers alternating with finely sliced green ginger, red chillies and black peppercorns, adding a sprinkling of salt. Fill up with fresh vinegar. Cork securely and use as desired.

ONIONS, STEWED

Ingredients	Method
Some Spanish onions	Peel the onions, flour them and fry them a light brown in some dripping, then put into a stewpan. Cover with stock and simmer gently over a low heat for 2½–3 hrs. until tender. Thicken the gravy with a little flour and season to taste. Serve on a hot dish with the gravy poured over.
Stock	
Dripping	
Flour	
Pepper and salt	

Onions with Mushroom Sauce

Ingredients	Method
6 large onions sliced	Place onions in greased casserole. Combine soup and water and pour over onions. Sprinkle with cheese. Cover and bake at 350° F. Therm. 4 for 1 hr. Canned mushrooms may also be added to the soup mixture.
1 tin condensed mushroom soup	
½ cup water	
½ cup grated cheese	

Onion Pie

Ingredients

3 large onions
2 oz. butter
3 tbsp. flour
½ pt. cream or evaporated milk
Salt and pepper
2 eggs

Method

Sauté onions, chopped finely, in butter until golden brown. Sprinkle in flour and stir in cream. Add salt and pepper and stir until mixture thickens. Remove from heat and add two well-beaten eggs. Pour this mixture into a pie-crust, add top crust and bake for 30 mins. at 400° F. Therm. 6. Serve hot with roast beef.

Onion Soup. See SOUPS.

Onions, Stuffed

Ingredients

6 large onions
8 oz. sausage meat
½ tsp. salt
1 tsp. mixed herbs
1 tbsp. butter
1 tbsp. flour
¾ cup milk

Method

Place onions in water and boil for 15 mins. Remove, and carefully scoop out centres without piercing bottom. Mix sausage meat, herbs and salt together, stuff centre of each onion with mixture and place on baking dish. Make sauce of butter, flour and milk, stir and cook till thickened, pour round onions and bake at 350° F. Therm. 4 for ½ hr. Baste during baking with the sauce.

Onion Sauce. See SAUCES (Soubise).

OPAH. This deep-sea fish, caught principally in the Atlantic Ocean, is commonly known as the King of Herrings, but as it has coarse flesh it is not much used for culinary purposes.

ORACH. French spinach or Mountain spinach. This annual was a popular pot herb from the sixteenth to the nineteenth century. The whole plant is used medicinally and the seed as an emetic.

ORANGE. The extensive family of citrus fruits to which this fruit belongs includes the lemon, the lime, the citron, the bergamot and the shaddock. Tangerines and Mandarins are the smallest oranges, Jaffas the largest.

ORANGE PEEL, TO CANDY. See LEMON (p. 314).

ORANGES, TO CANDY. See FRUIT (p. 325).

Orange Brandy. Into a brown mug put the rind of 8 lemons and the rind of 8 Seville oranges, peeled very fine, 3 lb. loaf sugar and a pinch of saffron. Steep all together for 3 days in a gall. of the best French brandy, stirring it well 3 or 4 times a day. Then strain it off into bottles, cork well and seal. It will be fit for use in 3 wks., but improves by keeping.

Orange Gin. Take the peel of 8 lemons and 8 Seville oranges cut thinly, add 3 lb. loaf sugar and 1 gall. unsweetened gin, and stir 3 times daily for 1 week. Strain through muslin and bottle. Keep at least 6 mths. before using.

Orange Marmalade, Seville

Ingredients

9 Seville oranges
2 sweet oranges
9 pt. water
9 lb. sugar
2 lemons

Method

Slice the fruit very thinly, place pips in cupful of water to soak. Place fruit in the water and allow to stand for 24 hrs. Next day boil until fruit is tender, add water pips were soaked in, and sugar, and boil

12*

Orange Marmalade, Seville (*continued*)

until marmalade thickens. Test for setting, pour into heated jars and cover when cool.

Orange Marmalade, Seville (Jelly)

Ingredients

12 Seville oranges
3 sweet oranges
2 lemons
12 pt. water
Sugar

Method

Peel the fruit thinly, cut into very fine shreds and place in large muslin bag. Place bag in preserving pan and cover with the water. Allow to stand for 12 hrs. Next day boil for 3 hrs., then remove muslin bag. Strain pulp, place contents of bag in liquid and measure. Add equal amount of sugar, and boil until it sets, about 30 mins. Allow to cool for 30 mins. before pouring into jars.

Orange Marmalade, Seville (Transparent)

Ingredients

6 lb. Seville oranges
6 qt. water
Sugar

Method

Slice the oranges very thinly, remove pips, and weigh fruit. Place in bowl with the water and allow to soak for 24 hrs. Next day boil until the rinds are quite clear. Allow to stand for a further 24 hrs. Then weigh the pulp and rinds and allow 1½ lb. sugar to every pound of pulp. Place together in preserving pan and boil until the rind is clear. Test for setting, pour into warmed jars and cover when cool.

Orange Marmalade, Sweet

Ingredients

20 oranges
5 lb. sugar
Water
Juice of 3 lemons

Method

Wash and dry oranges. Remove rind, grate or shred, place in pan of cold water and boil until tender. Prepare the pulp by removing "rag" in centre of core, and pips. Cook in separate pan until tender, then add to shredded rind and measure. Add sugar and boil for 20 mins., then add lemon juice. Test for setting, pour into warmed jars and cover when cold. (If desired, apple pulp may be added while the marmalade is still hot and thick).

Orange Marmalade, Tangerine

Ingredients

18 tangerines
3 lemons
Twice weight of oranges in sugar

Method

Wipe fruit with damp cloth and place in a preserving pan with water to cover. Boil until the rind can be pierced with a wooden skewer. Remove from water, cut

Orange Marmalade, Tangerine (*continued*)

each fruit into four and scoop out pulp with a spoon. Press the pulp through a sieve. Soak pips in basin of water for 24 hrs. Shred rind very thinly and place in a basin with pulp until next day. Then place rind, pulp, water from pips, sugar and lemon juice in preserving pan and boil gently to a syrup. Test for setting, pour into warmed jars and cover when cool.

Orange and Onion Salad. Take juicy oranges, peel them, removing as much of the white pith as possible. Slice them thinly, removing any pips; peel an onion (if you have home-grown ones, then your salad will be superb), slice to tissue-paper thinness and place on a flat dish in alternate layers. Dress with 3 tbsp. salad oil, combined with a seasoning of pepper and salt, small pinch of mustard, 1 tbsp. vinegar and lemon juice. Leave 2 hrs., serve garnished with finely chopped parsley. See also SALADS for **Orange Salad.**

Orange Pudding. Line a dish with puff paste (see p. 373). Take 6 oranges, pare peel very thin, boil, pound and rub through a sieve with the juice. Add 1 teacup breadcrumbs, 4 oz. sifted sugar, and yolks of 4 eggs. Beat the whites to a stiff froth and mix with the other ingredients at the last minute. Bake ¾ hr. at 350° F. Therm. 4.

Orange Sauce and Bigarade Sauce. See SAUCES.

ORANGE FLOWER. Though oranges are seldom grown in this country, the flowers grow profusely in greenhouses and have a strong perfume. The mock orange is erroneously called Syringa, the name which really belongs to the lilac. To candy flowers, see **FRUIT** (p. 235).

ORANGE-FLOWER WATER. Flavouring taken from orange flowers and used in both cakes and icings and in conserves.

OREGANO. Wild Marjoram. It has a more pungent flavour than Sweet Marjoram.

ORMERS or ORMER-SHELLS. This is the name given to certain shellfish which are found on the rocks round the coast of Jersey. They have but one beautifully coloured shell resembling in shape the human ear, hence they are commonly called Sea-ears or Ear Shells. They may be prepared and dressed as scallops or pickled.

ORRIS- or ORRICE-ROOT. The rhizome of a species of Iris (of which word "orris" is probably a corruption), which, when dried, develops an odour of violets and is used as a substitute for this flower in flavouring.

ORTOLAN (Fr. *ortolan*). This is the name given to a European singing bird about the size of a lark. It is a great delicacy.

OSTRICH EGGS. These are edible but rare.

OUNCE. The sixteenth part of a pound avoirdupois and the twentieth part of a pint.

OVAR. A Hungarian cow's milk cheese with a reddish brown crust and yellow-coloured inside; it has a mild and piquant taste.

OVEN TEMPERATURES. In the following table, the approximate oven setting is given for cooking both by Electricity and Gas. When the dial on the thermostat is set at a given reading the temperature inside the oven remains constant automatically. However, there are two zones in an oven. This enables you to cook a complete meal, the hotter or upper part being used for dishes requiring more heat while the base plate is used for dishes which require less heat.

[*Continued on page* 358

CHART OF GAS OVEN SETTINGS

(By courtesy of the North Thames Gas Board)

Having chosen the dish you want to cook, refer to column 1. If your dish is shown, then look in the column applicable to the make of cooker you have, and, opposite the dish you are preparing, you will find the setting—either a number or a letter—at which the thermostat should be set.

If your Cookery Book advises you to cook a recipe in a "cool" or maybe "moderate" oven, by referring to column 2 you will find in one of the adjacent columns the appropriate setting of the thermostat to be used with your particular cooker.

Finally, if you have a very modern or American Cookery Book you will find that the temperature at which the dish should be cooked is given. In this case, find the thermostat setting of your cooker opposite to the temperature given in column 3.

When the dial on the thermostat is set at a given reading, the temperature inside the oven remains constant, automatically. There are, however, two zones inside the oven, and it is this fact that enables you to cook a complete meal in the oven. Remember that you can use the baseplate or oven floor for dishes requiring less heat, while the upper—and hotter—part is used for dishes requiring more heat.

1	2	3	4	5	6	7	8	9	10	11	12	13	14	15	16	17	18	19	20	21
TYPE OF FOOD	HEAT OF OVEN	CENTRE OVEN TEMP. °F	CANNON			FLAVEL			GEN'L GAS	MAIN			PARKINSON				RADIATION			STOVES
			COTTAGE TALBOT	K.508	K.509	KABINEAT	37	45 SPEEDWAY	PRIMAX 4 27 C.31	57 1028 1228	177 14 177 16	GLC. 0 & 1 GLE. 0 & 1 290 291 292 293	CROWN A	RENOWN Mk. I	RENOWN Mk. II Mk. IV	CREST	F.202	545 548 1430 345 348	202 302 (side thermostats)	1478
Fruit Bottling		240°	½	½	¼	A		¼	¼	A	¼	2	1	0	0	1	¼	¼	¼	¼
Stews	Very Cool					B	1								1					
		260°																		
Custards			1	1	½		2	½	½	B	½	3	2			2	½	½	½	½
Egg Dishes		280°				C								1	2					
Milk Puddings			2	2	1		3	1	1		1		3	2		3	1	1	1	1
Rich Fruit Cake	Cool	300°								C		4								
Slow Roasting			3	3	2	D		2	2		2		4	3	3				2	
Soup & Stock		320°					4									4	2	2		2
Shortbread	Warm																		3	
Biscuits		340°		4	3			3	3	D	3	5					3	3		3
Madeira Cake	Moderate		4			E	5						5	4	4	5			4	
		360°		5	4			4	4		4						4	4		4
Queen Cakes			5			F	6					6		5	5				5	
Sponges	Fairly Hot	380°		6	5			5	5	E	5		6			6				
																	5	5		5
Plate Tarts		400°	6	7	6	G	7	6	6		6			6	6	7		6	6	6
Scones										F		7	7				6			
Roast Dinners	Hot	420°	7	8	7		8	7	7		7								7	
						H							8	7	7	8	7	7		7
Puff and Flaky Pastry		440°	8	9	8		9	8	8	G	8	8						8	8	8
	Very Hot	460°				I									8	9	8			
		480°																		

OVEN TEMPERATURES (*continued*)

Degrees Fahrenheit	Degrees Centigrade	Description of Oven	If You Have No Thermostatic Control on Your Oven
200–250		Very slow	Cool to the hand
250–300	121–149	Slow oven	Comfortably hot to hand
300–325	149–163	Very moderate oven	Comfortably hot to hand
325–375	163–191	Moderate oven	
375–400	191–204	Moderately hot	Uncomfortably hot to the hand; a little sprinkling of flour on the oven shelf should turn light brown in 2–3 mins.
400–450	204–232	Hot quick oven	Uncomfortably hot to the hand; a little sprinkling of flour on the oven shelf should turn brown in 2–3 secs.
450–500	232–260	Very hot oven	Tiny piece of paper turns brown in 5 mins.

OX. The cook uses this term in a limited sense, generally applied to offal only. It is the male of the beef-providing beast.

OX CHEEK
Ox Cheek, Braised

Ingredients

1 ox cheek
½ lb. sausage meat or veal stuffing
1 carrot
1 turnip
1 onion
1 sprig each parsley, thyme, marjoram
1 bay leaf
Pepper and salt
1 qt. stiff second stock
3 tomatoes or ½ head celery
Vegetables for garnish

Method

Remove all the bone, lay the forcemeat on the inside of the cheek, roll it up and secure it firmly with string. Cut the vegetables in pieces, lay them in the bottom of a braising-pan and put the meat on them. Add seasoning, pour in enough stock to come halfway up the meat, cover it with buttered paper, braise for 3 or 4 hrs. until the meat is tender. The meat should be basted constantly while cooking. Place on a hot dish in the oven. Strain stock into a saucepan and boil rapidly down to a glaze. Remove the string and, if necessary, place silver skewers in place. Pour over the glaze and garnish with vegetables.

OX KIDNEY. See **KIDNEY.**

OX MARROW. The fatty contents of the long bones of the ox are esteemed a great delicacy.

[358]

Ox Marrow Bones, Boiled

Ingredients	Method
½ marrow bone per person	Saw the bones to any size desired, and
Salt	cover the ends with a paste of flour and
Paste of flour and water	water. Tie each in a cloth and place in
Pepper	boiling water. Simmer gently for about
Toast	2 hrs. and when cooked take off the cloth

Ingredients / *Method*

½ marrow bone per person
Salt
Paste of flour and water
Pepper
Toast

Saw the bones to any size desired, and cover the ends with a paste of flour and water. Tie each in a cloth and place in boiling water. Simmer gently for about 2 hrs. and when cooked take off the cloth and serve the bone upright on a folded napkin on a hot dish and hand toast, salt, pepper and cayenne. A special fork or spoon should be supplied to each person for removing the marrow from the bones. Another method of serving is to take the marrow from the bones, spread it on small squares of toast, sprinkle with salt, pepper and cayenne, and serve at once. As the marrow chills quickly, it should be served directly it is spread on the toast. Some people use hot water plates or dishes on which to serve the marrow.

OX PALATE (Fr. *palais de bœuf*). The thick white linings of the upper jaw of the ox, consisting of the roof of the mouth and extending from the front teeth to the posterior opening of the nose. They may be sautéed in butter and then served in a blanquette sauce; thickened with an egg liaison or minced they may be used as fillings with chopped, cooked mushrooms and Béchamel sauce.

Ox Palates with Espagnole Sauce

Ingredients

2 ox palates
Stock
1 onion stuck with 2 cloves
1 blade of mace
Mashed potatoes
A macedoine of any appropriate vegetables
1 pt. Espagnole sauce (see p. 439)

Method

Soak the palates in salt and water, then wash them thoroughly, blanch for 10 mins. and scrape well. Place in a saucepan with the stock, onion and mace (the stock should be well flavoured with vegetables), simmer for 4 hrs. or longer, until the palates are quite tender, then press between two dishes, with a weight on the top, until cold. Stamp into very small rounds. Heat these in a little stock, then dish on a border of mashed potatoes, with the vegetables in the centre and the sauce poured round them. Ox palates may also be braised and served with half-glaze Tomato or any brown sauce.

OX PITH. Marrow taken from the spinal column.

OX TAIL

Ox Tail, Stewed

Ingredients

1 ox tail
Water
Flour

Method

Cut the tail into pieces and put into cold water. Bring to the boil and boil for 10 mins.; take out, flour and fry to a nice

Ox Tail, Stewed (*continued*)

Butter
1 carrot
1 turnip
1 onion
1 sprig each parsley, thyme and marjoram
½ head celery
1 bay leaf
Pepper and salt
Some good second stock
1 wineglass claret

brown colour. Put into a saucepan with the vegetables, seasoning and sufficient stock to cover, simmer gently from 3–4 hrs. When the tail is tender, remove it and place on a hot dish. Thicken gravy with flour, using about ¾ oz. flour to every ½ pt. gravy, add claret, remove all grease, strain or tammy the sauce and pour over the pieces of tail. Garnish with small glazed carrots, olives or mushrooms.

Oxtail Soup. See SOUPS.

OX TONGUE. When the tongues have been smoked and hung for some time, they will require quite 24 hrs. soaking in cold water to soften them. When not so long hung, only 6 hrs. will be needed. When fresh from pickle, they need not be soaked unless they have been very much salted or have remained longer than necessary in the pickle. Put a tongue fresh from pickle into lukewarm water, and simmer it until quite tender (3 hrs. or more). If a smoked tongue, put it into cold water and bring very gradually to simmering point; it will then probably take about 4 hrs. to cook. When cooked, remove it and take the skin carefully off. To truss it into shape, place a table close to the wall and put on it a board, place another on this, upright against the side of the wall. Trim the tongue carefully, then place it with the root against the upright board and with two forks fasten it to the under board, making it into a nice shape. When cold remove forks.

If to be used hot, place tongue on a baking-tin, well cover it with buttered paper, and heat thoroughly in the oven at 350° F. Therm. 4, making sure that the tongue does not get dry; or it may be heated in stock. Then put it on a dish, place a frill around the root and cover the tongue with glaze or raspings.

Any of these sauces—Italian, Piquant, Tomato, Tartare and Béarnase—may be served with hot dressed tongue; serve also new potatoes and mint sauce.

If it is to be served cold, put the tongue on to a dish, fix a frilled paper round the root with skewer, wet it with a little hot jelly and garnish with parsley and chopped aspic. Glaze well with light glaze, spread a thick layer of Aspic jelly over the tongue and garnish it on a dish with attelettes of jelly and mushrooms.

OYSTER (Fr. *huître*). The oyster is a bivalve mollusc which lives in shallow waters, sounds, bays and river mouths, where the saltiness of the water is reduced by the flowing of fresh water from tributary streams. The oyster has a single muscle which closes its rough shell. Oyster meat is succulent and oysters are in season when there is an "R" in the month. The Native, which comes from the Essex or Kentish beds (Colchester and Whitstable), should never be cooked. Add only a squeeze of lemon juice and serve. Oysters are sold fresh and also canned, and may be served in many different and attractive ways: they may be added to beefsteak pies and puddings and also used in stuffing. French oysters are usually small: the best among them are *Marennes* both *Blanches* and *Vertes* and *Belons*. Portuguese oysters and Blue Points or the large American oysters are the only ones which should be used for cooking. American oysters are sometimes very large. Never overcook oysters, they should only be cooked until the edges just curl up, or they will be tough.

TO OPEN. An oyster should be held in the folds of a cloth in the palm of the hand or in a hole cut out of a piece of wood; inserting an oyster knife between the shell, use a see-saw motion and force it inwards, cutting the oyster away from the flat shell. When the knife has done its work, the flat shell can be removed. It is usual to remove the beards or fringes of the oysters before using them, but it is not absolutely necessary. After cutting the body loose from the deep shell, they are ready to serve or use as desired.

TO SERVE. Serve on an oyster plate (this stands in cracked ice) with lemon quarters and brown bread and butter, also white or chilli vinegar.

OYSTERS, BROILED—I

Ingredients	Method
2 doz. large oysters in shells	Take the opened oysters and arrange them on shallow baking dish, sprinkle with minced garlic, chopped parsley and the chopped bacon. Season to taste with pepper and salt and place under pre-heated grill about 3″ from flame; grill until the bacon is slightly browned. Serve very hot on half shells with lemon quarters.
2 cloves garlic minced	
2 tbsp. chopped parsley	
2 bacon rashers diced	
Salt and pepper	
Lemon quarters	

OYSTERS, BROILED—II. Drain 1 doz. oysters on a cloth. Melt butter in omelet pan then drop in oysters separately, turning them constantly and shaking the pan. When done, serve on buttered toast with a slice of lemon.

OYSTERS, CREAMED. Make an oyster stew. Thicken the base with 2 tbsp. flour blended in milk with a dab of butter.

OYSTER COCKTAILS. Allowing ½ doz. oysters for each cocktail, put them into cocktail glasses with a dressing for each of 1 tbsp. each sherry and wine vinegar (or lemon juice), a few grains of salt, shake of cayenne pepper and a few drops of tabasco. (For Cocktail Sauce, see **COCKTAILS, SAVOURY.**)

Angels on Horseback. See individual entry.

Oyster Bisque

Ingredients	Method
1 pt. parcooked oysters	Chop onion, add water and simmer for 10 mins. Scald milk with seasoning and strain, rubbing oysters through sieve. Melt butter and flour, blend and add to strained oyster mixture. Cook until smooth and thick. Serve very hot. See also SOUPS.
½ pt. water	
1 pt. milk	
1 onion	
Piece of celery	
Parsley	
1 bay leaf	
½ tsp. mace	
Pinch of salt and pepper	
2 tbsp. each butter and flour	

Oyster Patties. Line some patty pans with a rich puff paste, and put some large oysters, bearded and chopped, in a stewpan with a little pepper and salt, and a scrape of nutmeg and morsel of lemon peel. Simmer for about 2 mins. Put a small quantity of chopped oyster into each patty pan, cover with puff paste, and bake in a quick oven (400° F. Therm. 6) for 10–15 mins. until lightly browned.

Oyster Sauce. See SAUCES.

Oyster Soup. See SOUPS.

Oyster Stew. Drain the oysters, strain the liquor through a fine sieve to remove any pieces of shell. Put the oysters in the liquor into the top of a double boiler, add sufficient milk to well cover, and a slice of onion, seasoning of pepper and salt. Heat gently and cook until the edges of the oysters begin to curl, thicken with a little blend of flour or cornflour. Add a little cream and a knob of butter just before serving. Serve in preheated bowls garnished with chopped parsley.

OYSTER OF A FOWL. These are the two succulent morsels found on the back of a fowl, in the concavity of the bone on either side of the lower part of the fowl's back.

OYSTER PLANT. This plant somewhat resembles an oyster when cooked. It is prepared by scraping and putting into cold water to which a little vinegar has been added, then boiled in a little salted water for about 20 mins., or until tender. Drain and serve with melted butter seasoned with salt and pepper. A little cream can also be added if desired. See also **SALSIFY.**

P

PADDY. A name given to unhusked rice.

PALESTINE SOUP. This name is given to a soup made with Jerusalem artichokes.

PALETTE KNIVES. These are made in different sizes and for different purposes. To the confectioner they are of great use for mixing and working sugar.

PALM KERNEL OIL. An oil obtained from the kernels of the nuts of the oil-palm. In West Africa, under the name of palm butter, it enters largely into the composition of savoury dishes. This oil resembles coconut oil. It is free from fatty acid, but soon turns rancid when exposed to the air.

PALMITIN. A fat substance exising in human fat, butter and olive oil. It is harder than oleine.

PALOMET. A species of mushroom.

PANADA. A culinary paste of flour and water used by all cooks to give consistency to forcemeat; generally flavoured, seasoned and sweetened.

TO MAKE—I. Soak in warm water the fine crumbs of bread. When the mixture is quite soft and moist, put in a cloth and wring out the water. Then put into a saucepan with a lump of butter and a little salt. Beat it smooth and dry over a very slow heat, taking care that it does not brown, then put aside to cool. If desired, milk or a little broth may be used instead of butter.

II. To 2 tbsp. each of breadcrumbs and sugar, add a little grated nutmeg, 1 pt. cold water. Place over a low heat and boil for 5 mins. Add 2 wineglasses of wine and serve immediately.

PANCAKE (Fr. *crêpe* or *pannequet*). Thin flat cakes made of batter and fried in an omelet pan.

METHOD I

Ingredients
  2 tsp. flour
  Pinch of salt
  4 egg yolks
  2 egg whites
  Few drops orange-flower
    water

Method
Mix flour and salt; beat egg yolks and whites, add orange-flower water, then stir them with the flour. Leave to stand 1 hr. Pour batter into a jug. Butter a small omelet pan. Put in a small quantity of the batter and cook for 1 or 2 mins. Then turn and cook the other side. Turn on to a piece of sugared paper. Roll up the pancake, sift sugar over, add a squeeze of lemon juice and put it on a hot dish. Keep warm until remaining pancakes are made. Arrange on ornamental dish paper or dish and serve with lemon quarters.

METHOD II

Ingredients
  4 oz. flour
  Pinch of salt

Method
Sift salt and flour into a bowl, make a hole in the centre of the flour, and first

[363]

METHOD II. (*continued*)

½ pt. milk (or milk and water)

1 egg

breaking the egg into a saucer (to see that it is quite fresh), drop it into flour. Add the liquid gradually until half has been blended with the flour (using a wooden spoon) and the mixture is smooth, without lumps; beat well for 10–15 mins., or until the mixture is full of air bubbles. Stir and add the rest of the liquid, and leave 1 hr. Pour into jug. Proceed as in Method I.

Jam Pancakes (Fr. *crêpe aux confitures*). Cover half the cooked pancake with jam before rolling up.

Crêpe Suzette

Ingredients

1 lb. sifted flour

1 pt. milk

½ pt. water

2 eggs

1 tsp. each salt and salad oil

1 tsp. brandy

Method

Add milk and water gradually to sifted flour, beating the whole time so that the batter keeps its smooth consistency. Add eggs separately, salt, oil and brandy; beat well, and then pour ¼ cup batter into a large, well heated, greased frying-pan, moving the pan so that the whole surface is covered with batter. This covering must be a thin one. Leave a moment or two to brown on underside, then turn with a large palette knife, and cook for a moment on underside. Spread with a little of the following filling: 4 tbsp. butter creamed with 4–5 tbsp. sugar, the finely grated rind of two oranges, and 2–3 tsp. curaçao, cointreau or brandy. Roll up and serve.

PAN DOWDY. This is the eccentric name given to a deep pie or pudding made of baked apples or of sliced bread and apples baked together with no bottom crust.

PAN FRY. To sauté.

PAP. Any soft food for infants.

PAP BOAT. A kind of sauceboat or dish.

PAPAW. This is a fruit found on the shores of the Gulf of Mexico, West Indies to Peru. When the fruit is green, it is peeled, boiled and cut, and served with oil, vinegar and seasoning. When ripe, it is eaten raw with sugar or pepper and salt.

PAPER. Kitchen paper is occasionally very useful. It is used to tie round delicate meals to be baked or roasted; for absorbing and draining the hot fat from fritters, fried fish, etc.; for covering pies and other pastries that require thoroughly cooking before browning; for lining cake-tins (see **CAKES**); for covering jams and for making cases for small birds, cutlets, etc., also frills for shank bones, haunches, etc.

[364]

TO MAKE FRILLS. Fold a thin strip of paper and cut it evenly and neatly a little way through the folded margin and by reversing single frill results. Two or three strips can be served in the same way, laid over each other, and so forming a very elegant ornamentation. When making incisions, they may be cut (instead of straight) slanting, zigzag or scalloped and will, when made up, have a very pretty effect according to the arrangement adopted.

TO MAKE PAPER CASES. These require somewhat stiffer paper with an even, smooth surface, and they can be formed into either round or square shapes.

PAPILLOTE. The French term for a curl paper, commonly applied to the papers used for wrapping cutlets and other dainties before cooking. Buttered paper answers the same purpose when twisted along the edges (this is the origin of paper-bag cookery).

PAPRIKA. Hungarian red pepper; a kind of sweet capsicum more pungent than Spanish pepper; a spice prepared from the dried fruit of Turkish peppers (sweet peppers) used with veal, stews, chicken and beef, and as a garnish. This spice is pungent and should be used with care, especially in sauces and salad dressings.

PARADISE, GRAINS OF. See **CARDAMOM.**

PARADISE APPLE. See **TOMATO,** sometimes called by this name.

PARASOL. An edible fungi with wide, bell-shaped cap 3–8″ across, white gills, thin scaly stem, gradually widening at base with large movable ring.

PARBOIL. To partly boil.

PARCH. To burn or roast the surface of as in drying grain.

PARKIN. The name of a flat, round, spiced gingerbread cake which is manufactured on the fifth of November in almost every cottage in the neighbourhood of Leeds. It is also usual to send slices of parkin as presents.

Ingredients	*Method*
4 oz. flour	Sift the flour, salt and bicarb. soda
Pinch of salt	together. Put the fat and treacle in a
$\frac{1}{2}$ tsp. bicarb. soda	saucepan and allow to melt slowly. Add
4 oz. fat	the sugar to flour, add beaten egg and
1–2 tbsp. treacle	spices. Add the heated liquid and stir
3–4 oz. sugar	till a stiff consistency. Beat well and pour
1 egg	into a prepared tin. Place in oven at
$\frac{1}{2}$ tsp. cinnamon	375° F. Therm. 5. Reduce to a slow oven
	250° F. Therm. $\frac{1}{4}$ after 10 mins. Cook
	according to depth for $\frac{3}{4}$–$1\frac{1}{2}$ hr.

PARMESAN CHEESE. The hardest cheese of all, made in Parma and Emilia from cow's milk. In Italy it is known as Grana. A fully ripened Parmesan cheese should exude a sweet sticky substance which looks rather like honey. For this reason Parmesan cheese of the finest quality is called "honeyed".

PARR. This is the name applied to a young salmon until the close of its second year, when it loses its dark transverse bands by the super-addition of a silvery pigment. See **SALMON.**

PARSLEY. Native plant of Sardinia introduced into England in 1548. Used as a pot herb, in salads, sauces and as a garnish.

PARSLEY, FRIED. Carefully pick the stems from the parsley, wash it dry it on a cloth, put into a frying basket and then into hot fat and fry for a few minutes, taking care that the fat is not too hot or the parsley will lose its colour and be spoiled.

Parsley Butter. See **BUTTER** (Maître d'Hôtel).
Parsley Sauce. See **SAUCES** (p. 437).

PARSNIP (Fr. *panais*). The parsnip is an edible aromatic spindle-shaped root. It is a native of England and Ireland but is also met with in many other parts of Europe and Northern Asia. In the Channel Isles, the parsnips frequently grow to 18″ long and 6″ in diameter.

PARSNIPS, BAKED. Peel and wash some large parsnips and cut them lengthwise into quarters. Steam them for 1 hr. Take them out, put them in a baking-dish with a little salt and meat dripping and bake until nicely browned. Drain and put on a hot dish to serve.

PARSNIPS, BOILED. Scrape 3 large parsnips and slice them ½″ thick and 2″ long. Boil in salted water until tender. Drain off water. Add to parsnips, 2 tbsp. butter and 1 teacup cream; season with pepper and salt. Reheat and serve.

Parsnip Pudding. Peel and wash 2 large parsnips. Cut into halves and boil until tender. Drain and mash them smooth with a piece of butter, sweetening to taste with caster sugar and flavouring with a small quantity of grated lemon peel or powdered cinnamon. Stir in a wineglass of brandy and sufficient beaten eggs to make a stiff batter. Turn into a well-buttered pudding basin, sprinkle with breadcrumbs, tie down securely and boil for 1 hr. Serve with sweet sauce.

PARSON'S NOSE or POPE'S NOSE. The extreme end portion of the tail of a fowl.

PARTRIDGE (Fr. *perdreau*). There are several species of the genus *Perdreaux*, which differ from each other in some few particulars, although all of them are ranked as partridge. The two kinds most frequently available are the European Grey and the French Red-legged bird (*bartavello*). The latter is sometimes found in the Eastern counties of Great Britain. The Grey partridge is considered best for table when young, whereas the Red-legged partridge is at its prime when mature. The partridge-shooting season opens on 1st September and continues until the end of January. See **GAME**.

TO PREPARE. Pluck and singe the bird and empty it (see **POULTRY**); wipe it inside and out. Cut the head off but leave sufficient neck skin to fasten back. Cross the legs upon the breast and keep them in position by tying them to a skewer passed through the body. Pass a skewer through the pinions and the breast, threading the skinned head upon the skewer. The bird is then ready for stuffing.

Partridges Braised with Cabbage

Ingredients	Method
2 or 3 partridges	Singe, draw and wipe the birds. Truss them with their wings turned inwards. Place in a roasting tin; cover with dripping and roast for 10 mins.; take up and drain. Wash cabbages, cut into quarters and remove stalks; cook for 10 mins. in salted water and drain. Take a large stewpan and put in some slices of pork or bacon, the carrot and onion cut into slices, cloves and bouquet garni. Lay the partridges on this; put the cabbage on top; then some more bacon or pork; add the wine and stock; season with pepper, salt and grated nutmeg; cover and cook slowly for 35–45 mins. Dress the cabbages on a dish to form a bed; place the partridges on this (whole or cut up); garnish with slices of carrot
2 oz. dripping	
2 small cabbages	
8 oz. salt pork or fat bacon	
1 carrot	
1 onion	
3 cloves	
Bouquet garni	
1 glass white wine	
1½ pt. rich stock	
Salt and pepper	
Nutmeg	
1 gill Espagnole sauce	

Partridges Braised with Cabbage (*continued*)

and bacon or pork. Skim and strain the gravy; add the sauce; boil up and pour sauce all over.

Chaudfroid of Partridge

Ingredients

2 roast partridge
¾ pt. Brown Chaudfroid sauce
½ pt. aspic jelly
1 crisp lettuce
1 hard-boiled egg
Ripe tomatoes
½ cucumber
8 stuffed olives
Mayonnaise
Watercress

Method

Cut the partridge into neat pieces, free from skin and trim. Mask each piece completely with sauce. When set, run over sufficient half-set aspic to mask them. Prepare a bed of mixed salad dressed with mayonnaise in the centre of a dish. Arrange the pieces of partridge neatly round the salad and garnish with chopped aspic and watercress.

Partridge Pudding

Ingredients

1 brace partridge
½ lb. rump steak
Suet crust as for beefsteak pudding
Pepper and salt
¼ pt. good stock (made from partridge bones if possible)

Method

Skin the partridges if they are old and cut into neat joints. Slice the rump steak thinly. Line a dish as for beefsteak pudding. Put steak in the bottom of the basin and lay the partridge joints on it, well seasoning them. Pour in stock and finish as for beefsteak pudding. Boil from 3–4 hrs., according to the age of the partridges. Mushrooms are a great improvement to the flavour of this pudding.

Partridge Roast

Ingredients

1 brace partridge
Bacon dripping or cooking fat
Flour
Pepper and salt
Croûtons of bread
Watercress

Method

Prepare the birds. Place in a baking tin, cover the breasts with dripping or bacon. Put into oven at 400° F. Therm. 6. Bake for 25–30 mins. Take two slices of lightly toasted bread (with crusts removed), put them under the birds so that they absorb the drippings. Place them on a hot dish, serve the birds on these, and garnish with watercress. Serve with brown gravy, browned crumbs and game chips.

Partridge Soup, Clear. Prepare some stock (see **STOCK**) using half beef and half partridge (old ones will do). Clarify as directed for clear soup (p. 472), and serve small quenelles of partridge in it. Other game soups may be made in the same manner.

PASQUE FLOWER. Anemone. The juice of the purple sepals yields a green colour which is not a permanent dye, but is used to colour "Pash" or Easter Eggs. The whole plant is used medicinally for asthma and rheumatism, etc.

PASSOVER CAKES. Unleavened cake made by the Jews from matzo or purified flour.

PASTA. A prepared flour mixture. See **MACARONI**.

PASTE AND PASTRY (Fr. *pâte, pâtisserie*). Successful pastry-making is dependent to a great extent upon the skill in manipulation; once the simple rules are mastered, such as the correct heat for cooking, with a little practice the art of pastry-making becomes an easy matter.

Always weigh the ingredients and sift flour with a little salt, and baking powder if used. When adding liquid take care not to make the dough sticky. Use a knife to mix.

Use for shortening, butter, margarine, lard or vegetable fat, or a mixture of these, dripping or suet.

Butter gives a specially good flavour, but usually used with lard.

Lard makes good pastry and especially good when used with butter.

Margarine, when used with lard or white fat, makes good pastry.

Dripping, when clarified, may be used for "short" pastry, but it does not make good "layer" pastry, as it is too soft in texture. The richer mixes with more fat are the lightest. In some mixes, e.g. suet and short pastry, baking powder (1 tsp. to $\frac{1}{2}$ lb. flour), is sometimes added to lighten the mixture.

Work in as cool a place as possible and keep the board or slab, rolling pin, and hands as cold as possible; when flouring the board and rolling pin, do not use too much flour, since a loose coating of flour on the pastry is apt to toughen the crust. Cold air occupies much less space than hot and consequently the colder the air the greater its expansion when it gets into a hot oven. The exception is when making choux pastry and hot water crust.

Always handle the dough lightly and roll lightly. Heavy rolling and handling expels the air.

Preheat the oven to the correct temperature and bake the pastry quickly and *never be tempted to peep to see how the pastry is cooking*. Do not open the oven door until the required cooking time is almost up.

GLAZES AND TOPS FOR PIES. *For shiny top* on pies, just before baking brush top lightly with milk.

For a sugary top, brush first with milk, then sprinkle with sugar.

For a glazed top (the brown polished finish), brush the top with a mixture of whole egg, or egg yolk and a little water, then bake.

For a lattice top, let the bottom pastry hang $\frac{1}{2}$" over edge of dish, roll pastry for top the exact size of dish and cut into strips $\frac{1}{2}$" wide. Lay some strips one way across filling about 1" apart, then place the same number of strips diagonally across (to make the diamond-shaped openings), seal ends to pastry on edge of pan, turn the pastry back over ends of lattice strips and build up fluted or crimped edge.

For interwoven lattice top, lay every other strip into which the round of pastry has been cut one way on a waxed paper, lay the other strips across the other way and weave them in and out beginning with the centre strips and working out to sides. Then transfer by turning lattice top on to top of filling. Adjust and finish edge.

TO COVER A PIE. Fill pie-dish and use a pie funnel, or inverted egg cup to hold up the crust. Roll out the pastry $\frac{1}{8}$–$\frac{1}{4}$" thick; cut a strip of pastry the width and length of the edge of the pie-dish. Damp the edge of the dish with a little cold water and place the strip of pastry on. Damp this pastry on top then place the large piece of pastry over the rolling pin, lift it gently and lay it on top of the pie. Care should be taken not to stretch it. Press down the edge and trim off any surplus, flute the edge by using a fork or flake with slashes horizontally with a knife, and then make a scallop pattern. Slit in the centre of the pie funnel. Brush with egg and milk or egg white and caster sugar. Bake at 400° F. Therm. 6 for about 30 mins. or according to type of pie.

One Crust Pies. Roll out the dough but do not divide it. Make the pastry circle 1" larger than the dish all round. Fit pastry loosely into dish, taking care not to stretch (this is to prevent shrinking of the pie shell while baking). Use scissors to

TO COVER A PIE (*continued*)

trim off ragged edges. Leave ½″ overhanging at edge of dish. Moisten the edge of dish with a little cold water. Fold the extra pastry back and under, press on to edge of dish to keep the pastry from shrinking or slipping. Build up a fluted edge to make it stand up. Place the left forefinger against the inside of the pastry rim and pinch the outside with tips of right thumb and forefinger, repeating until entire rim is fluted. Coat the bottom surface with melted butter to prevent the filling soaking in before the oven heat seals the crust. For a custard pie, brush the pastry with a little beaten egg white. Fill chilled and coated pastry-lined dish but be sure that the pie will not spill when carried, and bake according to directions for each pie's own recipe.

Two Crust Pies. Divide dough into half for the two crusts. Round up larger part of dough on lightly floured board. Roll it out for the lower crust, keeping it circular, to correct size to fill dish. Pat and fit pastry for the lower crust down into dish. Trim off any ragged edges, spread with melted butter and chill. Round up, and roll out the pastry for the upper crust to correct size of dish, fold, cut slits in it, unfold and chill. Preheat the oven, fill the pastry-lined dish, wet edge of pastry, lay top crust on filling. Trim, but leave ½″ hanging over edge of pan. Fold this under edge of bottom pastry, seal, make a fluted edge, and bake according to directions.

9″ Pie (1 lb. flour) cuts into 8 helpings; same ingredients will make 6 individual pies.

8″ Pie (12 oz. flour) cuts into 6 helpings; same ingredients will make 4 individual pies.

6″ Pie (8 oz. flour) cuts into 3 helpings; same ingredients will make 3 individual pies.

A plate fruit or jam tart. Allow 6 oz. short crust pastry for a plate pie. Grease a plate and line it with the pastry, cut and trim the edges and spread on the cold fruit, jam, etc. Moisten the edges and cover with pastry. Trim and decorate as desired. Brush with milk and dust with sugar.

TO LINE A FLAN RING. Well grease the flan ring and dust it with flour. Roll the pastry into a round 1″ larger than the ring. Lift this on to the rolling pin and place on the ring on the baking tin. Put into sides and run the rolling pin over to trim off edges; form into shape. Place a little rice or dry breadcrusts on a piece of greaseproof paper in the centre of the case, place in oven to bake blind at 400° F. Therm. 6. When the pastry is set and beginning to brown, remove the paper and return the pastry to the oven to finish cooking. Fill as desired.

RAISED PIES, TO MOULD. (See also **Veal and Ham Pie**, p. 508).

To mould with the hands. Cut off a quarter of the hot water crust for top and keep it warm in a covered basin standing over a pan of hot water. Knead the rest of the pastry into a barrel shape and press the centre in with the hands and work the sides to form a case. Pack with filling, pressing this down well, and keeping it level with the top of the edge of the pastry. Moisten the edge of the pastry with beaten egg or water. Roll out the remaining crust into a round for the top and cover, trim off any extra crust, press the edges together. Take a piece of folded double greaseproof paper and pin it securely round the sides of the pastry case to keep it in shape while cooking. Brush the top with beaten egg or milk. Decorate the top with leaves formed out of trimmings of crust. Make a hole in the centre. Bake at 425° F. Therm. 7 for 1½ hr. or longer, according to size. Remove paper (the pastry ought to be set by now), brush the whole pie with beaten egg or milk, and continue to cook a further ½ hr. at 375° F. Therm. 5 till the pastry is brown and the filling, when tested with a skewer, is tender.

To mould over a tin or jar. Make the hot water crust. Invert a tin or 2 lb. jam jar and flour well. Form the pastry into a flat cake. Place on the top of tin or jar. Work down the sides over the jar or tin till the required shape is moulded. Lift the pastry off carefully, use a knife to ease it if necessary. Fill and proceed as before.

When the pie is removed from the oven after cooking, fill with ⅛ pt. stock, ⅛ oz. gelatine, pepper and salt to season, *to make the jelly.*

RAISED PIES, TO MOULD (*continued*)

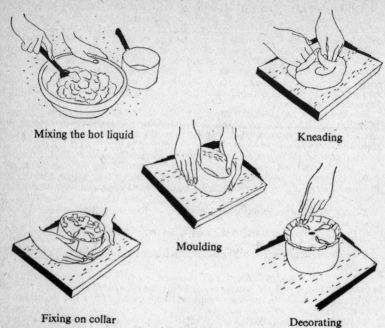

Mixing the hot liquid   Kneading

Moulding

Fixing on collar   Decorating

BISCUIT CRUST (RICH SHORT CRUST)

Ingredients
8 oz. flour
Pinch of salt
4 oz. butter or margarine
1 egg yolk
1 dsp. caster sugar
Cold water

Method
Sift salt and flour together (add baking powder if used), cut the fat quickly and lightly into the sifted flour, using the fingertips. Mix to a stiff paste, adding the yolk of egg to the cold water for mixing. For sweet dishes, add the sugar; for savoury, omit. Bake at 375° F. Therm. 5 (not 425° F. Therm. 7 as in short pastry; this is because egg yolk has been added to the mixture). Only just sufficient water should be used to bind the mixture, and it must be lightly kneaded and rolled out quickly until thin enough and of the right shape to use. This crust is used for fruit or custard tarts, flans, and apple dumplings (baked).

CHOUX PASTRY

Ingredients
¼ pt. water
1 oz. butter

Method
Boil water and butter in a saucepan. Sift flour and salt and quickly add to the

[370]

CHOUX PASTRY (*continued*)
3 oz. flour
Pinch of salt
2 eggs

liquid. Beat well over a low heat until the mixture is smooth and leaves the sides of the pan clean. Remove from heat. Cool the mixture before gradually adding the beaten eggs. Beat well, use as required, forcing through piping bag or dropping by spoonfuls on to a baking sheet.

Beating the hot roux

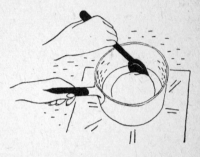

The mix when smooth

COLD WATER CRUST
Ingredients
4 oz. butter
1 lb. flour
1 tsp. salt
1 egg (optional)
Water

Method
Rub the butter into the flour; add salt and mix into a paste, with enough water, or egg and water, to bind.

CREAM PASTRY
Ingredients
3 oz. butter
12 oz. flour
1 tbsp. caster sugar
Cream (about ¼ pt.)
Pinch of salt

Method
Rub the butter into the flour; add the sugar and mix lightly but thoroughly with cream. If cream cannot be procured, use 3 egg yolks beaten with a little milk.

FINE CRUST
Ingredients
½ lb. butter
1 lb. dried and sifted flour
3 oz. caster sugar
3 egg yolks
2 egg whites

Method
Beat the butter to a froth in a basin. Mix with it by degrees the flour and sugar, then add the eggs well beaten and strained, taking care not to make mixture too moist to roll.

FLAKY CRUST
Ingredients
1 lb. flour
½ tsp. salt

Method
Sift the flour and salt. Divide the fat into four pieces. Rub one quarter into the flour

[371]

FLAKY CRUST (*continued*)
¾ lb. fat
Cold water
2 tsp. lemon juice

and mix to a dry dough with water and lemon juice. Roll out into an oblong about three times as long as it is wide. Spread into three: turn pastry once towards right and roll. Repeat until fat is all incorporated into the pastry. Leave for at least 15 mins. between each rolling Roll and fold once after adding fat, before rolling and using. Cover and stand in a cool place until required, then roll out to the size required.

FLAKY DOUGH CRUST
Ingredients
1 lb. bread dough
¼ lb. butter, lard or dripping

Method
Roll out the dough very thinly and spread with the fat. Fold in two, spread again with fat, fold in two and spread once more with fat. Fold again, and set aside for 1 hr., then roll out and use. This crust is very light and not at all like bread.

HOT WATER CRUST
Ingredients
¼ pt. water
4–6 oz. butter or lard
1 lb. flour
½ tsp. salt

Method
Boil the water and fat. Sift the flour and salt. Add the liquid to the flour and mix together with a wooden spoon. Knead together when the mixture is cool enough to handle. Cover and keep in a warm place until required. Mould into the desired shape whilst still warm and the dough is pliable.

PÂTÉ SUCRÉE
Ingredients
4½ oz. flour
Pinch of salt
3 oz. butter (scant measure)
2 egg yolks
1¾ oz. caster sugar

Method
Sift the flour and salt on to a slab; make a well in the centre. Put in the butter and add the yolks and sugar thus: with the right hand squeeze the butter and yolks of eggs together, working in with the finger-tips, and with the left hand draw in the flour, using a scraper or palette knife. Mix to a soft, smooth dough. Chill for at least an hour before use.

POTATO PASTRY
Ingredients
6 oz. flour
½ tsp. salt
1 heaped tsp. baking powder
1 oz. fat

Method
Sift together the flour, salt and baking powder. Rub in the fat and add the cooked sieved potato. Stir all together and add just enough water or milk and water

[372]

POTATO PASTRY (*continued*)

3 oz. cooked mashed potato
Milk or water to mix

PUFF PASTRY
Ingredients
1 lb. butter
1 lb. flour
1 tsp. salt

to make a stiff dough. Use this pastry for the crust of meat or game pie, brushing it with milk before baking.

Method

Wash the butter in very cold water, then place in a floured cloth and squeeze out all the moisture. Press the butter into a

Rolling out dough   Folding over fat

Rolling   Folding

Rolling out   Getting ready to make turn

PUFF PASTRY (*continued*)
Cold water
Juice of ½ lemon

slab (about 1″ thick). Leave in a cool place until required. Sift flour and salt. Mix to an elastic dough with the water and lemon juice. Turn on to a floured board. Roll into a strip three times longer than the width of the slab of fat and 1″ wider. Place the fat in the centre and fold over first the end nearest to you, then fold the end furthest away from you. Press the edges together lightly with the rolling pin (to seal in the air). Roll into a strip 3″ by 1″. This is called a "turn". Repeat this "turn" 6 more times, always keeping the open end towards you, putting it in a cool place for at least 5 mins. (if possible up to 1 hr.) between each turn to allow for shrinkage and rest. On the eighth rolling, roll into desired shape. While "resting", the pastry should be covered to avoid a skin forming.

TO MAKE PATTY-CASES. Roll the puff paste, when ready, to rather more than ¼″ thickness. Take a fluted cutter about the size of the top of a tumbler, and cut the paste into rounds with it. Mark the middle of these rounds with a cutter about three sizes smaller. Roll out the remainder of the paste to half the thickness of the cases. Stamp out some rounds for covers with a fluted cutter two sizes smaller than that used for the cases. Put the cases and covers on a baking-tin, and bake at 400° F. Therm. 6, for 10–15 mins. When cooked, lift the lid and scrape out the soft inside carefully.

TO MAKE A VOL-AU-VENT. Follow the directions given for cutting patty-cases, using vol-au-vent cutters. The paste should be rolled to about ¾″ thickness, and particular care must be taken that it is rolled very *evenly*. If this is not done, the case will not be shapely. After cutting the case, mark the centre with a small cutter that will come within ¾″ of the edge of the paste all the way round, and press this half through. The case will take about ½ hr. to bake at 400° F. Therm. 6 and must not be removed from the oven until the sides are quite set, or it will fall and lose its lightness. When nearly cooked, brush over the top with beaten egg to glaze it. When quite ready remove it from the oven, lift the lid, and then carefully remove the soft paste in the centre. Fill it just before serving and then replace the lid. If preferred, a separate lid may be cut as directed for patties. Care must be taken that the case does not take too dark a colour in baking.

ROUGH PUFF PASTRY

Ingredients
1 lb. flour
½ tsp. salt
6 oz. lard
6 oz. margarine or butter
2 tsp. lemon juice
Cold water

Method
Sift the flour and salt. Cut the fat into pieces (about the size of a walnut) and add to the flour. Add lemon juice and sufficient water to mix to a dough, leaving the pieces of fat whole. Roll and fold 5 times, "resting" for about 15 mins. between each rolling. Cover and leave in a cool place until ready for using.

[374]

SHORT CRUST PASTRY

Ingredients

1 lb. flour
1 tsp. salt
4 oz. lard
4 oz. margarine or butter
Cold water

Method

Sift flour and salt into a bowl; cut and rub in the fat until the mixture resembles fine breadcrumbs. Add sufficient cold water to make a dry dough. Mix with knife and press mixture together until it forms rough shapes. Gather together with fingertips, handling carefully. Let the rolled side of the pastry be uppermost in the dish or pie.

SUET PASTE (FOR BOILED PUDDINGS)

Ingredients

1 lb. flour
2 tbsp. baking powder
1 tsp. salt
6–8 oz. suet (finely shredded)
Cold water

Method

Sift the dry ingredients together, mix in the finely shredded suet. Add sufficient water to mix a stiff dough. Use first rolling.

Apricot Tartlets

Ingredients

½ lb. sweet short crust pastry
Tinned apricots
2 egg whites
4 oz. caster sugar

Method

Line some patty tins with the pastry and bake for 10 mins. at 400° F. Therm. 6. Put a small crust or a few rice grains on a piece of paper in the centre of each patty tin to prevent the pastry from rising during cooking. Remove after 8 mins. Fill each case with half an apricot with the cut side downwards. Whisk the whites of eggs until stiff and fold in the sugar. Put a spoonful on top of each apricot. Bake for a further 20 mins. at 200° F. Therm. ¼.

Assorted Pastries (allumettes glacés). Take a piece of good plain puff paste (see above) and roll out to about ¼″ thick; cut into long bands 3″ wide. Spread these with Royal icing, using a palette knife, then cut into pieces 1½″ in width. When cutting, always dip the knife in flour, then cut and push away the slice of pastry. Turn the knife back to lie flat on the table before pulling it away, otherwise it will stick to the icing and make the pastry look shabby. Leave to rest for a few mins., then bake at 350° F. Therm. 4.

Bakewell Tart

Ingredients

6 oz. short crust pastry
Jam
3 oz. butter or margarine
3 oz. sugar
1 egg
1 oz. ground almonds
2 oz. cake crumbs

Method

Line a 7″ sandwich tin with the pastry. Spread with jam. Cream the butter and sugar, beat in the egg; add the ground almonds and cake crumbs and spread the mixture over the jam. Bake for 40 mins. at 400° F. Therm. 6. Bakewell tart can be served either hot or cold as desired.

Bouchées-à-la-Pâtissière

Ingredients

½ lb. puff paste
Glacé cherries
Currant or apple jelly

Forming Rings

Method

Roll out the paste to the thickness of a penny, cut with fluted cutter into 15 pieces about 2½" in diameter and 1½" thick and damp them with water. Roll up the trimmings, roll out and cut 15 pieces 1" in diameter removing the centres with a small cutter, thus forming rings. Place them in the centre of the other shapes, damp them slightly, dip the tops into sifted sugar, put them on a greased baking sheet and bake at 350° F. Therm. 4 until they are a light colour. Remove from oven, fill the centre of the ring with jelly, decorate with halved glacé cherries and serve.

Bouchées of Lobster and Shrimps. To fill rings, cut the lobster and shrimps up into small pieces, and add White sauce only.

Bouchées with Game Purée (bouchées à Saint Hubert). Roll out 1 lb. puff paste to ¼" thickness and allow to stand for 5 mins. Cut into rounds with a 2" pastry cutter. Brush the baking sheet over with a pastry brush dipped in cold water, arrange the rounds of paste on it, brush over with beaten egg; then cut three parts through the centre of each flat of paste with a tin cutter 1" in diameter; mark three lines across inner circle of the paste with a sharp-pointed knife, and bake at 400° F. Therm. 6 for 20 mins. Remove from baking sheet by sliding a palette knife under each one, lift the lids and scoop out the underdone paste. Fill the patties with warm game purée, replace the lids, arrange on a hot dish, garnish with sprigs of parsley and serve.

Bouchées, Petites. Roll out ½ lb. puff paste to the size of half a sheet of foolscap; place on a floured board and cut the paste into 2" squares. Dip the paste brush into egg whites frothed, and touch the four corners and middle of the paste. Sprinkle with sugar and bake at 350° F. Therm. 4. Make a hollow in the centre of each and fill with raspberry jam or cherries.

Bouchées, Sweet. Roll out to $\frac{1}{12}$" thickness 12 oz. puff paste, cut into rings with a fluted cutter 2" in diameter, and from the rest of the paste form more rings with a plain cutter of 1¼" diameter, cutting out the centres with another cutter 1" wide. Damp the surfaces of the fluted pieces of paste, place the smaller rings over them, pressing together; dust with sugar and bake at 350° F. Therm. 4 until a light colour. Remove, allow to cool and mask the tops with white of eggs mixed with sugar; dust over some coarse grained sugar and return to oven for 2 mins. to dry the egg. Remove, cover rings with same mixture of egg and sugar, dip into chopped pistachios, dry again in oven and fill with any kind of preserve. Serve cold.

Cheesecakes

Ingredients

2 oz. sugar
2 oz. butter
1 egg
2 oz. flour
½ tsp. baking powder
4 oz. sweet short crust pastry or flaky pastry
Jam

Method

Cream the butter and sugar and add the egg. Fold in flour and baking powder sifted together. Line patty tins with pastry and spread with a little jam. Place 1 tsp. of the mixture on top and bake for 20 mins. at 400° F. Therm. 6.

Cream Horns
Ingredients
4 oz. puff pastry
¼ pt. cream
1 egg white
Caster sugar
Redcurrant jelly

Method
Roll pastry into an 8″ square, then divide into 8 equal strips. Brush with white of egg and twist each strip round the cornet moulds. Place on baking-tin, sprinkle with caster sugar and allow to stand about 10 mins. Place in a hot oven (400° F. Therm. 6) until set. Remove the cornet moulds and if necessary allow the pastry to dry in the oven for a further few minutes. Remove from oven; place the horns on cake tray to cool. When cool, drop about a tsp. of jelly into each. Pipe in whipped cream and decorate as desired.

Twisting pastry round cornets

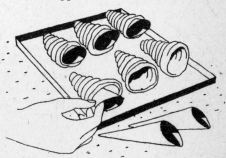

Removing cornet moulds

Éclairs
Ingredients
Choux pastry
Whipped cream
Chocolate icing or caramel

Method
Put some choux pastry into a forcing bag with a plain pipe. Force it on to a greased baking-sheet in lengths of 3½″ and not quite the 1″ width. Bake about 35 minutes. They require a quick oven, 400° F. Therm. 6 at first, to raise them up; afterwards reduce heat to 350° F. Therm. 4 to set them. When cooked, glaze with chocolate icing or caramel, and when cool, open them at the side and fill with whipped cream. Any glacé icing may be used instead of chocolate or caramel.

Sausage Rolls
Ingredients
Some puff or flaky crust
Sausages
1 egg
C.C.D.—13

Method
Parboil the sausages and skin them. Cut into halves and allow to cool. Roll out the paste and cut into squares. Brush the

Sausage Rolls (*continued*)

edges with beaten egg and lay a half-sausage on each piece of paste; roll the paste round it, pressing the edges together. Brush the rolls with beaten egg and lay them on a greased baking-sheet. Bake at 400° F. Therm. 6 for 15–20 mins.

Strawberry Tart
Ingredients
  Pastry
  Strawberries
  Sugar

Method
Roll out some puff, flaky or short crust. Line an open tart tin and fill the centre with strawberries which have been picked over well, the stalks removed, and the fruit rolled in sugar. Put them close together and bake the tart until the fruit and the paste are cooked.

Tartlets
Ingredients
  Puff paste
  Preserve

Method
Roll out the paste, and stamp into rounds with a fluted cutter. Lay the rounds on patty pans and place in the middle of each a dummy made of dough or bread. Bake at 400° F. Therm. 6 and when the pastry is cooked remove the dummies and fill the places with jam. Plainer tartlets may be made with short, flaky or other pastry.

Treacle Tart
Ingredients
  Short crust
  Treacle
  Breadcrumbs

Method
Line an open tart dish or ordinary dish that will stand the heat of the oven with the pastry and decorate the edges. Cover with golden syrup and dredge over some breadcrumbs. Bake at 400° F. Therm. 6 until the paste is baked.

Turnovers. Roll out some short crust and cut into rather large rounds. Wet the edges and put some fruit or jam in the middle of each round with 1 tsp. sugar. Fold the paste over and press the edges together. Decorate the edges with a fork or spoon. Put the turnovers on a greased baking-sheet and bake in a quick oven, 400° F. Therm. 6 for 15–20 mins.

PASTE ITALIAN. This is a mixture of fine wheat-flour and water. It is used chiefly in the manufacture of macaroni and vermicelli.

PASTRY CREAMS. Another name for éclairs.

PASTY. The name given to a sort of savoury pie, especially used in connection with game and venison. Also called Cornish Pasty.

PATIENCE. A vegetable which is similar to spinach. It has a specially mild flavour with a slight acidity like sorrel leaves.

PATTY (Fr. *pâté*). A small pie, a vol-au-vent of puff paste filled with oysters, game, fish, meat, etc., cut into dice, shreds or pounded.

PAUPIETTES. Lit. "little peeps" from Fr. *paupière*, an eyelid. This may be an allusion to the forcemeat peeping from between the rolls of material which encloses it. Nowadays, the cook is careful that the forcemeat shall not be exposed.

PEA, GREEN (Fr. *petit pois*). Today we have fresh green peas, dried or split peas, bottled, canned and frozen peas, also pea flour and pea meal. Young, tender, freshly cooked peas make an attractive garnish.

GREEN PEAS, BOILED

Ingredients

3 lb. peas in pod
½ tsp. sugar
Sprig of mint
½ oz. butter

Method

Shell peas; wash well and drain in colander. Cook in a small amount of boiling water with the mint and sugar for 8–10 mins. until just tender. Drain, turn on to a hot dish and toss in butter. Serve garnished with a little finely chopped parsley, or:

1. Finish with a little mayonnaise.
2. Use a spring onion instead of the mint when cooking.
3. Pass the peas through a sieve and season. Add a little sugar and butter and a spoonful or two of cream or white sauce and reheat before serving.

GREEN PEAS, BOILED (FLEMISH WAY). Prepare and slice ½ lb. young carrots and cook them very gently in butter or margarine. Add pinch of salt and 1 tsp. sugar. Use a saucepan with a tightly-fitting lid. When they are parcooked, add a pint of peas and simmer in the closely covered pan until the vegetables are tender. Add pepper and salt and a little more fresh butter and serve immediately.

GREEN PEAS, BOILED (FRENCH WAY). Put into a saucepan a little butter or margarine, two small onions, 1 qt. fresh peas (shelled), a bouquet (thyme, sprig of parsley and half a bayleaf tied together with thread) and ½ cup water. Cook very gently, adding more water if required. When peas are tender, remove the bouquet and serve.

GREEN PEAS, DRIED. Soak overnight in cold water, drain and place in a saucepan with a little water. Cook until tender over a very low heat.

Green Pea Salad. Take cooked green peas and arrange them on a bed of lettuce leaves; dress with French dressing and sprinkle over a little chopped tarragon and mint leaves. Toss lightly about.

Green Pea Soup. See SOUPS.

PEA, SPLIT. It is the common field pea that is generally used for this process of shelling when old, drying and then splitting. Sometimes these peas are ground into flour.

Pease Pudding. Put 1 lb. split peas into water and steep for 12 hrs. Tie them in a cloth, leaving room for them to swell, then boil for about 3½–4 hrs. Remove from cloth and rub through a hair sieve. Mix into them a little salt and add some butter. Put into cloth, tie up again, boil for ½ hr. and serve.

Pea Soup. See SOUPS.

PEA, SUGAR. The pods of this pea do not have the inner film, peculiar to all other pea-pods. They are consequently more fleshy and crisp, and admit of being cut and dressed like French beans.

SUGAR PEAS, BOILED. Put the required quantity of peas in a saucepan of water, leaving them in their shells. Boil for ½ hr., drain the water off the peas, put a lump of butter in with them, beat the yolks of 2 eggs with a small quantity of cream, then stir this in with the rest, adding a few drops of vinegar when hot. Do not reboil. Turn on to a dish and serve.

[379]

Sugar Pea Salad. Pick the pods when they are about 1" or so in length. Put into a dish with an equal quantity of garden cress. Arrange some slices of tomato on top, dress with oil and vinegar, season with salt and pepper and serve.

PEACH (Fr. *pêche*). There are two kinds of peach, the Clingstone or the firm-fleshed peaches, and the Fondant, which are soft and juicy as the mellowest apricot. Peaches are served for dessert (see FRUIT, p. 227), and also in fruit compôte or used in fritters; sometimes they are preserved in brandy or liqueur (see FRUIT).

Peach Jam

Ingredients	*Method*
12 ripe peaches Sugar	Peel and stone peaches and place in a preserving pan with enough water to cover bottom of pan. Boil very gently, mashing fruit against sides of pan. When tender, pass through a coarse sieve. Weigh and allow ¾ lb. sugar to each 1 lb. fruit pulp. Break the stones and remove kernels from 6. Pound in mortar or chop very finely and add to sugar and pulp. Boil all together for 30 mins., stirring frequently to prevent sticking or burning. Test for setting, pour into warmed jars and cover when cool.

Peach (Dried) Jam

Ingredients	*Method*
1 lb. dried peaches 3 pt. water 2¼ lb. sugar 1 lemon	Wash the fruit and soak in water for 36 hrs. Place fruit and water into preserving pan, bring to boil and simmer gently until fruit is soft. Add sugar and lemon juice and boil fast until the jam sets. Pour into heated jars and cover when cool.

PEAFOWL (Fr. *paon*). Peacocks and peahens do not often find their way to the table today, but our ancestors used to skin the bird alive, cook it and then send it to the table with all its feathers on.

PEAR (Fr. *poire*). The pear tree is of the same tribe as the apple, and is a native of Europe, Circassia, Central Asia, and the North of China. Pears, especially the more luscious varieties, are served for dessert, also crystallised and bottled (see FRUIT).

PEARS, BAKED. Peel, core and cut in halves 6 large pears and put them into a pan with a dozen cloves, ½ lb. sugar and just sufficient water to cover them. Bake at 350° F. Therm. 4 until tender. Keep the pan covered, then stew gently for 10 mins. over a low heat, adding a little grated lemon peel and extra sugar if desired.

PEARS, STEWED

Ingredients	*Method*
1 lb. pears ½ lb. syrup ½ pt. water Lemon peel	Put the sugar and water over a low heat and boil to a syrup. Then add some lemon peel (yellow part only). Pare and core the pears, cut them in halves and lay them in a deep dish. Stew gently until tender and of a good colour.

Pear Jam

Ingredients	*Method*
8 lb. pears	Peel and slice pears thinly; place in bowl
6 lb. sugar	and allow to stand for 12 hrs. Place in
4 oz. grated ginger	preserving pan with lemon rind and juice
Grated rind and juice of 4 lemons	and bring to the boil. Add sugar and ginger and simmer for 3 hrs. until clear. Pour into warmed jars and cover when cool.

PEANUT. The remarkable plant which bears peanuts is said to be a native of the Western Coast of Africa, but it is now cultivated elsewhere for the sake of its oil. The pods containing the seeds are usually found either on or under the ground. The external husk, something of a lobster shape with a waist or central depression, contains from 2–4 red-coloured seeds, about the size of field peas, having also much the same flavour. The African natives make a food from the peanut called Munduli, which they eat with much relish. The peanut is also known as the earth nut, ground nut, goober and monkey nut. These nuts are sometimes listed for use as a substitute for salted almonds.

Peanut Butter Loaf. Mix together 2 cups cooked beans and 1 cup breadcrumbs; add a grated onion and carrot and 1 tbsp. each parsley, diced celery and Worcester sauce. Then add salt and pepper to season, a beaten egg and 1 cup peanut butter. Mix all together, place in a greased tin and bake until browned at 375° F. Therm. 5.

PEARL MOSS. Another name for Carrageen (q.v.).

PECK. The fourth part of a bushel. A dry measure of 8 qts.

PECTASE. An enzyme which occurs in plants and ripe fruit juices and transforms pectin into pectic acid.

PECTATE. Salt of pectic acid.

PECTIC ACID. Derived from pectin; the acid formed as in vegetable jellies by the action of pectase on pectin.

PECTIN. The neutral substance which occurs in many vegetable tissues, as part of cell wall or sap. It is formed from pectose in the process of ripening and is used to stiffen jellies and jams (see JAM).

PECTINATE. Of comb-like formation, as in a leaf.

PECTOSE. A substance allied to cellulose found in unripe fruits and other vegetable tissue.

PELLOW or POOLOO. See PILAU.

PEMMICAN or PEMICAN. This is the name given by North American Indians to meat cut in thin slices, divested of fat and dried in the sun: it is mixed with melted fat and sometimes dried fruits and then compressed into cakes. Used by travellers and explorers.

PENGUIN. This bird's very large eggs are somewhat similar in texture and flavour to plover's eggs. They are imported from Cape Colony.

PENNYROYAL. There are two plants of this name; one is the English pennyroyal or the Pudding Grass, and the other is the Squaw Mint or American pennyroyal. They both have a very strong, clean, cool and refreshing minty odour and are used for infusions and medicinally.

PEPPER (Fr. *poivre*). What we term in our kitchen "black pepper" is the immature fruit or berry of the black pepper vine, an oriental climbing shrub which is found growing wild in the East Indies, but cultivated in other tropical climates. But the produce from Malabar is held in highest esteeem for the sake of the fruit. Peppercorns may produce either black or white pepper. *Black pepper* is the dried berry picked before it is ripe. *White pepper* is the produce of the ripe red berry

PEPPER (*continued*)

with skin and pulp removed; before grinding the corns are known as *mignonette pepper*. The unground black pepper retains the name which should be common to both peppercorns. Red pepper is found under **CAPSICUM**. *Long pepper* is composed of the immature fruit (dried female spikes) of the long pepper vine; the spikes are about 1½″ long, have an indented surface and are of a dark grey colour. It resembles black pepper but is less aromatic although of equal pungency. *Elegant pepper* is the larger variety of this species—the roots and stems when sliced and dried form the pippula moola of the East Indies. *Java* or *Tellichery pepper* is more pungent and delicate.

PEPPER, JAMAICA. See ALLSPICE.

PEPPER, NEPAUL. See under this main heading.

PEPPERMINT. A plant of the mint tribe. It is occasionally found growing wild in this country, but is more often cultivated for the sake of its volatile oil.
Peppermint Tea. Take 1 tsp. leaves and pour over almost 1 pt. boiling water. Leave to infuse for about 5 mins. (longer for a stronger infusion), then drink.
Peppermint Creams. Crush and sift some icing sugar and make a firm paste with the white of an egg. Add a few drops of peppermint essence to the desired strength and roll out thinly. Cut into small rounds, using a small sharp cutter. Place on a wire tray and leave to dry in a warm place.

PERCH (Fr. *perche*). The perch is found in most rivers, canals and lakes of Great Britain and numerous fish of the same tribe are found in other parts of Europe, also in America. The American perches are the Yellow perch and the White perch. The perch is one of the more delicate freshwater fish and in season from the latter end of May to the beginning of February. Perch may be cooked in any way suitable for trout or grayling.

PÉRIGUEUX SAUCE. See SAUCES.

PERIWINKLES (Fr. *bigorneaux* or *bigourneaux*). The small seasnail or fish in round black shells. They are abundant along the English shores and are in season all the year round. They require about 20 mins. boiling in salted water.
Periwinkle Patties. Pick them out of their shells and mince finely; then mix with pepper, salt, lemon juice and moisten with a little stock and cream. Put spoonfuls of this mixture into patty tins lined with puff paste. Cover, trim edges and press together. Brush with egg and milk and bake in a moderate oven, 350° F. Therm. 4, for about 15 mins.

PERRY (Fr. *poire*). A pleasant and wholesome liquor prepared from pears, in the same way as cider is from apples.

PERSIMMON. The fruit of the Virginian date palm. It is an inch or more in diameter, nearly round and of a yellowish-orange colour. The taste is rough and harsh, even when the fruit is quite ripe and it can only be considered eatable when softened by the action of frost. In the southern states of America, persimmons are pounded and made into beer and also into cakes with bran.

PETIT SUISSE. A French unsalted cream cheese; the smaller is known as *demi* and the larger as *gros*.

PETTITOES. See PIG'S FEET.

PHEASANT (Fr. *faisan*). There are several varieties of pheasants but the Common or English pheasant is now found over most of temperate Europe. Pheasants are in season during the winter months, commencing with October, and usually sold in pairs, called "braces". The young birds may be distinguished from the old ones by the shortness and roundness of the spurs. These birds require to be hung until the game flavour is pronounced. They should be hung upside down by the feet (tails up) and not by the necks, and are fit to eat when the flesh falls away at the tails. When preparing a pheasant for cooking, it should be carefully plucked of its feathers, the tail feathers being retained for garnishing when serving the pheasant. For carving see **CARVING**; for trussing, see **CHICKEN**.

PHEASANT, BRAISED

Ingredients

2 medium-sized young
    pheasants
1 carrot
1 small onion
3 or 4 slices fat bacon
2 oz. butter
1½ gills stock
Seasoning

Method

Take the pheasants, draw, singe, cut off
the neck and part of the legs, wipe the
inside with a damp cloth and truss as
usual for roasting. Put them in a fireproof
casserole with the carrot, onion and
bacon cut up in neat pieces. Season the
pheasants with the pepper and salt, and
place them on top of the vegetables.
Spread some butter on top of the
pheasants and roast at 400° F. Therm. 6
for 20 mins.; basting frequently. After
this, reduce the oven heat to 300° F.
Therm. 2, and cook for another 20 mins.
more slowly. When pheasants are done,
untruss, place them in a pan to keep hot.
Pour off the fat from the casserole, add
the stock, boil up, season and colour to
taste, strain. Pour round the pheasants.
Garnish with vegetables.

PHEASANT, ROAST

Ingredients

Brace of pheasants
2 oz. margarine or butter
2 rashers bacon
Watercress and a shallot

Method

Pluck, clean and draw the well-hung
pheasants. Preserve tail feathers for
garnish. Put margarine and shallot inside
the bird, wrap bacon round the breast.
Cover well with greaseproof paper and
roast for ¾–1 hr. at 350° F. Therm. 4,
according to the size of the bird. Then
dredge with flour, baste well, return to
the oven for a few minutes to crisp. Stick
the tail feathers into the bird and garnish
with watercress. Serve with Bread sauce,
chipped potatoes, thin gravy, fried
crumbs and green vegetables.

Pheasant Chaudfroid. Poach the pheasant and let it cool in its cooking liquor;
cut it up and clear the pieces of all skin; dip the pieces in Brown Chaudfroid sauce
flavoured with pheasant fumet. Glaze with cold melted jelly; trim the pieces and
leave to set; dish up and serve with Tartare sauce and some lettuce salad.
Pheasant, Cold. Roast the pheasant and keep it underdone. When it is quite cold,
raise its fillets and leave the legs and wings attached to the carcass. By means of
scissors, completely bone the carcass; garnish its inside with a parfait of foie gras,
and cover it with a thin coat of foie gras mousse. Replace the fillets upon this
mousse, after having sliced them, and fill any gaps that may exist between the
slices with some of the sauce mousse, thus reconstructing the bird. Let the mousse
set thoroughly and then glaze with aspic jelly. Meanwhile coat 8 boned,
stuffed, poached and cold quails with Brown Chaudfroid sauce; decorate with
pieces of truffle and glaze them with aspic jelly. Dish the pheasant on a low
forcemeat cushion; garnish with heaps of chopped and very clear aspic. Buy
fresh foie gras and use home-made liver pâté.

Pheasant Pie

Ingredients

1 well-hung pheasant
Some forcemeat and good gravy
Slices of fat bacon
Pastry
Pepper and salt

Method

Bone a well-hung pheasant, stuff it with some forcemeat and half roast it, basting well; leave to cool. Line a mould with pastry (raised pie crust) and lay slices of fat bacon at the bottom. Lay the pheasant on this and put in the remainder of the forcemeat. Cover with slices of bacon. Put a paste lid over and decorate. Bake from 2–3 hrs. at 310° F. Therm. 2. When cooked, pour through the hole in the centre of the pie some good gravy that will jelly when cold. The bones of the pheasant should be used for making the stock for the gravy.

FORCEMEAT FOR THE PIE

Ingredients

¼ lb. fillet veal
½ lb. fat bacon
6 oz. breadcrumbs
3 oz. lean ham
6 truffles or 4 medium-sized mushrooms
1 or 2 eggs
Pepper and salt

Method

Chop the veal, bacon and ham finely and mix them with the crumbs, the truffles or mushrooms, cut in pieces, add salt and pepper. Bind with beaten egg. Use half to stuff the pheasant.

Pulled Pheasant. Poach one or more pheasants, according to the amount required. Remove all white meat from the breast and pull into small pieces. Mix with a good creamy white sauce. Take the pinions and the legs, and devil them as follows:

DEVILLED PHEASANT

Ingredients

2 oz. butter warmed
1 dsp. dry mustard
1 tbsp. flour
1 tbsp. Harvey sauce
1 tbsp. Worcester sauce
Pinch pepper and salt
Eggs and breadcrumbs

Method

Mix seasonings and flour with warmed butter and coat joints. Dip in eggs and breadcrumbs and place under grill in tin to brown.

Salmi of Pheasant. Roast the pheasant, keeping it moderately underdone. Quickly cut into 8 pieces, 2 legs, 2 wings (separated from the pinions) and the breast cut into 4 lengthwise. Skin the pieces, trim them neatly and keep at a temperate heat in a covered vegetable pan, with a small quantity of burnt brandy and a little clear, melted meat glaze. Pound the carcass and the trimmings and add to them half a bottle of red wine (almost entirely reduced), three chopped shallots and a few mignonette peppers. Add ¼ pt. good Espagnole sauce; cook for 10 mins. and then strain through a strainer. Reduce this sauce to about one-third and remove all scum; strain it once more through a close strainer; add a small quantity of butter and pour the sauce over the pieces of pheasant, to which add a finely sliced truffle and 6 mushroom heads. Some croûtons fried in butter can be placed round the salmis, if desired. This dish should be very quickly prepared and served, so that it is eaten very hot and not allowed to stand.

PHILERNUM. The name of a West Indian liqueur which is suitable for cups, punch and flavouring and for use as a liqueur.

PICCALILLI. See **PICKLES.** The name given to an acid Mustard sauce or pickle.

PICKEREL. A young or small pike. In America this name very often is used for a particular pike, which is about two feet long and has a great reputation gastronomically. See also **PIKE.**

PICKLE. The name usually given in this country to the liquor (spiced vinegar sweetened and seasoned) in which substances used for food are soaked to give them certain flavours or to assist in their preservation. These are commonly known to French cooks as "marinades". Meat is preserved in brine. Large vegetables should always be cut into small pieces, and for this purpose an ordinary knife may be used on a chopping board. Salting or brining is an important part of the pickling process and this should be thoroughly effected or the pickles will be soft and flabby. Some pickles are merely covered with salt, having been freely pricked with a fork as in the case of green walnuts; others are soaked in strong brine. In order to soak them effectively they should be placed in an earthenware crock three parts filled with brine, with an inverted plate laid over the top and a brick or something heavy to keep the plate down. When pickles are served they are either left in their wide-mouthed jars or a small quantity of the pickle is placed in a flat dish.

PICKLE FOR EGGS

Ingredients	Method
1 doz. eggs	Boil the eggs for 20 mins., shell and take
$\frac{1}{4}$ oz. each cloves or mace	care not to break surface. Place in stone
$\frac{1}{2}$ nutmeg grated	or glass jars, adding seasoning to each jar.
1 oz. salt	Cover with boiling vinegar. When cool,
$\frac{1}{4}$ oz. whole peppers	seal jar.
2 bay leaves or pinch of dry thyme	
Vinegar	

PICKLE FOR FISH. To each 1 pt. vinegar, allow $\frac{1}{2}$ teacup beer, 3 bay leaves, $\frac{1}{2}$ oz. ground allspice, $\frac{1}{4}$ oz. each salt and pepper, and $\frac{1}{3}$ tsp. cayenne pepper. Mix together, pour over to cover the fish completely.

PICKLE FOR HAMS, TONGUES AND BEEF

Ingredients	Method
8 qt. water	Mix these together and put in a pickling-
2 lb. coarse sugar	pan with a close cover. Hang the meat as
2 lb. bay salt	long as possible, then well rub it with
$2\frac{1}{2}$ lb. common salt	coarse sugar; drain before putting it into
$\frac{1}{2}$ lb. saltpetre	the pickle. Let a small ham lie 2 wks. in
	pickle, a large one 3 wks., a tongue 12
	days, and beef in proportion to its size.
	They may be used from the pickle, but if
	dried let them drain well, then dry them
	thoroughly and smoke them for 8 hrs.

PICKLE FOR PORK. Mix 4 oz. saltpetre, 1 lb. coarse sugar, 1 oz. sal prunelle and a little common salt. Sprinkle the pork with salt and drain it for 24 hrs., then rub it with the mixture. Pack the pieces tightly together in the pickling tub and fill the spaces with salt. Put stones on the pork to keep it from rising as the salt melts.

13*

PIDDOCK. A bivalve mollusc or clam which bores and lodges itself in clay, soft rock and wood.

PIE (Fr. *pâté*). Meat, fish, or fruit covered with pastry and baked in a dish. One of the earliest types of pie is the pie made of all pastry (with filling) without a dish. See under individual headings.

PIG. From the flesh of the pig come pork, bacon, ham, and the fat makes a lard.

PIG'S CHEEK. A jowl, a face. These special parts require notice and are regarded as titbits. See BATH CHAPS. Wash the cheek and pickle for 3 days, then put it in lukewarm water and simmer gently until tender; this will take about 3 hrs., sometimes longer. When cooked, remove the rind and cover with browned breadcrumbs or raspings. If the cheek is dry, soak it for 4 hrs. before cooking.

PIG'S EARS. Esteemed for food principally on account of their crisp cartilaginous character. After singeing all hair off, they are scraped and blanched, and they may be braised, baked, stuffed or made into soup.

PIG'S FEET. Fastidiously known as Pettitoes, from the French *petit*, small. They are considered a great delicacy. Cleanse them very thoroughly and soak them for some hours. Boil until they are tender. Add a little vinegar and salt to some of the water in which they are boiled, and when cold pour this over them. When ready to use them, dry and cut the feet in two. Dip them in frying batter and fry in deep hot fat. Pour over them a little butter, just melted, into which a little mustard and vinegar and salt and pepper to season have been mixed.

PIG'S FRY. This term may be said to include almost all the internal organs of the pig; cooked with onion, potato, a little sage, pepper and salt to season, they make a tasty hot pot.

PIG'S HEAD. Used for brawn; only very seldom used as a substitute for a boar's head.

Brawn

Ingredients	*Method*
1 pig's head	Clean the head well and put it in pickle
2 or 3 hard-boiled eggs	for 3 days (see **PICKLE:** PICKLE FOR
2 onions	HAMS), then boil very gently from 3–4
6 cloves	hrs., until the flesh will leave the bones
1 blade of mace	easily.
1 doz. peppercorns	
1 sprig each parsley, thyme	
and marjoram	

PIGEON (Fr. *pigeon*). Pigeons can be used in innumerable ways. The season for them lasts from March to October. The flesh on the breast of a young bird should be light red in colour and the claws pinkish. Old birds can be detected by the thinness of their breasts and limbs and darkness of their skins. Wild or wood pigeons are usually larger than tame pigeons. The same rules for selecting and cooking apply equally to all. Pigeons should always, if possible, be cooked and eaten quite fresh.

PIGEON, ROAST

Ingredients	*Method*
2 pigeons	Flour the pigeons and put ½ oz. butter or
1 oz. butter or margarine	margarine in each bird. Bake for 30 mins.
1 oz. flour	at 400° F. Therm. 6, basting frequently.
2 large slices toast	Serve the pigeons on a piece of toast with
	a little of the gravy poured round and
	the remaining gravy served separately.
	Garnish with watercress.

[386]

PIGEONS, STEWED. Cut the birds in half and sauté them in a little melted butter or margarine. Then place in a casserole with mushrooms and seasoning and enough liquid to cover them. Put on the lid, place in a moderate oven 350° F. Therm. 4, and simmer until tender. Add 1 dsp. cornflour, blended with a little milk; return the casserole to the oven and allow the liquid to thicken before serving. Serve with a garnishing of watercress. If desired, a wineglass of red wine may be added 10 mins. before serving.

Compôte of Pigeons. Truss 2 fat tender pigeons as for roasting. Place them in a casserole or ovenproof dish with 2 oz. fresh butter and marjoram. Let them colour over a sharp fire, then add 2 oz. streaky bacon cut into small pieces, 6 or 8 small onions, carrots, a turnip and small button mushrooms. Fry all together for a few minutes and add a bouquet and some small green peas. Place the cover on the casserole and let it cook gently in the oven for about ¼ hr. at 300° F. Therm. 2, or until the contents are tender. Skim off the fat, and add 1 tbsp. Brown sauce and 1 tbsp. Tomato sauce. Let it simmer for 10 mins. Remove bouquet, but serve pigeons and vegetables together in the dish they were cooked in.

Pigeons and Mushrooms

Ingredients

3 pigeons
1 doz. medium sized mushrooms
Some good second stock
Flour
Butter or fat bacon
Pepper and salt

Method

Truss the pigeons for stewing and cut them in halves. Peel the mushrooms, cut off the stalks and rinse them. Fry the pigeons in butter or with the bacon. Place in a saucepan with the mushrooms; cover with the stock and add pepper and salt. Simmer very gently for ½ hr. or longer, until tender, then place the pigeons in a circle on an entrée dish, with the mushrooms round them. Thicken and strain the gravy and pour over them.

Pigeons with Truffles

Ingredients

3 pigeons
Little butter or slices of bacon
Some good stock
1 egg
Light brown breadcrumbs
Mashed potatoes
Truffles
Brown sauce
Flour

Method

Truss the pigeons as for boiling, cut them in halves, flour them, and fry them in butter or with a few slices of bacon. Place them in a saucepan, barely cover with good stock and simmer until tender. Drain them and, when cool, cover with beaten egg and light brown breadcrumbs; broil over a clear fire for a few mins. Dish them in a circle on a border of mashed potatoes. Put a few truffles, cooked in champagne, in the centre, and pour Brown sauce round. If truffles are too expensive, mushrooms, simply dressed, may be substituted, but the name of the dish must be altered.

PIGNOLIA (Fr. *pignons*). Kernels of pine cones of warm countries, frequently used in place of almonds and pistachio nuts.

PIKE (Fr. *brochet*). Commonly known as Jack, and sometimes as Luce, this is the king or tyrant of fish. The young are called Pickerel. They are in season during

PIKE (*continued*)

the winter months up to the beginning of March, their spawning season. Before cleaning or cooking, force coarse salt down the throat, and leave 12 hrs: this will help to tenderise. Horseradish sauce may be served with pike.

PIKE, BAKED

Ingredients	*Method*
3 lb. pike	Clean fish, but leave in backbone. Wipe with damp cloth. Place in baking dish. Combine all ingredients except watercress and spread mixture over the fish to cover thoroughly. Bake at 350° F. Therm. 4 for 30 mins. or until well browned. Serve very hot, garnished with watercress.
½ pt. sour cream	
2 oz. butter	
4 oz. grated cheese	
½ tsp. salt	
¼ tsp. pepper	
Watercress to garnish	

PIKELETS. A provincial name for muffins or cakes frequently used in the North country.

PILAU, PILLAW, PILAF. A dish common to Egypt and Turkey, made of fish, poultry or rice. Also an Indian dish of meat or poultry and rice.

Pilau of Fowl

Ingredients	*Method*
1 young fowl	Put the fowl, trussed for boiling, into the stock and half cook it. Stone raisins, blanch almonds, peel the onions and cut them into rings. Fry the onions in the butter very gently, taking care not to burn them. When these are fried, fry the raisins and almonds lightly. Well wash and dry the rice, and fry it in the butter until coloured. Then put it into the pan with the onions, raisins, almonds, etc. Make a well in the centre and put the fowl in it. Cover with stock and stew slowly until the chicken and rice are cooked and the rice has absorbed the stock. Place the chicken on a hot dish and the rice round it.
Stock	
1 lb. rice	
3 onions	
3 oz. raisins	
2 oz. almonds	
½ lb. butter	
1″ stick cinnamon	
Little cayenne	
Pepper and salt	

PILCHARDS (Fr. *royans*). The common name for the pilchard is the Gipsy Herring. It is a fat fish and is abundant on the Devonshire and Cornish coasts, but it may be found all over the Channel, even to the French coast where it is known by the name of "sardine". Pilchards are generally salted and preserved in oil in tins. Fresh pilchards are in season between July and Christmas but they are rarely found fresh in our inland markets. Pilchards may be grilled like herrings, when they are too large for tinning; they make good pies, especially when boned and placed in layers with pieces of leek, seasoned, covered with a good crust and baked at 350° F. Therm. 4. Just before serving, adding a cupful of cream under the cover to act as a sauce to the cooked fish.

PIMENTO. See ALLSPICE.

PIMIENTO. Red Spanish pepper pod of sweet and pungent flavour, used for garnish and in salads.

[388]

PINEAPPLE (Fr. *ananas*). The pineapple is the fruit of a tropical plant with rigid foliage, having sharp spines along the edges. It has long been acknowledged to be one of the most delicious fruits in existence. It can be used for many culinary purposes, as well as being a much esteemed dessert fruit (see **FRUIT**).

ANANAS À LA CREOLE (Hot or cold). Sliced pineapple, dressed on a border of cooked rice, garnished with angelica and glacé cherries and served with maraschino syrup.

ANANAS À LA CUSSY (Cold). Border shape of wine jelly set with pineapple slices, centre filled with whipped cream flavoured with apricot purée and suitably garnished.

ANANAS À LA REINE (Cold). Border of light genoese poached or steamed, with slices of pineapple ranged on top; the centre of the dish filled with pineapple, glacé cherries and apricots cut in dice and moistened with liqueur-flavoured hot syrup.

Pineapple Fritters. See **FRITTERS**.

Pineapple Ice Pudding

Ingredients
- ½ pineapple
- 3 oz. caster sugar
- 1 pt. double cream
- Juice of ½ lemon

Method

Peel the pineapple and cut into very small dice. Place in a saucepan with the sugar and half a gill of water. Simmer for ½ hr. then strain the syrup from the pineapple, mix it with the cream and add the lemon juice. Half freeze the mixture, mix in the pineapple, fill the pudding mould and place in ice till required.

Pineapple Jam

Ingredients
- 1 pineapple
- Sugar

Method

Peel pineapple and remove eyes. Mince twice and place in preserving pan. Allow 1 lb. sugar to each 1 lb. fruit. Add sugar and heat slowly to boiling point. Simmer gently for 1 hr., pour into hot jars and cover when cool.

Pineapple Mousse

Ingredients
- 10 egg yolks
- 5 egg whites
- ¼ pt. whipped cream
- 2 oz. caster sugar
- ½ gill pineapple purée (made by pounding the pineapple and rubbing through a sieve)

Method

Put the eggs, sugar and pineapple into a basin; beat over hot water until like batter, then put the basin on ice and whip until cold. Mix in the cream. Put in a mould and place in a cave or pack in ice for 3 hrs. Turn out like an ice pudding. By this recipe any mousse can be prepared, using other fruits instead of the pineapple.

Pineapple Salad. See **SALADS**.

Pineapple (Tinned) Trifle. Open a tin of pineapple and strain off the juice. Put the fruit in a mortar and mix with caster sugar and pound until smooth. Pass through a hair sieve and beat the juice with it. Sweeten, add 1 pt. cream to taste (or use evaporated milk with caster sugar); flavour with a few drops lemon essence. Put the pineapple pulp in a glass dish, pile cream over, decorate with a few halved cherries and serve.

PINIONS. The parts of a bird's wings which hold the long quill feathers. Pinions are usually cut away when trimming birds for cooking.

PINT. A measure of capacity containing the eighth part of a gallon.

PINTAIL (Fr. *canard pilet*). The name of a northern duck which is good eating. It is stuffed with sweet herbs, truffles and breadcrumbs bound with beaten egg, roasted and well basted with butter. Serve garnished with quarters of lemon.

PIPER. This European fish of the gurnet order is not often seen upon the table. It may be baked or roasted or fried, if filleted.

PIQUANT SAUCE. See SAUCES.

PISTACHIOS (Fr. *pistaches*). The tree which produces the edible pistachio nuts is a native of Western Asia. Each fruit is oval, about an inch long and contains a green-coloured kernel. Used for flavouring and garnishing. Also salted and used in savouries and cocktails.

PITCAITHLY BANNOCK. The name of a Scottish shortbread with peel, almonds and caraway seeds.

PLAICE (Fr. *plie*). This flat-fish is caught principally in European waters. It continues in season from about May throughout the best part of the year until Christmas; when in prime condition it should be quite white on the underside, the upperside dark with bright orange spots. The best are those caught between Dover and Hastings, known as Dover plaice. Plaice may be boiled, baked or fried, and when the fish is not too large it is best cooked in the oven at 350° F. Therm. 4 in a slightly buttered sauté-pan with mushrooms, shrimps, etc. Most recipes suitable for sole can be used for plaice.

    PLAICE, STEWED. Cut the plaice into small pieces, stew for ½ hr. in a little milk, thicken the liquor with flour, season with pepper and salt, chopped parsley and 1 tsp. lemon juice.

PLAIN CAKE, BASIC. See CAKES.

PLANTAIN. This fruit grows in bunches on trees, like the banana to which it is closely allied. Plantains are long, cylindrical, slightly curved, and when ripe, soft, fleshy and covered with a thick but yellowish skin. They are exceedingly nutritious, and they are used to brew a wine. They may be baked in their skins, sliced and fried in butter or floured and used in fritters.

PLOVER (Fr. *pluvier*). At one time plovers were much prized as game birds. The Golden, Grey and Green plovers are considered to be best for cooking.

PLUCK. The heart, liver and lights of an animal, so called because they are plucked out after slaughtering.

PLUM (Fr. *prune*). This name is applied to the succulent fruit of several species of the *prunus* family. There are both cooking and dessert plums, the choicest varieties being used for dessert. Plums are used in fruit pies. See also **PRUNE.**

    To BOTTLE. See FRUIT (p. 234).
    To CANDY. See FRUIT (p. 235).

Plum Cake

Ingredients	*Method*
½ lb. butter, lard or dripping	Rub the fat into the flour, sifted with the
¾ lb. flour	baking powder; add all the other dry
1 tsp. baking powder	ingredients and mix with the eggs one by
½ lb. sugar	one well beaten. Bake in a lined cake tin
½ lb. currants	for about 1¼ hr. at 200° F. Therm. ¼.
Grated lemon rind	
4 eggs	

Plum Cake (Plain)
Ingredients
  4 oz. dripping
  1 lb. flour
  2 tsp. baking powder
  ¼ lb. currants
  ¼ lb. sugar
  Pinch of salt
  ½ pt. milk

Method
Rub the dripping into the flour sifted with the baking powder. Add the other dry ingredients. Mix with the milk. Bake in a paper-lined cake tin for about 1½ hr. at 200° F. Therm. ¼. See **CAKES.**

Plum Chutney
Ingredients
  2 lb. plums
  1 lb. sweet apples
  2 lemons
  ½ oz. garlic or 4 oz. shallots
  1 oz. root ginger
  1 lb. sugar
  1 oz. salt
  1 oz. powdered ginger
  1 saltspoon cayenne pepper
  1 pt. malt vinegar

Method
Peel, core and cut the apples into dice; stone the plums; remove the rind and pips from the lemons and shred finely, slice the pulp; peel and mince garlic or shallots; bruise root ginger. Put all the ingredients together into an enamel pan, cover with vinegar, bring to the boil. Reduce heat and simmer until the mixture thickens, stirring occasionally to prevent burning. Put into jars and cover securely.

Plum Jam—I
Ingredients
  6 lb. Victoria plums
  6 lb. sugar

Method
Wipe over fruit with damp cloth; stone and place in preserving pan or large bowl. Sprinkle over half the sugar and allow to stand for 24 hrs. Then add further sugar and boil gently till jam thickens and sets. Stir occasionally to prevent sticking. Pour into hot jars and cover when cool.

Plum Jam—II
Ingredients
  3 lb. plums
  Water
  Sugar

Method
Wipe plums with damp cloth; place in preserving pan with enough water to cover. Simmer gently till fruit is pulp. Pass through coarse sieve, so that skins and stones are retained. Weigh and allow equal weight of sugar. Replace pulp in pan, heat and add sugar. Boil for 30 mins., stirring frequently. Test for setting, pour into warmed jars and cover when cool.

Plum Jelly
Ingredients
  6 lb. Victoria plums
  Water
  Sugar

Method
Wipe, skin and stone plums. Weigh them and place in preserving pan with water to cover. Boil up, pour off water and add

Plum Jelly (*continued*)

fresh boiling water. Allow to simmer until fruit is very soft. Strain through muslin, preferably overnight. Return to pan and reduce. Add sugar to pulp, allowing 1 lb. sugar to each 1 lb. pulp; stir until dissolved and boil for 20 mins. Skim and pour into hot jars. Do not cover until cold.

Plum Pudding—I

Ingredients

4 oz. flour
1 tsp. baking powder
Pinch of salt
12 oz. breadcrumbs
4 oz. caster sugar
4 oz. grated carrot
4 oz. grated apple
4 oz. currants
6 oz. mixed candied peel
12 oz. suet or butter
8 oz. each raisins and sultanas
Rind and juice of 1 lemon
2 oz. almonds
1 tsp. mixed spice
3 eggs
Milk
Wineglass brandy or sherry

Method

Sift together into a bowl the flour, baking powder and salt; add the breadcrumbs, caster sugar, carrot, apple, currants, chopped candied peel, chopped suet or melted margarine, raisins and sultanas, grated rind and juice of a lemon, blanched and chopped almonds and spice. Mix all the ingredients well together and stir in beaten eggs and sufficient milk to make the mixture moist. Add brandy or sherry. Put into 2 well-greased basins. Cover, tie up and boil for at least 4 hrs. at the first boil and 3 hrs. on day of use.

Plum Pudding—II

Ingredients

½ lb. finely chopped suet
¼ lb. raisins and currants
½ lb. flour
½ lb. brown sugar
½ lb. each grated potatoes and carrots
1 nutmeg
2 oz. candied peel
Little salt and cinnamon

Method

Grate the potatoes and carrots raw, and add them last. It is an improvement to use half flour and half breadcrumbs. This quantity makes two large puddings which must be steamed 9 hrs.

POÊLE. For this French culinary term there is really no English translation unless it be vaguely termed "white stew". The process is really boiling and stewing meat in unctuous, slightly acidulated white stock to preserve the whiteness of the meat.

POIVRADE SAUCE. See SAUCES.

POKEWEED. A North American plant which bears dark purple juicy berries, used for colouring wine. The young roots are sometimes eaten as a substitute for asparagus.

[392]

POLENTA. In Italy this word is more frequently spelt *polena* and signifies flour, prepared from chestnuts. The term has also been applied to a kind of special preparation of Indian corn meal.

Savoury Polenta. Put 1 cup polenta in a stewpan with some cold water and bring to the boil, stirring the whole time. When cooked, mix in 2 oz. grated cheese, 1 oz. butter; season to taste with salt and pepper. Stand the saucepan away from the heat. Make a pint of rich, hot gravy and add 2 tbsp. Tomato sauce. Turn the polenta on to a hot dish, pour the gravy over it, and serve.

POLLACK or POLLOCK. A seafish which resembles the cod. Also called Green Cod and Coalfish. Rock salmon is one variety of pollock. Cook in the same way as cod.

POLONY. A dry Italian sausage, made of partly cooked or smoked meat and cereal.

POMEGRANATE (Fr. *grenade*). The tree bearing this fruit is a native of North Africa and Western Asia. The name signifies an apple with many grains; made up of a quantity of grains or seeds packed closely and embedded in a very delicious red pulp. The rind is bitter, tough and leathery, of a golden brown colour tinged with red, and, as it contains a very large proportion of tannin, is used for curing skins, especially those known as Morocco leather.

Compôte of Pomegranates. Cut a small circle out of the skins of 5 or 6 pomegranates and with the point of a sharp knife, cut them down the sides. Take out the pips without injuring them (be sure there is none of the bitter yellow pith on them), put them into a compôte dish. Pour some syrup flavoured with maraschino or orange juice over and serve. Use also in mixed fruit salad.

POMMEL. An unsalted French double cream cheese.

POMPANA. Along some parts of the American coast this fish is regarded as a great delicacy. It has something of the flattened appearance of the sun-fish, and the brilliant silvery lustre of the mackerel. When broiled, it has a peculiar flavour which resembles pickled walnuts.

PONT L'ÉVÊQUE. A French semi-hard fermented cheese of delicate flavour, not unlike cheddar.

POONA. A cheese made in New York State.

POPCORN. See **INDIAN CORN.**

POPE. Also called Ruffe. A fish which resembles the perch in size, appearance and flavour.

POPE'S EYE. The name given to the small circle of fat found in the centre of a leg of mutton or pork. Also given in Scotland to a prime rump steak.

POPE'S NOSE. See **PARSON'S NOSE.**

POPPY (OPIUM). The seeds of this kind of poppy are used on cakes and breads, and also medicinally. The oil is used as a substitute for olive oil.

Poppy Seed Cake. See **CAKES.**

PORK (Fr. *porc*). The fresh meat of the pig; bacon or ham are the cured flesh. Pork is a good source of protein and vitamin B, but it must be carefully chosen, not kept too long and well cooked, because of the danger of disease. Never eat pork if the flesh remains pink after cooking: it should look white. A young pig or porker is divided into spare rib, leg, hand, belly, fore and hind loin. A chine of pork is cut from a bacon pig.

TO CHOOSE. The skin should be thin; a thick skin is a sign of age. Dairyfed pork is the best. The lean should be pale-pink rather than red, finely grained, and should yield to pressure, springing back readily; fat white and firm. Kernels in the fat indicate disease.

JOINTS OF PORK

Chine. Score with a knife, and roast or bake. Serve with Apple, Gooseberry, Piquant, Tomato or Robert sauce. Potatoes and any green vegetables may be served with it. The chine is also salted and boiled and may be served with turkey.

Spare Rib. This should be scored and then roasted or baked, and served as directed for chine of pork.

Hand. Soak it for 2 or 3 hrs. before cooking and then boil it. Serve pease pudding with it. For vegetables, carrots, turnips or parsnips. Cook these with the hand and garnish the dish with them. Potatoes may also be served and any green vegetables.

Leg. This may be roasted or baked and served as directed for roast chine or boiled and served according to directions given for hand of pork.

Loin. Score the skin. Brush it with salad oil, and roast or bake it. Serve Apple or Robert sauce with it.

Griskin. This may be roasted or baked. The basting must be very constant or the meat will be hard and dry. A plan sometimes adopted to make it tender is to put it in cold water and bring it to boiling point, then well dry the griskin and roast it.

Ham. See **HAM** and **BACON**.

PORK, ROAST. To make crisp crackling score the skin and brush it over with a little oil before placing in oven. Allow 25 mins. per lb. and 25 mins. over at 350° F. Therm. 4. Being very fat meat, pork usually needs no extra fat added for roasting, and little basting. Serve with sage and onion stuffing and Apple sauce, or as above according to the joint.

ROAST SUCKING PIG

Ingredients	*Method*
1 sucking pig	Stuff the belly of the pig with the forcemeat, and sew it in. Truss the legs like a hare. Brush well over with salad oil and roast quickly at 400° F. Therm. 6. Baste very constantly. It will take from 1½–2 hrs. according to its age.
Sage and onion forcemeat	
Salad oil	
Lemon	
Pepper and salt	

If more convenient the pig may be baked. For dishing it, remove the trussing string or cotton and cut it down the middle and place it back to back on the dish. Put half a head at each end, and the ears at the sides. The ordinary sauce served with it is made thus: Take the gravy from the pig and add to it some of the stuffing and the brains chopped fine and a little lemon peel and juice, pepper and salt and a little cayenne. Make hot and serve in a boat. Many other sauces, e.g. Brown, Apple, Tomato and Bread sauce with currants may be served instead.

NOTE. Sucking pig may also be stuffed with chestnut forcemeat mixed with sausage meat (see **FORCEMEAT**), also with truffles.

PORK CHOPS, GRILLED. Grill from 15–20 mins. according to size. They must be turned frequently to ensure they are cooked through.

Pork Pie, Raised

Ingredients

¼ lb. hot water crust (see p. 372)

¾ lb. lean pork

Salt and pepper

Nutmeg

Herbs and an apple (if desired)

Egg (for brushing)

1 tsp. gelatine

⅛ pt. stock

Method

Make the pastry. Mince or chop the pork. Grease the tin (5″ diameter), preferably one with a loose base. If this is not available, mould the pastry around a jam-jar turned upsidedown. When the pastry has cooled a little, line the tin or shape by hand. Fill with the meat and seasoning, a few herbs and peeled and sliced apple, and cover with a lid of pastry. Decorate the top with leaves and a rose, a hole in the centre. Bake the rose separately and replace when the pie is ready for serving. If the pie has been moulded by hand, a piece of greaseproof paper in a double band, to help to keep the shape, should be pinned firmly round. Brush the top over with egg before cooking. Remove paper half an hour before cooking is finished to brown pastry. Bake for 1½ hr. for the first 20 mins at 400° F. Therm. 6, then reduce to 310° F. Therm. 2, to continue cooking. When the pie is cooked, dissolve the gelatine in the stock and pour into the pie. Replace the rose in the centre and garnish with parsley.

Pork Pudding. Take ¼ lb. finely grated breadcrumbs and place in a bowl. Pour over ¾ pt. milk which has been mixed with 1 or 2 well-beaten eggs and leave to soak for an hour. Stir in 1½ lb. lean pork finely minced and seasoned with salt and pepper and a little grated nutmeg. Pour the mixture into a buttered oven-dish and bake at 310° F. Therm. 2 for about 2 hrs. Serve garnished with watercress and accompanied by Apple sauce.

Pork Sausage. Take 2 lb. fresh pork meat using equal proportions of fat and meat. Pass through a mincing machine and mix together with 4 oz. breadcrumbs, season with pepper and salt, add a sprinkling of grated nutmeg, grating of lemon peel, small pinch of thyme, savory, sweet marjoram and basil. Mix well together. Use as desired. If preferred, nutmeg and sage to season, may be added.

PORRIDGE. A Scottish dish made by boiling oatmeal in water or milk. See **OAT-MEAL.** It should be served with cream, milk and a pinch of salt, but some people prefer to eat it with sugar and butter, or even with golden syrup or treacle.

PORT. A dark red or purple wine made in the locality of Oporto, hence its name. Much used in cooking, particularly of game.

Port Wine Sauce. See SAUCES.

PORT DU SALUT or PORT SALUT. A fine French cheese of round, flat shape, firm, but creamy in texture and full of holes, originally made by the monks of the Trappist monastery at Port du Salut in the Mayenne Department, now made elsewhere in France and Belgium.

PORTERHOUSE STEAK. A steak cut from a sirloin of beef, including the upper and under part.

PORTUGUESE SAUCE. See SAUCES.

POSSETS. A beverage composed of milk, curdled by boiling with wine or cider.

POT AU FEU. This is the stock-pot of the French household; from it the cook makes her soups and sauces.

POT HERBS. A name applied to any kind of plant which can be boiled for food. It is generally used by the cook to signify a selection of vegetables suitable for flavouring soup or broth.

POT MARIGOLD. See CALENDULA.

POT MARJORAM. See MARJORAM.

POT ROASTING. This means cooking in a pan with a tight-fitting lid. Always use a thick saucepan, add 2 oz. dripping and a cupful water, allow 2–3 hrs. cooking time for a joint, 2½–3 lb. in weight. Turn the joint frequently to ensure even cooking.

POTASSIUM. See SALTPETRE.

POTATO (Fr. *pomme de terre*). The potato is one of the most universally esteemed vegetables. It has a high calorific value, but its vitamin content is relatively low. The Sweet potato of America is the tuber of a climbing plant to which the name "potato" was first applied. It was introduced by Sir Francis Drake and Sir John Hawkins and was grown at Formby, Lancashire. It forms a prime vegetable of the Southern and Central States of America. Another name for it is Spanish potato.

POTATOES, BAKED

Ingredients	Method
Potatoes Butter Salt and pepper	Choose large potatoes. Scrub well and remove eyes. Rub with olive oil or butter. Make a slit or two in each potato (with a knife) or prick with a fork. Bake at 375° F. Therm. 5 until soft, about 35–60 mins. according to size. Split and butter, season with pepper and salt and serve at once.

POTATOES, BOILED (NEW). Scrape or rub the skins off and put the potatoes into boiling water, to which a little salt is added. Boil them gently for 20 mins. or more, according to their age. When very nearly tender, pour off the water, cover with a cloth and set the saucepan by the side of the heat so that they may finish their cooking in their own steam. A small sprig of mint is sometimes boiled with new potatoes. Finish, if desired, with a small piece of butter and very finely chopped parsley.

POTATOES, BOILED (OLD). If to be boiled in their skins, scrub them perfectly clean, and put them into a saucepan with sufficient boiling water to cover them; add a little salt and boil gently for ½ hr. or more until *very nearly* tender, but not quite. Then pour away the water. Peel the potatoes, replace in the saucepan, sprinkle salt upon them, cover with a cloth and put the lid on the saucepan. Allow to stand by the side of the heat to finish cooking in their own steam. Care must be taken that the potatoes cooked in this way are free from disease. One tainted potato would destroy the flavour of the others. If cooked without skins, peel them thinly and treat them in the same manner; pour off the water when they are very nearly tender and finish cooking them in their own steam. If the potatoes are good and are cooked according to these directions, they will be perfectly dry and floury. Choose potatoes of the same size to cook together.

POTATOES, BROWNED. Peel the potatoes and allow a large one per head. Halve and quarter. Place in tin with beef, and roast brown in 1–1½ hrs. Turn well, season with salt and pepper.

[396]

POTATOES, FRIED. These may be cut in slices, straws or small fancy shapes. Throw them as they are cut into cold water to remove the outside starch. Before frying, dry them well in a cloth, otherwise they will not fry crisp. Fry them in hot fat (see **DEEP FRYING,** p. 239). Draw the fat to one side of the heat so that the potatoes may cook slowly without discolouring from 5 to 10 mins. according to size. Toss the potatoes frequently during cooking so that they do not stick together and those on the bottom do not become crisp and the top ones soggy. Use butter, fat or oil for frying. Then remove them and reheat the fat again. Plunge the potatoes in and fry to a golden-brown colour. When the potatoes are cut in very thin slices for potato chips, they may be fried crisp at once, allowing 1 large potato per person. In this case, cook the potatoes medium fast to prevent them sticking to the sides of the pan.

POTATOES, FRIED (SOUFFLÉ). Cut the potatoes in thin slices lengthwise, ¼″ thick. Throw into cold water and then dry in a cloth; put them into hot fat that has not quite risen to frying point, and allow them to cook in this for 7 mins. Then remove them and let them get cold. Heat the fat to frying point and put the potatoes in again; they will then inflate like small balloons and become a golden brown.

POTATOES, SAUTÉ. Cut the potatoes into olive or other shapes. Parboil them and dry in a cloth. Then sauté them in plenty of clarified butter until a golden brown.

POTATOES, STEAMED. Place the potatoes in a steamer and sprinkle them with salt. Keep the water in the saucepan underneath quickly boiling the whole time the potatoes are cooking. If the potatoes are cooked in their skins, peel them when very nearly tender, put them back into the steamer again, having first poured all the water from the under-saucepan, cover with a cloth and put them by the side of the heat to finish cooking in their own steam.

Steaming is one of the simplest and best ways of cooking potatoes. If the potatoes are good, and the water is kept briskly boiling, this method cannot fail to be successful.

Potatoes, Anna

Ingredients	*Method*
6 potatoes (raw)	Wash and peel the potatoes, slice into thin even slices. Take the butter and grease a round mould. Put a layer of potatoes at the bottom, placing them in evenly. Season with pepper and salt. Melt the rest of the butter and pour a little over the layer of potatoes. Then add another layer of potatoes and continue until mould is nearly full, adding butter and seasoning as before. Put the mould into a hot oven 450° F. Therm. 8 and bake for 1 hr. Then turn mould upside down on a platter to drain. Remove mould and the potatoes should be light brown and have the shape of the mould.
8 oz. butter	

Potatoes, Baked and Stuffed. Cook potatoes until soft; with a small knife cut a slice off one side of each potato, to make a long boat shape. Remove inside of potato and beat up with a little butter and 1 tbsp. cream or milk: then add chopped chives or parsley, pounded shrimps, chutney to taste or grated cheese, according to taste.

Potato Balls. Form some potatoes mashed (see p. 398), into balls. Brush them over with beaten egg. Place on a baking-sheet and bake at 400° F. Therm 6 until brown.

Potato Casserole

Ingredients

3 lb. potatoes
1 pt. condensed cream of mushroom soup (or cream of asparagus soup) ·
1 wineglass sherry
½ pt. milk
2 oz. butter (or margarine)
Pepper and salt
Grated cheese if desired

Method

Peel and slice potatoes thinly; place in a bowl, cover with water and leave 1 hr. Drain potatoes and place in layers in an ovenproof dish, dot with butter and season with pepper and salt. Add mixture of soup, sherry and milk; add grated cheese, and bake slowly at 210° F. Therm. ¼ for about 1 hr.

Potato Chips. See POTATOES, FRIED (p. 397). For *game chips*, see GAME.

Potato Croquettes

Ingredients

2 lb. potatoes
2 oz. butter
Pepper and salt
2 eggs
White breadcrumbs

Method

Boil the potatoes and rub through a wire sieve. Mash well with butter, pepper and salt, then mix in one well-beaten egg. Flour the hands lightly and form the mixture into balls or any other shape preferred. Brush them over with beaten egg and cover with crumbs. Slightly mould them again when the crumbs are on them. Fry in a frying basket in hot fat. Serve garnished with fried parsley.

Potatoes, Duchesse. See Potato Rosettes.

Potatoes, Mashed. Peel and cut into quarters 1 large or 2 medium potatoes per head. Boil in salted water till just tender and mealy, but not mushy. Drain and pass through a ricer or coarse sieve. Return to the pan and add 1 tsp. butter or dripping for each potato. Beat well with a fork or wooden spoon until perfectly free from lumps. Season to taste with salt and pepper, add scalded cream, or top off milk, beating until the potatoes are light and smooth. Garnish with chopped parsley or paprika before serving.

VARIATIONS

1. Add chopped parsley while whipping and sprinkle some on top before serving.
2. Add chopped chives according to taste and serve garnished with chopped chives.
3. Add grated cheese, dot with butter and place under hot grill before serving.
4. Add tomato sauce or purée.

Potato Ribbons. Peel the potatoes, and take very thin parings. Twist them into knots and fry them in hot fat until crisp and golden-brown colour. Drain on kitchen paper and serve at once.

Potato Rosettes (Fr. *pommes de terre à la duchesse*)

Ingredients

1 lb. potatoes
1–2 egg yolks
1 tbsp. cream
1 oz. butter
Salt and pepper
Nutmeg
Egg for brushing

Method

Cook and rub the potatoes through a sieve. Add eggs, butter, cream, seasonings and nutmeg. Pipe in rosettes on to a greased tin, brush lightly with egg and bake at 400° F. Therm. 6 until well-browned. Pile on a dish and serve hot.

Potato Rosettes (*continued*)

Piping creamed potato

Potato Salad. See SALAD.

Potatoes, Scalloped. Peel and slice thinly 1 medium large potato per head. Butter a baking-dish and arrange on bottom of this a layer of potatoes. Add salt and pepper to season and dot with butter, repeating the layers and seasoning and butter until they are all used. Add milk nearly to cover, dot top with butter; cover the casserole or baking-dish and place in a moderately hot oven, 375° F. Therm. 5 for about 30 mins. Remove cover, test for tenderness and continue to cook until done.

VARIATIONS

1. Sprinkle each layer with chopped chives and parsley mixed.
2. Sprinkle layers and top with parmesan cheese and dot with butter.
3. Alternate layers of potatoes with thinly sliced onion.
4. Mix 2 tsp. curry powder with the milk and alternate sliced onions with potatoes.

Potato Snow. Pass well-cooked floury potatoes through a wire sieve or ricer into a vegetable dish. Brown the top with a salamander or in a quick oven 400° F. Therm. 6 and serve very hot.

Potato Soup. See SOUPS.

POTTING. The process necessary for preserving various foods such as meats and fish in pots.

All meats may be potted in the same manner. The meat is cooked until quite tender, carefully rid of all bone, gristle and skin, and then scraped finely and rubbed through a wire sieve. Next, pound in a mortar with about 4 oz. clarified butter, to every 1 lb. meat or fish, seasoned well to taste. Put into jars with clarified butter poured over; keep in a cool place. Some meats may be potted together, such as chicken and ham, chicken and tongue, veal and ham, etc. Any bones may be made into stock in the usual way. This stock should be reduced afterwards to half-glaze which may be used in the place of butter. The quantity of butter and glaze must be determined according to the meat used. Dry potted meat is not agreeable, but on the other hand it must not be too moist. Sometimes a little spice is used, but it is safer to leave it out, as many people object to it. If not for immediate use, use butter only (no half-glaze) or the fat of ham, if ham is being potted.

Anchovies must be washed, filleted and dried, well pounded in a mortar with a little clarified butter, and rubbed through a sieve. Season nicely with pepper, pack closely in pots and cover with clarified butter. Bloaters, cooked dried haddocks and any fish suitable for potting, are all prepared in the same manner. Detailed instructions for potting will be found under individual headings.

POULARDES. These are young fowls which have been especially fattened. They may be regarded as the female of the capon.

[399]

POULETTE. French term for Henfowl.

POULETTE SAUCE. See SAUCES.

POULTRY (Fr. *volaille*). Under this heading are classified all sorts of domestic fowls reared for the table, and for eggs and feathers. This definition will include chickens, capons, ducks, turkeys and geese, to which some add guinea fowl and the peacock. See individual headings.

POUND. See COOKING TERMS.

POUTING. Also called Bill or Whiting Pout. A species of the cod.

POWAN. A white fish, a freshwater herring, found only in Lochs Lomond and Leck.

PRAIRIE HEN OR CHICKEN. The name given to an American grouse which frequents the prairies of the Central United States. It is very delicate when cooked. After plucking, singeing and drawing, cleaning and cutting the claws to about half their length, it may be baked, basting well, in butter at 400° F. Therm. 6. The bird should be kept rather underdone. When cooked, it should be split into halves. Put a squeeze of lemon juice into the dripping pan and season to taste with salt and pepper.

PRALINE. Any confection made with nuts and burnt sugar.

Ingredients	Method
6 oz. caster sugar 6 oz. whole almonds (unblanched)	Place the sugar and almonds together in a thick saucepan and set over a low heat to melt. Do not stir until the sugar is almost melted and turning colour. Then stir until a good caramel and the almonds are well toasted. Leave until cold and set. Break and grind or powder as desired, Keep in an airtight tin. Use for, or in, soufflés, ices, creams, etc.

PRAWN (Fr. *salicoque, crevette, rose*). The origin of the word is said to be unknown. The English prawn is caught when small in large quantities on most coasts and is sold in our markets sometimes as a "pink shrimp", being of a pinkish red when cooked. This varies from the brown shrimp, not only by colour but also by the shape of the body, which is narrower and slightly humped in the centre, and on account of the sawlike projection springing from between the eyes. Large prawns are caught singly and are much used for garnish. The black filament in the back of prawns should be removed before eating; it is poisonous to anyone who suffers from anti-shellfish intestinal complaints.

PRAWNS, BOILED. Throw them into quickly boiling water, with salt in it, and boil for 6 to 8 mins. Remove all scum from the water and drain them well when cooked.

Prawns Baked with Tomatoes (Shrimps may be substituted)

Ingredients	Method
1 lb. fresh prawns 4 firm tomatoes 3 oz. butter 1 small grated onion 1 diced celery stalk 1 bay leaf ⅛ tsp. chopped chives ⅛ tsp. mace ¼ tsp. salt	Choose fresh prawns. Shell and remove vein. Wash tomatoes, remove top, core and hollow out pulp, Reserve this. Melt 2 oz. butter in a saucepan over a low heat, add the onion and sauté for 3 mins. until light brown. Add celery, bay leaf, chives, tomato pulp, mace, salt and paprika. Cover and simmer for 15 mins, very gently. Add cream and 3 tsp. breadcrumbs

[400]

Prawns Baked with Tomatoes (*continued*)

Paprika
4 tbsp. cream
4 tsp. breadcrumbs

to make a thick sauce. Add prawns cut in half, lengthwise, simmer for 3 mins. Arrange tomato shells on a shallow baking dish, fill with the prawn mixture and cover each with 1 tsp. breadcrumbs. Dot with butter and bake at 350° F. Therm. 4 for 10 mins. until golden brown.

Prawns with Herbs
Ingredients

1 lb. freshly picked prawns
¼ pt. boiling water
½ tsp. salt
1 bay leaf
2 peppercorns
½ tsp. celery seed
2 oz. butter
¼ tsp. paprika
⅛ tsp. marjoram
Pinch of nutmeg
Juice of lemon
Salt and pepper
Watercress

Method

Melt the butter in a saucepan and add all ingredients except watercress. Cover and simmer for 3 mins. Serve on hot toast. Garnish with watercress.

Prawn Mayonnaise
Ingredients

1 cucumber
Vinegar
Water
1 cabbage lettuce
1 cup each cooked peas and French beans
4 tomatoes
½ pt. mayonnaise
12–16 shelled prawns
Chopped chives or grated beetroot

Method

Cut the cucumber into four blocks of equal size, scoop out centre; place in bowl with sufficient vinegar and water in equal portions to cover and leave 15 mins. Remove the leaves from the lettuce whole, and wash well in plenty of water, dry in a clean cloth and arrange on four individual plates. Mix the peas and beans together, add a portion to each plate. Blanch and peel the tomatoes, slice them and arrange on plates. Remove the cucumber, drain and place one block in the centre of each plate. Fill with mayonnaise and arrange the prawns in the cucumber cups and around the plates to form an even pattern. Garnish with beetroot or chives.

PRICKLY PEARS. Also known as Indian Fig. These are the fruit or berries of a cactus common to various parts of America, other varieties being found along the shores of the Mediterranean and in some parts of India.

PRIMROSE. The root and leaf are used medicinally. The leaves are also used in salads; the flowers, which have a delicate flavour, are used in puddings, salads, vinegar and wines.

[401]

PROFITEROLE. A kind of light cake which was originally baked in hot ashes and then filled with cream. Also a large pea-shaped fritter of the soufflé type made with choux paste, dropped in teaspoonfuls on to a baking-sheet and baked slowly at 200° F. Therm. ¼ until crisp and dry, then, when cool, filled with cream and served with thick Chocolate sauce.

PRUNE (Fr. *pruneau*). What are generally known as prunes or French plums are the dried fruits of a plum tree, cultivated in many parts of France, especially for the purpose. The fruits are also delicious fresh, when ripe, and are covered with a rich bloom, which makes them valuable for dessert.

PRUNES, STEWED. Well wash the prunes and put them in a saucepan with just sufficient water to cover them and sugar to taste. Simmer them for an hour or longer until perfectly soft.

Compôte of Prunes. Put 1 lb. prunes into a saucepan with ¼ pt. water, ¼ pt. white wine, and 1 oz. crushed loaf sugar. Set the pan at the side of the fire and simmer for 10 mins. Remove prunes, drain, arrange in a dish and then pour over liquor, adding a little cochineal to improve the colour, if possible.

Prune Drink

Ingredients
- 2½ oz. prunes
- 1 oz. sugar
- 1 qt. water

Method
Cut the prunes in two. Boil them with the sugar in the water for 1 hr. Strain and cover until cold.

Gâteau of Prunes

Ingredients
- ½–1 oz. gelatine
- ¼ pt. water
- 1 lb. prunes
- 3 oz. moist sugar
- Few drop cochineal (if desired)

Method
Soak the gelatine in ¼ pt. water. Well wash the prunes and put them in a saucepan with the sugar and ½ pt. water. Simmer until soft and rub through a wire sieve. Dissolve the gelatine and mix in thoroughly; add cochineal. Pour into wetted mould. When turned out, serve with boiled custard. This is a pretty dish if set in a border mould, and afterwards sprinkled with grated coconut, with whipped white of egg or cream in the centre of the dish.

Prune and Apple Jam

Ingredients
- 4 lb. prunes
- Water
- 9 large cooking apples
- Juice of 2 oranges and 2 lemons
- 1 lb. sugar

Method
Wash prunes and allow to stand all night in enough water to well cover them. Next day simmer in this water until tender, remove from heat and allow to cool. Remove stones and return to preserving pan. Peel, core and slice the apples, and with the orange and lemon juice and sugar, add to prunes. Cook slowly, stirring frequently but gently, until jam thickens. Test for setting, pour into warmed jars and cover.

PTARMIGAN. A kind of grouse which inhabits the Northern countries and high mountains of Europe, Asia and America. The European ptarmigan and some other varieties have brown plumage in summer which turns to nearly white in winter. The feet are usually feathered to the extremity of the outside claw. The ptarmigan can be cooked as grouse.

PTARMIGAN, ROAST. Pour 1 tbsp. sweet oil into a dish and roll the birds in this. Roasting time about 30 mins. in a moderate oven 350° F. Therm. 4. Dredge with flour when cooked and baste well. Return to oven sprinkled with breadcrumbs, to crisp and brown. Serve with Bread sauce, brown gravy and garnish with watercress.

PUDDINGS. Under this heading are a variety of recipes for the preparation of certain dishes which have no more definite name than "pudding". A pudding is a species of food which may be either soft or moderately hard in consistency and variously made: it is usually sweet, but may be savoury, as Pease Pudding. Steak-and-Kidney Pudding. The term "sweet" denotes the pudding course and "dessert" is also sometimes used, especially in America. The term "after" or "hereafter" is sometimes used to denote a pudding. Puddings can be grouped under the following headings:

Cereal (see MILK PUDDINGS), Pastry, Suet Crust, Steamed, and Steamed Sponge. See also under FRUIT, CUSTARD and JELLY.

TO PREPARE INGREDIENTS FOR PUDDINGS. Suet should be chopped finely, raisins stoned and cut in halves. Currants should be washed in lukewarm water, and then rubbed thoroughly in a cloth to dry them and rub off the stalks. Drop a few at a time on a plate to discover by the sound if there are any stones amongst them. Sultanas should be rubbed in flour and the stalks picked off. Candied peel should be cut in thin slices. Moist sugar is best for sweetening purposes, as less is required, but caster should be used for all light puddings.

TO BAKE PUDDINGS. Milk puddings require a moderate oven 350° F. Therm. 4, otherwise both the eggs and milk in them will curdle; the milk also will scorch (see MILK PUDDINGS). Any pudding of the nature of a soufflé will require a quick heat to throw it up. A batter pudding must also be baked in a hot oven 400° F. Therm. 6, or it will not be light. Custard puddings and all those containing custard must be very slowly cooked. The best way of cooking either large or small custards is to put them in a Yorkshire Pudding tin which contains sufficient hot water to come halfway up the dish or moulds. If they are placed thus in a slow oven 250° F. Therm ¼, they will cook without curdling.

TO BOIL PUDDINGS. A pudding which is to be boiled should be placed in a saucepan of *boiling water*. The water must boil all the time the pudding is cooking, and the pudding must be *under water* the whole time. If these directions are not attended to, the water will soak into the pudding and spoil it. A kettle of boiling water should be at hand to fill up the saucepan as may be necessary. A boiled pudding should be of a stiff consistency and may be cooked in a basin or mould, or in a scalded and floured cloth. There is no doubt that many puddings are much lighter when boiled in a cloth. When basins or moulds are used they must be thoroughly greased to prevent the pudding sticking to them, and a scalded and floured cloth must be tied over them. Fill the pudding-basin *quite full*. If this is not done the water will soak into the pudding. Scalding and flouring the cloth prevents this sticking to the pudding, and the flour also forms a paste which helps to prevent the water getting into the mixture. When a cloth only is used, it must be scalded and floured; the pudding mixture is then formed into a nice round shape and placed in the centre of the cloth, which must be tied securely, leaving room for the pudding to swell. It is advisable when a pudding is cooked in this way to put a plate at the bottom of the saucepan to prevent the pudding sticking and burning. The pudding-cloths should be quickly washed after using, in hot water without soap and hung in the air to dry. Keep them in a dry place. Badly washed cloths, or those that have been allowed to get damp will give an unpleasant flavour to the puddings. A 1-pt. basin full of mixture will require at least 2 hrs. to cook.

TO STEAM PUDDINGS. When a pudding is steamed it should be of a slack consistency and it must be placed in a well-greased mould or basin, and covered with buttered paper. If a steamer is not available for the purpose, put the pudding into a saucepan with just sufficient water to come half-way up the mould, and keep the water at *simmering* point until the pudding is cooked. A custard pudding, or any pudding containing custard, must be very carefully steamed, as extreme

TO STEAM PUDDINGS (*continued*)
heat would curdle the eggs and make the custard watery. A 1-pt. basin full of
mixture will require at least 3 hrs. to cook.

TO TURN A PUDDING OUT OF ITS MOULD OR CLOTH. First lift the pudding from
the saucepan by taking it firmly on a fork. Reverse the saucepan lid and let the
pudding rest on it, holding them both obliquely that the water may run away.
Then lift it on to a plate, untie the cloth and cut the string. Remove the cloth
carefully, then take the basin in the hands, holding a cloth round it to prevent it
burning them. Shake it gently to ascertain that the pudding is quite free from the
mould, then reverse it on to a dish and remove the mould carefully. In turning
out a pudding, guard against impatience or haste. Turning it out too quickly,
without being sure that it is free from the mould, will sometimes cause it to break
and have an unsightly appearance. When the pudding is in a cloth, untie the
strings and draw the cloth a little from the sides of the pudding, then reverse it
on a hot dish and draw the cloth carefully away. In turning baked puddings
out of the tins, cut them first into neat squares, and then slip a knife under them,
to be quite sure they are free from the tins before removing them.

SAUCES TO SERVE WITH PUDDINGS. The choice of the right sauce is dependent
upon the pudding itself, also the remainder of the meal.

With Cereal puddings, serve a plain sauce, such as custard, whipped cream,
plain cream or foamy sauce.

With Custard-type puddings, choose a harmonising sauce.

With Fruit puddings, serve cream, custard or sauces with spiced flavour.

With Plain puddings, choose a lemon or harmonising sauce.

With Rich puddings, serve plain sauces.

With Steamed or Baked puddings, serve a liquid sauce or well-sweetened whipped
cream.

Albert Pudding

Ingredients

3 eggs
Weight of eggs in:
   Butter or margarine
   Flour
   Sugar
Grated rind of 1 lemon

Method

Cream the butter or margarine. Mix in
gradually the flour and sugar, alternately
with the eggs, which should be well
beaten. Add the grated lemon rind, and
steam for 3 hrs. Serve with White sauce.

Amber Pudding

Ingredients

4 oz. butter
4 oz. sugar
3 eggs
4 oz. dry breadcrumbs
¼ tsp. salt
3 tbsp. orange marmalade

Method

Mix the butter and sugar together, add
the eggs well beaten, then the breadcrumbs, salt and lastly the marmalade.
Mix well. Pour into a buttered circular
mould, and cover tightly. Steam for 2
hrs. Serve with Orange sauce (see p. 45).
Sufficient for 4 persons.

Angel Pudding

Ingredients

4 oz. flour
1 oz. caster sugar
2 oz. butter or margarine
½ pt. milk
1 whole egg and 1 yolk

Method

Put the flour into a basin; add to it the
sugar. Melt the butter, add to the milk.
Make a well in the centre of the flour and
put in the eggs. Mix gradually, add the
milk by degrees, beat well. Partly fill
greased patty-pans. Bake for about 20
mins. at 400° F. Therm. 6. Serve with jam
or a sweet sauce.

[404]

Apricot Pudding
Ingredients
- 1 oz. isinglass
- 1½ pt. milk
- ½ pt. cream
- ½ lb. apricot jam

Method
Dissolve the isinglass in the milk over a low heat, and when it boils, stir in the cream and strain into a basin. Rub the jam through a sieve, add it to the cream and stir occasionally until cold, but not set, or the jam will sink to the bottom of the mould. Then pour into a moistened mould; when firm, turn on to a glass or silver dish. A few finely chopped pistachio kernels may be sprinkled over if desired,

Aunt Elizabeth's Pudding
Ingredients
- 1 cup stale breadcrumbs
- Knob of butter
- 1 pt. milk
- 1 tbsp. sugar
- Grated rind of 1 lemon
- 2 egg yolks

Method
Soak the bread in the milk for 30 mins. then beat well with a fork. Add the butter, sugar, lemon rind and well-beaten eggs. Bake in a good oven 375° F. Therm. 5, for 30 mins. Serve with a little jam poured over.

Aunt Susie's Pudding
Ingredients
- 4 oz. butter
- 2 tbsp. each ground rice and sugar
- 2 tbsp. flour
- Rind of 1 lemon chopped small
- 2 oz. candied peel
- ½ pt. milk
- 2 eggs
- Few drops almond essence

Method
Beat the butter to a cream. Add gradually the ground rice, sugar, flour, chopped lemon rind, peel, milk and the well-beaten eggs. Flavour with almond essence; pour the mixture into well greased mould, tie with a cloth and boil for 2 hrs. Serve with sweet sauce.

Batter Pudding, Steamed
Ingredients
- 8 oz. flour
- Pinch of salt
- 1 egg
- ½ pt. milk
- Fruit or spices or jam

Method
Sift the flour with a pinch of salt, make a well in the middle and break in the egg. Add half the milk, blend to a smooth paste and beat well for 5 mins.; add the remainder of the milk. Leave to stand for 30 mins., pour the batter into a well-greased pudding basin and steam for 1–1½ hrs. The basin may be lined with jam, or currants, fruit, spices or flavourings may be added to the batter.

Beaulieu Pudding
- 6 oz. butter
- 1 cup each flour and sugar
- Grated peel of ½ lemon

Melt the butter and beat until creamy, add the flour and sugar, grated lemon peel, candied peel and the almonds, blanched

Beaulieu Pudding (*continued*)

2 oz. candied peel
Few bitter almonds and twice the number of sweet almonds
½ wineglass brandy

and chopped. Mix the ingredients thoroughly, adding brandy. Butter some small moulds, fill them with the mixture and bake for 30 mins. in a moderate oven (350° F. Therm. 4). When cooked turn the puddings out of the moulds on to a hot dish and serve.

Bermuda Pudding

Ingredients

1½ pt. raspberries, strawberries or redcurrants
Sugar
2 tbsp. water
Arrowroot

Method

Place the fruit in a jar with some sugar and the water, cover and set in a cool oven (300° F. Therm. 2) and allow to remain until the juice runs freely. Strain and measure. To 1 pt. juice allow 3 tsp. arrowroot. Mix this in a cup with a little water or fruit juice. Pour the boiling fruit upon it, stir, return to the saucepan and boil until the mixture thickens. To improve the colour add a little cochineal. Pour into a wetted mould and next day turn out on to a dish and serve with cream.

Bernese Pudding

Ingredients

2 eggs
¼ pt. milk
2 oz. each breadcrumbs and flour
4 oz. each sugar, suet, chopped peel and currants
1 lemon
¼ tsp. grated nutmeg

Method

Beat the eggs in the milk, add the breadcrumbs and flour. Mix the finely shredded suet with the candied peel, sugar and currants, rind and juice of the lemon, grated nutmeg. Mix the ingredients for 10 mins. and allow to stand for 1 hr. Stir well, then put into a well greased basin, cover with floured cloth, place in boiling water and boil for 3½ hrs.

Boston Pudding

Ingredients

2 lb. cooking apples
Piece of cinnamon
3 cloves
1 lemon
Sugar
3 eggs
3 oz. butter
Grated nutmeg
Grated peel and juice of ½ lemon
Puff paste (see p. 374)

Method

Peel, core and cut the apples into small pieces. Put them into a saucepan with a small piece of stick cinnamon, the cloves and the thinly pared rind of the lemon. Moisten with a little water, allow to stew gently until reduced to pulp. When cooked, sweeten the apples with moist sugar to taste, and pass through a fine sieve. Beat the yolks of the eggs and the white of one with the warmed butter, grated nutmeg, grated peel and strained juice of half a lemon. Add the whole to

Boston Pudding (*continued*)

the apple mixture and beat thoroughly. Butter and line a pie-dish with puff paste, pour in the mixture and bake at 350° F. Therm. 4. When cooked, serve either hot or cold.

Bread Pudding
Ingredients
- ½ lb. scraps of bread
- ¼ lb. finely chopped suet
- 2 oz. moist sugar
- ¼ lb. currants
- 1 egg

Method

Soak the bread in cold water until soft; squeeze it quite dry. Beat it up with a fork. Add to it the suet, sugar and currants, which should be well washed and dried. Mix with the egg, well beaten. Boil in a greased basin for 1 hr.

Bread and Butter Pudding
Ingredients
- 2 slices thin bread and butter
- ½ oz. currants and sultanas
- 1 egg
- ½ pt. milk
- 1 oz. sugar

Method

Cut the bread and butter into small even-sized pieces and place in a buttered pie-dish. Sprinkle the fruit in between the bread and butter. Mix together the beaten egg, sugar and milk; pour over the bread; let it soak for ½ hr. or more. Sprinkle a little brown sugar on the top and bake at 350° F. Therm. 4, until brown and crisp (about 35 mins.).

Castle Puddings
Ingredients
- 2 oz. each sugar and butter
- 1 egg
- 3 oz. flour
- ½ tsp. baking powder
- 1 tbsp. milk
- Lemon juice
- Jam sauce

Method

Grease 3 or 4 small dariole moulds. Cream fat and sugar; add egg and beat well. Fold in the sifted flour and baking powder, then add the milk and lemon juice. Half fill each mould with the mixture (if steaming, cover with a piece of greased paper), and bake for 10 mins. at 400° F. Therm. 6, or steam for 25 mins. Turn out and serve with a little jam sauce round the dish. Serve remaining sauce in sauceboat.

Charlotte Russe
Ingredients
- Lemon jelly
- Cherries and angelica
- ¼ lb. sponge fingers
- ¼ oz. gelatine
- ⅛ pt. water
- ¼ pt. each cream and custard
- 2 tbsp. sherry
- 1 tsp. vanilla essence

Method

Pour a little jelly into the bottom of a soufflé tin. Decorate with cherries and angelica. Add a thin layer of jelly and set. Line the tin with sponge fingers, pressing them well together. Dissolve the gelatine in cold water. Half whip cream and add custard, lightly fold in other ingredients; add the gelatine last. When on point of

[407]

Charlotte Russe (*continued*)

1 or 2 tbsp. sugar

setting, pour carefully into prepared mould. Set, trim edges of sponge fingers level with cream. Turn out and arrange chopped jelly round. In hot weather always add good measure of gelatine.

Coconut Pudding

Ingredients

¼ lb. each coconut, sugar and butter
3 eggs
½ wineglass brandy
1 tsp. essence of lemon
Little nutmeg
Puff paste (see p. 373)

Method

Grate the coconut. Work the sugar into the butter, beat the eggs lightly and add. Sprinkle the coconut in and stir it well. Add the brandy and the lemon flavouring with the grated nutmeg. Line a pie-dish with puff paste, place the pudding into it, set it in the oven for ½ hr. at 375° F. Therm. 5. Have ready some of the paste, rolled thinly and cut into leaves. Make them into a wreath round pudding, and return to the oven for ¼ hr. at same temperature.

Date Pudding. As **Fig Pudding** below, with dates substituted for figs.

Fig Pudding

Ingredients

½ lb. scraps of bread
¼ lb. finely chopped suet
½ lb. figs
3 oz. moist sugar
1 egg

Method

Soak the bread in water until quite soft. Squeeze it quite dry. Add to it the suet, sugar and figs (chopped quite small) and mix with beaten egg. Boil in a greased basin for 1 hr.

Fruit Pudding

Ingredients

½ lb. suet pastry (see p. 375)
1½ lb. fresh fruit
Sugar

Method

Roll the pastry thinly into a circle large enough to cover the base and sides of the basin to be used. Cut out a section large enough to use as the lid. Ease the pastry into the greased basin, taking care not to leave any air bubbles underneath. Join, easing together with the finger tips. Fill the dish with the prepared fruit and add sugar between each layer, finishing with fruit. Damp the edges, fit on the lid and press the edges together. Cover with the greased paper and steam for 2–2½ hrs.

Ginger Pudding

Ingredients

3 oz. each flour, bread-crumbs, brown sugar and shredded suet

Method

Mix all dry ingredients together, add the beaten egg and sufficient milk to mix to a stiff consistency. Pour into a greased

Ginger Pudding (*continued*)
 ½ tsp. bicarb. soda
 1 tsp. ground ginger
 1 egg
 ⅛ pt. milk

pudding basin, cover with a cloth and boil for 2 hrs. Serve with syrup sauce.

Honeycomb Mould
Ingredients
 2–3 eggs
 1 oz. sugar
 1 pt. milk
 ½ oz. powdered gelatine
 ⅛ pt. water
 1 tsp. vanilla essence

Method
Make a custard with the lightly beaten egg yolks, the sugar and milk. Add the gelatine dissolved in the water. Allow to cool, add the flavouring; beat the egg whites very stiffly and fold into the custard. Stir occasionally, and when on the point of setting, pour into a wet mould and leave to set. Turn out. (For a 1½ pt. size mould, 3 eggs are used.)

Jam Roly-Poly Pudding
Ingredients
 1 lb. flour
 4–8 oz. finely chopped suet
 Pinch of salt
 1 tsp. baking powder
 Red jam

Method
Put the flour into a basin, and add to it the suet, salt and baking powder. Mix it with a little cold water, roll it out and wet the edges. Spread it with jam, and roll it up in the form of a bolster. Scald and flour a cloth and sew or tie the pudding securely in it. Boil for 2 hrs. Treacle roly-poly is made in the same way. If one uses the larger proportion of suet, the pudding will be richer. If no suet is available, use margarine or cooking fat.

Marmalade Pudding
Ingredients
 1 lb. marmalade
 2 tbsp. sugar
 ½ tsp. bicarb. soda
 ¼ cup milk
 1 cup flour
 Pinch of salt
 1 cup soft breadcrumbs
 1 cup butter (scant measure)
 1 egg

Method
Stir together the marmalade and the sugar. Dissolve the soda in milk. Add flour, salt, breadcrumbs and butter, and egg well beaten. Turn into well-buttered mould and steam for 3 hrs. Serve with Marmalade sauce. Heat marmalade to reduce to liquid, dilute with water or wine.

Milk Pudding. See under this main heading.

Orange Pudding
Ingredients
 2 oz. each caster sugar and cakecrumbs rubbed through a sieve
 The rind of 1 and the juice of 2 oranges
 3 egg yolks

Method
Place the crumbs and sugar in a basin. Add the orange rind and juice. Beat in the egg yolks, and add the milk or cream. Whip the egg white to a stiff froth, stir in lightly. Line a pie-dish with a little good pastry and pour the mixture in. Bake until

C.C.D.—14

Orarge Pudding (*continued*)
  1 gill milk or cream
  1 egg white
Peach Cream Dessert
Ingredients
  6 slices of sponge cake
  ½ pt. heavy cream (or whipped evaporated milk)
  1 tbsp. caster sugar
  ¼ tsp. almond flavouring
  6 whole fresh peaches halved (or canned peaches)
  ½ tsp. redcurrant jelly
  Ice cream (if desired)

set and of a light brown colour at 350° F. Therm. 4.

Method
Spread the sponge cake slices with cream, to which has been added the sugar and almond essence. Place halved peaches on top of each. Fill centre with red currant jelly and top off with cream or ice cream.

Queen of Puddings
Ingredients
  ½ pt. milk
  1 oz. butter
  2 oz. breadcrumbs
  1 oz. granulated sugar
  1 or 2 eggs
  1 lemon
  2 tbsp. jam
  1 oz. caster sugar (for meringue)

Method
Heat milk and butter together. Pour the milk and butter over the breadcrumbs. Separate the eggs. Add to the crumb mixture lightly beaten egg yolks and grated rind of lemon. Allow to stand for ¼ hr. or longer. Pour into a greased pie-dish and bake at 350° F. Therm. 4 until quite firm and set. Remove from the oven and spread with jam. Whip the whites of eggs very stiffly and fold in the caster sugar. Pile on to the pudding. Reduce heat to 200° F. Therm. ¼ and bake for about 15 mins. until the meringue is crisp and a pale brown colour.

Snow Pudding
Ingredients
  1½ oz. breadcrumbs
  ½ pt. milk
  2 tbsp. caster sugar
  3 eggs
  Grated rind of 1 lemon
  Short pastry (see p. 375)
  2 tbsp. strawberry or any other jam
  1 dsp. caster sugar (for meringue).

Method
Put the breadcrumbs into a basin. Boil the milk and pour over them. Mix in the sugar, one whole egg and two yolks well-beaten; add the lemon rind. Line a pie-dish with a little pastry, spread the jam at the bottom and pour in the mixture. Bake at 350° F. Therm. 4 until set. Beat the remaining whites to a stiff froth, with the caster sugar, and heap it lightly on the top just before serving.

Spotted Dick
Ingredients
  4 oz. flour
  2 oz. margarine or suet
  Pinch of salt
  1 oz. sugar

Method
Rub together the margarine or suet and the flour. Add salt, sugar, currants or raisins, mixed spice and a grating of lemon peel. Moisten with a little milk to

Spotted Dick (*continued*)

2–3 oz. currants or raisins

¼ tsp. mixed spice

Lemon peel

Milk

a stiff dough, place in a well-greased pudding basin and steam for 1½ hr. Serve with Lemon sauce (see p. 450).

Suet Pudding

Ingredients

8 oz. flour (or 4 oz. flour and 4 oz. breadcrumbs

4 oz. beef suet (margarine may be substituted)

1 tsp. baking powder

Pinch of salt

Cold water

Method

Sift flour, salt, baking powder. Remove the skin and the fibre from the suet and chop it finely (if using margarine, rub into the flour as in short pastry), and add just enough cold water to make a stiff paste. Dip a pudding cloth into boiling water, wring it out and flour it well; put the paste into it, roll up and leave enough room for the pudding to swell. Tie up the ends very securely and plunge it into a pan full of fast-boiling water and boil for 2 hrs.

Summer Pudding

Ingredients

1 lb. blackcurrants, redcurrants or blackberries

4 oz. sugar

Thin slices of bread

Cream

Method

Stew the fruit with very little water, until tender. Strain and put syrup back into pan with sugar. Allow to boil and simmer for 5 mins. Pass the fruit through a sieve into a basin. Add syrup. Mix well (use a wooden or silver spoon). Cut off thin slices of bread from a new loaf. Line a mould with these, then fill the mould with alternate layers of fruit pulp and thin slices of bread. Leave some hours. When well soaked, turn out and serve with whipped cream.

Treacle Pudding

Ingredients

1 lb. flour

¼ lb. finely chopped suet

½ oz. ground ginger

1 tsp. baking powder

2 oz. moist sugar

¼ lb. treacle

1 egg

1 gill milk

Method

Put the dry ingredients into a basin. Mix with the treacle and the egg well beaten with the milk. Turn into a greased basin and boil for 2½ hrs. (The egg may be omitted, if desired.)

Trifle

Ingredients

For Foundation. 1 round sponge cake, raspberry jam, fruit juice, or fruit juice and sherry, or sherry.

For Custard. ¾ pt. custard made with 3 eggs or 1 egg and 2 tsp. cornflour or custard powder.

Pulses	Preparation	Boiled in Water	Steamed	Pressure Cooked at 15 lb.	Soup	Baked	Uses
Butter Beans	Soak overnight in cold water	1 hr.	1 hr.	12–15 mins.	1 hr.	5–6 hrs.	Curry, Stews, Main dish, Soup, Vegetable.
Haricot Beans	Soak overnight in cold water	1 hr.	1½ hr.	15 mins.	1½ hr.	6–8 hrs.	Curry, Stews, Main dish, Soup, Vegetable.
Lentils	For boiling, wash in cold water. For steaming, soak 2 hrs.	20 mins.	Unsoaked: 1¼ hr. Soaked: 20 mins.	5–10 mins.	30–40 mins.		Curry, Meat or Fish, Paste, Soup, Vegetable.
Peas: Split Green	Soak overnight in cold water	1 hr.	1 hr.	10–15 mins.	1 hr.		Soup, Vegetable.
Peas: Split Yellow	Soak overnight in cold water	1 hr.	1¼ hr.	10–15 mins.	1¼ hr.		Curry, Pease Pudding, Soup, Vegetable.

Trifle (*continued*)

For Cream. ½ pt. cream, 1 oz. caster sugar, flavouring.

For Decoration. Cherries and angelica or pistachio nuts.

Method. Cut the sponge cake into even-sized slices, spread with jam. Place in a glass dish, soak with the fruit juice or sherry. Make the custard; pour over the sponge cakes when cool; allow to get quite cold. Whip the cream, add sugar and flavouring. Pile on the top and decorate as desired. See also **TRIFLE.**

PUFF PASTE. A rich paste used to cover pies and tarts and line tartlets. See **PASTE AND PASTRY.**

PULLAN, POLLAN. A freshwater herring which is netted during the spring and summer in the Irish Loughs Erne and Neagh, Derg and Ree. Very closely allied to Powan and Vendace.

PULLED BREAD. A term applied to small pieces of bread when the crumb part of a loaf is pulled into pieces while hot. Bake at 350° F. Therm. 5, until they become crisp.

PULLET. A young hen, a female fowl.

PULSE. A general term for leguminous plants or their seeds—beans, peas, etc. See table on p. 412 for preparation and uses.

PULTOST. An all-the-year-round Norwegian cheese.

PUMPKINS. Also called Pumpion. The pumpkin is a gourd of which there are several varieties differing in shape and size. It is used for soups and stews in America, and another favourite method of pumpkin cookery is pumpkin pie.

Pumpkin and Nut Pie

Ingredients	*Method*
2½ cups strained cooked pumpkin	Mix together the pumpkin, cream and eggs, add sugar, salt, flour, cinnamon and nutmeg and powdered mixed spice; mix well and then add lemon and vanilla essence and pour into unbaked pastry case. Bake at 425° F. Therm. 7 for 10 mins., then reduce heat to 350° F. Therm. 4, and cook for about 40 mins. until the mixture does not stick to the knife. Then cover pie with the nuts, brown sugar and melted butter, all previously mixed together, and place under the grill until the top is slightly caramelised.
¼ cup cream	
2 lightly beaten eggs	
1 cup sugar	
Pinch of salt	
1 tbsp. flour	
½ tsp. lemon and vanilla essence	
½ tsp. each cinnamon, nutmeg and mixed spice	
¼ cup melted butter	
1 cup each chopped nuts and brown sugar	

PUNCH. Hot or cold spiced drink.

PUNCHEON. See **WEIGHTS AND MEASURES.**

PURSLANE. At one time this plant was commonly grown as one of our garden herbs. The young shoots are sometimes put in salads and the older ones used as a pot herb.

Q

QUADRILLE. Checkered; the thin strips of paste laid across tarts to form a sort of net.

QUAHOG. An American round clam.

QUAIL (Fr. *caille*). The quail is a small brown migratory bird of the partridge tribe which arrives on the shores of the Mediterranean from Africa—and then disperses throughout Europe. Quail is regarded as a tasty bird and it is usually supplied plucked and trussed ready for cooking. In prime condition from September to January.

QUART. The fourth part of a gallon; two pints.

QUASSIA. Chips of quassia, a bitter wood, are used chiefly for making butters, or as a substitute for hops in inferior beers. Also used as an infusion for cups and other drinks and to give a bitter taste to marmalade.
Quassia Cup. An infusion of quassia chips flavoured with orange peel, spices and borage, sweetened and usually fortified with alcohol.

QUEEN CAKES. See CAKES.

QUEEN OF PUDDINGS. See PUDDINGS.

QUENELLES. Described in old cookery books as being delicate forcemeat, either forming a dish by themselves, or made into balls and used for garnishing. The art of moulding these consists principally in keeping them of equal size, and the surfaces quite smooth.
TO MOULD. This is accomplished with two spoons. One is filled with forcemeat, the piled surface being smoothed over with a knife which has been dipped into hot water; the second spoon is then dipped in boiling water, and pressed over the top of the quenelle, moulding it to its own shape; by a gentle rotary movement the shape of the quenelle is perfected. It is then slipped into a buttered dish and another quenelle is proceeded with. When as many are made as required, slip the balls from the dish into a saucepan of water, lightly salted, and let them boil until firm.
Quenelles, Fish. Take the skin from a thick slice of salmon or cod, scrape the flesh with a spoon, and rub it through a wire sieve upon a dish. Pound 6 oz. of the fish thus prepared with 3 oz. butter, and 4 oz. panada; season with salt and cayenne, and then add gradually one whole egg, and the yolks of two others. Pound the mixture again, and put it on ice or in a cool place until required. Any kind of fish forcemeat may be made in the same way.
Quenelles of Game. Take the remains of cold game or poultry, carefully remove the skin, bone, and sinew, then mince and pound the meat, and prepare the quenelles as follows:Mince 1 lb. meat finely, and pound it in a mortar, with butter, a little pepper, salt and grated nutmeg, 8 button mushrooms chopped small. Soak the crumbs of a French roll in gravy, and squeeze the moisture from it. Put it into a stewpan with as much gravy as it will absorb and stir it over a clear fire till it forms a smooth mass and leaves the sides of the saucepan. Mix with it the unbeaten yolk of an egg, and set it aside to cool, then pound it with the other ingredients till all are thoroughly blended. Leave in a cool place or on ice for 1 or 2 hrs., mould it into balls, dip these in egg and breadcrumbs and fry in hot fat until they are brightly browned. Drain on blotting paper, and serve on a hot dish, with good Brown sauce or Mushroom sauce poured over them.
Quenelles, German. These are made both sweet and savoury. When sweet, they are served with sugar and sauce; when savoury, they are either served in soups,

Quenelles, German (*continued*)

or as a garnish or piled high on a dish with vegetables. The following are made with flour, and may either be used as a garnish served with vegetables or, after being poached, may be dipped into clarified butter, then into egg and bread-crumbs, and fried till they are lightly browned, drained and served hot on a neatly folded napkin: Put ¼ lb. butter into a saucepan with 3 teacups milk. When the liquor rises in the pan, stir 6 oz. flour quickly into it, add a little salt, pepper and nutmeg and stir the paste briskly until it leaves the sides of the saucepan with the spoon. Turn it out and add gradually 3 whole eggs and a little grated parmesan. Mould the quenelles in the usual way and let them simmer gently until they are done through. The water or gravy in which these quenelles are poached should not be allowed to boil at all, or the balls will break.

Quenelles, Lobster (*for fish soups*). Take the meat, pith, coral and spawn of a small hen lobster, and pound it to a paste. Mix with it 2 tbsp. finely grated bread-crumbs and 3 oz. butter. Season the forcemeat with 1 tsp. anchovy, a little salt, nutmeg and cayenne and moisten with the yolks of 2 eggs and the white of 1. Test a little piece to be sure that it is properly seasoned and firm and, if necessary, add the yolk of another egg. Mould the forcemeat into small quenelles, and brown them in hot fat, or poach them in boiling water. They may be served with fish, soup or with good gravy poured over them as a breakfast or supper dish. Time to fry, according to size.

Quenelles for Poultry Garnish. Stuff a large fowl with veal forcemeat and roast it. Keep out a small quantity of the forcemeat and make it up into quenelles, about the size of small walnuts. Poach these in gravy, and warm with them as many slices of tongue as there are quenelles. Put a border of mashed potatoes round a large dish and place on this, alternately, the tongue and the quenelles. Put the roast fowl in the middle of the dish, and pour over it and the quenelles a qt. of good white stock. Serve very hot. The appearance of the slices of tongue will be further improved if they are brushed over with a little glaze.

Quenelles for Turtle Soup. Take about a ¼ lb. lean, white veal and cut it into long slices; scrape it with a knife until nothing but the fibre remains. Pound this to a smooth paste, and rub it through a wire sieve upon a plate. Make it into a ball, and take its bulk, not its weight, in panada and calf's udder. Many cooks substitute fresh butter for the udder: when this is used a smaller proportion will be required. Pound these ingredients and press them through a sieve, first separately and afterwards together; season the forcemeat with salt, pepper and grated nutmeg and add, gradually, the yolks of 2 and the white of 1 egg. After pounding the ingredients together, pass the whole again through a sieve, and before poaching the quenelles, test a little piece of the forcemeat by throwing it into boiling water. If, when it is taken out, it is not sufficiently firm, add the yolk of another egg. Mould it into balls of any size that may be preferred. Poach these in boiling water until they are sufficiently hard, drain them when done enough, put them into the tureen, and pour the soup gently over them. The quenelles may be made as small as marbles or as large as eggs; the former size is generally preferred for soup.

QUILLAIA BARK. This is obtained from a tree which is a native of Chile and is used in infusions to impart a soapiness to water; hence it is sometimes used by aerated-water makers to give a head to ginger ale, and other effervescing beverages.

QUILLET. A small alum cake. Dessert biscuit.

QUINCE (Fr. *coing*). The common quince takes its name from Cydon (now Candia) in the Isle of Crete. It is said the Romans had three sorts of quinces, one of which was called Chrysomera, from its yellowish-green colour, and they boiled them with honey, as we make our marmalade. The fruit is large, roundish or regular oval according to variety, and assumes a beautiful golden colour; but it has a strong odour and austere flavour which renders it unfit for eating raw. When used with apples, it greatly improves their flavour.

Quince Jam
Ingredients
4 lb. fruit
2 lb. sugar
1 cup water

Method
Peel, core and slice fruit, and simmer gently until soft. Add sugar and boil until jam sets on testing (about 20 mins). To improve the colour, place a tight-fitting lid on preserving pan after 10 mins. Pour into warmed jars and cover when cool.

Quince Jelly
Ingredients
5 lb. fruit
Water
Sugar

Method
Wash, peel, core and quarter quinces. Place peel and cores in a little water to soak. Place fruit in preserving pan, cover with water, and boil gently for 2 hrs. If the water should boil away, add water in which cores are soaking. When the fruit is boiled to a pulp, let it drip through muslin overnight. Next day, measure and allow an equal amount of sugar. Boil juice for 20 mins., add sugar, boil for a further 20 mins., test for setting, and bottle in warmed jars. Cover when cool.

QUINNAT. The Californian Salmon, known also as King Salmon, Chinnock Salmon and Sacramento Salmon, is one of the most important productions of that country. It closely resembles the European salmon, and can be prepared and cooked in the same way.

R

RABBIT (Fr. *lapin*). There are two kinds, the tame and the wild.

Tame rabbits are larger and have whiter and more delicate flesh than wild ones. They are bred and fattened for the table, but sometimes taste of cabbages on which they are usually fed.

Wild rabbit yields a well-flavoured flesh and when seasoned with thyme, wild thyme and marjoram, bearded with bacon, and properly cooked, makes a delicious dish. A young rabbit can be distinguished from an old one by compressing the underjaw, which should, in a young animal, snap or give way readily.

TO SKIN. Along the edges of the slit in the belly, the skin is readily stripped off

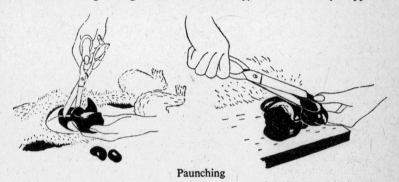

Paunching

the body and the extremities are pulled through, the feet being chopped off at the first joints.

TO TRUSS FOR ROASTING. The legs are pinned close to the body by means of skewers, and the head is thrust back and held there by a skewer passed through the mouth into the neck, or it may be tied with string passed under the forelegs and fastened over the shoulder.

TO TRUSS FOR BOILING. The head is drawn round to the side and fastened to the body with a skewer. The forelegs are then fastened backwards and the hind-legs forward.

TO JOINT. Always use a sharp knife and have a mallet or hammer handy. The head and legs should be removed first and then the back divided into neat,

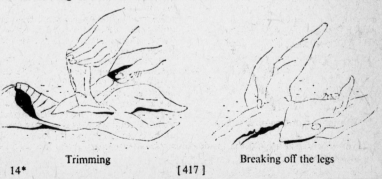

Trimming   Breaking off the legs

14*   [417]

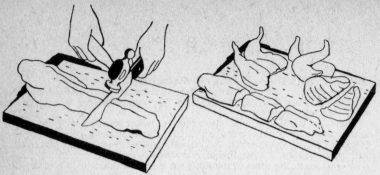

Jointing the back   The jointed rabbit

even-sized pieces. Rabbits may be stewed in milk, boiled or jugged, or used in pies. They are very good in casseroles.

Rabbit Casserole

Ingredients	*Method*

Ingredients
1 good-sized rabbit
4 strips of bacon fat
Butter
2 onions sliced
Bacon diced
Salt and pepper
1 dsp. flour
1 glass white wine
1 small bouquet garni
1 pt. stock

Method
Wash and wipe the rabbit. Divide into joints, lard the legs and breast portions with the strips of bacon fat, fry in butter, with the onions and bacon. When light brown in colour, season, sprinkle in the flour, and stir over a gentle heat until the flour is nicely browned. Turn into an earthenware casserole. Add wine, bouquet garni, and stock. Boil up, place the lid on pan, then cook over a low heat until the meat is quite tender. Remove the herbs, and any scum from the surface of the stew. Serve in the casserole.

RADISH (Fr. *radis*). Some of these pungent roots are long and tapering, others globular—the latter are commonly known as turnip radishes. Radishes are most commonly used in salads and for garnishing. The young green tops are sometimes chopped up and mixed with a salad; the old and large leaves are very tough.

RADISHES, BOILED. Radishes may be boiled for about 30 mins. in salted water, drained and served with Melted Butter sauce.

RADISH ROSES FOR GARNISH. The turnip radish with its red or reddish-purple colour and white flesh makes an attractive garnish. To make roses, use a sharp knife and make cuts all round the bottom edge; then repeat with a second set of cuts so they meet at the bottom. Holding the knife point

Cutting a radish into rose-shape

downwards, run it around the inside. This releases the cut pieces which are in separate leaves.

[418]

RAFFINADE. Refined sugar of the best quality.

RAGOÛT. The literal meaning of this French term is anything that restores the appetite, encouraging the epicure to continue his feast, even though the requirements of nature are satisfied. It implies a combination of materials used together to impart taste to each other, brought about during the cooking process.

RAIL. These small numerous wading birds are related to cranes. Their weight averages between 2½ to 3 lb. per dozen when plucked. One bird is only sufficient for 2 people. They are usually served split in two down the breastbone, through the centre of the breast. They may be braised, boiled, fried, grilled, etc., and used in a casserole.

RAISED CRUST. The traditional pie-crust for pork, veal and ham pies which do not need to be made in a dish. See **PASTE AND PASTRY** (p. 368).

RAISINS (Fr. *raisins secs*). These are commonly described as the prepared or dried fruit of the vine. Used for dessert, also cakes and puddings.

Raisin Pie

Ingredients	*Method*
½ lb. raisins	Cover the raisins with water and soak for about 30 mins., then bring to boil, add sugar and flour mixed together, salt and lemon juice, and cook until thick. Add apples and brandy and allow to cool. Fill an unbaked pastry case, dot with butter, cover with pastry, and bake for 15 mins. at 425° F. Therm. 7, then reduce heat to 325° F. Therm. 3 and cook for further 20 mins.
1 pt. water	
Sugar	
2 tbsp. flour	
Pinch of salt	
Strained juice of ½ lemon	
2 sour apples, peeled and diced	
1 tbsp. brandy	
Pastry	

Raisin Cake. See CAKES.

RAMEKIN. Originally, this word signified a mixture of cheese, eggs and other things formed in a mould, or served on bread. It is now used to signify, when used in the plural, almost any kind of cheese pudding or cheese cake, or cake containing cheese.

RAMPION. This root is used for culinary purposes, raw in salads, or the young shoots are blanched and eaten like asparagus, or boiled and eaten like parsnips. The leaf is used in raw dishes of salad, and cooked and eaten like spinach.

RAREBIT. See CHEESE (for Welsh Rarebit); also Buck Rarebit.

RASPBERRY. The plant from which this delicious fruit is gathered is a native of Great Britain and of most European countries. In some parts the fruit is called Hindberry and in others the fruit is generally known as "rasps". The juice of the raspberry is exceedingly luscious and possesses a peculiarly rich aroma, for which reason it is much used in cooking, confectionery and in the manufacture of liqueurs.

Raspberry Jam

Ingredients	*Method*
6 lb. raspberries	Pick over raspberries, removing all leaves and stalks. Place in preserving pan and allow to simmer for 30 mins. Add the warmed sugar, stirring gently until it dissolves. Boil for 3 mins., then pour into warmed jars and cover immediately.
6 lb. sugar	

[419]

Raspberry Jam

Ingredients

4 lb. raspberries
6 lb. sugar

Method

Place the fruit in a preserving pan, bring to boiling point, and let it boil gently for 3 mins. only; add the sugar, stirring until it is dissolved. Again bring just to boiling point, pour into warmed jars and cover at once.

Raspberry Jelly

Ingredients

4 lb. raspberries
Sugar

Method

Stem the fruit, place in a double saucepan and cook until quite pulped, approximately 50 mins. Strain through muslin overnight. Measure juice and allow 1¼ lb. sugar to each pint of juice. Boil up juice, add warmed sugar and stir until dissolved. Test for setting; pour into warmed jars but do not cover until quite cold.

RATAFIA. A liqueur flavoured with the kernels of various fruits—peaches, apricots, cherries. When used, it must be added with care to a mix.

RATAFIAS. Small biscuits made with almonds, taking their name from the liqueur. They are very useful for garnishes and in the preparation of many dishes.

RAVIGOTE. The literal meaning of this French term is a pick-me-up from the verb *ravigoter*, to revive, to strengthen. It is applied to a mixture of tarragon, chives, chervil and burnet minced very finely or used as a faggot. Minced ravigote is a favourite garnish for salads and is then served on a saucer by itself, each herb being kept separate, the whole constituting, therefore, four little heaps so that each may be used at discretion.
Ravigote Butter. See BUTTERS.
Ravigote Sauce. This is English "melted butter" or butter sauce with which chopped ravigote has been mixed. See SAUCES.

RAVIOLI

Ingredients

1 lb. flour
⅛ pt. olive oil
⅓ pt. water
Pinch of salt
Stock

Method

Mix all the ingredients to a smooth paste and, when ready for use, roll the paste very thinly and cut in two. Egg-wash half and then dot the stuffing on at equal distances (it is quick to use a forcing bag), cover with the rest of the paste and cut into circles with a pastry wheel, or cover with a sheet of greaseproof paper, mark into squares, remove paper and cut. Cook in boiling stock for 20 minutes.

FOR FILLING. Use minced meat, passed through a sieve, or spinach purée, with a little beaten egg added to bind. A grating of nutmeg or grated cheese may also be added if desired. They may be served after tossing in melted butter, adding a little grated parmesan. Sometimes they are served with parmesan cheese, grated nutmeg and Tomato sauce.

RAYFISH. See SKATE.

RECIPES. CHECKING AND BUILDING. In recipe building, the two main factors to take into account are the composition of the foods and the effect that heat will have on them. Heat melts fat and sugar and if too large a proportion of either of these are included in the mixture, it will be too moist and will not set properly.

If there appears to be a slight variation of ingredients or the addition of flavouring, e.g. if cakecrumbs are used instead of breadcrumbs, the fat and sugar proportions must be reduced as cakecrumbs contain these ingredients and the mixture would be too moist if they were not adjusted.

The method of cooking also has a bearing on the selection of the ingredient; for instance, in steaming, when no moisture is lost by evaporation, less liquid is needed than in the dry method of cooking. A soft consistency is only desirable when allowance has to be made for evaporation.

RED CABBAGE. See **CABBAGE.**

REDCURRANTS. See **CURRANTS.**

RED DEER. See **VENISON.**

RED HERRING. See **HERRINGS.**

RED MULLET. See **MULLET.**

RED PEPPER. See **CAPSICUM.**

RED WINES. See **WINES.**

REFORME SAUCE. See **SAUCES.**

REFRIGERATING. This term is applied to any process by which the temperature of an article is lowered considerably, sometimes to freezing point. Meat and other foods are preserved during hot weather by a system of refrigerating or storing in chambers kept cold by ice. Refrigerators are used to set jellies and freeze ices.

REINDEER. This native of the Arctic Regions is esteemed for its flavour. Reindeer flesh is said to be equal to our best venison.

REINDEER CUTLET. Small chops or steaks from the loin rib end or shoulder may be cut into suitable pieces for serving and prepared as cutlets. Wipe, dip into beaten egg to which 1 tbsp. water has been added, roll in fine breadcrumbs. Season well with salt and pepper and leave to dry. Cook in hot fat until golden brown, then lower heat and continue cooking. Allow 20–25 mins. total cooking time for cutlets 1″ thick. Drain on paper and serve garnished with sprigs of parsley.

RELISH. Pickles or a savoury spiced sauce.

REMOULADE. A name given to a salad dressing, taking its meaning from the French verb *rémoudre*, to grind, and referring to the process by which the hard-boiled egg yolks are worked down with oil and other ingredients.

REMOVES. This name is usually applied to large dishes such as joints, etc., which occupy the principal place on the table.

RENNET. Sometimes spelt "runnet" is the name given to the dried fourth stomach of the calf; when taken from the animal after it is killed it is freed from the outer skin, fat and superfluous membrane, and well washed. It resembles a piece of parchment and is commonly known as "vell". Rennet is employed to curdle milk (see **JUNKET**).

RHUBARB (Fr. *rhubarbe*). There are two or three varieties of rhubarb grown in this country for culinary purposes. In Queen Elizabeth's time, rhubarb leaves were used as a pot herb, and were considered superior to beet or spinach. Rhubarb is served stewed, and is also used for either one- or two-crust pies, and in suet puddings. The leaf and root ends are removed, the stalk wiped well with a damp cloth and the loose string (red skins) pulled off: the stalk is then cut into even-sized pieces.

RHUBARB, STEWED. Peel and cut the rhubarb into lengths. Put them into a jar with a very little water and some moist or lump sugar (the moist does as well for sweetening, but the lump will make the syrup clearer). Put the jar in a slow oven

RHUBARB, STEWED (*continued*)

250° F. Therm. $\frac{1}{4}$, or if preferred on the kitchener until the rhubarb is tender. An enamelled stewpan may be used instead and the rhubarb simmered slowly over a low heat.

Rhubarb Jam

Ingredients

4 lb. rhubarb
1 lb. stoned raisins
5 lb. sugar
Juice and rind of 1 lemon
  and 2 oranges

Method

Wash and wipe rhubarb and cut into 1″ lengths. Add juice and grated rinds of lemon and oranges, and raisins, and allow to stand for $\frac{1}{2}$ hr. Boil up gently with sugar, and keep boiling for 30 mins. Stir and skim. Pour into heated jars and cover.

Rhubarb Jam with Ginger

Ingredients

4 lb. rhubarb
4 lb. sugar
8 oz. candied peel
2 tsp. ginger

Method

Wipe the rhubarb with damp cloth, and cut into 1″ lengths. Place in preserving pan, sprinkle sugar over and leave standing until following day. Add ginger and peel and boil for $1\frac{1}{2}$ hrs. Pour into heated jars and cover at once.

Rhubarb and Raspberry Jam

Ingredients

3 lb. rhubarb
4 lb. raspberries
6 lb. sugar
6 tbsp. water

Method

Wash rhubarb, and cut into 1″ lengths Place in preserving pan with water and simmer until fruit is tender. Add raspberries and stir together. When mixture boils, add the warmed sugar and boil for 20 mins. Test for setting, place in warmed jars and cover when cool.

RIBOFLAVIN. The water-soluble Vitamin B_2 (Riboflavin) is known as Vitamin G in the United States. Found chiefly in offal (especially liver), and dairy products.

RICE (Fr. *riz*). An esculent grain, extensively cultivated in hot, moist climates. Although a useful food, it is not as nutritious as other cereals. Rice may be short-grained, of which there are several varieties, or long-grained and brightly polished (Patna). The former is used chiefly for puddings and moulds, the Patna rice to serve with curries, or for pilau.

RICE FOR CURRY. Wash some Patna rice and throw it into plenty of boiling salted water; boil quickly until nearly, but not quite, cooked. This will take from 7–10 mins. Strain through a sieve and pour hot water through it, rinsing thoroughly; finish cooking it either by putting it into a saucepan again over a low heat, or in the oven at 350° F. Therm. 4. Rice for curry should be dry, but not dried up. It should be firm, but not hard.

RICE, FRIED. Parboil the rice and allow it to swell, then brown in plenty of butter or oil. Add chopped green peppers and onions and fry all together.

Rice Pudding, Baked and Boiled. See **MILK PUDDINGS.**

Rice Pudding, Steamed

Ingredients

2 oz. whole rice
2 eggs
2 tbsp. sugar

Method

Wash the rice thoroughly and place in a saucepan of cold water. Bring to the boil then pour off the water, add milk and

[422]

Rice Pudding, Steamed (*continued*)

1 pt. milk

sugar. Simmer over a low heat until rice is soft. Remove from heat, cool a little, stir in egg yolks. Beat the whites to a stiff froth and stir in lightly. Pour into a well-greased mould and steam for 30 mins.

Rice and Sausages

Ingredients

2 cups cooked rice
1 medium-sized onion
¼ pt. milk
1 tbsp. grated cheese
1 lb. sausages
1 tin mushroom, chicken or tomato soup

Method

Place the rice and sausages in alternate layers in a greased casserole. Sprinkle with the grated onion; add the soup diluted with milk and sprinkle with cheese. Bake at 350° F. Therm. 4 for about 30 mins.

Rice Shape

Ingredients

7 oz. rice
1 qt. milk
¼ lb. sugar

Method

Cook the rice with the sugar in the milk until quite soft (use a double saucepan for best results). Put into a mould and turn out when cold.

Risotto. See under individual entry.

RICOTTA. The literal meaning of this term is "cooked again", a signification that seems to have been lost to some extent, seeing that it is now applied to a kind of cream cheese, prepared as follows: Put 2 qt. fresh strained whey into a flat lined pan, and place over a gentle heat. When the froth begins to rise, pour in 1 pt. milk, and stir lightly with a wooden spoon until the whole surface is covered with a thick froth. Skim the froth off and drain on a fine sieve. (*The milk and whey must not boil.*) When drained, the ricotta is ready for use.

RIND. The external covering or skin of fruit, bacon, etc.

RISOTTO. Brown some chopped onions, with minced beef and peeled sliced mushrooms. Add sufficient boiled rice for the number of persons to be served. Mix in fresh tomatoes to taste, add some stock; cook slowly for 15–20 mins. and serve with butter and grated cheese.

RISSOLES. This word is derived from the French *risoler*, to fry brown. A mixture of fish or meat which is sometimes enclosed in paste in half-moon shapes, or rolled in egg and breadcrumbs and fried.

RISSOLETTES. Similar to small rissoles, thin pancakes being used in place of paste.

RIZZARED HADDIE (Scottish). Sun-dried haddocks. See **HADDOCK**.

ROACH. A European freshwater fish common in English, French and European rivers. It is silver-white about the body with the red fins and dark green back of the carp family. It is not much valued as food fish, but can be boiled, stewed or broiled.

ROAST (Fr. *rôtir*). Roasting is one of the oldest methods of cooking meat. Originally it consisted of hanging the meat in front of a bright fire, suspended from a jack or spit. Today the meat is roasted in an oven by radiated heat. See individual headings.

ROCABOLE. An onion resembling garlic in flavour, but milder.

ROCKET (Fr. *roquette*). A salad plant.

ROCKFISH. A famous Californian food fish noted for its beautiful red colour. Boiled and served with egg sauce.

ROCK SALMON. See **POLLACK.**

ROE. See **FISH ROES.**

ROE BUCK (Fr. *chevreuil*). Known as red deer. This flesh is commonly eaten in France and Scotland and cooked as venison (see under this heading).

ROLLMOP. Soused herring fillets.

ROOK. The flesh of the rook is rather dry and somewhat coarse in flavour. Rooks can be baked, stewed, or put in a pie, but seldom, if ever, roasted.

ROOTS. A term generally applied to vegetables growing underground such as turnips, carrots, etc.

ROQUEFORT. A blue French cheese, from the district of Roquefort, made with ewe's milk. It should be well aged, crumbly and creamy.

ROSE. Apothecary's Rose de Provins, the Cabbage Rose, the Wild Brier or Dog Rose, and Damask Rose are used medicinally, also in conserves and industrially. The leaves are used in confectionery.

Rose Hip Jelly

Ingredients

3 lb. rose hips
Sugar
Water

Method

Prepare the rose hips by slitting them lengthwise and removing skin and hairs. Weigh fruit and place in a pan with enough water to float in. Allow 1 lb. sugar to each 1 pt. fruit. Bring fruit slowly to boil, add sugar and boil together until quite soft. Strain off liquor, return to pan and bring to boil. Pour into warmed jars and cover immediately.

Rose Petal Jam. Gather roses in full bloom. Pick off about 1 lb. of the largest petals; cut off white ends and put in a stewpan with some small petals. Reserve large petals. Pour ¾ pt. water in saucepan with white ends and small petals and place over low heat. Bring to boil; strain through a fine sieve, squeezing the petals well, then throw them away. Put the liquor with 3½ lb. caster sugar in pan and stir till dissolved. Add large petals and boil until reduced to a thick syrup. Test for setting, pour into jars and seal.

ROSE GERANIUM. The fragrant leaf of this plant is sometimes used in jellies and industrially for perfume.

ROSEMARY. The leaves of this herb have spicy, pungent, aromatic, warm and piny taste, and they are used to enhance the flavour of pickles, meat and rabbit stews, beverages, etc. Also used in some cakes for a variation of flavour.

ROUX. See **SAUCES** (p. 436).

ROWAN BERRIES. Ash Berries.

Rowan Jelly

Ingredients

3 lb. rowan berries
2 lb. preserving apples
1 qt. water
Sugar

Method

Peel, core and slice the apples. Stew in the water for 20 mins. until they are pulped. Strain well, add pulp only to the rowan berries in the preserving pan. Allow to simmer gently for 30 mins. until fruit is well pulped. Strain off juice, measure and allow 1 lb. sugar to 1 pt.

[424]

Rowan Jelly (*continued*)

juice. Boil up juice for 20 mins., then add warmed sugar, boil for further 15 mins., skim well, pour into heated jars and cover.

ROYAL. The name of an egg custard used for garnishing clear soups. Also applied to an icing (see **ICING**).

ROYAN. A fish very similar to the sardine, but smaller, less oily and more delicately flavoured.

RUDD. A European freshwater fish of the carp family. It is about the same shape and size as the roach, and is found in the same waters.

RUE. The leaf is used medicinally, industrially and for culinary purposes, chopped very sparingly for sandwiches, cocktails, with chicken and mushroom dishes and in salads and stews. Also called Herb o' Grace.

RUFF and REEVE. This bird is closely allied to the sandpiper, the male being called a ruff and the female a reeve. The male, during the breeding season, has a ruff of feathers round the neck. They are very rare, but, when cooked, are larded with bacon and roasted for 20 mins.

RUFFE or ROPE. A freshwater species of perch, which is found in the Midlands and South.

RUM (Fr. *rhum*). A spirit distilled from molasses of the sugar cane. In Westmorland and Cumberland, when a child is born, rum butter is spread on oatmeal biscuits and given for good luck to the mother and visitors who come to see her. Rum is used for culinary purposes for flavourings, also in a rum omelet, when a little rum is poured over cooked omelets and ignited, just as serving.

Rum Butter. Mix ½ lb. brown sugar, a little grated nutmeg and 3 oz. warmed butter together. Add ½ wineglass rum and beat the mixture. Pour on to a dish, and, when cold, sift over caster sugar.

Rum Sauce

Ingredients	Method
1 tbsp. cornflour	Mix cornflour, salt and sugar, add slowly milk and butter. When melted, stir until thick, add rum and serve with steamed pudding.
Pinch of salt	
4 oz. sugar	
½ pt. scalded milk	
2 tbsp. butter	
½ pt. rum	

RUSKS. Twice-baked slices of cake or milk bread, sweet or plain; in making them the dough is baked in a square tin, cut into slices when cold, and then rebaked in a slow oven 200° F. Therm. ¼, until crisp and browned.

RUSSIAN SALAD. See SALADS.

RYE. The seed of a cereal largely cultivated in Russia, Germany and Northern Europe generally. The rye flour is made into bread and cakes: these are not unlike the Scottish oatcake.

S

SACCHARINE. The commercial product has approximately 300 times the sweetening power of sugar and is used in diabetic cookery and for obesity. Saccharine does not supply nutrition to the body.

SACCHAROMETER. An instrument which is used for testing the degree of sweetness of syrups, etc.

SADDLE. A name given to that part of an animal containing a portion of the backbone, with ribs on each side, or double loin of mutton, venison, etc.

SAFFLOWER. American Saffron, False Saffron. The flower is used medicinally, and the seed industrially. The oil is used for culinary purposes.

SAFFRON. At one time saffron was used extensively in cookery for colouring both sweetmeats and broth but now its use has dwindled, being rarely met with except for colouring butter, cheese, confectionery and liqueurs. It has a rich orange colour, a bitter taste and aromatic odour.

SAGE. This herb is best known to us in sage and onion stuffing for pork, duck, and goose. It has a peculiar greyish-green leaf, powerfully aromatic; in some countries it is used to flavour cheese. The leaves may be dried and powdered for winter use as follows: Place the sage leaves on a sheet of paper and dry slowly in the oven at 200° F. Therm. ¼. When crisp, rub the leaves between the hands to obtain as fine a powder as possible. The powder must be kept in a tightly-covered bottle.

SAGO (Fr. *sagou*). See **MILK PUDDINGS.**

SAILOR'S PIE

Ingredients
- 1 lb. lean beef steak
- 1 dsp. seasoned flour
- 1 diced carrot
- 1 small turnip
- 1 diced onion
- 2 leeks or 1 stick celery
- ½ pt. hot water
- Suet crust (see p. 375)

Method

Cut meat into inch cubes and roll in seasoned flour. Put all ingredients into saucepan; add water to cover all, bring to boiling point, reduce heat and simmer until tender (2 hrs.). Three-quarters of an hour before using, make the suet crust; roll out to size of lid and lay on top of stew to cook. When serving out crust cut across into 6 portions and remove to a hot plate, re-season stew and serve on a dish with suet crust on top. Garnish with finely chopped parsley.

SAITHE. A name given in Scotland to the coalfish or pollock.

SALADS. The selection and choice of ingredients are of great importance in the preparation of salads. They must be fresh, clean, tender, well-chilled and crisp. The ingredients must combine and be palatable but not too strong in flavour; they must also harmonise with the flavour of the food, while contrasting in texture. When making salads, drain and toss ingredients lightly together; place in bowl or on individual plates. If marinated, marinate each ingredient separately. Dress as desired.

EGGS must be hard-boiled (cracking immediately prevents the dark line round the yolk), then cooled quickly under running water and shelled. They may be used whole, halved, sliced or sectioned or the whites minced and the yolks put through a ricer.

CHEESE must be grated, cut into cubes or, if cream cheese, put through a forcing bag, or made into balls.

CHICKEN. The skin and gristle must be removed and the meat cut into neat cubes and mixed with dressing and other ingredients just before serving.

MEAT. Cut into cubes.

NUTS must be shelled, blanched if necessary, used whole, chopped or shredded.

VEGETABLES. The shape, colour and flavour must be preserved when cooked.

Asparagus. Cooked and tips marinated, or else tossed in mayonnaise.

Beans (dry). Soaked, cooked and kept whole, dressed with French dressing or tomato purée.

Beans (string). Strings removed, beans cut, cooked and marinated.

Beetroot. Washed, cooked, peeled and cut into desired shapes.

Cabbage. Outer leaves removed, heart cut into quarters and centre stalk removed, shredded, tossed in French dressing or Sour Cream dressing.

Carrots. Peeled and grated or cooked and cut into shapes.

Cauliflower. Grated and served raw or leaves removed, or the flowerets separated, cooked and marinated.

Celery. Washed, trimmed, strings removed, shredded or cut into rings or curled.

Chicory. See *Endive* below.

Cucumber. Peeled, scored and sliced or diced.

Endive. Washed, dried and placed to chill wrapped in a cloth.

Green peppers. Washed, seeds removed and cut into rings or strips or diced.

Lettuce heads. Bruised leaves discarded and heads separated.

Lettuce leaves. Washed, drained and placed to chill: not dressed until just before use or the leaves will lose their crispness.

Onions. Skinned and wilted leaves removed; cut as desired.

Peas. Shells removed, peas cooked and marinated, or dressed with Sour Cream dressing.

Potatoes. Peeled, cut into cubes and cooked, or cooked, peeled and diced; or sliced and tossed in mayonnaise while still hot.

Spinach. Washed and used as lettuce.

Tomato. Blanched, peeled and used whole or sliced.

Watercress. Faded leaves removed, and cress broken into neat sprigs.

Artichokes (Globe) Vinaigrette. Boil artichokes (see **ARTICHOKES**) until tender. When the leaves come away easily, the artichokes are done. Strain and allow to cool. Make sauce of equal parts of salad oil and vinegar, salt, pepper and a very small amount of mustard. One artichoke should be allowed for each person. The sauce should be served separately.

Asparagus Vinaigrette. Cook the asparagus in water; place on a sieve and allow to become cold. Dish up and put the dish on ice until wanted. Serve with a vinaigrette sauce composed of 3 tbsp. best olive oil, 1 tbsp. best French tarragon vinegar, 1 tsp. chilli vinegar, 1 tsp. each finely chopped parsley, chervil and tarragon, 1 tsp. finely chopped gherkins. Season with salt and pepper; mix well and use as desired.

Bacon and Beetroot Salad. See **BACON**.

Beetroot. Peel, slice and cut into uniform strips, cold cooked beetroot, and marinate in French dressing for several hours or overnight. One hour before serving, drain and mix beetroot with Sour Cream dressing.

Cabbage with Sour Cream. Shred the cabbage (red or white) very thinly and soak in ice water for 1 hr. Drain well and combine with Sour Cream dressing.

Cauliflower Salad. Divide a boiled cauliflower into flowerets and remove the green leaves. Season with pepper and salt and arrange on a dish. Pour over mayonnaise or salad dressing. Garnish with beetroot.

Cauliflower Vinaigrette. Thoroughly clean a cauliflower and boil it. Divide into branches, and lay the pieces on a sieve to drain and become cold. Fry some breadcrumbs a golden brown in about 1 oz. butter, and set them on one side. Mix

Cauliflower Vinaigrette (*continued*)
in a basin 1 tbsp. vinegar and a little chopped tarragon and chervil; add this to the breadcrumbs, and pour over the cold cauliflower. Serve in a glass bowl.

Celery Salad. Wash 2 heads celery and cut it into $\frac{1}{2}''$ lengths. Put them in a bowl. Add salad dressing and garnish with a border of sliced or diced beetroot. See also **CELERY.**

Cherry Salad. Take 1 lb. cherries. If fresh cherries are used, remove the stalks and stones; crack the latter and take out the kernels; put them with the cherries in a bowl. Mix together 1 tbsp. salad oil, 1 tsp. lemon juice, few drops of tarragon vinegar, 1 tbsp. cognac or $\frac{1}{2}$ tbsp. Kirschwasser, a few tarragon and chervil leaves, chopped finely and 1 tsp. caster sugar in a small basin, and mingle with the cherries. Serve in a small salad dish or glass side dishes. An excellent accompaniment for roast game or duck.

Chicken Salad. Remove the skin from cold cooked chicken, and cut meat into dice. Cut celery into $\frac{1}{2}''$ lengths, taking half as much celery as chicken. Cut up some lettuce and mix the chicken, celery and lettuce together with $\frac{1}{4}$ pt. mayonnaise. Place in a salad bowl or heap on a dish. Decorate with endive, beetroot, and sliced hard-boiled eggs.

Chicory Salad. See **CHICORY.**

Chiffonade Salad. Slice 3 green peppers, removing seeds. Wash and dry a bunch of watercress and pull into neat pieces. Blanch, skin and quarter 4 tomatoes; remove skin and pith from 3 oranges and keep the quarters whole. Place the slices of green pepper on individual dishes, arrange tomatoes and oranges on top alternately. Dress with $\frac{1}{4}$ pt. French dressing.

Cos Lettuce Salad. Divide the lettuce into half lengthwise, or, if large, into four. Wash carefully in cold water, drain and place on ice, if a refrigerator is available, for about an hour for the leaves to become crisp. Dress as follows: Take 1 tsp. each chopped tarragon and chervil (or mint), pepper and salt to taste, 1 tbsp. oil and $\frac{1}{2}$ tbsp. vinegar or lemon juice. Serve the lettuce separately on a plate for each person and pour over a little dressing just before serving.

Cucumber Salad. Peel the cucumbers carefully and cut into two, lengthwise; remove seeds and slice finely; place in a bowl, sprinkle with table salt and leave to drain off their moisture for 25 mins. This done, press them in a cloth; place in a glass bowl and season with pepper, oil and vinegar, and sprinkle over a little finely chopped chervil.

French Salad. Chop finely some well-washed endive, lettuce, dandelion leaves, and mix them with a small quantity of shallot or garlic, chervil and tarragon. Mix together 1 tsp. salt, $\frac{1}{2}$ tsp. pepper, 2 tbsp. salad oil, 4 tbsp. vinegar. Put the salad herbs into a bowl; stir the mixture of oil, spice and vinegar; pour over the salad and stir all together. Add, if desired, cold fish or meat cut up small.

Haricot Bean Salad. Lay some cooked haricot beans in a dish, and sprinkle them with chopped parsley; mix equal quantities of oil and vinegar with the pepper and salt and pour over them. Garnish with parsley and grated cheese.

Lentil Salad. Lay some boiled lentils in a dish, sprinkle them with chopped parsley; mix equal parts of oil and vinegar with a little pepper and salt and pour over them. Garnish with chives or parsley.

Lettuce (Wilted) Salad

Ingredients	*Method*
1 lettuce	Wash and dry the leaves of the lettuce.
$\frac{1}{4}$ pt. white vinegar (cider if possible)	Blend oil, vinegar, salt and pepper, then add sugar. Put the leaves in a salad bowl,
$\frac{1}{8}$ pt. olive oil	add the dressing and leave for 1 hr.
$\frac{1}{2}$ tsp. salt	Garnish if desired.
2 tsp. sugar	
$\frac{1}{8}$ tsp. pepper	
1 hard-boiled egg, thinly sliced	

Mixed Salad. Cut equal quantities of boiled potatoes, carrots, turnips and beet-root into small dice and place in a salad bowl. Mix equal quantities of oil and vinegar, season with pepper and salt and pour over bowl.

Orange Salad. Remove the peel and pith from 4 oranges; divide the fruit into natural divisions, removing at the same time, all skin and pips. Put the fruit into a salad bowl; add a few thin slices of lemon, with skin and pips removed; pour over 1 tbsp. sweet salad oil and 1 tbsp. brandy and season with ½ tsp. caster sugar and pinch of cayenne. Add ½ tsp. each finely chopped tarragon and chervils. Mix thoroughly but carefully, and pile up neatly on a dish. Keep the dish on ice until required for table.

Pineapple Salad. Cut half a peeled, ripe pineapple into fine shreds (remove the core before shredding). Mix this with the white part of a small head of celery, cut into small shreds. Place on ice until required. A few minutes before serving, mix with sufficient Mayonnaise sauce to moisten and season the salad. Dress neatly on a deep glass dish; garnish with slices of lemon, and serve ice-cold.

Potato Salad. Slice boiled potatoes and 1 boiled onion (or a few chopped chives) thinly and lay them on a dish. Pour over a French dressing or mayonnaise; if preferred, the onion may be omitted.

Russian Salad. Take some cooked new potatoes, cauliflower, asparagus, turnips, peas, beans, parsnips, beetroot, and gherkins (pickled), lettuce and cress (uncooked). Cut the suitable vegetables in pretty fancy shapes. The cauliflower must be broken in flowerets. Set tastefully in aspic jelly.

Salmon Mayonnaise. Break some cold, cooked salmon into flakes, removing the bones: cut up a lettuce and mix this and the salmon with mayonnaise sauce. Heap lightly on a dish, decorate with endive, and some hard-boiled eggs cut into quarters; also, if desired, border with aspic jelly (see p. 38).

Spanish Sardine Salad. Remove the skin and bones from 12–16 sardines; cut them into short pieces and mix in a basin with 2 tbsp. capers. Season with salt, pepper and vinegar, and mix with some finely shredded lettuce leaves. Arrange in a salad bowl and garnish with stoned Spanish olives filled with anchovy butter.

Spring Salad. Wash a lettuce, some mustard and cress and watercress well; dry them quickly, then cut rather coarsely. Place in a salad bowl. Pour over some mayonnaise or dressing. Decorate with sprigs of endive, placing a large tuft at the top. Round the base place hard-boiled eggs, cut in quarters, alternately with slices of beetroot. Finish off with a border of chopped aspic jelly (see p. 38).

Tomato Salad. Slice a few ripe tomatoes and lay them on a glass dish. Mix equal quantities of oil and vinegar with pepper and salt and pour over them. Garnish with chopped parsley or chives.

Tomato Salad (American). Choose 6 or 8 even-sized, firm, tomatoes; hollow out as much as possible of the soft centre portions; remove the seeds and mix the pulp with an equal quantity of stiff Mayonnaise sauce; to this add some finely chopped celery and a very little chopped ripe pineapple. Fill the tomatoes with this mixture, and place them in a refrigerator for at least 2 hrs. When serving, place each tomato on a fresh lettuce leaf in a glass dish with small lettuce leaves ranged round the tomatoes.

Waldorf Salad. Peel and cut 1 ripe apple into thin slices; slice 2 cooked potatoes, peel and slice 2 bananas and 2 blanched tomatoes and place in salad bowl; add a few points of green asparagus. Make a dressing as follows: 1 tbsp. each mayon-naise and cream, a little sugar and salt to taste, 1 scant tsp. each chilli vinegar and tarragon vinegar. Mix well together to a thick white cream, then mix with the salad. Garnish with a little finely chopped parsley or chervil over the top.

SALAD BURNET. See HERBS.

SALAD CREAM. Rub a lump of sugar over the yellow rind of a lemon, then dissolve it in ½ tsp. white vinegar. Add sufficient sour cream to make the requisite amount of salad dressing. Stir well and season to taste with salt and pepper, either white or cayenne; use as desired.

SALAD DRESSINGS

SALAD DRESSING—I

Ingredients

Yolk of 1 hard-boiled egg
Pinch of caster sugar
¼ saltspoon salt
1 tbsp. vinegar
½ gill salad oil

Method

Rub the yolk in a bowl with the sugar and salt, and gradually mix in the oil and vinegar. A little mustard or cayenne may be added if desired.

SALAD DRESSING—II

Ingredients

1½ tbsp. dry mustard
1 tsp. caster sugar
½ tsp. cayenne pepper
Yolks of 3 hard-boiled eggs
4 raw yolks
½ pt. each oil and cream (or evaporated milk)
½ pt. vinegar

Method

Mix the dry ingredients and boiled yolks very thoroughly together. Then add the raw yolks, and mix very gradually with the oil and cream like a mayonnaise. Last of all add the vinegar.

Almond and Cucumber Dressing. See ALMOND.

Cream Cheese Salad Dressing

Ingredients

5 tbsp. cream cheese
½ tsp. salt
⅛ tsp. paprika
4 tbsp. vinegar
4 minced pickled onions
7 tbsp. salad oil

Method

Beat the cheese with a fork until soft and creamy, working in the salt, paprika and vinegar. Then add onion. Gradually beat in the salad oil. Serve with green salads or tomato salad or apple and grated beetroot salad. If preferred, the onion may be omitted, and the mixing basin rubbed with a clove of garlic instead.

Eggless Salad Dressing

Ingredients

⅜ pt. vinegar
¼ pt. salad oil
½ tsp. salt
½ pt. evaporated milk (undiluted)
1 tsp. dry mustard
Pinch cayenne pepper

Method

Blend together in a bottle, and shake vigorously for 5 mins.

French Dressing

Ingredients

2 garlic cloves
1 tsp. Worcester sauce
1 tbsp. each vinegar and caster sugar
Juice of ½ lemon
1 tsp. each paprika and dry mustard
¼ pt. oil

Method

Cut and crush the garlic and put into a pint jar. Add other ingredients and then add the oil gradually. Leave for 1 hr., remove garlic before using.

French Dressing for Green Vegetable Salads

Ingredients

½ small clove garlic or shallot
⅓ cup salad oil
1 to 2 tbsp. vinegar or lemon juice
¼ tsp. salt
⅛ tsp. pepper
¼ tsp. paprika
1 tsp. sugar

Method

Add garlic to oil and vinegar. Leave 20 mins. Combine salt, pepper, paprika and sugar with oil and vinegar in a glass bottle. Cover closely and shake vigorously.

Sour Cream Dressing (*for Cabbage*)

Ingredients

½ pt. sour cream
1 tbsp. horseradish
2 tbsp. grated Swiss cheese
¼ tsp. each salt and black pepper
1 tsp. dry mustard

Method

Beat all together with wooden spoon and use as desired.

SALAD OIL. It is best to use the purest olive oil that can be obtained. It should be a pale golden colour, almost odourless, and nearly tasteless, and should pour freely from the bottle.

SALAD ONION. Small onion seedlings which are used in salads.

SALAD VINEGAR. Lemon juice may be used as a substitute for salad vinegar when desired, and, if a variation of flavour is required, use one or other of the herb vinegars.

SALAMANDER. A thick plate of iron with a long handle, perforated or not, which is heated and held over a pudding or other dish to brown it.

SALAMI. An Italian sausage which is chiefly used in hors d'œuvres or for sandwiches.

SALLY LUNN. A sweet, light teacake raised with brewer's yeast. Sally Lunn was a well-known personage at Bath who, at the close of the 18th century, used to make and sell these cakes.

SALMAGUNDI. A dish of chopped meat, anchovies, eggs, oil, vinegar, etc., made in Yorkshire during Lent.

SALMI or SALMIS. The name given to a ragôut of partly roasted game, stewed with sauce, wine, bread and condiments to provoke the appetite.
Salmi of Game. Cut the birds into neat joints and place in a sauté-pan. Break up the remaining bones of the birds and place in a stewpan, with ½ pt. burgundy, 2 whole shallots, salt and pepper to season, and a grating of nutmeg. Reduce the wine, add ½ pt. Espagnole sauce (see p. 422) and simmer gently for about 25 mins. Strain; warm up the birds in the sauté-pan and then place them in a dish and pour the sauce over them. Garnish with croûtons of fried bread and cress.

SALMON (Fr. *saumon*). The True salmon, or Atlantic salmon, lives in the sea, except when it comes into European and North American rivers to spawn. The salmon caught in Norwegian waters is considered the finest, then comes Scotch salmon. Canadian salmon are at their best smoked. English and Scotch salmon are at their best from February to August. On the Tay the season opens on 1st January for rods and 4th February for nets.
Fry or *Parr* are the names given to salmon under two years old. A *grilse* is a young salmon on its first return to the river from salt water. A grilse weighing under 2 lb. is known as *Salmon Peel. Salmon Trout* is the sea-trout. *Black Salmon*

SALMON (continued)

is the Great Lake trout, and *Burnett Salmon* is a fish that has a reddish flesh like the salmon. The so-called *Cornish Salmon* (the pollock) is a member of the haddock family.

SALMON, TO POT. See **POTTING**.

SALMON, SMOKED. Serve sliced thinly with lemon quarters and a plate of brown bread and butter.

Salmon Broth

Ingredients

2 lb. salmon tails
3 pt. water
3 sticks celery
1 bay leaf
1 diced onion
1 carrot
6 peppercorns
2 tbsp. butter
½ tbsp. thyme
Salt and pepper
2 tbsp. vinegar

Method

Choose fresh tails and wash them well. Leave whole. Put into a deep pan, add water and all ingredients except vinegar. Bring to the boil, cover and simmer gently for about 30 mins., or until the fish will flake, but do not overcook. Remove salmon, strain the broth through muslin or hair sieve. Return to pan, add vinegar and fish. Reheat and serve piping hot.

Salmon Chowder

Ingredients

2½ lb. salmon
1 bay leaf
1 sprig parsley
3 peppercorns
Salt and pepper
¼ lb. pork bacon (diced)
2 large onions
2 large potatoes
3 pt. milk

Method

Put the salmon into a deep pan; cover with water; add bay leaf and parsley, peppercorns and salt and pepper to taste. Boil for 15 mins. or until the salmon will flake. Fry the bacon and onions over a low heat until tender, stirring occasionally. Heat a soup tureen, place salted pork in separate pan, with onion, potatoes and milk; simmer until tender but do not boil. Season with pepper and salt, pour over ingredients. Add the flaked salmon. Serve in preheated soup bowls and garnish with finely chopped parsley.

Salmon Mayonnaise. See SALADS.

Salmon Sauté

Ingredients

1½ lb. salmon steaks
Salt and pepper
3 oz. butter or margarine
1 wineglass Rhine wine
1 bay leaf
1 small minced onion
1 tbsp. chopped chives
¼ tsp. dill
4 sprigs parsley

Method

Wipe steaks with damp cloth. Cut into cubes, add salt and pepper to season. Put 1 oz. butter into frying pan, add fish, wine and bay leaf. Cover and simmer 10 mins. Melt 2 oz. butter in another pan, add onion, chives, dill and sauté for 3 mins. to a golden brown. Remove fish carefully from wine sauce and put on to hot dish. Pour over wine sauce, then butter and onion. Serve immediately, garnished with parsley.

[432]

Salmon Soufflé

Ingredients	Method
2 tbsp. flour	Mix flour, salt and cayenne with a little of the milk to a smooth paste. Add this to remaining milk and bring slowly to the boil, stirring constantly. Remove from fire and add salmon. Pour over beaten egg yolks and butter. When cool, fold in stiffly beaten egg whites. Pour into greased ring mould and set in baking tin of water. Bake at 325° F. Therm. 4 for 45–50 mins. or until set. Turn out and fill centre with peas. Garnish with parsley.
1 tbsp. salt	
Few grains cayenne	
1 cup evaporated milk	
1 cup flaked salmon (fresh or tinned)	
3 eggs (separated)	
1 tbsp. butter	
Peas and parsley	

SALMON TROUT (F. *truite saumonée*). The fish that is known by this name is a kind of Sea Trout (*salmo trutta*). It is similar to the salmon, but smaller and with much smaller scales. The European sea trout is in season from March to August only. Any recipe for trout can be used for salmon trout.

Salmon Trout with Vegetables

Ingredients	Method
3 lb. salmon trout	Clean fish, cut crosswise into 1″ steaks. Melt the butter and add onion; sauté to a light brown. Add marjoram, garlic, tomatoes and salt, and sauté. Add potatoes, milk and rice and cook 10 mins.; then add a little sauterne. Add beaten eggs, shrimps, cheese, blend well and cook for 5 mins. Remove from heat, season with chilli and keep hot. Fry the trout in melted butter for 3 mins. each side. Place in hot bowl and serve with mixture over.
4 tbsp. butter or margarine	
2 sliced onions	
¼ tsp. marjoram	
1 clove garlic	
2 lb. tomatoes sliced	
Salt	
2 diced potatoes	
1 gill milk	
2 tbsp. cooked rice	
Sauterne	
2 well-beaten eggs	
¼ cup minced shrimps	
3 tbsp. grated cheese	
1 dried chilli pepper	

SALPICON. A French name given to a mince of chicken or game, with tongue, mushrooms and truffles; sometimes foie gras is added. Generally used as stuffing with poultry or it can be used as a change in rolled beef steak.

SALSIFY (Fr. *salsifis*). The common name for this is the Oyster Plant, sometimes called a Vegetable Oyster, because of the oyster flavour of the cooked root. In some respects it resembles scorzonera, having a long tapering root, full of milky juice.

SALSIFY, BOILED. Well wash the roots and scrape them thoroughly. Throw them at once into a pan of cold water with salt and lemon juice to keep their colour. Cook in boiling water or stock to which some lemon juice and a little butter and salt have been added, for ¾ hr., or until tender. (Steam, if preferred.) Drain well and dish on a napkin. Serve accompanied by White or Brown sauce.

SALSIFY, FRIED. Cook the salsify as for boiled salsify, then drain and dry well. Egg and breadcrumb, and fry in deep hot fat. If preferred, the salsify may be covered with frying batter instead of the egg and crumbs. Dish on a folded napkin, and garnish with fried parsley.

SALSIFY À LA SUPRÊME. Cook the salsify as for boiled salsify. Cut into 1½″ lengths, and mix with sufficient Suprême sauce (see p. 447) to moisten well. Pile in the centre of a dish and garnish with fried croûtons of bread or sauté potatoes.

Salsify Patties

Ingredients	Method
Some patty cases made as for oysters	Cook the salsify in milk or water; cut it into small pieces. Melt the butter in a
½ lb. salsify	small stewpan, mix in the flour smoothly;
1 oz. each butter and flour	add the milk, stir and cook well. Mix in
½ pt. milk	the cream, and let it boil in the sauce.
2 tbsp. cream	Then add the lemon juice, seasoning, and
Few drops lemon juice	salsify. Fill the patty cases with the
Pepper	mixture, and put a lid on each.
Salt	
Cayenne	

Salsify Scallops. Prepare the salsify as for Salsify à la Suprême (above). Put it into buttered scallop-shells. Sprinkle with browned crumbs, and put little pieces of butter about it. Brown under a grill or in the oven at 400° F. Therm. 6.

SALT. Sodium chloride, a naturally occurring mineral, used for seasoning and preserving food. It is obtained from sea-water by evaporation or in crystalline form as rock salt in certain geological formations. Salt is indispensable in the diet and gives flavour to most dishes. The best salt is English.

Use with cereals	1 tsp. to 1 pt. liquid.
Use with dough	1 „ 1 lb.
Use with fish	½ „ 1 lb.
Use with meat	1 „ 1 lb.
Use with vegetables	¼ „ 1 pt. water.

SALT FISH. Fish which are salted when newly caught and kept in pickle or dried by air. The dried fish requires 24–36 hours' soaking; the pickled fish needs a few hours' soaking.

SALTING. See PICKLE.

SALTPETRE (Fr. *saltpetre*). Nitrate of potash, much used in pickling meats; it gives them the red appearance which is sometimes so coveted.

SAMPHIRE (Fr. *bacile*). A herb which grows wild amongst the rocks and along the sea coasts of this and almost any other country. It can be used in green salad or boiled and used as a vegetable.

SAND CAKE. See CAKES.

SAND EELS. These are small eel-like fish caught in large quantities at low tide on the sands of the Channel Islands and coasts of France. They are mostly used for bait, but dipped in batter or egg and breadcrumbs and fried, they are reckoned among the dainty dishes of Jersey. A squeeze of lemon juice after cooking is an improvement.

SAND GROUSE. A game bird related to grouse.

SANDERS. This name is given to a preparation of minced beef, or other meat.
TO MAKE. Season finely minced beef or mutton with salt, pepper and finely chopped onion, moisten well with good gravy. Take some scallop shells or saucers; three parts fill them with minced meat, fill up with boiled potatoes, mashed smoothly with a little cream. Add a dot of butter to the top of each and brown with a salamander, under a hot grill, or in oven at 400° F. Therm. 6. Serve very hot.

SANDWICHES. Any kind of bread may be used to make sandwiches, spread with butter, margarine (which should be soft enough to spread easily without crumbling the bread), or peanut butter. Brown and white bread may be used

SANDWICHES (*continued*)

together as a variation. The fillings should always be made a little moist either by the addition of mayonnaise, vinegar, or cream, so that they are easily managed and the contents not likely to spill out. In some cases it is best to blend the slightly warmed butter or margarine with the filling.

SUGGESTED FILLINGS FOR SANDWICHES

Cut slices of bread ¼″ thick into squares, rounds, stars, diamonds, etc. Spread with creamed butter or margarine, fill with:

Chopped ham and cheese
Lettuce and hard-boiled egg
Sliced cucumber and lettuce
Sliced tomatoes and cottage cheese
Jam
Grated cheese and lettuce

Hard-boiled eggs and pickles (moistened with mayonnaise)
Cold tongue and mayonnaise
Cheese and chutney
Dates, lemon juice and nuts (minced)
Sardines, moistened with a little vinegar or mayonnaise
Cream cheese and thin slices of beetroot
Grated cheese and carrot moistened with a little mayonnaise

Minced tongue and tomato
Chicken or shrimp salad
Chopped parsley, hard-boiled eggs (chopped finely and moistened with a little mayonnaise)
Honey and chopped nuts
Peanut butter and bananas, mixed together before spreading
Raspberry jam and cream cheese
Cheese, tomato and mayonnaise
Cream cheese and dates mixed before spreading
Chopped celery and mayonnaise
Cheese and very thin rings spring onions
Sardines minced with olives and moistened with lemon juice

TOASTED SANDWICHES. Remove crusts from slices of bread, toast and allow to dry before spreading butter, or, if preferred, split and fill unbuttered.

FOR FILLINGS:

Chicken salad
Sliced ham and mustard
Sweetbreads and mushrooms browned in butter
Goose liver, onion and mayonnaise

Sliced cheese, tomato and mayonnaise
Sardine and hard-boiled eggs, moistened with mayonnaise
Crisp bacon and sliced tomatoes

If desired the sandwiches may be served "open", without a top, and garnished with rings of stuffed olives, watercress, chopped parsley, mayonnaise, red or green peppers, radishes or nuts.

SANGAREE. A favourite West Indian drink, almost always made there with port wine. In America, spirits or beer are substituted for wine.

TO MAKE. Mix ½ pt. water with 3 pt. port or sherry. Sweeten with caster sugar and flavour with grated nutmeg and a small quantity of powdered cinnamon. Pour into a saucepan and bring to the boil. Remove from heat, cover until cold, strain, bottle and use as desired.

SAPODILLA. An American tree which bears the fruit called sapodilla, a plum about the size of an ordinary quince, with a rough, brittle, dull-brown rind. The flesh is of a yellowish-white colour, very soft and deliciously sweet. It is eatable only when it begins to be spotted, and is much used in desserts. Sometimes it is called Naseberry.

SAPUCAIA. A Brazilian tree which bears nuts, sometimes called Paradise Nuts. They are about 2″ long and 1″ wide, covered with a longitudinally-furrowed corky shell, and grow in large hard woody fruits, shaped like urns, measuring about 6 ft. in diameter, and having close-fitting lids at the top.

SARDINES (Fr. *sardines*). The true sardine is the young of the pilchard caught mostly off Sardinia and the coasts of Brittany, and generally preserved in oil and packed in hermetically-sealed tins or pots. Some of the cheaper brands are merely other small fish such as young anchovies or herrings. Sardines are used in bouchées, fritters, fried and served on hot buttered toast, or in salads and as sandwich fillings.

SARSAPARILLA. The root of the *smilax officinalis*. Used medicinally.

SAUCES. Sauces can be used to supply food value to a dish or to counteract richness. Both skill and knowledge are demonstrated in their preparation and to be able to make a perfect sauce is the height of the art of cooking. The simplest of dishes can be greatly improved by the addition of a good plain sauce, whilst the most excellent of dishes can be made superb by the still more succulent and palatable sauce. When using stock, it is essential that this be well strained, and the fat skimmed off the top. Sauces at all times should be smooth and even and contain no lumps or irregularities, except for such additions as capers, shrimps, etc.

When making any sauce with flour in it take care thoroughly to cook the flour, otherwise it will have a raw pasty taste. The consistency of a sauce is dependent upon its use. The richest sauces are simmered for some time after they are made and the butter is skimmed off as it rises to the surface. They are then rubbed or wrung through a tammy cloth to make them smooth and creamy. Tammy cloths must be carefully washed, and they must be kept thoroughly clean after use or they are liable to give an unpleasant taste to the sauce. Sauces must be carefully seasoned.

Special care is necessary, when making a sauce with a roux thickening, to see that the temperature is lowered before the liquid stock or gravy is added: this prevents the sauce getting lumpy. All roux must be stirred continuously during the process of blending and cooking.

The difference between a sauce and a gravy is not always known, but one may generally call liquids pure and simple, gravies, and the thickened liquids, sauces.

LIAISONS are for thickening or binding sauces and soups. There are various methods of thickening sauces:

1. *White Roux.* A mixture of equal quantities of flour and butter cooked in a saucepan over a moderate heat, without allowing it to attain any colour.

2. *Blond or Fawn Roux.* The mixture as above cooked over a low heat until it is light blond or fawn in colour.

3. *Brown Roux.* The same mixture cooked until it is russet brown. For Brown Roux mirepoix is sometimes used.

4. *Egg Liaison.* This thickening is composed of egg yolks, beaten.

5. *Blood Liaison.* For Hare.

6. *Arrowroot* and *Cornflour.* See **ARROWROOT** and **SAUCES**.

7. *Reducing.* One of the most valuable processes to sauce-makers is that which the cook terms "reducing", applying it to the reduction of bulk or quantity and the increase of quality. The sauce to be reduced should be strained quite clear, and then put into a broad, shallow stewpan, placed over a quick heat, and made to boil at a gallop. By leaving off the lid, the water in the sauce evaporates with extraordinary celerity. It should be remembered that as water only evaporates, the remaining bulk would, necessarily, contain a greater proportion of material in solution: this is sometimes overlooked when seasoning the original quantity with salt, etc., forgetting that, when reduced to half its bulk, there will be double the proportion of seasoning.

FOUNDATION WHITE SAUCE

Ingredients	Method
1 oz. butter 1 oz. flour Salt and pepper ½ pt. liquid (milk or mixture of milk, fish stock, meat stock or water)	Melt the butter, add flour and cook for a few mins. without colouring. Remove from the heat and add liquid gradually, beating well. Stir until boiling, cook for 5 mins., add seasoning, and use.

This recipe makes a sauce of *coating consistency*: for *pouring* use twice as much liquid; for a *panada* use half as much liquid.

[436]

VARIATIONS OF WHITE SAUCE

Anchovy Sauce	½ pt. white sauce, 1 tsp. anchovy essence, colouring if needed
Brain Sauce	½ pt. white sauce, 1 sheep's brain, cooked and chopped, 1 tsp. lemon juice
Caper Sauce	½ pt. white sauce, 1 tbsp. chopped capers, squeeze of lemon juice
Cheese Sauce	½ pt. white sauce, 2 oz. grated cheese
Egg Sauce	½ pt. white sauce, 1 hard-boiled egg chopped
Mustard Sauce	½ pt. white sauce, 1 tsp. dry mustard, added with flour
Onion Sauce	½ pt. white sauce, 2 large onions, blanched, boiled, drained and chopped
Parsley Sauce	½ pt. white sauce, 1 dsp. finely chopped parsley, few drops lemon juice
Velouté Sauce	½ pt. white sauce (made with stock), 1 tsp. lemon juice

SAUCES, SAVOURY

Admiral's Sauce

Ingredients
½ pt. melted butter
1 tsp. chopped capers
3 shallots chopped
2 pounded anchovies
Pepper and salt
Little thin lemon rind

Method
Add to the melted butter, capers, shallots and anchovies: season with salt and pepper, add lemon rind and place over a low heat. Simmer until the anchovies are dissolved. Sufficient for ½ pt. sauce.

Allemande Sauce

Ingredients
1 pt. Velouté sauce
3 egg yolks
½ oz. butter

Method
Reduce the Velouté sauce to one-fourth, add the yolks and butter, and stir over a slow heat until the yolks thicken. Strain through a tammy cloth. This sauce *must not boil* after the yolks are in it, or it will curdle.

Anchovy and Caper Sauce. See ANCHOVY.

Apple Sauce

Ingredients
6 good-sized apples
½ gill water
1 tbsp. caster sugar (or according to taste)
2 tbsp. whipped cream
1 oz. butter

Method
Wash and slice the apples, and cut them in pieces. Put them in an enamelled stewpan, or jar, with the sugar and water; cook gently, stirring occasionally, until quite tender; then rub them through a hair sieve. Make hot again and stir in the butter and 2 tbsp. very thick cream.

[437]

Asparagus Sauce. Cut the points from young asparagus, cook them until tender and mix them with Allemande Sauce (see p. 437) just before serving.

Aurora Sauce

Ingredients

Spawn of a lobster
Lump of butter
½ pt. Brown sauce
Juice of a lemon
Salt and pepper

Method

Pound the spawn and butter together in a mortar, then pass through a hair sieve. Add to sauce (thick enough to coat a spoon), add lemon juice season to taste and serve.

Béarnaise Sauce. Thick white sauce made from:

Ingredients

1 oz. butter
1 oz. flour
1½ gills milk
2 shallots or 1 onion
½ gill each tarragon vinegar and malt vinegar
2 egg yolks
1 oz. butter
¼ tsp. each chopped parsley and chopped chervil

Method

Make a white sauce with the butter, flour and milk. Simmer the chopped shallots or onion in the vinegar and reduce to 1 tbsp. Strain and add to the white sauce, mixing well. Whisk in the yolks of eggs separately in a basin over hot water. Remove from heat, whisk in the butter in small pieces to avoid oiling. Reheat if necessary and add the parsley and chervil.

Béchamel Sauce

Ingredients

½ pt. milk
Slice of carrot and turnip
2″ celery
1 blade mace
1 small onion stuck with cloves
6 white peppercorns
1 oz. butter
1 oz. flour
Salt
1 tbsp. cream

Method

Simmer the vegetables and flavourings gently in the milk for ½ hr., then strain. Melt the butter, add the flour and cook without browning, add the flavoured milk and boil well. Tammy, add salt to taste, and cream and reheat.

Bigarade Sauce

Ingredients

½ pt. Espagnole sauce using 1 shallot instead of onion
Juice and rind of 1 orange
½–1 tbsp. redcurrant jelly
Juice of ½ lemon
Cayenne pepper
1 gill port wine

Method

Make the Espagnole sauce and tammy. Add very finely shredded orange rind and redcurrant jelly and cook gently until tender. Add orange and lemon juice, cayenne pepper and port wine. Reheat and serve with wild duck.

Bordelaise Sauce

Ingredients

1 shallot finely minced
1 clove garlic bruised

Method

Blanch and chop the shallot and simmer it with the garlic, parsley, mignonette and

[438]

Bordelaise Sauce (*continued*)

1 dsp. finely chopped parsley
Little mignonette
Pepper and salt
1 wineglass Bordeaux
1 pt. Espagnole sauce

seasoning in the wine for ¼ hr. Add the sauce, then simmer for 20 mins. Tammy, and reheat before serving.

Bread Sauce (Fr. *sauce au pain*)

Ingredients
½ pt. milk
1 small onion
About 4 cloves
1 blade mace
2 oz. breadcrumbs
1 oz. butter
Seasoning
1 tbsp. cream (if desired)

Method
Infuse the onion, cloves and mace in the milk for about ½ hr. Strain over the breadcrumbs, butter and seasoning and cover with a saucer. When required add the cream, reheat and serve.

Brown Sauce

Ingredients
2 oz. butter
1½ oz. flour
1 pt. nicely flavoured stock
2 mushrooms peeled and sliced
1 slice each carrot, turnip and onion
1 tomato
Few drops lemon juice
Pepper and salt

Method
Melt the butter in a saucepan and fry the vegetables in it, but do not burn them. Remove from heat, add mushrooms and tomato, and stir well together, adding the stock gradually and lemon juice. Return to heat, reboil, strain, add blended flour and reheat to thicken.

Cardinal Sauce

Ingredients
½ pt. Velouté sauce
½ oz. lobster butter

Method
Make the Velouté sauce with fish stock, draw aside and whisk in the lobster butter (¼ tsp. at a time) until a delicate pink colour. Do not boil after the lobster butter is added, or it will curdle.

Celery Sauce

Ingredients
The white part of 5 heads of celery
2 oz. butter
Little white stock
Salt
1 pt. Velouté sauce
2 tbsp. cream

Method
Cut the celery in pieces, put them into a stewpan with the butter, enough stock to cover them, and a very little salt. Simmer very gently for ¼ hr., then add the sauce, and season to taste. Simmer for about 20 mins., skimming the butter off. Add the cream and tammy the sauce.

Champagne Sauce. Put 2 cloves, 6 peppercorns, 1 bay leaf and ½ tbsp. powdered sugar into a saucepan with a glassful of champagne. Place over low heat and reduce for 5 mins., then moisten with ¾ pt. Espagnole sauce. Cook a further 15 mins., strain and serve.

Chasseur Sauce

Ingredients

½ pt. Espagnole or good brown sauce
1 tbsp. redcurrant jelly
1 dsp. home-made glaze
Lemon juice to taste
½–1 gill port wine
Cayenne pepper

Method

Add all the ingredients to the prepared sauce, and reduce for 5–10 mins. Strain and serve with venison.

Chaudfroid Sauce (Brown)

Ingredients

1½ gills Espagnole sauce
1½ gills aspic jelly

Method

Proceed as for White Chaudfroid sauce (below).

Chaudfroid Sauce (Green)

Ingredients

1½ gills Béchamel sauce
1 tbsp. each chopped spinach, parsley, tarragon and chervil (after blanching)
Colouring if necessary
1½ gills aspic jelly

Method

Pound and sieve the green leaves and add the Béchamel sauce. Then proceed as for White Chaudfroid sauce (below).

Chaudfroid Sauce (Tomato)

Ingredients

1 gill tomato sauce
1 gill Béchamel sauce
1 tbsp. cream
½ pt. aspic jelly
Carmine if necessary

Method

Mix the two sauces together and proceed as for White Chaudfroid sauce (below).

Chaudfroid Sauce (White)

Ingredients

1½ gills Béchamel or Velouté sauce
1½ gills aspic jelly
1 tbsp. cream
Seasoning

Method

Add the liquid aspic to the hot sauce; bring to boiling point, season and tammy. Add the cream and use when beginning to thicken.

Chestnut Sauce

Ingredients

½ lb. chestnuts
Thin rind of 1 lemon
1 pt. each white stock and double cream
Seasoning

Method

Take off the brown skin and throw the chestnuts into boiling water; simmer for 2 or 3 mins., then drain and peel off the second skin. Put them into a stewpan with the stock and lemon peel, and cook them for 1 hr. or until they are quite soft. Rub them and the stock through a sieve.

[440]

Chestnut Sauce (*continued*)

Return to the stewpan again, add the cream, season to taste, and make quite hot.

Cocktail Sauce (*for fish*). **See COCKTAILS, SAVOURY.**

Colbert Sauce

Ingredients
- 1 cup concentrated stock
- 1 oz. butter
- Juice of a small lemon
- 1 tbsp. chopped parsley

Method
Put the stock into a saucepan and add the butter gradually. When boiling, strain, add the chopped parsley and lemon juice and serve.

Cranberry Sauce

Ingredients
- 1 lb. cranberries
- ½ gill water
- 4 oz. brown sugar
- ½ gill port

Method
Wash the cranberries, drain in a colander, place in a saucepan with the water, stew until tender. Rub through a hair sieve, add the sugar, reheat and, just before serving, add the port wine.

Creole Sauce

Ingredients
- 4 oz. melted butter or margarine
- 1 large minced onion
- 8 oz. minced green peppers
- 1 clove garlic minced
- Pinch of salt
- ⅜ tsp. pepper
- ⅛ tsp. each rosemary and paprika
- 2 pt. tomato pulp

Method
Melt the butter over a medium heat, add onion, green peppers and garlic. Sauté for about 10 mins. until tender. Add salt, pepper, rosemary, paprika and tomato pulp. Bring to boil, cover and reduce heat. Simmer slowly for 15 mins. (longer if possible to get the best flavour). Serve very hot. Pour over cooked macaroni, spaghetti, rice, or use as an omelet filling.

Cucumber Sauce

Ingredients
- 1 cucumber
- 1 oz. butter
- Seasoning
- Pinch of sugar
- Green colouring if necessary
- ½ pt. thick Béchamel or Velouté sauce

Method
Peel the cucumber, remove seeds, cut into 2″ pieces and boil for 10 mins. in salted water. Strain and rinse in cold water to preserve colour. Sweat in a saucepan with the butter, seasoning and sugar for 20–30 mins. Pass through a hair sieve and add to the hot Béchamel sauce. Tammy, season, colour of necessary, and reheat. See also **CUCUMBER**.

Cumberland Sauce (*for game, cold meats, boiled ham and tongue*)

Ingredients
- 1 lemon
- 1 orange
- ½ gill each water and port wine
- 2 tsp. each redcurrant jelly and vinegar

Method
Remove peel of orange and lemon without taking any of the pith; shred finely and simmer for 5 mins. in the water. Strain, return to saucepan and add port wine, redcurrant jelly, mustard, cayenne, salt, juice of orange and lemon and vinegar.

Cumberland Sauce (continued)
½ tsp. made mustard
Pinch salt and pepper
Glacé cherries

Simmer for a few mins., then add the chopped glacé cherries.

Curry Sauce
Ingredients
¾ pt. white stock
2 tbsp. coconut
2 oz. butter
1 medium-sized onion
1 medium-sized apple
1 oz. cornflour
1 tsp. each curry powder, chutney and curry paste
Redcurrant jelly
Lemon juice to taste
Seasoning

Method
Boil the stock, pour over the coconut, cover and infuse until needed. Melt the butter and sweat the chopped onion and apple together for 10 mins. Add the flour and curry powder and fry slightly for 10 mins. Add the strained stock, chutney and curry paste, bring to boiling point and cook gently for 1½–2 hrs. Add jelly, lemon juice and seasoning just before serving. The sauce may be tammied if required. Fish stock may be used for fish dishes.

Demi-Glace Sauce
Ingredients
½ pt. Espagnole sauce
¼ pt. well reduced gravy or 1 tsp. home-made glaze
Seasoning

Method
Prepare the Espagnole sauce, add the gravy or liquid glaze and seasoning. Reheat and serve.

D'Uxelles Sauce
Ingredients
Shallots
Mushrooms
Parsley
Butter
Brown sauce

Method
Blanch the shallots and thoroughly cleanse the mushrooms and parsley. Chop them all finely, using a double quantity of mushrooms. Cook them in a stewpan over a gentle heat in some butter for 10 mins., or until they are tender. Add the mixture to brown sauce in the porportion of 2 tbsp. to each 1 pt. sauce.

Egg Sauce. To 1 pt. Velouté or Béchamel sauce, add the whites of 4 hard-boiled eggs diced.

Espagnole Sauce
Ingredients
2 oz. butter
1 small onion
Piece each carrot and turnip
1½ oz. lean ham or bacon
2 oz. flour
1 pt. brown stock
Bouquet garni
2 tomatoes
2 mushrooms
Seasoning
1–2 tbsp. sherry

Method
Heat the butter and gently fry the onion, carrot, turnip and ham until lightly coloured; add the flour and cook slowly until brown; add the stock, bouquet garni, sliced tomatoes, mushrooms and seasoning. Bring to boiling point and simmer gently for 1–1½ hrs. Skim frequently. Tammy the sauce, add the sherry and reheat.

Fennel Sauce

Ingredients

1 handful fennel
½ pt. Velouté sauce or
  melted butter

Method

Pick the fennel from the stalk, wash
thoroughly and boil quickly until tender.
Drain, chop finely and mix with the sauce
or melted butter.

Financière Sauce

Ingredients

½ pt. Brown sauce
¼ pt. chicken broth
Truffle trimmings
4 mushrooms
½ glass madeira or sauterne
Seasoning

Method

Heat the Brown sauce and add chicken
broth. Add chopped mushrooms and
truffles, cook quickly to reduce. Lower
heat, add wine gradually, season, strain
and serve.

Gherkin Sauce. Make like Caper sauce, using chopped gherkins instead of capers.

Gooseberry Sauce. See GOOSEBERRY.

Green Sauce

Ingredients

1 handful parsley
Little chervil
1 sprig each tarragon and
  fennel
1½ oz. butter
1½ oz. flour
½–¾ pt. fish stock
½–1 gill sauterne
Seasoning

Method

Blanch the herbs by plunging into
boiling water for about 1 min., then into
cold. Drain and dry, then rub through a
hair sieve. Make a sauce with the butter,
flour and stock, add the sieved herbs,
sauterne and seasoning, tammy and
reheat.

Hollandaise Sauce

Ingredients

2 egg yolks
2 tbsp. water
½–1 dsp. lemon juice
Salt
Pinch of pepper
2 oz. butter

Method

Beat egg yolks, add water, seasoning,
lemon juice and half the butter melted.
Cook in basin over a pan of hot water
until thickened. Remove from heat and
beat in the remaining butter in small
pieces. Reheat if necessary and serve. If
the sauce is too acid, add a pinch of sugar.
If too thick, add a little hot water.

Horseradish Sauce (Cold)

Ingredients

4 tbsp. finely grated horseradish
½ tsp. dry mustard
½ tsp. caster sugar
¼ tsp. salt
1½ tbsp. vinegar
1 gill cream

Method

Scrub, peel and finely grate the horseradish; add the mustard, sugar, salt and
vinegar. Gradually stir in the cream. The
sauce should be of a dropping consistency.
If cream is not to be had, use milk
thickened with a little cornflour, but this
is not so good.

[443]

Horseradish Sauce (Hot) (Fr. *sauce raifort*)

Ingredients

½ pt. Béchamel sauce
2 tsp. caster sugar
1 tbsp. each cream and grated horseradish
1 tsp. vinegar
Seasoning

Method

Add vinegar to the horseradish. Add sugar and cream to the Béchamel sauce and heat thoroughly, then add horseradish and seasoning.

Italian Sauce

Ingredients

½ small onion or 2 shallots
3 mushrooms
1 oz. each butter and flour
1 sprig thyme
1 bay leaf
½ pt. brown stock
Seasoning
½ gill sherry

Method

Fry the sliced onion and mushrooms in the hot butter; add the flour, thyme and bay leaf and fry until brown. Add the stock and seasoning and boil and simmer for ¾–1 hr. Add sherry, tammy, reheat and serve.

Lobster Sauce I

Ingredients

1 small lobster
¾ pt. milk
Some spawn
1½ oz. butter
1 oz. flour
2 or 3 tbsp. cream or evaporated milk
Few drops lemon juice
Pepper and salt

Method

Remove the flesh from the body and claws of the lobster, and cut it into small pieces. Put the shell in a saucepan (broken small), cover with water, simmer quickly for 5 mins. then add milk, simmer for a further 5 mins. and strain. Rub the spawn with ¼ oz. butter through a hair sieve; melt the remaining butter in a small stewpan. Mix in the flour smoothly, and then add the liquid. Stir until it thickens. Put in the spawn butter, and continue stirring until the flour is well cooked. Add the cream. Do not let the sauce boil. Lastly, add the lemon juice, pepper and salt, and lobster meat.

Lobster Sauce II

Ingredients

Part of a tin of lobster
1 oz. each butter and flour
¾ pt. milk
Few drops lemon juice or ½ tsp. vinegar
Pepper and salt

Method

Cut up the lobster. Melt the butter in a small stewpan. Mix in the flour smoothly. Add the milk; stir and cook well. Then add the lemon juice, seasoning, and pieces of lobster.

Madeira Sauce (Fr. *sauce madère*)

Ingredients

¾ pt. Espagnole sauce
1 dsp. home-made glaze
Salt and cayenne pepper
2–3 tbsp. madeira

Method

Prepare the Espagnole sauce, add seasoning and glaze, and reduce slightly. Add wine, tammy and reheat.

Maître d'Hôtel Sauce. See p. 97.

Mayonnaise Sauce

Ingredients

1 egg yolk
1 tsp. dry mustard
¼ tsp. caster sugar
½ tsp. salt
Pinch of pepper
1 gill salad oil
2 tsp. malt vinegar
2 tsp. tarragon vinegar
1 tbsp. cream or milk

Method

Cream the dry ingredients with the egg yolk; add salad oil drop by drop, stirring in some of the vinegar when necessary to thin it down. Stir in the milk or cream just before serving.

Mayonnaise, Green and Red. See MAYONNAISE, Aspic (p. 327).

Melted Butter Sauce

Ingredients

3 oz. butter
1 oz. flour
½ pt. warm water
Pepper and salt

Method

Melt 1 oz. butter in a stewpan, put in the flour and mix it thoroughly. Pour in the water, stir and cook well. Then, just before serving, stir in the remaining butter off the heat, cut in small pieces. Season with pepper and salt to taste.

Mussel Sauce. Add chopped mussels to Hollandaise sauce.
Mustard Sauce. See MUSTARD.
Mustard Sauce (Brown)

Ingredients

½ pt. Brown sauce
1 tsp. English and French mustard, mixed
1 dsp. chilli vinegar
1 tsp. anchovy essence
Salt

Method

Heat all the ingredients together. Melted butter may be substituted for the Brown sauce.

Oyster Sauce

Ingredients

½ pt. Velouté sauce (made with fish stock and oyster liquor)
6 oysters
1 tsp. lemon juice
Cayenne pepper

Method

Strain the liquor from the oysters, simmer the beards in it and remove them. Use the liquid in the Velouté sauce. Add the oysters cut into small dice; flavour with lemon juice and cayenne pepper, reheat and serve.

Périgueux Sauce

Ingredients

1 pt. Espagnole sauce
4 mushrooms
Slice of lean ham
6 truffles

Method

Cleanse the mushrooms, add them and the ham to the sauce, and let it simmer by the side of the heat for 20 mins. Then strain through a tammy cloth and add the truffles, finely sliced or chopped.

Piquant Sauce

Ingredients

2 tbsp. each capers and chopped gherkins

Method

Put the capers, gherkins and shallot in the vinegar, and simmer until the

[445]

Piquant Sauce (continued)

1 dsp. of very finely chopped shallot
¼ pt. vinegar
1 pt. Brown sauce
Pepper and salt

shallot is quite soft. Pour in the sauce and let it boil up. Add pepper and salt to taste.

Poivrade Sauce

Ingredients

2 oz. butter
1 oz. lean ham
1 piece each carrot, turnip and onion
1 stick celery
1 large mushroom
1 sprig each parsley, thyme and marjoram
12 peppercorns
1 blade mace
1 wineglass sherry
½ wineglass vinegar
¼ pt. Brown sauce
1 tsp. Anchovy sauce
Pepper and salt

Method

Cut the ham, carrot, turnip, onion, celery and mushrooms into dice, and fry in the butter with the herbs, mace and peppercorns. Add the sherry and vinegar and reduce to half the quantity. Pour in the Brown sauce and add the Anchovy sauce. Let it stand by the side of the heat and boil gently until all the fat has been thrown up. This should be skimmed carefully off the surface as it rises. Add pepper and salt to taste and strain through a tammy.

Portuguese Sauce

Ingredients

1 pt. Espagnole sauce
¼ pt. sherry
1 blade mace
6 peppercorns
1 sprig of thyme
1 bay leaf
Thin rind of ½ lemon

Method

Put all the ingredients into a stewpan together, reduce gently and strain through a tammy.

Port Wine Sauce

Ingredients

2 wineglasses port wine
1 finely chopped shallot
Juice of ½ lemon

Method

Boil together and strain.

Poulette Sauce

Ingredients

1 pt. Velouté sauce
2 egg yolks
2 mushrooms finely chopped

Method

Simmer the mushrooms in the sauce for 15 mins., adding a little stock if it becomes too thick. Then thicken with the yolks of the eggs, taking care the sauce does not boil after they are added. Strain through a tammy cloth.

[446]

Ravigote Sauce

Ingredients
- 1 tbsp. each tarragon vinegar and finely chopped parsley
- 1 tsp. each mushroom ketchup and Anchovy sauce
- ½ pt. Béchamel sauce

Method
Put the vinegar, Anchovy and Mushroom sauces into a stewpan, and reduce to half the quantity. Add the Béchamel sauce and stir in the parsley. The Béchamel sauce used for this purpose should be made thick.

Ravioli Sauce

Ingredients
- 2 tbsp. butter
- 2 level tsp. flour
- 4 tbsp. Italian tomato paste
- ½ tsp. sugar
- ¾ pt. water

Method
Melt the butter, stir in the flour, add combined together the tomato paste, water and sugar. Stir and cook until the sauce bubbles.

Reforme Sauce

Ingredients
- 1 pt. Espagnole sauce
- 12 peppercorns
- 1 tsp. redcurrant jelly
- 1–2 tbsp. port wine
- Cayenne pepper
- Lemon juice to flavour

Method
Make the Espagnole sauce, adding peppercorns after boiling. Tammy and flavour; add the jelly, wine, cayenne and lemon juice; reheat and serve.

Remoulade Sauce. Mayonnaise sauce with chopped parsley, fennel and tarragon leaves, shallots and prepared mustard.

Shrimp Sauce

Ingredients
- 1 pt. Béchamel sauce
- 1 oz. lobster butter
- ½ pt. shelled shrimps

Method
Colour the sauce with the lobster butter and add the shrimps. Make quite hot before serving.

Soubise Sauce

Ingredients
- 2 Spanish onions
- ½ pt. milk
- 2 cloves
- 1″ stick celery
- 1 blade mace
- 6 peppercorns
- Small piece each carrot and turnip
- Salt
- 1 oz. each butter and flour
- 1 tbsp. cream
- Pinch of sugar

Method
Peel and blanch the onions and drain them; put the milk, onions, vegetables and flavourings into a saucepan and cook until the onions are tender. Lift out the onions and strain the liquid; rub the onions through a hair sieve. Cook the fat and flour together; add the strained liquid (this should have reduced to ¼ pt.), boil and cook thoroughly, add the onions, cream, sugar and seasoning. Reheat and serve.

Spanish Sauce. See Espagnole Sauce.

Suprême Sauce

Ingredients
- ½ pt. Velouté sauce
- 2 egg yolks

Method
Add the egg yolks to the hot Velouté sauce and thicken without boiling. Whisk

Suprême Sauce (*continued*)
  ½ oz. butter
  Juice of ½ lemon
  1 tbsp. cream
  Seasoning

in small pieces of butter and add lemon juice, cream and seasoning. Serve hot.

Tarragon Sauce. See TARRAGON.
Tartare Sauce (Cold).
Ingredients
  ½ pt. Mayonnaise sauce
  1 dsp. chopped capers
  1 dsp. chopped gherkins
  1 tsp. chopped blanched parsley

Method
Mix all the finely chopped ingredients with the mayonnaise.

Tartare Sauce (Hot)
Ingredients
  ½ pt. Béchamel sauce
  1 or 2 egg yolks
  1 tsp. each chopped gherkins, chopped capers, chopped parsley (blanched)
  Lemon juice
  Cayenne
  Salt

Method
Add the egg yolks to the hot Béchamel sauce and cook without boiling. Add the gherkins, capers, parsley, lemon juice and seasoning.

Tomato Sauce
Ingredients
  ½ pt. tinned tomatoes / ¼ pt. white stock *or*
  ½ lb. fresh tomatoes / ½ pt. white stock
  ½ oz. each butter and lean bacon
  1 small onion
  Small piece carrot
  ½ tsp. sugar
  Seasoning
  2 tsp. cornflour or crème de riz

Method
Melt the butter and sweat the carrot, onion and bacon for 5 mins. Add the sliced fresh or tinned tomatoes, the stock, sugar and seasoning. Bring to boiling point and simmer gently for about 45 mins. Rub through a hair sieve, add the blended cornflour or crème de riz and cook thoroughly. Tammy, if necessary, and reheat. See also **TOMATO**.

Velouté Sauce
Ingredients
  1 oz. butter
  4 button mushrooms
  6 peppercorns
  Few sprigs parsley
  1 oz. flour
  ½ pt. white stock
  ½ gill cream
  Pepper and salt
  Lemon juice

Method
Fry the coarsely chopped mushrooms, parsley, peppercorns in the butter without browning. Add the flour and cook well, add the stock and boil. Simmer gently 30–40 mins. Tammy and add cream, seasoning and lemon juice. If required to serve with fish, use fish stock instead of white stock.

Vinaigrette Sauce. Salad oil, vinegar, chopped shallots, parsley, chervil, gherkins, seasoned with pepper and salt, served cold with calf's head, asparagus, sea kale, etc.
Vin Blanche Sauce. Béchamel or Velouté flavoured with White wine, fish essence and lemon juice.

SAUCES, SWEET

Almond Sauce. Make according to the Vanilla Sauce recipe, using almond essence instead of Vanilla.

Apricot Sauce

Ingredients

12 apricots
3 tbsp. water
1 wineglass madeira
2–3 oz. sugar
About 1 tsp. arrowroot or cornflour

Method

Cut the apricots into halves, remove and break stones, blanch and pound kernels, and put fruit in saucepan with water. Add madeira and, when the fruit is soft, the sugar. Thicken with a little arrowroot or cornflour, moistened with a little water to a smooth paste. Stir until thickened and use as desired.

Arrowroot Sauce

Ingredients

1 dsp. arrowroot
½ pt. water
2 tbsp. sugar
Flavouring

Method

Mix the arrowroot with the water. Place in a saucepan and boil gently, stirring all the time. Add the sugar and flavouring. 1 tbsp. brandy may be added if desired. This sauce is suitable for rice, bread or plum pudding.

Brandy Sauce

Ingredients

1 oz. butter
¾ oz. flour
1½ gills milk or water
½ gill brandy
½–1 oz. sugar

Method

Make a sauce with the butter, flour and milk or water. Add the sugar and brandy, reheat and serve.

Chocolate Sauce

Ingredients

½ pt. water
2 oz. chocolate
3 tsp. crème de riz or cornflour
1 oz. icing sugar
¼–½ tsp. vanilla essence
1–2 tbsp. brandy

Method

Boil water and broken chocolate for a few mins. and stir until smooth. Add blended crème de riz or cornflour and cook thoroughly. Add sugar, vanilla and brandy; reheat and serve.

Custard Sauce I

Ingredients

½ pt. milk
Flavouring of lemon rind or vanilla if desired
2 egg yolks
1 tsp. sugar

Method

Heat the milk with lemon rind or vanilla and pour over the beaten yolks. Strain into pan, add sugar, stir until the custard thickens and remove instantly. Serve hot or cold. If desired the whites of eggs may be whisked stiffly and added when the sauce has cooled a little.

15*

Custard Sauce II

Ingredients

½ pt. milk
1 tsp. each cornflour and sugar
1 egg

Method

Blend cornflour with a little cold milk. Boil remainder of milk, add cornflour, stir well until boiling, then cook for 2–3 mins. Cool a little, add sugar and beaten egg. Return to heat and stir until egg thickens, but do not boil again.

Damson Sauce

Ingredients

1 pt. damsons
4 oz. lump sugar
¼ pt. water

Method

Stone the damsons, and place in a stewpan with the water and sugar. Stir occasionally until the damsons are cooked; rub through a hair sieve. All sauces made from stone fruit are prepared in the same manner.

German Sauce

Ingredients

4 egg yolks
2 wineglasses sherry
1 tbsp. caster sugar

Method

Put all the ingredients into a saucepan and stir with a whisk until the sauce froths. Care must be taken not to curdle it.

Hard Sauce

Ingredients

6 sweet almonds
2 bitter almonds
¼ lb. fresh butter
2 oz. caster sugar
1 tbsp. sherry
½ tbsp. brandy

Method

Blanch, chop and pound the almonds to a smooth paste in a mortar. Cream the butter and sugar, add almonds; add sherry and brandy gradually and mix well. Serve with Christmas, plum and brown puddings.

Jam Sauce I

Ingredients

2 tbsp. jam
Few drops lemon juice
¼ pt. water

Method

Boil together until reduced to two-thirds. Colour if necessary, strain and serve. This sauce may be thickened with a ½ tsp. blended arrowroot or cornflour instead of reducing.

Jam Sauce II. Make according to recipe for Wine Syrup sauce, using double the quantity of sugar and water, and omitting the wine.

Lemon Sauce

Ingredients

1 lemon (juice and rind)
1 pt. water
1 dsp. arrowroot
3 tbsp. caster sugar

Method

Put the water, with a little thin lemon rind, on the fire to boil. Mix the arrowroot smoothly with a little cold water. When the water in the saucepan boils, pour in the arrowroot, stir until it thickens, and add the sugar. Strain and

Lemon Sauce (*continued*)

add the lemon juice. Sherry or brandy may be used in this sauce, instead of lemon juice. See also **LEMON**.

Marmalade Sauce. As for Jam sauce, but omitting the lemon juice.

Melba Sauce I

Ingredients

¼ lb. raspberries or strawberries

3–4 oz. icing sugar

Method

Sieve and tammy the fruit through muslin. Beat in sufficient sugar to sweeten. Use as required.

Melba Sauce II

Ingredients

3 tbsp. raspberry or strawberry jam

¼ pt. water

Rind and juice of ½ lemon

2 tsp. cornflour

Carmine (if necessary).

Method

Boil the jam, water and lemon rind until reduced to half. Add blended cornflour, bring to boiling point and cook. Add colour if necessary. Add lemon juice, strain and cool. Use as required.

Mousseline Sauce (Sweet or Savoury)

Ingredients

3 egg yolks

1 or 2 egg whites

½ gill cream

Lemon juice to taste

  Pinch of nutmeg ⎫

  Salt and pepper ⎭

(For sweet sauce: substitute sugar and vanilla for seasoning and nutmeg.)

Method

Put all the ingredients except egg whites into a lined pan and whisk over a gentle heat until thickened and frothy. Fold in the stiffly whisked white of egg and serve at once.

Orange Sauce I

Ingredients

Juice ½ orange

Thin shreds of rind

1 or 2 tsp. lemon juice

1 tsp. cornflour

1 oz. sugar

¼ pt. water

Method

Boil the shreds or orange rind in the water, with orange and lemon juice, until tender. Blend the cornflour with cold water, add to the boiling liquid and stir until cooked. Add sugar and serve.

Orange Sauce II

Ingredients

5 large oranges

6 lumps sugar

1 wineglass curaçao

1 dsp. arrowroot

Method

Rub the sugar on the oranges to absorb the zest. Put it into a stewpan, and add the strained juice of the oranges. Mix the arrowroot smoothly with the curaçao, and mix in. Boil the sauce and serve. If too thick, add more orange juice.

Rum Sauce. See RUM.

Sabayon Sauce

Ingredients

1 gill sherry (or sherry and water)
2 egg yolks
½ oz. sugar
1 tbsp. cream (if desired)

Method

Heat the sherry, add beaten yolks and sugar. Whisk over a gentle heat until quite frothy and thick. Add cream and use at once. *Avoid using an aluminium pan.*

Strawberry Sauce. See **STRAWBERRY.**

Treacle Sauce

Ingredients

2 tbsp. syrup or treacle
1 gill water
1 tsp. lemon juice

Method

Boil together until reduced to two-thirds or thicken with 1 tsp. cornflour blended with a little water.

Vanilla Sauce. To ½ pt. plain white sauce, add a few drops of vanilla, ½ wineglass brandy and caster sugar to taste.

White Sauce (Blended)

Ingredients

½ pt. white sauce
2 tsp. sugar
Flavouring if desired
Small knob butter

Method

Mix the flour smoothly with a little of the milk; heat remainder of milk and add the blended flour. Stir until boiling, add butter, sugar and flavouring and serve.

Wine Syrup Sauce

Ingredients

2–4 oz. loaf sugar
½ pt. water
2 tbsp. marmalade
½ gill sherry
3 or 4 drops carmine

Method

Boil sugar and water together until reduced to half quantity. Add marmalade and cook for 10 mins. Strain, add sherry and carmine and serve.

SAUSAGE (Fr. *saucisse*). Sausages may be made fresh or of cooked meat and then dried or smoked according to taste. Some fresh meat sausages are apt to burst when cooking; to avoid this, either prick with a darning needle, or soak in boiling water for a few minutes before cooking. Sausage meat is used in forcemeat and stuffings.

SAUSAGES FOR HORS D'ŒUVRES. See **HORS D'ŒUVRES.**

Sausage Casserole. Grill the required number of sausages and place in a casserole. Cover with alternate layers of apple and onion, season with a little pepper; add 3 peppercorns and 2 bay leaves; add beer, cider or an undiluted tin of tomato or mushroom soup, to cover. Place on the lid; bake in the oven at 350° F. Therm. 4 for 30 mins.

Sausages, Fried. Prick the sausages. Place in a frying-pan with a little dripping and let them heat gradually. If the sausages are put into a hot pan, they will burst. Fry them until they are nicely browned, turning them so that they cook equally. They should be cooked for at least 20 mins. to ensure that they are really cooked through. Serve on toasted bread, with nice thick gravy in a sauceboat. Some people like the toast soaked in the fat, but this is a matter of taste. If desired, serve with bread sauce and mashed potato. Alternatively, parboil the sausages, then egg and breadcrumb and fry in hot deep fat. Serve with fried parsley.

Sausages, Oxford. Put sausage-meat in little heaps on a greased baking-tin and bake at 400° F. Therm. 6. Serve on toast with a good gravy.

Sausage Rolls. See **PASTRIES (Assorted).**

SAUTER. See **COOKING TERMS.**

SAVELOY (Fr. *cervelas*). A highly seasoned smoked pork sausage with the addition of saltpetre which gives the meat a red colour.

SAVORY. Two kinds of this aromatic plant, Summer savory and Winter savory, are used in cooking. Summer leaf is used for salads, sauce, meat dishes, sausages, poultry, stuffing, scrambled eggs, soup and as a garnish. Winter leaf can be used in a bouquet garni.

SAVOURIES. Delectable savouries may be quickly and easily made, and if served in larger portions than for a dinner menu, they will make good light luncheon dishes, especially when accompanied by a green salad. Remember that hot savouries must be served really hot, and see that the plates are piping hot. Many a good savoury has been ruined by being lukewarm. Cold savouries should always be served with a garnish. Savoury toasts may be made by spreading slips or rounds of toast with margarine, or frying bread in fat, and adding any of the following:

A pile of savoury scrambled egg, garnished with chopped olives or anchovy.

Asparagus tips with mayonnaise.

A tablespoonful of curry powder, mustard chutney and Worcester sauce, blended together. After spreading on the toast it should be heated through in the oven and served garnished with parsley.

Chopped ham or tinned meats pounded with a little margarine to soften, seasoned and garnished with paprika and chopped parsley.

Chutney, garnished with grated cheese.

Curried rice, garnished with shrimps.

Fillets of anchovy, garnished with chopped olives.

Flakes of cold or tinned fish and mayonnaise, garnished with chopped walnuts.

Fried apple rings with chopped pickled walnuts.

Grated or sliced beetroot, garnished with cream cheese.

Grilled mushrooms.

Mayonnaise and capers creamed together.

Shelled prawns with a little curry sauce, garnished with chopped parsley.

Prunes, cooked with a little spice in vinegar, stoned and pounded, and spread with a layer of thick cream cheese.

Raw cheese in a thin slice, sprinkled with pepper, salt and mustard and placed under the grill to heat through.

Small cubes of cheese dipped into batter and fried in deep fat.

Small amounts of creamed mushrooms.

Toasted cheese.

Tomatoes and grated cheese, placed under the grill and garnished with parsley.

Tomatoes, cut into halves and with the centres scooped out and filled with a mixture of tomato pulp and scrambled egg.

SCAD. A fish about the size of the herring found abundantly on the European coast. It is a very coarse-fleshed fish. Also called Horse Mackerel. The small fish are sometimes used as sardines.

SCALD. See **COOKING TERMS.**

SCALLION. A shallot or onion in which the bulb has not developed.

SCALLOP or SCOLLOP (Fr. *Coquille St. Jacques*). A shellfish with two shells, radially ribbed and with an undulating edge. After removing the black part and gristly fibre, leaving intact the red coral which is considered a delicacy, the whole of the scallop is edible. Scallops are at best in January and February. Remove the scallops out of their shells and trim off the beards and all the black parts. They may be boiled in milk and water and served in sauce, or used with celery and mushrooms and grated cheese in a casserole. Always keep the scallop shells after scrubbing and boiling, they can be used again and again for reheating left-over fish, etc.

Scallops, Baked

Ingredients	*Method*
2 cups boiled scallops	Parboil the scallops in milk and water,
¼ pt. milk and water	drain and save liquor, cut them into half if
2 oz. butter	large. Put half the butter into a saucepan

[453]

Scallops, Baked (continued)

4 tbsp. flour
2 tbsp. chopped onion
½ pt. cream
Salt and pepper
Breadcrumbs
Parmesan cheese
1 tbsp. parsley finely
chopped

and melt, add flour, blend together, add onion and cook for about 5 mins. Add scallop-liquor, cream and seasoning and cook until thick, stirring constantly. Add scallops. Heat together for a few minutes, turn into well-buttered oven dish, sprinkle with breadcrumbs and cheese and dot with butter. Bake at 350° F. Therm. 4 until brown. Garnish with parsley before serving.

Scallops with Wine

Ingredients
1½ lb. scallops
Breadcrumbs
4 oz. butter
¼ tsp. salt
⅛ tsp. pepper
Pinch of paprika
3 tbsp. white wine
4 slices toast
Squeeze lemon juice
4 tbsp. chopped mint or parsley

Method
Wipe scallops with damp cloth and roll them in breadcrumbs. Melt the butter in frying pan, season with salt, pepper and paprika. Heat butter but do not allow to smoke. Add scallops and cook over a low heat for 5 mins., turning constantly so that scallops brown all over. Remove from butter and add wine. Simmer for 2 mins., stirring whole time. Squeeze the lemon juice over the toast and arrange the scallops on the toast. Place on heated plates and garnish with chopped parsley or mint.

SCALLOP. See COOKING TERMS.

SCAMPI. Italian giant prawns which are closely allied to the Dublin Bay prawn.

SCARLET RUNNER. See BEANS.

SCHELLY or SKELLY. A white fish only found in Ullswater, Hawsewater and Red Tarn.

SCHNITZEL. See Escalope.

SCOLLOP. See COLLOP.

SCONE. A variety of teacake which was originally cooked on a griddle or hotplate.

Ingredients
1 lb. flour
Pinch of salt
3 oz. butter
½ tsp. bicarb. soda
¼ oz. cream of tartar
Milk

Method
Sift the flour and salt into a mixing bowl; rub the butter into it; add the bicarb. soda and cream of tartar, and mix with the milk into a dough. Handle the dough as lightly as possible. Divide into two parts. Form each into a ball, roll out to ¾″ thickness, divide into 4 pieces, and bake for about 20 mins. in hot oven 400° F. Therm. 6. Glaze with a little milk.

[454]

Girdle Scones

Ingredients

½ lb. flour
½ tsp. cream of tartar
1 saltspoon salt
½ tsp. baking powder
1 oz. butter
2 tbsp. golden syrup

Method

Sift flour, cream of tartar, salt and baking powder into a basin. Rub in butter with tips of fingers. Heat syrup until tepid. Stir in about ½ gill of milk and add to dry ingredients. Add more milk as required to make a soft dough. Turn on to a lightly floured pastry board, roll out thinly and cut into rounds with a cutter. Bake on a greased girdle or frying-pan. When brown on the underside, turn to top side and brown. Serve hot or cold with butter or margarine.

SCOTCH BROTH. See SOUPS.

SCOTCH WOODCOCK. Toast spread with anchovy paste, with a garnish of scrambled egg.

SEA BEEF. A name given to the flesh of young whales in the Western Isles of Scotland.

SEA GIRDLE. See SEAWEED.

SEA HEDGEHOG. The Sea Hedgehog or Sea Urchin is a shellfish greatly relished by gourmets. It is found on the coasts of the Mediterranean, the summer being the best season.

SEA KALE. This belongs to the same family as asparagus and is somewhat similar in flavour. It should be cut when the leaves are purple. If they are left until green, they will be found to be hard and bitter. The young shoots and unopened leaves are the best parts, but the largest leaves do very well for soups. Forced sea kale is good in midwinter.

TO BOIL. Tie in bundles, and put into boiling water with a little butter; add salt in proportion of ½ oz. to every 2 qt. water. Boil with the lid of the saucepan off until the sea kale is tender. Drain well before serving. White sauce or melted butter may be handed with it. Sea kale is sometimes boiled in milk which is used afterwards to make the sauce.

SEASONING. Seasoning can lift a dish to distinction, but it must not be overdone, as there is nothing more unpleasant to the palate than too much or too overwhelming a taste. Herbs must be used with care (see **HERBS**). A seasoning tray (made from a wooden knife and fork tray, or the bottom half of a half-sized biscuit tin) saves time by keeping together pepper and salt, mixture herbs, spices, celery seed, a bottle of caramel gravy, etc. Also keep all the flavouring extracts together in another tray.

SEASONED FLOUR. Flour, sifted with a seasoning of salt and pepper, used for coating fish, etc.

SEASONING OF HERBS AND SPICES

Ingredients

1½ oz. thyme
1 oz. bay leaves
1 oz. savory
1 oz. basil
1½ oz. marjoram

Method

Take the thyme, bay leaves, savory, basil and marjoram, dry thoroughly; pick the leaves. Pound in a mortar the cayenne, peppercorns, cloves, garlic, rind of lemon, mace and grated nutmeg. Mix all

SEASONING OF HERBS AND SPICES (*continued*)

¼ oz. cayenne	together, pass through a sieve, and keep
1 oz. peppercorns	in well-corked bottles.
1 oz. cloves	
Clove of garlic	
½ oz. mace	
Rind of 1 lemon	
1 nutmeg (grated)	

SEASONING TABLES (see also individual entries). Both seasonings and flavouring should be added before or during the cooking process. This ensures that they are properly blended. The exception to this rule is grilled meat when salt should not be added before or during cooking as it tends to extract the meat juice. In using seasonings and flavourings only very small amounts are needed.

From the following lists, it will be easy to choose any special seasoning or flavouring applicable to the dish you wish to cook.

TYPE OF SEASONING	USE
Capers: bottled in vinegar	In salads, sandwich spreads and sauces
Cayenne Pepper: pulverised	In savoury dishes
Celery Leaves: fresh	In salads and stews
Celery Seed: dried	In savoury dishes, soups and stews
Chillies: dried	As these are very hot and pungent they must be used sparingly. In savoury rice dishes, sauces, stews or pickles
Cinnamon: ground or stick	I n cakes and puddings, sauces, savoury dishes or stews
Cloves: ground or whole	In cakes, fruit pies, puddings, stews, soups
Curry powder	In curries or in very small amounts in sandwich fillings, scrambled eggs, stews and soups
Garlic: fresh	Bulb contains many cloves. In very small amounts in soups or savoury dishes or stews—from ¼-½ small clove is sufficient. Also in salads when the clove of garlic is cut and rubbed round bowl

Ginger:
  crystallised
  ground
  whole root
	In cakes, puddings and sometimes in stewed fruits
	Biscuits, cakes, puddings and some savoury dishes
	In sweet and savoury dishes—it is removed before serving—also in pickles

Horseradish: fresh root	Grated in sauces or as a garnish in cheese or meat sandwiches and some savoury dishes (can be obtained in bottle form)

TYPE OF SEASONING	USE
Lemons: fresh, dried, peel or juice	Grated in sauces, cakes, fish dishes, puddings, stuffings, and sweets
Mace: ground or whole in "blades"	In cakes, puddings, potatoes, sweet or savoury sauces, stuffings, stews, fish stock, pickles
Mustard: ground or whole, mustard seed. (Fresh mustard—see **HERBS**)	Ground mustard blended with water, milk or vinegar is used in savoury and meat dishes. Also pinch of dry ground mustard is added to some savoury dishes, the seed is used in chutneys and pickles
Nutmeg: ground or whole	Used grated on top of milk puddings, flavouring in custards, junkets and in some cakes and biscuits recipes, Christmas puddings and mincemeat
Onions: fresh or dried	In all savoury dishes and in many pickles
Orange: juice or rind of the fresh fruit candied rind	Grated or chopped in cakes, puddings, sauces, savoury dishes and pies Used in cakes or puddings
Paprika: ground	Sprinkled on dishes as a garnish, also used to colour and flavour
Pepper: ground or peppercorns	In all savoury dishes and some salad dressings
Sage: fresh leaves or dried	In stuffings with duck, goose or pork and in some savoury dishes
Salt	In most savoury dishes and a pinch in flour mixes and sweet dishes, also the smallest pinch in boiled milk. In salad dressings, cakes, sweet puddings, stewed fruits and other sweet dishes, soups, to enhance the flavour. Allow: 1–2 tsp. salt to each 1 lb. flour 1¼ tsp. salt to each 1 lb. meat 2 tsp. salt to each 1 pint water
Vinegar: elderflower, chilli, garlic, malt, tarragon, white, etc.	In sauces, stews and some other savoury dishes to give added flavour. Also to tenderise meat, in a marinade, and in the water when cooking fish to whiten it
Winter-keeping sauces:	Home-made winter-keeping sauces can be used in various ways to give added flavour to some foods

ESSENCES. Always use the best available. The following chart gives the approximate quantities for different uses, as some essences are stronger than others. All measurements are in teaspoonfuls.

	BISCUITS PER LB. OF BISCUITS	CAKES PER LB. OF CAKE	CUSTARDS, TRIFLES, MILK MOULDS PER PINT	FONDANTS, FUDGE, ETC. PER LB.	ICING PER LB.
Almond	2	2	$\frac{1}{2}$	$\frac{1}{2}$	$\frac{1}{2}$ (marzipan)
Banana	–	–	$\frac{1}{2}$	$\frac{1}{2}$–1	1
Caraway	2	2	–	–	–
Coconut	$1\frac{1}{2}$–2	2	–	$\frac{1}{2}$–1	–
Lemon	$1\frac{1}{2}$	1	$\frac{1}{4}$–$\frac{1}{2}$	$\frac{1}{4}$	$\frac{1}{2}$
Maraschino	–	2	$\frac{1}{2}$	–	–
Orange	–	2	$\frac{3}{4}$	$\frac{1}{2}$–1	1
Peppermint	–	–	–	1	–
Pineapple	–	–	$\frac{1}{2}$	$\frac{1}{2}$–1	1
Raspberry	–	2	$\frac{1}{2}$	$\frac{1}{2}$–1	1
Ratafia	2	$1\frac{1}{2}$–2	$\frac{1}{2}$	–	–
Rum	–	$1\frac{1}{2}$	$\frac{1}{2}$	$\frac{1}{2}$	$\frac{1}{2}$
Strawberry	–	2	$\frac{1}{2}$	$\frac{1}{2}$–1	1
Tangerine	–	–	$\frac{3}{4}$	1	1
Vanilla	3	2	$\frac{1}{2}$	$\frac{1}{2}$	$\frac{1}{2}$–$\frac{3}{4}$

HERBS, USES FOR. See HERBS.

SEA TROUT. See SALMON TROUT.

SEAWEED. There are several varieties of edible seaweed all more or less wholesome and nutritious. *Chondrus crispus*, or Carrageen, better known as Irish Moss Sea Moss (see **CARRAGEEN**); *Laminaria digitata* called Sea Girdle in England, Tangle in Scotland; Red Ware in the Orkneys; *L. saccharina* or Bladderlock, also called by the Scots, Henware or Honeyware; *Porphyra laminata* called laver in England, Stoke in Ireland and Stock in Scotland; *Ulva latissima* or Green Lavern. These seaweeds are easily prepared for eating, but are only fit for food in the cold season.

TO PREPARE. Wash in cold water and remove all salt and sand. Add a pinch of bicarb. soda to the last water and leave the weed seeping for some hours. This will remove some of the bitterness. Stew in milk until it is tender and serve strained like spinach or in the broth. Pepper, vinegar or lemon juice, salt and butter may be added as desired. If stored in earthenware jars, it will keep for 2–3 wks.

SEED CAKE. See CAKES.

SEED OIL. An oil expressed from cotton seed, said to be odourless and tasteless, and therefore a good substitute for olive oil.

SEIBLING. A freshwater fish resembling a trout, but having a red belly, and marked over the body with stars. It grows to a large size, and is found in the Bavarian lakes, but a species of it which is known as Star-fish is sometimes caught in the lochs of Scotland. Seibling are in season from September to January.

SEMOLINA (Fr. *semoule*). The large hard grains of wheat flour retained in the bolting machine after the fine flour has passed through its meshes. Granular wheat made from decorticated wheat by grinding pressure and heat, chiefly used for puddings and thickening soups; but in France, used for making the fine white bread known as *gruan*. See **MILK PUDDINGS**.

SEOUL. A kind of silvery trout caught in the lakes of Savoy. It is only obtainable in this country smoked.

SHAD (Fr. *alose*). This fish has been described as a freshwater herring: it migrates from the sea to the river like the salmon, and is caught in both European and some American rivers. The shad is not unlike the herring in shape; the body is compressed, the back rounded, and the skin is silvery with a reddish tinge. Shad is cooked and served like salmon.

SHADDOCK (Fr. *pamplemousse*). The citrus fruit of a tree called after Captain Shaddock, who introduced it from China to West Indies. Some varieties of pompoleons grown to a great size, often weighing from 10–20 lb. The smaller kind are known as Forbidden Fruit and resemble large oranges, with a smooth, thin, pale yellow rind; the pulp is either white or reddish and of a pleasant sub-acid flavour.

SHAGGY CAP. An edible fungi with a long, egg-shaped cap, white and scaly, but a smoothed yellow tip; gills are at first pink, turning to black on maturity, with a distinctly marked ring.

SHALLOT (Fr. *eschalotes*). In French cookery the shallot is considered invaluable, but in England it is somewhat disregarded, although there can be no doubt that it possesses a delicacy of flavour which no other of the onion tribe can boast. The shallot is red and smooth like a tulip bulb, and the common shallot which grows almost everywhere has cloves like garlic. When shallots are taken up from the ground they should be put in a net and hung up near the ceiling where the air can get to them but where they cannot taste other foods.

SHALLOTS, PICKLED. Top and tail the shallots, and scald with brine. Repeat again next day. Peel the shallots, then cover with vinegar (to preserve their colour). Pack into jars and cover with spiced vinegar. Cork securely.

SHALLOT VINEGAR. Peel and slice 3 oz. shallots, steep them in 1 qt. vinegar for 2 wks. Shake occasionally, strain and bottle. Cork securely.

SHELLFISH. The term shellfish includes both molluscs and the bivalve species with two valves which open and shut, e.g. oysters, clams, mussels, scallops; crustaceans are those shellfish whose bodies are covered with a crust or thin shell, which can be peeled off (after boiling), e.g. crawfish, crabs, lobsters, etc. Shellfish are alive until the moment they are cooked. The crayfish and spiny lobsters are usually bought in the freshly frozen form, the tails only being offered. Scallops are usually bought on the half-shell. (See also under individual headings for preparation and cooking of shellfish.)

TO SHUCK. When the oyster, or clams, are purchased alive, and have not been shucked (removed from their shells) at the shop:

Scrub shells thoroughly under running cold water and always discard broken or open shells. Hold oyster or clam in the palm of the left hand with shell hinge against palm. Insert thin strong knife between shells and cut around entire oyster or clam, twisting knife so as to pry shell open. Cut the muscle so that it is free from shell and remove oyster or clam. Wash oysters or clams well in salted water to remove sand. Remove small dark "beard" in mass. Snip off end of siphon. Wash again in salted water.

TO USE CANNED SHELLFISH. Shellfish are available both in cans and glass jars, when they are usually packed in brine. They are peeled or shucked and can be used in some recipes with great success. The meat may be "lump meat"—meat from large muscles and is all white; or "flake meat" which is also all white; the "claw meat" outside has a reddish colouring. It is useful for salads, soups, soufflés, etc.

SHERRY. A Spanish light-coloured wine, made in the district of Jerez in Andalusia, from which it takes its name. It varies considerably in quality (see **WINES**). A little sherry added to soup and some sauces greatly enhances the flavour. It is also added to jellies and some puddings and to grapefruit served before a meal.

SHORTBREAD

Ingredients	Method
6 oz. flour (or 4 oz. flour and 2 oz. ground rice) 4 oz. butter or margarine 3 oz. caster sugar Pinch of salt	Beat butter or margarine and sugar together in a mixing bowl until they are just mixed but not oily. Sift the flour with a pinch of salt and add to the mixture. Work with the hand until it just clings together. Roll out the shortbread keeping it in a round by pressing the edges towards the centre with the hands until it is a circle about 6″ in diameter and ¼″ thick. Thicken the edges slightly by pressing firmly from the centre. Mark the edge neatly all the way round with the back of a fork or pinch the edge with the finger and thumb, making a neat finish. Prick the centre of the shortbread all over with a fine skewer or fork. Place on a baking tray and leave in a very cold place for about ½ hr. before baking. Bake the shortbread at 375° F. Therm. 5 for 20 mins. until it is golden brown. Lower the heat to 350° F. Therm. 4 and continue cooking for another 10 mins. When ready, it will still be slightly soft in the centre, but it will harden as it cools. Leave the shortbread on the baking tray until it is firm enough to move without breaking, then slip it off with a palette knife on to a wire tray. Shortbread should be stored in an airtight tin and keeps very well. Traditionally, shortbread of this kind should always be broken, never cut.

SHORT CRUST. See **PASTE AND PASTRY.**

SHOULDER. The bladebone with the foreleg; usually applied in cookery to lamb, mutton and veal.

SHREWSBURY CAKES. See **BISCUITS** (p. 67).

SHRIMP (Fr. *crevette*). This peculiar little shellfish derives its name from a habit it has of curling up or shrinking when caught. There are several kinds, amongst

SHRIMP (*continued*)

which are the Brown Hornless shrimp, and the Horned shrimp or Prawn. Before cooking the shrimp is pale greenish grey and semi-transparent. Shrimps take about 6 mins. to boil After boiling they are reddish in colour. The tail meat is the only edible part of a shrimp.

SHRIMPS, TO POT. Take picked shrimps and place in a pot, adding salt, pepper and a grating of nutmeg to season. Place in the oven at 350° F. Therm. 4 for 10 mins.; remove from oven, leave to cool, and spread with softened butter to seal.

Shrimp Cocktail

Ingredients	*Method*
¼ pt. olive oil	Blend the oil, lemon juice, salt and pepper together. When smooth add onion, garlic and bay leaf. Place shrimps in a bowl. Cover with sauce, chill for 2 hrs. before serving. For a cocktail sauce for fish, see **COCKTAILS, SAVOURY.**
⅛ pt. lemon juice	
½ tsp. salt	
⅛ tsp. pepper	
½ onion sliced	
1 clove garlic (if desired)	
1 bay leaf	
1 pt. shelled shrimps	

Shrimp Creole. Sauté for 3 mins. 1 lb. shrimps (cooked and cleaned), or 1 package of frozen shrimps, with 4 tbsp. shortening. Lift out shrimps, add to remaining shortening a stalk of celery, small onion and green pepper (all diced), ½ lb. sliced mushrooms, a crushed clove of garlic (if desired). Sauté until lightly browned. Add 6 peeled, quartered tomatoes, crumbled bay leaf, 1 tsp. salt, a dash of cayenne pepper, and simmer 20 mins. or until thickened. Add shrimps, reheat and serve with fluffy cooked rice.

Shrimp Paste. Pound and grind 1 lb. cooked shrimps; add ¼ lb. creamed butter, salt to taste, a squeeze of onion juice, pinch of celery salt, a drop or two of Worcester sauce, and a dusting of cayenne pepper. Mix thoroughly; place in a covered bowl and if possible leave in refrigerator for several hours to chill thoroughly. Serve on a bed of lettuce leaves and eat with crisp hot toast.

SIBERIAN CRABS. Small apples about the size of cherries, which grow on a tree originally imported from Siberia.

SILLABUB. See SYLLABUB.

SILLOCKS. The fry of the saithe or coalfish.

SILVERSIDE. A fish related to the Grey Mullet, found along the coasts of America; it is delicate fleshed and must be cooked soon after catching. Cook as for smelts.

SILVERSIDE OF BEEF. See BEEF.

SIMNEL CAKE. See CAKES.

SIPPETS. Small pieces of bread usually toasted or fried in butter, cut into shapes and used to garnish dishes of hash or ragoût.

SKATE (Fr. *raie*). The skate is a somewhat coarse-fleshed fish, of which there are several varieties, known as Thorn-backs, Tinkers, Rays and Maids. It is sold cut into pieces and crimped, the thick middle cuts being the best buy. As the flesh is rather tough, skate should be parboiled or well marinated in oil and vinegar before frying.

TO BOIL. Remove the skin and boil or steam the skate according to the rules for boiling and steaming under **FISH.** Serve with Anchovy, or Shrimp sauce or Brown butter.

SKATE'S LIVER. This makes a good sauce for skate, and is a dish by itself.

SKEWER. See COOKING TERMS.

SKILLET. A very shallow frying-pan.

SKINK (Scottish). A strong beef soup.

SKIPPER. The saury or other allied fish; the larvae of the cheesefly which infests ham, cheese, etc.

SKIRRET (Fr. *chervis*). An umbelliferous plant, a native of China, introduced into this country about the middle of the 16th century. The roots, for the sake of which this plant is cultivated, consist of small fleshy tubers, about the size of the little finger. They are very white and sweet and considered by some to be the most delicious of all root vegetables. Skirrets make a good winter vegetable.

SKIRT. The midriff or diaphragm in beef.

SLAPJACK or FLAPJACK (Fr. *tôt-fait*). A kind of pancake.

SLAW. See CABBAGE.

SLIPCOAT CHEESE. A variety of white cheese, something resembling butter in consistency.

SLIP SOLE. A sole weighing about 6 oz.

SLOE. The dark purple fruit of the blackthorn.

Sloe Gin. Put 3 pt. sloes into 1 gall. jar with ½ oz. chopped or pounded bitter almonds and 1¼ lb. loaf sugar, and pour in ½ gall. gin. Shake the jar every 3 days for 3 mths. Strain off the liquor, bottle and seal. The gin is then ready for use. It keeps for some years, improving all the time it is kept. Sugar candy in equal quantity may be used for the loaf sugar if preferred.

Sloe Jam

Ingredients	Method
4 lb. sloes Sugar Water to cover	Wash sloes, place in preserving pan with enough water to cover and boil until tender. Pass through a coarse sieve, weigh and allow 1 lb. sugar to each 1 lb. pulp. Return pulp to pan, add sugar, stir until it dissolves. When jam thickens and sets, pour into warmed jars and cover immediately.

SMALLAGE. See LOVAGE.

SMELT (Fr. *éperlan*). This delicately-flavoured silvery fish allied to the salmon family is in season from September to April. The smaller kind are thought to be the best. The best way to cook this fish is in deep fat. It is usually served with lemon and thinly cut slices of brown bread-and-butter.

SMOKIES. Small smoked fish which are a favourite in the Stirling area of Scotland.

SMOKING. See under BACON (p. 42).

SMOLT. A young salmon about 2 years old. When it first descends to the sea, i.e., between the *fry* and *grilse* stages. The taking of smolts is illegal in the British Isles.

SMÖRGÅSBORD. The Swedish form of hors d'œuvres served buffet-style for luncheon.

SNAIL (Fr. *escargot*). The snail is a mollusc which lives in single, well-developed spiral shells. Snail meat is shucked from the shells and then seasoned and chopped. The edible snail is the member of a large family, nearly all, if not quite all, of which would be edible, provided they fed only on non-poisonous herbs. It has a very well-formed, handsome, pinkish-whitish brown shell and mottled body.

SNAP. A thin, crisp cake, usually small and flavoured with ginger.

SNIPE (Fr. *bécassine*). There are several varieties of this game bird, the most common being Jack-snipe, which delights in an assortment of synonyms such as Judcock, Jedcock, Juddock, Jed and Half-snipe. It is a small brown-grey bird, differing from the Common snipe and the Great or Double snipe in length of bill and size. The Dowitcher or Red-breasted snipe is another well-known variety.

SNIPE (continued)

All these are esteemed by epicures as the finest of game birds, excepting only the woodcock, to which it is akin (see **WOODCOCK**). They are in season from November throughout the winter months and are cooked without being drawn. In the young the feet are soft and tender; they thicken and harden with age. Young birds should have soft, downy feathers under the wing and pointed flight feathers. When the bills are moist and throats muddy they have been killed some time.. Snipes are trussed for roasting, broiling or baking by pressing the legs on to the thighs and fastening them close to the body of the bird. The head and neck should be skinned and the beak tucked and secured under a wing; the heads should be trussed all one way, or in such a manner thant they can be arranged symmetrically when serving. French cooks sometimes truss a snipe by crossing the legs and then drawing the head along the thigh, forcing the beak through the body of the bird under the thighs. Place the plucked bird on a slice of buttered toast in the roasting tin, and roast at 450° F. Therm. 8. Snipe take only 15–20 mins. to cook. Serve with sliced lemon and melted butter on the toast on which they were cooked.

SNOEK or SNOOK. Another name for the barracouta. Used as other tinned fish in hors d'œuvres, etc.

SNOW (Fr. *neige*). The name given to a froth of cream which is whipped up, or whisked white of egg and sugar, to which any desired flavour may be added if the colour is not altered. Snow is frequently used as a covering for sweet dishes.

SOLE (Fr. *sole*). The flesh of this flat-fish is both sweet and digestible. A sole may be cleaned and skinned for cooking by cutting away the gills, running the point of a knife into the belly, and making a small opening through which the gut is drawn, leaving the roe entire. The skin is next dissected off the head, and then stripped off by pulling it with one hand whilst holding the fish with the other. The fins require cutting off with a pair of scissors, or a sharp knife, and the fish should be washed. When it is desirable to remove the underskin, this is done in the same way as the upper or dark skin. Soles are filleted by passing the blade of a knife between the bone and the flesh, after cutting round the edge of the fish next to the fins, and making a long deep incision down the centre (see **FISH**). Soles may be boiled, steamed, baked or fried. A slip sole is one weighing about 6 oz.

SOLE, FRIED WHOLE. Cover the sole with beaten egg and fine white breadcrumbs; flatten these on with a knife, and fry in a deep frying pan. Reduce the heat when brown so that the sole may cook to the centre without drying or becoming too dark in colour. When cooked, drain well on kitchen paper, and serve garnished with fried parsley. A sole generally takes from 3–6 mins. to fry.

SOLE, FRIED FILLETS OF. As above. The fillets may be rolled before frying if desired. A frying basket should be used.

Sole à la Colbert. Fry the sole (see Sole, Fried). When cooked, carefully remove the bone by cutting down centre of fish, sliding the knife under flesh to loosen it from the bone, removing bone and then replacing fish in shape; put some Maître d'Hôtel butter (see p. 97) in the cavity and serve before it is melted. Garnish with fried parsley and cut lemon.

Sole à la Suprême

Ingredients	*Method*
Fillets or 2 or more soles ½ pt. Suprême sauce (see p. 447) Lemon juice	Roll or fold the fillets with the side from which the skin was taken inside. Place them on a buttered baking-sheet, sprinkle lemon juice over, and cover with buttered paper. Bake at 350° F. Therm. 4 for 7–12 mins., according to the thickness of fillets. Dish in a circle, and cover with the sauce. Maître d'Hôtel, Italian, Cardinal and many other sauces may be used with

Sole à la Suprême (*continued*)

Sole à l'Orley
Ingredients
Some fillets of sole
Juice of 1 lemon
1 small onion sliced
Little pepper and salt
Some frying batter (see p. 50)
Few sprigs parsley

Method
Put the fillets in a basin with the lemon juice, onion and pepper and salt to marinade for 2 hrs., then draw each fillet through the batter, and fry in hot deep fat. Drain, and garnish with fried parsley. Serve with Hollandaise, Tomato or any other suitable sauce.

fillets of sole in the same manner, and the sauce will give its name to the dish.

Sole au Gratin
Ingredients
1 tbsp. chopped parsley
1 shallot very finely chopped
6 button mushrooms finely chopped
Lemon juice
Pepper and salt
1 sole
½ oz. butter
1 oz. good glaze
Few browned breadcrumbs
1 wineglass sherry or white wine

Method
Butter a gratin dish and sprinkle on it half of the parsley, shallot and mushrooms, with a little lemon juice, pepper and salt. Fillet the sole and remove the dark skin. Notch the white skin of the sole here and there to prevent contracting. Lay the prepared sole on the mixture and sprinkle the remainder of the parsley, etc., over it. Put the butter about it in small pieces. Add sherry and sprinkle breadcrumbs over. Bake from 10–15 mins., according to the size of the sole, and serve on the dish on which it was cooked (this should be placed on another), with the glaze poured over it.

Sole with Brandy
Ingredients
8 fillets lemon sole
Water
1 small onion sliced
1 bay leaf
1 clove garlic
2 tsp. thyme
Salt and pepper
Paprika
5 oz. butter
¼ lb. chopped mushrooms
½ wineglass cognac
Rich cream
1 tsp. lemon juice
Few sprigs parsley

Method
Put fish in water with onion, bay leaf, garlic, thyme, salt and pepper and paprika and simmer for 20 mins. Strain through sieve and set aside. Melt 1 oz. butter in saucepan, add mushrooms and sauté well for 15 mins. until tender and then add to strained liquid. Melt remaining butter in frying pan until hot but not smoking, and fry fillets for 3 mins. on both sides. Remove from heat, pour over cognac, quickly set alight with match and let blaze for ½ min. Remove fillets and arrange on preheated platter. Keep hot. Blend butter and cognac mixture in saucepan with cream and lemon juice. Heat and pour over fillets. Serve very hot with finely chopped parsley to garnish.

[464]

Sole (Lemon or Plain) with Sauterne Sauce

Ingredients	*Method*
1½ lb. fillets of sole	Wipe the fillets with damp cloth. Place in
1 clove garlic	steamer with garlic and bay leaf; pour
1 bay leaf	water into saucepan but do not allow to
Water	touch fish. Cover and steam for 15 mins.
3 oz. butter	Turn on to a hot dish. Melt butter in
4 tbsp. flour	saucepan, blend flour and mustard, cook
¼ tsp. dry mustard	1 min., stirring constantly. Add milk
1 pt. milk	gradually, stir until the sauce thickens;
4 hard-boiled eggs	add chopped eggs, Worcester sauce, salt
½ tsp. Worcester sauce	and pepper and blend in wine. Reheat
¼ tsp. salt	but do not boil, and pour over fish.
⅛ tsp. pepper	Serve and garnish with parsley.
¼ pt. sauterne	
4 sprigs parsley	

SOLFERINO. A brilliant deep pink analine colour with a purplish tinge used for colouring confectionery.

SOP. Anything dipped in liquid food and intended to be eaten.

SORBET. (French for Sherbet.) An ice flavoured with fruit juice or spirits.
    Sorbet of Rum. Make a lemon water ice, add sufficient rum to flavour, half freeze and serve piled high in a sorbet glass.
    Sorbet of Strawberries. Make a strawberry water ice, add a liqueur glass of noyau. Half freeze and pile high in a sorbet glass.

SORREL. A herb with acid leaves. There are two varieties to be noted: French and Garden Sorrel. The leaf is used in soups and salads.
    Remove the stalks from the sorrel; wash leaves well in several waters. Put into a saucepan; cover with boiling water; boil gently, stirring occasionally until tender. Then drain thoroughly and chop finely. When used for a garnish, mix with some Allemande sauce (see p. 437).

SOUFFLÉ. Soufflés are the lightest of sweet or savoury "puffed-up puddings". There is a cold or uncooked soufflé or mousse, which is not a real soufflé but a gelatine mixture. A true soufflé is based on a thick well-cooked sauce called a panada. The liquid or the added flavour decides the name. The eggs are added separately; the whites must be stiffly whisked and, when possible, exceed the yolks by one. Well-beaten eggs always form a good medium for introducing and retaining air in the mixture. In soufflés the egg yolks must be added individually, each beaten in; the stiffly whisked whites are folded lightly into the mixture with a metal spoon. If a wooden spoon is used, the air bubbles get broken up and the mixture will not be so light. Decide upon the method of cooking and prepare the necessary pans before starting the soufflé. Always preheat the oven or pan.

    TO PREPARE THE TIN OR CASE. Grease the tin or case and place a round of greaseproof paper in the bottom. If steaming, place a piece of thick cartridge or folded double greaseproof paper round the outside of the tin, tie it securely to project 3 or 4″ above the top of the tin in case the soufflé rises higher than the tin. (This will hold the mixture in place until it sets and cooks.) The paper is, of course, removed just before serving. A round of greased paper is also placed on top of the uncooked soufflé.

    FLAVOURINGS. Cook basic ingredients and only add raw flavourings which take very little cooking. They should be shredded or finely grated, pounded or reduced to purée. Nothing solid or heavy must be added, or the soufflé will be ruined.

FLAVOURINGS (*continued*)

For a *savoury soufflé*, the following flavourings may be used:

- 2 oz. grated cheese, dash cayenne and mustard.
- 1 gill tomato purée, ½ tsp. chopped chives.
- 4 oz. of any of the following, cooked, shredded finely or pounded: bacon, crab, crayfish, chicken, game, ham, lobster, mushroom, salmon and shrimp.

Serve masked in sauce, if desired, garnished with finely chopped parsley or a sprig of watercress.

For *sweet soufflés*, see section on pages 468–9. Most fruit flavourings can be used.

TO BAKE. Put in a moderately hot oven (400° F. Therm. 6) for about 30 mins. or place tin in hot water and bake at 200° F. Therm. ¼. Baked soufflés are served in the tin which is slipped into a silver case, or a napkin is folded round it.

TO STEAM. Place in a pan or fish kettle with sufficient water to reach three-quarters of the way up the side of the tin or case. Steamed soufflés are turned out of the tin they are cooked in and served with a sauce poured round them.

BASIC RECIPE

Ingredients	Method
2 oz. each butter and flour	Cream butter and flour; gradually pour
¼ pt. each scalded milk and	on scalded milk (and cream if used). Cook

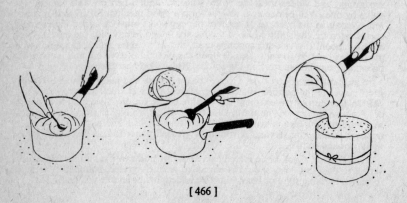

BASIC RECIPE (*continued*)

cream (if available, otherwise use extra milk)

3–5 eggs

gently in a basin standing in a pan of water, or in a double saucepan. Carefully add the egg yolks, beat until thick and pale yellow in colour. Remove from heat and fold in stiffly beaten whites. Pour into a well-buttered tin or mould (or individual cases) and stand in a tin of hot water. Bake at 200° F. Therm. ¼ for about ¾ hr.

SOUFFLÉS, SAVOURY AND SWEET

Chicken Soufflé

Ingredients

The white meat from a cold chicken (boiled)

1 slice of cooked ham

2 oz. each butter and flour

1 gill each white stock and cream

5 eggs

Method

Pass the chicken and ham twice through a mincing machine and pound them in a mortar. Melt the butter in a stewpan and mix the flour in smoothly. Add the stock and cream and well cook the sauce. Mix it with the chicken and ham, and season well with lemon juice, pepper and salt, and rub through a sieve. Add the yolks of egg, and beat them well in. Then mix in lightly the stiffly whisked whites of the eggs, turn into a prepared soufflé tin and bake at 400° F. Therm. 6 for about ½ hr. Serve immediately.

Lobster Soufflé

Ingredients

2 whitings

1 hen lobster

2 oz. each butter and flour

¼ pt. milk

3 eggs

½ lemon

Pepper and salt

Little cayenne

¼ pt. cream

Method

Pound the flesh of the whitings and the lobster coral together in a mortar, and rub them through a wire sieve. Melt the butter in a saucepan. Mix in the flour and add the milk, stir and cook well. Cut the lobster up finely, pound it in a mortar with the panada, whiting, eggs, lemon juice, pepper, salt and a little cayenne. Rub through a hair sieve. Beat the cream stiffly, mix it lightly in, pour into a prepared soufflé tin, cover with buttered paper and steam for ½ hr. Serve with a Suprême sauce (p. 447) poured over. The soufflé tin may be decorated with lobster coral and truffle if desired.

Oyster Soufflé

Ingredients

3 small whiting

1 oz. butter

2 oz. flour

Method

Remove the flesh from the bones of the whitings and rub through a wire sieve. Melt the butter in a saucepan and mix in

Oyster Soufflé (*continued*)

1 gill oyster liquor
3 eggs
Pepper
Salt
Cayenne
14 oysters
1 gill cream
Few drops of lemon juice

the flour smoothly. Add the oyster liquor, which should be strained through muslin. Stir and cook the mixture well. Take the bead and hard white part from the oysters and cut each one into four. Pound the panada and whiting meat with the eggs, pepper, salt, cayenne and lemon juice. Mix in the oysters, then whip the cream stiffly and add lightly. Pour the mixture into a prepared soufflé tin, cover with buttered paper and steam for about ½ hr. or until the soufflé is firm in the centre. Decorate with chopped truffle and powdered lobster coral and pour round Oyster sauce (see. p. 445).

Spinach Soufflé. See SPINACH.

Chocolate Soufflé. Make as **Coffee Soufflé,** substituting chocolate for coffee. Use with it a few drops of vanilla essence.

Coffee Soufflé

Ingredients

1 oz. each butter and flour
½ gill each strong coffee and milk
1 oz. caster sugar
3 egg yolks
4 egg whites

Method

Melt the butter in a saucepan and mix in the flour smoothly. Add milk, coffee and sugar and stir in, cook thoroughly. Remove from heat and add three egg yolks. Stir in lightly the whites of four eggs beaten to a firm froth. Pour the mixture into a prepared soufflé tin and bake at 400° F. Therm. 6, until well thrown up and firm in the centre. This will take approximately 25 mins. Little cases may be used for this mixture, filling 12. These cases should be well oiled and dried before using.

Lemon Soufflé

Ingredients

1 lemon
½ pt. milk
1½ oz. butter
1½ oz. potato flour
2 oz. caster sugar
2 egg yolks
4 egg whites

Method

Peel off the yellow part of the lemon rind (without pith), and allow to soak in the milk for 1 hr. Melt the butter in a saucepan and mix in the flour smoothly. Add the milk, strained from the peel; stir and cook thoroughly. Add the sugar. Remove from heat and add egg yolks. Whip the whites to a stiff froth and stir them lightly in. Pour into a prepared mould and steam or bake at 400° F. Therm. 6 for about ½ hr.

[468]

Orange-Flower Water Soufflé

Ingredients	*Method*
2 oz. each butter and flour ½ pt. milk 4 dsp. caster sugar 7 egg yolks 2 dsp. orange-flower water 8 egg whites	Melt the butter in a small saucepan. Mix in the flour smoothly. Add the milk, and stir and cook thoroughly. Mix in the sugar and beat in the yolks of 7 eggs one by one. Add the orange-flower water. Beat the whites of the eggs to a stiff froth, stir them in lightly, turn the mixture at once into the tin, cover it with buttered paper, and steam carefully for about 1 hr. When cooked it will be firm in the middle. Turn it quickly on to a hot dish and serve at once, with Wine Syrup sauce (see p. 452) poured round it. This soufflé may be baked, if preferred, at 400° F. Therm 6.

SOUPS (Fr. *potages*)

GENERAL RULES FOR SOUP-MAKING

Use well-flavoured stock which is free from fat.

Use a strong pan with a tight-fitting lid.

Always expose as much surface of meat and bones as possible and begin cooking with cold liquid and a little salt.

Bring slowly to boil and skim well.

Season well.

Serve very hot and free from grease.

Serve toasted or fried croûtons with all vegetable and meat soups which have no garnish.

Cream is an improvement to many soups if it is obtainable. Evaporated milk may be used in some soups. A little sherry greatly enhances the flavour of most soups.

Soups may be grouped as follows:

1. Soups made with stocks:
   Clear meat or fish soup
   Consommé
   Bouillons
   Broth
2. Reinforced stock soups
3. Clear vegetable soups:
   Vegetable broth
   Vegetable bouillon
4. Thickened soups made without stock
5. Milk soups:
   Cream soup
   Chowder
   Bisque
   Purée
6. Leguminous soups
7. Jellied soups

SOUPS, GARNISHES FOR. Among the garnishes used for soups are vegetables cut into fancy shapes with different sizes of vegetable cutters; lettuce, carrot and cabbage, used raw, finely shredded; macaroni, noodles, spaghetti, all broken into small pieces; barley, rice, sago and tapioca; finely chopped parsley and other herbs.

SOUPS, ACCOMPANIMENTS FOR. A small bowl of finely grated cheese (parmesan if possible), sippets or croûtons; small squares of dry toast; dry fried onions; savoury custard.

Almond Purée

Ingredients
3 oz. sweet almonds
6 bitter almonds
3" white celery
1 small onion
1 pt. milk
1½ oz. each butter and flour
1½ pt. white stock
¼ pt. cream
Salt and white pepper

Method
Blanch, chop and pound the almonds. Put the almonds, celery, onion and milk into a 2 qt. saucepan and simmer gently for about 1 hr. Strain through a hair sieve, pressing the almonds to extract flavour. Prepare the roux, add the white stock and boil. Add the strained milk, seasoning and cream. Reheat and serve with croûtons of fried bread.

Artichoke Purée

Ingredients
1½ lb. artichokes
1 oz. butter
2" celery
1 very small onion
1½ pt. white stock
Salt and pepper
½ oz. cornflour
¼ pt. cream

Method
Wash, peel and slice the artichokes in water containing a few drops of lemon juice or vinegar. Melt butter, add the artichokes, celery and onion, and sweat for 5 mins. Add the stock and seasoning and cook gently until the artichokes are tender. Rub through a hair sieve, add blended cornflour and boil for 5 mins. Cool slightly, add cream, reheat without boiling, and serve.

Asparagus Cream Soup

Ingredients
25 asparagus heads
¼ lb. green peas or spinach
1½ pt. white stock
1 lump of sugar
Seasoning
1 oz. each butter and flour
1 gill each milk and cream
Green colouring if necessary

Method
Wash and prepare asparagus, reserving 12 tips for garnish, cook separately. Cut remainder into 1" lengths, cook in the boiling stock with peas or spinach, sugar and seasoning until tender. Rub through a hair sieve. Make a roux with the butter, flour and milk, add purée and boil well. Cool slightly, add asparagus tips, cream and colouring if necessary. Reheat and serve.

Barley Cream Soup

Ingredients
1½ oz. pearl barley
1 qt. white stock
¼ pt. cream
1 oz. butter
Nutmeg
Seasoning

Method
Blanch the barley, simmer in the stock for 2½–3 hrs. Pass through a hair sieve, add the cream, a grating of nutmeg, seasoning and butter in small pieces. Reheat and serve.

Beetroot Soup. See BEETROOT.

Bonne Femme Soup

Ingredients
4 lettuces
1 cucumber finely chopped
1 teacup chervil leaves
Small lump of butter
Grating of nutmeg
Pepper and salt
1 tbsp. flour
3 pt. veal stock
Yolks of 4–6 eggs
½ pt. cream
2 tsp. sugar

Method
Wash lettuces and chop finely, place in saucepan with the cucumber and chervil, butter, nutmeg, salt and pepper. Cover saucepan and cook quickly for 10 mins., then stir in flour. Add veal stock and stir over heat until boiling. Reduce heat and simmer for ½ hr. Beat egg yolks and add cream and sugar; stir gradually into soup. Turn soup into a tureen, and serve with sippets of toast or croûtons of fried bread.

Brown Vegetable

Ingredients
2 small carrots
2 small turnips
2 small onions
Bouquet garni
2 oz. each flour and dripping
1 qt. brown or bone stock or water
Seasoning

Method
Prepare the vegetables and cut them into rough pieces. Fry the thinly sliced onion in the hot dripping until slightly browned. Add flour and cook until brown; add stock and vegetables and stir until boiling. Simmer for 1–2 hrs. until tender. Sieve if required, reheat and season. Serve with croûtons of toast.

Cauliflower Purée

Ingredients
1 large cauliflower
1½ oz. butter
1 stick celery
½ leek
1 oz. lean ham
1 bay leaf
1 pt. white stock
½ pt. milk
1 oz. flour
1 egg yolk
½ gill cream

Method
Boil or steam the cauliflower and reserve 3 small neat sprigs for garnish. Sweat together in ½ oz. butter, the celery, leek, chopped ham and bay leaf. Add the roughly chopped cauliflower, stock and milk. Simmer gently for ½ hr. and pass through a hair sieve. Make a roux, add purée and boil well. Cool, add strained egg yolk and cream. Reheat with garnish of cauliflower sprigs.

Celery Cream

Ingredients
1 or 2 heads of white celery
1 pt. white stock
Small piece onion
Bouquet garni
Pepper and salt
1 oz. each butter and flour
1 pt. milk
¼ pt. cream

Method
Wash celery thoroughly and cut into 2 pieces. Put into stock with onion, bouquet garni and seasoning. Cook for about 1–1½ hrs. until tender. Rub through a hair sieve. Make a roux with butter and flour; add purée and milk gradually and boil well. Cool slightly, add cream, and reheat.

Celery Purée

Ingredients
- 1 or 2 heads of celery
- 1 pt. white stock
- Bouquet garni
- 1¼ oz. butter
- 1½ oz. flour
- 1 pt. milk
- Pepper and salt
- Cream if desired

Method

Wash celery thoroughly and cut up sticks (use green portions for other flavouring purposes). Cook in stock with bouquet garni until tender—about 40 mins. to 1 hr. —then rub through a hair sieve. Make a roux with the margarine and flour, add purée and milk gradually. Stir until boiling and add seasoning. (2 tbsp. cream is an improvement.) Serve in a hot tureen, garnished with croûtons of toast.

Cheese Soup. See CHEESE.

Chestnut Purée

Ingredients
- 1 lb. chestnuts
- 1 onion
- 2 cloves
- 1 qt. white or bone stock
- 1 oz. flour
- Pepper and salt
- Few drops carmine if necessary

Method

Prick chestnuts well and roast at 400° F. Therm. 6, until shells crack. Remove shells and inner skin, pound slightly. Put into pan with the onion, cloves and flavoured stock and simmer until tender for about 1½ hr. Rub through a sieve, add flour blended with milk and seasoning. Reheat but do not boil. Add carmine, if necessary.

Chicken Broth

Ingredients
- 1 small carrot
- 1 small turnip
- 1 chicken
- 3 pt. water
- 2 oz. lean raw ham
- Salt and pepper
- Bouquet garni
- White end of a leek (or 1 small onion)
- 1 oz. rice or pearl barley
- 1 tsp. finely chopped parsley

Method

Cut fine dice of carrot and turnip for garnish. Joint the chicken and simmer gently in the water with trimmings of vegetables, ham, seasonings and flavourings for 2–3 hrs. Strain, remove breast of chicken and cut into fine dice. Return the liquid to the pan, add diced vegetables, chicken and rice or barley. Cook until the vegetables are tender, season carefully. Pour into tureen and sprinkle with parsley. If barley is used, tie loosely in muslin and cook with chicken. If rice is used, add it with the diced vegetables. If using veal or rabbit broth, substitute for the chicken, 1 small knuckle of veal or 1 rabbit.

Consommé (clear soup)

Ingredients
- 1 qt. brown stock
- ¼ lb. gravy beef shredded finely
- Whites and shells of 2 eggs

Method

Heat stock and remove every trace of fat with kitchen paper. Season carefully and put into a scalded pan with all ingredients except sherry. Bring slowly to boiling

[472]

Consommé (*continued*)

Vegetables for flavouring if necessary
2 tomatoes
Seasoning
2 tbsp. sherry

point and simmer gently for 30–45 mins. with the lid tilted. Pour gently through scalded cloth, add sherry through the cloth, reheat and serve with required garnish.

Consommé à la Jardinière. Clear soup with the following garnish: Turnip and the red part of carrot cut into pea shapes; green peas, small sprigs of cauliflower, white leaves of cabbage cut into rounds the size of a shilling; a few sprigs of tarragon and chervil; these must all be cooked carefully. Allow $\frac{1}{4}$ pt. these vegetables measured together for 1 qt. soup.

Consommé à la Portugaise

Ingredients

1 qt. consommé (see above)
1 tbsp. diced tomato
1 dsp. tiny rounds of firm prune
1 tbsp. $1\frac{1}{2}''$ strips of leek

Method

Cook the leek, heat the rest of the garnish and pour soup over.

Consommé à la Russe

Ingredients

1 qt. consommé (see p. 472)
1 tbsp. green peas
Sprigs of chervil
1 dsp. truffle cut into fancy shapes

Method

Mix all the ingredients together and strain into another mould. Steam until firm, cool, cut slices and stamp out into fancy shapes.

CUSTARD FOR GARNISH:
1 whole egg and 1 yolk
$\frac{1}{2}$ gill stock
Carmine
Seasoning

Consommé aux Trois Fillets

Ingredients

1 qt. consommé (see p. 472)
1 dsp. each strips of cooked ham, strips of cooked chicken, strips of cooked tongue

Method

Heat the garnish and pour the soup over.

Consommé Brunoise

Ingredients

1 qt. consommé (see p. 472)
1 tbsp. each diced carrot, diced turnips, diced leek, diced celery
1 tsp. fine sprigs of parsley

Method

Cook the vegetables separately in boiling salted water until tender. Pour the soup over.

C.C.D.—16   [473]

Consommé Carmen

Ingredients

- 1 qt. consommé (see p. 472)
- 1 dsp. boiled rice
- 1 tbsp. diced tomato
- 1 chilli cut into fine strips
- 2 doz. leaves chervil

Method

Heat the garnish and pour the soup over it.

Consommé Fromage Royale

Ingredients

- 1 qt. consommé (see p. 472)

For Garnish

- 2 tbsp. stock
- ½ tbsp. parmesan cheese
- 1 egg
- Seasoning

Method

Mix all ingredients together, steam until firm after straining into a buttered mould. When cold, cut into thin slices and stamp out with fancy cutters. Reheat and pour the soup over.

Consommé, Iced. Thoroughly chill consommé and serve in cups.

Consommé Julienne. Clear soup garnished with inch-long shreds of cooked carrot and turnip.

Consommé Royale. Clear soup garnished with fancy shapes of savoury custard, made as follows:

Ingredients

- 1 whole egg and 1 yolk
- Pepper and salt
- ½ gill clear stock

Method

Beat the eggs and stock together and season carefully. Strain half the mixture into a well-greased dariole mould. Colour remainder pink and strain into another mould. Place on a folded paper in a saucepan and add sufficient cold water to come halfway up the moulds. Steam slowly until firm. Cool slightly before turning out. Cut into thin slices, then into small fancy shapes.

Consommé Tomate

Ingredients

- 1 qt. clear stock
- ¼ lb. tomatoes
- 1–2 tsp. carmine

Method

Proceed as for consommé with the addition of tomatoes and carmine.

Consommé Tomate Royale

Ingredients

- 1 qt. consommé

For Garnish

- 2 egg yolks
- 2 tbsp. sieved tomato
- Carmine
- Seasoning

Method

Mix all ingredients together, colour carefully and strain into buttered dariole mould. Steam until firm. When cold, cut into thin slices and stamp out with fancy cutters. Reheat and pour the soup over.

Court Bouillon. See under own heading.

Crécy Soup

Ingredients

- 4 large carrots
- 2 onions
- 2 sticks celery (or ¼ tsp. celery seed)

Method

Prepare and slice the vegetables and sauté for 10 mins. with the margarine. Add stock, rice, ham and flavourings, and simmer for 1½–2 hrs. Rub through a wire

Crécy Soup (continued)
1 turnip
1 oz. butter
1 qt. second stock
Rice
1 oz. ham or a ham bone
Seasoning
12 peppercorns

sieve. Add seasoning, reheat and serve.

Cucumber Cream Soup

Ingredients
2 large cucumbers
½ oz. butter
Pepper and salt
Pinch of sugar
1½ oz. each butter and flour
1½ pt. white stock
¼ pt. cream
2 egg yolks
Green colouring

Method
Peel the cucumbers, remove seeds, cut into 2″ pieces and boil for 10 mins. in salted water. Strain, rinse in cold water to preserve colour; sweat in a pan with butter, pepper and salt, and pinch of sugar for about 20–30 mins. Make a roux, add stock and boil thoroughly. Add sieved cucumber, strain in cream and egg yolks, colour if necessary, reheat but do not boil.

Green Pea Purée

Ingredients
1 lb. green peas
Few mint leaves
1 lump of sugar
1½ pt. white stock
1 tsp. cornflour
1 gill cream
Pepper and salt
Green colouring, if necessary

Method
Put green peas, a few of the pods, mint and sugar into the boiling stock and cook until tender with the lid tilted. Rub through a fine hair sieve, keeping back the mint leaves and pods. Thicken with blended cornflour, boil well and cool slightly. Add cream, seasoning and colouring, reheat and serve.

Hare Soup

Ingredients
½ hare
2 oz. butter
1 onion
1½ lb. shin of beef
3 oz. lean ham
3 qt. water
Carrot, turnip and leek to flavour
Salt and cayenne pepper
Bouquet garni
10 black peppercorns
3 or 4 cloves
1 oz. flour
2 tsp. redcurrant jelly
1–2 gills port wine

Method
Skin and paunch the hare, remove blood, add a few drops of vinegar and stand aside. Joint the hare, heat the butter, fry onion and remove, then fry hare, beef and ham. Add the water, vegetables and flavourings, bring slowly to boiling point and simmer gently until the liquid is reduced to half and the hare tender. Keep well skimmed. Strain through a hair sieve, reserve 2 tbsp. diced meat from best joints. Pass as much meat as possible through the sieve. Add the blended flour, boil thoroughly, add the redcurrant jelly and cool slightly. Strain in the blended blood and wine, season, reheat and serve with garnish of diced hare.

[475]

Hollandaise Soup

Ingredients   *Method*

FOR GARNISH:

1 tbsp. carrot cut in pea shapes
1 tbsp. cucumber cut in pea
  shapes
1 tbsp. green peas

FOR SOUP:

1 oz. each flour and butter
1½ pt. white stock
2 egg yolks
¼ pt. cream
½ tsp. each chopped tarragon
  and sugar
Seasoning

Cook the garnish in boiling salted water, using separate pans. Melt butter, add flour, cook thoroughly without discolouring. Add stock gradually, boil well, cool slightly; strain into the soup the egg yolks and cream mixed together; cook gently without boiling until thickened. Add finely chopped tarragon, garnish of vegetables, sugar and seasoning, and serve.

Italian Soup

Ingredients   *Method*

1½ oz. vermicelli
1½ pt. white stock
2 large tomatoes
3 egg yolks
¼ pt. cream
Carmine
Seasoning

Break vermicelli very finely, drop into boiling stock and simmer gently for about 20 mins. Sieve tomatoes, tammy the pulp through muslin and add to the soup. Strain in egg yolks and cream, add carmine and seasoning, cook and stir until thickened.

Kidney Soup

Ingredients   *Method*

½ lb. ox kidney
1 oz. butter or margarine
1 small onion
1 qt. bone or brown stock
1 small carrot
½ turnip
Bouquet garni
1 oz. cornflour
Seasoning
½ gill sherry (if desired)

Remove all fat from kidneys, wash, dry and cut them into slices. Fry quickly in hot margarine, fry onion; drain and add to stock with vegetables and herbs. Simmer for 2 hrs., then strain and cut the kidneys into dice, or rub through a sieve. Return stock to pan, thicken with cornflour and boil for a few mins. Add kidney, seasoning and sherry, and serve hot.

Lentil Soup (White)

Ingredients   *Method*

¼ lb. lentils
1 blade mace
12 white peppercorns
1 sprig parsley
1 stick celery
1 thinly sliced onion
2 pt. water
1½ oz. each flour and butter
1 pt. each milk and cream
1 lump of sugar
Seasoning

Put the lentils, flavourings, vegetables and water to cook until tender (2–2½ hrs). Pass through a hair sieve. Make a roux with the butter, flour and milk, add purée of lentils and boil well. Cool slightly, add cream and sugar, reheat, season and serve.

Lobster Soup (Plain). Proceed as for Oyster soup, using a small tin of lobsters instead of oysters.

Lobster Bisque

Ingredients

1 small lobster or ½ large one
1 oz. butter
1 bay leaf
1 sprig parsley
Seasoning
1½ oz. crème de riz or corn-flour
1½ pt. fish stock
1 gill cream
Lemon juice
1 oz. lobster butter

Method

Remove lobster from shell and reserve best claw pieces for garnish. Wash and pound the shell with the butter and put into a saucepan with the bay leaf, parsley, seasoning and crème de riz. Cook without discolouring for 10 mins.; add stock and roughly chopped lobster and simmer gently for 30–40 mins. Pass through a hair sieve and add cream and garnish of neatly diced claws. Add lemon juice and lobster butter in small portions until correct colour is obtained. Do not boil.

Milt Soup

Ingredients

2 sheep's or ½ ox's milt
1 onion
1 carrot
2 cloves
1 qt. water
Seasoning
½ oz. fine sago

Method

Wash the milt, cut into small pieces and put into a saucepan with vegetables, cloves, water and salt. Bring slowly to boiling point, remove scum; simmer for about 2 hrs. Strain, return to pan, and add the washed sago. Stir, boil gently until it is transparent, season and serve.

Mock Turtle Soup

Ingredients

½ calf's head
2 lb. knuckle of veal
2 oz. lean ham
Bouquet garni
2 qt. water
1 carrot
1 turnip
1 onion
1 leek
2 sticks celery
½–1 oz. cornflour
2 tbsp. sherry
Lemon juice
Cayenne pepper
Seasoning

Method

Wash, soak and blanch the head and put into a pan with the cut-up knuckle of veal, ham and bouquet garni. Add water, bring to boiling point and simmer gently for about 3 hrs.; skim thoroughly; lift out head and set aside for garnish. Add vegetables and simmer stock for 2 hrs. longer. Strain through a hair sieve, leave until cold and remove fat. Heat the stock and thicken with cornflour; add sherry, lemon juice, cayenne and seasoning. Garnish with ½″ cubes of calf's head. If desired, poached forcemeat balls may also be added.

Mulligatawny, Clear

Ingredients

½ oz. butter
1 onion
1 apple
White part of a leek

Method

Melt the butter and sweat the chopped onion, apple and leek for 10 mins. Add curry powder, paste, chutney, sugar, seasoning, lemon juice and stock. Simmer

[477]

Mulligatawny, Clear (*continued*)

2 tsp. curry powder
1 tsp. each curry paste and chutney
1 lump of sugar
Salt and pepper
½–1 tsp. lemon juice
1 qt. brown stock
2 whites and shells of eggs
3 oz. boiled Patna rice

for 2 hrs.; strain and cool; remove the fat and clear as for consommé. Serve rice separately, garnished with lemon, parsley and chilli.

Mutton Broth

Ingredients

¼ lb. lean middle neck of mutton
1 qt. water
Bouquet garni
1 oz. pearl barley blanched
Seasoning
1 small leek
1 onion
1 small carrot
½ turnip
1 stick of celery or ¼ tsp. celery seed

Method

Remove *all* fat from meat, then put into the cold water with the bouquet garni, blanched barley, seasoning, chopped onion, leek and vegetable in small dice. Simmer for 1½ hr., then lift the meat out; remove the meat from the bones and cut into small pieces. Return meat to the broth, reheat and remove fat with soft paper. Re-season and serve sprinkled with chopped parsley.

Onion Soup

Ingredients

1 lb. onions
Pinch of celery salt
1½ oz. dripping or margarine
Pepper and salt
Rasher of lean bacon
1 qt. stock
1½ oz. cornflour blended with cold milk

Method

Peel and slice onions and toss in melted dripping but do not brown. Add salt and pepper. Heat stock in another pan, then pour over onions. Bring to boil, simmer gently for 1–1½ hrs. Long, slow cooking is essential to bring out the flavour. Add blended cornflour, reboil and serve very hot with croûtons of fried bread.

Oxtail Soup

Ingredients

1 qt. oxtail stock
2 oz. margarine or dripping
3 oz. flour
¼ lb. oxtail meat cut into tiny dice
2 tbsp. port wine
1 tsp. redcurrant jelly
Seasoning

Method

Remove all fat from stock. Make a brown roux with the fat and flour; add stock and stir till boiling. Add remainder of ingredients and seasoning. Reheat and serve.

Oxtail Soup, Clear

Ingredients

1 qt. oxtail stock
4 oz. gravy beef

Method

Clear as for consommé. Cook garnish separately.

[478]

Oxtail Soup, Clear (*continued*)
  2 whites and shells of eggs
  Flavouring of vegetables if necessary
  Pea-shapes of carrot and turnip
  Dice of oxtail as garnish

Oyster Bisque

Ingredients

  1 doz. oysters
  1½ oz. each butter and crème de riz
  1½ pt. fish stock
  Seasoning
  2 egg yolks
  1 gill each milk and cream
  Squeeze of lemon juice

Method

Cut the oysters into quarters after removing beards. Melt the butter, add crème de riz, and cook for a few mins. without discolouring. Add the stock, oyster beards and seasoning, and simmer for 20 mins. Sieve, add the strained yolks, milk and cream, oysters and lemon juice, and cook until thickened without boiling.

Oyster Soup (Plain)

Ingredients

  12 fresh oysters or ½ pt. tin of oysters, quartered
  1 qt. fish stock
  2 oz. flour
  ¼ gill milk or a little cream
  1 tsp. anchovy essence
  Juice of ½ lemon
  Seasoning

Method

Strain the liquor from the oyster tin through muslin and add to the stock. If fresh oysters are used stew the beards for 5 mins. in the liquor from the oysters then strain and add to stock. Bring to boiling point, add the blended flour to milk, stir and boil well for 5 mins. Add oysters, anchovy, lemon juice, seasoning.

Partridge Soup.   See PARTRIDGE

Pea Soup

Ingredients

  ¼ lb. split peas
  1 large onion
  1 large carrot
  ½ turnip
  ½ lb. peeled potatoes
  1 oz. dripping
  Seasoning
  Bouquet garni
  1 qt. water
  1 gill milk

Method

Soak the peas for 12–24 hrs. Prepare the vegetables and cut into small pieces. Put all into the pan with the dripping, stir occasionally and cook for 5 mins. (lid on pan). Add water and herbs, and boil gently for 2 hrs. or until reduced to a pulp, then rub through a sieve or colander. Season, add milk, reheat and serve, sprinkled with dried mint. Serve also croûtons of toast or fried bread.

Potato Soup

Ingredients

  1 lb. peeled potatoes
  2 small onions
  ½ oz. dripping
  1½ pt. stock or water
  ½ oz. sago
  ½ pt. milk

Method

Slice potatoes finely and cut onions into thin slices, then cook in the dripping for 5–10 mins. without discolouring. Add the stock and simmer gently from 1–2 hrs. or until reduced to a pulp. Rub through a wire sieve, return to pan and

[479]

Potato Soup (*continued*)

add the washed sago and milk. Cook until sago is transparent. Season and serve. The soup should be the consistency of thick cream.

Scotch Broth
Ingredients

2 tbsp. barley
2 qt. stock or water
1 lb. lean neck of mutton
2 sticks celery
1 each carrot, turnip, onion, leek
Pepper and salt
½ tbsp. chopped parsley

Method

Wash and blanch barley and put in saucepan with stock, meat and seasoning. Put over a low heat, bring slowly to the boil and simmer for 1 hr. Add diced vegetables and simmer further 1½ hr. Take out meat, cut into neat squares and return to pan. Reheat, skim off any grease with tissue paper and add chopped parsley just before serving.

Shrimp Soup. Proceed as for **Oyster soup**, using ¼ lb. picked shrimps instead of oysters. Wash the shrimp skins and simmer them for 20 mins. in the stock before using it. Strain carefully before thickening the soup.

Summer Soup
Ingredients

2 tbsp. each shredded spinach, shredded lettuce
Shredded cucumber
½ oz. butter
1¼ pt. white stock
2 tbsp. green peas
4 leaves tarragon
4 sprigs chervil
Seasoning
1 lump of sugar
1 gill cream
2 egg yolks

Method

Sweat the shredded vegetables in the butter until it is absorbed. Add the boiling stock, green peas, herbs, seasoning and sugar, and cook gently until the peas are quite tender. Cool slightly, strain in cream and yolks, cook until thickened without boiling.

Tapioca Cream Soup
Ingredients

1½ pt. white stock
1 oz. French tapioca
Seasoning
2 egg yolks
¼ pt. cream

Method

Bring stock to boiling point, sprinkle in the tapioca and stir until it thickens, cool slightly and season. Beat the yolks and add the cream, strain into pan and cook carefully. The eggs are cooked if the tapioca floats on the surface.

Tomato Soup
Ingredients

1 pt. tinned or 1 lb. fresh tomatoes
1 pt. white or bone stock
1 small onion
Bouquet garni

Method

Put tomatoes, stock, onions and bouquet garni into a pan. Simmer till tender for ¾–1 hr., then rub through a hair sieve. Make a white roux with the fat and flour, add the purée gradually and stir until

[480]

Tomato Soup (*continued*)

1½ oz. each butter and flour
Seasoning
1 gill milk
1 tsp. sugar
Few drops carmine, if necessary

boiling. Add seasoning, milk, sugar and carmine, if necessary; reheat and serve with croûtons.

Tomato and Rice Soup

Ingredients

1 onion
½ oz. butter
1 pt. tinned or 1 lb. fresh tomatoes
1 qt. stock or water
1 oz. rice
Pinch of sugar

Method

Chop onion finely and sauté in the butter. Remove skins from tomatoes and cut into dice; add to the onion with stock, washed rice and sugar, if desired. Simmer gently until cooked for ½–¾ hr.; season and serve.

Turtle, Clear

Ingredients

¼ lb. dried turtle
3 qt. brown stock
Flavouring of carrot, turnip, onion, celery and leek
Lemon juice
Cayenne and salt
   FOR CLEARING:
¼ lb. gravy beef
Whites and shells of 2 eggs
½ gill sherry
1 tbsp. brandy

Method

Wash and soak the turtle for 4 days, changing the water each day. Rinse and cut turtle into 1″ pieces and cook with the stock and vegetables gently for 4–5 hrs. until the turtle is tender. Strain through a hair sieve, remove turtle and reserve for garnish. Cook stock and clear as for consommé. Add garnish of turtle cut into ¼″ pieces or cubes.

Vegetable Soup, White

Ingredients

1 carrot
1 small turnip
1 stick celery
1 small onion
½ oz. dripping
1½ pt. white stock or water
1 bay leaf
2 oz. flour
¼ pt. milk
Seasoning

Method

Prepare the carrot, turnip and celery, cut into inch-long blocks, then into strips the thickness of a match. Chop onion finely, sweat with the vegetable strips for 5 mins. in the hot dripping. Add stock and flavouring, then simmer until tender for about 1 hr. Mix flour and milk smoothly, add to soup and stir until boiling. Simmer for 5 mins., season and serve.

SOUR CREAM DRESSING. See SALAD DRESSINGS.

SOUR CROUT (Fr. *choucroute*: Germ. *sauerkraut*). Cabbage pickled in brine. It can be bought from delicatessen shops and is good served with frankfurter sausages.

SOUSE. A liquid in which fish or meat is soaked.

SOUTHERNWOOD. Also Old Man or Lad's Love. Leaf used medicinally and as a moth preventative.

SOY, SOJA, SOYA. A preparation made from the soya bean. It is a dark brown, and treacle-like, and gives both colour and flavour to soups. A flour is also made from the soya bean; it gives added nutriment to pastry, cake and pudding mixes if 1 oz. in every 8 oz. is replaced by soya flour. Also used in almond paste when ground almonds are not available.

SPAGHETTI. A very small macaroni made in cords. Cook as for macaroni, but not for quite so long.

WAYS OF SERVING SPAGHETTI

Plain, with butter, grated cheese and tomatoes.
With cooked diced celery and grated cheese.
With fried onion and cheese.
With curry sauce and parboiled vegetables.
With parsley sauce, garnished with tomatoes.
With grated beetroot and onion.
Cold, dressed with mayonnaise.
In a milk pudding.
As garnish in a clear soup.
Garnish all spaghetti dishes with cress, parsley or shredded spinach.

Spaghetti with Cheese and Ham

Ingredients

½ lb. butter or margarine
¾ lb. cooked spaghetti
½ tsp. breadcrumbs
1⅓ cups thick tomato pulp
1½ cups tomato juice
1¼ cups parmesan cheese (grated)
¾ lb. smoked ham cubes
1½ cups fresh mushrooms diced
1 large onion chopped fine
1 tsp. salt
¼ tsp. pepper
3 eggs beaten
1½ cups milk or cream

FOR TOPPING:

2 tbsp. parmesan cheese (grated)
2 tbsp. each butter and breadcrumbs

Method

Butter a casserole and sprinkle with breadcrumbs. Put a layer of spaghetti then tomato pulp and juice; dot with butter, add cheese, ham and mushrooms, onion, salt and pepper. Repeat layers until three-quarters full. Pour in beaten eggs and milk, loosen with a fork, top with cheese and breadcrumbs and dot with butter. Bake at 350° F. Therm. 4 for 20–25 mins. Serve in casserole.

SPANISH NUTS. Small nuts of the filbert kind, imported from Spain, principally Barcelona. They are sometimes used in confectionery.

SPANISH ONIONS. See ONIONS.

SPARE RIB. See PORK.

SPATCHCOCK or SPITCHCOCK. A process of splitting open and grilling or broiling an eel or fowl. The word is a compound of "spit" and "cock" or "cook", denoting the mode of trussing by means of small spits or skewers. It is said that the distinction between the two is that Spatchcock is applied to fowls or other birds, and Spitchcock to eels.

SPEARMINT. See MINT.

SPICE (Fr. *épice*). Aromatic vegetable substance used for flavouring or seasoning. See under individual headings.

SPINACH (Fr. *épinard*). A green vegetable rich in vitamins A and C. Allow ¼ lb. spinach to each person as it cooks down so much.

TO PREPARE AND BOIL. Pull off the stalks and wash the spinach well in several waters to remove the grit. If young, put it into a saucepan without any water other than that which remains on the leaves after washing. If old, put it into boiling water with salt. Cook with the lid off the saucepan until tender, stirring occasionally if hot water is used. Drain in a colander and wring dry in a cloth. Then chop, or rub through a wire sieve. To dress, mix spinach in a saucepan over the heat with a little butter, pepper and salt. Cream may be used also, taking care not to make the spinach too moist. Press it into a mound or pyramid in a vegetable dish, and garnish with fried croûtons of bread or sauté potatoes.

Spinach Soufflé

Ingredients	*Method*
1 tbsp. butter	Put butter into a saucepan; when warm,
1 cup strained spinach	add spinach and seasoning; stir till hot
Pepper and salt	then add egg yolks one at a time. Remove
2–3 eggs	from heat; when cool beat in cream or
⅛ pt. whipped cream, evaporated milk, or thick white sauce	sauce. Beat whites of eggs to a stiff froth and fold lightly in with a metal spoon. Turn the mixture into a buttered soufflé case. Bake at 375° F. Therm. 5 for 1 hr. or until puffed up.

SPINY LOBSTER. See CRAYFISH.

SPLEEN. A gland-like organ found near the stomach in almost every animal. It is usually known as the milt, and sometimes eaten when fried or boiled.

SPLIT. A bun split almost in half and filled with whipped or clotted cream. Banana split is a banana filled with whipped cream.

SPONGE CAKE. The name given to a kind of light cake, that is made with eggs, sugar and flour. See **CAKES.**

SPRATS. A small, inexpensive, useful fish, allied to the herring. Usually served grilled whole, with lemon or mustard sauce and brown bread and butter.

SPRING OF PORK. The thin flank or breast and belly.

SPRING ONION. An onion lifted while still quite young and before the flavour becomes too strong. Spring onions are frequently used in salads.

SPROUT TOPS. See BRUSSELS SPROUTS.

SPRUE. The thin stalks of asparagus in season January to July.

SQUAB. A young pigeon. Squab pie is young pigeon pie; Devonshire squab pie has apples added to it. A squab chicken is a young chicken.

SQUASHES. There are two kinds of squashes, summer and winter. The winter one usually means the Hubbard, or small acorn, or the Danish Squash. Among the summer squashes are included the white, scalloped variety, and the dark green Italian zucchini. The latter is least likely to have large seeds, or to be watery. Winter squash are good when baked or steamed. Remove seeds and stringy portions. See **VEGETABLE MARROW.**

STACHYS. See CHINESE ARTICHOKE.

STARCH (Fr. *amidon*). Starch is an organic substance occurring in the rounded or oval grains in the cellular tissue of certain parts of plants. The seeds of the cereals contain it in large quantity and it is also present in great abundance in leguminous

STARCH (*continued*)

plants, such as beans, peas, lentils, etc. Wheat and potatoes also contain a percentage of starch. All starches are said to have the same nutritive value, but differ in digestibility. Starch is not soluble in cold water, but when heated swells considerably.

STEAK. Mostly used for beef, but any piece of meat cut as for broiling may be a steak even though it be used in a pie or a pudding.

STEARIN. A constituent of many animal and vegetable fats and oils which raises the melting point.

STERILISE. See COOKING TERMS.

STERLET. A small sturgeon found in the Caspian Sea. Caviare is made from its roe.

STILTON CHEESE. A full-cream, well matured, green-veined cheese which takes its name from Stilton. Originally made in Rutland, now made in Leicestershire.

STOCK (Fr. *fond*). The liquid or broth in which meat and bones have been boiled, and of which soups and sauces are made. See **SOUPS**.

GENERAL RULES FOR STOCK-MAKING

Use a *very clean* strong pan with tight-fitting lid. Chop bones into small pieces, wash well and remove all fat and marrow. Cut up meat very finely.

Put ingredients into pan with cold water to well cover and allow $\frac{1}{2}$ tsp. salt for every quart. Bring slowly to boiling point and carefully remove all green scum. Boil bone stock for 5–9 hrs. Simmer meat stock for 3–5 hrs.

All vegetables should be cleanly scraped or peeled, cut into rough pieces and added when the stock is half cooked. Strain stock through a sieve and *never* leave stock in pot all night. Remove all fat before use. Use meat or bones for a second time. Water from the boiling of meat, rice, macaroni or potatoes may be used as a substitute for bone stock. Avoid use of turnips for flavouring in hot weather. Never use remains of thickened sauce, potatoes or bread.

STOCK TABLE

TYPE OF STOCK	AMOUNT OF INGREDIENTS REQUIRED	LIQUID	COOKING TIME	USE
Bone	2 lb. fresh meat bones	2 qt. water	6–7 hrs.	Gravies, Soups and general use
Brown	2 lb. shin beef bones and vegetables	,,	$3\frac{1}{2}$–5 hrs.	Consommé Purées
Fish	$1\frac{1}{2}$ lb. fish and bones, heads and skins	,,	$1\frac{1}{2}$–2 hrs.	Fish dishes or soups
Game and Poultry	2 lb. giblets, trimmings and carcases	,,	3 hrs.	Broths and soups
Household Stock	$2\frac{1}{2}$ lb. scraps, meat and vegetables	,,	2 hrs.	General purpose and soup
Vegetable	$1\frac{1}{2}$ lb. assorted vegetables and trimmings	,,	$1\frac{1}{2}$ hrs.	Gravies, sauce and soups
White	$2\frac{1}{2}$ lb. knuckle veal or veal trimmings and bones and vegetables	,,	5 hrs.	Sauces, soups and general use

Bone Stock

Ingredients

4 lb. raw or cooked bones
3 qt. cold water

Method

Prepare bones, place in stockpot with cold water and salt. Bring to boiling

Bone Stock (*continued*)

2 onions
¼ turnip
2 stalks celery (or ¼ tsp. celery seed or salt)
1½ tsp. salt
Bouquet garni

point, skim thoroughly, then boil for 3 hrs., skimming frequently. Add vegetables and herbs and boil gently for 2–3 hrs. longer. Strain, remove fat the following day. Continue cooking the bones until they are soft and porous. If desired, the stock can be browned by frying the onions.

Brown or Clear Stock

Ingredients

2 lb. shin of beef
½ lb. knuckle of veal or chicken bones
¼ lb. raw lean ham
Bouquet garni
2 sticks of celery or ½ tsp. celery seed or salt
2 qt. cold water
2 tsp. salt
1 oz. dripping or butter
1 large onion
1 carrot
½ turnip

Method

Place prepared meat and bones into stock-pot with cold water and salt. Bring slowly to boiling point; simmer gently for 3 hrs. Skim carefully. Fry finely sliced onion until golden brown. Add to stock with vegetables and flavourings, and simmer for 2 hrs. Strain through a hair sieve and remove all fat the following day. Use as required. The meat and bones can be used for second stock.

Court Bouillon. See also under this heading.

Ingredients

2 lb. fish trimmings
1 qt. water
1 bay leaf
¼ lb. butter
2 chopped carrots
3 stalks celery
1 qt. wine (sauterne or Rhine)
8 peppercorns
1 tsp. thyme
3 sprigs parsley

Method

Put all ingredients into large pan; bring quickly to the boil, then simmer gently for 1 hr. Remove fish and strain. If preferred, juice of 1 lemon may be used instead of wine.

Fish Stock

Ingredients

1 lb. whiting or good fish trimmings
Bouquet garni
12 white peppercorns
1 qt. water
1 small piece each carrot, turnip and onion
Seasoning
2″ celery

Method

Remove eyes from whiting and cleanse it. Divide into pieces and simmer gently with vegetables, flavourings and water for 20 mins. Strain and use for soups and sauces.

[485]

Ox-tail Stock

Ingredients

1 oxtail
1 lb. shin beef
2 qt. water
1 carrot
1 turnip
1 onion
Bouquet garni
1 stick celery
12 white peppercorns
2 tsp. salt
3 oz. white dripping

Method

Slice and fry the onion in the dripping and drain well. Wash the tail, joint it and remove fat; cut the beef up and fry with oxtail in dripping until brown. Cook as for brown stock. Simmer for 5 hrs., strain and reserve best joints of oxtail for garnish. When cold, remove fat.

Vegetable Stock

Ingredients

2 qt. water
1 medium carrot
½ turnip
1 onion
2 sticks celery (or ¼ tsp. celery seed or salt)
Bouquet garni
2 cloves
2 oz. pulse vegetables
Seasoning
1 leek (in season)

Method

Simmer all ingredients together gently for about 4 hrs. If required brown, fry the thinly sliced onion.

White Stock

Ingredients

1–2 lb. knuckle of veal
¼ lb. lean ham
2 onions
2 sticks celery (or ¼ tsp. celery salt or seed)
3 qt. cold water
½ turnip
20 peppercorns
1 blade mace
Bunch of herbs
4″ lemon rind
1½ tsp. salt

Method

Put the prepared meat and bones into the stock pot with salt and cold water and proceed according to rules given. Skim carefully; simmer for 3 hrs. Add vegetables and flavourings and simmer for another 2 hrs. Strain through a hair sieve and remove fat when cold. Use bones and meat for second and third stock.

STOKE. See SEAWEED.

STRAWBERRY. A soft fruit of delicious flavour and rich in Vitamin C, in season during the height of summer. It is very seldom cooked as it is more attractive in flavour and appearance if served raw; also used widely in jam which is always popular.

STRAWBERRIES, TO PRESERVE. See FRUIT.

[486]

Strawberry Delight. Other fruit, or marrons glacés may be used in place of strawberries.

Ingredients
- ¾ lb. strawberries
- ¼ gill cream or mock cream
- ¾ pt. stiff jelly flavoured with wine

Method

Take a little of the jelly and pour enough into a pint mould to fill it an inch. Place the mould in a basin on ice. When it begins to set, make a design with half strawberries putting half the red side and half the white side down. Pour in just enough jelly to cover. After this has set, add a little more fruit and place a lining or empty round bottle exactly in the middle. Fill up with alternate layers of fruit and jelly. When the mousse has set (which should take about 20 mins.) pour a little hot water into the lining (or bottle) and lift it out. Fill the empty space with whipped cream, flavoured with vanilla or strawberry, or maraschino. Turn out and decorate with cream.

Strawberry Jam I
Ingredients
- 6 lb. strawberries
- 6 lb. sugar

Method

Pick over fruit and remove stems. Boil sugar in preserving pan until it candies when dropped into cold water. Add fruit and boil for 10 mins. Pour into heated jars and cover immediately.

Strawberry Jam II
Ingredients
- 8 lb. strawberries
- 8 lb. sugar
- 1½ pt. redcurrant juice
- 1 pt. cold water

Method

Place the strawberries in preserving pan with half the sugar and allow to stand overnight. Next day add the redcurrant juice and water to remaining sugar and boil for 30 mins. Place the strawberries and syrup into this and stir gently, taking care not to break them, until the jam sets. Pour into heated jars and cover.

Strawberry Jelly
Ingredients
- 4 lb. strawberries
- Sugar

Method

Place fruit in preserving pan and stand over gentle heat until juice is extracted. Strain through muslin, measure and allow 1 lb. sugar to 1 pt. juice. Heat juice in slow oven 200° F. Therm ¼ then place in preserving pan with the warmed sugar and stir until dissolved. Boil for 15 mins., pour into warmed jars and cover when cold.

Strawberry Sauce

Ingredients

4 oz. butter
8 oz. sugar
1 egg
½ lb. crushed strawberries

Method

Cream butter and sugar, separate yolk and white of egg, add egg yolk and strawberries, and fold together lightly through the stiffly whisked egg white.

Strawberry Tart. See **PASTE AND PASTRY** (p. 378).

STUFFINGS

Chestnut Stuffing

Ingredients

½ lb. chestnuts
2 oz. breadcrumbs
1 oz. chopped suet or margarine
1 tbsp. lemon juice
1 tbsp. finely chopped parsley
Salt
1 egg

Method

Prick the chestnuts, place under grill and leave until the skin splits. Shell and blanch them; place in a pan, cover with boiling water (or milk and stock) and simmer until tender. Pass through a hair sieve. Add the other ingredients, bind together with the egg and use for turkey.

Thyme and Parsley Stuffing. See **FORCEMEAT** adding sprinkle of thyme. Use for chicken.

Sage and Onion Stuffing

Ingredients

½ lb. onions
2 oz. breadcrumbs (dry)
Seasoning of pepper and salt
1 tsp. powdered sage

Method

Peel and place onions in saucepan. Cover with boiling water and cook until tender. Drain and chop finely. Mix all ingredients together and use for stuffing as desired.

Sausage Stuffing

Ingredients

1 lb. sausage meat
2 oz. breadcrumbs
½ tsp. mixed herbs
1 tsp. chopped parsley
1 egg

Method

Mix all the ingredients well together in a basin, then add the egg to bind.

Veal Stuffing

Ingredients

2 oz. breadcrumbs
1 oz. chopped suet (or dripping or margarine)
Squeeze of lemon juice
1 egg or milk to bind
1 tbsp. chopped parsley
½ tsp. mixed herbs
Grating of lemon rind
Pepper and salt

Method

Mix all the ingredients well together, adding a little extra milk to bind if necessary. If desired, add two or three oysters.

STURGEON (Fr. *esturgeon*). A fine-flavoured fish which was at one time considered exclusively royal property. The roe is made into caviare. Before cooking, the skin must be removed, as the oil in it is apt to give an unpleasant flavour.

SUCCORY. See CHICORY.

SUCCOTASH. An American dish of beans and whole corn boiled together.

SUCKING PIG (Fr. *cochon de lait*). An unweaned pig roasted whole. See **PORK.**

SUCROSE. Cane sugar or saccharose.

SUET (Fr. *graise*). The fat from round the kidneys of any animal, especially from the bullock, calf, sheep and lamb. In a literal sense the term has a wide signification being applied to almost any kind of fat from which tallow is made. For most purpose, beef suet is preferable. Veal suet is harder and less strongly flavoured. Suet should be quite fresh when used, but it can be kept for 12 mths. by removing all the membrane and veins and melting down gradually at a slow heat, and then pouring in a large basin of cold water; it should then set hard and firm, requiring to be scraped before use. Suet is usually chopped after shredding, using plenty of flour in the operation.

For *Suet Pastry* or *Suet Crust*. See **PASTE AND PASTRY.**

For *Suet Pudding*. See **PUDDINGS.**

SUGAR (Fr. *sucre*). Sugar is a substance sweet to taste which is obtained from various plants, especially from the sugar cane and sugar beet. When submitted to different changes of temperature, it takes on different forms and characteristics.

First, it is in a crystalline condition; by boiling or manipulation, it is changed to fondant; then by further heating it becomes a clear brittle substance and can be spun. It dissolves in water and, when concentrated by heat, a syrup is obtained, of varying degrees according to requirements.

Beet Sugar is the produce of sugar beet.

Cane Sugar is the concentrated produce of the sugar cane.

Caster Sugar, being finer-grained, dissolves more rapidly than *granulated sugar*, but its sweetening power is not as great.

Brown and Yellow Sugars consist of the coarser part of sugar and are suitable for some candies. Avoid sugars which are very dark in colour for cookery purposes, because they burn more rapidly during boiling.

Honey is the natural form of invert sugar.

Icing Sugar is specially pulverised sugar which is suitable for icings and for sweet-making. It must be kept in a dry place.

Lump Sugar is best for preserving.

Maple Sugar is obtained from the juice of the Sugar Maple tree. It is largely imported from Canada.

Treacle, Molasses, and *Golden Syrup* are sticky fluids which are extracted during the refining of sugar.

TO BOIL. With careful attention and practice some knowledge may be obtained by the following directions:

When using a sugar-boiling thermometer, stand it in hot water before use, and return it to hot water immediately it is moved from the syrup. Always stand it upright in the saucepan, and be sure there is no direct heat playing on the back of the thermometer. Read the thermometer at eye level with the top of the saucepan to ensure a correct reading.

During sugar-boiling, one danger must be guarded against—sugar, being a crystalline substance, tends to form a syrup, to crystallise out and change from syrup into crystals and water. To guard against this:

(*a*) Add to the syrup some substance such as glucose, cream of tartar—this "greases" the sugar and it is therefore less likely to granulate. The proportions are 3 oz. glucose to 1 lb. sugar at 240–250° F., 2 oz. per 1 lb. sugar at 280–310° F. Use ½ oz. cream of tartar to 14 lb. of sugar.

(*b*) Melt the sugar very thoroughly before boiling.

(*c*) Brush round the sides of the pan during boiling to dissolve any crystals which form.

(*d*) Remove any scum on the surface then boil briskly until the required degree is reached.

[489]

TO BOIL (*continued*)

First or Small Thread	216° F.	Let the sugar boil a few minutes then dip the thumb and finger quickly into cold water and then with them touch the syrup on the skimmer. Press them together and if on pulling them apart a small thread is formed which will break at a slight distance, the sugar has reached its first degree.
Second or Large Thread	218° F.	Boil a little longer, then test as before, and if a rather longer thread will form without breaking, the second degree is reached.
Small and Large Pearl	220°–230° F.	The small pearl is when the thread will not break when the thumb and finger are some distance apart, and the large pearl when they can be extended as far as possible without the thread breaking.
Small Blow	230° F.	Continue boiling, dip in the skimmer, and when, on blowing through the holes, little bubbles appear on the other side, the sugar has reached the small blow.
Feather or large Blow	233° F.	After a little further boil the mixture bubbles more and feathers when shaken.
Soft Ball	240° F.	The sugar forms a soft ball when tested.
Hard Ball	250°–255° F.	The sugar forms a large hard ball.
Crack	290° F.	The sugar when tested with cold water breaks between finger and thumb.
Hard Crack	312° F.	When sugar breaks and is brittle when test on a finger dipped in cold water is made.
Caramel	350° F.	The sugar colours slightly and when it is yellow, add lemon juice and a little water—reboil until brown, then "black".

TO CLARIFY. Break the sugar into lumps and to every 2 lb. allow 1 pt. water, and to every 10 lb. 2 egg whites. Beat the eggs slightly as for jelly clearing, add them to the water; mix thoroughly together and pour on to the sugar. Allow to dissolve over a gentle heat then bring to the boil, and instantly throw in a little cold water. Bring to the boil again, and again throw in cold water. Do this three times, and then boil it again. Skim it now thoroughly, dropping in, if necessary, a little cold water now and again, then strain through a hair sieve.

Great care must be taken in testing the hot syrup, owing to the danger of accidents.

SUGAR TEMPERATURES AND TESTS FOR CANDIES AND SYRUPS

	SEA LEVEL DEGREE OF CONCENTRATION REQUIRED		CONCENTRATION STAGE
	°F.	°C.	
Barley Sugar	320	160	Clear liquid, the sugar is reclarified.
Brittle Glacé	300–310	149–154	Hard crack; the syrup when tested by dropping into very cold water separates into threads; these are hard and brittle.
Butterscotch	270–290	132–143	Soft crack; the syrup when dropped into very, very cold water separates into hard but not brittle threads.
Caramel	388	170	Brown liquid.
Caramels	244–248	118–120	Firm ball; the syrup when dropped into very cold water should form a firm ball which retains its shape on removal.
Fondant Fudge	235–240	112–116	Soft ball; the syrup when dropped into very cold water forms a ball which flattens when removed.
Marshmallow Nougat	250–265	121–129	Hard ball; the syrup when dropped into very cold water forms a ball which is hard enough to retain its shape yet it is plastic.
Syrup	230–235	110–112	Thread; the syrup when dropped from a spoon or fork can be spun into a 2″ thread.

Spun Sugar

Ingredients

½ lb. loaf sugar
¼ pt. cold water
Small pinch cream of tartar
2 drops acetic acid

Method

Dissolve the sugar in the water and boil for a few minutes. Add the cream of tartar and acetic acid. Boil to 310° F., then plunge the pan into cold water immediately to prevent the temperature of the syrup from rising. Grease a rolling pin with olive oil and put a clean sheet of paper on the floor. Remove the pan from the water. Dip a fork in the syrup and allow most of the syrup to trickle off so that only a little remains. Shake the fork quickly backwards and forwards over the rolling pin held over the paper. Keep the fork high above the rolling pin so that long threads are spun. Gather up the threads and use immediately as they will not keep more than 2 hrs. If desired, the syrup may be coloured and flavoured just before the temperature reaches 310° F.

SUGAR CANDY (Fr. *aphenie*). Made by suspending strings in a strong solution of sugar. These are left until cool and the candy is deposited on the strings.

SUGAR PEA. A variety of pea without the tough inner lining of ordinary peas, cooked and served in their pods. See **PEA, SUGAR.**

SULTANA (Fr. *sultana*). A small seedless raisin, light in colour. Used extensively in cakes, puddings, mincemeat, pickles, etc.

SUNDAE. A mixture of fruit, ice and sugar, sometimes garnished with nuts.

SWEAT. See **COOKING TERMS.**

SWEDE or SWEDISH TURNIP. A coarse, root vegetable of a yellow colour with an excellent flavour. It should be peeled thickly, sliced and boiled in salted water until tender, then mashed with butter, pepper and salt.

SWEET BALM. See **BALM.**

SWEET BASIL. See **BASIL.**

SWEET CICELY. See **CICELY.**

SWEET CORN. See **INDIAN CORN.**

SWEET HERBS. See **HERBS.**

SWEET MARY. See **COSTMARY.**

SWEET PEPPERS. See **CAPSICUM.**

SWEET POTATO. A vegetable not allied to the potato from the West Indies and other tropical countries. These sweet potatoes are prepared and cooked as white potatoes.

SWEETBREAD (Fr. *ris de veau* or *d'agneau*). There are two kinds of sweetbreads known respectively as the throat sweetbread and the ordinary or heart sweetbread. The former is a large thymus gland, situated round and along the windpipe and the latter is anatomically the pancreas. Either may be used in this recipe. The throat sweetbread is reckoned the more dainty, and the sweetbreads of calves and lambs the best of all.

SWEETBREADS, STEWED

Ingredients

1 calf's sweetbread
1 teacup light stock
1 tsp. cornflour
Seasoning
Little cold water
1 tbsp. cream
1 tsp. chopped parsley

Method

Steep the sweetbread in cold water for 1 hr. Put into a saucepan of cold water, bring to boil; boil 3–4 mins. Drain, put again into cold water, remove skin and fat and break into pieces. Put sweetbread into saucepan or casserole; add stock and seasoning, simmer until tender, about 1 hr. Blend cornflour with water. Remove sweetbread, keep hot; add cornflour to stock; stir until boiling, boil 5 mins., add cream and parsley; pour over the sweetbread. Garnish with sippets of toast.

SWISS ROLL. See **CAKES.**

SYLLABUB. Also spelt Sillabub. A dish made by mixing wine or cider and new milk to form a soft curd; also sweetened cream flavoured with wine and beaten to a stiff froth.

Ingredients

1 pt. cider
Sugar to taste

Method

Place the cider, brandy and sugar into a bowl and pour into it a quart of milk, or

[492]

SYLLABUB (*continued*)

1 wineglass brandy (or
sherry or light French
wine)

1 qt. milk

Little grated nutmeg if
desired

pour in warm milk from a teapot held
high over it.

SYRUP. A solution of sugar, usually flavoured, and used for various culinary
purposes. For **Stock Syrup,** dissolve 1 lb. granulated sugar in 1 pt. water. For
Syrup Crystallising see FRUIT.

T

TABASCO. A pungent Indian pepper sauce.

TAMARIND (Fr. *tamarin*). The fruit of the tamarind tree is usually imported into this country as a preserve in syrup. The fruit or bean consists of a brittle brown shell, within which is a soft acid brown pulp, transversed by strongly woody fibres. The pulp is used as a laxative. Before preserving tamarinds the outer skins are removed.

TAMMY. A kind of woollen cloth, also known as "taminy", used for straining fruit syrups, liquid jellies, etc.

TANGELO. A hybrid between the tangerine orange and the grapefruit.

TANGERINE. See ORANGES.

TANGLE. See SEAWEED.

TANSY. An aromatic, bitter-tasting plant at one time used much in English cookery to flavour omelets, puddings and cakes. A variety with curled leaves is sometimes used as a garnish.

TAPIOCA (Fr. *tapioca*). A starch or fecula obtained from the root of the cassava, a tropical plant. It is most commonly sold in flakes or pearls. See also CASSAVA. Pure tapioca is insipid, inodorous, only slightly soluble in cold water, but quite soluble in boiling water, when it forms a nutritious jelly. For **Tapioca Cream Soup**, see SOUPS; for **Tapioca Pudding**, see MILK PUDDINGS.

TARRAGON (Fr. *estragon*). An aromatic plant with long narrow leaves of a bright green colour, used especially in sauces, salads and vinegar.
Tarragon Butter. See BUTTERS.
Tarragon Sauce. Put a few branches of green tarragon, and a wineglass of white wine vinegar into a saucepan and boil for 10 mins. Then add 4 tsp. Velouté sauce (see p. 448) and 2 egg yolks to thicken. Pass through a sieve into a basin; add a squeeze of lemon juice, a little finely chopped tarragon and salt and pepper to taste. This sauce is good with boiled fowl.
Tarragon Vinegar. Fill a large bottle with leaves of tarragon (when in flower), pour vinegar over them and leave 2 wks. Strain through flannel into small bottles. Cork well.

TART AND TARTLET. An open pastry case, large or small, filled with fruit, jam, treacle, custard, etc.

TARTAR. See CREAM OF TARTAR.

TARTARE SAUCE. See SAUCES.

TARTARIC ACID. An acid obtained in crystals from cream of tartar; it is very soluble in water and usually sold in a powder, which renders it exceedingly liable to adulterations. It is used in conjunction with bicarbonate of soda as a raising agent, and also in place of citric acid or lemon juice in setting jams.

TARTINE. Literally this is the French for a slice of bread and butter of which, as may be supposed, several varieties are known according to the nature of the bread and what is spread on the slices.

TEA (Fr. *thé*). Tea was first introduced into England about the year 1661. It is divided into two great classes, known as black and green teas, the colour depending upon the mode of manufacture. Black tea is allowed to turn colour in the sun before it is curled and dried; green tea is dried in its freshly picked state and is not much drunk in this country.

TO MAKE AND SERVE. When making tea it is of the first importance that the pot should be well heated before adding the required amount of tea, that the water should be freshly drawn and boiling as it is poured on the tea. But the infusion itself must not be boiled or a larger proportion of the tannin contained in the leaves would be extracted than would be either pleasant or desirable. Allow the tea infusion to stand for a few minutes before pouring. Tea can be used for other purposes than a simple beverage served with milk or cream and sugar. With the delicately flavoured China teas some people prefer a slice of lemon instead of milk and sugar.

ICED TEA. Half fill tumblers with strong cold tea, without cream or milk. Add to each the strained juice of half a lemon; sweeten well and fill each glass with broken ice.

TEAL (Fr. *cercelle* or *sarcelle*). One of the smaller wild ducks. The varieties best known in this country are the Common European Teal and the Blue-winged Teal or Garganey; their flesh is much esteemed by epicures. Teal is best during the winter months. The legs should be soft and pliable, indicating freshness.

TO TRUSS FOR ROASTING. Pluck, draw and singe the teal. Wash and wipe it well inside. Give each of the legs a twist at the knuckle and bring the claws to each side, letting them rest on the breast. Pass a skewer through the thighs and wing pinions.

TEMPERATURES. The degree of heat or cold, critical in the cooking of food.

EQUIVALENT TEMPERATURES FAHRENHEIT AND CENTIGRADE

° F.	° C.
32	0·00
65	18·3
86	30·0
100	37·7
122	50·0
150	65·5
167	75·0
176	80·0
200	93·3
212	100·0

See also OVEN TEMPERATURES and COOKING TERMS (for boiling and simmering temperatures).

TENCH (Fr. *tenche*). A European freshwater fish of the carp family. When caught in fresh clear water it is a very good fish for eating, but otherwise it is apt to be muddy in taste. It is in season from December to February. Tench requires to be thoroughly washed and soaked in salt water and the gills, which always give a muddy flavour, should be removed. It may be boiled, steamed, baked, fried or grilled (see FISH), and served with Melted Butter or other suitable sauce. Tench may also be stewed in stock with a little port wine and some mushrooms and oysters and served with sippets of fried bread.

TENDON. The long, tough, inelastic sinews or gristle into which the fibres of muscles are inserted, are usually known by this name, but the French cook extends the signification to the cartilages at the end of the ribs of a breast of veal.

TERRAPIN. A cross between a turtle and a land-tortoise, about a foot long, found on the sea-shore or in the salt marshes of America. Its flesh is esteemed a great delicacy but it is little known or used in England.

TERRINE or TERRENE. Vessel made of earthenware that will slow-heat. It is fitted with a lid the edges of which are sometimes hermetically sealed with a flour and water paste, thus preventing the escape of steam. The process of cooking resembles braising, with the exception that the food is often served in the terrine in which it was baked.

THUNNY. See TUNNY.

THYME. There are many varieties of thyme, but the common Garden thyme and Lemon-scented thyme are the most common, the latter having, as its name suggests, a strong lemon-like odour that limits its use as a seasoning. The leaves, both in green or dried state, are employed for seasoning soups, stews, sauces and stuffings, to which they give an agreeable and highly aromatic flavour. See also HERBS.

TIMBALE. A mould of meat, fish, game, vegetables, etc.

TINNED FOODS, TO USE. Whether the foods are home-canned or bought from a shop, they help to give variety to the menu and make out-of-season foods everyday fare. When using tinned foods it is always advisable to combine them with less expensive food to make them go further and also to add fresh vitamin foods to supplement the vitamins that cooking and canning may have partially destroyed. Nearly all recipes which call for fresh, cooked fish, fruit or meat or vegetables can be made up with the tinned counterpart. In most recipes which call for milk, evaporated or powdered whole milk may be substituted. After opening, *never* leave canned food standing in the tin; turn it out at once. Most canned foods are greatly improved if they are left in an uncovered dish for about half-an-hour before use; they re-oxygenise on exposure to the air.

SUGGESTIONS FOR THE USE OF TINNED FOODS

FISH. Any canned fish is greatly improved if boiling water is poured over it before use and then drained off.

Herring. For sandwiches, salads and reheated.

Kipper. Grilled or flaked in sandwiches.

Lobster or Crab. Creamed in sauces, salads, soufflés, Newburg patties, vol-au-vent, toast.

Mackerel
Salmon
Snoek   } Creamed for sauces, croquettes, patties, salads, sand-
Tuna or   wiches, soufflés, soups, vol-au-vents and warmed in butter.
Any flaked fish

Sardines. Canapés, sandwiches, salads, hors d'œuvres, on toast.

Shrimps. Canapés, creamed in sauces, devilled, salads, sandwiches, toasts, curry, fish cocktails.

FRUIT. To revive canned fruit, drain off syrup, heat this well (but do not boil), turn into basin; add fruit and leave to cool.

Apricots
Cherries
Loganberries
Oranges
Peaches   } For flans, fruit tarts, fruit whips, fritters, ices, jellies, in
Pears   salads and stewed.
Pineapple
Plums
Strawberries

GAME. Cold or reheated or in salads or sandwiches, creamed in sauces or soups.

MEAT AND OFFAL

Corned Beef. Cold with salads, in hash and stews, sliced and reheated, in sauce or butter, creamed, croquettes, rissoles, curry.

Ham. Cold with salad, grilled, reheated in sauce, with scrambled eggs, in savoury rice.

Lamb's Tongue. Sliced and served with salad, steamed, sliced and served with gravy or sauce.

Pressed Meat. Sandwiches, sliced and served with salad, steamed, in meat loaf, in pasties, heated in sauce.

Tongue. Sandwiches, in hot sauce, with salad, chopped in cream or tomato sauce, served on toast.

POULTRY
Chicken } Cold, heated in a cream sauce (or with mushroom sauce and
Turkey } rice), in salads, in sandwiches, casseroles, pies, in aspic.

SOUPS. As soup, as the basis for sauce, soufflés, cream fillings for vol-au-vent, etc.

SPAGHETTI. Reheated, in salads, on toast, as a border.

VEGETABLES
Asparagus. Reheated or served cold with French dressing or mayonnaise. Also as a snack served on toast or in a sandwich.
Baked Beans. Reheated, in sandwiches, salads, on toast, as a garnish.
Beans. Reheated with butter, pepper, salt, parsley and chopped chives; in any way fresh beans are used.
Beetroot. Reheated with butter, pepper and salt.
Carrots. In any recipe where carrots are used, in salads, casseroles, soups, stews.
Corn. Reheated with butter, cream or milk, as a vegetable, in a soufflé, in soup.
Peas. In any way fresh peas are served, salads, reheated in sauce.
Spinach. In any recipe as for fresh spinach, soufflé, salad.
Tomatoes. Escalloped with rice and cheese, in omelets, soups, stewed.

TIPPAREE. The fruit of the Cape Gooseberry. It has a slightly acid taste, is eaten as dessert in Arabia, Germany and Spain, and also made elsewhere into jelly and preserve.

TIPSY CAKE. Tipsy cake is a sponge cake, soaked in sherry or fruit juice, to which the juice of half a lemon has been added. Decorate with chopped almonds.

TISANE. A decoration, or infusion, usually of herbs.

TOAD IN THE HOLE. Pieces of sausage or meat baked in a batter pudding (see p. 51).

TOAST. Grilled or toasted slices of bread.

TOASTS. A variety of savoury meats spread or laid upon pieces of toasted bread. Several of these are described under special headings such as **ANCHOVY**, etc.

TOFFEE

Ingredients	*Method*
5 oz. butter 1 lb. brown sugar	Melt the butter in a sugar-boiler or other suitable pan. Stir in the sugar, keep stirring until the toffee is ready (about 10 mins.). Test by dropping a little of the toffee into cold water; if when bitten it breaks clean between the teeth it is ready. Pour it then without any delay on to a buttered tin or dish.

TOMATO (Fr. *tomate*). A soft, pulpy fruit, South American in origin, which is in season all the year round as it can be grown both out of doors and in hothouses. There are several varieties known to horticulturalists, different in size, shape and colour (red or golden). Tomatoes are better baked than boiled as boiling destroys the flavour, but best of all eaten raw.

TO BLANCH. Put the tomatoes into a basin and pour over sufficient boiling water to cover. Leave for a minute or two. Pour away the hot water and cover with cold. The skin will be easily removed.

TO BAKE. Put the tomatoes on a greased baking-tin with a little butter or dripping. Sprinkle with pepper and salt and cover with greased paper. Bake at 350° F Therm. 4 for 10–15 mins.

[497]

TOMATOES, TO BOTTLE. Tomatoes may be bottled skinned, unskinned or pulped.

1. *Skinned.* Blanch the tomatoes in boiling water; then plunge them into cold water and remove the skins. Pack them tightly with their own juice, either whole or in quarters, and press them down well. Sprinkle with salt and sugar, allowing ½ oz. salt and 1 tsp. sugar to each jar.

2. *Unskinned.* Remove the stalks and wash the fruit carefully in cold water. Pack into the jars, cover with brine made with ½ oz. salt to 1 qt. water.

3. *Pulped.* Heat the tomatoes in a pan and add a little sugar and salt; then proceed as for fruit pulp. Choose any of the methods of sterilisation given for fruit bottling.

TOMATOES, TO STEW. Cut the peeled tomatoes into quarters, season with salt and pepper. Cook very slowly until just tender. Add butter and a pinch of sugar.

VARIATIONS

1. Add a little chopped onion.
2. Add a few leaves of basil.
3. Add crisp buttered breadcrumbs if desired.
4. Add little pieces of garlic, some finely chopped parsley and a little grated cheese.

Tomato au Gratin

Ingredients

1½ lb. tomatoes
2 oz. butter
1 pt. breadcrumbs
Pepper
Salt

Method

Slice the tomatoes and put a layer of them in the bottom of a buttered dish. Cover with crumbs, season with pepper and salt and dot with butter. Put another layer of tomatoes in covering them with crumbs in the same way. Use up all the tomatoes and crumbs. Bake at 400° F. Therm. 6 for 20 mins.

Tomatoes Canapés. Mix 3 tbsp. flour with 2 tbsp. butter. Add 1 cup tinned tomatoes, ½ cup each minced green pepper and celery, 2 tbsp. grated onion, and ¼ lb. bacon chopped and sautéed. Season with salt, paprika and cayenne. Cook until thick. Spread on toast rounds, top with grated cheese and bake at 350° F. Therm. 4 until cheese melts. Serve hot or cold.

Tomato Chutney

Ingredients

2 lb. tomatoes (green or red)
½ tsp. each salt and chillies
¼ tsp. each ground cloves and ground ginger
1 pt. vinegar
¾ lb. sugar
Few peppercorns
Mustard seed

Method

If ripe tomatoes, blanch and skin them, then slice. If green, slice and place in dish in layers with salt between each; cover with water. Leave overnight, next day drain off liquid and wash tomatoes thoroughly in running cold water. Put all ingredients into a saucepan, simmer gently until soft, cool a little, pot and seal.

Tomato Jam

Ingredients

4 lb. sound tomatoes
4 lemons
2 pt. water
4 lb. sugar

Method

Blanch tomatoes (see above). Cut them into pieces and place in preserving pan. Boil lemons in the water until tender, then slice thinly, removing pips. Add slices to tomatoes with the water in which the lemons were boiled, boil for 15 mins.

[498]

Tomato Jam (*continued*)

then add sugar and boil for further 20 mins. Test for setting, pour into warmed jars and cover when cool.

Tomato Pie
Ingredients
8 oz. flour
1 tbsp. shortening
1 tsp. salt
Scant ½ pt. milk
5 or 6 tomatoes
Seasoning
Little sugar
½ pt. mayonnaise
8 oz. grated cheese
2 tbsp. grated onion

Method
Make a pastry crust with flour, shortening, salt and milk, and line a greased pie-plate. Cover with blanched, sliced tomatoes, season with salt, pepper and sugar; mix together the mayonnaise, cheese and onion, and spread on top of tomatoes. Bake at 375° F. Therm. 5 for about 1 hr.

Tomato Salad. See SALADS.

Tomato Salad Dressing
Ingredients
1 tin tomato soup
4 oz. sugar
2 tsp. each prepared mustard and Worcester sauce
½ tsp. black pepper
¼ saltspoon salt
8 oz. salad oil
4 oz. vinegar
1 clove garlic (minced finely)

Method
Combine all ingredients and beat well with hand or electric beater. Dressing keeps well in refrigerator for months. Shake well each time before using. Excellent on tossed green salads.

Tomato Sauce
Ingredients
2 tbsp. butter or margarine
1 tbsp. flour
Pepper and salt
½ pt. milk
½ tsp. grated onion
¼ pt. strained cooked tomato

Method
Put the margarine or butter, flour and seasoning together in a double boiler. Stir constantly. When the mixture is smooth and creamy, add the milk, onion and tomato. Leave to simmer on a low heat for 10 mins. Use as desired. See also **SAUCES.**

Tomato Sauce (Winter-keeping)
Ingredients
2 lb. tomatoes
¼ lb. grated apple
1 shallot
1 bay leaf
Small clove garlic (if desired)
¼ tsp. paprika
Salt
¼ lb. sugar
⅓ pt. vinegar

Method
Slice tomatoes, put into a saucepan with apple, shallot and bay leaf. Place over a low heat, stir gently until the mixture is pulp, then rub through a hair sieve. Add paprika, salt, sugar and vinegar. Reboil until a smooth and heavy consistency. Then pour into hot sterilised bottles.

Tomatoes, Stuffed I

Ingredients

6 large tomatoes
1 cup cooked diced vege-
tables
4 tbsp. breadcrumbs
¼ tsp. pepper
1 tsp. salt
1 tsp. herbs mixed
1 egg
2 tbsp. grated cheese
2 tbsp. butter
1 tin vegetable soup

Method

Scoop out centre of tomatoes; place pulp in mixing bowl; add diced vegetables, breadcrumbs, seasonings, and lightly beaten egg. Mix well together and fill tomatoes. Sprinkle grated cheese on top and dot with butter. Arrange tomatoes on baking-dish. Pour round soup and bake at 350° F. Therm. 4 for about 40 mins., basting with soup every 10 mins.

Tomatoes, Stuffed II

Ingredients

1 oz. butter
½ oz. flour
1 gill milk or stock
Some white crumbs browned
1 tsp. each chopped ham and parsley
1 large cooked mushroom chopped finely
1 dsp. grated parmesan cheese
Few drops lemon juice
Pepper and salt
6–8 ripe tomatoes

Method

Melt the butter in a small saucepan. Mix in the flour smoothly. Add milk, stir and cook well; then add sufficient breadcrumbs to slightly thicken the mix. Add parsley, mushroom, ham, cheese, lemon juice and seasoning. Scoop out the top of each tomato. Pile a little stuffing on each and sprinkle a few browned crumbs on it. Put the tomatoes on a slightly greased baking sheet and bake at 350° F. Therm. 4 for 15 mins.

Tomato Soup. See SOUPS.

Tomato Toasts

Ingredients

2 bacon rashers diced
3 tbsp. flour
2 tbsp. butter or margarine
½ pt. tomato pulp
¼ pt. chopped green peppers
8 oz. shredded celery
2 tbsp. grated onion
Pepper, salt and paprika
Toast
Finely grated cheese

Method

Sauté the bacon; add flour and butter, mix well together and cook for about a minute. Add tomato pulp and green peppers, celery and onion, add seasoning and stir all well together. Spread on toast rounds, sprinkle with grated cheese and bake at 350° F. Therm. 4 until the cheese melts.

TONGUES (Fr. *langues*). See **OX, LAMB,** etc.

TORBAY SOLE. A name given to the lemon sole.

TOURNEDOS. Fillet steaks are cut laterally from the thickest part of the fillet of beef. They should be about 1½″ thick and weigh 6–7 oz. Tournedos are half fillets as to weight. The thickness of tournedos should be about 1¼″; they should be cut into a round shape.

Tournedos Béarnaises. Season the tournedos and grill them. Place on round crusts ½″ thick fried in clarified butter, taking care not to overcook them. Cut off a nice piece of fat to lay on top of each tournedos. Arrange neatly in a dish (or on a silver grid). Arrange some sautéed potatoes (see p. 397) in the centre of the dish and serve with Béarnaise sauce (see p. 438) in a sauceboat.

TREACLE. A thick, dark-coloured syrup, a by-product of sugar refining. Both treacle and syrup have the same food value.

Treacle Cake. See CAKES.

Treacle Sauce. See SAUCES.

Treacle Tart

Ingredients	*Method*
2 tbsp. golden syrup or treacle	Put the syrup or treacle into a basin with the breadcrumbs. Add the grated lemon rind and strained lemon juice. Mix well. Line a round open tin or plate with the short crust; prick the bottom, turn in the treacle mixture, cover with crossbars of pastry and bake at 400° F. Therm. 6 for about 20 or 30 mins., or until the pastry is cooked. Serve hot or cold.
2 tbsp. breadcrumbs (or cake crumbs)	
1 lemon	
½ lb. short crust pastry (see p. 375)	

TRIFLE

Ingredients	*Method*
1 large and 6 small sponge-cakes	Cut the cake into slices about 1″ thick and lay on the bottom of a glass dish. Spread with jam and lay the macaroons on them. Cover with spongecakes. Soak them with sherry and brandy for an hour or more. Cover with custard. Beat cream to stiff froth. Strain through a hair sieve and heap on the custard. See also **PUDDINGS** (p. 411).
Strawberry or other jam	
½ lb. macaroons	
1 wineglass each sherry and brandy	
1 pt. rich custard (see p. 188)	
1 pt. double cream	

TRIPE (Fr. *tripe*). The large stomach of ruminating animals, prepared for the cook. There are various kinds of tripe, such as Blanket, Honeycomb, etc., according to which part of the stomach is used. Tripe is usually bought ready prepared, in which case it simply requires washing and blanching. In the North of England it may be sold parcooked, tripe dressed in the South of England usually takes longer to cook tender. If, however, the tripe is not prepared, wash it well in tepid water, scrape with a knife, then rinse very thoroughly. Put into a pan with cold water to cover, bring to the boil, pour the water away, wash again, and continue this washing and blanching until it loses its unpleasant smell. When cold, return to the pan with fresh cold water, bring to the boil and simmer gently for 6 or 7 hrs., or until quite tender. The tripe must always be covered with water, adding more if necessary during boiling. When cooked, put the tripe with the liquid in which it was cooked into a basin and leave until the following day, when it can be used as desired.

TO BLANCH DRESSED TRIPE. Put the tripe into a saucepan with cold water to cover, bring to the boil and then strain. Again cover with water, or half water and half milk, and simmer very gently for about 2 hrs. when it may be used as desired.

Fricassée of Tripe

Ingredients	*Method*
2 lb. tripe	Prepare and cook the tripe, then cut into small squares. Wash, peel and trim mush-rooms, and cut into slices. Melt half the
½ lb. mushrooms	
1½ oz. butter or margarine	

[501]

Fricassée of Tripe (*continued*)

Stock
1 gill Tomato sauce
Salt and pepper
2 oz. breadcrumbs

margarine in a pan, add mushrooms and tripe and sauté together for about 10 mins. Pour in enough stock to just cover. Put the lid on the pan and simmer gently until mushrooms are tender. Add Tomato sauce and heat. Arrange neatly in a casserole or fireproof dish. Season well, sprinkle with breadcrumbs and brown in the oven or under a griller.

NOTE. Should no Tomato sauce be available, a few tomatoes rubbed through a sieve may be added to the sauce. Tripe may be curried by warming the cooked tripe in Curry sauce: serve in the centre of a border of boiled rice.

Tripe, Fried

Ingredients

1 lb. cooked tripe
Frying fat
Salt and pepper
Flour
Frying batter
Parsley
Maître d'Hôtel sauce (see p. 97)

Method

The tripe must be carefully prepared and cut into strips about 3″ long and cooked until tender. Drain well, dry with a cloth, sprinkle with salt and pepper and dip into flour. Have some frying batter ready; heat the fat in a deep saucepan to blue-smoke degree; dip pieces of tripe in batter, then drop into fat and fry until pale brown. Drain on soft paper and dish, piled on one another, on a doily on a hot dish. Garnish with fried parsley and serve with Maître d'Hôtel sauce.

NOTE. If desired, the pieces of tripe may be brushed over with egg and dipped in breadcrumbs instead of using the batter.

Tripe and Onions

Ingredients

2 lb. tripe
1 oz. flour
1 pt. milk
Salt and pepper
4 large onions
1 oz. butter

Method

Prepare the tripe as directed, then dip the pieces in the flour. Place them in a pan with milk and water and salt and pepper. Bring to boil and simmer gently for 15 mins. Peel, slice and parboil° onions in salted water, strain and add to the tripe, simmer all very gently for about 15 mins. or until onions are cooked. Add butter. Season well. Arrange neatly on a hot dish and garnish with sippets of toast.

Tripe, Spiced. Cut the tripe into small even-sized squares, and place in a deep pie-dish; add 2 or 3 cloves, a few peppercorns, a little grated onion and a spoonful or two of vinegar or wine. Leave for a few hours to marinate; then dip the tripe into batter and fry in deep fat to a golden brown. Serve garnished with crisply fried onions and watercress or parsley, accompanied by chutney.

TRITURATE. See COOKING TERMS.

TROTTERS. See LAMB'S FEET or PIG'S FEET.

TROUT (Fr. *truite*). Next to salmon the trout ranks the highest as a game fish. It belongs to the salmon tribe and the Salmon-trout or Sea-trout can only be distinguished from the salmon by its slighter gill cover and more numerous teeth. The Bull or Grey trout is distinguishable from the Salmon-trout by its teeth being larger and stronger, and flesh paler and not so delicate. The name covers the Salmon Peal of Devonshire and the Sewin of Wales. The Grey or Lake trout grows to a great size and is nearly equal to salmon in flavour. It is caught in Loch Leven. The best known species in Europe is the Rainbow trout. All trout should be cleaned and cooked as soon as possible after catching, as the extremely delicate flesh soon deteriorates. This delicious fish may be broiled, steamed, baked, grilled or fried. When the fish is preferred simply dressed, it is better to bake it (see FISH), as boiled trout is rather insipid. Serve with Hollandaise, Caper, Melted Butter, Mushroom, Piquant or other sauce as desired.

TROUT, BOILED. Thoroughly cleanse and dry the trout, split it down the back, season with a little salt, pepper, cayenne, lemon juice, and rub it over with a little salad oil. Place under a red-hot grill for 5–10 mins. or more, according to the size of the fish. Serve browned butter or any sauce as desired.

TROUT, FRIED. Split the fish in half and remove the bones; egg and breadcrumb, and fry in hot fat (see FISH, DEEP FRYING). Serve any sauce suitable for fried fish with it. Garnish with fried parsley.

TRUCKLE. This name is given to two different cheeses:
1. A blue-veined cheese made in Wiltshire from skimmed milk and similar to Blue Viney.
2. The full-cream loaf Cheddar, which is known as Truckle in the West of England.

TRUFFLES (Fr. *truffes*). There are three varieties of this fungus, black, red and white, which grow underground in England, France and Italy. They have an insidious individual flavour and perfume (smelt out by pigs and dogs). They grow underground, usually near a certain type of oak tree. Much used for cocktail savouries and garnishing.

TRUSSING. The appearance of certain foods depends very much upon the trussing, and the convenience in carving or serving is of the first importance. The simplest mode of trussing resembles that adopted by our ancestors, the Ancient Britons, who threaded pieces of meat on long wooden sticks or stakes upon which they toasted them in front of the fire. The French *aiguillette* and *attereau*, and the Turkish *kebob* are the present-day examples of this, and the same treatment is used for small birds which are threaded on long skewers or spits. When cooked in this way, they are termed *à la brochette*. Trussing means holding together, also transfixing in a certain position, e.g. kidneys for grilling, a spatchcock on which a fowl is split open. For methods of trussing, see individual entries of poultry, game, meat and fish.

TUNNY or TUNA. The largest fish of the mackerel family reaching 10 ft. in length. It lives in most warm seas and is caught in the Mediterranean, also for sport with rod and line off California and New Zealand. The flesh is firm, with a delicate flavour, and usually preserved in oil. Used mostly for hors d'œuvres.

TURBOT (Fr. *turbot*). The turbot, the king of flat-fish, is highly prized by epicures and deservedly so, for its flesh is white, delicate and deliciously flavoured. It weighs up to 40 lb. It is in season all the year round in some fisheries, but prime from March to August. It is a broad flat fish, thick and fleshy, with a gelatinous skin, the upper skin being dark and studded with shell-like bony tubercules and the under-skin usually white: the flesh should be firm and curdy without being hard or woolly. Cook according to rules for boiling, steaming or baking fish (see p. 213). Cook a small turbot in the oven. Dish on a folded napkin garnished with cut lemon, parsley and lobster coral. Serve Lobster, Shrimp, Hollandaise, Tartare, Horseradish or any other suitable sauce with it.
NOTE. The fins are not removed; they are considered a delicacy.

TURKEY (Fr. *dinde*, *dindon*). This large species of domestic fowl is really a native of North America; it was introduced into Europe in the 16th century and into England during the reign of Henry VIII. The turkey-poult (*dindon neau*), the young turkey with black, smooth legs and moderate size, is better flavoured than the large one. Old birds are known by the roughness and redness of their legs. A full-grown turkey will weigh from 8–12 lb.

TO PLUCK AND DRAW. Pluck the feathers—use a knife to remove fine feathers, and singe off all the down with a lighted taper or piece of lighted brown paper. Chop off the head and, should the turkey be for roasting, slip the skin back from the neck and chop off the neck close to the body, leaving skin long enough to fold over on to the back. Take out the windpipe, then pull the crop away from the skin on the neck and breast and cut off close to the opening into the body, taking care not to injure the skin. The crop should always be pulled out from the end of the neck rather than a cut in the skin which will have to be sewn up if made. Cut through the skin at about 2″ below the leg joint, bend the leg at the cut and by pressing it on to the table or board, break off the bone, and pull out the tendons (which must never be cut) one at a time, by pushing a finger through under them, or they may be taken out all at once by holding the foot of the bird in a door and pulling the leg, when the tendons will come out with the foot. The advantage gained by cutting the leg below the joint is that there is more length of bone left for tying and after the bird has been cooked, the pieces of bone are easily removed, leaving a clean, unburnt joint. Cut out oil bag at the tail and remove the inside.

TO TRUSS. For *roasting*, adopt the same method as under **CHICKEN**.

For *braising* or *boiling*, trussing differs from the former in that the legs are tucked under the apron as follows: Singe and draw the bird, cut the legs off at the first joint, pass the finger into the inside, raise the skin off the legs and tuck them under the apron of the bird. Pass a skewer through the joint of the wing and the middle of the leg and run it through the body and other leg and wing. Clean the liver and gizzard and tuck them in with the pinions. Turn the small end of the pinion on the back and fasten some twine over the ends of the legs to keep them in their place.

TO BONE. See **CHICKEN**.

Turkey, Roast

Ingredients	*Method*
1 turkey	Prepare and cook as roast chicken. Roast
Veal, Chestnut or Sausage	at 300° F. Therm. 2 for the times stated
stuffing (see **STUFFINGS**)	below. Serve with bread sauce, bacon
2 rashers of bacon	rolls and thick brown gravy.
Lemon	
½ lb. small sausages	

DRESSED TURKEY WEIGHT	OVEN TEMPERATURE	COOKING TIME
About 10 lb.	325° F. Therm. 3	3–3½ hrs.
,, 12–14 ,,	,, ,, 3	3½–4 ,,
,, 14–17 ,,	300° F. ,, 2	4–4½ ,,
,, 17 ,,	,, ,, 2	4½–5 ,,
,, 20 ,,	,, ,, 2	5–6 ,,

Turkey with Noodles and Rice

Ingredients

- 6 oz. noodles or rice
- 1 lb. diced cold turkey
- 1 oz. butter
- 2 oz. onion
- ¼ lb. mushrooms
- ½ lb. cooked green peas
- 2 pt. turkey cream sauce
- Breadcrumbs
- Butter
- Pepper and salt

Method

Cook the noodles or rice; cook the onion in butter, add the diced turkey, noodles or rice, mushrooms and peas. Blend with the sauce; add seasoning; pour into individual greased dishes or a casserole. Sprinkle with crumbs, dot with butter, and bake at 350° F. Therm. 4 for 20 mins.

TURMERIC. Powdered turmeric root or root stock is the ingredient to which curry powder owes its deep yellow colour. The tubers yield a resinous powder.

TURNIP (Fr. *navet*). This white bulbous root was introduced into England from Hanover during the reign of George I.

TO BOIL. Peel the turnip and cut into sections. Place into boiling salted water and cook until tender. This will take about 30 mins. (according to age and size). Drain and mash or rub through a sieve and mix the butter, pepper and salt. When turnips are served with boiled meat, cook them with it.

Turnip tops may be boiled for 15-20 mins., drained and served as a green vegetable.

TURTLE (Fr. *tortue*). The edible marine or sea tortoise. Green turtle, the large sea turtle, is the most highly prized delicacy. In addition to turtle soup, many other dishes are made from it. The turtle was first brought to England in the 17th century.

TUTTI FRUTTI. A confection of ice cream served with or flavoured with various fruits.

U

UDDER. The udder of a young cow or heifer is used in cooking for the purpose of wrapping up cromeskies. The udder of the cow, although more plentiful, is somewhat coarser and more strongly flavoured, but it is sometimes used especially for making a stew or ragoût when tripe is unobtainable.

UMBLES. See **HUMBLES.**

UNLEAVENED BISCUIT. A biscuit without raising agent.

UNLEAVENED BREAD. Bread that is made without any kind of leaven in it. See **YEAST.**

UTENSILS, for all kitchen utensils. See **KITCHEN UTENSILS.**

V

VALENCIA ALMONDS. See ALMONDS.

VANILLA. The vanilla plant, the pods of which are used for flavouring, belongs to the orchid tribe. The pod, bean or fruit is very long and thin, exhaling a powerful odour which has an intoxicating effect upon those who climb the trees to gather it. When ripe, the fruit forms two to six drops of liquid, having pungent aromatic odour and soft, spicy flavour. It is found in Mexico, also Honduras, Guinea, Brazil, Peru and Ceylon.

The uses of vanilla for flavouring are many. If the pods are used, they are simmered in the liquid, then removed, washed in cold water and carefully dried and put away for further use. The essence is used according to the type of mix (see SEASONING, p. 548). A few drops of vanilla added to any chocolate mix greatly enhances the flavour of the chocolate. For *Vanilla Sauce*, see SAUCES.

VEAL (Fr. *veau*). Veal is the flesh of a calf. When selecting, see that the fat over the kidneys is plentiful and white and firm; when this fat softens, the meat is stale. The veins of the shoulder should be blue or bright red; when they are any other colour, the meat is not freshly killed. If the flesh is clammy and spotted, it is unwise to use it. Veal is in season from May to September.

JOINTS OF VEAL. The calf is usually cut into the following joints:

The hindquarter is cut up into:
1. The knuckles.
2. The fillet.
3. Loin with its chump.
4. The best end containing the kidney and the kidney fat.

The forequarter is cut into:
5. The breast with its best end.
6. The brisket, which contains the sweetbread.
7. The neck with its best end.
8. The scrag.
9. The shoulder or oyster.
10. Fore-knuckle.
11. Head.

TO ROAST. Allow 25 mins. per lb. and 25 mins. over.

Veal Cutlets Baked with Sweet Herbs. Put into a saucepan some chopped mushrooms, sweet herbs, winter savory and shallots with 1½ oz. butter and some salt and pepper. Stir over a low heat until well mixed and hot. Trim the cutlets and then spread them over with the mixture. Brush with beaten egg and coat with grated breadcrumbs. Lay the cutlets on a baking dish and bake them at 350° F. Therm. 4 until lightly browned. Pour into a saucepan a cup of white wine, add a little blended flour and the remainder of the herbs and bring to the boil. Skim and, when cooked, lay the cutlets on a hot dish, pour sauce round and serve.

Veal with Chestnuts

Ingredients	*Method*
2 lb. veal trimmed and chopped into even-sized pieces 1 pt. stock or milk 2 shallots	Brown the veal in a little butter, add half the stock to pan, add shallots cut up, the bay leaf and basil. Season with salt and pepper and cover. Turn into a casserole and bake slowly for an hour at 260° F.

[507]

Veal with Chestnuts (*continued*)

1 bay leaf
Pinch of basil
Salt and pepper
¾ lb. peeled and sliced large
mushrooms
1 tbsp. butter extra
1 lb. chestnuts
2 tbsp. flour and butter
2 or 3 tbsp. sherry
1–2 tbsp. cream

Therm. ½. In the meantime peel and slice the mushrooms, and sauté in the tbsp. butter; prick the chestnuts, blanch them in boiling water, then peel and cut into slices, and cook in a little milk. Blend flour and butter, add second cup of stock (including mushroom liquid); add sherry, stir until almost thickened. Add to casserole, and cook very gently for a further half-hour. Before serving, stir in a spoonful or two of cream if desired.

Veal and Ham Pie

Ingredients

1½ lb. veal fillet
¼ lb. bacon or ham
1 hard-boiled egg
1 tsp. salt
1 tsp. chopped parsley (if
desired)
Pepper
Stock
6 oz. flaky or rough puff
pastry (see pp. 371 & 374)
Gelatine

Method

Cut the meat into pieces, dice bacon or ham, slice egg, place in pie dish in layers, with seasoning. Add sufficient stock to half fill the dish. Cover with pastry and cook 1½ hr. in a moderate oven (350° F. Therm. 4). Fill up with stock. If the pie is to be served cold, add gelatine to stock, allow ¼ oz. gelatine to ½ pt. stock.

Veal and Ham Pie (Raised) may be made if desired, allowing 6 oz. hot water crust; 8 oz. veal; 2 oz. bacon; 1 hard-boiled egg; grating lemon rind; salt and pepper; 1 tbsp. water. See **PASTE AND PASTRY** (p. 369).

VEGETABLES (Fr. *légumes*). The distinction between vegetable and fruit is sometimes difficult to make. In a culinary sense, vegetables are usually cooked savoury and fruits are associated with sweets. Amongst the fruits which are called vegetables in the kitchen are tomatoes, vegetable marrows, peas, beans, etc. Some vegetables have a special appeal when served with a specific dish, and today vegetables are frequently used dressed in varied forms as the main dish. Vegetables must be fresh. When they are stale they lose both bulk and flavour.

Cooked vegetables as accompaniments require to be served hot (hence the necessity for dishes with tight-fitting lids). Those made of metal retain heat longer, as well as the steam, which keeps the vegetables moist and well-flavoured.

Root Vegetables. These offer scope for the exercise of skill and ingenuity as they may be cut into numerous shapes and designs for both soups and garnishes, e.g., flowers, rounds, olives, lozenge shapes, ovals, spirals and curls. These require special tools for their production, scoops, stamps and cutters (see p. 306).

Fresh vegetables are at their best at certain seasons of the year, but bottled, canned, frozen or dehydrated vegetables can be obtained all the year round (see individual headings).

TO CLEAN VEGETABLES. Soak in salted water, always turning cabbages and cauliflowers upside down. All grit and dirt must be removed and a wire sieve is used for this purpose. It can be dipped again and again into a vessel of deep water, the vegetables in it being shaken and rinsed. A colander is used for draining vegetables.

VEGETABLE COOKING TIMES

VEGETABLE	METHOD OF COOKING	TIME	PRESSURE COOKING TIME 15 LB. PRESSURE
Artichokes: Jerusalem Globe	Boiled Boiled	30–40 mins. 15–20 mins.	10 mins. 6–10 mins.
Asparagus	Steamed	About 20–30 mins	2–4 mins.
Aubergine	Boiled	About 15 mins.	3 mins.
Beans: Broad French Runner	Boiled do. Stewed Boiled	15–20 mins. do. About 30 mins. 20–25 mins.	3 mins. do. 2 mins.
Beetroot	Boiled	According to size 1¼–1½ hrs.	According to size 10–15 mins.
Broccoli	Boiled	10–15 mins.	2–3 mins.
Brussels Sprouts	Boiled	10–15 mins.	2 mins.
Cabbage	Boiled Steamed	10–15 mins. 20–25 mins.	2–3 mins.
Carrots	Boiled	20 mins.	3–8 mins.
Cauliflower	Steamed Boiled Steamed in flowerets	30–40 mins. 30–35 mins. 15–20 mins.	2–5 mins.
Celeriac	Boiled	20–30 mins.	3 mins.
Celery	Boiled Stewed or Braised Steamed	20–30 mins. 30–40 mins. 40–45 mins.	3 mins.
Chicory	Boiled Braised or Stewed	20–30 mins. 35–40 mins.	3 mins. 3 mins.
Corn on the Cob	Boiled	15 mins.	4 mins.
Cucumber	Boiled or Stewed	20–30 mins.	1 min.
Curly Kale	Boiled	15–20 mins.	2–3 mins.
Endive	Boiled	15–20 mins.	2–3 mins.
Kohl-Rabi	Boiled	15–20 mins.	8 mins.

VEGETABLE COOKING TIMES (*continued*)

VEGETABLE	METHOD OF COOKING	TIME	PRESSURE COOKING TIME 15 LB. PRESSURE
Leeks	Boiled Braised or Stewed	15–20 mins. 20–30 mins.	3 mins.
Lettuce	Boiled Braised	Young—about 10 mins. Old—20–25 mins. 20–30 mins.	
Onions	Boiled Braised or Stewed Baked Fried	20–30 mins. 30–40 mins. About 30 mins. A few mins.	6 mins.
Parsnips	Boiled Baked or Steamed	20–30 mins. 30–40 mins.	3–8 mins.

Peas:
  fresh
  dried
	Boiled
	Boiled
		10–15 mins.
		15 mins.
			$\frac{1}{2}$–$1\frac{1}{2}$ mins.

Potatoes:
  new
  old
	Boiled
	Boiled
	Baked in jacket
	
	Baked
	Steamed
	Fried (Shallow)
		15–20 mins.
		30–40 mins.
		According to
		  size 1–1$\frac{1}{2}$ hrs.
		$\frac{1}{2}$–1 hr.
		45 mins.–1 hr.
		10 mins.
			3–8 mins.

Salsify	Boiled	30 mins.	5 mins.
Sea Kale	Boiled Braised or Stewed Steamed	20–30 mins. 30–40 mins. 40–45 mins.	3–6 mins.
Spinach	Boiled	10–15 mins.	1 min.
Spring Greens	See CABBAGE		
Swedes	Boiled Steamed	About 30 mins. 45–50 mins.	
Tomatoes	Boiled Baked Stuffed and Baked Fried Stewed	About 5 mins. 10–15 mins. 15–20 mins. About 5 mins. 15–20 mins.	$\frac{1}{2}$–1 min.

VEGETABLE COOKING TIMES (*continued*)

VEGETABLE	METHOD OF COOKING	TIME	PRESSURE COOKING TIME 15 LB. PRESSURE
Turnips	Boiled	35–40 mins.	3–8 mins.
Vegetable Marrow	Boiled Steamed Baked	15–20 mins. About 30 mins. About 35 mins.	2 mins.
Zucchini	Boiled Steamed	About 5 mins.	2–3 mins.

VEGETABLES, TO PRESERVE. See under **FRUIT** (p. 229-238).

VEGETABLE SALAD SUGGESTIONS (FOR DRESSINGS SEE SALAD DRESSINGS):

ASPARAGUS
Slip 3 cooked asparagus tips through a ring of green pepper and arrange on lettuce leaf with diced carrots and celery. Dress with mayonnaise.

BEANS, COOKED, FRENCH OR RUNNER
Mix together cooked whole or sliced green beans, diced carrots, celery, chopped parsley. Dress with French dressing and mayonnaise mixed.
Mix together cooked sliced green beans, finely chopped spring onions and sliced radishes. Dress with a thick French dressing.
Mix green beans (cooked) finely shredded cabbage, chopped onion, diced celery. Dress with French dressing with little minced onion, chopped parsley and red and green pepper.
Mix cooked green beans, small pieces of cauliflower and sliced carrot. Dress with French dressing with little minced onion, chopped parsley, red and green peppers.

BEETROOT
Mix diced cooked beets (previously marinated in vinegar), with chopped celery, green pepper, little onion, salt, pimento and paprika. Dress with half French dressing and half mayonnaise.
Mix chopped beets, previously marinated, with finely shredded cabbage, diced celery, sweet pickle, salt and paprika. Dress with Sour Cream dressing.
Mix diced beetroot, cucumber, little onion, sweet pickle, salt and pepper. Dress with mayonnaise, adding a little Worcester sauce, dash cayenne and onion juice.
Mix diced beetroot, chopped pickles and little salt on bed of shredded cabbage. Dress with French dressing and mayonnaise, in equal quantities.
Mix chopped celery, sweet pickle, onion and mayonnaise and stuff large cooked beetroots. Dress with mayonnaise.
Mix diced beetroot, rings of spring onion, and hard boiled egg, coarsely chopped. Dress with mayonnaise with minced onion, little chopped hard-boiled egg.

CABBAGE
Mix shredded cabbage, hard-boiled eggs and nuts. Dress with mayonnaise and French dressing mixed.
Mix shredded cabbage, chopped green peppers, diced carrots and salt. Dress with mayonnaise.
Mix shredded cabbage, diced celery and raw shredded beetroot. Dress with mayonnaise.
Mix shredded cabbage with diced raw apple. Dress with French dressing and mayonnaise mixed.
Mix shredded cabbage with vinegar, salt and sugar, adding, if desired, a little grated horseradish.

CARROT

Mix fine strips of raw carrot, celery, cucumber and green pepper. Dress with mayonnaise.

Mix diced cooked carrots, chopped cucumber, celery, little onion and salt. Dress with mayonnaise and French dressing in equal proportions.

CAULIFLOWER

Mix cooked cauliflower, diced cooked carrot, cooked green peas, sliced stuffed olives. Dress with a thick French dressing.

Arrange marinated raw cauliflower and sliced tomatoes on bed of lettuce. Dress with French dressing.

Arrange marinated raw cauliflower and rings of carrot on lettuce and sprinkle with grated cheese. Dress with French dressing.

CUCUMBER

Arrange ½″ wedges of cucumber with sections of tomatoes. Dress with French dressing on mayonnaise.

Slice thinly a cucumber and place on bed of watercress. Sprinkle with paprika. Dress with French dressing or Sour Cream dressing.

LETTUCE

Mix shredded lettuce with sliced cucumber, sliced tomato, rings of spring onions and rounds of radish. Dress with French dressing or mayonnaise.

PEAS

Mix cooked green peas, diced celery, cheese and pickle and place on lettuce leaves. Dress with mayonnaise and French dressing mixed.

POTATO. See SALADS.

SPINACH

Serve raw spinach leaves coarsely chopped. Dress with mayonnaise with little onion juice, chopped parsley, red and green peppers and finely chopped, hard-boiled egg added.

TOMATO

Stuff tomatoes with cottage cheese, accompany with curls of celery. Add Sour Cream dressing.

Mix diced celery, salt, chopped green pepper and mayonnaise, and stuff large tomatoes. Add Sour Cream dressing or mayonnaise.

Remove tops of tomatoes, place piece of cauliflower in top. Dress with mayonnaise with finely chopped, hard-boiled egg, minced onion, chopped parsley and dash of cayenne added.

Thick slices of tomato on bed of lettuce, with diced celery and apple on top. Cover with French dressing.

Vegetable Soups. See SOUPS.

VEGETABLE MARROW (Fr. *courge*). The earliest vegetable marrow plants bore fruits shaped somewhat like an egg. By cultivation, however, they have assumed quite a different character. They are watery without much nutriment, but have a fine mellow flavour. Marrows are in season from June to August.

VEGETABLE MARROW, BOILED. Cut, peel and remove seeds and pith. To each 1 lb. prepared marrow, allow pinch of salt, 1 oz. butter or margarine, and 3–4 tbsp. water. Cover with well-fitting lid, or add piece of paper and shut lid on it. Bring to the boil and simmer until tender, about 20 mins. Thicken and use liquid for sauce, adding a little extra milk.

VEGETABLE MARROW WITH BACON. Peel, clean and cook in butter until soft (this will take about 50 mins.). Season to taste, add 3 tsp. butter, mash well and serve with crisp rashers of bacon.

VEGETABLE MARROW SAUTÉD WITH SOUR CREAM. Peel and cut 4 lb. marrow into match-like strips. Sprinkle with 2 tsp. salt, leave 1 hr. Drain and sauté in 2 oz. butter until almost soft (this will take about 15 mins.). Stir in 2 tsp. flour mixed to a paste with sour cream. Add more sour cream, about 1 pt. in all, then add 2 finely chopped onions and simmer for 5 mins. Stir carefully. Serve at once, garnished with dusting of paprika and a little chopped parsley. Sufficient for 6 persons. Peeled and dried tomatoes may be added to the pan during simmering, if desired.

Vegetable Marrow Jam

Ingredients	Method
12 lb. marrow	Peel marrow and cut into 2″ cubes.
4 lemons	Squeeze juice from lemons and cut rind
12 lb. sugar	very thinly. Place marrow and lemon
3 oz. bruised ginger	juice and rind in large bowl with the sugar
8 oz. candied peel, finely	and allow to stand for 24 hrs. Place
chopped	mixture in preserving pan, add ginger and
	boil for 1½ hrs. Add peel, pour into
	warmed jars and cover when cool.

VEGETABLE MARROW FLOWERS. These can be gathered in full bloom and treated in the following way. Wash the flowers thoroughly and fill with a mixture of half-cooked rice, chopped veal, onions, and sweet herbs formed into a paste with egg. Place in a saucepan, cover with stock and simmer gently for 30 mins. Remove, drain and serve.

VELOUTÉ SAUCE. See SAUCES.

VENDACE. A white fish or freshwater herring found only in the Lake District and Dumfriesshire.

VENISON (Fr. *venaison*). Under this title might be included the flesh of all kinds of deer. Of these the Fallow, or Park deer of England is considered superior to all. The buck comes into season in May and continues prime until September, when the doe venison comes into season, continuing until Christmas. In Scotland the Roebuck abounds, and in Ireland the Red deer.

TO CHOOSE. When purchasing venison, care should be taken to see that the fat is clear, bright and thick, and the cleft of the hoof smooth and close. To ascertain if the meat is fresh, run a sharp narrow knife or small skewer into the shoulder or haunch close to the bone. The smell of the skewer will give the necessary information, as it is customary to keep venison a long time to bring out the game flavour. In venison which is carefully treated and hung, the vein in the neck should be bluish, not green or yellow. A faint smell in the hindquarter or under the kidney indicates stale meat.

JOINTS.

The hindquarters are cut into:
1. The leg.
2. The loin.
3. The leg and loin together constitute the haunch.

The forequarters are cut into:
4. The neck.
5. The best end of the neck.
6. The breast.
7. The head.
8. The shoulder.
The feet are usually thrown away.

TO KEEP. If received fresh in the first instance, wipe it dry, dust over with a floury cloth and hang it end upwards in a cool, airy place. If desired to keep it a long time, use a little powdered ginger instead of flour. Should the meat be a little musty, wash it first with lukewarm water and then lukewarm milk and water. Wipe it perfectly dry and dust with powdered ginger, as before.

Venison Steak, Broiled

Ingredients	Method
Venison steak	Marinate the venison in salad oil and
Salad oil	lemon juice—the stronger the venison the
Lemon juice	longer the marination. Drain without

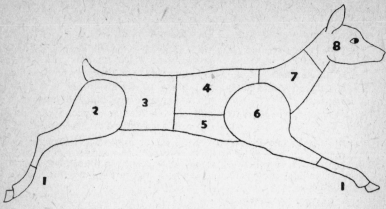

1. The Feet are usually thrown away
2. The Leg
3. The Loin. The leg and loin together constitute the haunch
4. Back Ribs
5. The Breast
6. The Shoulder
7. The best end of the Neck
8. The Head

Venison Steak, Broiled (*continued*)

Salt and paprika

wiping and broil. Turn over. This takes just a few minutes longer than broiling beefsteak. Sprinkle with salt and paprika. Serve on a very hot platter with wine sauce made as follows:

Simmer together for 5 mins., 1 tbsp. butter, 4 oz. redcurrant jelly, juice of ½ lemon, 5 oz. water, 3 cloves, 1 tsp. salt, dash of cayenne. Strain and add 4 oz. port wine and a little of the meat gravy.

Venison Stew. Heat 1 tbsp. lard in a saucepan, add 2 diced onions, 4 red peppers, chopped, and a small piece of garlic. Cover, and cook for 5 mins. Add 2 lb. venison cut into neat small chunks, and fry till golden brown, then add sufficient hot water to cover. Cook very slowly over a low heat, season with a little salt to taste and thicken the gravy with a little flour blended with milk; reheat until thickened. Add, if desired, half a wineglass of sherry or claret.

VERMICELLI (Fr. *vermicelle*). The literal meaning of this term is "little worms", which vermicelli resembles. It is made of Italian paste (a dough of wheat flour), forced through cylinders or pipes until it takes a slender, worm-like form when it is dried. Principally used in soups and milk puddings. See **MACARONI** for cooking method.

VICTORIA SANDWICH. See CAKES.

VINEGAR (Fr. *vinaigre*). Literally "sour (or acid) wine". Made in various countries from apples, sugar, grain, or from cheap and inferior wines. Malt forms the chief substance from which the ordinary table vinegar is made in England.

[514]

Vinegar, Spiced Pickling

Ingredients	*Method*
1 qt. vinegar	Place all together in a saucepan; bring to
½ tsp. cloves	the boil, remove from heat and leave to
Small piece root ginger	infuse for 3 hrs. Strain and use.
2 chilli pods	
2 blades mace	
1″ stick cinnamon	
½ tsp. each peppercorns and	
allspice	

Vinegar Whey. Put ½ pt. each milk and water into a saucepan with 1 tbsp. caster sugar and boil. Pour sufficient vinegar in the milk to form a curd. Boil it up again then strain through a jelly bag and serve the whey while hot.

VIOLETS. These sweet-smelling and pleasantly flavoured flowers hold a prominent position in confectionery. The petals are also used in salads.
Candied Violets. Choose double violets and pick off the green stalk. Clarify and boil some loaf sugar to the "blow degree" (see **SUGAR**), then put in the violets and let the sugar again boil to the blow. Draw the pan from the heat and rub the sugar against the sides of the pan until the sugar separates from the violets. Sift and put them in a gentle heat to dry.

VITAMINS. See FOOD VALUES.

VOL-AU-VENT. A round or oval case which is made of puff pastry filled with a rich ragoût of cooked meat, game, chicken, sweetbread, shellfish, oysters and sometimes fruit. See **PASTE AND PASTRY** (p. 374).

W

WAFER. Thin crisp, sweet biscuit eaten with ice cream.

WAFER PAPER. Used in cookery for covering some kinds of sweetmeats or to form a basis upon which sugary biscuits, such as macaroons, are laid.

WAFFLE (Fr. *gaufre*). A waffle is a soft, indented cake made in irons or tongs specially constructed for the purpose.

TO MAKE. Take 2 cups warm milk. Place in a basin and mix in 2 oz. butter, 2 beaten eggs, a little grated nutmeg, crushed loaf sugar and sufficient flour to form the whole into a stiff paste. Add 1 lb. yeast and put into warm place to rise. Let it remain for 2–3 hrs. Work it softly and lightly and then leave to rise again for ½ hr. longer. Put about 2 lb. of this paste into waffle irons which should be hot and well-greased. Close the irons and bake for a few mins. Turn the waffles out when they are a light colour. Serve with sugar or syrup, maple syrup preferably.

WALDORF SALD. See SALADS.

WALNUT (Fr. *noix*). This nut was originally imported from Persia. It is a prime favourite for dessert or as an accompaniment to wine. The trees sometimes grow to an enormous size and age, bearing prolifically season after season. If the green fruit is picked for pickling, those nuts left to ripen greatly increase in size. Of the varieties of walnuts best known to our markets are, the oval, egg-shaped one, the large square with small fruit, and the elongated nut, but the kernel of this is not very fine in flavour. The Titmouse walnut is soft-shelled and a small bird can peck through it. The Long-beaked walnut has an elongation at the flower end of the shell. Walnut oil soon turns rancid and the refuse matter left after the oil is extracted is eaten in Switzerland and known as *pain amen*.

Walnuts can be preserved from one year to another by removing the green husks, drying the shells thoroughly and then packing the nuts in layers in boxes and covering with dried silver sand. When wanted for use, wipe them with a clean cloth. If the walnut kernels are shrivelled, soak them in milk for an hour or two.

WALNUTS, TO KEEP

1. Fill an earthenware pot with them and cover with clay 1″ thick. At Christmastime they will be found as fresh as when first gathered.

2. Put the walnuts into a common earthenware jar with an earthenware lid, and bury the jar in the earth about 1 ft. deep in a place not too wet or too dry.

3. Gather the walnuts on a dry day, and directly the walnuts are taken out of the rind, put them into large flower-pots holding two pecks (any pans, however, will do as well), and when nearly full cover the pots 2″ thick with sawdust. Place the pots on the floor in a wine cellar.

TO FRESHEN OLD NUTS FOR DESSERT. Place the nuts into an earthen pan and pour over them as much cold water, slightly salted, as will cover them. Leave until the next day and rub them dry before using them.

TO USE WALNUT VINEGAR. The vinegar covering pickled walnuts is useful for flavouring the gravy used for hashes of cold meat. It is also excellent when used in pickle.

WALNUTS, BRANDIED. Choose rather under-ripe walnuts; shell and peel them carefully so as not to break them. Plunge into cold water to blanch and harden them. Then put them into a pan of fast-boiling water to scald them (leave just long enough for the water to reboil). Drain and place in cold water, adding a squeeze of lemon juice. Have a syrup ready boiled to "thread" (see SUGAR), put into a bowl, and pour this over them. Leave overnight, drain off syrup and reboil to thread. Pour over walnuts, leave overnight and repeat on third day. Fourth day boil syrup to strong thread and put nuts into another pan. Add syrup and brandy in equal proportions. Boil up and turn into jars. Cork securely.

WALNUTS, PICKLED. (To be made from the beginning to the middle of July.) Be very particular to gather the green walnuts when they are in a proper state for pickling, neither too soon nor too late. If they are too young, they will dissolve in the pickle, if too old, they will resist the action of the vinegar. They ought to be taken before the shells have begun to form; they are right if a large pin can, without difficulty, be pushed through them in every direction. If once the shell can be felt, they are no longer fit for pickling. Wipe the walnuts separately with a coarse cloth; put them into an earthen pan, and pour on them a strong brine that will float a fresh egg. This brine may be made by boiling 6 oz. salt with 1 qt. water. It should be skimmed carefully and allowed to get cold before being put to the walnuts. Lay a thin board upon the walnuts to keep them under the brine. Turn them about with a wooden spoon every day, and let them remain for 6 days. Then drain them and pour fresh brine on them. Leave them from 3–6 days longer, drain in a colander, and put them in the sun in a single layer on a large dish covered with coarse sackcloth. They will turn black in a few hours. Turn them over once or twice, handling them gently. Boil as much vinegar as will entirely cover the walnuts, with spices in the proportion of 2 oz. whole ginger bruised, 2 oz. black pepper, 4 blades mace, 2 oz. mustard seed, 8 cloves stuck into 4 shallots, or small onions, and 1 tsp. salt to ½ gall. vinegar. 1 dsp. scraped horseradish and 2 capsicums are sometimes added, but they destroy the flavour of the pickle. Boil the vinegar for 10 mins. put the walnuts into unglazed jars or wide-mouthed bottles and when the vinegar is cool, pour it upon them and divide the spices equally amongst the bottles. When cold, tie them over with moistened bladder or with strong brown paper. As the walnuts soak up the vinegar, boil a little additional vinegar without spices, and pour it cold upon them. They must be kept entirely covered with vinegar. They will be ready for use in 3 months, but will improve with keeping. If wanted for early use, pierce once throughout both ways with a needle, leave them in the brine fully 12 days and pour the vinegar upon them boiling hot. Allow about a fortnight to make this pickle.

WALNUTS FOR SALAD. Gather the young walnuts when the nut is just formed, and when they can be pierced easily with a pin. Pare them down to the kernels, put them into a salad bowl, pour a little good salad sauce over them, toss them lightly in it, and serve immediately. This salad, though very agreeable, can only be had in places where walnuts grow abundantly.

Walnut Cake. See CAKES.

Walnut Jam. Take 50 walnuts in which the shell has not begun to form, prick them all over, and boil in water until they are quite soft. Strain off the water, put a clove in each and sprinkle over them 2 oz. bruised ginger. Make a syrup of ½ pt. water to 2½ lb. coarse brown sugar, stirring over heat until all is dissolved; then put in the walnuts and boil for 20 mins., stirring to prevent them burning. This jam forms an excellent laxative and may be elevated to the position of a pleasant domestic medicine.

Walnut Ketchup

Ingredients
100 green walnuts
¼ lb. shallots
3 garlic cloves
2 qt. vinegar
¼ lb. salt
3 oz. anchovies
2 oz. whole pepper
½ oz. cloves
½ oz. mace

Method
Bruise the walnuts thoroughly in a mortar, then put them into a pan with the shallots sliced, the garlic, vinegar and salt, and let it stand for 2 wks., stirring 2 or 3 times a day. Strain away the liquor after this time and put into an enamelled saucepan with anchovies, whole pepper, cloves and mace. Boil for ½ hr., skimming well. Strain and bottle when cold.

WASSAIL or WASTLE CAKE. (Scottish). An oat cake. It is baked on a girdle which is analogous to the griddle, or English girdle.

WATER. A transparent fluid composed of oxygen and hydrogen. Water produces neither heat nor energy, so it cannot be classified as food, though without it all vital action would cease.

WATERCRESS (Fr. *cresson de fontaine*). An aquatic plant which is used for salads and garnishing, etc. Originally found growing wild, but since 1808 it has been cultivated. There are three varieties of watercress—the Small Brown-leaved, the Large Brown-leaved, and the Green-leaved. The Large Brown-leaved is thought to be the best. See also CRESSES.

WATER RAIL. Also known as Water Crake or Spotted Gallimus; it is dressed and served like widgeon.

WATER SOUCHET. Name derived from the Dutch word *waterzoetje*. A fish stew served in a vegetable dish or soup tureen, and eaten with a spoon.

WEDDING CAKE. See CAKES (p. 107).

WEEVER (Fr. *vive*). A sea-fish of the perch family with a number of sharp spines along the back and which cause painful wounds if they pierce the skin. Other names for weevers are Stingbull and Seacat. It is mostly found in the Mediterranean but sometimes as far north as Scandinavia.

WEIGHTS AND MEASURES. Accurate measurements are essential to consistently good cookery: the maxim of "a little of this" and "a little of that" may, sometimes, prove successful, but it is very uncertain. In standard measurements the spoon should be *level*, not rounded. If cups are used, instead of scales, proper measuring cups should be used as household cups vary in size. Careless measuring usually means not only a failure, but waste of money and ingredients, loss of time and energy.

To measure for accuracy, either use scales and weigh up the ingredients and measure the liquid, or else use a half-pint measuring cup, teaspoons and tablespoons, always with level measurements, levelling or scraping them with a knife. To measure a part of a cup, follow the numbers on the cup.

All dry ingredients should be sifted before measuring as they are apt to lump.

Fats which are solid, like butter, lard, margarine, and dripping, must be packed down before levelling off. When the word *melted* follows the word *fat*, it means measured and then melted; when it is melted fat, it means the fat is melted before the measuring.

For half-spoonfuls of any dry ingredients or solid fat, fill the spoon *quite full*. If it is a dry ingredient, *level it off*, then measure it lengthwise of the spoon into halves, scraping off the unused half. When measuring solid fat, pack it into the spoon then level it off. For a fourth or quarter of a spoonful, first measure a half and then divide it. This simplified table (spoon measurements level) will help when measuring dry ingredients.

> 1 saltspoon equals ¼ teaspoon
> 1 wineglass equals 4 tablespoons or ¼ cup
> 2 teaspoons equal 1 dessertspoon
> 2 dessertspoons equal 1 tablespoon
> 4 teaspoons equal 1 tablespoon
> 1 gill equals ½ cup
> 16 tablespoons equal 1 cup (8 fluid oz.)
> 2 cups equal 1 pt.
> 4 cups equal 1 qt.
> 16 cups equal 1 gall.
> Standard measuring cup: 10 oz.–20 oz.
> American measuring cup: 8 oz.–16 oz.

When adjusting a recipe work out the difference in ingredients and note them in the margin for future reference.

Avoirdupois Weight

16 drachms	=	1 ounce
16 ounces	=	1 pound
14 pounds	=	1 stone
28 pounds	=	1 quarter
4 quarters	=	1 hundredweight
20 hundredweights	=	1 ton

Dry Measure

2 pints	=	1 quart
8 quarts	=	1 peck
4 pecks	=	1 bushel
3 bushels	=	1 sack
12 sacks	=	1 chaldron
8 bushels	=	1 quarter
5 quarters	=	1 load

Liquid Measure

4 gills	=	1 pint
2 pints	=	1 quart
4 quarts	=	1 gallon
$31\frac{1}{2}$ gallons	=	1 barrel
2 barrels	=	1 hogshead

AMERICAN WEIGHTS AND MEASURES. An American measuring cup — 8 oz. or $\frac{1}{2}$ lb. and the following table of equivalents will help you to translate the required amount of ingredients given in the recipes. All measurements are level unless otherwise stated.

		Cups		*lbs.*
Almonds	chopped	1	=	1
Apricots	dried	3	=	1
Butter		2 ($\frac{1}{4}$ cup = 2 oz.)	=	1
Cocoa		4	=	1
Coconut		5	=	1
Cheese	dry	4	=	1
,,	freshly grated	5	=	1
Cottage cheese		2	=	1
Fat		2	=	1
Dates		2	=	1

Eggs	whole	5	=	1 cup
Egg white	about	8	=	1 ,,
Egg yolk	about	16	=	1 ,,
Figs	chopped	3 cups	=	1 lb.
Flour or bread		4 ,,	=	1 ,,
Cake	sifted	$4\frac{1}{2}$,,	=	1 ,,
Lemon juice		1	=	2—3 tablespoons
Macaroni (Long)		4 ,,	=	1 lb.
Margarine	level	2 ,,	=	1 ,,
Meat	diced	2 ,,	=	1 ,,
Milk		2 ,,	=	1 ,,
Noodles	raw	1 ,,	=	$1\frac{1}{4}$ cups cooked
Orange juice		1 ,,	=	6—8 tablespoons
Prunes	dried	$2\frac{1}{2}$,,	=	1 lb.
,,	cooked	4 ,,	=	1 ,,
Raisins	seedless	3 ,,	=	1 ,,
Rice	raw	1 ,,	=	3—4 cups cooked
Sugar	brown	$2\frac{1}{4}$,,	=	1 lb.
	(finely packed)			
,,	granulated	2 ,,	=	1 ,,
Syrup		1 ,,	=	1 ,,
Walnuts	shelled	2 ,,	=	$1\frac{1}{4}$,,
Water		2 ,,	=	1 ,,

$\frac{1}{8}$ pt. = $\frac{1}{2}$ gill = 4 tablespoons.
$\frac{1}{4}$ pt. = 1 gill = 8 tablespoons.

Cheese grated Rolled oats Flour	4 level tablespoons = 1 oz.
Cocoa Cornflour Butter	2 level tablespoons = 1 oz.
Fat Margarine	2 level tablespoons = 1 oz.
Jam Syrup	1 level tablespoon = 1 oz.

1 oz. — approximately = 30 grams.
1 lb. or 16 oz. — approximately = 454 grams.

$\frac{1}{2}$ cup less 1 tablespoon butter (7 tablespoons) = 100 grams.
$\frac{3}{4}$ cup less 1 tablespoon all purpose flour (11 tablespoons) = 100 grams.
$\frac{1}{2}$ cup less 1 tablespoon sugar (7 tablespoons) = 100 grams.

French Weights and Measures. In France and other parts of the Continent, a system of weighing and measuring is used based upon the decimal or multiple of ten plan.

MEASURES OF CAPACITY are calculated from the LITRE which is about 1$\frac{3}{4}$ (1·7598) British pints.

the	10th part of a litre	..	..	..	..	1 decilitre
	100th part of a litre	..	..	..	..	1 centilitre
	1,000th part of of a litre	..	..	..	..	1 millilitre
	10 litres	..	..	..	..	..	1 decalitre
	100 litres	..	..	..	..	..	1 hectolitre
	1,000 litres	..	..	..	..	..	1 kilolitre
	10,000 litres	..	..	..	..	..	1 myrialitre

MEASURES OF WEIGHT are calculated from the GRAMME which is nearly equal to 15 (15·43235) British grains.

the	10th part of a gramme	..	..	..	..	1 decigramme
	100th part of a gramme	..	..	..	..	1 centigramme
	1,000th part of a gramme	..	..	..	..	1 milligramme
	10 grammes	..	..	..	..	..	1 decagramme
	100 grammes	..	..	..	..	..	1 hectogramme
	1,000 grammes	..	..	..	..	..	1 kilogramme
	10,000 grammes	..	..	..	..	..	1 myriagramme

Scotch dry measure

4 lippies	..	..	..	..	..	..	1 peck
4 pecks	..	..	..	..	..	..	1 firlot
4 firlots	..	..	..	..	..	..	1 boll
2 bolls	..	..	..	..	..	..	1 quarter
A boll of meal	..	..	..	..	..	140 lb.
2 bolls	..	..	..	..	..	1 sack
On the bower a boll	..	..	..	..	6 firlots

Special Weights

1 stone of butcher's meat	..	..	..	..	..	8 lb.
1 firkin of butter	..	..	..	..	..	56 lb.
1 barrel of butter equals 4 firkins equals 224 lb.						
1 box of fish about	..	..	..	..	..	90 lb.
1 barrel of raisins	..	..	..	..	..	112 lb.
1 sack of flour	..	..	..	..	..	280 lb. or 5 bushels of 56 lb. each
1 sack of potatoes	..	..	..	..	..	168 lb. or 3 bushels of 56 lb. each
1 peck or stone of flour	..	..	..	..	..	14 lb.

1 gallon of flour .. .. 7 lb.
1 quart of flour .. .. 32 lb.

Beer Measures
1 Tun .. .. 3 barrels
1 Firkin .. .. 9 gall.
1 Anker .. ..7½–10 gall.
1 Kilderkin .. .. 18 gall.
1 Barrel .. .. 36 gall.
1 Hogshead (rarely used) .. .. 54 gall.
1 Puncheon .. .. 72 gall.
1 Butt .. .. 108 gall. or 3
                                                    barrels

Wine Measure
Aum or Hoill of Rhenish .. .. .. 30 gall.
Hogshead of Claret .. .. 46 gall.
Pipe of Madeira or cape .. .. 92 gall.
Pipe of Marsala .. .. 93 gall.
Pipe of Teneriffe .. .. 100 gall.
Butt of Sherry or Tent .. .. 108 gall.
Pipe of Port or Masden .. .. 115 gall.
Butt of Lisbon or Bucellag .. .. .. 117 gall.

WELSH ONION. This onion does not form bulbs, but is used in salads and for flavouring; it is ready in early Spring, before chives.

WELSH RAREBIT. Commonly called Welsh Rabbit. A slice of toasted bread covered with melted cheese and butter, and seasoned with pepper and mustard. Sometimes a little beer is added, or vinegar. See **CHEESE**, also **BUCK RAREBIT**.

WHALE. This warm-blooded viviparous mammal of which there are many species is true air-breathing and suckles its young. It is hunted chiefly for its oil and whale-bone but the flesh may be eaten. A whale steak should be well marinated before cooking.

Whalemeat with mushrooms

Ingredients

2 lb. whalemeat fillet
¼ lb. butter
1 lb. mushrooms sliced
Salt and pepper
Water
1 tbsp. flour
2 tbsp. lemon juice

Method

Cut the whalemeat into steaks or fillets and wipe with a damp cloth; season with salt and pepper to taste. Melt 2 oz. butter in frying pan, arrange fillets carefully, fry over low flame ½ hr. each side, turning only once. Melt other 2 oz. butter in another pan, add mushrooms and sauté over low heat for 3 mins.; add seasoning and water and simmer until mushrooms are tender. Remove whalemeat, pour off butter into pan, blend with flour, add lemon juice, stir in mushrooms, blend well and keep hot. Arrange whalemeat on a hot dish, serve immediately with mushrooms arranged as garnish and sauce poured over.

WHEAT. This is the grain of a cereal grass which, when ground, yields a fine white flour. There are many varieties of wheat all closely resembling each other. See **FLOUR** and **STARCH**.

WHELK (Fr. *buccin*). The Common whelk, much used as a food in Europe, is one of the many species of spiral-shelled marine gasteropods which go by this name. This shellfish is indigestible. It should be plain boiled in salted water and then

WHELK (*continued*)

removed from its shell and served with lettuce and French dressing in a salad, or used in soups with onions, cloves, mace and pepper to give added flavour. The Red whelk is found and gathered in large quantities on the Cheshire coast and chiefly sold in the Liverpool area.

WHEY (Fr. *petit lait*). The serum or part of milk that is watery separated from the curd. The uncoagulated portion of milk used as a cooling beverage: it has laxative properties.

WHITEBAIT (Fr. *blanchaille*). Whitebait is frequently met with under its English name on the Continent. English whitebait are said to be the fry or the young of the common herring; the whitebait of Italy is said to be the young of the Anchovy and sardine; in Canada it is said to be the young of the flying-fish; the Norwegian whitebait (*bergylt*) is mostly miniature rise-fish; the whitebait of Canton in China is a young, small, transparent fish not unlike the smelt. Whitebait are at their best from March to August. Before cooking the whitebait should be thoroughly washed in a washing-basket, with a largish mesh. They must then be carefully picked over and all intruders among them taken out—such as small flounders, gobies, etc. Any weed should also be removed.

WHITEBAIT, FRIED. Always avoid touching the whitebait more than necessary. To fry well it must be perfectly fresh and it should be kept perfectly cold with a lump of ice in the cold water. Put the oil or fat into a deep saucepan. Lay a cloth upon a tray; put a heap of flour in the centre. When the fat is sufficiently hot, throw a small handful of whitebait into the flour, then taking hold of the cloth at each end, shake it rapidly until the bait is well floured. Then empty the bait into the frying-basket; shake vigorously to let the loose flour drop out and plunge into the hot fat. Fry until crisp, then drain and serve at once with thin brown bread and butter and lemons cut in quarters then lengthwise. If a large quantity is to be served, after they have all been fried, make the fat very hot and plunge them in again for a few seconds. For success, quick flouring and *very hot* fat are essential. If the flouring is a lengthy process, the moisture on the bait makes a paste with the flour. Properly fried whitebait is perfectly crisp and each fish distinct and separate.

WHITE FISH. Another name for this fish is Silver Salmon. White fish are caught in the lakes and rivers of Scotland, but the largest kind of all are caught in the colder lakes of North America.

WHITE PERCH. A small edible fish closely related to the Yellow Bass.

WHITE SAUCE. See SAUCES.

WHITE PUDDING (Fr. *boudin blanc*). The continental white puddings differ from the black puddings; they are sometimes made in long coils. There are various recipes with assorted ingredients.

WHITING (Fr. *merlan*). The true whiting is a pale silvery fish of the cod family. The flesh is delicate, quite free from oil and very digestible. Whiting seldom weighs more than 1½ lb. or exceeds 10–12 ins. in length. In winter this fish is sometimes sold under the peculiar name of Buckhorn, which is simply whiting caught in Cornwall, salted and dried. Whiting are usually trussed with the tail passing through the eyes or skewered in the mouth.

Whiting may be boiled, steamed, baked, fried, or broiled, but they are rather insipid when boiled.

WHITING, BAKED WITH CUCUMBER

Ingredients	Method
2 lb. whiting fillets	Wipe fillets with a damp cloth and place
Salt and pepper	in a shallow fireproof dish, sprinkle with
⅛ tsp. dill	salt, pepper and dill. Peel cucumber and
2 cucumbers	onion and cut into cubes. Add to fish

[522]

WHITING, BAKED WITH CUCUMBER (*continued*)

1 small onion   with chicken broth and bake at 350° F
Chicken broth   Therm. 4 for 20 mins. Serve very hot,
6 stuffed olives   garnished with chopped olives.

WHITING, FRIED. Skin the whiting, fasten the tail between the jaw with a small wooden skewer. Egg and breadcrumb the fish and fry in hot deep fat. Garnish with fried parsley. Any suitable sauce may be handed with them: Oyster, Lobster, Shrimp, Hollandaise, Maître d'Hôtel, etc. If preferred, the whiting may be dipped in beaten egg, and then in flour instead of crumbs, before frying.

WHITING, BAKED, WITH RAVIGOTE SAUCE. Skin some small whiting, and fasten the tails in the jaws with a small wooden skewer. Lay them on a buttered sauté-pan or baking tin and cover with buttered paper. Bake at 350° F. Therm. 4 for about 20 mins.; then dish them up. Make a Ravigote sauce (p. 447) and pour a little over. Serve the remainder in a tureen.

WHITING POLLOCK or WHITING POUT. See POLLOCK.

WHORTLEBERRY or HUCKLEBERRY. See BILBERRY.

WIDGEON (Fr. *macreuse*). A species of wild fowl, common to many countries, seasonable October to February. The widgeon belongs to the same family as the wild duck. A native of the northern regions of Europe and Asia it begins its polar migration early in March. It is sometimes incorrectly called *sarcelle* in French, but that is the teal. Widgeons may be grilled or roasted.

WIDGEON, ROAST. Pluck and singe a pair of widgeons; cut off the heads and claws, draw the birds without breaking the entrails, wipe them with a wet cloth. Rub them all over with cold butter, dredge with flour, place in baking tin and roast at 400° F. Therm. 6 for about 20 mins. Carefully preserve all the gravy that flows from them. When nearly done, dust with salt and pepper and serve at once with redcurrant jelly, and their gravy, adding a wineglass of port and the juice of an orange and half a lemon to this, reheating and serving at once.

WILD BOAR. The flesh of the wild boar is finer than that of the pig. Found in the temperate regions of Europe and Asia it seeks its food at night, feeding on roots which it digs with its snout. Where truffles abound, its flesh is of a delicate flavour. See **BOAR.**

WILD DUCK (Fr. *canard sauvage*). In this country this usually means the Mallard. It is distinguished from the tame duck by the colour of its bill, this being red, whereas in the tame duck it is yellow. It is trussed like an ordinary duck.
Fillets of Wild Duck with Orange Sauce (*au bigarde*). Fillet 3 wild ducks, score the skin and put them in a bowl with onions cut in halves, a few sprigs of parsley, and a little sliced mushroom. Season with salt and pepper, cover with oil and leave for an hour, then fry, and serve with Orange sauce (see p. 451) in a sauceboat.

WILD FOWL and WATERFOWL. There are many varieties of "wild fowl". The peculiar flavour, for which they are so much prized, is entirely lost if they are not kept hung for sufficient length of time after being killed, though if the weather is particularly close and damp, it is unwise to keep them too long. The plainer the cooking, the better game is said to be liked and it makes an appetising meal with all its accompaniments. See individual entries, also tables under **GAME.**

WILD GOOSE. The flesh of the wild goose has a more gamey flavour than the domestic goose.

WINDSOR BEANS. See BEANS.

WINE (Fr. *vin*). The fermented juice of the grape. Next in importance to the service of food is that of the beverage which accompanies it. Wines of the different countries vary greatly depending chiefly upon the soil and climate. Wine is used in some cookery recipes to enhance the flavour. See **HARE (Hare, Jugged), SAUCES,**

WINE (*continued*)

etc. Sometimes food is marinated in wine, or it is added to a cold sauce or jelly to give added flavour.

TO SERVE WITH FOOD. Wine and food are good partners. Wine not only aids the digestion and helps to enhance an insipid dish, but it contains certain beneficial body-aids. The art of marrying wine and food is a delicate matter and affords a great variety of pleasurable sensations.

Wines can be classified in three groups:

Beverage Wines which, when taken in moderation, are healthful and stimulating. Among this group are Bordeaux, Burgundies, Hocks, Moselles, the Rhine wines and Sauternes.

Fortified wines to which brandy is added. Australian Madeira, Marsala, Port, Sherry and the South African Dessert wines.

Sparkling wines. Among these are Champagne, Saumur and Sparkling Moselle. It is not generally realised that wine may be obtained at a very reasonable price for everyday use. The vintage wines, of course, are more expensive.

Some wines are served at room temperature while others are slightly heated, as will be seen from the list at the end of this entry.

Avoid the refrigerator or ice in the wine itself.

Remember a light and delicate wine must always come before and not after a strong wine. Some wines such as champagne may be served from the beginning to the end of the meal. But a varied scale of wines makes a most successful dinner. "Rest" your wines at least 8 days ahead of serving and take the greatest care in handling fine vintage bottles. Be on the watch for deposits, use cradles and decant old wines with great care.

Sherry is decanted and served at room temperature in a glass smaller than a wineglass. It is often served instead of a cocktail and is enjoyable with soup, even if half a glass only is served to be added to the soup. Sherry is also served as a midway drink, or at any other time when it is desired to extend hospitality. Never serve a delicate wine in a thick glass; serve a great wine in a large glass, one-third full.

Red Wine means Red Bordeaux, Burgundy, Claret, Chianti and similar wines which are partners with roasts of beef, venison and game, but not with fish or with chicken. These wines are best served at room temperature in their own bottle in a straw-handled cradle which holds the bottle on its side with least disturbance and ensures full flavour. Due to their low alcoholic content, they spoil very readily when opened and exposed to air. The claret glass is easily recognised by the more bulb-shaped glass on the taller stem, though not as broad as a champagne glass. Burgundy is served at room temperature, and in the same glass as claret, though it is a fuller-bodied and stronger wine. It is a good partner with duck and all game.

White wine is served chilled and kept in its own bottle wrapped in a napkin and if desired it may be served throughout the entire meal, the "extra dry" is best with oysters and fish, the slightly less dry goes well with fowl or entrées, while a sweeter white wine is served with dessert (pudding) course, if champagne is not being drunk throughout the meal. Glasses for white wine have a smaller and more contracted bowl than claret glasses. For *Rhine* wines, the glasses have their own specially long stems and are either crystal or coloured.

Champagne is distinctly a wine for the more formal occasions. Should it be served throughout a meal, "dry" is more preferable to the "sweet" wine. If a sweet champagne is to be served just before dessert, it must be well chilled, and it is not served or uncorked until just before the course. Like all the white wines, champagne remains in the bottle and is wrapped in a napkin. Champagne glasses should be of thin crystal, they may be of the saucer type or have hollow stems. When champagne is served at a reception or large party it usually passes amongst the guests in small, narrow-topped glasses or flaring-topped tumblers which are less liable to upset. (These can be obtained from caterers.)

WINE (continued)

When planning a menu, before deciding upon the wine, the different courses and food must be taken into consideration:

With Caviare	Serve Champagne
,, Hors d'œuvres	,, Chablis or Sauterne
,, Oysters, Shellfish and Crustaceans	,, Chablis, Champagne, or a special White Burgundy
,, Soup	,, Sherry or Marsala
,, Fish Soups	,, Hock or Moselle
,, Fish (especially salmon, sole and turbot)	,, Rhine Wine, Sauterne, Dry White Wine
,, Entrées } Removes }	,, Burgundy, Light Claret
,, Poultry and White Roasts	,, A light Red Wine, fine White Wine, but not a full-blooded wine.
,, Roasts (Red Meats, Venison, Game)	,, A strong Red Wine of aromatic flavour
,, Entremets	,, Champagne
,, Foie Gras	,, French sparkling wine
,, Cheese	,, Natural Sweet Wines, Red Wine, Great Red Wines and Sauterne
,, Dessert	,, Champagne, Claret, Port, Madeira

WINE, TO MULL. Break a fresh egg into a basin and put in 1 tbsp. caster sugar and a wineglass of wine. Beat well together then pour in gradually ½ pt. water, stirring to keep it firm; pour the mulled wine into a glass, grate a little nutmeg over and serve.

Wine Whey. Put 1 pt. milk into a small lined saucepan and place over a low heat until boiling. Add 2 wineglasses port and 1 tbsp. caster sugar. Stir until the sugar has dissolved, then strain through muslin into a jug. Add a grating of nutmeg and serve very hot.

WINE SYRUP SAUCE. See SAUCES.

WINKLES. See PERIWINKLES.

WITCH FLOUNDER. Also known as Pole Flounder and Fluke. A deep-water flounder of the North Atlantic.

WOLF-FISH. This fish is sometimes sold as Mock Salmon.

WOODCOCK (Fr. *bécasse*). This bird arrives in England about the middle of September for a short and fleeting stay. By gourmets its flesh is regarded as choice. The woodcock is a bird of the snipe variety, having a long beak which by some cooks is fancifully used for trussing purposes. The flesh is dark and very delicate, especially when the bird has been hanging for a sufficient time to assume a game flavour. To tell if a woodcock has been hung long enough for cooking, lift by one of the tail feathers and if sufficiently mature the body will detach from the feather by its own weight. There are three varieties of woodcock known to the game seller: large, which is about the size of a partridge but not so heavy, with brown plumage tinted with black and grey stripes; middle size which is of a chestnut colour, equally striped with black and grey, the belly being spotted with black on a brown ground; and the smallest, which has a plumage that is almost exclusively reddish brown or russet.

TO CHOOSE. Feel the vent; if this is thin, the bird is not in prime condition. The mouth and throat should be clean and the feet supple and soft. Reject woodcock with dry stiff feet and foul mouth.

TO PREPARE FOR COOKING. Pluck feather by feather and skin the head and neck. The inside or trail is left untouched. Fix the thighs close to the body and bring the beak under the wing, or pass it through the body to

TO PREPARE FOR COOKING (*continued*)

transfix the thighs. Sometimes the head is tucked under the skin of the breast, leaving the beak protruding.

TO ROAST. Truss the birds and brush with melted butter; place on slices of buttered toast in a roasting tin. Season lightly with salt and pepper. Roast at 450° F. Therm. 8 for about 15 mins. for a rare bird, or leave from 20–25 mins. but NO LONGER. Baste constantly and serve garnished with watercress, accompanied by orange salad (p. 429) and gravy.

TO CARVE. See CARVING.

WOOD HEN. The gourmets do not think the female bird as well flavoured as the male. The mode of preparation and trussing is the same in both cases. See WOODCOCK.

WOOD PIGEON (Fr. *mansard*). Hang for a few days. Cook as PIGEON.

WORMWOOD (Fr. *absinthe*). This plant is closely allied to Southernwood and Tarragon. At one time it was largely cultivated in this country for the purpose of producing bitters for beer. Known as Crusader's Herb.

WURST. The German for fresh or smoked sausage.

Y

YAM (Fr. *igname*). There are many species of this root vegetable, best known in America; that best known to us is a large fleshy tuberous root which resembles Jerusalem artichokes in peculiarity of irregular growth, and potatoes in constitution; it contains a large quantity of starch. It is used for cakes and puddings, etc. Yams are commonly sliced and dried in the sun in order to preserve them. The yams bear close resemblance to the Spanish sweet potato.

YAMS, BAKED

Ingredients	Method
1 lb. small yams	Wash the yams, dry in a cloth and bake
Salt and pepper	at 400° F. Therm. 6 until they are soft to
Butter	touch. Spread a folded napkin on a dish, arrange yams on it and serve with salt, pepper and butter.

YAMS, BOILED. Peel and wash the yams. Soak in cold water for a short time then place in cold salted water and boil slowly until soft. Drain and serve.

Yams, Creamed. Cut ½ lb. cold boiled yams into small pieces of about ½" square and put into a flat baking-dish. Cover with cream, place in a moderate oven (350° F. Therm. 4) and bake until nearly all the cream is absorbed. Add 1 tbsp. butter, sprinkle with finely chopped parsley, season with pepper and salt, return to oven. Place in hot vegetable dish and serve.

YARROW. This asteraceous strong-scented plant with small white flowers is used medicinally.

YEAST. Yeast is a plant, a small piece of which contains thousands of tiny single cells so small that they cannot be seen by the naked eye. Yeast is used for biological aeration. To keep it alive and to start it growing, warmth, food and moisture are essential. When these are supplied, the yeast grows and multiplies rapidly, and through this activity bubbles of carbonic acid gas are given off, which are released in the dough; these help it to separate and become lighter. Because yeast is a living organism, time is necessary for growth and multiplication, and it is for this reason that plenty of time must be allowed for the yeast to "work" before putting the dough into the oven. Remember that time is a vital factor when using yeast, and that the success of a yeast mixture is to thoroughly understand its use, preparation and cooking. Too cold a temperature retards the growth of yeast, and too great a heat can kill the yeast plant (see **BREAD**). Yeast is also called "barm" when added in small quantities to flour for making dough so that it ferments and quickens.

TO USE FRESH. With a large amount of flour, it is quite safe to use 1 oz. yeast to each 3½ lb. flour (quartern). For small quantities, never use less than ½ oz., as the yeast will not work satisfactorily. The amount of yeast depends upon the time required for the dough to rise: for a quick rise, more yeast is needed.

Approximate proportions to use:

½ oz. yeast to 1 lb. flour (this small quantity of flour is seldom used).
1 oz. yeast to 3–7 lb. flour.
1½ oz. yeast to 7–13 lb. flour.

Fresh yeast should smell fresh, be firm and yet crumble easily, be fawn in colour and when creamed with a little sugar, it should become liquid. For the tepid liquid used in breadmaking, allow 1 part boiling water to 2 parts cold.

TO USE DRIED. See **BREAD**.

Yeast Cake

Ingredients

¼ lb. flour
Pinch of salt
¼ lb. butter or fat
¼ pt. hot milk
1 small tbsp. fresh yeast
2 well-beaten eggs
6 oz. currants
4 oz. caster sugar
1 oz. candied peel
Little grated nutmeg

Method

Sift flour and salt into a bowl. Dissolve butter or fat in hot milk and leave to cool a little; when lukewarm stir into flour. Add crumbled yeast and eggs and knead to a smooth dough. Make 2 or 3 gashes across surface with knife; cover bowl with cloth, and leave to rise in warm place. When light, knead again; add currants, sugar, and peel and nutmeg. Turn into a good-sized cake-tin, lined with buttered paper, to rise 4″ above tin, and leave to rise 30 mins. Protect surface with a sheet of paper and bake at 350° F. Therm. 4. for 1½ hr.

Yeast Dumplings. Beat ¼ lb. butter to cream, add 4 or 5 eggs; when well-mixed, pour in ¼ pt. milk, 2 oz. each yeast, sugar, grated lemon peel, and little pinch cinnamon, adding as much flour as will make it of a proper consistency. Make the dough into dumplings, and let them remain an hour in a warm place to rise, then boil them in boiling water. Serve with melted butter and sugar or Wine Syrup sauce.

Yeast Fritters

Ingredients

½ oz. yeast
2 oz. sugar
1 pt. water
1 lb. flour
Small pinch of salt
1 tbsp. olive oil

Method

Crumble the yeast with sugar; dissolve in the lukewarm water; add flour, salt and oil. Mix well together and leave 1 hr. before use. For savoury batter use a little less sugar.

YORKSHIRE PUDDING. There are variations to the Yorkshire pudding which is traditionally served with roast beef, and which should be only ½″ thick and not turned during cooking. In some Yorkshire families this pudding is made in individual dishes and served before the meat, with a good thick gravy.

Ingredients

Plain

4 oz. plain flour
¼ tsp. salt
1 egg
½ pt. milk
2 oz. dripping

Rich

6 oz. plain flour
Pinch of salt
Dusting of red pepper
2 eggs
½ pt. rich milk
2 oz. dripping
1 tbsp. hot water

Method

Sift flour and salt, make a well in centre and add egg and seasoning; mix to a smooth paste with half the milk. Beat for 5 mins., add remaining milk, beat for a further 5 mins., then stand in cool place for ½ hr. Melt dripping in baking tin (10″ × 6″), add hot water to rich mixture, pour batter into tin and bake pudding at 400° F. Therm. 6 for 30 mins. Cut into 2″ squares and serve round meat on hot dish.

YORKSHIRE SPICE CAKE. These traditional cakes are made in large quantities in Yorkshire at Christmas-time. Also called Yule Cake.

TO MAKE

Sift 8 lb. flour with 1 tbsp. salt; rub into it $1\frac{1}{2}$ lb. butter and 2 lb. lard. Scoop a hole in the centre of the bread without touching the bottom, and pour in $\frac{1}{2}$ pt. fresh sweet brewer's yeast mixed with water. Stir flour into yeast until it is like batter, sprinkle flour over the top, and set the bowl in a warm place. When the yeast rises in bubbles through the flour, knead the dough thoroughly as for common bread, and let it rise until it is light. When risen, work in with it 6 lb. currants, picked and dried thoroughly, 2 lb. sugar, some grated nutmeg and 8 well-beaten eggs. Divide into loaves of various sizes, put these into tins which they will half-fill, lined with buttered paper, and bake at 375° F. Therm. 5. The yeast must on no account be bitter. Time to bake the cakes is according to size.

Z

ZABAGLIONE. A frothy mixture composed of wine, egg yolks, and sugar, thickened over heat, and served hot in glasses. See also **Sabayon Sauce (p. 452).**

ZANDER or ZANT (Fr. *sandre*.) A freshwater fish of the perch tribe, found in some of the North European continental rivers and lakes and frequently attaining the size of a salmon. It is greatly esteemed for the quality of its flesh which is very white and said to be almost equal to the whiting. In different countries this fish is known under different names.

ZEPHYRS

Ingredients	*Method*
1 oz. gelatine ½ pt. milk 3 heaped tbsp. grated parmesan cheese 1 cup thick cream	Put the gelatine and milk into a small lined saucepan. Place over a low heat and stir until dissolved. Remove from heat, add cheese, whisk cream to a stiff froth, then add to the other ingredients and mix. Fill some small moistened moulds or cups with the mixture and place in a refrigerator or in a very cool place until it has set. When ready to serve, turn out of the moulds on to a dish and garnish with small croûtons or aspic jelly.

ZEST. The yellow surface of oranges and lemons, containing the essential or flavouring oil of the peel. A term commonly used in this sense, but it has a more extensive signification and might be applied to all sorts of spices and flavourings.

ZUCCHINI. A young vegetable marrow.

Zucchini with Melted Butter or Sauce. Slice (but do not peel) into ½″ slices. Soak in cold water 15–20 mins., then cook in a small amount of boiling salted water in covered saucepan. Drain and serve with butter or Hollandaise sauce. Do not overcook.

Zucchini with Cheese

Ingredients	*Method*
4 small zucchini ⅛ pt. olive oil 3 eggs ½ tsp. salt 1 tsp. coarsely ground pepper ¼ lb. grated parmesan cheese	Cut the zucchini into ½″ slices. Place in large frying-pan containing the heated olive oil. Sauté gently for 4 or 5 mins. Beat eggs well, add salt and pepper and parmesan cheese. Pour over zucchini and cook slowly until eggs are set. Serve hot or cold, cut into wedges. Sufficient for 4 persons.

NOTES

NOTES

NOTES

NOTES

NOTES

NOTES